Bihar
General Knowledge

Dr. Manish Rannjan
(IAS)

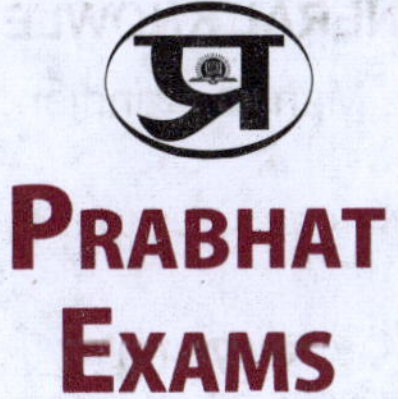

PRABHAT
EXAMS

Publisher
PRABHAT EXAMS
An imprint of Prabhat Prakashan
4/19 Asaf Ali Road, New Delhi–110002
Ph. 23289555 • 23289666 • 23289777 • Helpline/ 7827007777
e-mail: prabhatbooks@gmail.com • Website: www.prabhatexam.com

Price
Five Hundred Seventy Five Rupees

ISBN 978-93-5488-490-0

Printed at
Siddhi Press, New Delhi

BIHAR GENERAL KNOWLEDGE 2026
by Dr. Manish Rannjan, IAS

ISBN 978-93-5488-490-0

₹ 575.00

Dedicated to Millions of Students of Bihar who with the Strength of their Boundless Energy and Talent are Willing to Take the State to its Zenith.

Preface

he land of Bihar, brimming with its illustrious history and inspiring traditions, has the distinction of being the birthplace and the place of action of great personalities. Encompassing otality of nature's beauty and historical legacy, Bihar has not only been a witness to the ıtion of culture but is also the place where the first democracy of the world was founded. : has since ancient times been moralising the world on governance, peace, truth and non-nce. Bihar has been the birthplace and place of action of various ancient sages like Buddha, avira, Aryabhata and Chanakya as well as great legends like Lok Nayak Jai Prakash Narayan Deshratna Rajendra Prasad of modern times. Since ancient times, Bihar has played a leading n nation's development and provided a new direction and novel message to the world. The has registered its presence at national and international levels on account of its intellectual natural resources. Reviving the ancient Nalanda University as an international university is test example of the same.

t's a fact that Bihar, basking in golden moments of history, lagged behind and failed to keep with other states on national and international levels during subsequent years. However, the lecade has seen the state, on the strength of its performance, regain its place among the fast loping states.

Besides being my birthplace, I have special fondness for Bihar, and I have been harbouring for ; the desire and ambition of authoring a book on Bihar. Intellectual affluence of Bihar, aided nple availability of resources like land and water, is capable of making the state economically essful. I have felt, based on personal experience, that all the books written on Bihar have been le to reflect honestly the natural and socio-cultural diversity of the state. Books and guides able on Bihar have not proved to be useful to provide simple, comprehensible, factual, and vledgeable information to candidates appearing for competitive examinations. As a result, have to face failure even after making lots of efforts. Even in the context of my book, it may id that 'यदिहास्ति तदन्यत्र यन्ने हास्ति न तत् क्वचित' meaning that whatever is available in this book may und elsewhere also but what is not available in this book cannot be found anywhere else. An ıpt has been made to exemplify this very concept in the book.

'न हि ज्ञानेन सदृशं पवित्रमिह विद्यते'....Gita

Vith this purpose, the analytical aspect of information has been kept in mind while finalizing ook.

This presented book has been divided into 38 chapters. Various chapters present factual and endious analysis of history, art, and folk culture and geographical, economic, and political itions of Bihar.

Historical Sources: Socio-cultural perspective of history of Bihar has been detailed ;orically in the book. Attempt has been made to present a meticulous analysis of cultural formation and its impact on people's lives. A systematic analysis of historical resources and ts is the mainstay of the book.

Pre-historic Period and Ancient Period: This chapter describes cultural evolutio prehistoric and historical Bihar and social and religious reform movements as well as its pol history including Magadh Empire, post Maurya and Gupta periods of Bihar. These details are useful for readers to understand the historical legacy of the state.

Medieval Period: In this chapter, a meticulous analysis of medieval era has been prese by dividing the same into various periods. Details have been provided for the impact of r of Delhi Sultanate during pre-medieval as well as medieval periods. Shershah, the Af ruler of Bihar had made the greatest impact on the history of India, both administratively economically, during medieval period, this chapter covers a pragmatic analysis of his emerg and his policies. It presents a realistic portrayal of Mughal administrative structure and mys Islamic Sufi tradition of medieval period that provided the foundation for the Indo-Islamic cu of brotherhood to bloom in Bihar as well as across India.

Modern Period: This chapter provides details of the reasons for emergence of regional po and their impact in the state as well as across the country after downfall of centralised Mughal Also, arrival of European companies in Bihar, struggle among them for control of the state ultimate triumph of the British has been analysed. A minute analysis of people's movements were launched in the state against establishment of the British rule has also been presented.

Freedom Movement: Bihar has always been a place of revolutionary ideology. Several t and farmer movements had taken place even before the revolution in the year 1857. Resic of Bihar had overwhelmingly contributed to various movements like 'Champaran Satyagr 'Khilafat Movement', 'Non-cooperation Movement', 'Civil Disobedience Movement' and India Movement' during the course of freedom movement. It was the land of Champaran where Mahatma Gandhi had experimented truth and non-violence and started his mover Besides these revolutionary nationalist movements, revolutionaries from Bihar had also playe important role in Azad Hind Army. Detailed analysis has also been presented in this chapter c contributions of women, farmers, and people with socialist ideology to the freedom moven Additionally, details of the policies relating to development of education in Bihar and grow educational institutions during the British rule have been provided.

Separate Bihar Movement: This chapter contains systematic description of the mover launched for the current political structure of Bihar. Bihar was constituted as a separate stat 1st April, 1912. It was constituted as a separate province right from the period of Maurya to t of Shershah and Akbar. However, it was merged with Bengal and Orissa as a separate state du the British rule. But, western education helped emergence of intellectuals in Bihar also, and became aware of their rights. They felt that constitution of a separate state of Bihar only w be able to bring about transformation in social, economic, and political structure of the pe of Bihar. Sachchidananda Sinha, Mahesh Narayan, Deepnarayan Singh, and Ganesh Sha Vidyarthi were some of the notables among those intellectuals.

Architecture and Painting: A detailed analysis of different styles of architecture and pair like Maurya art, Pal art, Patna Kalam, Madhubani painting, and Manjusha style that bloomed flowered in Bihar right from ancient times to modern period has been presented in this chapte

Folk Culture: An attempt has been made in this chapter to understand special featur social framework and cultural complexity of Bihar. A state or a country is typically defined b cultural heritage. This only determines its soul and independent identity. The chapter also con comprehensive analysis of folk songs, folk dances, folk plays, and tribal culture that reflec inherent harmony of cultures.

Fairs and Festivals: Important fairs, carnivals, and festivals that reflect common people's lives in the state have been given in detail in this chapter. Many such events like Sonpur fair, the largest cattle fair of the country, and the pious Chhath festival have been explored.

Literature and Litterateur: A detailed observation has been presented on language, literature, journalism, litterateurs, etc. of Bihar in this chapter. There are many languages and dialects used in Bihar. Hindi, Urdu, Sanskrit, Maithili, Bhojpuri, Angika, Vajjika and Magadhi, etc., are the most popular ones. Hindi is the main language of expression in Bihar. Many dialects of Hindi language are found in different regions of Bihar. The state has a long history of journalism and writing in literature. Bihar is the birthplace of Rashtrakavi Dinkar and Acharya Shivpujan Sahay who highlighted regional characteristics of the state, and Vidyapati, the great poet of regional languages.

Bihar's Luminaries: Right from historical times, Bihar has always enlightened the whole world in every field from time-to-time. This land has been home to various great personalities right from ancient times. It has been the place of birth and place of action for many of them right from ancient sages like Buddha, Mahavira, Aryabhata, and Chanakya to luminaries of modern times like Lok Nayak Jai Prakash Narayan and Deshratna Dr. Rajendra Prasad. In the present chapter, these personalities who helped Bihar take a place on the world human stage have been discussed.

Education, Health and Sports: This chapter covers description of main educational institutions and important museums in the state; this is quite significant and interesting from the point of view of readers. Health and sports are the essential pre-requisites for all-round development of people. Health services and sports-related activities in the state have been analysed here. The state has achieved unparalleled national and international feats in sports.

Location and Relief: A minute and factual analysis of geographical features like geographical boundaries, geographical structure and relief and geographical regions of the state has been presented in this chapter. The state is blessed with captivating landscape and is equally rich in water and soil resources. Scientific methods have been used to present maps and statistics, etc. in this book.

Drainage System: Analytical details of rivers, hot water springs, waterfalls, lakes, humid lands, etc. have been presented in this chapter. The state has a network of rivers having water throughout the year. They originate from Himalayas and flow through Bihar irrigating and enriching the land on their way. This network of rivers has made invaluable contribution to the development of human civilisation in Bihar.

Climate and Soil: This chapter covers details relating to Bihar's broad-based tropical climate, distribution of rains, soil types, features, etc.

Forests and Wildlife: Detailed description of the forest resources and bio-diversity in the state has been provided in this chapter. Flora and fauna of the state is quite diverse having several species and suitable efforts are also being made for their protection. Remarkable efforts are being made for protection of forests and wildlife in the state through various institutions like The State Forest Development Corporation, and Environment Forest and Climate Change Department.

Agriculture: Land use model, farming intensity, farm pooling, agriculture regions, agro-climatic conditions, main crops, animal husbandry, pisciculture, and land reforms are described in this chapter. Agriculture is the main foundation pillar of development of the state. Development of the state cannot even be imagined without development of agriculture.

Means of Irrigation: This chapter covers details relating to important means of irrigation, various projects like Kosi Project, Gandak Project, Son Project, etc., Rainbow Revolution launched for agricultural development, Accelerated Irrigation Benefits Programme and ICAR Research Complex for Eastern Region, Patna.

Minerals and Industries: Mineral resources, industries like agro-based industries, forest-based industries, mineral-based industries and food processing industries available in the state have been described in this chapter.

Basic Infrastructure: This chapter covers details relating to basic infrastructure available in the state, viz., transport, communication, power, etc. The Bihar Policy for Promotion of New and Renewable Energy Sources, implemented for development of energy sources has been described in detail in this chapter.

Population and Domicile: Population density and distribution have been discussed in this chapter. The population policy formulated for regulating the population of the state has also been included in this chapter. Human development index and rural and urban demography of the state have also been included.

Tourism and Tourist Destinations: Various kinds of tourist places have been covered in this chapter. The Bihar Tourism Policy formulated for promoting tourism in the state has also been included in the chapter.

Disaster Management: Different kinds of disasters that the state encounters like flood, drought, earthquake, cyclone, etc. have been described in this chapter. Disaster management related activities, regulations and authorities in the state for prevention of disasters have also been included here. The state has developed the 'Bihar Disaster Risk Reduction Roadmap, 2015–30'. This also has been described in detail in this chapter.

Governance Structure: The chapter covers details relating to the political framework and system in the state. This includes discussion on the positions of the Governor, Legislative Assembly, Cabinet of Ministers, Chief Minister, Attorney General, and Lokayukta. Various commissions set up in the state have also been covered for discussion in this chapter.

Administrative System: This chapter includes discussion on administrative framework in the state like divisional administration, district administration, sub divisional administration, block administration, etc. Additionally, social, political, and economic profiles of various districts of the state have also been described here.

Judiciary: The structure of judiciary in the state comprising high court and subordinate courts has been detailed in this chapter. The process of appointment of judges in the high court, their roles and jurisdiction of subordinate courts has been described in detail.

Local Self Governance: The Panchayati Raj system and urban self-governance structure existing in the state have been discussed in this chapter. Discussion on the Panchayati Raj system covers details relating to the constitution of gram panchayat, panchayat samiti and district boards as well as their functions and jurisdictions.

Important Economic Indices: The chapter covers discussion on the primary economic indicators of the state, including demography, state domestic product, economic framework, regional disparity, fiscal policy, poverty, and unemployment with the help of statistics. The present situation of Bihar and its developmental potentials have been presented in the chapter. Despite facing economic backwardness at the moment, Bihar has potentials for development, and the same has been presented in a logical manner.

Union and State Sponsored Programmes: Centre and State sponsored projects that have been implemented for inclusive development of the state and for the benefit of scheduled tribes, the poor; the backwards; women and other deprived classes have been discussed in detail in this chapter. An information-based analysis has been presented on the way these projects are being implemented and the results they have been able to achieve in the state.

Financial System: Banking infrastructure existing in Bihar has been described in this chapter. This includes details relating to the branches, credit deposit ratios and other functions of commercial banks, state cooperative banks, regional rural banks and private commercial banks. Various financial institutions functioning in the state have also been included in the chapter.

State Policies: Various policies like industrial policy, start-up policy, information and technology policy, advertisement policy, Right to Public Service Act, Bihar Agriculture Land (Conversion for Non-Agriculture Purposes) Act, Bihar Right to Public Grievance Redressal Act and Bihar Prohibition and Excise Act, formulated for social, economic and political development of the state have been described in this chapter.

Economic Survey 2025–26 and Bihar Budget 2026–27: Bihar Budget, 2026–27 has been detailed sector-wise in this chapter. Allocations made to different sectors have also been presented in this chapter. The chapter also contains detailed evaluation of Bihar Economic Survey 2025–26.

Partition of Bihar: The chapter has discussions on economic, political and social impacts on Bihar after its bifurcation. This also includes impact of bifurcation on resources, assets and liabilities. The demand made by Bihar for grant of special category status to the state on account of its special circumstances has also been explained in this chapter. Additionally, the special package provided by the Prime Minister has also been detailed here.

Naxalism: The chapter contains discussion on naxalism, its current status, reasons and impacts in Bihar.

Good Governance and Seven Resolutions: The concept of good governance with the outlook of development with justice taking along people from all regions and classes and 'seven commitments' for attaining the same for a developed Bihar have been discussed in this chapter.

Bihar Foundation Day: Bihar government celebrates Bihar Day to arouse and demonstrate Bihari spirit. This chapter contains details of the same.

Statistical Presentation: All the information related to Bihar have been presented in the form of statistics and diagrams in this chapter. This would be quite helpful for competing students and readers desirous of understanding Bihar. Anybody who wants to have a comparative study of Bihar against other states would find this chapter extremely useful.

Appendices: This chapter presents a compendium of different kinds of information relating to Bihar.

The contents listed above indicate that the book 'Bihar General Knowledge' has been written keeping in mind the competitive examinations being conducted in Bihar. This has been purposefully made comprehensive to help you prepare well for competitive examinations. We aim to equip you in such a way that you feel comfortable at every stage of the examination, be it Prelims or Mains or even when you are appearing before the interview board. And to attain the same, we have attempted to gather available facts relating to all aspects of a matter, viz., ideological, conceptual, and factual (up to date), at one place in the book. We believe this book would prove to be the ultimate dependable testament for resolution of every factual and conceptual issue.

I am an administrator and an integral part of the government. My impartiality is my identity. Hence, my responsibility is also quite sensitive. It has not been my aim to put blame on the state, or the central government, or to make an adverse remark or criticise them. Even if any such matter is found appearing anywhere in the book, that does not reflect my view but just an innocent articulation of the media or the feelings of common people. If still that hurts anybody's sentiments, I present my apology for the same.

Lastly, in the context of language, style and appeal of this book, I would definitely like to mention that the predicative form of language has been used here. The language is simple, comprehensible and easy to understand which, I strongly believe, would be able to delight students as well as common people.

The following shloka from Bharat Muni's Natyashashtra confirms the significance of this book.

न तद् ज्ञानं न तच्छिल्पं न सा विद्या न सा कला।
न स योगो न तत्कर्म नाट्येस्मिन यन्न दृश्यते।।

There is no form of wisdom, art, knowledge, craft, yoga or karma that cannot be found in this book.

I acknowledge the active support received from Deepak Kumar, Sunil Kumar, Noor Alam Khan, Ashish Kumar, Priyaranjan, Praveen Kumar, Arvinda Kumar and Pradyumna Kumar while drafting and writing this book and extend my heartfelt gratitude to them for the same.

— Dr. Manish Rannjan
(IAS)

Contents

Historical Sources

- **Archaeological Sources**
- **Literary Sources**

The history and culture of Bihar has been the bearer of its illustrious and magnificent traditions right from ancient times to the modern age. The land of Bihar has been witness to emergence, amalgamation and development of different cultures and tenets. We may notice, in the context of historical affairs, that all major events that took place around the world were somehow or other linked to Bihar. The land of Bihar has been blessed to be the birthplace of great sages, scholars, and kings and emperors who were instrumental in taking not only Bihar but also India to heights of glory in the whole world. Bhagwan Mahavira and Mahatma Buddha who preached truth, morality and non-violence were born on this very land of Bihar. Emperors like Chandragupta Maurya and Ashoka the Great provided strength and development to the state.

History of any place or period is constructed based on the sources or evidences available. There are plenty of sources available for studying the history of Bihar. They include archaeological as well as literary sources.

ARCHAEOLOGICAL SOURCES

Evidences relating to prehistoric era have been found at many places in Munger, Saran, Vaishali, and Patna. They include Neolithic Age bone tools found in Chirand in Saran and Chalcolithic Age tools in Sonpur in Gaya and Maner in Patna. Inscriptions on stone pieces, pillars, and copper plates, monuments, remains of buildings, coins, etc. are among various archaeological evidences found at different places in Bihar. Notable among them are pillar inscriptions of Ashoka found in Lauria-Areraj, Lauria Nandangarh and Rampurva, stone inscriptions found in Chandanpir Hills of Sasaram, and cave inscriptions of Ashoka and his grandson Dashrath found in Barabar and Nagarjun Hills. The language and script used in Maurya inscriptions are Prakrit and Brahmi respectively. There are two inscriptions on the Yaksha idol found in Patna. Two inscriptions of Mahadevi Prabhudaya have also been found in Basarh in Vaishali District. The inscriptions relating to Gupta Period are in Brahmi script in Sanskrit language. Two earthen seals with engravings have been found in Basarh. One seal found in Basarh belongs to Mahadevi Dhruvaswamini, which reveals that Dhruvaswamini was the second wife of Chandragupta and the mother of Govinda Gupta. One of the inscriptions located in Bodh Gaya has references to Mahamana II, a bhikshu from Sri Lanka. It mentions that Mahamana II had built a palace near Vajrasana in Bodh Gaya. Gupta genealogy can be found out from Gupta Period seals found in Nalanda. Gupta period stone inscriptions of Adityasena found in Aphsad village near Nawadah provide good amount of historical information relating to rulers right from Krishna Gupta, the founder of the later Gupta Dynasty to

Adityasena. Adityasena's inscriptions have been found in Mandar Hills at Baunsi of Banka District. These inscriptions mention activities like digging of ponds and installation of Vishnu's idol. The genealogy of the later Gupta rulers can be found in stone inscriptions of Jivitagupta found in Deo-Barunark near Arrah. Inscriptions of Pala rulers of pre-medieval period that have been found at many locations in south and central Bihar are written in Sanskrit. The stone inscription of Dharmapala, found in Bodh Gaya, refers to a person named Keshav who had built a Shiva temple at Bodh Gaya. The copperplate engraving of Dharmapala found in Nalanda clearly indicates that Dharmapala had offered a village in Gaya as donation. Devapala's stone inscriptions found at Dhensrava in Nalanda has mention about appointment of Viradeva of Nagarhara, presently in Afghanistan, as head of Nalanda University. We find out from Mahipala's stone inscriptions in Nalanda that Baladitya had burnt Nalanda Mahavihara.

Devapala's copper plate inscriptions found in Munger also throw some light on the history of ancient Bihar. Buchanan and Hamilton have studied the fortified walls and Barabar caves built by Ajatashatru in Rajgir. Hotgaon was the first to report Kesaria stupa and Areraj pillar. Major Kitto has made a mention of the cave built by Ashoka and his grandson Dashratha on the Barabar Hill, and he only was instrumental in carrying out excavations at Kurkihar (Kumharar). Cunningham, also known as the father of Indian Archaeology, had identified various archaeological sites in Bihar in 1861. It was Cunningham only who had first reported Bodhi temple in Bodh Gaya and had discovered granite railings. Cunningham also discovered Bardgaon where the ancient Nalanda Mahavihara is located, around 11 km away from Rajgir. Two inscriptions with the name of Nalanda engraved thereon, have been found there. From Nalanda region only, famous stone engravings of Kumaragupta and Skandagupta have been excavated.

After independence, the Department of Ancient Indian History and Archaeology was established in Patna University; this speeded up search for archaeological sites in Bihar. Mr. K Deo and Dr. Altekar had led excavations at Vaishali in 1950 and at Kumhrar in 1951. The Bihar State Directorate of Archaeology was set up in 1962.

Study of coins is known as numismatics. Coins are vital sources for study of history. Coins belonging to periods right from Vedic era to Gupta era have been found in Bihar. The early coins are known as 'Aahat' coins. In the Later Vedic Period, when Aryans started wielding influence, coins came into usage in Videha, Anga, and Magadh regions. According to the Brihadaranyaka Upanishad, Videha King Janak had offered 'Nishk' (gold) coins as gifts. The Jataka tales of Buddha era have references to 'Nishk' as gold coins; however, no ancient gold coins have been found anywhere in Bihar till date. Such coins have, of course been, found in Takshashila in North-western India (existing Pakistan). Nine such coins are in the safe custody of the museum of Department of Archaeology of Patna University. The ancient coins found in Bihar are primarily Aahat coins only, known with several names like 'Karshapana', 'Dharana', 'Poorna' and 'Parna'. Silver and copper coins have been found at many Northern Black Painted (NBP) sites in Bihar. 'Silver Aahat' coins have been recovered from Lohanipur, Kumharar, Maner, Mayaganj, Rajgir, Bodh Gaya, Nalanda, Vaishali, Fatuha, Bhabhua, Supaul, Motihari, Nandangarh, Munger, Patna City, Gaya, Chirand, and Buxar. Gold, silver and copper coins of Gupta era have been found at many places in Bihar. Coins of Pratihara King Bhoj have been recovered from Nalanda. Gold coins of Shashank have been found in Nalanda and Gaya districts.

LITERARY SOURCES

Among literary sources, we may find both religious and non-religious materials to understand the history of Bihar. Vedic, Jain and Buddhist literature are foremost among religious sources. Some of the most important sources in Vedic literature are Rigveda, Atharvaveda, Shatapatha Brahmana and Brihadaranyaka Upanishad. The term

'Bihar' has been first mentioned in Atharvaveda, though the term 'Magadh' has been first used in Rigveda. 'Anguttara Nikaya', 'Digha Nikaya' and 'Vinaya Pitaka' in Buddhist literature and 'Bhagavati Sutra' in Jain literature are some of the primary literary sources that provide information relating to the history of Bihar. First reference to the 16 mahajanapadas can be found in the Anguttara Nikaya and the Bhagavati Sutra. Magadh, Lichchavis and Anga out of the 16 mahajanapadas were located in Bihar. The books 'Tabaqat-i Nasiri' of Minhaj-i-Siraj, 'Basateen ul-Uns' of Abdoosi Akhsitan Dehlavi, 'Afsana-i-Shahan' of Shaikh Kabir, and 'Tarikh-i-Sher Shahi' of Abbas Khan Sarwani are the primary literary sources relating to the medieval period. 'Tabaqat-i Nasiri' is the earliest record of the arrival of Turks in India. This is the first book written in Persian language in India. 'Tarikh-i-Sher Shahi' is the only source to learn about the rule and history of Sher Shah. 'Waqiat-e-Mushtaqi' by Rizq Ullah, 'Riyaz-us-Salatin' by Ghulam Husain Salim Zaidpuri and 'Siyar-ul-Mutakhkherin' by Ghulam Husain Khan are also great sources to learn about the medieval history of Bihar. Besides them, 'Kirtilata' and 'Kirtipataka' written by Vidyapati, 'Varnaratnakar' by Jyotirishwar Thakur and 'Rajniti Ratnakar' by Chandreshwar are also notable sources to explore medieval history of Bihar. Books authored in the context of Indian history like 'Arthashastra' by Kautilya, 'Ashtadhyayi' by Panini, 'Tarikh-i Firoz Shahi' by Ziauddin Barani, 'Tuzuk-e-Babri' by Babar and 'Akbarnama' by Abul Fazal are also great sources for studying the history of Bihar.

In addition to the archaeological and literary sources, even foreign literature and travellers' accounts are important sources. Among them, travelogue 'Indica' of Greek traveller Megasthenes and those of Fa-Hien and Hiuen Tsang are notable. Europeans like Rolf Finch, Edward Terry, John Marshall, Peter Mundy, Monrick, Manucci and Tavernier, who visited India during the Mughal period, have also narrated in their travelogues the details of socio-economic landscape of 'at the time' Bihar.

Prehistoric Period and Ancient Period

- **Prehistoric Period**
- **Historic Period**
- **Social-Religious Reform Movements in Ancient Bihar**
- **Political History of Bihar**
- **Emergence of Magadh Empire**
- **Post-Maurya Bihar**
- **Bihar during Gupta Dynasty**

The history of human civilisation in Bihar is studied by dividing the same into two segments:

- Prehistoric Period
- Historic Period

PREHISTORIC PERIOD

It was some 30,000 years ago when the 'wise men', known as 'Homo Sapiens' came into existence on this earth. Evidences that have been recovered at some sites in Bihar indicating habitation of primitive men are almost 100,000 years old. These evidences belong to the Palaeolithic era which also include stone tools. These remains have been recovered from excavations in Nalanda and Munger districts. The initial period of prehistoric era is referred to as Stone Age. During this period, man developed his culture based on stone tools. Based on the changes in varieties and peculiarities of the stone tools, the Stone Age is divided into Palaeolithic, Mesolithic and Neolithic ages. Evidences of different stages of human civilisation of prehistoric period are found even in Bihar at various locations.

Palaeolithic Age: Stone tools belonging to Lower, Middle, and Upper Palaeolithic ages have been found in Nalanda, Gaya Munger, and Bhagalpur districts in Bihar. These tools have been recovered from the Jethian Valley in Nalanda, the Pemar Valley in Gaya, Bhimbandh, and Paisara in Munger, Rajpokhar and Bhalijor in Bhagalpur and Valmiki Nagar in Champaran. All the tools found at above-mentioned sites are of Acheulean type. Axes, cleavers, scrapers, blades, engravers, knives, and segmental chopping tools are prominent among those tools. These tools were used for hunting animals and for removing their skin. During that period, the main source of livelihood for man was hunting and fishing and collecting root vegetables. Man used to lead the life of a vagabond and live in natural habitat like hill rocks and caves. Remains of two rock shelters of prehistoric Homo sapiens have been found in Sherghati in Gaya District.

Neolithic Age: The Neolithic Age is known as the age of first revolutionary change in human life on account of adoption of agriculture. Agricultural activities led to development of permanent settlements during this period. Man, having taken up cultivation, started to come out of caves and started living in plains. Important Neolithic sites in Bihar have been found in Chechar (Shwetpur) and Kutubpur in Vaishali, Chirand in Saran, Maner in Patna, Senuar in Rohtas and Sonpur, Taradih and Keur in Gaya. Neolithic bone tools have been recovered from Chirand in Saran. Chirand is located some 11 km southeast from Chhapra on the banks of the Ganges. It is believed that Chirand was named after the name of Chero ruler. Excavations were carried out here during 1962. Besides the Neolithic bone tools, black painted ceramics belonging to the period around 2500-1345 BC have also been recovered from this site. Neolithic remains have been found in Chechar village located east of Hajipur City in the doab between the Ganga and the Gandak in Vaishali District. Taradih is situated on the western bank of the Falgu River in Gaya District whereas Senuar is located on the bank of the Kurda River in Rohtas District. All the above mentioned sites have been found to be in doabs or on the banks of rivers; this indicates that during the Neolithic Age, adoption of cultivation prompted humans to colonise in these regions due to availability of water and fertile land.

Human civilisation underwent a lot of changes during the period of transition from the Palaeolithic Age to the Neolithic Age. Permanent settlements were developed for the first time during Neolithic Age on account of adoption of cultivation. This led to changes in material life of humans, which later resulted in development of chalcolithic culture.

Chalcolithic Age: Man, for the first time, started using copper as metal. Copper was used along with stone. Hence, this age is referred to as 'Chalcolithic Age'. Evidences of the chalcolithic culture have been recovered in Bihar from Sonpur, Taradih, Maner, Senuar, Chirand, Chechar and Ariyap. Human life depended on agriculture and hunting even under chalcolithic culture. Evidences have been found that iron was discovered at Atarajikhera (Uttar Pradesh) in the valleys of the Ganges around 1050 BC. Discovery of iron resulted in the Iron Age taking the place of the Chalcolithic Age.

Iron Age: The Iron Age is the Later Vedic Period when human settlements had already expanded to North Bihar in the valleys of the Ganges. Iron was the primary material for building tools during this period. The second stage of the Iron Age, which is also known as the Northern Black Pottery ware Age, saw iron being used for agricultural activities also. Villages started getting gradually transformed into towns. Evidences of first urbanisation in Bihar have been found.

HISTORIC PERIOD

Use of iron brought about wide-ranging transformation in human culture. A new material culture developed. Vedic culture expanded up to North Bihar in East India during the Later Vedic Period (1000-600 BC). The Shatapatha Brahmana, authored by Yajnavalkya, is the oldest and the greatest Brahmana scripture and contains details of growth of Aryans. According to the Shatapatha Brahmana, Aryans first entered India in its north-western region. The Saraswati River was their centre of activities and large-scale worship ceremonies and rituals used to be performed there. The Shatapatha Brahmana contains stories of Madhava Videha and Gautam Rahugana, according to which it was Madhava Videha who had expanded the Aryan culture up to North Bihar. By the time the later Vedic Period entered its middle phase, the Aryans had already expanded to Magadh, Anga, Vajji, Videha, Anguttarappa and Kaushiki regions in Bihar. King Madhava Videha and his priest Gautam Rahugana marched from the bank of the Saraswati River, keeping Agni the fire god burning, towards East India and reached the Gandak River in Videha region of Bihar. Agni was doused in the Gandak River and that's how the Gandak is also known as 'Sadaneera'. Thus, evidences of expansion and settlement of the Aryans in Mithila Videha region is found in the Shatapatha Brahmana. References to Videha during the final phase of the Later Vedic Period are found due to creation of the Upanishads. King Janaka of Videha was a scholar and philosopher and had got the Upanishads developed. Details of dialogues between scholar Yajnavalkya and Gargi and Yajnavalkya and Maitreyi are available in the Brihadaranyaka Upanishad. Maitreyi was King Janaka's wife and sage Yajnavalkya used to visit his court.

A major reason of expansion of the Aryans towards the east of the Ganges Valley was the development of iron technology, and iron tools had been found in abundance there. Availability of iron led to growth in the field of agriculture, and this further resulted in urbanisation in ancient Bihar also.

SOCIO-RELIGIOUS REFORM MOVEMENTS IN ANCIENT BIHAR

Use of iron in the field of agriculture during the Later Vedic Period resulted in improvement in production that in turn led to complexities in socio-economic life of people. Expansion of agriculture created fresh demands for animals whereas during the Later Vedic Period, animals were actually being sacrificed with large-scale rituals

In the last phase of the Rigvedic Period (1500-1000 BC), i.e., by the time it was 1000 BC, social life was gripped by many kinds of evils. The Purusha Sukta of the 10th mandala of the Rigveda has the first reference to Varna system that took a complex form by the end of the Later Vedic Period. Social evils like untouchability had taken firm shape by sixth century BC. Women enjoyed good position during the Rigvedic period but their status turned miserable by the time the Later Vedic Period entered its last phase.

Socio-religious reform movements started to appear in protest of social complexities, rituals, untouchability etc. in the last phase of the Later Vedic Period (6th century BC). The primary reasons for these movements were :

1. Complexities of the Varna system and tense social life
2. Dissatisfaction with religious life
3. Emergence of new religious beliefs
4. Impact of new economy.

Many disbeliever and atheist communities or sects emerged during that period to oppose the Vedic religion. Some 62 such sects came up in North India alone; Buddhist sect and Jain sect are the prominent ones among them. The place of birth and place of action of both the sects have been Bihar only.

Buddhism

The founder of Buddhism, Gautam Buddha, was born at Aamraking of Lumbini Village in Kapilvastu (presently Piprahwa) he was the son of Suddhodana, Kshatriya king of Kapilavastu belonging to Shakya Dynasty, and Mahamaya Devi, Koliyan princess of Kaushala. Buddha's mother Mahamaya Devi died within a week of his birth. Hence, he was brought up by his maternal aunt and his stepmother Prajapati Gautami. Gautam Buddha was known as Siddhartha in his childhood. 'Gautama' means the rules of upbringing, and his family name also was 'Gautama'. As per Chinese literature, Buddha was born in 563 BC and he died at the age of 80 years in 483 BC. One fortune teller named Kaladevala had told Suddhodana at the time of Buddha's birth that the child would grow to be an ascetic. Hence, the king had imposed ban on his moving out of his palace, and arrangements for food and other facilities were made inside the palace itself. He was married at the age of 16 years to Shakya princess Yashodhara, also known as Bimba, Gopa, Bhadrakachcha, etc. He was blessed with a son at the age of 29 years; he named his son as Rahul. In the course of his city visits, he encountered 'four sights', viz., an old man, a diseased man, a decaying corpse, and an ascetic. As per Digha Nikaya, Gautama Buddha encountered all four signs during the same trip, but other sources indicate they were sighted during separate trips. Gautama Buddha got disillusioned towards worldly life after looking at the ascetic, and he decided to abandon his family life. At the age of 29 years, he left his palace in the middle of the night; this is referred to as 'Mahabhinishkramana' (the great departure). Siddhartha had left his palace in the middle of the night along with his horse Kanthaka and his charioteer Chhandaka. Birth, death and enlightenment of Buddha— all had happened on the day of the full moon of the month of Vaishakha whereas he had left his house on the day of the full moon of the month of Ashadha. At a place known as Anuvin close to the Anoma River, Buddha removed his robes. For his enlightenment, Buddha underwent learning under two initial gurus—first, in Vaishali, Sankhya philosophy scholars Alara Kalama and his disciple Marandu Kalama and later, Rudrak Ramaputra, in Rajgriha. However, Buddha was not satisfied with their teachings, and he reached Uruvela (Bodh Gaya) forest. He performed rigorous meditation there along with his five followers namely Kaundinya, Aja, Assiga, Vappa and Bhadiya. When even that meditation did not help attain enlightenment, all his followers abandoned him pronouncing him to be a hypocrite. Gautama Buddha started deep meditation afresh at the bank of the Niranjana River (Falgu) near Gaya. It was at the age of 35 on the 49th day of his meditation when he accepted milk and rice pudding (Kheer) from a girl named Sujata that he attained enlightenment, and he came to be known as Bodhisattva. The incident of enlightenment is referred to as 'Nirvana' in Buddhism. Two wanderers Trapusa and Bhallika were the first to be taken as Buddha's disciples in Bodh Gaya. After enlightenment, Gautama Buddha went to Sarnath (Rishipattana). Five of his followers there were the first to be taught by him. This first teaching is known as 'Dharmachakra Pravartana'. At Sarnath itself, Buddha established the first Buddhist Sangha. After this, Buddha reached Varanasi and stayed with Yasha, son of a rich man. Yasha, along with his parents and wife, turned Mahatma Buddha's disciple. Yasha's mother and his wife were the first female disciples of Mahatma Buddha. In the course of his journey from Varanasi to Uruvela, Buddha met 30 rich youths led by Bhadra. They all became Buddha's followers. After Uruvela, he went to Rajgriha where King Bimbisara offered him Venuvana Vihara as gift. He got some new disciples like Sariputra, Modglayan, and Upali in Rajgriha. After Rajgriha, Buddha arrived at Lumbini where he brought in female disciples into Buddhist Sangha. His step-mother Prajapati Gautami was the first woman to join Sangha. Buddha had agreed to take in women under Buddhism only at the request of his disciple Ananda. While permitting women to join Buddhism, he had remarked that Buddhism that would have run for thousand years would now vanish in just 500 years. His cousin brother Deodutta also joined him as his disciple in Lumbini. In his eighth year after enlightenment, Buddha reached Vaishali where Lichchavis offered him a Vihara named Kutagrashala. At Vaishali, Amrapali, the royal courtesan of Vaishali joined Gautama Buddha as his disciple. Kshema, wife of Magadh king Bimbisara, also became his disciple. In his 20th year after enlightenment, Buddha reached Shravasti, capital of Kosala, where dacoit Angulimala became his disciple. Shravasti was the place where Buddha lived most after his enlightenment and taught his disciples. At the age of 80, Buddha died in 483 BC due to stomach disease after consuming pork at the house of a goldsmith named Chund at Pava, capital of South Malla. The event of his death is known as Mahaparinirvana. At the time of Buddha's death, his disciple Ananda asked him as to who would be his successor after him. Buddha replied that his teachings only would be their guide after him. The last words of Buddha were, 'Appo Deepo Bhava'.

As per the Buddhist literature 'Mahaparinirvana Sutra', eight rulers had come to collect his remains after Buddha's death. Thus, his remains, including his bones were divided into eight portions. Stupas have been built over those eight portions.

Given are the list of the rulers who had collected the mortal remains of Buddha and built stupas over the same.

Name of Ruler	Name of Kingdom	Name of Ruler	Name of Kingdom
Ajatashatru	Magadh	Buli	Alakappa
Shakya	Kapilavastu	Malla	Pava
Lichchavi	Vaishali	Moriya	Pippalivan
Brahman	Vethadweep	Koliya	Ramgram

Prominent disciples of Gautama Buddha and followers of Buddhism:

1. Sariputra
2. Ananda
3. Modglayan
4. Upali
5. Sunit
6. Anuruddha
7. Anath Pindak
8. Bimbisar
9. Prasenjit
10. Ajatshatru
11. Jivak
12. Mahakashyap

Prominent women followers of Buddhism:

1. Mahaprajapati Gautami
2. Yashodhara
3. Nanda
4. Kshema or Khema
5. Amrapali
6. Vishakha

Principles of Buddhism:

Gautama Buddha's teachings were quite simple. He first of all propounded four noble truths:

1. Dukkha (Pain and misery)
2. Samudaya (Origin of dukkha)
3. Nirodha (Cessation of dukkha)
4. Marga (Path leading to cessation of dukkha)

Gautama Buddha propounded noble Eightfold Path for cessation of dukkha. These eight practices are:

1. Right View, i.e., understanding of truth and untruth
2. Right Resolve, i.e., resolve devoid of desire and violence
3. Right Speech, i.e., speaking truth and being soft-spoken
4. Right Action, i.e., acting truthfully
5. Right Livelihood, i.e., leading a simple life
6. Right Effort, i.e., working in the right direction
7. Right Mindfulness, i.e., being mindful of one's actions
8. Right Concentration, i.e., being focussed.

Buddhism suggests 10 precepts in order to follow the Eightfold Path and observe rightfulness in life. These 10 precepts are the moral basics of life. They are also referred to as 'Shiksha Pad'. They are as following:

1. Non-violence
2. Truth
3. Asteya (non-stealing)
4. Aparigraha (non-possessing)
5. Observing brahmacharya
6. Not indulging in adultery
7. Not drinking
8. Not eating without routine
9. Keeping away from song and dance
10. Renunciation of comfortable beds

Truth, non-violence, asteya, aparigraha and brahmacharya were mandatory for everybody in Buddhism; the other five were mandatory for Buddhist bhikshus.

In Buddhism, the origins of dukkha are referred to as 'Pratitya Samutpada'. There are 12 chakras in Pratitya Samutpada and they are known as 'Dvadasa Nidanas'. They are as following:

1. Avidya
2. Samskara
3. Vijnana (Consciousness)
4. Namarupa

5. Sadayatana (Collection of five senses and mind)
6. Sparsa
7. Vedana
8. Trishna
9. Upadana (Attachment to worldly materials)
10. Bhava (Becoming)
11. Jati (Birth)
12. Jaramarana

Buddhism is an agnostic religion. Buddhists believe in reincarnation but do not believe in a soul. They believe the principle of karma and that karma leads to future consequences. In Buddhism, it's possible to attain nirvana while still alive but mahaparinirvana is possible only after death.

After Gautama Buddha, Buddhism was protected and promoted by Ashoka, Kanishka, Harshavardhana and Pala rulers. Not only in India, but Buddhism also spread to places like Southeast Asia, Sri Lanka, China, Tibet, Japan, and Central Asia. Following were the main reasons for Buddhism being successful in India:

1. Buddhism being simple and populist religion
2. Use of popular language Pali
3. Religion of middle path
4. Royal protection, e.g., Bimbisar, Ajatashatru, Kalashok, Ashoka, etc. provided protection to Hinayana school while Kanishka, Harshavardhana and Pal rulers protected Mahayana school of Buddhism.
5. Contributions of Buddhist educational institutions, e.g., Buddhist educational institutions like Nalanda, Vikramashila and Odantapuri made significant contributions towards promotion of teachings in Buddhism.
6. Absence of aggressively competitive cults
7. Buddhism laid emphasis on the notion of equality and freedom.

However, Buddhism started declining by the onset of third to fourth century. The most important factor for its decline was the corruption and moral degeneration prevalent in Buddhist monasteries.

Following were the prominent factors for decline of Buddhism:

1. Corruption and moral degeneration rampant in Buddhist monasteries
2. External invasions, e.g., Bakhtiar Khilji had burnt and destroyed Nalanda and Vikramashila universities.
3. Absence of royal protection.
4. Resurgence of Hinduism.
5. Power of communion and unification in Hindu religion.

Buddhist Councils (Sangiti)

Gautama Buddha died in 483 BC. A monk named Subhadra remarked at the time of Gautam Buddha's death that we had got liberty. His remarks had made Gautama Buddha's followers sensed a danger of division in Buddhism. Hence, Buddhist councils started getting organised in order to avoid the same. As a result, four Buddhist councils were organised.

Council	Year	Place	Presided by	Ruler	Main Activities
First	483 BC	Saptaparni cave, Rajgriha	Mahakashyapa	Ajatashatru	Compilation of Sutta and Vinaya Pitakas
Second	383 BC	Vaishali	Sarvakami	Kalashok	Division of Sthaviras and Mahasanghikas
Third	249 BC	Pataliputra	Mogaliputta Tissa	Ashoka	Compilation of Abhidhamma Pitaka
Fourth	95 CE	Kundalavana (Kashmir)	Vasumitra Vice-president - Ashvaghosh	Kanishka	Division of Hinayana and Mahayana

Buddhism has had significant impact on Indian culture and civilisation. Following are the main contributions of Buddhism to Indian culture:

1. Buddhism provided a simple, understandable and popular religion to Indian lifestyle.
2. Buddhism facilitated arrival of high moral standards.
3. Sangha system was started. Sangha system was based on democratic structure.
4. A new philosophical ideology emerged.
5. It helped, beginning of idol worship.
6. Folk literature developed.
7. There was development of stupa, chaitya, etc. in Indian art.

Buddhist Scriptures

Buddhist scriptures are referred to as 'Tripitaka Grantha'. They are in Pali language. These three pitakas are Sutta Pitaka, Vinaya Pitaka, and Abhidhamma Pitaka.

Sutta Pitaka: Gautama Buddha's teachings and religious discourses are compiled in Sutta Pitaka. Ananda was instrumental in compiling this. There are five sections in Sutta Pitaka.

1. Digha Nikaya: This comprises Buddha's discourses and details of Mahanirvana Sutta and Eightfold Path. Buddhaghosa has written commentaries titled Sumangalavilasini and Samantapasadika on Digha Nikaya.
2. Majjhima Nikaya.
3. Anguttara Nikaya: 16 Mahajanapadas have been mentioned for the first time here.
4. Samyukta Nikaya.
5. Khuddaka Nikaya: This has compilation of 549 jataka tales related to former lives of Buddha.

Vinaya Pitaka: This comprises rules of Buddhism and was compiled by Upali. It has three sections.

1. Suttavibhanga
2. Khandhaka
3. Parivara.

Abhidhamma Pitaka: This was compiled during third Buddhist Council and is in the form of questions and answers. It contains philosophical explanation of Buddhism, and was compiled by Mogaliputta Tissa. It's most important part is Kathavastu.

Other Important Scriptures

Buddhist Literature	Author	Details
Jataka Tales	–	They are 549 in number. They have stories of former lives of Buddha.
Milinda Panha Language - Pali	Nagasena	It's a record of the dialogue between Buddhist sage Nagasena and Bactrian ruler Menander.
Vishuddhi Magga	Buddhaghosa	It is a philosophical treatise on Buddhism.
Nidana Katha	Buddhaghosa	It is the sole biography of Gautama Buddha in Pali language.
Attha Kathas		A commentary on Tripitaka.
Abhidhamma Kosha	Vasubandhu	It provides information related to computation of time and period.
Sudarbha Pundarik	Vasubandhu	It is related to Mahayana Buddhism. Bhagwan Buddha has been referred to as Amitabh, sitting in paradise.
Prajnaparamita	Nagarjuna	It provides details of the doctrine of emptiness.

Akutomaya	Nagarjuna	
Lalit Vistar	Vasumitra	It is known as 'Light of India'.
Vibhasha Sutra	Vasumitra	It is related to the fourth Buddhist Council that was held at the time of Kanishka.
Sounderananda	Ashvaghosha	It contains details about Sounderananda, stepbrother of Buddha, accepting Buddhism.
Buddha Charita	Ashvaghosha	It is referred to as the 'Mahakavya' of Buddhism.
Deepavansha		It contains history of Sri Lanka.
Mahavansha	Bhadanta Mahanama	It has details about the third Buddhist Council that was conducted by Ashoka. A commentary named 'Vanshanapatha' has been written on this work.
Divyavadana	-	A Nepali literature that has two parts, viz., 'Ashokavadana' and 'Kunalavadana'.

Buddhist Sect

A difference of opinion in Buddhism had surfaced during second Buddhist Council (383 BC). The Buddhist bhikshukas who believed in basic teachings and precepts and who were called Sthaviras or Theravadis or Hinasanghikas, expelled those who had difference of opinion, from Buddha Sangha. Those Buddhist bhikshukas who were expelled and were in favour of changes were called Mahasanghikas or Sarvastivadi. Mahakachchayana was the founder of Sthavira Sect and Mahakashyapa was the founder of Mahasanghika Sect.

After the third Buddhist Council that was organised in 249 BC, Sthaviras gradually disappeared from India, and there was emergence of Sarvastivada or Vaibhashika Sect in their place.

After the fourth Buddhist Council, Buddhism was clearly divided into two sects—Hinayana and Mahayana. Hinayana was basically the sect of Sthaviras whereas Mahayana belonged to Mahasanghikas. Hinayana is the Sect that believes in Buddha's pure religious principles like Four Noble Truths, Eightfold Path, 10 Precepts etc. 'Arhat' is the ideal for this Sect. 'Arhat' is referred to the one that makes effort for his own Nirvana only. Hinayana Sect believes Buddha to be a human and opposes idol worship.

Mahayana sect professes changes in basic ideology of Buddha. It was in Mahayana only that Buddha was believed to be God and idol worship was started. Sanskrit is the language of Mahayana's literature. Mahayana believes in Sarvamukti, and they refer to Buddha as Bodhisattva.

Buddhist Sangha

Buddha had established the Sangha in Sarnath with the help of his five disciples. Buddhist Sangha is based on democratic system. A minimum age of 15 years was required for anybody to join the Sangha. Nobody could join the Sangha without his parents' consent. The following people were prohibited from entering the Sangha:

1. A person with age less than 15 years
2. Thief
3. Murderer
4. Borrower
5. Royal Servants
6. Soldier
7. Sick.

Jainism (Jain Dharma)

The word 'Jain' comes from the Sanskrit word 'Jina' that means conqueror. A victorious person is referred to as 'Veetaraga' in Jainism. Jainism is an ancient religion, and its promoters or leaders are referred to as 'Tirthankaras'. There were 24 Tirthankaras in Jain Dharma. The first Tirthankara Rishabhadeo (Adinatha) is known as the founder of Jainism. Out of 24 Tirthankaras, historical evidences of only the 23rd Tirthankara Parshvanatha and 24th and the last Tirthankara Mahavira are available. Historical evidences for the earlier 22 Tirthankaras have not been found.

Parshvanatha was the son of Kashi ruler Ashvasena. He renounced the world when he was just 30. He meditated for 83 days at Samveta Hill before he attained omniscience. He was critic of vedic rituals and polytheism. His followers were called 'Nigranthi'. Nigranthi means free from shackles. His main follower was Keshi. His four primary teachings are:

1. Truth
2. Non-violence
3. Asteya (non-stealing)
4. Aparigraha (non-possessing).

The parents of 24th Tirthankara Mahavira were followers of Parshvanatha. Mahavira was born in 540 BC at Kundagram in Vaishali. His mother Trishala (Videhadatta) was the sister of Lichchavi ruler Chetaka. His father Siddhartha was a Kshatriya of Ikshvaku Dynasty. Mahavira was married to Yashoda of Kundian Dynasty. He had a daughter named Priyadarshana who was married to Jamali. Mahavira died at the age of 72 in 468 BC at Pavapuri. His childhood name was Vardhamana. After the death of his father, he renounced the world and left his home at the age of 30, after taking permission from his elder brother Nandivardhana. Thirteen months after leaving his house, he discarded his clothes. After 12 years of rigorous penance, at the age of 42, he attained omniscience under a Sala tree on the bank of the River Rijupalika near Jambhika Grama. After that omniscience, Mahavira was known as Kaivalya. Kaivalya means the person attaining the highest knowledge. His followers are called Jainis and his chief disciple was Indrabhuti Gautama. After omniscience, Mahavira delivered his first teaching at Rajgriha. Jamali was his first disciple. Among his contemporary rulers, Bimbisara, Ajatashatru, Udayan, Pradyotsena, etc., were his followers.

Teachings of Jain Dharma

Jainism has the principle of 'Triratna', also known as 'Three Jewels'. The principles of Triratna include:

1. Right conduct
2. Right knowledge
3. Right faith.

Out of the three, maximum emphasis has been laid on the 'Right Conduct'. Jainism is also an agonistic religion. This religion believes in soul and reincarnation but does not believe in God. In order to maintain moral conduct, five mahavratas (vows) have been propounded under Jainism. They are:

1. Truth
2. Non-violence
3. Asteya (non-stealing)
4. Aparigraha (non-possessing)
5. Brahmacharya (sexual continence).

First four of the above vows were put forward by the 23rd Tirthankara Parshvanatha, whereas Bhagwan Mahavira added the last one—Brahmacharya. Strict rules to follow five mahavratas have been framed for the Jain ascetics. However, it has been made lenient, in the form of 'Anuvratas', for householders.

Besides the five mahavratas and various anuvratas, a lot of emphasis has been laid in Jainism also on observing and following three 'Gunavratas' and four 'Shikshavratas'.

Three Anuvratas

1. Every householder should determine the limits of his responsibilities as per his convenience.
2. Only just and exemplary activities should be performed.

3. Limits of food and enjoyment should be prescribed, and they should not be crossed.

Four Shikshavratas

1. Deshavirati—vow not to cross the boundary of a territory.
2. Samayika vrata—meditate at least four times a day, free from worldly worries.
3. Propodyopavas—fasting.
4. Vaiyavritya—vow to donate, worship.

Kaya klesha has an important place in Jainism. A provision to leave body by fasting exists in Jainism; this is known as Sanlekhana Process (Santhara) and Nisiddhi. As per Jain legend, Chandragupta Maurya had left this world by following this very process in Shravanabelagola (Mysore).

Jain Philosophy

Jainism believes in soul and reincarnation. Sankhya philosophy and Jainism are closely related. Jain Dharma accepts existence of deities but their position has been kept below Jina/Mahavira. As per Jain philosophy, God is not the real power behind existence of this world. The world is real and true and is divided into several chakras. Every chakra has two periods—Utsarpini, i.e., period of growth and progress and Avasarpini, i.e., period of decline. There is no place for cataclysm or end of the world in this Dharma. This world is made of living and non-living beings. Living beings are conscious elements, and non-living things are inanimate and senseless.

Five kinds of knowledge have been described under Jainism.

1. Mati meaning sensory knowledge
2. Sruthi meaning knowledge acquired by listening to others
3. Avadhi meaning divine knowledge
4. Mahaparyaya meaning knowledge gained by reading the minds and thoughts of others
5. Kaivalya meaning attainment of the ultimate knowledge.

Jainism provides the principles of Anekantavada and Syadvada. Syadvada is also referred to as 'Saptabhangi'. Jains have developed the concept of 'Saptabhanginyaya' to explain the Supreme Element. This is referred to as 'Syadvada' philosophically. Syadvada means possibly or 'may be'. Seven elements of Syadvada are the following:

1. Syad-asti—'in some ways it is'
2. Syad-nasti—'in some ways it is not'
3. Syad-asti-ch—nasti-'in some ways it is and it is not'
4. Syad-avaktavyam—'in some ways it is indescribable'
5. Syad-asti-avaktavyam—'in some ways it is and it is indescribable'
6. Syad-nasti-avaktavyam—'in some ways it is not and it is indescribable'
7. Syad-asti-nasti-avaktavyam—'in some ways it is, it is not and it is indescribable'.

Karma and bondage have been explained in Jainism. Eight kinds of karma have been listed. Mutual intermingling of soul and karma is bondage. With the help of knowledge, all the eight kinds of karmas may be destroyed and moksha may be attained. As per Jain Dharma, body and soul are by nature free but the soul gets entangled in karmic bondage because of ignorance. Five states of union and disunion between karma and soul have been explained in Jainism. These five states have been referred to as 'Tattva'. They are as follows:

Astava—Karma getting attracted to soul.

Bandhan (Bondage) - Karmic matter enters the soul and grabs it.

Samvara—Stoppage of influx of material karmas into the soul consciousness to prevent them from entering the soul.

Nirjara—Removal, with the help of knowledge, of karmas associated with the birth of a being.

Moksha—When all material karmas get destroyed, the soul attains true and pristine nature of infinite bliss, infinite knowledge and infinite perception. This is called Moksha or Kaivalya.

Jain Councils

Council	Year	Place	Presided by	Ruler	Main Activities
First	322–298 BC	Pataliputra	Sthoolabhadra	Chandragupta Maurya	12 parts were compiled and Jainism divided into two parts— Digambara and Shwetambara.
Second	512 BC	Vallabhi	Devardhi Kshamashravan		Jain religious texts were compiled in their final form.

Jain Literature

Jain literature is known as 'Agam Grantha'. Its language is Prakrit. Some Jain literatures have been written in Magadhi and Ardhamagadhi languages also. They include 12 Angas, 12 Upangas, 10 Prakirnas, 6 Chedasutras, 4 Mulasutras and Anuyogasutras. Following are the prominent literary works in Jain Dharma:

1. **14 Purvas:** This work is the sole literature of Digambara Jain.
2. **12 Angas:** This work was authored by Sthoolabhadra. Its main parts are:
   - **Acharang Sutra:** It describes the rules relating to conduct and behaviour of Jain bhikshus.
   - **Bhagawati Sutra:** It describes the doctrine of swarga (heaven) and naraka (hell) and also contains the life sketch of Jain Tirthankaras. About 16 Mahajanapadas have been detailed for the first time in this Bhagawati Sutra.
   - **Uttaradhyayan Sutra:** This work contains details of the dialogue between Indrabhuti Gautam and Kesi Prajapati. It only was instrumental in developing Jain sect.
3. **Kalpa Sutra:** Authored by Bhadrabahu, this sork describes 11 Ganadharas. Ganadhara is a person who is equal to Mahavira. A Ganadhara in Jainism has the same position as that of Ananda in Buddhism.
4. **Parishishtaparvana:** This work was written by Hemachandra. Hemachandra was a scholar in the court of Chalukya Dynasty in Gujarat. He was equivalent to Bhadrabahu in 1200 CE, and after Bhadrabahu, he was the greatest scholar of Jain Dharma. Parishishtaparvana is a short history of Jainism. As per this work, there was a 12-year-long famine during the period of Chandragupta Maurya. Chandragupta Maurya was a follower of Jain Dharma. He went to Shravanabelagola (Mysore) along with Bhadrabahu; he died there after long fasting.
5. **Avasadagao:** This work contains stories of 13 wealthy businessmen who had accepted Jainism.

Various Sects in Jainism

1. **Shwetambara:** During the famine in Magadh, Sthoolabhadra stayed in Magadh with his followers, and he started using white dress. Shwetambara Jains are called 'Yati', 'Sadhu', and 'Acharya'. They are liberal in following the rules. Shwetambara followers treat food as essential, and they believe that Mahavira Swami was married and had a daughter also.
2. **Digambara:** There was a severe famine in Magadh during the reign of Chandragupta Maurya. After the famine, Bhadrabahu, along with his followers, left for South India and he discarded his clothes. Digambara followers abide by the rules very meticulously. They treat directions and the sky as their clothes

(dik+ambara). Digambara Jains are called 'Jhullaka', 'Aillaka' and 'Nirgrantha'. Digambara Jains believed that food is not a necessity after omniscience. They believed Mahavira to be unmarried.

In due course, Shwetambara and Digambara further divided into many sub-sects.

- Sub-sects of Shwetambara—Pujera or Deravasi and Dhundhia or Sthanakavasi.
- Sub-sects of Digambara—Bisapanthi, Terapanthi and Samaiyapanthi or Taranapanthi.

Pujera Jains visit temples and worship Jain Tirthankaras. Dhundhia or Sthanakavasi Jains only follow the principles. Bisapanthi and Terapanthi Jains worship idols of Tirthankaras, whereas Taranapanthi do not worship idols.

Atheist sects, other than Buddhist and Jains, that emerged during sixth century BC are the following:

- **Akriyavadi Sect:** This was founded by Puran Kashyapa. According to this sect, acts do not have any consequences.
- **Ajivaka Sect:** This was founded by Makkhali Gosala. This was a group of religious people. Maurya ruler Bindusara, Ashoka, and his grandson Dashratha had provided protection to the Ajivaka Sect.
- **Bhautikavadi Sect:** This was founded by Ajit Keshakambali. It was also known as Lokayata Sect. It was the one to propound the Charvak philosophy. Charvak means group of people adept at pleasant speaking. As per Charvak philosophy, Vedas were created by liars and wicked and non-vegetarian people. This sect does not believe in God and reincarnation. Out of dharma, artha, karma and moksha, it accepts only artha and karma. The famous saying of this sect is –

यावत् जीवेत् सुखं जीवेत् ऋणं कृत्वा घृतं पिबेत् ।
भस्मीभूतस्य कर्तारौ भण्डधूर्तनिशाचाराः ।।

- **Meaning:** As long you live, live happily; drink ghee even if you have to incur debt for that. In other words, you do whatever you need to do for your happiness.
- **Anishchayavadi Sect:** This was founded by Sanjay Velatthaputra. According to this sect, no definite answer is possible for any question. This is a sceptical sect.

POLITICAL HISTORY OF BIHAR

An attempt to determining the political history of India has been first made by Portziter. The people dependent word 'Jana' is found to have been used as a political unit during Rigveda period. Region dependent word 'Janapada' came into usage in the Later Vedic period. Around 600 BC, Mahajanapadas were created by uniting multiple Janapadas. Reference to 16 Mahajanapadas can be found in Buddha period. The first mention of 16 Mahajanapadas is found in Buddhist literature 'Anguttar Nikaya' and Jain literature Bhagawati Sutra'. Following were the 16 Mahajanapadas:

Sl No.	Mahajanapada	Capital	Present Position
1	Kashi	Varanasi	Uttar Pradesh
2	Kosala	Ayodhya or Shrawasti	Uttar Pradesh
3	Anga	Champa	Bihar
4	Magadh	Rajgriha or Girivraj	Bihar
5	Vajji	Vaishali	Bihar
6	Malla	North Malla - Kushinagar, South Malla - Pavapuri	Uttar Pradesh & Bihar

7	Chedi	Shuktimati	Uttar Pradesh
8	Vatsa	Kaushambi	Uttar Pradesh
9	Kuru	Indraprastha	Haryana
10	Panchal	North Panchal - Ahichchhatra, South Panchal - Kampilya	Uttar Pradesh
11	Matsya	Virat Nagar	Rajasthan
12	Shoorasena	Mathura	West Uttar Pradesh
13	Ashmaka	Patan/Potan	Andhra Pradesh
14	Avanti	North Avanti - Ujjain, South Avanti - Mahishmati	Madhya Pradesh
15	Gandhar	Takshashila	Afghanistan
16	Kamboj	Hatak	Afghanistan

Out of the above 16 Mahajanapadas, 2 Mahajanapadas Gandhar and Kamboj are located in Afghanistan, but Takshashila, the capital of Gandhar, is presently located in Pakistan. Out of the above 16 Mahajanapadas, 3 Mahajanapadas, viz,. Magadh, Anga and Vajji are located in Bihar. The capital of Anga, which is mentioned first time in Atharvaveda, was Champa, near present Bhagalpur. Anga has also been referred to as Vanga, Kalinga and Pundru in 'Ashtadhyayi' written by Panini. Anga Mahajanapada extended from the Eastern part of Bihar up to the Bay of Bengal. Regions of Manbhum, Veerbhum, Murshidabad and Santhal Pargana were parts of this Mahajanapada. As per Mahabharata and other Puranas, one of the 6 sons of King Bali had established the Anga Mahajanapada. According to the same sources, Champa town was established on the name of Champ, son of Prithulaksha, and this very town was chosen as the capital of Anga. When Anga ruler Brahmadutta defeated Bhatti, father of Magadh ruler Bimbisara, Bimbisara got angry and attacked Anga and was able to kill Brahmadutta with the help of Nagaraja, ruler of Chhotanagpur region. After taking over Anga, Bimbisara appointed a Brahmin Shenadanda as the jagirdar of Champa. Thus, Brahmadutta was the last ruler of Anga Mahajanapada. Anga was fully merged into Magadha during the reign of Magadha emperor Ajatashatru. Five out of 16 Mahajanapadas emerged stronger on account of their geographic and economic conditions.

Vajji Mahajanapada was established around 725 BC. This was a Sangha (union) of 8 states. The states included in this Mahajanapada were Lichchavi, Videha, Gyataka, Vajji, Ugra, Bhoga, Kaurava, and Ikshvaku. The capitals of Lichchavi, Videha, Gyataka and Vajji were Vaishali, Mithila, Kundagrama and Kollaga, respectively.

Vaishali was the capital of entire Vajji sangha. Lichchavi was the most famous among the 8 states. Hence, Vajji sangha is also known as Lichchavi sangha. Vaishali had established a democratic set up and hence, it is also known as the first democracy of the world. Vaishali was named after King Vishal. Magadha ruler Bimbisara had married Chellana, daughter of Lichchavi king Chetaka; hence, during the reign of Bimbisara, there was good friendship between Magadha and Lichchavi sanghas. However, when Bimbisara's son Ajatashatru took over as the ruler, Vajjis, protesting against Ajatashatru, had colluded with Malla and Kosala to establish a Mahasangha. This Mahasangha included

9 Ganarajyas of Lichchavi, 9 Ganarajyas of Malla and 18 Ganarajyas of Kashi and Kosala. According to Buddhist scholar Buddhaghosa, Vajjis had formulated a constitution for its governance system and their Raja (the ruling chief) was elected through the same. There used to be 7707 Rajas to govern Vajji sangha. Along with the Raja, even Uparaja (the deputy chief), Senapati (the chief of the army) and Bhandargari (the chancellor of exchequer) were elected. Meetings of Lichchavi sangha used to be held in assembly hall known as Santhagara. The council of Lichchavi Rajas was called Sanstha, and it was the highest council of the ganarajya. Besides this sanstha, there was another sanstha named Ashtukula comprising of representatives of all 8 ganarajyas of Vajji sangha; this sanstha used to function as judicial Mahasamiti. Gramini and Purnagamik were appointed for supervising administration of village and town administrations. The Gramini was the head of a village. Purnagamik was the head of industrial production units. In reference to the democratic system of the Vajjis, Gautama Buddha had remarked that Vajji sangha would never be defeated till the time their people keep following their 7 necessary dhammas. The meetings of Vajji sangha were presided by Ganapramukha (head of democracy) and ganapurti (quorum) was essential for those meetings. The requirement of number for ganapurti was set as 20. All decisions in Vajji sangha were taken on the basis of votes. The ballots, made of wood in different colours, used to be provided to all the members.

The periods of all the 4 rulers, Bimbisara, Udayin, Pradyotasena and Prasenajit fall in the latter half of 6th century BC. They were all contemporary to Buddha and Mahavira. All the 5 fought for their domination and finally, Magadha was victorious.

EMERGENCE OF MAGADHA EMPIRE

The first mention of the word 'Magadha' is found in 'Atharvaveda'. Magadha is the region in Bihar to the south of the Ganges. It basically comprises the areas of Patna, Gaya, Nalanda, Nawadah and Aurangabad. Rajgriha and Pataliputra were the focal points of Magadha Empire. Magadha was able to establish its supremacy over other Mahajanapadas on account of its geographic location and its affluence in economic resources.

Reasons Behind Ascendance of Magadha Empire

1. **Geographic Location:** The capital of Magadha was surrounded by hills from all sides. Hence, it was secured from external aggressions. The Ganges and the Son rives passing through Magadha provided means of water transport. The southern basin of the Ganges was quite fertile and was perfect for agriculture.
2. **Availability of Mineral Resources:** Iron, copper and forest resources were found in abundance in the southern part of Magadha. Availability of iron helped in making the best weapons and implements and agricultural productivity reached great heights.
3. **Decline of Other Ganarajyas:** Both Buddhism and Jainism emerged in Magadha region and rulers in this region supported them. The rulers enjoyed large-scale support from the people in this region because of their support for Buddhism and Jainism.

Vrihadratha Dynasty

Though historically, the first dynasty to rule Magadha was Haryanka Dynasty under which the Magadha Empire arose, puranic sources mention Vrihadratha Dynasty as Magadha's first Dynasty. Vrihadratha was the initiator of this dynasty. His father was Chediraja Vassu. Its capital was Vasumati or Girivraja or Kushagrapur. Jarasandha was the most famous king of this dynasty. Description of the malla-yuddha between Jarasandha and Bhim is found in the Mahabharata. According to legend, signs of this yuddha are available even today on the rocks of Rajgriha. He had also defeated the kings of Kashi, Kosala, Chedi, Malwa, Videha, Anga, Kalinga, Kashmir and Gandhar. After Jarasandha's death, his son Sahadeo took over the reins. The last ruler of the Vrihadratha Dynasty was Ripunjaya. His minister Pulaka had killed Ripunjaya and installed his own son as ruler. Later, a courtier Maheeya killed both Pulaka and his son and installed his own son Bimbisara on the throne.

Haryanka Dynasty

The first mention of the words 'Magadha' and 'Bihar' has been made in Atharvaveda. The Magadha Empire established by Bimbisara or Shrenika of the Haryanka Dynasty is considered to be the first empire of India.

Bimbisara (544–492 BC): As per Buddhist scripture Mahavansha, Bimbisara, the founder of the Haryanka Dynasty, occupied the throne at the age of just 15 years, and it was in his reign only when the Magadha Empire started expanding. He established Rajgriha as his capital and rule Magadha for 52 years. Mahagovinda was the architect of Rajgriha.

Ajatashatru (492–460 BC): Like his father Bimbisara, Ajatashatru was also a ruler with imperialistic temperament. He was a follower of Jainism. He was also known with his nickname Kunika. There were three major revolts during his regime, and all of them ended in his favour.

War against Kosala: After Bimbisara's death, his wife Kosala Devi also met with her end unable to bear the grief. This infuriated Prasenajit, and he recaptured many of the villages of Kashi that had been earlier passed on to Magadha. This act resulted in a war over Kashi between Ajatashatru and Kosala ruler Prasenajit, in which Prasenajit was defeated. He fled and took refuge in Shrawasti. In their second war, Ajatashatru was defeated; however, he managed to bring an end to their dispute by marrying Prasenajit's daughter Vajira. Kosala was completely merged with Magadha while Ajatashatru was still in power.

Conflict with Vajji Sangha: After his victory over Kosala, Ajatashatru managed to disunite Vajji Sangha with the help of his minister Vassakara. Later, after 16-year-long battle, he was ultimately able to conquer Vaishali and merge the same into his Empire. Ajatashatru had used weapons like Kantaka Shila and Rathamusala in this war. He had built an army camp at the confluence of the Ganges, the Gandaka and the Son rivers to fight the Vajjis; this place was later known as Pataliputra. Keeping in mind the possibility of attack by Avanti ruler Paradyota, Ajatashatru had built a secured fort in Rajgriha; it is the oldest example of architecture in India.

War against Mallas: After defeating Lichchavis, Ajatashatru attacked and conquered the Malla Sangha and got the same merged into his empire. He befriended Vatsa using marital relationship. During the first 10 years of his regime, Ajatashatru built a stupa at Rajgriha over the remains of Gautama Buddha after his Mahaparinirvana. The nagaravadhu of Vaishali, Amrapali was in love with Ajatashatru. It was during his reign only when the first Buddhist Council was organised in the Saptaparni Cave at Rajgriha under the chairmanship of Mahakashyapa. Ajatashatru was killed by his own son Udayin, who took over the reigns after him.

Udayin (460–444 BC)

Udayin was the governor of Champa when his father Ajatashatru was in power. He established the town of Pataliputra at the confluence of the Ganges and the Son rivers and shifted the capital of Magadha from Rajgriha to Pataliputra. Udayin was a follower of Jainism. He built a Jain Chaityagriha at the centre of Pataliputra. Udayin was killed by Avanti ruler Palaka.

Kashi amatya Shishunaga had established the Shishunaga Dynasty after killing Nagadashaka, the last ruler of the Haryanka Dynasty. Nagadashaka is also referred to as 'Darshaka' in Puranas.

Shishunaga Dynasty (412–344 BC)

Shishunaga, governor of Kashi, occupied the throne of Magadha in 412 BC. He shifted the capital of Magadha from Pataliputra to Vaishali. Shishunaga registered victories over Vatsa, Avanti and Kaushambi. Shishunaga, after his death in 394 BC, was succeeded by his son Kalashoka (Kakavarna). He re-established Pataliputra as the capital of Magadha. Kalashoka was the greatest ruler of the Shishunaga Dynasty. It was during his reign only that the second Buddhist Council was organised in 383 BC at Vaishali. Nandivardhana was the last ruler of the Shishunaga Dynasty.

Nanda Dynasty (344–322 BC)

Mahapadma Nanda, after exterminating the Shishunaga Dynasty, took over the Magadha Empire and established the Nanda Dynasty. Magadha reached the pinnacle of its glory under the Nanda Dynasty. Under this dynasty, Nanda and his eight sons ruled over Magadha. Mahapadma Nanda and Dhanananda were the greatest rulers of this dynasty. Mahapadma Nanda has also been described as 'Kali Ka Ansh', 'Sarvakshatrantaka', 'Second Parshurama', 'Bhargava', 'Ekarata', etc. In the Indian history, this was the first time that Mahapadma Nanda had established such a great empire the boundaries of which made intrusion in the basin of the Ganges. It was Magadha ruler Mahapadma Nanda only who had first hoisted the victory flag to the south of Vindhya Hills. Mahapadma Nanda conquered Odisha and built canals there. A monarchical regime was established in this vast empire.

Nanda rulers followed Jainism and were related to Shudra caste. Mahapadma Nanda had shifted a Jain idol from Odisha to Magadha. After his reign Dhanananda was the last ruler of Magadha. It was during Dhanananda's period when the Greek ruler Alexander invaded India in 326 BC. The Nanda Dynasty met its end when Chandragupta Maurya defeated Dhanananda in 322 BC.

Maurya Dynasty (322-184 BC)

Chandragupta Maurya established the Maurya Empire after overthrowing the last ruler of the Nanda Dynasty and sat on the throne of Magadha. Chandragupta Maurya and Ashoka were the greatest rulers in this dynasty.

Chandragupta Maurya

Chandragupta Maurya was the founder of Maurya Empire. There is difference of opinion among scholars with regard to his birth and caste. According to Brahmana Granth, Vishnu Purana and Mudra Rakshasa, Chandragupta Maurya was a Shudra, whereas Spooner claims him to be a Parsika. Jain and Buddhist scriptures treated him to be related to a Kshatriya and Moriya Kshatriya family. Chandragupta Maurya is also known with names like Sandrocottus, Androcottus and Sandrocoptus.

Chandragupta Maurya, first of all, conquered north-western states of Punjab and Sindh with the help of Kautilya. He then attained victory over the Magadha Empire. Seleucus I Nicator had succeeded Alexander as the King of Babylon. Having a desire to conquer India, he marched towards the Sindhu River through Kabul; there, he had to face the army of Chandragupta Maurya. Seleucus was defeated in this battle, and he entered into a treaty with Chandragupta Maurya in 303 BC. Seleucus married off his daughter to Chandragupta Maurya and offered him Herat, Kandahar, Makaran Tat and Kabul as dowry. In return, Chandragupta Maurya offered 500 elephants to Seleucus as gift. Seleucus had sent an envoy to the court of Chandragupta Maurya; that envoy had authored the book 'Indica'.

Chandragupta Maurya is called the 'Liberator of India'. In the last year of his rule, Chandragupta Maurya relinquished his throne and left for Shravanabelagola (Mysore) along with Bhadrabahu to meditate at Chandragiri Hill. He died there following the Jain Sallekhana process.

Bindusara (298–73 BC)

After the death of Chandragupta Maurya, his son Bindusara ascended the throne of Magadha Empire in 298 BC. Greeks have called him 'Amitrochates' or 'Amitraghata' that means slayer of enemies. He also had another name 'Singhasena'.

Ashoka, the governor of Ujjain or Malwa was deputed to suppress the revolt in Takshashila during Bindusara's period. Syria ruler Antiochus I had appointed Diemachus and Egyptian ruler Ptolemy Philadelphus had sent Dionysius as ambassadors to the court of Bindusara. Just like his father, Bindusara was controlling administrative functions. He divided his empire into provinces and appointed a 'Kumar' as Uparaja in every province. He set up a council of ministers to attend administrative responsibilities. He also appointed several mahamatras. Bindusara was on the throne for 25 years before he died in 273 BC.

Ashoka (273–232 BC)

Bindusara was succeeded by Ashoka the Great, who ascended the throne of Magadha in 269 BC. As per Sinhala literature, Ashoka killed his 99 brothers to become the emperor, though there is difference of opinion in this regard. Ashoka definitely had fight with his brothers running for almost 4 years, as he was designated as the ruler in 273 BC itself whereas his coronation took place only in 269 BC.

Ashoka, as per Nepali literature, was the governor of Takshashila before being crowned, whereas as per Sri Lankan literature, he was the governor of Ujjain. Ashoka was earlier called Chandashoka or Kalashoka. The name Ashoka is found mentioned on his four inscriptions at Maski, Gurjara, Nettur, and Udegolam. He has been referred to as 'Priyadarshi' in Bhabru inscription whereas at Maski, he is called 'Buddha Shakya'. The only war that Ashoka fought in his life was the Kalinga War, which is detailed in his 13th Major Rock Edict. This war was fought in the 8th year of his reign in 261 BC. The horror of the Kalinga War changed Ashoka's heart. He abandoned his policy of war and embraced Dhamma and became the world's first promoter of peace. According to Kautilya, Kalinga war was fought for capturing the region having elephants whereas Pliny has indicated that the purpose of the war to gain control over the seacoast for business and commerce. 'Rajatarangini' authored by Kalhan mentions that Ashoka was a staunch Shiva devotee before embracing Buddhism. Ashoka was initiated in Buddhism by monk Upagupta or Moggaliputta Tissa. Ashoka had divided his empire into five provinces as below:

Province	Capital	Province	Capital
Uttarapath	Takshashila	Kalinga	Tosali
Dakshinapath	Swarnagiri	Prachi/ Eastern State	Pataliputra
Avanti	Ujjain		

Pataliputra was the capital for the entire Maurya kingdom. Ashoka had established the towns of Srinagar in Kashmir and Lalitapatan in Nepal. The Junagarh rock inscription of Rudradamana mentions the construction of water reservoir named Sudarshana at the Ujayanta Hill by Pushyagupta during the reign of Chandragupta Maurya. This was later renovated by Tushaspa during the reign of Ashoka, by Suvishakha during the reign of Rudradamana and by Chakrapalita during the reign of Skandagupta. Tushaspa was the governor of Avanti along with Ashoka. He was a Greek. After Ashoka, the Maurya Empire got divided into many parts. The eastern part covered Bihar, Bengal and Uttar Pradesh; this region was ruled by Dashratha who retained Pataliputra as his capital. The western region included Rajasthan, Gujarat and western Madhya Pradesh, which was ruled by another grandson of Ashoka, Samprati. Samprati is considered to be the best ruler of the Maurya Empire after Ashoka. As per Rajatarangini, Jalauka became the ruler of Kashmir region. The last ruler of the Maurya Dynasty, Vrihadratha, was killed in 185 BC by his Brahman Commander Pushyamitra, and the Shunga Dynasty was established.

Ashoka is famous not for his victory march but for his Dhamma policy. The word 'Dhamma' is Prakrit version of the word 'Dharma' in Sanskrit. Ashoka is considered great in the world history for his concerted efforts for moral upliftment of common people. Those very principles that may make moral upliftment possible have been referred to as Dhamma in Ashoka's inscriptions.

As per Ashoka, Dhamma is righteousness, doing a lot of good and welfare activities, being free from sin, being courteous to others, practising donation, kindness, non-violence, respecting parents, elders, relatives, and friends, behaving properly with servants and subordinates, etc. Additionally, Ashoka's Dhamma has some negative aspects also. Thus, violence, cruelty, anger, hatred etc. are barriers to a person's development. Hence, every person should keep away from them. Ashoka laid emphasis on self-check by every person on daily basis. According to Ashoka, man takes note of all his good works only; he never reflects on what immorality he has committed. He should ensure that his temperament of violence, cruelty, anger, and hatred does not lead him to a wrong path and make him commit a crime.

The above principles of Dhamma leaves nothing in doubt with regard to the fact that this is a dharma for common people, and its fundamental values are acceptable to all communities. This concept is not limited to a place or period. Ashoka was a follower of Buddhism. He worked for promotion of Buddhism, but Ashoka's Dhamma is not Buddhism, and he exhorts his people to follow Dhamma in their routine. His Dhamma is acceptable to all, is universal and the best; it establishes relationships, opposes external ostentation and laid emphasis on internal purity. Ashoka's inscriptions are classified into three parts:

1. Rock Edicts
2. Pillar Edicts
3. Cave Edicts

Rock Edicts

Famously known as '14 Major Edicts of Ashoka', this is a collection of 14 different rock edicts, which have been recovered from 8 different locations. They are as following:

1. Girnar (Near Junagarh in Kathiawad, Gujarat) (In Brahmi script)
2. Dhauli (Puri, Odisha) (In Brahmi script)
3. Jaugarh (Ganjam District, Odisha) (In Brahmi script)
4. Kalsi (Dehdradun) (In Brahmi script)
5. Yerragudi (Kurnool District, Andhra Pradesh) (In Brahmi script)
6. Sopara (Thane District, Maharashtra) (In Brahmi script)
7. Shahbazgarhi (Peshawar, Pakistan) (In Kharosthi script)
8. Mansehra (Hazara, West Pakistan) (In Kharosthi script)

Minor Rock Edicts

These rock edicts are not included in the main class of 14 Major Edicts. They are hence known as minor edicts. They have been recovered from the following locations:

1. Sasaram (Bihar)
2. Rupnath (Jabalpur, Madhya Pradesh)
3. Gurjara (Datia, Madhya Pradesh)
4. Bhabru (Vairat) (Jaipur, Rajasthan)
5. Maski (Raichur, Karnataka)
6. Brahmagiri (Chtaladurga, Karnataka)
7. Siddhapur (Brahmagiri)
8. Jatingarameshwar (Brahmagiri)
9. Yerragudi (Kurnool District, Andhra Pradesh)
10. Gavimatha (Mysore)
11. Palkigundu (Raichur, Karnataka)
12. Rajul Mandagiri (Kurnool District, Andhra Pradesh)
13. Aharaura (Mirzapur, Uttar Pradesh)

Pillar Edicts

There are 7 major pillar edicts of Ashoka. They have been found mainly at 6 different locations.

1. **Delhi-Topra Pillar Edict:** This has been recovered from Ambala (Haryana) and Sirsava (Uttar Pradesh). This was installed in Delhi by Firozshah Tughlaq.
2. **Delhi-Meerut Pillar Edict:** This was earlier in Meerut and was brought to Delhi by Firozshah Tughlaq.
3. **Lauria Areraj Pillar Edict:** This is installed at Lauria Areraj in West Champaran District of Bihar.

4. **Lauria Nandangarh Pillar Edict:** This is located in West Champaran District of Bihar.
5. **Rampurva Pillar Edict:** This is located in West Champaran District.
6. **Prayag Pillar Edict:** This was earlier located at Kaushambi. It was later relocated to the Allahabad Fort by Akbar.

Ashoka's seventh pillar edict was his longest one and his shortest edict was the Rummindei Pillar Edict. In his short pillar edict of Kaushambi, Ashoka directs his Mahamatras to stop divisions in Sanghas. The pillar inscriptions at Kaushambi and Prayag have mention of the donations made by Ashoka's queen Karuvaki. This is also referred to as Queen's Edict. Rummindei Pillar Edict has description of Ashoka's pilgrimage to this place, and the same edict also has words on taxation. Ashoka had travelled to Lumbini 20 years after his coronation and had reduced land tax rate there to 1/8 of existing rate. 'All men are my children'—these words have been found in edicts at Dhauli and Jaugarh. The Girnar Edict reflects that Ashoka had established separate hospitals for men and animals. Huntsmen and fishermen had renounced hunting after getting influenced by the Kandahar Edict. The inscriptions found at a place named Shar-i-Kuna near Kandahar are in Greek and Aramaic scripts. The Allahabad Pillar has inscriptions belonging to Samudragupta and Akbar's courtier Birbal in addition to that of Ashoka. In his short pillar edicts of Sanchi, Sarnath and Kaushambi, Ashoka directs his Mahamatras to stop divisions in Sanghas. The Bhabru Rock Edict is the only inscription that is engraved on stone plates. The language used for Ashoka's inscriptions was not Sanskrit but Pali that was the common people's language at that time. Brahmi script was written left to right whereas Kharosthi script was written right to left. However, Ashoka's Yerragudi Rock Edict has been written right to left in Brahmi.

Cave Edicts

Ashoka's edicts are found engraved on walls of three caves on the Barabar Hill located in Gaya District of South Bihar; they contain details of donation of caves by Ashoka to the sages of Ajivika community for their settlement. All these inscriptions are written in Prakrit language using Brahmi script. Smith had referred the borders of the Maurya Empire as the scientific or geographic borders of India. The vast empire of the Mauryas was called a nation from the point of view of governance. The entire empire was divided into 4 states or chakras during the period of Chandragupta Maurya and Bindusara and into 5 provinces during the period of Ashoka. Following were those 5 provinces:

1. **Uttarapath:** Its capital was Takshashila. It covered Afghanistan, Jammu-Kashmir, Himachal Pradesh, Uttarakhand, Pakistan, and Punjab.
2. **Avanti:** Ujjayini was its capital. This province included Rajasthan, Gujarat, and West Madhya Pradesh.
3. **Dakshinapath:** Its capital was Swarnagiri. This province covered South Madhya Pradesh, Maharashtra, Goa, Karnataka, and Andhra Pradesh.
4. **Prachi:** Its capital was Pataliputra. This province included Delhi, Uttar Pradesh, Bihar, Bangladesh and Tarai region of Nepal.
5. **Kalinga:** Tosli was its capital. This province covered Odisha region and was the smallest province.

Village (Grama) was the smallest unit of administration. Components of Maurya administration may be depicted as below.

Nation -> Province -> Mandala (Commissionerate) -> Janapada -> Sthanika (800 villages) -> Dronamukha (400 villages) -> Kharvatika (200 villages) -> Sangrahana (100 villages) -> Village (the smallest unit).

Higher officials have been referred to as 'Tirtha' in Kautilya's Arthashastra. The 18 Tirthas (Departments) have been mentioned in the Arthashastra; head of these departments was called

Mahamatra. Following are the prominent ones among those 18 Tirthas:

1. Minister
2. Purohita
3. Senapati
4. Yuvaraj
5. Samaharta
6. Sannidhata (Treasurer).

Samaharta was responsible for collection revenue and maintaining law and order in district. Samaharta was the head of a Janapada, and he also used to attend to legal issues. i.e., he also had semi-legal authority though revenue collection was his primary job. Additionally, Samaharta would keep record of income and expenses and prepare annual budgets. Revenue collected from a village area was called 'Rashtra', and that collected from town was called 'Durga'. Samaharta used to send both kinds of revenue directly to the centre. A land having state ownership was called 'Sita', and Samaharta would also collect income generated by 'Sita'. He would ensure coordination among district police officers, Rajukas and city administrative officers. Samaharta, directly appointed by the king, was the most important official in Maurya administration. The district Samaharta would remit revenue to the central Samaharta who in turn would deposit the same with the Sannidhata.

Judicial System

There were two kinds of courts during Maurya period:

1. Dharmasthiya (Court of Civil Law)
2. Kantakashodhana (Court of Criminal Law)

The emperor himself was the highest authority of the judicial system. There were village courts at lower level. Higher to them were Sangrahana, Dronamukha, Sthaniya, and Janapada level courts. At the top was the central court of Pataliputra. The entire 4th chapter of the 'Arthashastra' deals with the subject of Kantakashodhana court.

The Maurya administration had a strong espionage system. The spies were known as Goorha Purush. Kautilya has referred to them as the eyes of the king. As per the Arthashastra, there were two kinds of arrangements for spies:

1. Sanstha (Permanent)
2. Sanchar (Mobile).

Agriculture was the main source of economy during Maurya period. Agriculture, animal husbandry, business, commerce, etc. have together been referred to as 'Varta' in the Arthashastra. The rate of tax was 1/6 part. The state had ownership rights over forests, textile industry, etc. As per the Arthashastra, Kashi and Pundru were famous for silk industry and Bang was famous for muslin production. Silk used to be imported from China during Maurya period. Punch-marked silver coins were prevalent during the period. They generally had seal marks of peacock, mountain or half-moon. 'Bali' was a kind of land revenue whereas 'Hiranya' was salt tax that was collected in cash. When people created their own coins, they had to pay interest at the rate of 13.5 per cent in the form of 'Rupika' and 'Parikshan'. Merchant tax, boat and port tax, tax on grasslands and roads and revenues collected from other sources were known as 'Rashtra'. Income received from lands owned by the Empire was known as 'Sita'. A landowner was called 'Kshetraka' and a farmer 'Upavasa'. Provision of irrigation by the state was known as 'Setubandha' for which a separate tax ranging from 1/5th to 1/3rd of the produce was levied. 'Pinda Tax' was collected from the entire village once whereas 'Vivita Tax' was collected for security of animals. Forced labour during Maurya period was known as 'Vishti'. Sales tax was levied at the rate of 4 per cent on domestic goods and 10 per cent on imported goods.

Following were 4 main roadways during Maurya period:

- **Uttarapath:** This connected Rajgir to Pushpakalawati, i.e., it linked Pataliputra to Takshashila. This was the busiest road.
- **Himavanta Road:** It went north towards the Himalayas.

- Road from Pataliputra towards western coast through Kashi and Ujjain.
- Road from Pataliputra to Tamralipti or Tamraluk.

An another road originated at Kashi and went up to Mysore via Pratishthan. Chanakya assigned more importance to southern roadways as compared to northern roadways, as most of the valuable items like metals, precious wood, ivory and gold were available in south.

Two primary means of business during Maurya period were the following:

1. Water routes
2. Land routes

For Chanakya, water routes were more useful and secured as there was much lower risk of theft there, though there was arrangement for payment of compensation by the state in the case of a theft. For the Mauryans, Takshashila was the main centre for international business.

The following were the main ports during Maurya period:

- On west coast-Bharukatchha or Bharuch, Sopara, Barberikam, Munjarish
- On east coast-Tamralipi.

The following were the taxes collected on trade:

1. Shulk (Chungi Tax)
2. Vartani (Road Tax)
3. Gulmadeya (Tax on security against robbers)
4. Ativahaka (Carriage Tax)

Kautilya has described 7 organs of state, referred to as 'Saptang Theory', in his Arthashastra. They are as below:

1. The Ruler
2. Amatya
3. Janapada
4. Durga
5. Kosha
6. Danda
7. Mitra.

Military Administration

Military was an important part of the central administration. As per Pliny, Chandragupta's army included 6 lakh infantry, 30,000 cavalry and 9000 chariots. This department had a total of 30 members divided into 6 committees having 5 members each. The Senapati was the chief of this department. The officer operating the army in war field was known as 'Nayaka'. 'Navadhyaksha' was the head of warships and commercial ships. Permanent army was called 'Maula', forest army was called 'Atavi Bala' and a hired army was known as 'Bhritaka'. The person in-charge of management and security of arms and ammunition was called 'Ayudhagaradhyaksha'.

Social and Economic Life

In the Arthashastra, Kautilya has made mention of all the 4 varnas in society-Brahmin, Kshatriya, Vaishya, and Shudra. Ashoka's inscriptions have references to dasas and karmakaras. The status of women in family was much better as compared to smritikaal. They were permitted to remarry or take up employment but were not free to go out. Kautilya has referred to such women as 'Anishkashini'. There are references to 'Ganika' or prostitutes in Maurya period. Women engaged in prostitution independently were called 'Rupajiva'. Marriage of widows was accepted in the society. Widows who lived independently were called 'Kshandavasini'.

Takshashila, Ujjain and Varanasi were considered to be the most famous centres of education during Maurya period. There was growth of even technological education during that time; that was imparted to students based on rankings. 'Nata', 'Nartaka', 'Gayaka', 'Vadaka', etc. provided entertainment to people in the society. The means of entertainment included even gambling, liquor, hunting, etc. The economy of the state depended on agriculture, animal husbandry, and trade and commerce. All these together were referred to as 'Varta'. In the Arthashastra, paddy crop has been termed as the best and cane as the worst crop.

The official currency in the Maurya Empire was 'Pana'. This was silver coin weighting 3/4 tolas. This only was used for payment of salaries, etc. to officials. The coins during that period were generally made of gold, silver, and copper. The gold coins were known as 'Nishka' or 'Suvarna', silver coins as 'Pana' or 'Karshapana' and copper coins as 'Masaka' or 'Kakini'. These coins were also called 'Aahat coins'.

Decline of the Maurya Dynasty

There were various causes for the decline of the Maurya dynasty.

1. According to Mahamahopadhyaya Hari Prasad Shastri, Ashoka's religious policy was the primary cause for the decline. His policy favoured Buddhists and opposed Brahmins. Killing of Vrihadratha was just a reaction of Brahmin dharma. However, Hemchandra Roy Chaudhary does not agree to this theory. According to him, animal killing was entirely prohibited and even the Pradhanmantri and Senapati Pushyamitra Shunga were Brahmins, implying that Ashoka's policy was not against Brahmins. Vrihadratha's assassination was an army revolt and not a religious reaction.
2. According to Hemchandra Roy Chaudhary, the real reasons for the decline of the Maurya Empire were Ashoka's pacifism and his policy of non-violence, as that had lowered the spirits of the army. The successors started to lay more emphasis on Dhammaghosh (Sound of Peace) than on Yuddhaghosh (Sound of War Drums). Neelkanth Shastri opposed Roy Chaudhary's version and asserted that there was fanaticism in Ashoka's peaceful policy. He had maintained his army and had renounced his war policy only to a certain extent.
3. Incapable succession system.
4. Dismal condition of economy–Economy was facing lot of problems after Ashoka due to his indulgence in distribution of largesse.
5. Centralisation of administration–Romila Thapar considers this to be primary cause of decline, as this resulted in lack of a system of trained officials.
6. As per Nihar Ranjan Ray, Maurya rulers started to embrace foreign customs that people rejected.

POST MAURYA BIHAR

The end of the Maurya Empire resulted in emergence of the tendency for decentralisation in India. Different dynasties established separate states in different regions. Thus, Shunga and Kanva dynasties established their rule in Magadha and Bihar regions, Kushan Dynasty in Central Madhya Pradesh, Andhra Saatvahana Dynasty in Deccan region, Shaka Dynasty in West India and Chaitra dynasty in Odisha region. All these dynasties, in some way or other, influenced the history of Magadha and Bihar.

Shunga Dynasty

Pushyamitra Shunga established the Shunga Dynasty in 185 BC after killing Vrihadratha, the last ruler of the Maurya Dynasty. Information relating to the Shunga 'Dynasty may be found in Ayodhya inscription' of Dhanadeva, Besanagar (Vidisha Madhya Pradesh) Garuda pillar inscription, 'Malvikagnimitram' of Kalidasa and 'Mahabhashya' of Patanjali. Pushyamitra, by claiming his right over the Magadha Empire, not only defended the country against Greek invasion but also enshrined Vedic Dharma and Vedic ideals by establishing law and order in the country. This is the reason why his period is known as the period of Vedic reaction or Vedic Renaissance. Pushyamitra fought against Vidarbha and the Greeks and secured victory in those wars.

After the death of Pushyamitra Shunga, his son Agnimitra Shunga became the king of the Shunga Dynasty. He ruled for a total of 8 years (140 BC). He is the hero of Kalidasa's play 'Malvikagnimitram'. The last ruler of the Shunga Dynasty was Devabhuti, who was killed by Vasumitra. The empire of the

Shunga Dynasty was spread over the area right from the Himalayas in the north to Barar in the south and from Punjab in the west to Magadha in the east. Pataliputra was the capital of the empire. There was a cabinet of ministers to assist the king. 'Grama' was the smallest unit of administration. Pushyamitra had destroyed 84 thousand Buddhist stupas but had made the stupas at Sanchi, Bharhut and Bodh Gaya more magnificent.

During the reign of the Shunga Dynasty, gold coins were known as 'Nishka', Dinar, Suvarna and Swarna Masika, etc. Copper coins were called 'Karshapana'. For silver coins, words like 'Purana' or 'Dharana' were used. During this very period, there was emergence of Bhagavata Dharma. Maharshi Patanjali had made the major contribution towards revival of Sanskrit; he had authored 'Mahabhashya'. Excellent samples of architecture existing during the Shunga period can be found at Bodh Gaya. A small stone platform has been found around the grand temple at Bodh Gaya; this was built during the Shunga period.

Kanva Dynasty (73-27 BC)

Devabhuti, the last ruler of the Shunga Dynasty, was killed by his amatya Vasumitra who then established a new dynasty Kanva. He was a Brahmin like the Shungas. Vasumitra ruled for a total of 9 years and he was succeeded by Bhumimitra, Narayana and Susharma. Susharma was the last ruler of this dynasty; he was killed by the Andhra slave Simuka. With Susharma's death, the Kanva Dynasty also came to an end.

Kushan Dynasty

The Kushan Dynasty was established by Kujula Kadphises. However, Kanishka, who became the king in 75 BC, was the greatest ruler of this dynasty. Kanishka had established his capital at Kanishkapura (Kashmir) or Purushapura. In the course of his empire expansion efforts, Kanishka conquered regions up to Magadha and brought the famous Buddhist scholar Ashvaghosha from Pataliputra to his own capital Purushapura. It was Ashvaghosha who had presided over the Fourth Buddhist Council organised by Kanishka. Archaeological remains of the Kushan period have been recovered from many locations in Bihar. After fall of the Kushan Dynasty, Lichchavis of Vaishali ruled over Magadha, though historians do not agree to the same. Some historians believe that after the end of the Kushan Dynasty, Magadha region was ruled by Shaka-Murundo.

BIHAR DURING GUPTA ERA

After fall of the Maurya Empire, Magadha that was the focal point of Indian history was rules by weak Brahmin dynasties like Shunga and Kanva. Magadha was even attacked and ruled by Kushan, Shaka, etc. during that period, but with establishment of the Gupta Dynasty in the beginning of 4th century, Magadha had regained its glory. Initial Gupta rulers retained Pataliputra as their capital and established the focal significance of Magadha and Pataliputra in the Indian history.

The Gupta Dynasty was established by Maharaja Shrigupta in 240 CE. He had a son Ghatotkacha. Chandragupta I was the son of Ghatotkacha. Chandragupta I is considered to be the real founder of the Gupta Dynasty, which is believed to have ruled from 319 CE to 335 CE. The Gupta Samvat started in 319 CE; this is related to Vallabhi Samvat. Chandragupta I for the first time assumed the title of 'Maharajadhiraja'.

Chandragupta I was succeeded by Samudragupta (335–375 CE). Prayag Prashasti is the primary source for information relating to Samudragupta. Samudragupta is also known as the 'Napoleon of India'. First of all, he defeated the rulers of Ganga-Yamuna valley region and annexed their kingdoms. He even annexed Punjab, Assam, Nepal, Bengal and Tamilnadu regions. He also defeated Shaka and Kushan rulers and took control of western and north-western India.

Chandragupta II, successor to Samudragupta, conquered and annexed Saurashtra and Malwa.

His period is referred to as the golden period of the Gupta era. He ruled from 380 CE to 415 CE. Successors of Chandragupta II had to face foreign invasions, where in the Hunas attack was the most important. The Huna ruler Mihirakula invaded Pataliputra and defeated Narsinhagupta Baladitya. The successors of the Gupta Dynasty held control over Magadha region till the middle of 6th century whereas the Maukhari Dynasty had established its rule over some regions of eastern Uttar Pradesh and Bihar by that time. The Gupta era is believed to be the era of outstanding achievements in art and culture. The era is also known as the golden period of the ancient Indian history on account of political calm and soundness, economic prosperity and cultural development. Varahamihira, Aryabhata and Brahmagupta are the most noteworthy names among the eminent scholars of that time. Their contributions in the field of mathematics, astronomy and philosophy are unforgettable. The Nalanda Mahavihara was established during the Gupta period only. Kumaragupta was its founder. In the course of time, this became a prominent centre of education where even foreign students used to come for study in large numbers. The Chinese traveller Fa-Hien visited India the regime of Chandragupta II. He came to Bihar region and stayed back in Pataliputra for three years. The Mahabodhi Temple at Bodh Gaya and the Nalanda Mahavihara are examples of the outstanding achievements made in the field of art during this period.

Later Gupta Rulers of Magadha

Some inscriptions recovered from Gaya and Shahabad districts provide details about reigns of the later Gupta rulers in some parts of Bihar during 6th century. Krishnagupta was the founder of this dynasty. These inscriptions have details of Kumaragupta III expanding his reign up to Prayag and defeating the Maukhari ruler. The Maukhari ruler later defeated Damodaragupta, the successor to Krishnagupta and captured a major part of Magadha. Magadha region was attacked by Shashanka who badly vandalised Buddhist religious places and also damaged the Mahabodhi Tree at Bodh Gaya. Devagupta entered into an agreement with Shashanka and defeated Grihavarma, the Maukhari ruler of Kannauj. Thus, the History of Bihar was witness to serious conflicts during the period between fall of the Gupta Empire and beginning of the Harsha Empire.

In the beginning of 7th century, when Harshavardhana expanded his empire in North India, some parts of Bihar also came under his control. After Harsha's death, Bihar again went into a state of anarchy. Some local ruler of Bihar named Arjuna inflicted harm on Chinese travellers and in retaliation of the same, the rulers of Tibet and Nepal jointly attacked Bihar. Possibly, even Tibet's sovereignty was established over some parts of Bihar for some time. This was ended by Madhavagupta's son Adityasena. His reign included the regions of Magadha and northern and eastern Bihar. Shortly after his death, this dynasty came to an end. Jivitagupta II was the last ruler of this dynasty. This dynasty was brought to an end by his killing by Kannauj ruler Yashovardhana around 725 CE. Pataliputra also had lost its glory by that time. By the time the Chinese traveller Hiuen Tsang visited this region during Harshavardhana's period around 635 CE, Pataliputra town was already ruined.

Date Sequence	Ancient Period
2300–1750 BC	Harappan civilisation period
1500–1000 BC	Rigvedic period
1000–600 BC	Expansion of Aryan culture in Ganga valley
800 BC	Mention in Shatapatha Brahman about Aryans' settlement in Gandaka basin (Videha)

600–500 BC	Period of second urbanisation and 16 mahajanapadas
563–483 BC	Life period of Mahatma Buddha
544–492 BC	Reign of Magadha king Bimbisara, ascendance of Magadha
540–468 BC	Life period of Vardhamana Mahavira
500 BC	Establishment of first ganarajya in Vaishali
492–460 BC	Reign of Ajatashatru over Magadha, victory over Vaishali
490 BC	Establishment of Pataligrama by Ajatashatru
483 BC	The First Buddhist Council organised in Saptaparni Cave at Rajgriha
460–444 BC	Reign of Udayabhadra (Udayin) over Magadha
455 BC	Pataliputra declared as capital by Udayin
413–344 BC	Reign of the Shishunaga Dynasty over Magadha
383 BC	The Second Buddhist Council organised in Vaishali
344 BC	Establishment of the Nanda Dynasty by Mahapadma Nanda
322 BC	End of the Nanda Dynasty after defeat of Dhanananda by Chandragupta Maurya
322–298 BC	Period of Chandragupta Maurya
305 BC	Arrival of Megasthenes in Pataliputra
298–273 BC	Reign of Bindusara
272–232 BC	Reign of Ashoka the Great
261 BC	Kalinga victory, Ashoka embraced Buddhism
251 BC	The Third Buddhist Council organised in Pataliputra; promotion of Buddhism by Ashoka in neighbouring countries
185 BC	Pushyamitra killing Vrihadratha and bringing the Maurya Dynasty to an end; attack on Pataliputra by Demetrius
185–73 BC	Reign of the Shunga Dynasty
73–27 BC	Reign of the Kanva Dynasty
319–335 CE	Reign of Chandragupta I in Magadha; ascendance of the Gupta Empire
319 CE	Beginning of the Gupta Samvat
335–375 CE	Reign of Samudragupta; beginning of expansion of his empire
380–415 CE	Reign of Chandragupta II (Vikramaditya); Golden Era on account of cultural progress

405–411 CE	Period of visit of the Chinese traveller Fa–Hien
415–455 CE	Reign of Kumaragupta I; establishment of Nalanda Vihara
455–467 CE	Reign of Skandagupta; attack by the Hunes
467–494 CE	Reign of Buddhagupta; beginning of decline of the Gupta Empire
500 CE	Attack on Magadha region by the Hunes
495–510 CE	Reign of Bhanugupta; end of the Gupta Dynasty
530 CE	Ascendance of the Later Gupta rulers of Magadha
606–647 CE	Expansion of empire in East India by Thaneshwar and Kannauj ruler Harshavardhana
629 CE	Arrival of the Chinese traveller Hiuen Tsang in India
673 CE	Arrival of the Chinese traveller I–tsing in India

❑❑❑

Medieval Period

- Pre-medieval Period
- Emergence of Afghan Power
- Sufism in Bihar
- Medieval Period
- Bihar during Mughal Era

The medieval period is considered to begin after the death of Harshavardhana in 647 CE. From the point of view of convenience of studying it, medieval history is divided into two periods:

- Pre-medieval period—Period from 8th century to 12th century
- Medieval period—Period from 12th century to the beginning of the 18th century.

PRE-MEDIEVAL PERIOD

Bihar was primarily ruled by the Pala Dynasty, the Karnata Dynasty and the Sena Dynasty during the pre medieval period. Turkish invasion during that period also had left its impact on Bihar.

Pala Dynasty

Subsequent to the fall of Harshavardhana in North India and that of Shashanka in Bengal region, the Pala Dynasty emerged as powerful dynasty in Bihar and Bengal region. Gopala was the founder of the Pala Dynasty; he ruled from 750 CE to 770 CE. Gopala was elected as ruler by the Samantas and common people of Bengal. According to the Tibetan historian Taranatha, Gopala belonged to a Kshatriya family of Pundravardhana (Bengal) in Bogra district. He established his reign in Bihar. After Gopala, Dharmapala ruled from 770 CE to 810 CE. He attacked Kannauj in the last quarter of 8th century, and after appointing Chakrayuddha as the king of Kannauj, he organised a grand durbar and assumed the title of 'Uttarapatha swamin'. Gujarati poet Soddhala, in his book 'Udayasundari', written in 11th century, has referred to Dharmapala as the 'Master of north'. Dharmapala was defeated by Pratihara king, Vatsaraja and Rashtrakuta king, Dhruva.

The greatest ruler of the Pala Dynasty Devapala ascended the throne after Dharmapala. The Pala Dynasty was at the pinnacle of its glory during his period. He adopted an expansionist policy and expanded his kingdom to Pragyajyotishapura in northeast, Nepal in north, and Odisha on the east coast. He defeated the Pratihara ruler Nagabhata II and the Huns of Kamboj. According to some historians, he even had encounters with Deccan states. There was cordial relation with Southeast Asia during his period. He had even offered villages as grant at the request of the Java ruler Velatthaputra for maintenance of a Vihara at Nalanda. Devapala was famous for providing patronage to Buddhism. Arab traveller Sulaiman regards Devapala as the greatest among all Rashtrakuta and Pratihara rulers.

After the death of Devapala, the Pratiharas took control of majority of regions in Eastern Uttar Pradesh and Bihar during the reigns of Mihira Bhoja and Mahendra Pala. During 11th century, Mahipala I became the king; he is known as the second founder of the Pala Dynasty. Mahipala conquered the entire

Bengal and Magadha regions, but his successors proved to be weak. Rajendra Chol attacked Bengal during his reign. As the successor was weak, the Kaivartas went on gaining strength, and the Sena rulers established their kingdoms in some regions of North Bihar and Bengal. The sovereignty of the Palas was reduced to some parts of Magadha. Ramapala was the last ruler of the Pala Dynasty. The book 'Ramacharitram' by Sandhyakar Nandi is related to Ramapala.

After the death of Ramapala, the Gahadavalas also expanded their reign up to Shahabad and Gaya in Bihar. The Sena rulers Vijaya Sena and Ballat Sena also continued with their expansionist design and extended their control up to the east of Gaya. In the midst of this situation of anarchy, the Turks had started their attacks on Bihar, towards the end of 12th century. References to a tax named 'Turushka Danda' are found in Maner copperplate of King Govinda Chandra of the Gahadavala Dynasty. This tax was recovered from the farmers in this region and the same was used for procuring means for stopping Turk invasions.

Pala rulers were followers of Buddhism. They supported educational institutions. Dharmapala had established Vikramashila Mahavihara. He only had donated 200 villages to Nalanda Mahavihara. Odantapuri and Jagadala Universities were also established during the reign of the Pala rulers. Tibet was very closely related to the Palas. Among the Buddhist scholars, Shantarakshita and Atish Dipankara visited Tibet during this period. Subsequent to Bakhtiar Khilji's campaigns, Buddhist Bhikshu Dharmaswami came from Tibet to Bihar for the purpose of studying at Nalanda Mahavihara. Cordial relations were also established with the islands in Southeast Asia. A ruler of the Shailendra Dynasty in that region had obtained permission from Devapala for building a Buddhist temple at Nalanda. Devapala even offered financial assistance for maintenance of that temple. The Pala rulers also provided ample support to sculpting. Beautiful idols of Gautama Buddha and Hindu deities have been made with shining black stones. The best period for making copper idols was the Pala period.

Sulaiman called the Pala Dynasty as 'Ruhaiya'. Devapala and Dharmapala were the greatest rulers of the Pala Dynasty. The reign of the Pala Dynasty in East India was contemporary to the reigns of Gurjara-Pratihara Dynasty in West India and Rashtrakuta Dynasty in South India. Kannauj had become the focal point of power during the reign of Harshavardhana. Hence, there was fight among the Pala, the Pratihara and Rashtrakuta dynasties for control over Kannauj this was also called the 'Tripakshiya Sangharsh' (Tripartite Struggle). This struggle had taken place in five stages. Dharmapala was the first to participate in this on behalf of the Pala Dynasty. He had to fight against the Pratihara king, Vatsaraja and Rashtrakuta king, Dhruva; Dhruva had come out victorious in this fight. After Dharmapala, Devapala, Vigrahapala, Narayanpala, and others also participated in this struggle. In this tripartite struggle, it was the Gurjar Pratihara Dynasty who was the ultimate victor. However, out of the above 3 dynasties, it was the Pala Dynasty who had the longest reign. Inscription of the Gurjar Pratihara ruler Mahendrapala related to that period have been recovered from Bihar and Bengal regions.

Karnata Dynasty

Right when the Pala rulers were getting weak towards the end of 11th century, there was a beginning of Turkish invasions on India. There were two phases of Turkish invasions on India. The first phase was the invasion by Muhammed Ghazni and the second one was that by Muhammed Ghori. Bihar was being ruled by the Pala king Ramapala at that time. It was during his reign when the Karnata Dynasty emerged in Tirhut region in the north plains of the Ganges. This dynasty was established by Nanyadeva. The 11th century stone inscriptions of Mithila king, Nanyadeva also indicate that he only had founded the Karnata Dynasty. Information about this dynasty can also be found in the inscriptions of Maladeva recovered from Bhit Bhagwanpur in Darbhanga district.

Nanyadeva made Simraongarh, the capital of Karnata. The reign of the Karnata rulers is also referred to as the golden period of Mithila. Mithila had experienced stability and development till the reign of the Vainavara Dynasty. Nanyadeva had regular conflicts with the rulers of the Sena Dynasty. The Karnata ruler Narsinha Deva also kept on fighting with the Sena rulers of Bengal. This was the reason that Narsinha Deva supported the Turks. Narsinha Deva's kingdom extended to Tirhut and Darbhanga regions. Karnata rulers were in constant touch with the Delhi Sultans. Normally, the Prantapati of Delhi Sultanate, who was appointed in Bihar and Bengal regions, used to accept gifts from Karnata rulers. Control over this region was secured during Bengal campaign of Ghiasuddin Tughalaq. Harisingh Deva was the ruler of Tirhut at that time. He could not withstand the attack by Turk army and fled to Nepal Tarai area. This way, north and central Bihar regions got merged. Harisingh was the last ruler of the Karnata Dynasty. By 1378 CE, the Karnata Dynasty was completely finished. Harisingh Deva was active as a great social reformer. 'Panji Prabandh' was developed during this very period. As a result, a new class of panjikars got mobilised. Even books comprising memoirs and essays were written in large numbers during this period and the form of the Maithili society that has been retained till today, actually had its features fully developed during this very period. The famous Maithili poet Vidyapati was a court scholar under Darbhanga king Kriti Singh and Shiva Singh. Vidyapati was born in Bisapi village in Benipatti Police Station area of Darbhanga district. Ganapati Thakur was Vidyapati's father and Hasini Devi his mother. He had a son named Harapit and daughter named Dulahi, who have been mentioned in Vidyapati's writings. This village was offered to Vidyapati as gift by his protector King Shiva Singh. According to legends, Vidyapati was born in 1350 CE and he died at the age of 90 in Bajitpur village in 1497 CE. A Shiva temple was built over his funeral pyre. Hari Mishra had taken over the responsibility of imparting education to Vidyapati. There was a Brahmin named Karmaditya Tripathi in Garh Bisapi; he was a state minister in the court of Karnata. Karmaditya Tripathi was the grandson of Vishnu Sharma Thakur, the primogenitor of Vidyapati's family. Most of the people in this family were connected to king's court and were working at different positions. Veereshwar Thakur of this very dynasty was state minister of the Nanya Dynasty ruler Shatru Singh and his son Harisingh Deva. He had authored the book named 'Chhandogya Dashapaddhati'. His brother Dhireshwar Thakur is known as 'Mahavartika Naibandhika'. Chandreshwar, the son of Dhireshwar Thakur, had written the set of books called Sapta Ratnakar that included 'Krityachintamani', 'Vivad–Ratnakar', and 'Rajniti Ratnakar'. Chandreshwar was the minister and Mahamahattaka Sandhivigrahika of Harisingh. Vidyapati's father was the sabhapandita and state minister of King Ganeshwara; he had written the book titled 'Vyadhibhakti Evam Tarangini'.

Vidyapati is also known as 'Abhinava Jayadeva'. He wrote the book titled 'Kirtilata' based on the name of Kirti Singh. Presently, this book is preserved in the state library of Nepal. The languages Sanskrit, Prakrit, and Maithili have been used in this book. These mixed languages have been named as 'Avahatta' by Vidyapati. Vidyapati also wrote the book 'Bhooparikrama'. He wrote this with the approval of King Deva Singh. This is a collection of moral stories, and it has an expanded version titled as 'Purush Pariksha'. This was translated into English in 1830 CE by the King Kalikrishna Bahadur, with support from Lord Bishop Turner. This book is also included in the curriculum of Fort William College, Kolkata.

The fourth book authored by Vidyapati is 'Kirtipataka' that is a collection of love stories written in Maithili language. He also wrote the book 'Likhanawali' in Sanskrit language. He had written the book 'Shaiva–Sarvasva–Sar' after the death of Raja Shiva Singh, under the supervision of Maharani Vishwas Devi. This contains description of the reigns of Bhava Singh up to Vishwas Devi.

Vidyapati had also written the books titled 'Ganga Vakyavali', 'Dan Vakyavali', Durgabhakti Tarangini', Vibhag–Sar', 'Varshakritya', 'Gaya–Patan' etc. 'Ganga Vakyavali' is about Vishwas Devi and 'Dan Vakyavali' is about Narsinha Deva's wife Dhiramati. The books 'Vibhag–Sar', 'Varshakritya' and 'Gaya–Patan' are written in Sanskrit language.

Sena Dynasty

After the fall of the Pala Dynasty, the Sena Dynasty was established under the leadership of Samanta Sena. Samanta Sena was a samanta under the Palas. During the period of Hemanta Sena, the Sena Dynasty became completely independent. The rulers like Vijaya Sena, Ballala Sena and Lakshamana Sena ruled over Bihar and Bengal regions. Vijay Sena was a powerful ruler of the Sena Dynasty. Information relating to Vijaya Sena is also found in copperplate inscriptions recovered from Devapara (Bengal). Vijaya Sena had defeated the Karnata dynasty ruler, Nanyadeva. He was a follower of Shaiva Dharma. He had written two books titled 'Danasagar' and 'Adbhutsagar'. Lakshamana Sena was the last ruler of this dynasty. Jayadeva, author of the book, 'Gita Govinda', was a courtier under Lakshamana Sena. Lakshamana was a follower of Vaishnava Dharma. Sena rulers had established their capitals in Nadia and Lukhnauti. The Sena rulers had conquered regions up to Gaya, though they had to fight Gahadavala ruler Govinda Chandra for the same.

Around the same time when Bihar and Bengal regions were under control of Lakshamana Sena, military operation of Bakhtiar Khilji, commander of the Turk Muhammed Ghori, was going on-stream in India up to Bihar–Bengal. In the same campaign, Bakhtiar Khilji had defeated Lakshamana Sena and brought this region under the control of the Turks.

Turkish Attacks on Bihar

A Turkish attack was launched on India in the beginning of 11th century, under the command of the Ghazni Dynasty ruler Mahmud Ghazni. Details of the Turkish attack are available in the book 'Shahnama' written by Firdausi. 'Shahnama' is the first and the most famous book in Persian literature. Belonging to the Yamini Dynasty, Mahmud Ghazni, who was the son of Subuktigin, assumed the title of Ghazi. Mahmud Ghaznavi had launched an attack for the first time in 1001 CE on Jayapala, the Hindushahi Dynasty ruler of Udbhandapur. After that, he attacked Chandraswami Temple of Thaneshwar in 1011–12 CE and then attacked Punjab in 1021–22 CE. The primary purpose of the attack on Punjab was to establish a military centre. The Somnath Temple in Gujarat was attacked in 1025–26 CE. Ghaznavi's last attack was against the Jat rulers in 1027 CE. The sole purpose of Ghaznavi's attacks was to loot riches. Hence, these attacks did not have any material impact on the political history of India and Bihar.

The second phase of Turkish attacks on India started with the attack by Muhammed Ghori in the second half of 12th century. Muhammed Ghori, whose original name was Muizz ad–Din Muhammad Ibn Sham, launched multiple attacks on India between 1175 CE and 1194 CE. The primary aim of his attacks was to establish political sovereignty and he was quite successful in the same. His attacks had impacted Eastern India up to the regions of Bihar and Bengal. The basic reason for his success was lack of political unity in India. Just like India, decentralised powers were quite influential in Bihar also during his attacks. Bihar also was not an organised and close-knit political unit. At that time, most of the North Bihar was ruled by the Karnata Dynasty whereas the remaining part was having several small kingdoms. At the same time, the situation in Bihar had turned extremely miserable on account of the attacks by the Sena Dynasty rulers of Bengal.

Three commanders of Muhammed Ghori were running the victory campaign in India; one of them, Ikhtiyar al–Din Muhammad Bakhtiar Khilji was conducting his campaign in East India up to Bihar and Bengal. Bakhtiar Khilji is also known as 'Ghazi Ikhtiar'. Thus, the credit for installation of Turk rule in Bihar goes to Bakhtiar Khilji. When Bakhtiar Khilji attacked Bihar and Bengal regions, he was confronted by the Sena dynasty ruler Lakshamana Sena and the Pala dynasty ruler Indradumna Pala. Bakhtiar Khilji registered his first victory in Bihar in 1198 CE, by taking control of Odantapuri (Bihar Sharif) and burnt the educational institution Nalanda University located there. Next, he attacked the capital Nadia of Lakshamana Sena in 1203–04 CE and defeated him. After conquering the regions of Bihar and Bengal, Bakhtiar Khilji organised them in the form of a province and established Lukhnauti as its capital. Bakhtiar Khilji was killed by Alimardan Khilji in 1206 CE. After Bakhtiar Khilji, this region was ruled by Qutb al-Din Aibak, another commander of Muhammed Ghori.

After the death of Muhammed Ghori in 1206 CE, Qutb al–Din Aibak established an independent Turkish rule in Delhi that is now known as 'Delhi Sultanate'. Even the regions of Bihar and Bengal were directly or indirectly brought under the control of Delhi Sultanate after the death of Bakhtiar Khilji. Establishment of Delhi Sultanate brought an end to the pre–medieval period; this was the beginning of the medieval period.

MEDIEVAL PERIOD

Beginning of 13th century witnessed establishment of the Delhi Sultanate by Qutb al-Din Aibak in the year 1206 CE. The following five dynasties ruled under the Delhi Sultanate:

1. Mamluk or Slave dynasty: 1206–1290 CE
2. Khilji dynasty: 1290–1320 CE
3. Tughlaq dynasty: 1320–1414 CE
4. Sayyid dynasty: 1414–1451 CE
5. Lodi Dynasty: 1451–1526 CE

After the death of Bakhtiar Khilji in 1206 CE, Qutb al–Din Aibak established an independent state in north India that included Bihar. Qutb al–Din Aibak was engaged in conflicts with local rulers in Delhi and nearby regions and Muhammed Ghori's other successors Yalduz and Kubacha. Besides, because of the geographical distance and lack of transport facilities also, Aibak was unable to pay good attention to Bihar and Bengal. Hence, taking advantage of the situation, the local samantas started making efforts to get free. In the circumstances, Bengal rulers launched attacks on Bihar repeatedly and strengthened their position; they kept on launching revolts against the sultans of Delhi. Thus, Bihar became a battleground for Turkish rulers of Delhi, Bengal rulers and local rulers in Bihar. After Qutb al–Din Aibak, during the period of Iltutmish (1210–1236 CE), Ghiasuddin established his independent rule over Bengal and started collecting tax from Tirhut region in Bihar. In 1225 CE, when Iltutmish had made his position strong, he took control of Bihar and appointed an administrator there and defeated and chased the Bengal ruler Ghiasuddin away from Bihar. When Iltutmish returned back to Delhi, Ghiasuddin regained control over Bihar after dislodging the administrator Malik Jani. After that, Iltutmish himself launched campaign to suppress revolts in Bengal and after defeating the Bengal ruler Hisabuddin, constituted two separate provinces of Bihar and Bengal. After return of Iltutmish, his successors were not capable of retaining their rule over Bihar. Revolts erupted again in Bengal during the period of Balaban (1266–1286 CE). Balaban was able to suppress the revolts under the leadership of Tugaril.

After Balaban, the Turks had established their rule over South Bihar as well as North Bihar (Tirhut) during the period of Tughlaq. Evidences of establishment of rule of the Tughlaq Dynasty and information relating to their administration are found in the books 'Malfuzat' and 'Manakibul Asafia' written by Sufi saint Hazarat Sharfuddin Yahia Maneri and Tughlaq era coins recovered from Tirhut region. When Ghiasuddin Tughlaq was returning to Delhi after Bengal campaign in 1324 CE, he had defeated the Karnata ruler Harisingh Deva and annexed Tirhut (Mithila) state to the Tughlaq Empire; he named this area as 'Tughlaqpur'. Muhammed Bin Tughlaq had built a fort and a Jama Masjid at Darbhanga. After getting defeated, Harisingh Deva had taken refuge in Nepal region with the help of the poet Vidyapati. Amatya Amiyakar of Harisingh Deva had gone to the court of Ghiasuddin Tughlaq and successfully convinced him to restore the state to Harisingh Deva. That time, even the Prantapati (Makta) of Bihar Majadul Mulk had defeated Harisingh Deva. During the period of Tughlaq, the capital of Bihar was Bihar Sharif that was a famous centre of Buddhism. After Ghiasuddin Tughlaq, Firozshah Tughlaq launched his Bengal campaign in 1359 CE; mention of this campaign is found in 'Sirat–e–Firozshahi'. The conflict between the Karnata dynasty and the Turkish rulers existed right from the beginning. However, during the period of Bakhtiar Khilji, Karnata ruler Narsinha Deva had adopted the policy of conciliatory cooperation with the Turks. He had even sent najaraanaa (present) to placate Bakhtiar Khilji. After Narsinha Deva, even during the period of Ramsinha Deva, Tugril Tugana had launched attacks on Mithila.

EMERGENCE OF AFGHAN POWER

During the period of the Tughlaq dynasty, the central authority of the Delhi Sultanate weakened after the invasion of Taimur in 1398 CE; this resulted in the beginning of a spate of disintegration. Several regional dynasties, the Sharqi dynasty of Jaunpur and the Hussain Shahi dynasty of Bengal being the notable ones, emerged during the period of Sayyid, and Lodi dynasties. During that period, the western part of Bihar was under the control of Sharqi rulers of Jaunpur and the eastern part was under the control of the Hussain Shahi dynasty of Bengal. Hence, fighting started among Jaunpur, Bengal, and Lodi dynasties for control over Bihar. Delhi was being ruled by famous rulers Bahalol Lodi and Sikandar Lodi of the Lodi dynasty. Jaunpur ruler Hussain Shah Sharqi launched a revolt in Uttar Pradesh region but the same was crushed by Sikandar Lodi. In the same sequence, Sikandar Lodi established his sovereignty over Bihar and compelled the ruler of Tirhut to pay taxes. Mubarak Khan was appointed to collect taxes. In 1504 CE, Sikandar Lodi and the Nawab of Bengal Alauddin engaged in a war, though that ultimately resulted in reconciliation under which Alauddin accepted Sikandar Lodi's sovereignty over North Bihar region of Saran and Tirhut. Bihar Subedar Daria Khan Nuhani revolted during the period of Lodi ruler Ibrahim Khan Lodi. After the death of Afghani Daria Khan Nuhani in 1523 CE, his son Muhammad Shah Nuhani (Bahar Khan) declared Bihar as an independent state.

In 1526 CE, the Mughals led by Babar defeated Ibrahim Lodi in the first battle of Panipat and established the Mughal dynasty in Delhi. When the Afghans attempted to take control of Jaunpur, Babar sent his army under the command of Humayun, which quelled the subversive attempts of Afghan Nuhani rulers. During this period, south Bihar was being ruled by Afghan ruler Muhammad Shah and north Bihar by Bengal ruler Nusarat Shah. Both these rulers were Afghans and were joining hands against the Mughals. After the death of Babar in 1530 CE, the Afghan power started to rise again. However, Humayun defeated the Afghans in Daura battle in 1532 CE and ensured the fall of the Nuhanis. After the fall of Nuhanis, Afghan power saw its resurgence under the leadership of Sher Shah.

Sur Dynasty

After the fall of the Nuhanis, there was resurgence of Afghan power under the leadership of Sher Shah Suri. Sher Shah was originally named as Farid Khan. He was the grandson of Ibrahim Khan Sur and son of Hassan Khan Sur. He was born in Punjwara near Delhi in 1472. His grandfather Ibrahim Khan and father Hassan Khan had left Punjab and gone to serve Bihar subedar Jamal Khan. Pleased with Hassan Khan's dedication, Jamal Khan handed over to him the estate of Sasaram, Khwaspur and Tanda parganas. Farid spent his childhood at the bank of the Son River in Sasaram. His childhood was not that joyful. As his father and stepmother were neglecting him, he moved to Jaunpur in 1494 CE at the age of 22 years. Jaunpur was a major centre of Islamic religion and culture in 15th century. It was known as the 'Shiraz of India'. Farid very diligently attained good knowledge of Arabic and Persian languages. Impressed by his merits, Jamal Khan succeeded in bringing about conciliation between him and his father Hassan Khan. Hassan Khan handed over the estate of Sasaram to his son Farid Khan in 1497 CE. Farid Khan very ably managed the estate of Sasaram from 1497 CE to 1518 CE and succeeded in systematising its administration. After overcoming the revolting zamindars, he made all possible efforts to provide amenities to common people. Again, after having some discord with his father and his stepmother, Farid moved to Agra. After the death of Hassan Khan in 1520, Ibrahim Lodi restored Hassan Khan's estate to Farid Khan. Farid Khan returned back to Sasaram. Immediately after his return, his stepbrothers started fighting among themselves for partition of the estate of Sasaram. Farid Khan got fed up with the same and again, in 1522 CE, he left Sasaram and took refuge under Bahar Khan Lohani, the ruler of South Bihar. Once, when he along with his master Bahar Khan was in a forest for hunting, he had killed a lion with a single blow. Impressed by his bravery, Bahar Khan had rewarded him with the title of 'Sher Khan'. Not happy with the growing influence of Sher Khan, the Afghan sardars, using Bahar Khan, dispossessed him of his inherited estate and made him leave South Bihar. Sher Khan then reached Agra and met Babar. Babar provided Sher Khan a job in his army. Observing Sher Khan's loyalty, Babar restored his ancestral estate of Sasaram to him. He moved back in 1528 CE to Sasaram where he functioned as the teacher and guardian of Bahar Khan's son Jalal Khan. After the death of Bahar Khan, Jalal Khan's mother Dudu Bibi became his guardian. She appointed Sher Khan as her Nayab (assistant). As her nayab, Sher Khan managed to remove the deficiencies existing in the army and made a significant contribution in making the administration robust. Sher Khan became the real ruler of Bihar after the death of Dudu Bibi. He assumed the title of 'Hazarat–e–Aala'.

In 1530 CE, Sher Khan married Lad Mallika, widow of Chunar's earlier Subedar Taj Khan. This significantly augmented his economic and military power. Sher Khan assigned his son, Kutub Khan the responsibility of Chunar's security. After the death of Babar in 1530, Humayun ascended the throne of Delhi. He dispatched a huge army to launch attack on Chunargarh. Demonstrating his political foresightedness, Sher Khan asked his son Kutub Khan to surrender. After Kutub Khan's surrender, Humayun entered into a deal with Sher Khan on simple terms and went back. Thus, Sher Khan succeeded in saving Chunargarh.

Bengal's new rulers Mahmud Shah and Jalal Khan formulated a plan again to launch an attack on Sher Khan. A fierce battle ensued between the armies of Sher Khan and Mahmud Shah in Surajgarh in 1534 CE. Sher Khan emerged as winner in this fight. After this victory campaign, Sher Khan got well convinced that Afghan rule could be re–established in India. Hence, he started recruiting Afghan soldiers at different places.

With the objective of taking a revenge for his defeat, the Bengal ruler Mahmud Shah, in collaboration with the Portuguese, attacked Sher Khan again. However, he was defeated in two battles–one at Teliagarhi and the other at Sikri Gali. Mahmud Shah requested Humayun for help. Humayun was then engaged in a battle with Bahadur Shah of Gujarat. At the request of Mahmud Shah, he set out for Bengal and laid siege to Chunar for six months. During the period, Sher Khan had secured victory over Bengal and Rohtasgarh.

Conflict with Humayun

Concerned with increasing strength of Sher Khan, Humayun decided to launch an attack on Bengal. Sensing a threat of attack, Sher Khan shifted his treasury from Gaud to Rohtasgarh. He allowed Humayun to enter Bengal without any resistance and he returned to Bihar. Humayun conquered Gaud and stayed back there for almost eight months. In the meantime, Sher Khan captured regions like Jaunpur, Varanasi and Kannauj.

Battle of Chausa (26 June 1539)

After securing victory over Gaud, Humayun's army stayed back there for almost eight months. While returning from Gaud, they decided to camp near Buxar at Chausa. Sher Khan, who was tracking their movement, reached there and attacked Humayun's army. Taken by surprise, the army started to flee. Humayun himself jumped in the Ganges to save his life. A bheesty named Nizam saved him. While Chausa victory on one hand emboldened Sher Khan, it had an adverse impact on the strength and reputation of Mughal army.

Battle of Kannauj (17 May 1540)

Humayun somehow managed to save his life after losing the battle at Chausa and reached Agra. He planned to launch another attack on Sher Khan and, gathering his courage, marched to Kannauj to confront Sher Khan. The armies of Humayun and Sher Khan came face to face in Bilgram. However, Humayun had to face defeat again without any fight because of the plots of his own samantas and soldiers. He fled to Punjab.

The battles of Chausa and Bilgram elevated Sher Khan to the status of the emperor of India. His unflinching courage and bravery dethroned the Mughal Empire and he established the Sur Dynasty in India. Sher Khan came to be known as the founder of the second Afghan Empire.

Expansion of Sher Shah's Empire

1. **Gakkhar Province (1541 CE):** Northwest border province was populated by Gakkhar community that was loyal to the Mughals. In order to weaken them and make northwest border secured, he built the Rohtasgarh Fort. Army was deployed there under the command of Haiwat Khan and Khwas Khan.
2. **Bengal (1541 CE):** Khizra Khan revolted in Bengal but the revolt was crushed by Sher Shah. After this, the governance structure was revamped to avoid any revolt in far-off and wealthy regions. He divided Bengal into 19 districts. He also created a new post of Amin-e-Bengal (non-military officer). Every district was assigned to a Shikadar for governance.
3. **Malwa (1542 CE):** After the death of Bahadur Shah, Mallu Khan assumed the title of 'Kadir Shah' and declared himself independent. He surrendered after Sher Shah's campaign and Shujat Khan was appointed the subedar of Malwa.
4. **Rayasin (1543 CE):** Rayasin province (Madhya Pradesh) was under the control of Puranmal, son of Chauhan Rajput Rai Singhalji. Sher Shah laid siege to Rayasin for several months and finally, Puranmal surrendered and handed over the fort to Sher Shah. This was a battle in line with his victory policy, but he launched large scale massacre in this battle that is considered to be a black spot on the reputation of Sher Shah.
5. **Rajasthan (1544 CE):** Marwar was being ruled by Maldev who was quite competent, brave and ambitious. Sher Shah wanted to wipe out the increasing power of the Rajputs. He for once used his cunningness instead of his valour and succeeded in taking control of Marwar. After winning Jodhpur, he defeated Chittor ruler Uday Singh also and within no time, captured four important forts like Ajmer, Jodhpur, Mount Abu and Chittor. But this victory proved to be too costly for him. He had himself accepted that he could have lost entire Hindustan for a fistful of millet.
6. **Kalinjer (May, 1545):** This was Sher Shah's last campaign. The main reason behind this campaign was the non-submission of King Kirat Singh to Sher Shah. Not only that, he had even provided protection to Maharaja Virbhan Singh of Rewa. In 1544, Sher Shah laid siege to the fort of Kalinjer. When he could not capture the fort even after six month's siege, Sher Shah ordered the wall of the fort to be demolished

using canon; however, the canon ball hit Sher Shah himself and he died. Sher Shah was operating the firearm 'Ukka' just before he met his end.

Sher Shah was a great ruler and administrator; rising from the status of the son of a simple jagirdar, he had attained the position of an emperor. When he was working for Mughal army, he had made a statement during the Chanderi battle—'If fate favours me and good fortune stays as my friend, I will one day chase the Mughals out of Hindustan.'

Sher Shah's Administration

Sher Shah was one of the greatest administrators of the medieval period. He had got the first experience of administration while managing the estate of his father. Later, he attained further experiences in administration when he worked as trustee of Jalal Khan and when he came in contact with the Mughals. He would work for 16 hours a day and manage all the jobs like managing army, recruiting soldiers, ensuring adjudication, and collecting taxes on his own. From the point of view of administration and military skills, Sher Shah was the greatest among the Afghans and was a great nation builder having creative intelligence even more than Akbar. Sher Shah is called the forerunner of Akbar. Sher Shah was considered the most famous ruler in the medieval history for his governance reforms. Historians believe but for the unexpected death of Sher Shah, India would not have seen resurgence of the Mughals. According to Sher Shah, the state was responsible not only for police administration but also for common welfare. He implemented reforms in army as per Alauddin Khilji, tax and revenue system as per Muhammad Bin Tughlaq, public services as per Firoz Shah Tughlaq and religious policy as per Kashmir Sultan Jainul Aabadin. Sher Shah implemented governance in the form of central and provincial structures.

Central Administration

All the powers of the centre were vested in Sher Shah, but he used the power for the welfare of his people. He organised all the departments of the central administration. His revenue policy was a mixture of those of the Turks and the Afghans. There were ministers and high officials in his administration also, but contrary to the Mughals, he had not provided them too much of power. Instead of taking their own decisions, they just followed instructions of Sher Shah. For his administrative structure, he built several departments just like those existing during the Sultanate period, as below:

- **Diwan-e-Wazarat:** This department was related to taxes and economy. Its head was known as Wazir. His job was a combination of the jobs of a finance minister and a prime minister and he also monitored other ministers. Maintaining record of income and expenses also was the responsibility of this department.
- **Diwan-e-Ariz:** This was the head of military organisation. Recruitment and management of army and maintenance of its discipline were included in its responsibilities.
- **Diwan-e-Rasalat:** This department was also known as Diwan-e-Mohatsib. This controlled foreign ministry that handled foreign affairs.
- **Diwan-e-Insha:** This was the department for handling official edicts and correspondences. This very department was responsible for communicating with subedars and other local officials.
- **Diwan-e-Kazi:** This was the judiciary department. Head of the department was known as Kazi. This department also heard appeals against subedars.
- **Diwan-e-Barid:** This was secret service department that supervised secret agents. These secret agents delivered all kinds of information to the king. Management of posts also was the responsibility of this department.
- **Khan-e-Sama:** The job of managing all the works of the royal palace was assigned to this department.

Thus, the central departments under Sher Shah had the same structure as that exited under the rulers of the Delhi Sultanate.

Provincial Administration

There is difference of opinion among historians with regard to the management of provincial administration under Sher Shah. Kanungo believes that there was no department above states during the period of Sher Shah. The entire empire was divided into 47 sircars. There was no administrative unit like province or suba during his period. However, Parmatma Sharan indicates that there was a system of provinces and military governors, though, after the revolt in Bengal in 1541 CE, some special arrangements were made and Bengal was divided into 19 sircars. Thus, the number of sircars during the period of Sher Shah had gone up to 66. This way, every suba was divided into sircars and every sircar had two officers–one being Shikdar-e-Shikdaran and the other Munshif-e-Munshifa.

Shikdar-e-Shikdaran: Besides being the chief officer of the sircar, he used to be an army officer also and took care of the law and order. He also supervised criminal cases.

Munshif-e-Munshifa: He used to be the chief judicial officer and adjudicated civil cases. Additionally, he also supervised the works of subordinate munshifs.

Every sircar (district) was divided into several parganas. Key officials of a pargana used to be Shikdar, Khazanchi (Fotedar), Amin, Munshif, one Hindi and one Persian clerk (Karkoon). Gram was the smallest unit of administration. Officials in a gram included Patwari, Chawkidar, Chaudhary, Mukkadam, and Pradhan. They discharged jobs related to administration, security, education, sanitary, etc.

Lagaan System of Sher Shah

During the period of Sher Shah, primary means of central income was land revenue or lagaan. Other means included unclaimed assets, loot, jizya tax, etc. Sher Shah paid special attention to farmers' wellbeing and their prosperity. He implemented the lagaan system similar to that of Alauddin; this was known as Raiyatwari. This had a system of making direct contact with farmers. Sher Shah got land survey done in order to implement land reforms. Land was divided into bighas, one bigha being an area of 3600 Sikandari Gaj. He classified lands into three categories:

1. Good land
2. Middling land
3. Bad land

Sher Shah used 32-digit sikandari gaj and jute stick for measurement of land. One-third of the crop was recovered as lagaan. Lagaan was recovered in the form of cash as well as crop, but cash was preferred. Sher Shah introduced the practice of patta and qabuliyat. The government provided each farmer a patta that had record of all details relating to his land. The farmer executed the qabuliyat to undertake payment of a definite amount as lagaan. The farmers would deposit lagaan directly into the royal treasury. After Firoz Shah Tughlaq, it was Sher Shah who paid more attention to the interest of farmers during the medieval period. He even directed his army not to destroy standing crops of the farmers and also not to harass them. There was a provision of compensation in the case of a crop being destroyed. Sher Shah also provided loans to the farmers on easy terms for land development or improving land fertility. Lagaan was waived in the case of a crop getting destroyed by natural calamities. Besides lagaan, he also imposed taxes like Zaribana (Survey fee) and Muhasilana (Tax collection fee). The lagaan system of Sher Shah later became the basis of the Dahsala system of Todarmal and Raiyatwari system of the British. As per Kanungo, had Sher Shah lived for another 10–20 years, he would have completely eliminated the zamindari system.

Judiciary and Secret Services

Sher Shah himself was the highest judge. He would sit in his court every Wednesday to adjudicate.

The cases relating to lagaan were disposed off by munshifs in parganas and by munshif–e–munshifa in sircars (districts). The cases related to army were handled by Kazi whereas criminal cases were heard by the shikdar-e-shikdaran. The criminal law was quite stringent and applied equally to everybody. All kinds of punishments were meted out, like imprisonment, whipping, dismemberment and fine. Sher Shah was a justice–loving ruler and used to say, 'Justice is the most excellent of religious rites'.

The secret service and information department of Sher Shah was quite advanced. 'Harakaras' were appointed for important towns, markets and inns. Two horses were always kept ready for secret services. Sher Shah kept control over his public administration with the help of secret agents and messengers. 'Daroga–e–Dak Chowki' was the head of postal and secret service department.

Monetary System

Sher Shah implemented several reforms in monetary system. He stopped circulation of old outworn coins and issued mainly coins of silver termed as 'Rupiya' (178 grains) and copper termed as 'Dam' (380 grains). Good quality metals were used for all the coins. The name of the mint of Sher Shah was printed on the coins in Arabic–Persian and Devanagari scripts. There were 23 mints at that time. Sher Shah was the first ruler who issued silver coins. His silver Rupiah was in circulation till 1835 CE. One Rupiah of silver was equivalent to 64 copper dams. The gold coin issued by Sher Shah was known as Ashrafi that contained 167 grains of gold. The coins were round and quadrangular. Being a Sunni, he got first four Khalifas of Islam printed on his coins.

Trade and Business

Sher Shah took several steps to develop trade and business. He instructed his officers to behave properly with businessmen. Many of the excise duties were scrapped. Excise duty was levied only at two locations—first, at Sunar village border in East Bengal or Rohtasgarh border in Punjab or specific borders of border provinces where goods for sale were first unloaded, and second at the places where goods were sold. Strict surveillance was maintained on smuggling trade. Efforts were made to keep prices of goods in the market consistent.

Building Projects of Sher Shah

Sher Shah took many initiatives in the field of architecture. He built the Rohtasgarh Fort in Sasaram. He got the old fort constructed in Delhi after demolishing the Dinpanah built by Humayun. Qila–e–Kuhna mosque was built inside the same in 1542 CE. This mosque was an example of a mixture of Indian and Islamic architecture. Sher Shah re–established Pataliputra in the name of Patna in 1541 CE. He also demolished Kannauj town and gave it a new shape. The best construction work of Sher Shah is the tomb of Sher Shah in Sasaram, built in the middle of a lake. Kanungo has made a comment in this regard, 'It is an example of Islamic architecture from outside and Hindu architecture from inside'. Cunningham has regarded this tomb to be even more beautiful than Taj Mahal.

Public Welfare Activities

Important public welfare activities undertaken by Sher Shah included construction of roads, inns and wells, planting shady trees and setting up postal services. He built four major roads in his empire. The longest and the most famous road was the 'Sadak–e–Azam' (Grand Trunk Road) originating at Sonar in the east and going up to Atak (Sindh) in the west. This is also known as 'Sher Shah Suri Road'. The second road is from Agra to Burhanpur, third from Agra to Jodhpur–Chittor and fourth from Lahore to Multan. Sher Shah arranged horses for making the postal system efficient.

Sher Shah was a very kind-hearted person. He established a number of religious institutions, arranged free meals for the poor, arranged houses for orphaned refugees, and even provided facilities for free houses and education.

BIHAR DURING MUGHAL ERA

The credit for establishment of the Mughal dynasty goes to Zahir ud-Din Muhammad Babar, a descendent of Timur Lang and Genghis Khan. He defeated the Delhi ruler Ibrahim Lodi in the first war of Panipat in 1526 CE and captured a major portion of India. In Bihar, Sultan Mohammad Shah Nuhani and sardars (heads) of Farmuli tribes challenged him. In the course of his military campaign, Babar compelled Farmuli sardars to surrender at Buxar, in Bihar, in 1529 CE, and appointed Murshid Iraqi as Diwan of Bengal. He defeated Muner sardars on 27 April, 1529. Even Sher Shah had accepted Babar's sovereignty. After the death of Babar on 30 December, 1530, his son Humayun occupied the throne. Sher Shah challenged the sovereignty of Humayun and defeated him comprehensively near Chausa on 26 June, 1539. Humayun somehow managed to save his life by crossing the Karmanasa River. Sher Shah defeated Humayun again in the battle of Kannauj in 1540 CE. Humayun had to go in exile and he took refuge under Iran ruler Tahamasya. With the help of the Iran ruler, he managed to capture Delhi again in 1555 CE and established the Mughal Empire. However, in 1556 CE, Humayun died after falling from the stairs of a library. After Humayun, his young son Jalal ud–din Muhammad Akbar ascended the throne of Delhi at the age of 14.

In fact, Akbar is considered to be the founder of the Mughal Empire in India. He demonstrated his foresightedness and established a mighty empire. In the initial years of Akbar taking over the reigns, the Afghans retained their sovereignty over Bihar. In 1564 CE, one Safaleman Karrani declared his independent rule over Bihar. After his death in 1572 CE, Daud Khan became the ruler. He made people read Khutbah in his name and also launched new coins. Daud Khan demolished the Patna fort. In order to crush the increasing power of Daud Khan, Akbar sent Munim Khan to Bihar. At that time, Daud Khan was in Hajipur and his minister Lodi Sardar was in Rohtas. After Munim Khan failed to defeat Daud Khan Emperor Akbar himself had to come to Patna. He attacked Hajipur fort, and Kiledar Fatah Khan, along with Barha defeated the other Afghans badly. Thus, Akbar succeeded in capturing the Hajipur fort.

Akbar sent his army captain Shahbaz Khan to confront king Vairishal of Chhota Nagpur. Shahbaz Khan defeated Vairishal and made him accept the sovereignty of Emperor Akbar. In 1579 CE, King Man Singh attacked Chero state of Palamu and compelled it to accept the sovereignty of the Mughal Empire and pay lagaan. Akbar defeated the Rajput king of Mithila in 1574 CE and Maḥesh Thakur, a Maithili Brahmin, was assigned the responsibility of collecting revenue from the region. Man Singh provided strength to the Mughal Empire during the period from 1587 CE to 1594 CE. He defeated local sardars of Giddhaur, Kharagpur, Bhojpur etc. He made Rohtas his capital. For some time, Man Singh used Raj Mahal also as his capital and he renamed it as Akbar Nagar.

Jahangir appointed Rajkumar Parvej as Governor of Bihar in 1621 CE. During Jahangir's rule, the Mughals were able to establish their control over the region of Khokhradesh (Chhota Nagpur). He succeeded in taking control of diamond mines in Chhota Nagpur. Jahangir's autobiography 'Tuzk–e–Jahangiri' has mention of gold also being recovered here. Shahjahan took away the region of Bihar from Parvej and crushed his revolt in 1623–24 CE. There was peace in Bihar during his rule. Aurangzeb, in 1702 CE, appointed his grandson Rajkumar Azim as Subedar of Bihar. Rajkumar Azim renamed Patna as Azimabad and spent ₹1 crore for beautification of the city. Murshid Kuli Khan was the Diwan of Bengal at that time. He established his independent kingdom in Bengal in 1704 CE and stopped paying taxed to the Mughal Emperor. Azim's son Farrukhsiyar was born in Patna. He defeated Emperor Jahandar Shah and ascended the Mughal throne. In Patna itself, Farrukhsiyar got his formal coronation performed and became emperor after securing victory in

Agra battle. He was the first Mughal emperor who was crowned in Bihar. Farrukhsiyar's successors Shuza–ud–Din and Sarfaraz Khan continued to rule up to 1740 CE. A new post of Nayab Nazim was created for efficiently managing the administration in Bihar. Aliwardi Khan was made the first Nazim. In 1740 CE, Aliwardi Khan killed Sarfaraz Khan and declared himself as the Nawab of Bengal; he ruled up to 1756 CE. He appointed Zainuddin Haibat as Nayab Nazim of Bihar to ensure smooth administration there. Right from the beginning, Aliwardi Khan had to face attacks from the Marathas and the Afghans. In 1743 CE, Maratha Peshwa Balaji Rao attacked Bihar again and reached Bhagalpur via Munger. In 1748 CE, the Afghans, under the command of Mustafa Khan, killed Haibat Jung. Aliwardi Khan defeated him in a battle at Patna. In 1751 CE, Aliwardi Khan defeated the Marathas in a battle near Fatuha, but majority of the regions in Odisha remained under control of the Marathas. Siraj ud-Daulah succeeded Aliwardi Khan after his death in 1756 CE.

Bihar Administration During Mughal Period

During the Mughal period, the administration in Bihar was split into several levels. In the initial years, especially between 1526 CE and 1540 CE, the old structure of administration was retained. Babar had defeated the Afghans of Bihar in the Battle of Ghaghra in 1529 CE. He visited Bihar many times but did not make any changes in the administrative structure there. In 1540 CE, Sher Shah established his rule over Bihar and implemented a new administrative structure there. He separated the north region of the present Bihar from Bengal and merged the same completely into Bihar. He split his administration into multiple levels that was later followed by Akbar also.

Akbar constituted Bihar in the form of a suba or province and this tradition was continued till the reign of Aurangzeb. As per Ain–i–Akbari, Bihar province (suba) was divided into seven sircars (districts). These sircars were Tirhut, Hajipur, Saran, Champaran, Munger, Bihar, and Rohtas. Sircars were further divided into 199 parganas, Mithila being the prominent one. Bettiah and Hathua were under the control of sircars of North Bihar. Munger, Bihar and Rohtas were the prominent sircars (districts) in South Bihar. They were under the control of Patna and Gaya Bihar sircars. Sircars were placed under zamindars. During the reign of Aurangzeb, there were 8 sircars and 245 parganas in Bihar. The Mughals had assigned Bihar the status of a very important suba. Among the subedars appointed were Kutub ud–Din Kokal, Sulaiman Shikoh, Azam, Azim–us–Shan, Man Singh, Saif Khan, Mir Jumla and Daud Khan. Diwans were appointed to assist the subedars; they helped subedars in managing administration in the suba. The diwan had the primary job of collecting revenue. Sadra used to be the head of religious department whereas Kazi was the judge. Bakshi was the military head and Fauzdar was the commander of the provincial army. Kotwal was the head of police department. Mirbahar had the primary task of recovery of taxes at ports, custom duty, and taxes on boats. Wakai was the officer that collected information related to rivers.

There were many officers for running the administration smoothly at sircar (district) level. Fauzdar was the chief administrative officer of the government and was the main assistant of subedar. Fauzdar had revenue, police, and army powers. He may be compared to present day District Magistrate. Amalguzar was the officer responsible for collecting revenue. Every sircar had a Kaudi or Kadi who had good knowledge of religious scriptures. Muftis were appointed to assist Kaudi. He would hear criminal cases also. He was assisted by Mir Adil. Kotwal had the responsibility of maintaining law and order in the town as a municipal officer.

There were many parganas under every sircar. There were 200 parganas during the period of Akbar and 246 parganas during the period of Aurangzeb. Pargana was smallest unit of administration.

Shikdar was the chief administrative officer in a pargana. Amil was responsible for revenue-related administration. Karkoon's job included maintenance of records for the pargana and deposit of revenue into government treasury. Fotedar was the officer of the local treasury. Chaudhary was the officer responsible for collecting revenue whereas Kanungo did safekeeping of revenue-related documents.

The Mughal rulers carried on with the impartial and justice loving administration established by Sher Shah. Jafar Khan, an officer of Viceroy Daud Khan, had established such judicial courts at many locations like Khajekala, Sadargali, Bhagalpur, and Rajmahal. Local administration in Bihar suba was quite robust during the period of the Mughals. A pargana covered many villages. The Mughal Emperor did not interfere at all in administration of these villages. Mukhia was the chief officer of a village. Mukhia of a village resolved all kinds of disputes at village level. A panchayat worked as a court.

Main sources of income for the suba of Bihar mainly included land revenue, trade, mint, gifts, monopoly, salt, mines, jizya, zakat and khams. Besides these, there were revenue receipts from market taxes. Land was classified into Khalsa, Jagir, and Sayurgal. They were left under the ownership of the king. Land revenue was collected by Shikdar. Navisinda and Mukaddam were there for his assistance. During the reign of Akbar, Todarmal conducted a measurement of land in Bihar and determined land revenue of around ₹25 lakhs. Wuzuhat, Zihat, and Sairzihat were among the main taxes levied on businessmen. Faruat was the tax recovered from zamindars. Besides above, Ikharazat, Abab, Hububat etc. were other prominent taxes. Taxes were also collected from brothels.

Special attention was paid towards army administration in Bihar province. The position of wrestlers was important in the army. People from Mahcshi in North Bihar and Buxar in Central Bihar were dominant among them. There were three kinds of army. First, it was the army organised by high officials. They were classified according to mansab. Second, it was the provincial army in which zamindars played key role. Provincial army assisted the subedar when required. Third, it was cavalry constituted at local level.

Thus, it may be said that the Mughal rulers established an organised administrative structure in Bihar suba. They instructed their provincial officials to serve for public welfare without any discrimination. Maintaining law and order and ensuring justice to people were their primary duties. There was provision for stringent punishment to convicts in civil and criminal cases.

Social Environment in Medieval Bihar

Bihar was divided into several religious communities and castes during medieval era. Hindu society was primarily divided into four varnas viz. Brahman, Kshatriya, Vaishya, and Shudra. The Brahmans enjoyed the highest position. Next was the position of the Kshatriyas in society. The Vaishyas, as usual, were engaged in economic and commercial activities. The position of the Shudras had not undergone any specific change. Just as before, they were involved in activities related to farm production and manual labour.

In medieval Bihar, primarily Brahma, Vishnu and Mahesh were worshipped in the form of a trimurti. Shakti was specially worshipped in Mithila. Among the notable saints and devotees there, reference to the names of Devaditya Mandal Mishra, Gangesh Upadhyay and some other tantrics have been found. Vaishnava dharma has made impact on the people of Bihar for a long time. The Vishnupada Temple of Gaya is a famous religious place for Vaishnava community. It is said that Chaitanya was initiated into Vaishnava dharma in Gaya by Vaishnava saint Ishwarpuri. A large number of Vaishnava followers of Chaitanya Dev belong to Bihar. His main disciple Raghupati Upadhyay was born in Tirhut. Vishnupuri, another disciple of Chaitanya, was a Maithili Brahman.

The Shaiva dharma has also been quite popular in Bihar. Famous religious centres related to the Shaiva dharma here are Baidyanath Dham, Baikunthapur (Patna), Bodh Gaya Math (Bodh Gaya) and Bazidpur (Samastipur). The largest number of the followers of the Shaiva dharma was in North Bihar. 'Hariharnath Temple' of Sonepur is a leading example of combined puja of Lord Vishnu and Lord Shiva. Arrival of the Muslims in Bihar in 11th century resulted in several changes in social structure here. Hindus initially protested against Islam with full force, but this protest slowly turned into compromise and there were a lot of exchanges at various levels between the two religions. People started using Persian and Arabic words in courts. This trend continued till 18th century. Both Hindu and Muslim saints were equally forthcoming in singing devotional songs in praise of Lord Rama and Lord Krishna. Bihar was an important centre of Sufi saints in medieval era. A lot of similarity was noticed in the philosophy of the Sufis and that of Shankaracharya.

During the medieval period, emergence of Kulinism in the social structure of Mithila was an important event. Instead of providing a progressive outlook, this resulted in development of conservative and rigid outlook. Credit for reorganising the society of Mithila on the basis of kulinism goes to King Harisingh Deva, who was the last ruler of the Karnata Dynasty of Mithila. Ancestry records were created in Mithila at a large scale, and record maintenance was provided an institutional shape. Under the registration process, purity of blood became the basis of marriage and also a means to maintain one's importance in society. The society, instead of getting united, split into many classes. Many gotras emerged in the Brahmans and the Kshatriyas also. Jyotirishwar has, in his book 'Varna Ratnakara', provided a list of Rajput castes, the major ones being Parmar, Chauhan, Kachhwaha, Chandel, Gahlot and Gandarbh. Malik Muhammad Jayasi has also mentioned about 36 Rajput castes. Some people from lower castes also acquired political power and declared themselves to be Kshatriya. Once they became rulers, they got their ancestry created and linked themselves to the lineage of 'Chandra' and 'Surya'.

The status of women in the medieval period remained quite miserable as before. The customs of polygamy and child marriage were still prevalent. Parents started to sell their daughters just for a few pennies. The condition of education was quite pathetic. Prostitutes became an object of ridicule in this period. Evidences showing women committing sati during that period have also been found. Proof of the wives of the Karnata king Shiva Singh Deva and Mithila king Bhava Singh committing sati are available. Sati practice was prevalent only among high castes of society. This practice was banned during the period of Akbar by enacting a law. There was also a practice of slave labour in Medieval Bihar. The master or owner could buy or sell slave labours whenever they wanted. Clear evidences of this practice of slave labour are found in Vidyapati's books. It may be understood from Vidyapati's 'Kirtilata' that the condition of Hindus in 13th and 14th centuries was quite miserable.

Economic Condition of Medieval Bihar

In Medieval Bihar, people were entirely dependent on agriculture. Agriculture only was the backbone of economy. Farming methods during medieval era were possibly similar to those exiting today. The most notable feature of the ancient village system was production of all the items of use at local level. Food crops cultivated by the farmers at that time included rice, pulses, oilseeds, barley, millet, sugarcane, cotton, and wheat. Tobacco and opium also were cultivated; they were used for medicines and as intoxicants. Besides above, that period also had production and even export of products like sugar, oil, perfumed oil, scent, etc.

In the second half of the medieval period, a new class of zamindars, jagirdars and middlemen emerged and they made the condition of farmers extremely miserable. The feudalistic system started collecting lagaan at high rates, adversely impacting the development of agriculture as well as growth of the farmers. Farmers were excessively exploited in the feudalistic system and they were turned landless. Many kinds of industries had developed in medieval Bihar. Especially notable among them were textile industry, silk industry, sugar industry, dairy industry, leather industry, wood industry, and handicraft industry. Tirhut region was famous for dairy industry. Mithila region was famous as a textile market. The book 'Varna Ratnakara' of that period has mention of 30 kinds of cloth. Though silk worms are found in Bengal, silk cloth was produced in Bihar. Besides, many small and cottage industries had also developed in medieval Bihar.

Thus, it may be said that though the condition of farmers was not very good in Medieval Bihar, many kinds of small and large industries were developed at that time. Trade and business were the most important economic activities after agriculture.

SUFISM IN BIHAR

The trend of cultural development continued during Medieval Bihar and a synergic tradition emerged in which the contribution of Sufi saints was quite significant. Among the initial Sufis, the name of saint Imam Taj Fakih who resided in Maner during 12th century was quite prominent. Many Sufi orders were active in Bihar during 13th century. They mainly included Chisti, Kadri, Suhrawardi, Firdausi and Nakshabandi. In Bihar, Sufi saints of Chisti and Suhrawardi orders had contributed the most towards synergic cultural development. Firdausi order has been the most popular Sufi order among all above.

Sufi saints laid emphasis on practical aspects of life and described innocence and simplicity as the greatest ornaments of human life. They acclaimed Hindu dharma and affirmed that a perfect society can be established in India only on the basis of harmony between Islam and Hindu dharma. They had faith in monotheism and they treated God as their lover. Instead of hatred and revulsion, they laid emphasis on infusing people's mind with honour and respect for each other.

Among the saints of Firdausi community in Bihar, Makhdum Sharfuddin Yahiya Maneri has been assigned the highest position. He was born in 1263 CE. His father was Makhdum Yahiya Maneri. Even today, his dargah is present in Maner in the name of 'Badi Dargarh'. He stressed on accepting the sovereignty of God and devotion towards Him instead of accepting the sovereignty of people of this world. He died in 1381 CE. The Firdausis in Bihar stressed on Hindu–Muslim unity. They did not support religious conversion. Still, Hindus impressed by his ideology, and accepted Islam.

The mausoleum of Makhdum Yahiya Maneri, father of Makhdum Sharfuddin, is known as Bari Dargah. The dargah of Ahmad Chirampos, another famous saint of Firdausi order, is located in Ambai near Bihar Sharif. He was a disciple of spiritual guru Sheikh Alauddin Chirampos (Bhagalpur).

The famous Suharawardi order had two sub–branches–first, Firdausia order and second, Sattaria order. Sattaria order was founded in Bihar by Abdullah Sattar. Even Kadri and Nakshabandi orders were widely promoted on large-scale in Bihar province. Kadri order in fact emerged in Bihar relatively later. Ali Sher was the first saint of this order. He was buried in Kutumb in Aurangabad. The most respected and dominant saint of Kadri order was Makhdum Shah Mohammad Munnam. He was born in Pachna village near Bihar Sharif. He built the Mir Taki Mosque in Mitan Ghat Mohalla of Patna City. The tomb of the main Sufi saint of Nakshabandi order Sahakale is located at Paschim Darwaza in Patna. Aurangzeb was a disciple of Mulla Mohan who was a famous saint of Nakshabandi order and was a resident of Bihar Sharif. Famous saints of Chishti order Shaikh Fateh and Shaikh Burhan came to Bihar during the reign of Firuz Shah Tughlaq.

Thus, Sufi saints of various orders preached religious tolerance, social compassion, public welfare and peaceful co-existence in Bihar. They disapproved bigotry, discrimination, inequality, and hatred.

Education in Medieval Bihar

Traditional way of imparting education was prevalent in medieval Bihar. Education centres were located in Tolas, Pathshalas, and temples. Teachers used to teach at their own residences. They imparted education in grammar, theology, jurisprudence and astrology. Sanskrit was the medium of education. Besides Sanskrit, other languages like Pali, Prakrit, Hindi, Bangla, Odiya, and regional languages of Bihar were also taught in Tolas. Educating students in Tolas was more popular. Muslims were educated in Makhtab, Madrasa and Khanqah. The main subjects of education used to be primarily religious. Makhtabs were usually centres of primary education. Madrasas were similar to the present day universities. Khanqahs were established in places like Bihar Sharif, Phulwari Sharif, Sherghati, and Bhagalpur.

Mithila was the main education centre of medieval Bihar. Along with the students of Bihar, students from outside Bihar were also imparted education here in jurisprudence and other subjects in addition to general studies. Ganesh Upadhyaya of Mithila had written the book titled 'Tatvachintamani' in 13th century. Dhayot test was quite popular in Mithila. This was brought into practice by Darbhanga Maharaj. Under this, royal pandits would conduct interview of the educated students and a debate on literature and other subjects would be arranged in presence of the Maharaja. Raghunandan Das Rai, a disciple of the founder of Darbhanga Raj Mahesh Thakur, was a great scholar of the science of reasoning. Impressed by his erudition, Akbar had gifted him the Mithila region.

The scholars of Bihar were highly respected during the reign of Shahjahan. These scholars were pundits of Persian, Arabic, and Sanskrit languages and grammar. Prince Dara Shikoha had honoured Bhavdeo Mir of Patna, who had written a number of books on Yoga and Vedantas. Patna, Bhagalpur, Bihar Sharif, Maner, etc. were the main education centres in Medieval Bihar. Detailed discussion on the subjects of intellectual and cultural activities taking place in Ajimabad (Patna) is presented by Mohammad Sadiq and Abdul Latif in the book 'Afsana–e–Shasan' written by Shaikh Kabir. Raja Ram Mohan Roy had come to Patna to learn Persian language. The famous Iranian traveller Ahmad Bahani (1807 CE) had visited the madrasa (Patna) of Saif Khan. Naib Nazir of Bihar Raja Ram Narayan, who was a disciple of the famous poet Shaikh Ali Ajin, had written a book titled 'Diwan' in Persian language. Another notable personality Maharaja Kalyan Singh had authored the famous historical book 'Khulasat–ut–Tawarikh'. Francis Buchanan had visited Patna in the beginning of 19th century. A famous personality of Wahhabi Movement Maulwi Ahmadullah had established a madrasa named Islah–al–Musalin in Patna.

Architecture in Medieval Bihar

Medieval Bihar is well recognised from the point of view of architecture prevalent during the period. There was a large-scale development of Islamic architecture during that period as replacement of the Hindu architecture. Islamic architecture was nothing but a mixture of Arabic, Afghani, and Hindu styles. The most important feature of Islamic architecture was construction of minarets, arches, domes, etc. Sculpting idols was prohibited in Islam and hence, sculpting could not progress during the medieval period.

Bihar mostly remained under the rule of Delhi Sultanate, Shirke, Lodi, Sur and Mughal kings during the medieval period. Hence, impact of these dynasties on the architecture in Bihar is clearly visible. A beautiful example of the royal style of the Delhi Sultanate is the tomb of Malik Ibrahim constructed in 1353 CE in Bihar Sharif. The tombs of Hazrat Mohammad Sibastani and Malik Bayan in Bihar Sharif, and the Sangi Mosque located in Patna are some of the important structures of the same style. There was an impact of Bengali style in the field of architecture in Bihar during 15th century.

The Bengal style developed well during the reign of the Shirke dynasty. An important structure of this style is the tomb of Shah Nafi located in Munger.

The best example of Sur style or Afghan style is the tomb of Sher Shah in Sasaram. Built in 1545 CE, this tomb is believed to be the last in the series of octangular tombs. This is a great and beautiful example of the blend of Hindu and Muslim architectures. Percy Brown and Cunningham have profusely appreciated the tomb of Sher Shah. The Rohtas Fort in the district of Rohtas in Bihar was built by Sher Shah. This fort is located on Kaimur Hill range at 40 km south of Dehri. Ganesh temple, Elephant door, Hanging House, Hathia Pole, Aaina Mahal, tomb of Habsha Khan, Jami Masjid. Diwan–e–Khas, Diwan–e–Aam etc. are some of the notable structures within this Rohtas fort. Among the structures under earlier Mughal architecture style are those built in Bihar during the reign of Akbar and Jahangir. Two prominent examples of architecture built during the reign of Akbar are Khan Mosque and Saki Sultan Tomb at Rohtasgarh. Among the structures built during the reign of Jahangir, the tomb of Makdum Shah Daulat at Maner, which is also known as Chhoti Dargah, is notable. This was built with red stone in 1617 CE. Another important structure of that period is the Sangi Mosque at Phulwari Sharif. Among the structures having later Mughal architecture style, the tomb of Makdum Saheb located at Champanagar near Bhagalpur is noteworthy. Jami Mosque of Hajipur, Tola Mosque of Mir Sahib at Bhagalpur, Shershah Mosque of Patna, Madrasa Mosque at madrasa ghat at Patna and tomb of Munaruddaula are prominent among structures of this style. Even artistic Hindu temples were built at several locations during medieval Bihar. The Shiva Temple at Baikunthapur near Patna, which was financially supported by King Man Singh, is famous for its ornamental sanctum sanctorum, miniatures on its walls etc. The Harishchandra Temple in Rohtasgarh was built by King Man Singh only. The Ganesh Temple also is one of the prominent temples of that period. Arrival of European businessmen also had left some impact of European architecture styles in Bihar. The Patna Museum and Patna College buildings are impacted by Holland style. Footprints of European style can be clearly observed on the structures of Raj Bhavan, Central Secretariat, High Court, etc.

Early Medieval Period

Date Sequence	Event
750–1175 CE	Reign of the Pala Dynasty
750–770 CE	Reign of Gopala, founder of the Pala Dynasty; Odantapuri Vihar established
770–810 CE	Reign of Dharmapala; Vikramshila Vihar established
810–855 CE	Reign of Devapala; period of cultural development of the Palas
858–912 CE	Reign of Narayanpala
912–936 CE	Reign of Rajpala
1095–1197 CE	Reign of the Sena Dynasty in Bihar; decline of Buddhism
1097–1098 CE	Emergence of the Karnata Dynasty in Mithila and Tirhut regions
1180 CE	Arrival of Imam Taj Fakih at Maner.

Medieval Period

Date Sequence	Event
1197 – 98 CE	Establishment of the reign of the Turks by Bakhtiar Khilji in Bihar. The last Pala ruler Indradhanu defeated.
1203 – 04 CE	Occupying of Lakshmanvati (Lucknauti) by Bakhtiar Khilji, Lakshman Sena defeated, Expansion of reign of the Turks in Bengal, Kamarupa campaign of Bakhtiar Khilji.

1290 – 1381 CE	Life period of the famous Sufi saint Makhdum Sharfuddin Maneri of Bihar.
1324 – 25 CE	Campaign of Gyasuddin Tughlaq in North Bihar, end of the Karnata Dynasty, annexation of Bihar to the Tughlaq Empire, establishment of provincial capital in Bihar Sharif.
1359 – 60 CE	Jajnagar (Odisha) campaign of Firozshah, Military pursuit of the Turks in Bihar (Jharkhand).
1504 CE	Arrival of Sikandar Lodi in Bihar.
1528 – 1532 CE	Growth of Nuhani Afghans in Bihar.
1529 CE	Nuhani Sardar defeated by Babar in Ghaghra battle.
1536 CE	Sultan of Bengal defeated by Sher Khan (Shah) in Surajgarh battle.
1539 CE	Humayun defeated by Sher Shah in Chausa battle, beginning of revival of the Afghans.
1540 CE	Humayun defeated again by Sher Shah in Bilgram (Kannauj) battle, occupation of Delhi by Sher Shah, establishment of the Sur Dynasty.
1540 – 55 CE	Reign of the Sur Dynasty.
1540 – 45 CE	Reign of Sher Shah.
1541 CE	Reconstruction of Patna by Sher Shah and its development as provincial capital.
1545 CE	Construction of the tomb of Sher Shah in Sasaram.

1556 – 1576 CE	Reign of the Karrani Afghans in Bihar.
1574 – 76 CE	Akbar's attack on Bihar, Daud Karrani defeated, beginning of the reign of the Mughals in Bihar.
1580 CE	Constitution of Bihar province under the Mughal Empire.
1585 – 1587 CE	Bihar journey by British traveller Raulf Fitch and Iranian traveller Mulla Takia.
1608 CE	Bihar journey by Iranian traveller Abdul Latif.
1616 CE	Construction of the tomb of Shah Daulat in Maner.
1619 CE	Arrival of Iranian traveller Muhammad Sadiq in Bihar.
1621 CE	Rajkumar Parvej appointed as Subedar of Bihar.
1623 CE	Revolt by Shahjahan, attempt to take control of Bihar.
1651 CE	Establishment of factory (commercial centre) by the British in Patna.
1666 CE	Birth of Guru Govind Singh in Patna.
1665 – 66 CE	French traveller Tavernier's journey to Bihar.
1671 – 71 CE	British traveller John Marshal's journey to Bihar.
1702 CE	Rajkumar Ajim appointed as Subedar of Bihar, Patna renamed as 'Ajimabad'.
1713 CE	Coronation of Mughal Emperor Farrukhsiyar in Patna.
1733 CE	Complete control of nawabs of Bengal established over Bihar.
1734 – 40 CE	Aliwardi Khan appointed as Nayab Nawab in Bihar.

1740 – 48 CE	Haibat Jung appointed as Nayab Nawab in Bihar.
1748 CE	Revolt of Rohilla Afghans in Bihar, Haibat Jung killed.
1751 CE	Maratha's attack on Bihar.
1757 CE	Victory for the British in the Battle of Plassey, Siraj–ud–Daulah killed, Mir Jafar appointed Nawab of Bengal and Raja Ramnarayan Singh as Nayab Ajim of Bihar.
1759 – 1760 CE	Unsuccessful campaign of Rajkumar Ali Gauhar against the British; subsequently, his (Shah Alam II) coronation at Patna under the patronage of the British.
1764 CE	Victory of the British in the Battle of Buxar.
1765 CE	Diwani rights for Bihar, Bengal and Odisha granted to the British East India Company by Shah Alam II, sole right of the East India Company over lagaan collection.
1769 CE	British administrator appointed for Bihar
1770 CE	Constitution of Bihar Council, growth of the British rule, suppression of protest of Nonia community, severe famine in Bihar and Bengal.
1774 CE	Constitution of the Provincial Committee in Bihar as per provisions of the Regulating Act.
1781 CE	Revolt by zamindars in Patna and nearby regions, first Santhal Rebellion.
1786 CE	Construction of Golghar in Patna by John Augustus.
1789 – 94 CE	Tamar Rebellion.
1793 CE	Permanent Settlement introduced in Bihar.
1809 – 10 CE	Bihar trip of Iranian traveller Bahbahani.
1821 CE	Beginning of Wahabi Movement in Bihar.
1831 – 32 CE	Kol Rebellion.
1832 – 33 CE	Bhumij Revolt.
1855 – 56 CE	Santhal Rebellion.

❑❑❑

Modern Period

- **Arrival of European Companies**
- **Establishment of the British Rule**
- **People's Movements against the British Rule**

ARRIVAL OF EUROPEAN COMPANIES

European trading companies arrived in Bihar in the 17th century. Bihar was an important centre for international trade at that time. The Portuguese were the first to arrive in Bihar region; they set up their business centre in Hugli. They used to come to Patna via boats. They would bring with them spices, porcelain pots, etc. and take back cotton clothes and other kinds of clothes on return.

By the middle of 17th century, the Dutch had established shora (saltpetre) godowns at many locations in Bihar. First of all, the Dutch set up a Dutch factory in the north building of Patna College in 1632 CE. They were interested in trades involving cotton clothes, sugar, saltpetre, opium, etc. In 1662 CE, Nathias Vagden Baruk, chief of Dutch affairs in Bengal, had obtained a trade related farman from Mughal Emperor Aurangzeb in respect of Bengal, Bihar and Odisha. The Dutch traveller Tavernier arrived in Patna on 21 December, 1665. He then travelled to Chhapra. Chhapra was a centre for refining saltpetre at that time. There would be always some tension among the East India Company, French and Dutch companies for control over saltpetre. Rebellious Afghan Sardar Shamsher Khan attacked Patna in 1848 CE and looted the Dutch factory located at Fatuha. The position of the Dutch turned even more miserable after victory of the British in the Battle of Plassey. The British East India Company secured exclusive rights over saltpetre trade in Bihar in 1758 CE. In the decisive battle of Bedara in 1759 CE, the Dutch were defeated by the British and their existence almost came to an end. They were somehow able to secure their warehouses at Chinsura Kasim Bazar and Patna.

The eruption of war between Britain and Holland in Europe around 1780–81 CE resulted in strained relationship between the two companies in Bihar also. On 10 July, 1781, Patna militia commanding officer Major Hardy seized the Dutch warehouse at Patna. The Dutch factories at Chhapra and Sindhia were also taken under control. On 5 August, 1781, Patrick Whitley received command of the Dutch factory from Maxwell. The warehouse was returned to the Dutch company on 8 October, 1784. Again in 1795, as a result of Franco Dutch war, the Dutch locations in India were taken over by the British government. However, the warehouses were again returned to the Dutch in 1817 CE. Eventually, in 1824–25 CE, the Dutch commercial establishments were permanently merged with the British East India Company.

Arrival of French Companies in Bihar

The French East India Company was established in India in 1664 CE under the leadership of Francois Martin. Martin established Pondicherry in 1674 CE and very soon, set up French commercial centres at Mahi, Karaikal and other locations. The French entered Bengal after a few years and established Chandra Nagar. Immediately after that, they built a warehouse at Patna in 1734 CE. The primary interest of the French company was to acquire saltpetre in Bihar. An atmosphere of tension between the British East India Company and the French East India Company used to be always there—both trying to gain supremacy and control over trade. The British captured Chandra Nagar in March 1757. M. Jianlaw, head of the French company at Kasim Bazar was compelled to leave Bengal. Jianlaw reached Bhagalpur on 2 May, 1757 and Patna on 3 June, 1757. He was welcomed at Patna by Bihar Deputy Governor Raja Ramnarayan who provided him land for building a barrack. After attaining victory in the Battle of Plassey, the then Bihar General of the British East India Company Eyre Coote externed Jianlaw from Patna and captured the French warehouses. The French lost Pondicherry also in 1761 CE. Under the Dairif agreement of 1763 CE, the lost regions were restored to the French company. During the period of Lord Cornwallis in 1793 CE, commercial activities of the French in India got restricted to Pondicherry. After that, French activities gradually started disappearing from Bihar and India and by 1814 CE, it was almost non–existent.

Arrival of Danish Company in Bihar

The name of Denmark comes last in the list of European companies coming to India. A factory of Denmark Company was established in Patna in 1774–75 CE. In May 1775, Head of Patna Danish factory George Warner demanded a farman from the Governor General of the East India Company and its board for doing business in Bihar. Danish Company also was primarily engaged in the business of saltpetre.

A war erupted between Great Britain and Denmark in 1801 CE, resulting in an atmosphere of tension between the two companies in India also. The British seized the Danish factory in Patna and the mansion in Serampur. A treaty was signed in the city of Amiens in 1802 CE, according to which the properties owned by Denmark in India were returned to them. By 1845 CE, all the warehouses and locations belonging to Denmark were in control of the British.

Arrival of the British East India Company

There is difference of opinion among scholars with respect to the establishment of permanent warehouses of the British East India Company in Bihar. Most of the historians believe that the permanent warehouse of the East India Company was constructed at Gulzarbagh in Patna in 1691 CE. The company was interested in trading in calico cloth and raw silk. Besides, they considered saltpetre and opium also an inseparable part of their business. Calico cloth was produced on large-scale in Lakhbar near Patna.

In 1664 CE, Job Charnock was appointed as head of the British factory at Patna; he continued there till 1680–81 CE. Irked by the imposition of 3.5 per cent tax on the business of the British company by Bihar Subedar Shaista Khan in 1680 CE, Job Charnock looted the city of Hoogly in 1686 CE. As a result, Shaista Khan issued an order to seize all the properties of the British in Bengal and Bihar; however, after an agreement in 1690 CE, the British were allowed to carry on with their business again. The death of Mughal Emperor Aurangzeb brought about interruptions in trading activities of the British. During the reign of Farrukhsiyar, the Patna factory was closed in 1713 CE; however, in 1717 CE, he provided the British the freedom to do business in Bihar and Bengal again. Thus, the British reopened the Patna factory in 1718 CE. Under pressure from Nawab Aliwardi Khan, the Patna factory was closed again in 1750 CE, but Hallvel managed to restart the factory in 1755 CE. The Battle of Plassey in 1757 CE and the Battle of Buxar in 1764 CE resulted in Bihar coming under complete control of the British. Subsequent to the Battle of Buxar, Lord Clive and Mughal Emperor Shah Alam II entered into in agreement at Allahabad on 12 August, 1765, according to which the Company was provided Diwani rights over Bihar, Bengal, and Odisha.

ESTABLISHMENT OF THE BRITISH RULE

Bihar has been a bustling business centre since the beginning. Bihar was a major business centre during the medieval period also. Businessmen like Edward Terry, Ralph Fisch, Peter Mundy, and Tavernier travelled through Bihar and presented detailed description of business activities there. During the reign of Nawab Murshid Khan and Aliwardi Khan of Bengal, foreign trading companies essentially kept themselves busy with their business activities in Bihar and their political aspirations remained suppressed. Siraj–ud–Daula defeated Shaukat Jung in the battle of Manihari on 16 October, 1756. Siraj–ud–Daula still had the risk of attack from the British. The officers of the British East India Company started fortification of Fort Williams in Kolkata. This created friction between Siraj–ud–Daula and the British, finally resulting in the Battle of Plassey on 23 June, 1757, where the British emerged victorious. They appointed Mir Jafar as Nawab of Bengal and his son Miran as Deputy Nawab of Bengal; however, Raja Ramnarayan got the real control of Bihar. In 1760 CE, Mir Qasim, with the help of the British, became Nawab of Bengal, but his relationship with the British did not continue to be cordial for a long time. In 1761 CE, Mir Qasim shifted his capital from Murshidabad to Munger. He built a fort to keep Munger secure. His relationship with the Nawab of Bihar Diwan Ramnarayan was also not so cordial. Mir Qasim made an attempt to take him into custody accusing him of indiscipline, but Ramnarayan joined hands with the British. Mir Qasim wrote a letter to the Company Governor Vansittart asking him to hand over Ramnarayan. Vansittart handed over Ramnarayan to him and he got Ramnarayan executed.

Mir Qasim imposed a ban on misuse of the 'Dastak' facility by the Company officials. This enraged the British East India Company. Mir Qasim put Seth Hirachand and his brother Swaroopchand, both sympathisers of the British, under house arrest at Munger. The British agent at Patna Alice was instructed to attack the town. Alice took control of Patna on 24 June, 1763, and after overrunning the town, got many innocent people killed. With no other option in sight, Mir Qasim launched military action against the British agent Alice. Alice was brought to Munger in captivity. Several British officers were massacred by Mir Qasim in Patna; this incident later came to be known as 'Patna Massacre'. A conflict between Mir Qasim and the British became inevitable after this bloodbath. Mir Qasim was defeated by the British in the battle of Udaynala of Rajmahal in Bihar on 2 September, 1763. The British could not capture Mir Qasim and he managed to escape to Avadh state after crossing the Karmanasa River on 4 December, 1763.

The British named Mir Jafar as Nawab of Bengal again. They also took control of the mandis at Colonelganj and Marufganj in Patna. Even the timber mandi of Purnia was captured by the British and deprived the Nawab of the annual income of ₹50,000 generated there. After being defeated at Patna, Mir Qasim, in alliance with Avadh Nawab Shuza–ud–Daula and the Mughal Emperor Shah Alam II, started preparing for a war against the British. He set out for Patna along with the combined army of Avadh Nawab Shuza–ud–Daula and the Mughal Emperor Shah Alam II. This unnerved Carnac, chief of the British army. Calcutta Council appointed Hector Munro as Commander–in–Chief. Munro arrived in Patna in July 1764 and enticed Rohtas Fort governor Sahumal to join hands with him. Munro crossed the Son River and reached Buxar, where he had to fight a war against the three prominent powers of India on 22 October, 1764. The British were the ultimate victors. While this defeat at Buxar brought an end to the fortunes of Mir Qasim, at the same time, this also resulted in complete control of the British over Bihar. Considering the prevailing situation, the Mughal Emperor granted Diwani rights to the British over Bihar, Bengal and Odisha in 1765 CE.

PEOPLE'S MOVEMENTS AGAINST THE BRITISH RULE

An atmosphere of discontent had developed here right from the moment the Company entered this region in 1767. Tribal lifestyle was already hard and over and above that, natural famine, and disasters had created severe crisis for them. Financial problems and shortage of food grains had shattered these tribals to the core. Above all the Mughals, Marathas and local zamindars, by their acts of oppression and exploitation, turned the tribals rebellious.

The rights and interest, of tribal population were being impaired and suppressed at administrative level. In addition to that, these people could also see the danger hovering over their culture and civilisation. The tribals started fearing loss of their identity and freedom after arrival of the British. All these various reasons gave rise to the tribal revolt. Tribal revolts had started towards the end of 17th century even though the British had been here for just two decades. Discriminatory policies of the British had also played a role in fomenting these tribal rebellions. There were in all 13 tribal rebellions that occurred during the British rule. The major rebellions are described below.

Tamar Revolt

The British had attained control over Chhotanagpur in 1771 CE and the kings and zamindars in the region were enjoying the Company's patronage, thereby giving them enough leverage for exploitation of common people. The zamindars had started to grab the lands of farmers. This policy of exploitation had ignited the fire of rebellion among the people of Oraon tribe. This tribe started to demonstrate its revolutionary intentions in 1789 CE and started assailing zamindars. By 1794, these rebels made the zamindars so fearful that they urged the British government for their protection.

The British assessed the situation and suppressed the rebellion with full force. This gave rise to a number of new arrangements and there was peace for some time. When the incidents of land grab started again, the revolt became widespread.

Chero Revolt

This movement was launched by Chero farmers against British ruler in 1800 CE. This revolt was later targeted against the discriminatory policy of the British when the Company plotted to dethrone Jainath Singh and install Gopal Rai as the new ruler in his place. After some time, Gopal Rai joined hands with some rebellious *Chero sardars*; which angered the British. The British arrested Gopal Rai and imprisoned him in Patna Jail. They then installed Chudaman as the new ruler of that region. Chudaman Rai took every action in consultation with the British only and this adversely impacted the interest of the tribals. This resulted in rise of discontent among the people and an open rebellion was launched under the leadership of Chero sardar Bhushan Singh. Chudaman Rai made an appeal to the British for help and swooped on the rebellious group. Colonel Jones made all possible efforts to suppress this rebellion but he failed to attain the expected success. Chero rebels kept dodging the British and Chudaman Rai for two years. Eventually, Bhushan Singh was arrested. This revolutionary Chero leader was hanged to death in 1802 CE and that gradually brought this rebellion also to an end.

'Ho' Revolt

This revolt was launched by 'Ho' people of Chhotanagpur in 1821–22 CE against Jagannath Singh, ruler of Singhbhum. Ho people were generally neutral towards Jagannath Singh and they were not fighting for any issue. The Nag Ruler had attacked them on one or two occasions but they were on friendly terms with the ruler of Singhbhum. When the ruler of Singhbhum later accepted the sovereignty of the British and started to mistreat his own Ho friends following the policies of the British, the Ho people got infuriated. Major Russej also used these people to serve his own interests and kept making fool of them by giving them false assurances.

Ho people were quick to realise that they were being duped and their simplicity was being exploited. When they raised objections to the same, Major Russej realised that they were turning rebels. A glimpse of their revolt was visible when there was an incident of a group getting looted and some people getting killed. Russej immediately dispatched an army contingent to take on the Ho rebels. The Hos got together and thrashed the army badly. This made Russej nervous and he sent his army to Gutialor village that was inhabited by majority of Ho people. The British ransacked and burned the village and inflicted heavy damage there. The Hos also did not surrender and they kept on fighting with full force. Russej started to feel the situation was getting worrisome. Hence, he called for additional army. After continuous fighting for over a month, the Ho rebels had to finally surrender. Thus, eventually an environment of peace was created after some taxes and conditions were agreed upon.

Kol Rebellion

This widespread uprising was a combined revolt of several tribes of Chhotanagpur, Palamu, Singhbhum, and Manbhum regions; this was a reaction against their exploitation because of the rising interference of the British. The zamindars supported by the British were exploiting these people, especially the farmers to such an extent that they were even getting deprived of food. Innumerable unwanted taxes and forced recoveries were making their hearts bleed. In order to collect arbitrary taxes from these people, who depended on agriculture and hunting, they were tortured in various ways and in the case of their inability to pay taxes, their lands were given to dikus (outsiders). The zamindars would subject them to forced labour. These zamindars would themselves move in 'Palkis' and the tribals would work as 'kahars'. Even the animals of the zamindars were taken care of by these tribals only.

Cuthbert has said, "These zamindars oppressed the farmers to the extent that many of the villages turned deserted. In this feudal system, the zamindars would never care for the interest of the peasants and additionally, the ruling class was also busy exploiting these people. As a result, the population was on the decline and people were just somehow managing to sustain themselves."

W. W. Blate has, in respect of the same, made the following remark, "The administrative system of the ruler was extremely pessimistic and grievous towards these oppressed classes. Lands of the peasants were being grabbed by force and handed over to outsiders. The attitude of none of the rulers or the administrators was sympathetic towards their complaints. This loot, oppression, and exploitation had resulted in many lives being lost."

Besides, there were some ethical reasons also that had created rebellious feeling in the mind of the tribals. Hence, there was a sense of discontent among these people and this could have exploded like a volcano any time. The Munda community called for a meeting of tribals at Bandagaon. Around seven members of Kol tribe attended that meeting and this marked the beginning of this great rebellion. Dikus, the British, and the zamindars were all gripped by this revolt. The rebels burnt many of the villages completely. The consequence of all this was that the rebellion and the immediate causes lit the fire of revolt in other regions also like Singhbhum, Tori, Hazaribagh, and Manbhum. This uprising took the lives of around 1000 people.

The British government assembled their army at Ramgarh with the purpose of suppressing this widespread uprising. They even sought some army from outside. Buddhu Bhagat, Singh Roy and Surya Munda were leading the rebels. Captain Wilkinson was the commander–in–chief of The British army. There was large-scale loss of life and property when the British army faced the rebels. Budhu Bhagat was killed along with his 150 supporters. The uprising continued for almost five years and the number of rebels killed during the period was quite large; this upset the Company.

The Company conducted an investigation of the causes of the rebellion and introduced some basic changes in the governance system of Jharkhand. The need for a better judiciary and transparent system was felt. Till that time, the British government had implemented the same common rules that were prevalent in Bengal; however, after looking into the complexities of the current situation, they enacted a new law in the name of 'Regulation XIII' according to which, Ramgarh was divided. A new separate administrative region was constituted with Jungle Mahal and the Tributary Mahal, a non–regulation province. This new administrative region was placed under a Governor as the first Agent of the General. In this governance system, Wilkinson, who was earlier a captain in the army and was sent for suppressing the rebellion, was made the first governor. 'Kol Rebellion' has a special place in the history of Jharkhand as it had far–ranging consequences. It was this revolt only that laid the foundation stone for reforms in the governance system.

Bhumij Revolt

Bhumij Revolt is also known as 'Ganga Narain Hungama'. This was a joint revolt of tribal zamindars and tribal people and was led by Ganga Narain, the grandson of the Badabhum's ruler Belak Narain. While there were definitely some political reasons behind this revolt, this had basically emanated out of the oppression of the tribals. Madhav Singh, brother of Ganga Narain, had plotted to grab the properties belonging to Ganga Narain at Badabhum. Madhav Singh was a Diwan. He had exploited people badly. When Ganga Narain protested against the same, he turned to the Company army for protection. Ganga Narain also perceived seriousness of the situation and made contacts with the zamindars that were already anguished with the British system. Besides them, Ganga Narain also received support of the tribals, as they were also quite frustrated with the system. Those from Kol and Ho tribes were particularly very unhappy. Thus, a precursor of a joint revolt under the leadership of Ganga Narain was set, with the tribals playing a significant role in the same. In the year 1832 itself, when an attempt was being made to suppress the Kol Rebellion, Ganga Narain along with his group of rebels launched the revolt. The British termed this revolt as 'Bhumij Revolt'. Very soon, the revolt turned widespread and the Company army set out under the command of Lt. Bendon and Timor for suppressing the same. Thakur of Kharsawan took the side of the British in this fight.

Ganga Narain was killed in this fight and Thakur of Kharsawan cut his head and sent the same as a gift to Captain Wilkinson. The rebellion was already suppressed, but this uprising had made Wilkinson ponder over something more. He explained the reality to his senior officials and sought their advice on the need for some administrative reforms in Jungal Mahal. Under Regulation XIII, the district of Jungal Mahal was suspended and its Diwani court was closed. New constitution policy was implemented according to which, Shergarh, Vishnupur and Sonpahadi were merged with Burdwan and a new district Manbhum was created with the rest of the regions. This new district covered many of the important regions including Jhaldah, Dhanbad, Supur, Raipur, Ambika Nagar, Badabhum, and Shyam Sundarpur. Man Bazar was made its immediate headquarters; this was later shifted to Purulia in 1838 CE.

Thus, 'Bhumij Revolt' also turned to be a cause for reforms in governance system. The British officers had understood that lack of transparency in justice delivery to the tribals and their exploitation in any form were the reasons for giving rise to revolts. Bringing the governance structure under direct control of the governor was a positive step in this direction.

Santhal Rebellion

The Santhals persecuted by the zamindars of Birbhum, Dhalbhum, Singhbhum. Manbhum and Bankura had started to relocate to Santhal Parganas, also known as 'Damin–i–koh', right from the year 1790 CE. The rebellion raised by these very Santhals has been the most talked about revolt in the history of Jharkhand, as this inflicted large-scale damage to life and property of the Company and its employees and officers and the zamindars supported by it. Exploitation of the peasants was the primary reason behind this rebellion. The Santhal tribe was also dependent on agriculture and forests, but the zamindari system had started to dispossess them of their own lands. The zamindars supported by the British were exploiting them blatantly and additionally, the Company had unfairly raised agriculture taxes beyond the capacity of these Santhals to pay. Besides, movement of the outsiders in their region had compelled the Santhals to get restricted to their own lands and made them very poor. The Santhals just for their subsistence were getting trapped in the cycle of exploitation, unleashed by these money-lenders and zamindars. These exploiters provided loans at high interest rates and then indulged in mental and physical oppression in the name of recovery. The judicial system also sided with these very rich and wealthy exploiters. The Santhals, unable to find a way to wriggle out of this network of exploitation, were going to the extent of committing suicides.

Common people would wish for an incarnation of God only to help them in such a grave situation. God also heard their prayers, and that's how two young brothers named Sidhu and Kanhu came forward to oppose this atrocious exploitation of the Santhals. The two brothers worked round the clock to instil the courage of revolt among the Santhals and encouraged them to come together.

In the year 1855, thousands of Santhals organised a meeting under the leadership of four sons of Bhognadih resident Chunnu Manjhi—Sidhu, Kanhu, Chand and Bhairav vowed to launch a sustained fight against their persecutors. Sidhu and Kanhu were successful in instilling a new spirit in these people. They unitedly served an ultimatum to the dikus (outsiders) to get away from their lands. These dikus included Britishers and their supported employees, officers and zamindars. A proclamation was made for disobeying government orders, setting up self–governance structure in Damin region and discontinuing payment of taxes. In the meantime, police inspector Maheshlal was killed. Two days after issuing their ultimatum, the Santhals started hunting their exploiters and killing them. The haveli of the zamindar of Amber was burnt. The rebels made an attempt to take control of Maheshpur in Rajmahal. The officers and zamindars were their primary targets, though houses and shops of the outsiders were also vandalised. This was an open armed rebellion that had spread right from Kahelgaon up to Rajmahal. This uprising further spread to Birbhum, Bankura, and Hazaribagh also by 1856 CE. This made the Company worried and attempts were made to persuade the Santhals through dialogue. However, the Santhals, whose hostility had taken shape after crossing the limits of patience, were not ready to listen to anything. The Santhals had already vowed to remove the Britishers and their supporters from their lands. British offices were getting burnt one by one. Even the Britishers were being killed wherever the Santhals could find them. The Santhals had turned 'Kaal' incarnate. They went on killing even the British women and children.

The upheaval caused by the Santhals unnerved the British administration. The Company allowed full freedom to its army to suppress the rebellion. The Britishers also demonstrated extreme brutality towards the Santhals and burnt many of their villages. The British army was busy round the clock hunting down Santhal leaders and they were successful also to a great extent. Most of the rebel leaders were either killed or arrested. Chand and Bhairav attained martyrdom. Sidhu and Kanhu were arrested; they were hanged to death in Barhet. The rebellion had still been successful to some extent as the Santhals were able to either kill or oust most of the Britishers and their supporters from their regions. Even those who were left behind lived under the cloud of terror for a long time. The people of Jharkhand started treating Sidhu and Kanhu, founders of this revolt, as their God, and even today, they are remembered as revolutionary leaders of Jharkhand. The legends of Sidhu–Kanhu are still sources of inspiration for the people of Jharkhand.

The Santhal Rebellion was suppressed in Santhal Pargana region by January 1856. However, the goverment did come to realise the bravery and valour of the Santhals. The government had to accept the need for reforms in governance.

As a consequence of this Santhal rebellion, Santhal Parganas was formally constituted as a separate district on 30 November, 1856, and Ashley Eden was appointed as its first District Magistrate.

Sardari Movement

Acceptance of Christianity by many of the tribals in this region after 1850 CE had made the issue of land ownership still worse. Tribal reform movements were launched in protest against widespread promotion of Christianity. Sardari movement, launched from 1859 CE to 1881 CE was one among them. This has been mentioned by Sharat Chandra Roy in his book 'The Mundas and Their Country'. In fact, this was a struggle for land. The primary aim of this movement was to oust the zamindars, stop the system of forced labour and protest aganist the restrictions imposed on lands. This movement generally ran in three stages.

Kharwar Movement

The Kharwar Movement, launched by Bhagirath Manjhi, was primarily aimed towards re–establishing the ancient values and traditions of the tribals. The impact area of this movement was Santhal Parganas. Additionally, they also promoted reforms in land related issues and sanctity in social rituals. Hence, they protested against drinking etc. Those who fully supported this movement were called Safa Hor and those who were neutral to the same were known as Babjiya. Those who supported half–heartedly were called Melbaragar.

Birsa Munda Movement

This has been regarded as the most organised and widespread movement in the tribal regions of Bihar. The founder of this movement, Birsa Munda has been recognised as an incarnation of God. Munda tribe, just like other tribes, was also depending on agriculture and forests and preserving its traditions and beliefs. This was one of the major tribes of Chhotanagpur region and people of this tribe never figured in the headlines of any kind of disputes. The oppression and looting by the British made even the peace–loving Mundas turn to revolt. Another major reason for their revolt was also the sense of their own culture getting contaminated by other cultures. Some common internal disputes that generally exist in every caste and tribe were existing among the Mundas also. They were friendly to the Hindus also and hence, some of the Mundas had started following Hindu traditions. The disputes had also led some Mundas turn to Christian missionaries. As the zamindars and rulers in Chhotanagpur were indulging in their cycle of oppression, these tribals also had got caught in that cycle. Their lands were being grabbed and the burden of taxes on them was also continuously growing. Hence, they were also getting squeezed into the cobweb of loans. The judiciary was there just for namesake and the Mundas faced the hardest shock when neither their Hindu friends not the Christian missionaries, who had enticed them to abandon their own traditions, came to their rescue when required. All these things had made the Mundas quite demoralised and they were worried about protecting their own existence. In that moment of anxiety, young Birsa Munda came forward avowing upliftment of the Munda tribe. He asserted that he had come as an incarnation of God with His permission and power to rid the Mundas of external forces and restore their rights. There was energy in his voice and it also had the capacity to hit hard the system existing at that time. Very soon, some more young Mundas got influenced and joined him. Using religious discourses, he tried to bring about renaissance among the people. That was the reason people started believing him to be an angel. His thoughts had the power to contemplate on all subjects. He would organise meetings and exhort people to keep away from social evils and give importance to self–sufficiency in their life and also explain to them the strength of his organisation. His group of friends also soon established him as a 'Divine Power' among the people.

Birsa Munda was able to get together around 6000 Mundas by 1895 CE. This was the largest group till date. Though this was a myth, people did recognise Birsa Munda as an incarnation of God. He made people aware of their objectives that made the Munda tribe rejuvenated. His most important objectives were as following:

- Crush the British government completely.
- Oust 'Dikus' from all the regions including Chhotanagpur.
- Establish a free Munda state.

Birsa Munda did not shy away from using even violent means for attaining the above objectives. He called upon all the Mundas to join his crusade with courage and started attacking moneylenders, zamindars, missionaries and dikus in a planned way. Though this attack was forceful, the administration did not allow this to be as successful as Birsa Munda had expected. He was arrested by the Company army in Ranchi. However, he was released after some time and he joined his group again.

This time, Birsa Munda gave a concrete shape to his plans and chose 25 December, 1897, when the Christians would be busy celebrating Christmas, to launch his attack. They vowed to kill Christians as many as possible this time. On the designated day, The Munda rebels created mayhem all around and killed the Christians busy with their celebrations and also the Mundas who had accepted Christianity. This was a large-scale massacre that shook the British government. The local police force also had to face the wrath of this Munda revolt. There was chaos all around; the Company dispatched its army to Ranchi and suppressed the revolt with all brutality. Birsa Munda and his companion Gaya Munda were arrested and sent to jail.

While still in jail, some incurable diseases and lack of adequate treatment for them led to the demise of Birsa Munda. At the same time, this rebellion proved to be a lesson for the Company. It implemented some changes in its policies. The British formulated new regulations with respect to land ownership and 'Mundari Khuntkari System' was implemented for the first time under the Tenancy Act. The administrative services were made still better. Attempts were made to remove the feeling of aversion in the mind of the tribals towards the administration. Gumla sub–division was constituted in the year 1908 whereas Khunti was already upgraded to a sub–division in 1905. These were measures to create an atmosphere of trust between the administration and the tribals.

The Birsa Movement is considered to be a successful movement in real terms. While it prompted the tribals to safeguard their rights and self–respect and protect their religious beliefs, the movement also inspired them to keep away from social evils and superstitions. This very movement compelled the British government to be sensitive towards the tribals. Birsa Munda had awakened people in his brief span of life and even today, he is remembered as an incarnation of God.

Tana Bhagat Movement

This movement was an offshoot of the Birsa Movement. This also was a multi–dimensional movement, as its leaders also had come forward with the issues of their social existence, religious traditions and human rights. The movement started in 1914 CE. Tana Bhagat was not a person but a branch of Oraon tribe that had adopted Kurukh Dharma. They were in a very pitiable condition and they were engaged mostly in manual labour only. They would toil from morning to evening carrying bricks and stones for construction of roads, buildings, etc., but would be paid nothing special for their labour. In a way, they were being used just like mules. One youth named 'Jatra Bhagat' was recognised as the leader of this movement; he used to be busy trying to attain supernatural powers. According to rumours, this very Jatra Bhagat had a vision of 'Dharmesh' the supreme Oraon deity who had ordained him to lead this movement.

After being ordained by 'Dharmesh', the supreme God, Jatra Bhagat abandoned his activities related to taming of ghosts and spirits and turned vegetarian. He exhorted people not to believe in superstitions and advised them to inculcate moral values in their character. Also, he enjoined those working as forced labour or low–paid labour to stop doing the same. Very soon, he became quite popular among people and they started to follow every word coming from him. This unnerved the British and they arrested Jatra Bhagat. This created a lot of resentment among the Oraons. The British started arresting all prominent leaders connected to this movement. This resulted in violent incidents and there was social awakening all around. The British crushed the movement with all brutality; however, the movement was still able to awaken social consciousness among people.

Thus, these tribal movements against the British rule played an important role in restoring the rights of the downtrodden to some extent. These movements had all the elements like aggression, brutality, anger, strong organisation, and tactical reasons that gave rise to revolts. The condition of Bihar at that time was pitiable and the irony was that the outsiders who had come to exploit and take advantage of this naturally rich region had almost dispossessed the original tribes of the region of their lands and properties. Away from formal education and deprived of facilities, this tribal society was leading a peaceful life. All their pleasure and happiness revolved around their festivals, rituals, and their social structure. These tribals have been able to safeguard their existence even after withstanding 300 years of instability, anarchy, exploitation, oppression, insult and poverty; it was a demonstration of nothing but their strong desire to live. Despite all this, people of Bihar did their duty towards their nation. The unparalleled contribution that they have made to the freedom struggle of India cannot be forgotten.

Nonia Rebellion

This revolt had taken place between 1770 CE and 1800 CE in the regions in Bihar like Hajipur, Tirhut, Saran, and Purnia that were producing shora (saltpetre, also known as Potassium Nitrate). Bihar was a major centre for production of saltpetre at that time. Saltpetre was produced for making gunpowder. The production activities related to saltpetre were mostly handled by people from Nonia community. There were people who worked as middlemen between the British Company and the Nonias; they would buy raw saltpetre from the Nonias and supply the same to the British factories. The British Company would pay these middlemen one–fourth of the price of saltpetre as advance. These middlemen received ₹2 to ₹4 per maund of Kalmi shora (saltpetre) and one to four annas per maund of crude shora from the Company and paid just 12, 14 or 5 annas to the Nonias. On the other hand, other businessmen who were not connected with the Company used to pay ₹3 per maund of shora to the Nonias. Thus, the Nonias were being badly exploited by the company and hence, the Nonias started selling shora to those businessmen surreptitiously. When the British government came to know of the same, they started taking brutal action against the Nonias.

Wahabi Movement

The Wahabi Movement also has an important place among movements of Indian people against the British rule. Arabian Abdul Wahab was the founder of this movement. He launched this movement with the aim of eradicating the evils prevalent in Muslim society. Syed Ahmad Barelvi was the leader of this movement in India. He was born at Rai Bareli in Uttar Pradesh in 1776 CE. He regarded the British government responsible for the fall of the Mughal Empire in India and used the term 'Dar–ul–Harb' to refer to the territory of India occupied by the British. They vowed to convert this territory into 'Dar-ul-Islam'. They established an independent state in Sitna with the help of tribal Afghans of the north–western border areas.

Ahmad Barelvi visited Patna in 1821 CE where he came in contact with many people including Vilayat Ali, Inayat Ali, Muhammad Hussain and Farhat Hussain and established Patna as the main centre for the Wahabi Movement. The Wahabi movement was a religious movement in the beginning, but later took the shape of an economic and political movement. This movement turned into a freedom movement against the British government and a class struggle against the officers, zamindars and moneylenders. Muslim peasants in Punjab revolted against Sikh zamindars. Inspired by Syed Ahmad, Titu Mir launched movement against wealthy Hindu and Muslim zamindars.

In 1853 CE, the British army was dispatched to Sitna to suppress the Wahabis; however, it had to face defeat. The British army was sent again to Sitna in 1858 CE; this time it was successful in defeating the Wahabis and making them flee the place. In Patna, the Wahabi movement was led by Vilayat Ali and Inayat Ali. Inayat Ali had made Hyderabad in South India as his headquarters while Vilayat Ali had made Sitna as his centre of activities. In 1844 CE, while on his way to Afghanistan along with 80 followers, Vilayat Ali was arrested in Lahore and sent to Patna. In 1851–52 CE, he went to North-western Frontier Province (present Pakistan) where he was killed while fighting the British army.

The people connected with the Wahabi Movement had taken part wholeheartedly in the rebellion of 1857. After the death of Vilayat Ali and Inayat Ali, the Wahabi movement was spearheaded by Maksood Maulvi Abdullah. He made Malka his centre of activities in 1861 CE. In 1864 CE, Navil Chamberlin defeated the Wahabi leader Ahmadullah and sent him to the jail in Port Blair. Other leaders of the Wahabi movement like Mubarak Ali, Ibrahim Mandal, Mohammad Ismail and Amir Khan were arrested and sentenced to life imprisonment. By 1868–69 CE, the Wahabi Movement almost lost its energy and the movement came to a standstill. Thus, it may be said that while the Wahabi Movement started as a religious movement, during the course of time, it turned into a political movement. This was a rebellion of the Indians to end the British rule in India and make India an independent country. In fact, this was a fight against imperialism.

Lota Rebellion (1856 CE)

Even before the rebellion of 1857, people's anger against the British was on the rise in Muzaffarpur region during 1856 CE. Discontent among the people was getting aggravated because of continued exploitation and atrocities by the British. Around that very time, the inmates of Muzaffarpur Jail launched their revolt that came to be known as 'Lota Rebellion'. The inmates in the jail were being provided brass lotas at that time; the government abruptly changed their decision and started providing earthen lotas instead of brass lotas. Hence, the inmates started protesting against the same. Apprehending the possibility of this revolt getting spread even outside the jail, the decision was reversed and inmates started getting brass lotas.

Freedom Movement

- The Revolt of 1857
- Khilafat Movement
- Civil Disobedience Movement
- Role of Revolutionaries in Azad Hind Fauj
- Role of Women in Independence Movement
- Labour Movement
- Communist Movement
- Champaran Satyagraha
- Non-Cooperation Movement
- Quit India Movement
- Revolutionary Nationalist Ideology
- Peasant Movement
- Socialist Movement
- Development of Education during the British Period

THE REVOLT OF 1857

The British power had to face most strong mass movement in India in 1857. Before the rise of nationalist feeling, the movement of 1857 was the most important in the series of anti-British movements. Bihar played a significant role in this movement. This movement started in Bihar on 12 June, 1857 at Rohini in Deoghar at the headquarters of 32nd Infantry Regiment. Three English officers, Commandant, Major Macdonald, Lieutenant Norman Leslie, and Assistant Surgeon, Dr. Grant, were attacked. Leslie was killed, and other two officers were wounded. On 16 June, 1857, the three mutineers Amanat Ali, Salamat Ali and Sheikh Haro were court-martialled and hanged under the supervision of Major Macdonald himself.

On 3 July, 1857, struggle began against the Britishers is Patna City. It was led by bookseller Pir Ali of the Gurhatta locality. Under the leadership of Pir Ali, around 200 rebels came out on the roads of Patna with flag of Mughal Emperor Bahadur Shah in their hands who were confronted by British officer Loyle and his soldiers. Pir Ali gunned down Loyle. Therefore, Pir Ali along with 16 rebels was apprehended and hanged. On getting this information, revolt spread in three battalions of Danapur.

The revolt of 1857 spread rapidly in Saran, Tirhut, Arrah, Shahbad, etc. apart from Patna. The revolt began under the leadership of brave zamindar Babu Kunwar Singh of Jagdishpur Estate in Shahbad District. Among the associates of Babu Kunwar Singh, his brother Amar Singh, nephew Rathbhanjan Singh, Nishan Singh Harikishan Singh, Jaikrishna Singh and four zamindars of Shahbad Narhanan Singh, Johan Singh, Thakur Dayal Sing and Vishveswar Singh were prominent. Veer Kunwar Singh along with 10 thousand soldiers proceeded towards Arrah, and they were joined by soldiers who revolted in Danapur cantonment. Around 500 European and Sikh soldiers were sent to Danapur under the leadership of Captain Dunbar, but they were defeated in 29–30 July. Major Vincent Ayer of Bengal artillery attacked Biwiganj on 2 August and was successful in getting released soldiers. He captured Jagdishpur on 12 August. Kunwar Singh in association with Nana Saheb defeated the English on 26 March, 1858 and badly defeated British Army led by Captain Lee Grant on 23 April, 1858. Kunwar Singh himself got injured in this battle and died after two days. This struggle was continued by Amar Singh and was successful in wresting control on Shahbad area.

The revolt of 1857 spread extensively in Gaya and Muzaffarpur regions too. The Europeans began to retreat from Muzaffarpur. The revolt there became famous by the name of 'Lota Rebellion', which was crushed later. The rebel soldiers attacked a prison in Gaya and released a number of rebels. A revolt occurred in canton Rajgir under the leadership of Namdar Khan. In this area, Mama Singh, Haidar Ali Khan, Ghulam Ali Khan, Nanku Singh, Fateh Singh, etc. led the revolt. The revolt of 1857 spread in almost the entire state although the Munger region was untouched by this revolt.

After Queen Victoria's proclamation of pardon in 1858, rebels in India largely surrendered, and British power was restored by 1859. However, the 1857 mutiny sparked a new awareness among Indians of their own identity and a sense of national unity. The mutiny was a turning point marking the beginning of the struggle for Indian independence.

Foundation of Congress (1885)

Congress was founded on 28 December, 1885 at Gopudas Sanskrit School of Mumbai by retired English civil servant, Allan Octavian Hume with its first President as Womesh Chunder Banerjee. This session was attended by 72 representatives, but these did not include any representative from Bihar. The second session of Congress held in 1886 in Kolkata was participated by 31 representatives from Bihar prominent among whom were Maulvi Sayyed Sharfuddin, Visheshwar Singh, Guruprasad Sen, Gajodhar Prasad, Maulvi Ahsan, Jai Narayan Vajpeyi, Kuldip Sahay, Ishwari Prasad, Tej Narayan Singh, Parameshwar Narayan, Shah Raza Hussain, Sheikh Barish Ali, Kishori Lal Haldhar, etc. The third session of the congress in 1887 has organized—Madras/Chennai in which only two representatives, namely, Shaligram Singh and Guruprasad Sen participated. The first session of Congress was held in 1912 in Bankipur of Patna. This was 27th session of Congress, which was presided by Ragunath Narsinh Madholkar. Sachidanand Sinha was general secretary of this session and Maulana Mazrul Haque was chairperson of reception committee.

The 31st Congress session was held in 1916 in Lucknow, which was joined by Rajkumar Shukla as representative from Bihar. He had requested Gandhiji to come to Champaran. Peasants were forced to practise indigo cultivation in Champaran which led to their exploitation. So, two resolutions relating to Bihar were passed in the 1916 Congress session—

1. Patna University Bill
2. Investigation of relation between indigo criskos and their raiyyats of Champaran.

The 37th session of Congress was organized in 1922 in Gaya which was presided by Deshbandhu Chittaranjan Das. It was decided to boycott legislature in this session. Chitaranjan Das was not in favour of this bill.

The 53rd session of Indian National Congress was held in Ramgarh (in present-day Jharkhand) in 1940, which was presided by Maulana Abul Kalam Azad. Bihar peasant leader Sahajanand Saraswati and Subhash Chandra Bose had organized a meeting protesting against conciliatory policy towards Britishers in Ramgarh session.

Home Rule Movement

Under the leadership of Bal Gangadhar Tilak and Annie Besant in 1916. Home Rule Movement was started in the entire country the effect of which was seen in Bihar on a large scale.

The Home Rule League was established in a meeting organized in Bankipur, Patna on 16 December, 1916. Maulana Mazrul Haque was made its president and Khan Bahadur Sarfraz Hussain and Rai Bahadur Purnendu Narayan Sinha were made vice-presidents. Vaidanath Narayan Singh and Chandravanshi Sahay were appointed as secretaries. Rajendra Prasad, Mohd. Azam, S.A. Sami, Shambhunarayan, Harinarayan Prasad, A. Sen, B. Basu, Parameshwar Lal and Sh. Krishna Sinha were members of first meeting of Home Rule. On 18 April, 1918, Annie Besant came to Patna who was accommodated in Narayan Sinha's house located on Bikhna Hill. Home rule was published in whole Bihar except Champaran District.

CHAMPARAN SATYAGRAHA

Mughal ruler Shah Alam II gave diwani rights of Bihar and Bengal to the East India Company in 1765. During this time, Champaran area of Bihar was famous for indigo cultivation. Then, Champaran was a part of Bettiah and there 36 English contractors of indigo and 23 indigo businessman resided. In this area, indigo cultivation was done by two ways–

1. Jeerat
2. Asamivaar

Jeerat was land under the occupation of bungalow owners and under the system, farmers used to plant indigo with the help of their plough and ox but used to get very less wages. In case of Asamivaar, bungalow owners made arrangements for getting cultivation of indigo by ryots. Before 1867, it was made compulsory for ryots to cultivate indigo in 5 katthas per bigha. But in 1867, rule was made for compulsory cultivation of indigo in 3 katthas per bigha. Hence, it was also refered to as tinkathia system. Tinkathia system was the main reason for exploitation of farmers of Champaran. Farmers used to get ₹6.50 per acre for indigo cultivation before 1867, which was increased to ₹13.50 since 1909 based on Gorley Report.

In fact, even before Champaran Movement, indigo cultivators had raised voice against the exploitation. The indigo producers had launched a movement under the leadership of Harish Chandra Mukherjee in 1860 in Bengal. The indigo producers of Jaisore region in Bengal had revolted against the exploitation in 1889–90.

The government had been given representation regarding exploitation of farmers due to cultivation of indigo in Champaran region. The ryots of bungalow owners had given a representation to the collector of Champaran and also in 1907 on which no action was taken. So, the ryots stopped sowing indigo for the bungalow owners. As a result, the owners started charging ₹3 per acre for water since 1908, which is called pan charges. Many other types of taxes were also imposed on the farmers other than pan charges which made their condition quite worse. The additional taxes imposed during this time were as follows–

1. **Pan charges:** This tax was imposed in return for canal water supplied for irrigation, which was at the rate of ₹3 per bigha.
2. **Salami:** This was also levied at the rate of ₹3 per bigha, which is also called as tinkathia or agricultural rent.
3. **Bandh Behri:** It was a tax at the rate of 1 anna for each 1 rupee of land revenue, which was levied similar to pan charges for irrigation.
4. **Beth Maafi:** It was a tax of ₹3 levied on the farmers on a yearly basis.
5. **Baphi-Puthi:** It was a type of succession tax which was taken from the heir of ryot after his death for purpose of property transfer.
6. **Madwan:** It was levied by bungalow owner at the rate of ₹1 during the marriage of daughter.
7. **Sagora:** This tax was levied at the rate of ₹5 in case of betrothal of a widow.
8. **Kolhuaavan:** It was a tax levied at the rate of ₹1 from mill owners for crushing oil seeds or sugarcane.
9. **Chulhiaavan:** Turmeric was produced on a large scale in this region. Hence, a tax at the rate of ₹1 was levied for each stove owned to boil turmeric.
10. **Baatchhapi:** This tax was levied at the rate of ₹1 per year from shopkeepers who sold milk and oil.
11. **Bechai:** This tax was levied at the rate of ₹1 per year from shopkeepers who sold grains.
12. **Hathiaati:** The bungalow owners used to levy takes on farmers for purchase of elephants which was called hatiaati.
13. **Haavhi:** Ryots had to give this tax for meeting the expenses on illness of bungalow owners.
14. **Aamdi Salami:** It was a greeting tax that was to be given by ryots at the rate of ₹1 person whenever any officer or government official visited a village.
15. **Saridawan:** This tax was collected along with the land revenue receipt at the rate of 1 anna per receipt.

Apart from these, various other taxes had also been imposed, like singarhat tax, It was levied in the condition when a women went astray and starting living with some other man owing to which that man had to pay this tax.

Thus, farmers were being exploited a lot in Champaran region by giving various types of taxes and doing cultivation of indigo, thereby resulting in their pathetic condition. Under the Tinkathia system, even the police and officers were also excessively exploiting the farmers. They used to help the indigo merchants. Fed up by this persecution, the farmers launched movement many times, but they were suppressed.

A secret organization was formed by farmers in 1907-08 against the tyrany of indigo planters. Mahesh Narayan tried to draw the attention of government through a newspaper named 'Bihari' but it was of no use. Finally, peasant leader of Bihar, Rajkumar Shukla, began the work of highlighting this problem before the Congress and Gandhiji. Rajkumar Shukla, Ganesh Shankar, Vidyarathi, editor of newspaper 'Pratap' in Kanpur and told him about the exploitation of farmers. On 4 January, 1915, Ganesh Shankar Vidyarathi published an article called 'Champaran mein Adhera' (Darkness in Champaran) in Pratap. It was on the advice of Ganesh Shankar Vidyarathi, Rajkumar Shukla went to Sabarmati Ashram to meet Gandhiji, however could not meet Gandhiji there.

In the Lucknow session of Congress in December 1916, Brij Kishore Prasad, Harivansh Sahay, Gorakh Prasad, Ramdayal Prasad Sahu, Pir Mohammed Munis and Pandit Rajkumar Shukla participated as representatives from Bihar Rajkumar Shukla requested Gandhiji to come to Champaran to realize the problems faced by the farmers. Raj Kumar Shukla was born in a village named Satbaria located near Chanpatia Bazaar in West Champaran. But his life was spent in Belva Kothi which came under Murli Barhwa. His land existed in Murli Barhwa Kothi and its indigo planter AC Ammon was a ruthless person.

The resolution related to Champaran was passed in Lucknow session, and Gandhiji also accepted Rajkumar Shukla's invitation of coming to Champaran. Gandhiji has written in his autobiography that Rajkumar Shukla was determined to remove blemish of indigo from thousands of people living in Bihar. Gandhiji as per his schedule of going to Calcutta proceeded towards Patna along with Rajkumar Shukla on 9 April, 1917. Gandhiji at this time said about Rajkumar Shukla that "uneducated determined farmer won me." Gandhiji reached Muzaffarpur at first where Acharya J.B. Kripalani took him to his house. Gaudhiji met Bihar Planters' association of Muzaffarpur minister J.M. Wilson on 11 April, 1917, but refused to help Gandhiji. Gandhiji again met Commissioner of Tirhut Division, L.F. Mosherd, J.M. Wilson and District Magistrate of Champaran imposed prohibition on Gandhiji to go the Champaran from Muzaffarpur, but Gandhiji along with Ramnavmi Prasad reached Champaran (Motihari) on 15 April, 1917 where chief barrister of Motihari, Gaurav Prasad, took Gandhiji to his house. Gandhiji toured Jasauli swathe in Champaran first on 16 April. At that time, section-144 was imposed there. So Gandhiji was prosecuted for violating section-144. Gandhiji was asked to give ₹10 towards bail, but be refused to do so. Gandiji's surety bond was paid by magistrate himself, and he was set free. After that Gandhiji reached Bettiah. Brij Kishore Prasad also accompanied him. Gandhiji reached Belwa Kothi via Kudiya Kothi along with Rajkumar Shukla. In this series of activities, Gandiji's popularity kept on increasing and crowd of people was also growing. Therefore, to lower the effect of agitation, the government appointed an investigation committee on 10 June, 1917 in which Gandhiji was also one of the members. The investigation committee submitted its report on 4 October, 1917, and the government after going through the report published it on 18 October, 1917. It is on the basis of this report that Champaran Act was framed on 4 March, 1918 as a result of which Tinkathia system was abolished, taxes on ryots were decreased and other taxes were declared illegal.

In this way, large-scale presentation of farmers of Champaran that was being done by indigo planters ended in which Rajkumar Shukla played a big role along with Gandhiji. Rajkumar Shukla kept on fighting in this agitation from beginning to end, and he died in Motihari on 20 May, 1929. In this way, first Satyagraha of truth and non-violence carried out by Gandhiji in India succeeded.

KHILAFAT MOVEMENT

Turkey had fought against the Allied powers during the First World War. Allied powers won in the war, and they divided the empire of Turkey amongst themselves. The Allies insulted the caliph of Turkey too who was considered as religious leader of the Islamic world. Even the Indian Muslims were hurt by the action of the Allies, especially by the action of the British government. Therefore, they started Khilafat Movement as a protest. An All-India Khilafat Conference was held on 24 November, 1919 in Delhi under the chairmanship of Gandhiji in which it was decided to non-cooperate with the government. A meeting was held on 30 November, 1919 in the Anjuman Islamic Hall of Patna to consider taking part in peace celebration. Hasan Imam proposed the name of Maulana Shah Resid-ul-Haque as president and Rajendra Prasad seconded it. A similar resolution was passed in Ranchi under the leadership of Maulana Abdul Kalam Azad which related to non-cooperating with the British. The Muslims held a strike in entire Bihar on 19 March, 1920. Its extensive effect was seen in Munger, Bhagalpur, Arrah, and Daltenganj. Maulana Shaukat Ali, a prominent leader of Khilafat Movement came to Patna in April. His meetings were organized in a number of places in Bihar. The prominent supporters of Khilafat Movement were Maulana Mazhar-ul-Haque, Brij Kishore Prasad, Rajendra Prasad, Mohammad Shafi, Maulana Nurul Hasan, Dharnidhar Prasad, etc.

NON-COOPERATION MOVEMENT

Muslims decided to start Khilafat Movement in protest of ill treatment of caliph of Turkey by the British. The congress under the leadership of Gandhiji also decided to start non-cooperation movement to express its dissatisfaction. The 12th session of Bihar Provincial Conference was held in Bhagalpur on 18-19 August, 1920 under the chairmanship of Rajendra Prasad. The resolution on non-cooperation was put forward by Babu Dharnidhar of Darbhanga, and it was seconded by Shah Mohd. Jubair of Munger, Gulam Imam of Patna and Babu Gorakh Prasad Motihari. The resolution was approved with huge majority, and it was decided to begin non-cooperation movement in the whole country. Gujarat and Bihar were the only two provinces of the country in the provincial conference of which non-cooperation was invoked before the Calcutta session itself. In this session, to implement the non-cooperation programme suggested by Gandhiji, a practical plan was prepared and a committee was constituted whose members were Rajendra Prasad, Mazhar-ul-Haque and Shah Mohd. Jubair.

Gandhiji's non-cooperation program was accepted in the special session held in Calcutta in September 1920 under the presidentship of Lala Lajpat Rai, and in the, annual session of Congress in Nagpur, non-cooperation movement was approved. The election of councils was boycotted under it. Consequently, Mazhar-ul Haque, Rajendra Prasad, Brij Kishore Prasad, Gorakh Prasad, Dharnidhar Prasad and Mohd. Safi withdrew their candidature from the council.

Arugrah Narayan Singh, Brij Nandan Prasad, Mathura Prasad, Deep Narayan Singh, Shree Krishna, etc. gave up their advocary, Honorary Magistrate of Chhapra, Mahendra Prasad, resigned from his post.

The leader of farmers' movement of North Bihar, Swami Vidyanand, criticized the government policies. Patna Law College Student, Syed Mohd. Sher and Bihar National College students, Abdul Baari and Mohd. Saki left the college, and later, Abdul Baari proved to be an extremist leader. As a result of Gandhiji's short-term Bihar visit in December 1920, national schools were opened in 1921.

In accordance with the wish of Gandhiji, National College was established on 5 January, 1921. When Gandhiji came to Bihar on 6 January, 1921, he formally inaugurated National College and Bihar University. Mazhar-ul Haque and Brij Kishore Prasad respectively occupied the post of chancellor and pro vice chancellor and Rajendra Prasad became the principal of National College. By July 1922, in Munger itself 6 national schools were opened. Tilak Swaraj Fund was created after the death of Bal Gangadhar Tilak. For this, a Tilak Swaraj Fund was created by the Bihar Provincial Congress Committee whose convener Shri Krishan Babu was appointed. By the end of 1921, the revolutionary movement of India had reached its height. The movement had an extensive effect on Bihar along with that on the Indian people. The British imperialists sent Prince of Wales to India to curtail this opportunity. When the Prince of Wales came to pathar on 22 December, 1921, the whole city observed strike. In the 16th session of Bihar Students' Conference in Hazaribagh, under the presidentship of Sarla Devi, it was decided to boycott Prince of Wales. A number of leaders of Bihar were apprehended in this act of protest, and harsh atrocities were committed on them. This has been described by Mazhar-ul Haque in his paper 'The Motherland'.

The agitating farmers attacked a police station in a place called Chauri Chaura in Gorakhpur of Uttar Pradesh on 5 February, 1922 and consigned to fire many policemen there. This incident shocked Gandhiji, and he immediately withdrew Non-Cooperation Movement. In this way, the Non-Cooperation Movement became weak both in Bihar and India.

CIVIL DISOBEDIENCE MOVEMENT

Many factors like the failure of Simon Commission, increasing atrocities by British imperialists, rising communal riots in the country, and movement launched by nationalist revolutionaries played an important role in giving birth to the Civil Disobedience Movement. A II-point proposal was submitted by Gandhiji to Viceroy Irwin important amongst which were complete prohibition, reducing agricultural rent by half, abolition of salt tax, reducing the exchange rate to one schilling four pence, cutting defence related expenditure by 50 percent, stoppage of import of British clothes, cut in salary, release of political prisoners, granting licence to keep arms for self-defence, etc. Lord Irwin did not heed to these requests of Gandhiji due to which Gandhiji decided to launch Civil Disobedience Movement.

Gandhiji began Dandi March from Sabarmati Ashram along with 78 followers on 12 March, 1930. Reaching Dandi on 6 April, 1930 after covering a distance of 24 miles in 24 days, Gandhiji broke the salt law by making salt. Biriwardhari Chaudhary alias 'Karo Babu' from Bihar participated in the Dandi March along with Gandhiji. Soon, this movement spread like a wild fire in almost all the regions of the Bihar.

This movement was led by people like Jagat Narayan Lal in Patna, Satya Narayan Sinha and Chaturanan Das in Darbhanga, Shri Krishna Singh and Nand Kumar Singh in Munger, Girish Tiwari, Chandrika Singh, Bharat Mishra and Shri Narayan Prasad Singh in Saran, and Ramdayalu Singh, Kanakdhari Prasad Thakur and Ramnandan Singh in Muzaffarpur.

'Civil Disobedience Movement' spread rapidly from urban areas to rural areas, and villagers also actively participated in this movement. Bonfire of foreign-made clothes, picketing before liquor shops and other constructive works were important programs of this movement. Women also participated in this movement. The Tana Bhagats of Chhotanagpur held demonstrations against the government on a large scale non-violently. Whereas the movement was supported through giving up of schools by students, resignations by many people from government jobs, renunciation of their advocacy by lawyers and relinquishing of government titles by numerous people, they expressed their protest against the government thus. The British administration ruthlessly crushed the movement. Around 13 thousand agitators were arrested in Bihar, and a lot of atrocities, were committed on them. The agitators had occupied Badhi city during this movement in 1930.

Gandhiji was arrested on 4 May, 1930, and other prominent leaders including Shri Krishna Singh were taken into custody in Bihar. Rajendra Prasad and Abdul Bari sustained serious injuries. Bihar Congress Committee under the chairmanship of Anugraha Narayan Singh approve Civil Disobedience Movement on 9 May, 1930. During this movement, sentinel tax cessation campaign in Bihar became very famous. 'Nakhaspind Movement' of Patna played an important role in salt satyagraha. A place named Nakhaspind in Patna was selected for violating the salt law on 16 April, 1930 and slogan 'Nakhaspind Chalo' was raised. Under the leadership of Secretary, Patna City Congress Committee and Ambika Kant Singh, a procession of satayagrahis advanced toward Nakhaspind. At the time, another procession under the leadership of Ramvriksha Benipuri was heading towards Nakhaspind. The demonstrators were being stopped at different places in Patna, and they were being imprisoned. They were lathicharged at many places in which professor Abdul Bari got injured. Benipuri, Ramnath and Ambika Kant Singh were arrested and given six months' imprisonment. A meeting was organized in Bhawar-Pokhar ground of Patna as a protest under the chairmanship of Hasan Imam, which was convened by Rajendra Prasad, Ali Imam and Sachidanand Sinha. Sentinel tax cessation movement (1930) was first started in Munger, Bhagalpur, Siwan, etc. People in these districts stopped giving sentinel tax and compelled sentinels to give resignations.

This movement spread in Darbhanga, Shahabad, Champaran, Munger, Purnia, etc., also where people stopped giving sentinel tax. A regular training camp of volunteers started in Bihpur Village of Bhagalpur in protest of sentinel tax on 31 May, 1930, which was declared illegal, and police occupied the Congress Ashram. Dr. Rajendra Prasad and Adbul Bari organized a huge rally in Bihpur in protest, which was lathicharged by police. Rajendra Prasad and Adbul Bari were greviously hurt in the police lathicharge. Congress was declared an illegal organization on 30 June, 1930, and Rajendra Prasad was arrested on 5 July, 1930. Around 130 sentinels of Bihpur police station resigned in protest of this incident.

Bihar State Congress Committee passed a resolution for picketing before shops of foreign clothes and liquor on 9 May, 1930. Inpired by this resolution, prisoners of Chhapra jail refused to wear foreign clothes and demanded indigenous clothes. On not getting indigenous clothes, these prisoners decided to remain bare for many days, which is referred to as 'naked strike' (1930). Compelled by this conduct of the prisoners, the jail administration had to make available for them indigenous clothes.

An assembly was held under the chairmanship of Rajendra Prasad on 12 March, 1931 in which demand for immediate release of Political prisoners was raised. A widespread remonstrance was held in the entire state, including Patna due to execution of Bhagat Singh and his associates on 23 March, 1931. A complete strike was observed in Patna on 26 March. Mahatma Gandhi returned to India on 28 December, 1931 with the 'Round Table Conference' and exhorted to intensity the movement again. Leaders like Rajendra Prasad, Brij Kishore Prasad, Krishna Vallabh Sahay, Jagat Narain Das, Mathura Prasad, Prajapati Mishra were arrested on 4 January, 1932. On 7 January, Shri Krishan Singh, Namdhari Singh, Tejasvi Prasad and Ram Prasad Gupta, and on 9 January, Nirapan Mukherjee was arrested. On 26 January, independence day was celebrated in the whole province.

British Prime Minister MacDonald with the intention of creating dissension in Hindu society, announced communal award, which was opposed by Mahatma Gandhi who began fast unto death. Poona Pact was signed between Bhimrao Ambedkar and Gandhiji on this subject, and the communal award was withdrawn. Gandhiji established 'Harijan Sevak Sangh' to ameliorate the condition of harijans, many branches of which were opened in Bihar also. Leaders from Bihar like Jagjivan Ram and Jaglal Chaudhary played an important role in Harijan Sevak Sangh. The 'Civil Disobedience Movement' began to became ineffective by onset of mid-1933 due to which it was being considered for withdrawal. Accordingly, Congress postponed its movement in Bihar on 18 May, 1933.

Individual Satyagraha

The 53rd session of Indian National Congress was conducted under the presidentship of Maulana Abul Kalam Azad in a place called Ramgarh in Bihar. Mahatma Gandhi gave the slogan of individual satyagraha in this session. Vinoba Bhave became the first individual satyagrahi. This movement had a very good effect on Bihar. Shri Krishan Singh became the first individual satagrahi on 27 November, 1940. Tana Bhagat of Chhotanagpur also actively participated in this satyagraha. On 27 November itself, Shri Krishna Singh was arrested, which had an intense reaction in Bihar. Anugrah Narayan Singh become second satyagrahi who was arrested in Patna city while delivering lecture. The satyagraha was led by Gaur Shankar Singh in Gaya and Shyam Narayan

Singh in Shilar. Some women were also arrested on the charges of Satyagraha in Gaya among which prominent were Priyavanda Devi, Jagatrani Devi, Janki Devi, etc.

QUIT INDIA MOVEMENT

Congress had resigned in 1939 after running the government for 28 months in various provinces. With this, background for a big movement against the Britishers was created. Although efforts were made to get their demands fulfilled by individual satyagrah in 1940 but these were not successful. America and other allied countries put pressure on Britain asking it to win confidence of Indians at the earliest for the Second World War. In order to pacify the conditions arising out of war period, a mission led by Cabinet Minister Sir Stafford Cripps visited India on 22 March, 1942, which is also called Cripps Mission. Cripps assured Indian leaders that India would be granted status of colonial state after the end of war, but Mahatma Gandhi declined the offer of Cripps Mission saying that is a 'Post-dated Cheque'. Pandit Nehru also said at this time that "My old friend Cripps has come as the devils' advocate".

In this way, the failure of Cripps Mission and continual success of Japan in the Second World War compelled Indian masses to launch a big movement. A meeting of congress executive was convened in Wardha on 14 July 1942, and it was decided to end soon the British rule in India. On 8 August, 1942, a session of All-India Congress was held in the Gowalia Tank Maidan of Mumbai, which is now referred to as August Kranti Maidan in which a resolution was passed to begin 'Quit India Movement' under the leadership of Gandhiji. At this time, Congress President Maulana Azad commented, "they community cannot keep watching idly when its fate is going to be decided". Quit India Movement resolution was proposed by Pandit Jawahar Lal Nehru and Sardar Vallabh Bhai Patel seconded it. At this time, Gandhiji remarked that this is the last struggle, and Britishers need to leave India. He raised the slogan of 'Do or Die'. Although Jawahar Lal Nehru was the last to agree on this movement.

Bihar had an important role in the 'Quit India Movement'. Bihar and Eastern Uttar Pradesh were the most affected regions in this movement. Rajendra Prasad had asked congress workers on 31 July, 1942, to be prepared for the future struggle. On that day, students and youth gave their support to Rajendra Prasad by organizing a meeting in Anjuman Islamia Hall in Patna. Mahatma Gandhi was arrested on 8 August within few hours after passing of the 'Quit India Resolution'. Soon, the movement intensified in the whole country. Protest demonstrations and meetings began swiftly. In this movement, the agitators from Bihar were given an imprisonment of maximum 51 years, and a fine realization of ₹40 lakh collectively was imposed on the whole state.

Rajendra Prasad was arrested under the Defence of India Act on 9 August, in Patna, and was detained in Bankipur Central Jail. Shri Krishna Singh was arrested and detained in Bankipur Jail on 10 August on the orders of Patna Commissioner W.G. Archer. Then, Baldev Sahay had resigned from the post of Solicitor General. A procession was taken out on 10 August in Danapur, under the leadership of Sitaram Kesri and Hare Ram Krishna Singh. Female members of the Women Charkha Committee organized a meeting under the chairpersonship of Rajendra Prasad's sisters, Bhagwati Devi in Kadamkuan located in Patna, in which wife of Jagat Narayan Lal, Rampyari Devi and Sundari Devi also participated. On this day, an assembly was convened in Gandhi Maidan (Bankipur Maidan) in which decision to hoist flag on secretariat building was taken. A procession of students tried to hoist flag on secretariat building on 11 August, 1942. Collector of Patna District, W.G. Archer ordered to open fire on them as a result of which Umakant Sinha, Satish Prasad Jha, Devipad Chaudhary, Ramanand Singh, Rajendra Singh, Ramgovind Singh and Jagpati kumar were martyred.

The first agitators, Ramanand Single to get martyred on 11 August was a resident of Shahadat Nagar Village coming under Dhanria Police Station of Patna District. His father's name was Laxman Singh and mother's name was Smt Anantiya Devi. He was studying in 11th class in Ram Mohan Roy Seminary, Patna during 1942. Martyr Umakant Prasad Singh, who is also known as Ramanji, was born on 4 April, 1923 in Narendrapur village of Saran District. He was studying in 11th class in Ram Mohan Roy Seminary, Patna during 1942. Martyr Satish Prasad Jha was born in Khadhara village of Bhagalpur District. His father's name was Jagdish Prasad Jha and mother's name was Smt. Tripura Devi. He was acquiring education in Collegiate School located in Patna. Martyr Jagpati Kumar was born in 1923 in Kharati Village which came under Obra Police Station of Aurangabad District. His father's name was Sukhraj Bahadur and mother's name was Devrani Kunwar. Martyr Jagpati Kumar was studying in BN Collegiate School of Patna.

Martyr Devipad Chaudhary was born in Silhat Village, Jamalpur on 16 August, 1928. His uncles Rakesh Chandra Chaudhary, Jai Shankar Chaudhary and Yogendra Chandra Chaudhary were freedom fighters. Another member of his family, Kalipad Chaudhary was sentenced for 2 years for the crime of setting fire to a police station, Devipad Chaudhary was a student of Miller High School of Patna. 'Country Servant Father and Martyr Son' is a book written on Devipad Chaudhary and his father. Martyr Rajendra Singh was born in Banwarichak Village under Sonpur Police Station of Saran District on 5 December 1924. His father's name was Shiv Narayan Singh and mother's name was Smt. Jeera Devi. He was a student of Miller High School Patna. He used to listen independence related stories from Nathuni Sharma living in Sadakat Ashram which left an imprint of country's independence on his life. Martyr Ramgovind Singh was born on 1925 in Village Dashratha of Patna District. His father's name was Devkinandan Singh and mother's name was Smt Ram Kunwar Devi. He was a student of Punpun High School located in Patna District. During independence struggle, leaders like Mahatma Gandhi and Abdul Gaffar Khan came to this school whose sight had an effect on his life.

As a result of this cowardly act of the Britishers, whole of Bihar got more severly agitated. It was exhorted by passing 12 resolutions to completely shut down government establishments. People got violent in many places and drove away officers of British Army. Shri Jagannath Mishra, Shri Kailash Ram and Shri Mai became a victim of police gunshots on 13 August in Gaya. In continuation of the movement Kapil Muni, Ramdas Vishvakarama, Gopal Kahar, Sadhusharan Ahir and Baleshwar Dubey died of police gun shots in Dumrao of Buxar District on 16 August, 1942.

Phulena Prasad Srivastava died from police fire in course of this movement while hoisting, his wife, Tara Rani hoisted flag on the police station building after which she was arrested. Phulena Prasad Srivastava was born in Pachlakhi Village of Siwan District in 1914. He began to live with Gandhiji along with his wife Tara Devi in Wardha Ashram in 1933. He went to Lucknow in 1936 to gain higher education, where he began to awaken common people against the exploitist policies of the government as a result of which Phulena Prasad and his wife had to go to jail. After the release from prison, a disruptive committee was formed on 16 August in Mahrajganj during the Quit India Movement of 1942 which organized a big procession. Phulena Prasad Srivastava who tried hoisting flag on the police station, in accompaniment of procession destroying government symbols died of police bullets. This incident has been described by his wife Tara Devi in a book, titled 'His Memories' Shri Maheshwar Prasad was martyred as a result of police bullet on 15 August, 1942 near Sonpur Railway Station of Saran District.

Shri Jubba Sahni of Chainpur Village, Sitamarhi attacked Minapur Police Station on 15 August, 1942 along with the agitators, and the mob burnt alive Inspector Bollar. After the incident, Jubba Sahni was arrested for assassination Bollar and was executed along with Banwari Lal in Muzaffarpur.

Jubba Sahni was born in 1906 in Chainpur Village. His father's name was Pachu Sahni. Initially, he worked as a labourer in Bhikanpur Sugar Mill. He had a scuffle with English supervisor in the sugar mMill. So, a warrant was issued against him on the charges of manhandling the supervisor. He actively participated in the Civil Disobedience Movement started by Mahatma Gandhi. He was sentenced to jail in 1932, 1934 and 1942.

He ran a campaign related to Satyagrah Movement, picketing at liquor shops, protesting sentinel tax, boycott of British clothes by going from village to village. Police attacked him with lathis when he was picketing before a liquor shop in 1932 in Muzaffarpur. At that time, when Pandit Jawahal Lal had come to Muzaffarpur, then he had remarked that "Jubba bhai, you are not alone in this fight, we all are with you, the whole of India is with you". When a warrant was issued against him during the Quit India Movement, then he had surrendered to save the lives of his 56 associates. He was hanged on 11 March, 1944 at the age of 38 years.

A mini newspaper called 'Azad Hindustan' was published in Munger on 13 August, in which government repression was protested. In return, a newspaper named 'Munger News' came to be published by the government from 26 August, 1942 through which the government started publicizing its achievements.

During this movement, son of Shri Amir Roy died of gunshot. In a series of continual efforts to hoist national flag on government buildings in Madhubani on 14 August, 1942, Shri Aklu Shah, Ganeshji Thakur and Nathuni Shah got martyred. Yogendra Narayan Singh, Parameshwar Das, Sheikh Idahaq, Moti Mandal, Sukhdev Bhagat, Kutai Sahu were leading in the act of hoisting flag on the collectorate building on 27 August, 1942 in Purnia. In this course, all these people attained martyrdom as a result of police firing. On this day, a procession laid siege on a police station in Katihar and burnt the registry office. Enraged by this incident, the government ordered to open fire on the mob which resulted in death of Dhruv Kumar Kundu, Ramasheesh Singh, Bihari Shah, Ramadhar Singh, Kaland Mandal, Damodar Singh and Munshi Shah. Six youths lost their lives in Saharsa as a result of gunfire on agaitators on 29 August, 1942. Kaleshwar Mandal was leading these protesters. Kedarnath Tiwari of Nariyar Village in Bhagalpur priosn and Dheero Roy of Ekaad Village, Saharsa died in Bhagalpur prison as a result of police beating.

Socialists from Bihar like Jai Prakash Narayan, Rammanohar Lohia, Aruna Asaf Ali, Achyut Patwardhan, Shaligram Singh, Suraj Narayan Singh, Sitaram Singh, Gulabi Sonar, Yogendra Shukla, Ramanandan Mishra, Gangesharan Singh and other played an important role in 'Quit India Movement'. In 1942 itself, the government arrested Jai Prakash Narayan and jailed him. On 8 November, 1942 in the night of Deepavali, Jai Prakash Narayan, Yogendra Shukla, Surya Narayan Singh, Gulali Prasad, Shaligram Singh and Ramanand Mishra absconded from jail by crossing over its wall. Famous litterateur Ramvriksha Benipuri was also imprisoned in Hazaribagh Central Jail along with these people, who helped them in absconding from the jail. Jai Prakash Narayan along with his associates reached Gaya at first. In this sequence of reaching Gaya, people of Tatra Village helped them. From Manpur in Gaya, they reached Orail Village in Rajgir. From Rajgir, they reached Benaras. They look shelter in lowland of Nepal along with some of their comrades from Benaras. In Nepal they formed 'Azad Dasta' and led the movement remaining underground. 'Azad Dasta' adopted the mechanism of gorilla warfare. The youth were given training of arms in the Azad Dasta and were sent for sabotage of government buildings, means of communication and rail transport and movement against the British government. With the arrest of prominent leaders in the 'Quit India Movement' during its last phase, this movement was steered by socialists resulting in increased participation of peasant and worker class. By the end of 1943, a number of arrests were made in Bihar.

'Siyaram Dal' of Bihar played an important role in a 'Quit India Movement'. This army was constituted by Siyaram Singh of Tilakpur, Bhagalpur District. Prominent members of this group were Parthasarthy (Instructor of Khagaria Gymnasium), Nityanand Singh (had resigned from army) and Bindeshwari Singh (Shooter). Diha and Bhuvaneshwar Thakur did the task of provisioning of arms. 'Siyaram Dal' was a secret weapons society which used to train youth in use of arms and ammunition and which had the objective of establishing village self-government by uniting the people. Siyaram Dal prepared a gorilla walfare squad which adopted gorilla tactics and ran the movement for two years. Chief of this group, Siyaram Singh toured many districts of Northeast Bihar. On the advise of Jai Prakash Narayan, a meeting was organized in the house of Chaturanan

Singh on 12 December, 1942, in Nepal which was presided over by Shiv Shankar Prasad Mandal. Siyaram Dal constituted a peace brigade and soldier's brigade on 5 December, 1942 in Bihpur of Bhagalpur by organizing a meeting.

Thus, 'Quit India Movement' was the result of resentment of Indian people from British policies. In a way, this movement was a symbol of end of freedom struggle because after this, a round of parleys occurred for transfer of power towards freedom attainment.

ROLE OF REVOLUTIONARIES IN AZAD HIND FAUJ

During the Second World War, Japan had occupied Singapore by 15 February, 1942. The condition of Allies was worsening in the war. A number of Indians were made captive. Rash Bihari Bose conducted a conference of all these Indian prisoners of war in Tokyo on 28 March, 1942 during which decision to constitute 'Indian National Army' (INA) was taken. Rash Bihari Bose formed 'Indian Independence League' in Bangkok on 23 June, 1942, and it was decided to recall Subhash Chandra Bose from Germany to Japan. Captain Mohan Singh first mooted the idea of formation of INA and he was appointed its commander. Subhash Chandra Bose assumed its leadership on 4 July, 1943 in Singapore.

Subhash Chandra Bose formed a provincial government called 'Provisional Government of Azad Hind' in Singapore on 21 October, 1943 and made a radio broadcast from there. Anand Mohan Sahay of Bihar was the general secretary in the ministry of provinicial government. He was born in a landlord family of Bihar on 10 December, 1898. His father's name was Lalmohan Sahay. After qualifying matric and ISC examination from Bhagalpur, he took admission in Patna Medical College but be gave up his studies in 1921 under the influence of Non-Cooperation Movement going on in the country. Therefore, he worked as personal secretary of Dr. Rajendra Prasad up till 1922.

He met Subhash Chandra Bose during the Gaya Congress Session of 1922. President of Congress, Chittaranjan Das was the personal secretary of Subhash Chandra Bose at this time. After meeting Netaji, Anand Mohan Sahay remained in Japan until 1922-25. During this period, he came in contact with the revolutionary Rash Bihari Bose and Raja Mahendra Pratap.

Rash Behari Bose had come to Japan after throwing a bomb on viceroy in Delhi. Raja Mahendra Pratap had constituted a provincial government in Afghanistan during the First World War due to which the British government had arrested him along with his family, but he escaped from the custody to Japan. During this time, Anand Mohan Sahay organized a conference of Nagasaki Slave Citizens in which it was decided to unite youths of all the slave countries for the movement and Anand Mohan was entrusted to accomplish this work. Anand Mohan Sahay reached India in 1925 in the disguise of a trader after crossing many countries and contacted Gandhiji, Pandit Nehru, Chittaranjan Das, Rajendra Prasad, Maulana Azad and Subhash Chandra Bose and apprise them with his plan. His marriage was solemnized with Sati Devi, maternal niece of Chittaranjan Das in 1926. He reached Japan again in 1927 and started publishing newspaper 'Voice of India' through which he began the work of highlighting the conditions in India.

The newspaper was published both in English and Japanese languages. During this time, Anand Mohan Sahay established, 'Independence League' in Japan and created a guest house for Indians in Kobe. At this time, Subhash Chandra Bose was under house arrest in Calcutta, and it was difficult to meet him. So, in sending information secretively, he was assisted by two brothers named Mubarak and Murtaza, residents of Narga (Nathnagar, Bhagalpur), who worked as lascars in a ship. When Anand Mohan Sahay was in Japan in 1939, the Second World War had started. During world war itself, he escaped house arrest and went to Afghanistan via Germany. Azad Hind Fauj in Japan had been organized by Rash Behari Bose with first commander as captain Mohan Singh, but under the pressure of Anand Mohan Sahay, Subhash Chandra Bose made leader of Azad Hind Fauj after his recall from Germany to Japan.

By 1943, Azad Hind Fauj had occupied Andaman and Nicobar Islands and Anand Mohan Sahay and Subhash Chandra Bose together observed independence by hoisting flag on this island on 30 December, 1943. During this time, Rangoon had became headquarters of Azad Hind Fauj. The position of Japan started weakening gradually in the war and Rangoon had been encircled by the British army to counter which a team was formed under the leadership of Colonel Chatterjee, Mohd. Khan and Anand Mohan Sahay. During the war period itself, Anand Mohan Sahay reached Vietnam via China and met its chief leader to Ho Chi Minh. After the end of Second World War, he was arrested in Saigon of Vietnam. He was released in 1946 along with other officers of Azad Hind Fauj on whom lawsuit was instituted after independence, his wife, Sati Devi, opened a girls school in Nath Nagar and he opened Sundarwati Girls College in Bhagalpur. Anand Mohan Sahay worked in Indian Foreign Service and was posted to Thailand, Mauritius. He died on 13 February, 1991.

REVOLUTIONARY NATIONALIST IDEOLOGY

The period from 1858 to 1885 in the history of independence movement is the period of development of nationalism in India. Indian National Congress was formed in 1885. After that, there was an influence of liberalist ideologies on nationalist movement 1905. The initial nationalist movements failed to influence the youth causing resentment in this class. In this sequence, Lord Curzon announced partition of Bengal in 1905, which angered the youths and a class of nationalist revolutionaries came into existence. Bihar too did not remain untouched by this revolutionary nationalism. The credit of starting nationalist movement in Bihar goes to Dr. Gyanendra Nath Mishra, Babaji Thakur Das, Kedarnath Bannerjee, Khudiram Bose, Prafulla Chaki, etc. Gyanendra Mishra was born in 1870. He completed his medical studies from Calcutta University. Later on, he was known by the name of Swami Brahmanand. Babaji Thakur Das was born in Gaya. He had established Ram Krishan Society in Patna in 1906-07. He began editing newspaper, 'The Motherland'.

A revolutionary incident occurred in Muzaffarpur of Bihar on 30 April, 1908 in which Khudiram Bose and Prafulla Chandra Chaki tried to assassinate district judge named Kingsford. Both of them threw bomb on the Fiten car of Kingsford, but unfortunately, the wife and daughter of Barrister Pringley Kennedy who were seated in that car died. Judge Kingsford was presidency magistrate of Calcutta during swadeshi movement. He had given stringent punishment to seditious articles written by members of disruptive group during the swadeshi movement. So, revolutionaries had decided to kill him. After getting information about this plan, the government had transferred Kingsford to Muzaffarpur from Calcutta as district judge. Members of disruptive group, Khudiram Bose and Prafulla Chandra Chaki had thrown a bomb on his horse carriage to assassinate him.

Prafulla Chandra Chaki committed suicide after this incident, whereas Khudiram Bose was arrested in Pusa Baini, Samastipur, and was hanged on 11 August, 1908. Shri Kalidas Bose had fought the case for Khudiram Bose. Khudiram Bose was the youngest revolutionary to be hanged in the nationalist movement. He was born on 3 December, 1889 in Midnapore District of Bengal. Mahant Bhagwan Das was slayed in 1913 in Nanakshah Temple, Nibheji, Shahabad. Mahant Dad had also played a role in revolutionary movement.

The revolutionaries had set up Anushilan Samiti in Calcutta and Dacca in protest against Bengal Division. This organization used to give training to revolutionaries. The influence of Anushilan Samiti had spread even in Bihar also. Rewati Nag, Phanibhushan Bhattacharya, Nalini Baagchi, etc. of Bihar along with prominent leader of Anushilan Samiti namely Sachindra Sanyal Rasbehari Bose, etc. spread revolutionary activities.

The contribution of Sanyasi Baikunth Shukla and Yogendra Shukla in revolutionary movement is immemorable. Baikunth Shukla was born in Jalalpur Village of Vaishali. He in association with Yogendra Shukla, conducted revolutionary activities in areas around Hajipur. Baikunth Shukla was sentenced six months imprisonment for joining non-cooperation movement. Baikunth Shukla was entrusted with the task of killing Phanindranath Ghosh, who became public witness in Lahore conspiracy, whom he killed in Bettiah. In the sequence of coming to Hajipur, police after arresting Baikunth Shukla, had kept him in Motihari Jail. He was sentenced to death and kept in central jail, where he was hanged on 14 April, 1934. Before getting hanged, Baikunth Shukla had met Pandit Jawahar Lal Nehru and Rajendra Prasad in Gaya.

Yogendra Shukla was born in 1898 in Jalalpur Village of Vaishali. His father's name was Shri Nanku Shukla. In 1917, he met J.B. Kripalani and Professor Malakani, who was professor in G.B.B College of Muzaffarpur. Yogendra Shukla became further active in revolutionary activities after coming into contact with Phanindra Nath Sanyal and Satyadev Parivrajak. When demonstrations were being carried against the arrival of Prince of Wales in India in 1921, Shri Yogendra Shukla was arrested during it. After meeting Sardar Bhagat Singh, Chandrasekhar Azad and Rajendra Lahiri, Shri Yogendra Shukla became an important member of Hindustan Socialist Republican Army'. An arrest warrant was issued against Shri Yogendra Shukla on 3 July, 1929 in Maulniya Political Dacoity Case. When the 'Hindustan Socialist Republican Army' had made a plan for escape of Sardar Bhagat Singh from Lahore Central Jail, Yogendra Shukla was also a part of it. Public arrested Shri Yogendra Shukla from Malkhachak Village of Saran District on 11 June, 1930, and he was awarded 22 years of rigorous imprisonment with internment in Bhagalpur, Hazaribagh, Calcutta and Andaman respectively in series. He was again arrested in 1942 during the 'Quit India Movement' and was kept in Hazaribagh Jail where Jai Prakash Narayan, Ramanand Mishra and Suraj Narayan Singh were also imprisoned.

All of them were successful in fleeing from the Hazaribagh Jail. Yogendra Shukla was elected as a member of legislative council for 5 years a candidate of 'Praja Socialist Party' in 1948. He died on 19 November, 1966.

Revolutionary activities had increased in Bihar after 1924. Bihari Student Conference was held in Motihari in 1928 in which 'Bihar Youth Federation' was formed under the leadership of Professor Gyan Saha. Thousands of copies of photo and placard of Bhagat Singh and Butukeshwar Dutt were distributed in Patna in 1929, which were written by Gyan Saha. Gyan Saha was declared by the government as a revolutionary with extreme ideology.

Revolutionary leader of Bihar, Batukeshwar Dutt was an active member of 'Hindustan Socialist Republican Army'. He was born in Kanpur in 1910, but his plan of action has been Bihar. Owing to coming in contact with revolutionaries like Sachin Sanyal and Suresh Bhattacharya during the early days of life, the flame of resolution was lit in him. Sachin Sanyal and Suresh Bhattacharya introduced him to the biggest revolutionary leaders of the time namely, Bhagat Singh and Chandrashekhar Azad. The Indian revolutionaries formed Hindustan Republican Army at that time inspired by Russia Revolution of 1917. As a member of this organisation, he along with Bhagat Singh threw bomb in Central Hall of Delhi Assembly on 8 April, 1929. The time when both of them threw bomb, two block acts were being passed in the assembly. Both of them were arrested after this incident. Case for the assassination of police officer Sanders who lathicharged Lala Lajpat Rai was also instituted against them. Bhagat Singh was sentenced to be hanged and Batukeshwar Dutt was imprisoned in Andaman Jail (Kaalapani). He was relieved from the Andaman Jail in 1938. He was again imprisoned during the 'Quit India Movement' in 1942. He died after independence on 20 July, 1965 is All-India Institute of Medical Sciences New Delhi.

Gaya is the main place of conspiracy in the history of revolutionary nationalist movement of Bihar. This conspiracy is linked to revolutionary leader Keshav Prasad Sinha. Keshav Prasad Sinha was born on 7 June 1906 in the house of an engineer, Ayodhya Prasad. Keshav Prasad received his initial education in the district school of Gaya, Again, he started taking education in B.Ed college of Patna. At the mere age of 12 years, he reached to join the annual session of Congress in Calcutta in 1918. On his way, he met Motilal Nehru. He was arrested for the first time in 1928 on the grounds of engaging in anti-national activities and was arrested thrice within one year. Inspired by Hindustan Republican Association that was formed in Kanpur in 1924, Keshav Prasad Sinha established. 'Youth Federation' in T. Model School of Gaya in 1929, which was linked with 'Socialist Republic Association'. Its objective was to establish Federal Republic of United States of India. To fulfil this purpose, Keshav Prasad started making fire arms at Brahmyoni mountain and Ramshila mountain in Gaya and started looting government treasury. Plan to rob Imperial Mail in 1930, plan to loot cash of post office at Pamarganj Railway station, Rail decoity scheme in Daltenganj, plan to kill Moredith and his associate in 1932 in Gaya, etc. were the main activities of 'Gaya Conspiracy Case'. Fearing terror unleashed by these people, superintendent of Gaya Jail, Major Borke, who was persecuting revolutionary captured in the jail, namely Mahant Bhagwan Das, committed suicide in April 1931. During this time, Tekari Raj Ki Pehsi Kothi, which was also called 'Saat Aana Raaj' Kothi, served as centre of revolutionary activities. A person named Bageshwari Sharma was helping the revolutionaries in this Kothi. The police raided Pehsi Kothi on 3 August, 1931 from where cartridges, firearms, etc. were recovered. Again, after the arrest of Bengal revolutionary leader, Prabhat Chakravorty and on the basis of documents recovered from him, police again raided this kothi on 16 January, 1933. Keshav Prasad and his 16 comrades were arrested on 21 January, 1933 and they were subjected to inhuman treatment in Gaya jail.

Advocates Baldev Sahay of Patna, Devki Nandan Sinha of Calcutta, and Avdhesh Nandan Sahay, Laxmi Narayan Sinha and Dhyan Chand of Gaya, etc. defended the case on behalf of these people. In this case, Keshav Prasad Sinha, Shyamcharan Bathewar and Vishwanath Mathur were sentenced for seven and half years and Keshav Prasad Sinha was put in Hazaribagh Central Jail and then again in Dum Dum Jail located in Calcutta. He was sent to Cellular Jail of Andaman in 1934 where his name is inscribed on the walls along with other revolutionaries. After release in 1937, he was again arrested on 13 August, 1942 in the 'Quit India Movement'. He formed 'Gandhi Seva Mandal' in Gaya after independence and was elected as member of legislature in 1952. He died on 3 September, 1975.

Another revolutionary leader, Basawan Singh, had played an important role in the independence of country by associating himself with 'Hindustan Socialist Republican Association'. He was born on 23 March, 1909 in Subhai Village of Jalalpur, Vaishali. He actively participated in the non-cooperation movement started in 1920 and met Gandiji in Hajipur. Basawan Singh became an active member of 'Hindustan Socialist Republic Army' after 1925. Basawan became underground after the Lahore Conspiracy of 1929, but he was arrested in 1930 and held captive in Bankipur Central Jail, Patna. He fled three days after the arrest. He was arrested again after seven days and kept in Gaya Central Jail. He went on hunger stike for 57 days in Gaya Central Jail protesting against the arrested. He was released on June 1936. After release, he joined 'Congress Socialist Party'. He joined 'Gaya Cotton Mill Union' on coming in contact with Subhash Chandra Bose. He formed 'Labour Union' in 1937 in Japla and 'Jamalpur Rail Workshop Labour Union' along with Shivnath Bannerjee in 1937. He became associated with 'All India Railway Federation', in year 1936 and was also elected as chairman of 'Northwest Railway Union' he was arrested in 1937 along with Jai Prakash Narayan and Beni Prasad and was sentenced for six months.

Basawan Singh was in touch with prominent leaders of socialist movement like Acharya Narendra Dev, Jai Prakash Narayan, Sampoornanad, Ram Manohar Lohia, Achyut Patvardhan, Yusuf Mehar Aami, Kamla Devi Chattopadhyay and Mr. Masani. He was arrested from Husainabad area of Palamu on 26 January, 1940. He had gone to Afghanistan and Rawalpindi with the objective of establishing coordination amongst revolutionaries. He had participated in the session of congress held in Mumbai on 9 August, 1942 during 'Quit India Movement'. He was sent to Jail after arrest in Delhi on 8 January 1943 and was released from jail on 3 April, 1946. He remained associated with socialist and workers movement even after independence and established 'Hind Mazdoor Sabha'. He was eleced as member of legislative assembly from Dehri-on-Sone in 1952. He served as leader of opposition in Bihar Legislative Assembly from 1952 to 1962 and was member of Bihar Legislative Council from 1962 to 1968. He worked as Labour, Planning and Industry Minister in 1967 and died on 7 April, 1989.

ROLE OF WOMEN IN INDEPENDENCE MOVEMENT

In the national movement, not only students, youth, labours, farmers, etc. of Bihar made a contribution, but the woman of Bihar also participated actively.

The contribution of women in national movement continually increased after the Champaran Satyagraha. Women movement had taken the form of an organization by 1919 under the leadership of Kasturba Gandhi and her followers Smt. Sarla Devi, Prabhavati Devi, Rajvanshi Devi, etc.

Hundreds of students had boycotted government schools and colleges under the leadership of Sarla Devi in 1921 during the non-cooperation movement. That year, Savatri Devi had organised a function in protest against arrival of Prince of Wales in India. Women in Bihar had constituted a 'Charkha Committee' during non-cooperation movement. Smt C.C. Das and Smt. Urmila Devi of Patna played major role in the formation Charkha Committee when Mahatma Gandhi was on tour of Bihar in 1921, then he did the job of collecting money for the Deshbandhu Memorial Fund. He was helped most in this task by wife of Loknayak Jai Prakash Narayan, Smt. Prabhavati Devi.

During the Civil Disobedience Movement also woman of Bihar played an important role in breaking the Salt Law. On this chain of events, Smt Shailbale Roy inspired hundreds of woman in Santhal sub-division. Wife of Shri Ram Bahadur of Shahabad District went to Sasaram Police Station and opposed Salt Law. President of District Congress Committee Smt Saraswati Devi and Smt. Sadhana Devi were arrested in Hazaribagh during the movement and sentenced to six months imprisonment. Smt. Meera Devi was arrested in July 1930 in course of doing satyagraha woman satyagrahis held picketing in Patna before shops of foreign clothes. This program was conducted by woman organization whose leaders were Smt. Hasan Imam and Smt. Vindhyavasini Devi. Smt. Hasan Imam and her daughter Sami and Smt C.C. Das and her daughter Gauri Das actively participated in boycott of foreign clothes. These people held demonstration in 3 different places. Smt. Shah Mohd. Jubair of Munger had also jumped into movement by getting influenced with these agitating women. During Civil Disobedience Movement, Ramswarup Devi went from village to village and inspired women to join the movement. She was kept in Central Jail after her arrest in Bhagalpur in 1931. She was released from prison after the Gandhiji Irwin Pact. Chandrawati Devi, resident of Gaya, campaigned against Chaukidari tax due to which she was arrested.

When Bhagat Singh was hanged on 23 March, 1931, then Kusum Kumari Devi had organized a large assembly in protest in Arrah on 30 March, 1931 and had exhorted, "Youths, why do you lag? Why do don't you come forward like Bismil, Bhagat Singh and Khudiram to sacrifice yourself? The pyre of Bhagat Singh hasn't cooled down and go forward to kindle its spark." Mahatma Gandhi was arrested on 4 January, 1932. So, Mahatma Gandhi Arrest Day was observed in the whole country on 4 January, 1933 in protest, and independence day was celebrated on 26 January. Seven women of Patna city were arrested on account of this program amongst which Rajvanshi Devi and Chandravati Devi were also present. Rajvanshi Devi was the wife of Dr. Rajendra Prasad. Chandravati Devi was famous by the name 'Dictator' Both of them were sentenced to 15 months' imprisonment.

Mahatma Gandhi had started individual satyagraha in 1941. Many women of Bihar gave their arrest in this satyagraha, which included Priyavanda Devi, Jagat Rani Devi and Janki Devi of Gaya. These woman were sentenced to four months' imprisonment each. Members of Charka Committee actively participated in Bihar during the Quit Indian

Movement of 1942. A large procession of women was taken out in Patna on 9 August which was led by Smt. Bhagwati Devi, Sister of Dr. Rajendra Prasad. A Similar large procession was taken out on 11 August, 1942 in Hazaribagh under the leadership of Saraswati Devi. That very day, Saraswati Devi was arrested and kept in Hazaribagh Jail, and she was being taken to Bhagalpur Jail on 12 August, but the agitating students got her released in the way itself. Again, she was arrested on 14 August while delivering a lecture before an assembly.

Maya Devi was arrested in Bihpur Village of Bhagalpur. Again, in Govindpur village of Bhagalpur, wife of Shri Narsinh Gop, Jiriavati was shot dead. A large assembly was convened in Town Hall under the Presidentship of Shanti Devi in Chhapra on 15 August, 1942. In this series of events, Sharda and Saraswati of Malkhachak Village of Dighvar Block in Saran District were punished at the mere age of 14 and 11 years for the crime of unfurling the tricolour. Pyari Devi of Mohammadpur Village, Gaya District was arrested during the movement of 1942 and send to Camp Jail where she died. A number of women took active participation in 'Quit India Movement' in which Sumiti Devi, wife of Kishori Prasann Singh and Radhika Devi, wife of Baikunth Shukla from Vaishali, under the disguise of men, went from village to village to motivate people to join the movement. Tara Devi, wife of Phulena Prasad Srivastava, also actively participated in the movement. Viraji Madhiyain of Ghodmara Village and Akli Devi of Lashadi Village, Bhojpur District became victims of police bullets.

PEASANT MOVEMENT

Where on one had the nationalists and revolutionaries played an important role in India National Movement, the farmers also actively participated on the other hand. It was the farmers, who were the most affected by British imperialist exploitative policies. Farmers had a pentahedral classification condition due to British divisive policies. English East India Company and later the British administration exploited the farmers here at many levels in order of generate maximum revenue. Landlords, agents, moneylenders, etc. also fully exploited the farmers, Lord Cornwallis of the British Company implemented Permanent Settlement System in Bihar. Bengal, Orissa and Benaras region in 1793 for collective exploitation of the farmers, and it was primarily a zamindari practice. Under this practice, 89 percent of the land revenue went to the company and 11 percent share was give to zamindars. The farmers from the initial stage itself opposed their exploitation and persecution, but their voice was suppressed.

Farmers from Bihar also played an important role in the 'Indian National Movement'. During the latter half of the 19th century, Indigo plantation owners from Bengal victimized farmers on a large scale after coming to Bihar. Farmers revolted against them at a place called Pandaul in 1866-67. Farmers launched a big movement against the Raja of Darbhanga in 1883-84. The real beginning of peasant movement in Bihar is considered to the 'Champaran Satyagraha'. Champaran movement was initiated under the leadership of Mahatma Gandhi in 1917 which ended the longstanding Tinkathia System. Encouraged by Champaran movement, Swami Vidyanand led farmers Movement in Madhubani District. Kisan Sabha was formed by Shah Mohd. Jubair and Shri Krishna Singh in Munger in 1922-23. Chief personality of peasant movement in Bihar was Swami Sahajanand Saraswati. He was born in 1889 in Devagram Village of Gajipur District, Uttar Pradesh, but he devoted himself towards the problems faced by farmers of Bihar. His childhood name was Navrang Rai. He became a recluse in 1906 after death of his wife. He became an active member of Bumihar Brahman Mahasabha established in Bihar and stated working as peasant worker leader through this organization. He started publishing a monthly magazine 'Bhumihar Brahman' from Kashi in 1915 in which the casteist feeling among the Brahmans was opposed. He worte a book name 'Bhumihar Brahman Parichay' name of which was later changed to 'Brahmrishi Vansh Vistar'. Apart from this, he also wrote 'Brahman Ki Stithi' and 'Jhootha Bhay Mithya Abhiman'. He also wrote a book related to rituals and astrology called 'Karma Kalaap'.

On getting influence with Gandhiji, he met him in Patna in December 1920 and decided to join Congress. He made Sitaram Ashram, located in Bihta near Patna, as the centre of his political struggle. He participated in the Congress session of 1924 held in Ahmedabad, and after returning back, ran campaign in Buxar to promote congress membership. Apart from these activities, he wanted to make an organisation for the farmers for which he created a society called 'Western Patna Farmers Committee' on 4 March, 1928 in Bihta, which proved as a milestone in the history of farmers movement. He decided to form 'Bihar Provincial Farmers Committee' in association with Ram Dayalu Singh and Yamuna Karzi and later organized it on the eve of Sonpur festival. Swami Sahajanand Saraswati was appointed as its chairman and Shri Krishna Singh as its secretary. In this meeting, it was also decided that Kisan Sabha (Farmers Committee) shall not oppose the Congress in political matters. Farmers movement became more intense after the arrival of Sardar Vallabh Bhai Patel in Bihar in 1929 and beginning of 'Civil Disobedience Movement' by Gandhiji in 1930. Swami Sahajanand Saraswati was arrested and sentenced for six months for breaking salt law at the Vikram Ashram in Patna during the 'Salt Satyagraha'. He was first detained in the Bankipur Jail and later in the Hazaribagh Central Jail. He started living in the Bihta Ashram after his release in 1930 and did the work of activating farmers movements.

During this time, the effect of worldwide recession manifested on the farmers movements too, taking advantage of which landlords formed 'United Political Party' to preserve their interests, and Maharaja of Darbhanga has its President and Shivshankar Jha the secretary. The objective of this party was to protect itself from the farmers movement. A committee was formed during the working committee meeting of the provincial farmers assembly on 18 June, 1933 to know the problems faced by the farmers whose members were Yamuna Karji, Chand Nandau Sharma, Yugal Kishore Singh, Badri Narayan Singh, Yadu Nandan Sharma and Swami Sahajanand Sharma. This committee compiled the problems faced by the farmers of Gaya region, which was given the shape of a book, 'Gaya Ke Kisanon Ki Karuna Kahani' (Story of pathos of the Gaya farmers) by Sahajanand Saraswati Purushottam Das Tandan gave suggestion to Sahajanand Saraswati in 1934 to constitute a farmers assembly at national level. Ultimately, All India Kisan Sabha was formed under the chairmanship of Swamiji in Lucknow in 1936.

After the election of 1937, Kisan Sabha started getting disenchanted with the Congress because Congress started making alliances with landlords. It was felt that Congress was becoming a protection agency of capitalists, landlords and moneylenders. At last, Swami Sahajanand Saraswati started satyagraha movement against congress due to which he was expelled from Congress. He was arrested in 1940 and sent to Hazaribagh Jail. During this time, he wrote books 'The other side of the shield and 'Rent Reduction in Bihar: How it Works'. He gave the slogan 'We have the stick, how will you take tax'. He resigned from the congress membership on 6 December, 1948. He died on 26 June, 1950. One of the main personalities associated with farmers movement in Bihar was Shilbhadra Yaji. He was born on 22 March, 1906 in Bakhtiyarpur of Patna District. His father's name was Shivtahal Yaji and mother's name was Reshmi Devi. He was one of the active members of Kisan Sabha and even served as its minister in 1941. Swami Sahajanand Saraswati had form units of All-India Kisan Sabha in all the districts. Leadership of Patna District Kisan Sabha was entrusted to Shilbhadra Yagi.

Shilbhadra Yaji worked along with revolutionary leaders like Bhagat Singh, Chandra Sekhar Azad and Yogendra Shukla, including leaders Such as Acharya Narendra Dev, Jai Prakash Narayan and Achyut Patvardhan. When he had gone to Calcutta in 1928 during the annual session of congress as a representative from Bihar, he came in contact with Subhash Chandra Bose. In continuation of non-cooperation movement, he was arrested in 1930 in Patna and was kept in Bankipur Central Jail for 8 months. During the 'Quit India Movement' of 1942, he was largely influenced by the policies of Forward Block and its ideas underwent radical change. He participated in the meeting of All India Congress

Committee held in Mumbai in 1942. On coming into contact with Subhash Chandra Bose, he helped him in formation of Azad Hind Fauj. On the charges of contacting Netaji Subhash Chandra Bose in Mumbai, he was arrested in the guise of a hermit and faced trial in 1944 at Red Fort, Delhi. Shilbhadra Yagi remained in custody in different prisons for seventeen and half and years from 1930 to 1947 and spent two and half years in anonymity. He died on 28 January, 1966.

Congress Socialist Party was formed within the congress by progressive youth in 1934 under the leadership of Jai Prakash Narayan and Acharya Narander Dev. Leaders of this party gave full support to the 'farmers movement' started by Swami Sahajanand Saraswati. Congress got huge success in the elections of 1837. Encouraged thus, leaders like Abdul Bari and Ramvriksha Benipuri proposed for zamindari abolition before the government, but no significant progress occurred in this front. After independence, Zamindari System was ended constitutionally in 1952; however, still, the upper caste Hindus with higher social status had control over the land. Under the leadership of Swami Sahajanand, around 50,000 farmers laid siege of legislative assembly and shouted slogans against Prime Minister, Shri Krishna Singh and Congress President, Rajendra Prasad. 'Bakasht Movement' was launched in place called Badhiya in Central Bihar under the leadership of Karyanand Sharma. This movement was an effort by exploited and persecuted farmers towards getting their ryot land, which got changed into babash land, back from the landlords.

Initially, the peasant movement started in Patna, Shahabad, Saran, Muzaffarpur, Darbhanga, etc. districts, which later spread to whole Bihar. Congress adopted a conciliatory policy towards the landlords. Leaders like Shri Krishna Singh and Rajendra Prasad asked farmers to withdraw their movement, but the farmers movement continued. Yadunandan Sharma in Gaya, Ramanandan Mishra in Darbhanga, Rahul Sankrityayan in Chhapra and Yamuna Karji in Saran provided their leadership. Swami Sahajanand Saraswati began getting drafted towards the Marxit ideology during the Second World War and decided to take peasant movement on the line of class struggle. For this reason, Jai Prakash Narayan formed 'Red Kisan Sabha'. 'Farmers movement' became weak due to separation from the socialists.

In this way it can be said that many important farmers movements arose in Bihar after 1930 and lent strength to the Indian freedom struggle. It is due to the farmers movement that state government framed a number of legislation related to land reforms after independence.

LABOUR MOVEMENT

After the end of First World War workers began to retrenched on a large scale from most of the machine factories and industries due to which their status and working conditions became deplorable. To protect the economic interests of the workers, labour movement was started in the second half of the 19th century by labours and intellectuals. Initially, this movement was reformist in nature but later it took political form. During this time, Bolshevik Revolution occurred in Russia under the leadership of Lenin, which impacted learned and worker class in India. It was in 1918 that labours under leadership of V.P. Wadia at first launched strike in Winni Cotton Mill, Madras to secure their rights. The same year workers of Tata Iron and Steel Works in Jamshedpur also went on strike and in 1919, about 40 thousand labours took to strike in protest against the Rowlatt Act.

MN Roy established Communist Party in India in 1925 in Kanpur and put forward the principle of obtaining rights based on struggle. Biggest strike in India (around three and half months) occurred in Jamshedpur in 1928 which was led by labour leader Manik Homi. Even with the effort of C.F. Andrews, N.M. Joshi and Yamunadas Mehta, this strike could not be ended. It ended on 18 August, 1828 after agreement between Subhash Chandra Bose and Managing Director of the company. 'Jamshedpur Labour Federation, constituted by labour leader Manik Homi was given recognition by the company. Workers of Tinplate Company in Golmuri also went on strike many times in 1929. Here too, Subhash Chandra Bose and Rajendra Prasad along with their associates toured many times.

Pandit Jawahar Lal Nehru presided over 'All India Trade Union Congress session held in coal mining region of Jharia. 'Congress Socialist Party' was established by leaders like Jai Prakash Narayan and Abdul Bari in 1934. These leaders paid special attention to problems faced by the workers. In 1937-38, 11 significant strikes took place in Bihar. Strikes occurred in Rohtas Industry, Dalmia Nagar, Gaya Cotton Mill, India Copper corporation Mugabani, Singhbhum, Indian Cable Company, Gulmuri, Jamshedpur, Tata Nagar Foundary Company, Jamshedpur, Japla Cement Works, Tinplate Company of India, Jamshedpur and other factories. A labour federation named 'Tata Workers Union' was formed under the leadership of Abdul Bari, Satya Narayan Singh and Yogendra Shukla.Bermo provided leadership to workers of coal mine. Abdul Bari and Ramvriksha Benipur addressed a meeting of Bihta Sugar Mill in December 1938 and formed a labour federation. Riyasat Hussain and Major Rayjeesh held a meeting with workers of Dehri on 16 December 1939 and laid emphasis on making a united front of workers.

Revolutionay leaders like M.N. Roy and Batukeshwar Dutt during their address in Jamshedpur exhorted workers to take part in freedom struggle. Jai Prakash Naryan was arrested and awarded 9 months' rigorous imprisonment under the Defence of India Act for his speech delivered before workers in Jamshedpur on 18 February 1940. Strikes and picketing was done in many places, including Patna in protest of this act. 'Jai Prakash Day' was observed in whole province on 14 March.

Consequent to August revolution of 1942, strikes occurred in Jharia and Katras and an assembly of thousands of workers was held in Jamshedpur. During this time, strike was also observed in Katihar Flax Mill. A mob of around 10 thousands workers attacked Registry office in Katihar on 13 August, 1942. A meeting of Bihar Trade Union Congress' was held in Giridih on 10 June, 1944 in which around 30 persons participated along with 40 state representatives. A meeting of central committee of AITUC was held on 16 January, 1947 in which it was decided to observe 'Demand Day' in whole India to solve the problems faced by the workers. As per this decision, a public assembly was held by CPI in Bankipur 18 March 1947 under the chairman of Gayan Vikas Maitra.

Assistant Secretary of 'Bihar Trade Union Congress', Habibur Rehman along with student leaders Kanta Singh and Brij Kishore Prasad held a public assembly in Parade Ground on 5 March, 1947 and advised policemen too to go on strike. Slogans like 'Blood will be revenged with blood, and gun will be replied by gun' were raised during the procession on 26 March, 1947. Similarly, unions affiliated to AITUC declared strike on 26 March, 1947, and workers raised slogans like: 'Hail Red Flag,' we will rule this time' and 'labour state be established' conference of different workers organizations was held in Patna from 17-20 June 1947 under the leadership of CPI. Gyan Vikas Maitra and Jagnnath Sarkar addressed workers associated with coal and rail industries in this conference. Two CPI members, Shri Kedas Das and Nihal Singh were arrested for violating prohibitive order in Jamshedpur and engineering strikes in tin plate industry and TISCO.

In this way, it can be said that workers movement took a strong political form in Bihar after its beginning as a liberal entity.

SOCIALIST MOVEMENT

The sudden postponement of Non-Cooperation Movement by Congress and the failure of Civil Disobedience Movement had created a feeling of frustration in the youth of the country. They seemed to be getting perturbed with the national movement. They had the feeling that Congress was working on the directions of right-wing feudalists and that it had become completely unprogressive and orthodoxical. It had become a need of the hour to bring changes in the congress in line with the circumstances. Youth of Bihar were also restless, similar to those of the country, to make congress progressive. At the same time, Bolshevik Revolution of Russia in 1917 had inspired youth to treat the path of socialism. In this way, revolutionary socialists and international socialist movements did the work of propagating socialist ideology in Bihar.

The youth of Bihar first established 'Bihar Socialist Party' in 1931 with the aim of providing impetus to freedom struggle in India. Its main founders were Gangesheran Sinha, Ramvriksha Benipuri, Ramanand Mishra etc. Later, formal proclamation of 'Indian Socialist Congress Party' was made in 1934 in Anjuman Islamia Hall of Patna. Acharya Narendra Dev was made its president and Jai Prakash Narayan the Secretary. Jai Prakash Narayan was born on 11 October, 1902 in Sitab Diara Village of Saran District, Bihar. He is also known by the name of 'J.P.' and 'Loknayak'. His father's name was Harshal Dayal Srivastava and mother's name was Phoolrani Devi. He received his initial education from Patna Collegiate School, Patna. He was married to Prabhavati Devi in 1920. Prabhavati Devi spent many years with Kasturba Gandhi in the Gandhi Ashram. Jai Prakash Narayan first enrolled himself in Patna College but influenced by national movement, he left college and studied in Bihar University up till 1922. He went to America in 1922 to gain higher education where he studied in Berkeley University. He returned to India from America in 1929. At this time, national movement had intensified in Indian and Jai Prakash Naryan had come in contact with Jawahar Lal Nehru and Mahatma Gandhi. He was arrested in Madras and put in Nasik Jail in 1932 during the 'Civil Disobedience Movement' where he came in contact with leaders possessing socialist ideology, such as Achyut Patvardhan, Ashok Mehta, M.R. Masani, M.H. Dantewala and CK Narayan Swami, and under the influence of these leaders, he formed 'Congress Socialist Party'.

When the Indian National Congress decided to contest elections in 1934, then Jaiprakash Narayan opposed this idea on the behalf of Congress Socialist Party. He was arrested and sentenced to 9 months imprisonment during the 'Quit India Movement' of 1942 was kept in Hazaribagh Jail. During the movement itself, he fled from the jail along with Yogendra Shukla and other associates and kept the movement going remaining underground in Nepal region. At this time, he formed 'Azad Hind Squad'. Even after the independence, he played an important role in nation building. He took retirement from politics in 1957, but again in opposition of the Congress policies became actively involved in politics during the emergency. He was conferred Magsaysay Award for social service in 1965 and was felicitated by 'Bharat Ratna' in 1998 after his death. He launched a movement against the emergency launched in 1975 and raised the slogan of 'total revolution'. He died in Patna on 8 October, 1979.

Other people also made valuable contributions to development of 'Indian Congress Socialist Party' movement amongst whom were Gangasharam Sinha, Ramviksha Benipuri, Abdul Bari, Ramanand Mishra, Yogendra Shukla, Avdeshwar Prasad Sinha, Ambika Kant, Phulan Prasad Verma, etc., Where India Congress Socialist Party helped congress in making anti-British government on the one hand, it did the work of creating political consciousness in workers, and farmers, on the other. During the Quit India Movement of 1942, leaders of congress socialist partly displayed unprecedented nationalism. They led the movement remaining underground. They were arrested and subjected to physical and mental torture in many ways, but they were not perturbed. Socialist made an unprecedented contribution to the national movement.

COMMUNIST MOVEMENT

Communist movement also has a special important in Bihar similar to the other movements. This movement mainly played the role of creating political awakening amongst farmers and workers in Bihar. The Bolshevik Revolution of 1917 helped in creating awakening in people of Bihar also, including that in the world. Singar Velli Chettiyar was the first to propagate communist ideas in Bihar in 1921 by putting them forward before coal mines of Jharia. He acquainted the workers with communist ideology in his address made before them. Communist leader M.N. Roy expressed his idea in the Gaya session of Congress in 1922. He was successful in attracting workers, farmers and youth of Bihar.

M.N. Roy formed communist Party of India in 1925 in Kanpur but it had its influence over the youth of Bihar too. They became inseparable part of the movement by getting inspired with communist ideas. Communist youth like Anil Mitra, Sunil Mukherjee, Ratan Roy and Vishwanath Mathur were arrested in 1930 on the charges of engaging in terrorist activities. After his release from prison, he formed Patna branch of the 'Communist Party of India' in Munger on 20 October, 1932. Prominent amongst the founder of party were Sunil Mukherjee, Rahul Sankrityayan, Gyan Vikas Mitra, Vinod Biheri Mukherjee, Anil Mitra, etc. Other revolutionary leaders who played important role in this movement were Ali Ashraf, Krishna Chand Chaudhary, Chandrashekhar Singh, Gangadhar Das, Rajkumar Purve, Vishwanath Lal, Kishori Prashna Singh, Tej Narayan Jha, Mohd. Shafi, Jagannath Sarkar etc. Under the leadership of Karyanand Sharma a Rahul Sankrityayan. 'Bakasht Movement' started in Bihar, which was related to surrendering land of marginalized farmers. Youth like Kedar Das, Chaturanan Mishra, Phanindra Nath Dutt, Teja Singh, and Mangal Singh did a lot of constructive work among the farmers and workers of Bihar and formed many communist labour organisations. The British administration banned the communist organization for its revolutionary activities. Consequently, communist leaders went underground and kept leading the movement. During the Second World War the communists cooperated with British government to defeat the Nazi forces. Thus, communists played an important role in making the mass movement effective in India and inspiring for a struggle towards rights of farmers and workers.

DEVELOPMENT OF EDUCATION DURING THE BRITISH PERIOD

Modern Education

British has been an important centre of education since ancient time itself. Nalanda University situated in Bihar was considered one of the major educational centres not only in India but also the world. The real beginning of Western education is considered to be form 1835 onwards. It is also considered as the beginning of western education in Bihar, including the country. The development of Western education was emphasized under the Lord Macaulay Plan. At the same time, it was announced that educational institutions imparting English education will be provided financial assistance. A number of intellectuals supported in promoting English education. Maharja Minnijit Singh of Tikari, Maharaja Chhatradhari of Hathua, Maharaja Rudra Singh of Darbhanga etc. gave financial assistance liberally to popularize English education. Governor General of India Lord William Bentick took many government efforts to encourage western education. Schools were established for this purpose in Purnia in 1835, Bihar Sharif in 1838 and Bhagalpur in 1840. Later, one school each in the district of Patna , Arrah, Chhapra, Muzaffarpur, Munger, Deoghar, Harazibagh, etc. was established, Bhagalpur Hill school was opened in Bhagalpur for imparting education to children of soldiers. St. Joseph School was established in Patna in 1847 and St. Michael School in 1856.

Earlier, people of Bihar had a number of misconceptions regarding western education due to which its advantage was taken only by the Bengalis. W.S. Atchinson, Education Director of Bengal reviewed educational backwardness of Bihar in 1861 and remarked that Biharis, due to ignorance and orthodoxical thinking, kept themselves away from modern education, leading to their deprivation from recruitment in government services.

Syed Nawab Rizvi established B.N.R. Teachers Training College Guljarbagh, Patna in 1909 and the same year, Patna Law College was established. Establishment of Patna University on 1 October, 1917 paved the way of higher education Bihar. J.G Jevings was made the first vice chancellor of Patna University. Ram Bahadur Idal Singh established Nalanda college in 1920 in Bihar Sharif. Panta Science college was founded in 1917 as an independent college. With the establishment of Chandradheri Mithila College, Darbhanga in 1938-39 and Rajendra College Chhapra, propagation of modern education in Bihar got valuable assistance. Basic Education Board was created in 1938 with the objective of providing impetus to Western Education. Decidedly, propagation of modern education in different parts of the state was possible gradually. This led to creation of social and political consciousness in people and movement for a separate Bihar state heralded.

Technical Education

Technical Education got spread very late in Bihar. Except few technical educational institutions, formation of most institutes occurred only after organization of a separate Bihar province that is after 1912. Beginning of higher education in Bihar is considered to be after established of Patna College in 1863. Animal Breeding and Dairy farm was founded in 1902 in Samastipur, Pusa. Load Curzon established Agricultural Research Laboratory in 1904, which came to be known as Imperial 'Agricultural Research Institute' in 1919. Few years after the formation of Bihar Province, Patna University was established in 1917 and Prince of Wales Medical College was established in 1925, which later became famous by the name of 'Patna Medical College'. Syed Imdad Ali founded 'Bihar Scientific Society' in Muzaffarpur in 1972. This institution proved quite helpful for studies in engineering. A 'Survey School' relating to studies in engineering was established in Patna in 1874, which later came to be known by the name of 'School of Engineering'. Later, it became famous as Bihar College of Engineering', the 'Bihar College of Engineering' was given the status of National Institute of Technology (NIT) by the Government of India in the year 2004.

Bihar Legislative Council by passing a resolution started Ayurvedic Education System in the year 1921. Resultantly, Government Ayurvedic School was opened in Patna in 1926. with the objective of promoting arts in Bihar, Government College of Arts and Crafts was established in Patna in 1939. 'Patna Science College', by separating it from Patna college, was formed in 1927 with the aim of encouraging studies of science in Bihar. Governor of Bihar, Sir Henry Miller, founded Bihar Veterinary School in 1927 in Patna, which took the form of a college in 1947. Darbhanga Medical School was established in the 1940 decade, and this school later became famous as Darbhanga Medical College and Hospital.

A number of technical institutes were formed by the central and state governments, after getting independence. A branch of B.I.T extension was formed in Patna in 2006 for engineering education. As a management institute, 'Chandragupta Management Institution' was formed in Patna in year 2008, and 'Indian Management Institution' was established in year 2015. Engineering and medical colleges were opened at many places in Bihar. IIT was established in Patna in year 2008. Similarly, in the year 2008, engineering colleges were opened in Darbhanga, Nalanda, and Gaya. The state government opened medical college in Bettiah in 2009 and in Madhepura in 2010, keeping in view providing medical facilities. AIIMs was established in Patna in the year 2012 by the central government.

Currently, agriculture has been given the status of an industry in Bihar, and a number of research centres have been opened for its development. The eastern regional office of Indian Agricultural Research Council has been established in Patna. Agricultural Research Centre is situated in Muzaffarpur. Maiza Research Centre has been established in Begusarai. Water Management Research Centre has been established in Patna with the objective of promoting agriculture.

In this way, it can be said that development of modern technical education that began in the British period is continuing in present times also.

Date Sequence	Incident
1857 (12 June)	Revolt by soldiers in Rohini (Deoghar).
1857 (3 July)	Revolt by masses in Patna under the leadership of Pir Ali.
1857 (25 July)	Revolt in Danapur and Arrah, Revolt of Kunwar Singh in Jagdishpur.
1858 (23 April)	British General Le Graw defeated by Kunwar Singh.
1858	End of East India Rule, Direct rule of Britain established.

1860	Sardari Battle.
1865	Arrest of Behawi Leaders of Patna.
1870	Kharwar Movement.
1894	Publication of Bihar Times.
1895	Movement by Birsa Munda.
1906	Demand to separate Bihar from Bengal begins.
1908	Muzaffar Bomb Case, Spread of revolutionary nationalist in Bihar through Prafulla Chaki and Khudiram Bose, organization of Bihar Regional Conference in Patna.
1911 (12 September)	Declaration by King George V in Delhi Durbar to make Bihar a separate province.
1912 (22 March)	Proposal for separation of Bihar and Orissa from Bengal accepted.
1912 (1 April)	New provinces of Bihar and Orissa established.
1912	Session of Indian National Congress in Bankipur, Patna; Pandit Nehru present in Congress session for the first time.
1913-13	In sequence of Balkan Wars, display of support by Muslims of Bihar in favour of Sultan of Turkey (Caliph).
1913-14	Tana Bhagat Movement.
1916	Establishment of Patna High Court, Sir Edward I appointed first Chief Justice; Beginning of Home Rule Movement in Bihar under the leardership of Maulana Mazhar-ul Haque.
1917	Successful satyagraha by Gandhiji in Champaran against indigo planters; Establishment of Patna University.
1919	Beginning of Khilafat Movement in Bihar, Beginning of Peasant Movement under the leadership of Swami Vidyanand.
1919	Beginning of the system of Dyarchy introduced by 1919 Act (Montague Chelmsford Reforms) in provinces including Bihar), Foundation of Bihar Hindi Conference.
1920	Beginning of Non-Cooperation Movement in Bihar, Establishment of Sadakat Ashram by Mazhar-ul Haque.
1921 (6 February)	Establishment of Bihar University, Maulana Mazhar-ul Haque appointed as Vice Chancellor and Dr. Rajendra Prasad as Principal.
1921	Bihar visit by Prince of Wales.
1923	Formation of Swaraj Party in Bihar.
1925	Establishment of Patna Medical College (Prince of Wales Medical College).
1928	Arrival of Simon Commission in Bihar.
1929	Constitution of Bihar Provincial Farmers Committee by Swami Sahajanand in Bihar.
1930 (15 April)	Beginning of Salt Satyagraha in Bihar.
1931	Formation of Bihar Socialist Party.

1934 (7 April)	Call for individual Satyagraha by Gandhiji in Patna.
1936 (1 April)	Orissa separated. Re-organisation of Bihar Province, Sir James David Sifton appointed first Governor of Bihar, formation of Triveni Sabha.
1937	Elections in Bihar under the 1935 Act, Majority to Congress.
1937 (7 July)	Leader of Bihar Muslim Independent Party, Mohd. Yunus appointed as first Prime Minister of Bihar.
1937 (20 July)	Shri Krishna Singh appointed as Bihar Prime Minister and organisation of Congress government.
1938	Formation of Momin Conference by Abdul Qayyun Ansari.
1940	Formation of Bihar branch of Forward Bloc.
1942	Quit India Movement, Seven students martyred in Patna shootout on 11 August.
1942-43	Freedom squad organized by Jai Prakash Narayan.
1946	Interian government formed in Bihar under the leadership of Shri Krishna Singh.
1946-47	Hindu-Muslim riots in Bihar.
1947 (15 August)	India becomes independent, Jairam Das Daulat Ram becomes governor and Shri Krishna Singh the chief minister of Bihar.
Important Chronology of Events after Independence	
Date Sequence	Incident.
1950 (26 January)	Bihar becomes a state in place of province.
1950	Abolition of Zamindari System law in Bihar promulgated.
1952	First legislative assembly elections in Bihar in which Congress got full majority.
1961	Death of Shri Krishna Singh, Deep Narayan Singh becomes acting chief minister.
1964	Oil refinery established in Barauni.
1967	Congress defeated for the first time in elections to legislative assembly, formation of government under the leadership of United Legislative Party, Mahamaya Prasad Sinha appointed as chief minister.
1974	Total Revolution Movement started under the leadership of Jai Prakash Narayan, Students movement in Bihar, Declaration of emergency in the country.
1975	Urdu declared the second official language of Bihar.
1977	Congress defeated in legislative assembly elections, Janata Party government under the leardership of Karpuri Thakur.
2000 (15 November)	Division of Bihar, formation of Jharkhand state.
2005	Coalition government by Janata Dal (United) and Bhartiya Janata Party under the leadership of Nitish Kumar.
2007	Global meet organized for the first time in Bihar.
2010 (22 March)	First time Bihar Day observed.
2012	Bihar Centenary Year celebration organized.

❑❑❑

Separate Bihar Movement

The popularity of Western Education led to rise of the intelligentsia in the state of Bihar. Consequently, they became aware of their rights and privileges. They realized that only after the formation of a separate Bihar province, there could be an improvement in the social, economic, and political conditions of the Biharis. For the first time in 1876, in a publication/magazine from Munger, called 'Moordh-e-Sulaiman', talked about the idea of Separate Bihar Movement through its title, 'Bihar for Biharis'. This letter demanded that Biharis should be appointed in place of Bengalis for government jobs in Bihar. On 22 January, 1877, the Urdu subject 'Qaseed' strongly advocated the separation of Bihar from Bengal. It stressed that the association of Bengal and Bihar is incompatible, as both have different traditions, customs, cultures, and practices. Where Bengalis were getting benefiting from this, the situation/condition of Biharis was worsening or becoming pathetic. 1894, the movement for a separate Bihar became more intense. The credit for initiating this movement is Bihar actually attributed to Satchidanand Sinha and Mahesh Narayan. Other prominent contributors were Nand Kishore Lal, Krishna Sahai, Ali Imam, Maulana Sharfuddin, Maulana Mazharul Haque, Deepnarayan Singh, Parmeshwar Lal Mahtha, etc. Mahesh Narayan provided a solid foundation to the 'Bihar Separate Movement' through the "Kayastha Gazette". Through his letter, he highlighted and stressed upon the backwardness of Biharis. It was through the efforts/endeavours of Deepnarayan Singh, that the second session of the Provincial Congress was convened in Bihar.

Subsequent to the great revolution of 1857, there was a revival/renaissance in Bengal leading to great intellectual development. The Bengali intelligentsia resorted to adopting a critical approach towards British rule and gradually the seeds of nationalism started growing. The British government in India did not consider this development favourable and efforts were made by them to weaken and limit their voice.

The Biharis were openly supported by the British authorities with the aim of weakening Bengal. Lt. Governor Campbell asserted that unless the people of Bihar were provided with an opportunity of livelihood, Bihar cannot progress. He advocated the creation of a separate Bihar. The Anglo-Indian newspapers deliberately raised the issue of Bengal-Bihar rift and created a feeling of animosity and competition in the minds of Biharis against Bengalis.

Anglo-Indian newspaper, the 'Englishman' contributed hugely in kindling and airing this issue. In 1880, Campbell's successor Ashley Aiden visited Bihar and demanded reservation for Biharis in government jobs in Bihar. British officials encouraged the institutes set up by Muslims and Kayastha comities in Bihar. Among these institutions the 'Sadar Anjuman-e-Hind' founded by Munshi Pyarelal and the 'Scientific Society' formed by Imam Ali were prominent.

Satchidanand Sinha, Mahesh Narayan and other leaders demanded for the formation of a fully autonomous local government in Bihar. The formation of a new through the medium of language gained momentum. In fact, this was the first movement in India to create a separate province on the basis of 'language'.

By the last decade of the nineteenth century, Bengal had become a refuge for nationalists, extremists, and revolutionaries. This was a matter of great concern for the British administration. They wished to partition Bengal at the earliest with a view to weakening the revolutionaries. Satchidanand Sinha and Mahesh Narayan, observing the emerging environment as a favourable one, handed over a memorandum to Governor Charles Elliot and Alexander Mackenzie for the creation of a separate Bihar, but no special attention was paid to their demand.

Architecture and Painting

- Mauryan Art
- Patna Kalam
- Manjusha Style
- Pal Art
- Madhubani (Mithila) Painting

MAURYAN ART

The Mauryan period in Indian history was the time of the initiation of Indian art. In the Harappan era, a high level of art and architecture existed. In the pre Mauryan era, wood, clay and thatch were used in the manufacture of artistic objects, due to which those objects are not available at the present time. In the Maurya period, for the first time, Paashan (stone) was widely used in the field of art; these artifacts became everlasting. The Maurya period is comprised of two forms of art, namely—'Provincial or court art' and 'Folk art and sculpture'

Provincial or Court Art: The best example of this is Rajprasad of Magadha Emperor Chandragupta found in Kumhrar in Pataliputra. The remains of this hall determine its importance and greatness. This assembly premises was a giant hall supported with several pillars. About 84 stone pillars have been found in this hall. This hall measured 140 feet long and 120 feet wide. Emperor Ashoka expanded this wooden palace using stones. Famous Chinese traveller Fa-Hein praised this place as "God built palace". Many more remains of Mauryan art during Emperor Ashoka's reign have been found. The artifacts of the period of Emperor Ashoka can be divided into four parts:

(a) Pillars: Pillars are the best examples of Mauryan art. The number of these columns and pillars is not fixed. Possibly, they might have been ranging between 30 to 40. Of these, 15 are secured. These pillars are of two types:

1. **Dhamma Scripts Pillars:** Etched with Dhamma Script, these type of pillars have been received from locations like Delhi-Meerut, Delhi-Topra, Allahabad, Lauria-Nandangarh, Lauria-Areraj, Rampurva, Sanchi, Sarnath, Lumbini, etc.
2. **Plain Pillars:** These types of pillars have been found from places like Rampurva (bull head), Basadh, Kosai, etc. All these pillars are shiny, long, shapely, and monolithic. They have been shaped progressively thinner from bottom to top. The weight of each pillar is 50 tonnes and the maximum length is 50 feet. All these pillars are independently standing by themselves under the open sky. They are coated with such a shiny polish even today, they impress with illusion of being made of metal to spectators. The central part of the pillar is made of red stones of Chunar. Various animal figures (swan, lion, elephant, bull, etc.) are found at the top of the pillar. Among these pillars, the lion head pillar of Sarnath is the best, which was declared as the state emblem of India. This pillar is seven-feet high with four grand lions standing with their back to back on top. These lions symbolise the power of Chakravarti (of vast empire) Emperor Ashoka.

(b) Stupas: These stupas were solid domes made of brick or stone. These were constructed bythe people of Buddhist and Jain communities as a monument at a holy place. Emperor Ashoka himself was a great builder of huge stupas. According to a tradition, he had built 84 thousand stupas, of which only a very small number have survived till the present time. The Great Stupa of Sanchi was also built by Emperor Ashoka. Besides, the Dharmarajika Stupa at Taxila wasalso erected by Ashoka.

(c) Stone Vedika: Mauryan stupas and parks were surrounded by Vedikas (altars). The ruins of some of them have been found. Remains of Ashokan era have been found from Bodh Gaya and Sarnath. Fragments of three altars have been found in the excavation of Pataliputra; these are supposed to be of Mauryan period due to their bright polish.

(d) Guha Park: Emperor Ashoka and his grandson Dasaratha built viharas (Parks) in the form of caves for the monks to live in. A group of these beautiful caves has been found at 16 miles north of Gaya in Barabar and Nagarjuni hills. Sudama Cave, Karna Chaupar, Vishwa Jhompadi (Hut) caves are renowned among the caves found here. Another name for Sudama cave is Nyagrodha cave, which was built in the twelfth year of the accession of Ashoka. The cave of Lomesh Rishi built during the time of Dasharatha is also well known. Still, important is the Gopika cave found in the Nagarjuni group, which was built by Dasharatha in his consecration year. Following these Mauryan caves, many Chaitya Grihas were built in Western India over a period of time.

Folk Art and Sculpture

In the Mauryan period, there was a wonderful development of art by the general public outside the royal court, which has been called folk art. The best specimens of sculptures are the evidence of this folk art. Yaksha-Yakshini statues were the mainstay of folk art.

All these statues were brilliantly polished. A Chamar Grihini idol has been found from Didarganj in Patna, which has been christened as 'Streeratna' or 'Yakshi'. A female idol has been found from Bulandi Bagh, which is standing and tall in shape and rotates. An idol of a Jain Tirthankara has also been found in Patna. The idol of Yaksha obtained from Parakham village and the idol of Yakshini procured from Besnagar are the best evidences of Mauryan folk sculpture. Besides, a big number of idols of various animals, birds, men, and women have been found from many locations viz Sarnath, Mathura, Hastinapur, Basadh, Kaushambi, Kumhrar, etc. Mauryan art was perfect in various dimensions and very rich in its imagination, craft, scientific methodology and creativity.

Post Mauryan Art

Art continued its journey to develop during the Shunga and Kushan periods, but Mauryan artistry does not get reflected from the samples in this period. The development of architecture again took place on a vast scale in the Gupta dynasty and it was inspired by the style and the pattern developed in the region of Sarnath and influenced by Mathura art. Its samples were obtained from places like Rohtas, Bhojpur, Nalanda, Rajgir, Gaya, Vaishali, Sultanganj, Patna etc. The Gupta art was influenced by the Mathura style in which the influence of Hinduism is more visible than that of Buddhism.

The copper statue of Buddha, 7.5 feet high, during obtained from Sultanganj in Bhagalpur is one of the best creations in the early works built in the Gupta period. This idol adores transparent dresses, which are clinging to the body. A statue is currently preserved in the Burmingham Museum in England. Besides, many Gupta period idols have been found, which are very beautiful. The natural expression of the feminine beauty of the Gupta era represented by these idols. Idols of Buddhist and mythological gods and goddesses were also made in this period using moulds.

PAL ART

In the areas of Bihar and Bengal, Pal Art was developed between 8th and 12th centuries by the Pal rulers and the contemporary saints. During the Pal era, an advanced style of making idols of stone, bronze, and Ashtadhatu developed, which has been named 'Pal Art.' Dhiman and his son Bithpal contributed significantly in the development of the Pal style of making bronze idols. They were residents of Nalanda. They were the contemporaries of the great Pal rulers Dharmapal and Devpal of the 9th Century AD. The following are the different forms of Pal Art:

Architecture

In the field of architecture, many Mahaviharas, stupas, chaityas, temples, and forts were built duringthe Pal period. There could be seen an absolute influence of religion on architecture in this period. The credit for the establishment of Odantapuri, Nalanda, Vikramshila and Somapur Viharas in various Mahaviharas goes to the Pal rulers namely—Dharmapala and Devapada. The Odantapuri Buddh Vihara, which is the second ancient Buddh Vihara in India, was founded by the Pal ruler Gopal I. It emerged as a major centre of education. The Pal rulers have been a major contributor to the temples, stupas, and viharas built in different eras in Nalanda. During this period, houses for Buddhist monks were built under a meticulous plan. The remains of Vikramshila Mahavihara explain the uniqueness of the architecture in this period. The remains of a temple and stupa made of bricks have been found there. Apart from this, the cave temple of Kahalgaon, Ardhmandapu of Vishnupad temple at Gaya, Surajgarha, Indapai, Jaimanglal Garh, etc. are vivid examples of Pal Art. The influence of Buddhism and Vaishnavism on the architecture of this period is evident.

Sculpture

The art of sculpture was highly developed in the Pal era. In this period the idols of stone, bronze, and Ashtadhatu started being made. Dhiman and his son Bithpal are considered to be the founders of the style of making bronze statues. The style of Pal Art sculpture is popularly known as the "East Style" of medieval sculpture. Bronze statues of this period were cast, samples of which have been obtained from places like Nalanda and Kurkihar (near Gaya). The samples from Nalanda belong to the time of King Devapala, while those from Kurkihar belong to the later period. Most of the sculptures of this period are influenced by Buddhism. Maximum statues of Buddha have been found. Idols of Hindu gods and goddesses were also constructed in this period, among these are idols of Vishnu, Balarama, Surya, and Ganesha.

Stone statues of this period have also been found, which present an illustration of artistic beauty. These idols are made of black basalt stone. These stones must have been procured from the hills of Santhal Parganas and Munger. In these sculptures, only the front portion of the body is shown. Ornamentation is predominant. The beauty of these sculptures reflects the artistic maturity of the artist. These idols mainly depict the deities.

Pottery Art

The beautiful and artistic forms of pottery were developed in Pal Art. The development of this art is mainly for decoration. In this art, idols are created on the walls. Scenes of religious and normal life are mainly seen in this art. A classic example of artistic beauty is a plank on which a woman is depicted in a sitting posture. She has rested her right foot on the left foot and the bodyis bent.

With a mirror in one hand, she is beautifying her form and with the fingers of the other hand, sheis filling vermilion in her head/hair space. The beauty and innocence of the face is a successful depiction of her physical beauty. Her beauty has been made more attractive by covering the body with ornaments.

PATNA KALAM

During the decline of the Mughal Empire, artists had started migrating to other regions due to lack of patronage in the royal court. After the displacement of art from the court by Aurangzeb, various artists took shelter with the regional Nawabs. As a result of this, painting and artistry developed in different regional forms. One of these is Patna Kalam or Patna style. The development of this style took place from the middle of the 18th century to the beginning of the 20th century. Some scholars also call it "Company style" having developed during the Company period.

Patna Kalam continued from the late 18th century to the early 20th century. The history of the ancestors of the artists of this style is unclear, as no authentic records are available about this pattern. Based on the informative statements given by former president and art lover of Patna Museum, Shri P.C. Manuk and Mildred Archer, and the last successor of Patna style of painting, Ishwari Prasad Verma, have been accepted as the proof thereof.

The development of Patna School of Painting or Patna Kalam in Murshidabad and its early artists being trained in Delhi Kalam is the reason for no fundamental improvement in Patna Kalam. Nonetheless, a few of the local characteristics are definitely ingrained in its development.

The painting of Patna Kalam (Pen) was done on paper, mica (abrakh) and ivory. All types of paintings have been included in the collection of Patna Museum. Actually this pattern was market oriented.

The drawings were made on the subjects the buyers demanded. Unlike the Mughal pattern and other styles derived from other patterns, this pattern became an example of folk art. Characters like Bhishti, chobdar, concierge, washerman, maid, carpenter, blacksmith, goldsmith, comb bangle maker, jardon, weaver are mostly seen in Patna Kalam, associated with various jobs. Minerals, chemicals, and the botanical colours have been used in Patna Kalam. Goat's milk was also applied before colouring in paintings, made on ivory and mica. The painters of Patna Kalam (pen) used brushes made from the hair of squirrels, pigs, etc. They used handmade self-developed paper, which they used to prepare by coating.

The Mughal empirical pattern and British art have had a strong influence on this style. Besides, local specialties are also reflected in it. Along with the blend Mughal elements, European elements and local Indian elements, this pattern has its own distinct characteristics.

The main features of Patna Kalam are as follows:

Miniature Paintings

Patna Kalam's paintings come in the category of miniatures, which are mostly made on paper and elsewhere on ivory.

The main theme of the paintings of this pattern is the depiction of the normal life of common man. The paintings of this pattern lack the grandeur of Mughal paintings. They usually depict a carpenter, a carrier carrying a palanquin, a woman selling fish, a farmer ploughing the field, a tonga driver, a dyer, a blacksmith, a goldsmith, and a hermit. A few paintings of this pattern have also been engraved on leather, metal, and glass. The use of bright colours is negligible in the paintings of this pattern.

Portrait of Common Man's Life: The portrait of a common man's day-to-day life in the paintings ofthis pattern, of the hitherto Bihar has been depicted. The traditional Indian painting pattern has been well expressed in this style. Paintings of this pattern encompass working class (coolie, maid, bhishti, kahaar, butcher etc.), handicraft class (carpenter, goldsmith, dyer, blacksmith etc.), means of transport (bull cart, palanquin, tonga, elephant, horse etc.), market scenes (sweet shop, fish shop, toddy shop, tobacco shop etc.), which have been featured prominently. In addition, madrasas, schools, cremations, festivals, and saints have also been depicted.

Speciality of Fineness and Ornamentation: The painters of this pattern had perfection in miniature and ornamentation. The fine depiction of birds in the paintings is a testament to the artist's in-depth knowledge of bird physiology. In this style, at some places, the suppressed imaginations of artists have been articulated with ornamentation, such as Ragini Gandhari painting by Mahadev Lal, a painting based on Ragini Todi made by Madho Lal, a picture of Muslim wedding by Shivlal, and the pictures of the drunken queens by Yamuna Prasad are prominent ones.

Less Use of Backgrounds and Landscapes

There is minimum use of backgrounds and landscapes in paintings. The use of backgrounds and landscapes costs the artists dearly, which was not compensated. As a result the artists thought it fit to resort to low-cost styles in this pattern. Human portraits of this pattern depict high noses, heavy eyebrows, dark eyes, thin faces, and thick moustaches.

Personal Style of Painting

The painters of this pattern worked very hard to make their paint brushes. Artists used to tie the tail of a squirrel or the hair of a camel, boar, deer, etc. to the feathers of a pigeon or an eagle to make paint brushes. In this pattern, colours used in painting were extracted from flowers, fruits, stones, metals, and clay. In this pattern, white colour was prepared by burning Kashgari clay and oysters, yellow colour from Hartal and Ramras, red colour from lacquer vermilion, cinnamon and ocher, blue colour from blue and laju stones and black colour from porter of the lamp.

Pattern Different from Mughal Style

Unlike the Mughal pattern, the paintings of this art lack the grandeur of the Mughal pattern. The vitality and closeness to general life are the salient features in the paintings of this pattern. This pattern also differs from the Mughal style in the use of colours and the methodology to shade. Prominent Artists:

Two of the original artists are known as Nohar and Manohar, who used to paint in the courts of Akbar and Jahangir. Sevak Ram also figures in the known artists of this pattern. They stayed between 1770 to 1830. Hulas Lal (1785 to 1865) is also observed among his contemporary painters. Among his famous paintings are pictures from the Hindu festivals–Holi and Diwali.

Other prominent painters of this pattern are Jairam Das, Shiv Dayal Lal, Shiv Lal Sahib, Daksho Bibi, Sona Bibi, Munshi Mahadev Lal, Gur Sahai Lal, etc. The last eminent painter of this pattern was Ishwari Prasad Verma. Radha Mohan Babu, a connoisseur of this pattern, is called the master of creation of portraits. Radha Mohan Babu died in 1997. Among the patrons of the Patna Kalam pattern were British Commissioner Taylor, Patna Collector W.B. Archer and his wife Mildred Archer, Patna based lawyer P.C. Manuk, Sir Charles D. Aayali, Rai Sultan Bahadur etc. were prominent. The collection of paintings of this pattern is in Khudabakhsh Library and Patna Museum.

Eminent Portraits

1. **Ragini Gandhari:**This portrait has been created by Mahadev Lal. A visual depiction of the depression and frustration of the heroine's isolation is presented in this picture.
2. **Picture of a Virani (dejected) heroine holding a Veena:** Her portrait has been created by Madho Lal. This picture is based on Ragini Todi.
3. **Picture of Muslim Nikah:** This portrait has been created by Shiv Dayal Lal.
4. **Picture of Begums' drunkenness:** This portrait has been created by Yamuna Prasad.

Calcutta (now Kolkata) was the work place of Ishwari Prasad, the last painter of this pattern. For this reason, the Patna pattern has a clear influence of artists like Rabindranath Tagore and Avanindra Nath Thakur.

MADHUBANI (MITHILA) PAINTING

The history of Madhubani painting is quite old. The culture of Mithila flourished the most in the tenure of Vidyapati of the Karnata dynasty. His songs also had an impact on the paintings here. Before this effect, Ram Chitravali was composed here. Subsequently, the influence of Vidyapati's songs led to the initiation of Krishna and Shiva Chitravali. In present times, the painting of Mithila is being created on the basis of many new and traditional folk beliefs and assumptions. It is a folk art, wherein there is great participation of women. Madhubani district has been the heart of Mithila culture. This painting is also called Mithila painting. This painting is the art of folk life of Madhubani, Darbhanga, Saharsa and Purnia.

There are two patterns of Madhubani painting: Bhitti Chitra and 'Aripan'.

Bhitti Chitra

Bhitti Chitra is a sophisticated ornamental art, which women paint on the paved surface of their homes mainly through mineral colours at various festivals and celebrations of social life. In this, on the basis of mathematical measurements of ornamentation, the gods and their footprints and human shape are depicted. At times, tantric symbols and narratives are also painted. Their form is varied at different festivals. There are primarily two forms of it–

(a) **Gosni home decoration:** It contains pictures of religious importance. In religious depiction, the prominence of Shiva-Parvati, Ram-Sita, Vishnu-Lakshmi, Radha-Krishna, Dashavatar, Durga-Kali is observed.Women from Kayastha and Brahmin families play a major role in the creation of these paintings.

(b) **Kohbar home decoration:** The depiction of Kohbar in Mithila's painting or "Kohbar writing" in the local language, embraces the deep meanings of the life of people here. These paintings done in caves during the Gupta Dynasty or the Middle Ages are different from realistic depictions.Kohbar writing is a geometric and tantric method of Mithila painting, in which the configurations and symbols of many forms are indicated. Kohbar is actually said to be the location where the Kuldevta (Family God) is established at the time of marriage. With this establishment of the Hindu marriage system, paintings and decorations are performed in a quadrilateral or rectangular area on the walls of the place where the totem is placed. This is builtin an area of up to 20 square feet.

Before starting the writing of Kohbar, women worship their totem and start drawing, wishing the newly wed couple a happy life. Before this process, the wall is whitewashed with cleansing lime. Later on, the drawing is done with the colours of ocher or turmeric. Symbols like bamboo, parrot, lotus leaf, tortoise, fish etc. are primarily depicted in Khobar. Among these, bamboo is a symbol of male organ and progeny growth, parrot is a symbol of knowledge, lotus leaf is a symbol of female genitals. Similarly, the tortoise represents the long life of the couple (bride and groom) and the fish for their bearing a son.

Aripan (Bhoomichitra)

The tradition of Aripan is predominantly prevalent in Mithila painting. In Mithila, during rituals like Janeu, Mundan, marriage, etc., Aripan is created and in art form performed at various fests and festivals compulsorily. Practice of Aripan has been prevalent as per ancient books of Mithila since the post Vedic era. Subsequent to this, the rituals of the Brahmin era also had the primacy of Aripan, whose tradition is still seen today. At the timeof Vidyapati, the unmarried girls of Mithila used to make Aripan every day near Tulsi Chaura in their house.

There were also some traditions along with this creation. During the era of Vidyapati in Mithila, Krishnalila (Krishna dance) has been painted mainly in Aripan. In this, women make special use of chaurath (rice flour), vermilion, wheat flour, ocher and ramras. It reflects the culture of Mithila. This tradition has been carried on by women as a culture from generation to generation. There in paintings are ritually made in front of the courtyard or door frame, in making these paintings, grinded rice mixed with water and colour is used. These pictures are made with the finger. There are five types of these pictures found:

(a) Pictures depicting humans, animals, and birds
(b) Pictures of fruits, flowers, and trees
(c) Pictures based on tantric symbols
(d) Pictures of gods and goddesses
(e) Pictures of suspicious symbols of Swastika, lamps, etc.

In this pattern, different forms of aripan are prevalent in the context related to different occasions. Geometric shapes (triangular and rectangular) are used more in the aripans made on the occasion of Tulsi Puja for unmarried girls. There is an abundance of leaf shapes in the aripan made on the occasions of weddings and other festivals.

Stylistic Features

Only the symbolic form of the objects depicted in the paintings is made in this pattern is creation. The paintings of this pattern are mainly made on the walls. The trend of drawings on cloth and paper has enhanced in recent times. In this pattern, instead of physical beauty and fitness, only in the portrait of a man, his business, qualities and philosophical aspects are depicted deeply. In this, the picture is drawn with fingers or bamboo sticks.

The prominence of folk imagination, deep emotional attachment to art and the use of beautiful natural colours are the main features of these paintings in the absence of advanced pattern.

Natural colours are used in this painting, but nowadays artificial colours are also used commercially. The colours used in this art are procured from plants. Colours like green, yellow, saffron, orange, etc. are primarily used. Green colour is obtained from leaves of beans, red from saffron flowers, orange from palas flowers, blue from indigo and black from kajal. In this art, yellow colour is used for earth, white colour for water, red color for fire, black colour for air and blue colour for sky.

Main centres: The main centres of this art are Madhubani, Laheria Sarai, Bhawanipur, Simri, Ranchi, etc.

Major artists: The prominent artists of this art are Siya Devi, Kaushalya Devi, Ganga Devi, Mahasundari Devi, Jagdamba Devi, Bhagwati Devi, Maina Devi, Lal Baba and Sasikala Devi. Exhibition of this art is also organized abroad. An exhibition of Sasikala Devi's paintings had also been organised in Japan. Hasegawa, a prominent Japanese figure played important side in carrying Mithila art to international fame. The Mithila Museum has been built with the support and cooperation of Hasegawa in the city of Tokamanchi in Japan. Rare paintings of Mithila art have been assembled and displayed in this museum. The famous German researcher Eric Smith has also conducted research on these paintings. At present, efforts are on to make this pattern of paintings business-oriented and professional to generate jobs. For this, innovation is being incorporated in the traditional pattern. Mithila Painting Institute, Saurath (Madhubani) has been established by the Government of Bihar for the protection, promotion, and development of Mithila folk painting.

MANJUSHA STYLE

A folk festival celebrated for centuries in Manjusha style in Anga Janpad (i.e. Singh Nakshatra) of old Bhagalpur division is famed as Bihula Puja, Bishari Puja or also known as Mansa Puja. In this puja, the shape of a temple made of paper, Sunai and Shola is used. This is called "Manjusha".

In regional language, it is called Manjosa. Manjusha painting is an incarnation of the society standing on the lowest pedestrian of caste hierarchy. This art is considered to be the result of the folk culture that grew out of struggle and coordination between the Aryans and the non-Aryans.

In this, the oppressed people are seen creating inspiring images of their gods and goddesses for the existence and identity of their society.

At present in Bhagalpur, attractive pictures are made on the box which is used in worshipping during the festival. According to folk belief, Mansa i.e. 'Shiva' has five Manas daughters—Maina, Bhavani, Devi, Padma and Jaya. They are called Bishari. According to folklore, the five Bishari sisters went to Shiva with their wish.

Shiva pronounced that if the last Shiva devotee Chando on earth worships them, he will be worshipped in the world of dead bodies, but Chando humiliated these serpentine girls. Then the angry sisters drowned Chando's six sons along with the boat. Chando's seventh son BalaLakhindra was married to Bihula, the daughter of Basu Saudagar of Ujjaini, by the illusion of Goddess Bishari.

Just ahead of this, Bishari, having got enraged at some mistake of Bihula, had cursed her to be a widow on the honeymoon itself. According to the legend, Bihula along with her husband was kept under strict guard in the iron and bamboo house built by Vishwakarma for the honeymoon, but no one could stop Bala from Bishari's wrath. Saddened by the death of her husband, Bihula vowed that she would go to Indraran and bring back her husband's life. For this Vishwakarma Lohar created a special type of Manjusha. Lahsan gardener decorated it with colours. Despite suffering immensely, she was able to get Bala alive. Then she forced Chando to worship Mansa Bishari. Eventually the worshipping of Bishari became prevalent in the world of death. In Manjusha painting, the characters of this story are shown through various symbols and sketches. The depiction of love of nature imparts uniqueness to this art. The salient character of the story Chando merchant is always depicted with the moon.

In this, the human figure is of'X' shape of English letter i.e. right foot and left hand and in the same way the left foot and right hand are separately in linear state. The facial features are one dimensional and the craniums are earless. The eyes are bigger in 'that' proportion. Male figures 'must' have moustaches and crests. Curve line is used to show women's upper part of the body. The neck of males is thick and that of females is relatively thin. The snake in the picture is marked with a coloured line and a dot. Folk artists impart more attention to impression perception rather than geometric perception. In the paintings of this art, the woman is often depicted with her husband. The hair of women remains tightly tied. The main character of the story, Bishari, who was later revered as a goddess, is always depicted with a snake.

The credit for keeping these arts and their pattern alive in present-day Bihar, is accredited to Chakravati Devi and her ancestors. Despite their poverty and deprivation, this art has survived for years due to their tireless work. Painter Shekhar drew the attention of people on this art by making a slide film named 'Manjusha Shilp'. There are limitless possibilities and hopes still present and alive in Manjusha Art.

INDIA'S LARGEST RECLINING STATUE OF LORD BUDDHA

The largest reclining statue of Lord Buddha in India is being built in Bodh Gaya, Bihar. India's Buddhist pilgrimage circuit is being proactively revived and Bodh Gaya is an integral part of it. Hence, the site of Gautam Buddha's enlightenment will soon be home to his largest reclining statue. Built by Buddha International Welfare Mission, the statue is 100 feet long and 30 feet high. In the statue, Lord Buddha is in the sleeping posture. The giant statue's construction began in the year 2019. This statue is being made with fiberglass and is being built by sculptors who are from Kolkata. The reclining statue of Lord Buddha is open to all visitors. Bodh Gaya is the place where Lord Buddha attained enlightenment, hence, the statue is being built here.

Lord Buddha's idol is in the Mahaparinirvana Mudra is very important in Buddhism as he preached to his followers in this pose before attaining Mahaparinirvana. Kushinagar in Uttar Pradesh also has an idol of Lord Buddha in this posture as this where he attained Mahaparinirvana.

❑❑❑

Folk Culture

- Folk Songs
- Folk Plays
- Folk Dance
- Tribal Culture

FOLK SONGS

The place of folk songs in the cultural environment of Bihar is very important. On the basis of regionalism in India, songs have their own identity. Each state has its own tradition of folk songs. In these folk songs, there are songs played on occasions like festivals, marriages, births, mundan, janeu, etc. These songs include melody and sentimentality. Despite the diversity in linguistic folk songs, there is a wonderful harmony of sensitivity, which are not melodious on the basis of verses, but on the basis of rhythm. Angika folk songs describe a pleasing description of natural beauty, while Magahi folk songs describe the mutual behaviour of family relations, love, hatred, humour, etc. In these some songs of detachment are also sung. The place that Bhojpuri songs have made in Bihar is probably not even possible for other folk songs. At present, Bhojpuri folk songs have made their identity at the national level. The folk song culture of Bihar is divided into following classes:

Sanskar Songs

There are two forms of sanskar songs – classical and cosmic. Sanskar songs are related to cosmic rituals. These songs are recited in all castes and tribes on all major occasions from birth to death of a human being. These songs, played on occasions like birth, mundan, marriage, gauna, dviragamana, are full of gaiety and joy. Songs like Sohar at the time of birth, Khelauna at the time of shaving of head and farewell song at the time of marriage are prevalent in the society here.

In Bihar, some Muslim ritual songs are sung under Magahi region. In Bihar, "Sohar" is sung on the occasion of son's birth anniversary. In these songs, the expressions of joy and congratulation related to the birth of a son are included. In Bhojpur and Magadha region, Pavadia dance takes place on this occasion. Pavadia people congratulate the birth of a child through songs and ask for congratulations. The Sohars sung in Bihar and Eastern Uttar Pradesh are bound by a particular Raga, Laya and Chhand, which is known as Soharch and. Soharch and has been composed by Tulsidas in earlier times. There is a lack of rules of rhyme and pingal scripture in Sohar folk songs.

There is a trend of singing playful songs in the categories of these songs. The only difference in songs playing with Sohar is that Sohar is sung on the occasion of the birth of the son, the folk song is sung after the birth anniversary, after the celebration of the birth, the inclusion of folk songs in the rituals of marriage remains integral. The maximum number of songs in the entire cultural music is marriage songs. The themes of Shiva marriage and Ram marriage are described in these songs. In the songs of Shiva marriage, there is a debate between Shiva and Parvati and the description of Shiva's wedding procession. In the songs of Ram marriage, there is a description of the sarcasm of friends while decorating the procession, leaving the procession, door worshipping, parichhawan (shelter of umbrella), marriage and entering the Kohbar (entry gate). In Mithilanchal it is customary to sing "Sammari Song" on this occasion. At the time of marriage, the house in which the Kuldeity (community Goddess) is worshipped and where the auspicious work is performed, is called Kohbar and there is a widespread custom of singing Kohbar songs relating to it. In Bihar, 'Domkachkh' is a theatrical folk music, which is sung on the occasions of wedding with the joint cooperation of the women of the groom's side. In the past, after the boy's wedding procession in the rural society, it was named Domkachh (because of the dom-dominos folk song) played by it. References to this tradition are also found in the theatrical compositions of Bhikhari Thakur. In Mithila, a special pattern of song is played at the time of the farewell of a daughter. This is known as 'Samadauni'. This is pronounced as 'Samdavan' and 'Samdan' in Bhojpur Province and Magadha respectively.

Ritu Geet (Seasonal Songs)

There is a tradition of singing folk songs in the state in accordance with the weather prevailing at that time. As the seasons alter, the folk songs also change. Songs like Fagua, Chaita, Kajari, Hindola, Chaturmasa, Barhamasa etc are played in this song-tradition. Kajari is an important song pattern in this singing. It originated in Bihar and Eastern Uttar Pradesh. Kajari is sung in Thumri style in the rhythm of Kaharwa and Dadra. A form of Kajari is famous in Mithila as Malar. Sawan (Rainy season), Jhoola (Swing), Hindola (Ropeway) are prevalent in the folk tunes of the rainy season. In these, the tunes of Sawan have now remained in the form of the ecclesiastical lyrical genre, 'Phaag' or Holi is the song of the spring season. It is mainly played in groups. The elements of love and affection predominate in Phaag songs. It is customary to sing 'Hori' or 'Jogida' in Bihar. There is often participation of males in the Hori song. In this, the euphoria is made to be seen. in the Chaitra month along with makeup, there is a blend of compassion and poignant sorrows. It consists of folk verses and is sung in both solo and group form. The song became more popular among thumri singers and was played by them in the sub-classical Jama (form). The practice of singing Chaita is mainly found among men in Magahi and Bhojpuri-speaking regions of Bihar. Chaita sung on dholak and cymbals is called 'Ghato', which is mainly sung in Bhojpur region. 'Barahmasa' folk song is famous among seasonal songs. This is in fact a folk song detailing all twelve seasons. This is a song presenting separation. It has expanded in the dialects of Bhojpuri, Magahi, Maithili, Angika, Bajjika, etc. These songs culminate with the first rain of Ashadh (March) and conclude in the scorching sun of Jeth (June). Short form of Barhamasa songs (twelve months folk songs) and Chhamasa (six months) songs are also played in Bihar. In the four months, these songs are prevalent from Ashadh to Ashwin and Sawan to Kartik.

Parv Song (Festival Songs)

Many festivals and fests are celebrated in Bihar. In all the festivals like Deepawali, Chhath, Teej, Nagpanchami, Godhan, Nihura, Madhushravani, Ramnavami, Krishnashtami, there is glee and gaiety in the state and men and women sing festive songs on these occasions. The description of the worship of the Sun in Chhath festival due to the nature of the sun, the materials of Chhatpuja, the difficult rituals of worship, the plight of the Vandhyas and lepers is described in the folk songs of Chhath festival. After the end of Chhath, women-oriented theatrical songs 'Sama-Chakeva' are specifially sung in Mithilanchal region in the Shukla Paksha of Kartik (October) month. In addition to Mithila these songs are organized in some Bhojpuri speaking regions also.

Caste Based Songs

There is special importance of every class and caste of social system in India. There are folk deities of every caste living in the village, whose folk songs with heroic tales come in the category of ethnic songs. Each caste has a different song, which has different characteristics. Ahir, Dusadhu, Chamar, Kahar, Dhobi and Luhar all have their own songs. The song sung by the Ahirs is known as Birha Geet. Loriki is also a song of Ahirs.

Pesha Geet (Profession Related Songs)

Songs played at the time of execution of any work, fall into the category of labour songs, fun songs or action songs. In Bihar, "Lagni" is sung by women while grinding flour by running a mill. This song is also known as Jantsaar. There is a practice of digging or tattooing among rural women. The woman who conducts the ditch also sings the song along with the tattooing, which is called the song of Khoda Phadne. The agricultural labourers while planting paddy in the fields also sing folk songs called 'Chonchar'. Elsewhere it is also christened as "Ropani Geet."

Balkrida Geet (Kids Play Song–Lullaby Or Baby Songs)

Songs related to child life are called children's songs or baby songs. The song, which is for entertainment purposes, is a sports song, e.g. Atkan-Matkan, Chora-Mukki, Atta-Patta, Kabaddi songs. There are lullabies in Sleeping Shishu Geet and 'Uptoni Geet' for children to apply Ubtan. Besides, some songs are sung by women when their wards are playing in a group. In these songs 'Oka-boka teen tadoka' etc. are famously sung.

Bhajans or Shruti Geet (Devotional Songs)

These songs relate to the worshipping of gods and goddesses or come under the category of Shruti songs. These songs have religious and spiritual significance as well as auspicious importance. They describe both Saguna and Nirguna forms of God. Among the Saguna songs, Gosauni Geet, Nachari, Maheshvani, Kirtan, Vishnupad, Parati, Saaj, Ganga Geet, Sheetla's Geet, Devi's songs are prominent. There is no separate song category for Nirguna songs, but in some folk hymns, Nirguna Upamanas are directed.

Gatha Geet (Ballad Songs)

This form of songs is played by the Indian public because of their innate attachment to heroism and patriotism. The way Aalha is sung in Bundelkhand, Bihar has a tradition of singing the tales of Veer Ras. These are songs sung with zeal, fervour and aggressive expressions in memory of the heroic heroes of folklore. According to the legend, they also include Karun, Vatsalya and Shringar Rasa, which mesmerizes the listeners. The song sung by the agricultural labourers while planting paddy in the fields is called 'Chonchar'. Somewhere it is also named Ropani Geet. In Bihar, these ballads also have some titles most of which are related to the name of the hero of the saga.

Nayaka Banjara: The hero of this saga is a Vaishya-son named Shomyanik, who is immensely engrossed to love his wife. As a sequel to unavoidable reasons, the husband has to be away from his wife and the great pain of separation engulfs the hero-heroine. Based on this story, the singers present love and separation in a very touching manner. This story is sung all over Bihar giving a poignant form to the story. According to regional tradition and culture, there is a change of place and hero in the story and hence in related songs.

Mirayan: The occurrence of this saga is the princely state of Nunjagarh. Harphool of Dehri city attacks this princely state and in this war he is killed along with his sons. Harphool's wife was pregnant at that time and is blessed with a son on delivery, He is christened "Meera". Meera fulfills the dream of her dynasty by conquering Nunjagarh as a young man, showing extraordinary valour and enhances its pride. This story is very popular, which is sung all over Bihar. Elsewhere it is also sung with the title of 'Battle of Nunjagarh'

Raja Harichan: This saga became synonymous with truth in the world and is related to King Harishchandra, the king of Ayodhya who was the flag bearer of religion. It is primarily attributed to the emergence of this story in Bihar. Rohtas, the son of King Harishchandra, had been the king of Rohtasgarh. Although the saga has been linked to the incident of Raja Mordhwaj in Bihar, who had ripped off his son with a saw, yet its poignancy and sensitivity remain intact. Its singers are many in number, who sing their songs according to different characters. The singers of this song are called "Netua". Such a poignancy is created in these songs as tears come in the e yes of the listener-society. This saga of King Harishchandra awakens a unique feeling in the society in its poignant and message form. The specialty of this saga is that the number of women listeners in its audience excels over men.

Lorikayan: This is a very famous and widely spread song ballad and is famous by the name of 'Lorik Maniyaar'. Veer Ras is predominant in this and it is sung all over Bihar. Most of its singers are people of Ahir caste. The hero of this story, Lorik, was also from the Ahir caste. This saga is language-based in Bihar, which is also sung in Maithili, Magadhi, and Bhojpuri. It describes the life-struggles of the protagonist of the story. The ups and downs of life and relationships in this tale of Lorik's family are sung in a simple and eloquent expression.

Dina Bhadri: It is the sad saga of Dina and Bhadri, two brothers of the Musahar caste who led their lives as the poorest of Bihar. These two brothers, living in dire deprivation and calamities, had lived by their heroic deeds to confront very difficult times very boldly and with valour. The saga of these two brothers, residents of Jogiyanagar, is sung all over Bihar.

Nunachar: This is the music ballad prevailing in Mithila region whose hero is King Karnu. He falls prey to his maternal uncle's devious conspiracies and atrocities, but he attains his glory by exposing his uncle's conspiracies with his valour and courage. In the beginning of the story there is a poignant description of the pathetic conditions of the hero and it concludes with a scintillating rendition of his valour that is well and highly hailed.

Chhatri Chauhan: This saga is sung in the area of Magarhi and it seems as if the Nunachar of Maithili were inspired by this in a transformed form and sung therein. In this saga too, the protagonist Chhatri Chauhan takes revenge from his maternal uncle for his atrocities. Possibly both the above tales have evolved from Krishna-Kansa episode. In Chhatri Chauhan saga, Veer rasa predominates.

Dhudhali Ghatma: This saga is seems to be the extension for above sagas. The protagonist Dhudhali and his maternal uncle Ghatma are its characters, but the number of maternal uncles in this is seven. Hero (Nayak) Dhudhali's father is murdered by Dhkudhalis maternal uncles, whose vengeance is bravely fought by Dhudhali. This saga is sung under different titles in Champaran and Darbhanga.

Vijaymal: This interesting saga is of Vijaymal, son of Dhurmal Singh, the king of Dhundhuniya. The marriage of minor Vijaymal is fixed with the princess of Bawangarh. Raja Dhurmal Singh takes the wedding procession to Bawangarh, where a fight breaks out over some trivial issue. Vijaymal somehow manages to escape and flee away from there, but King Dhurmal Singh and many of his relatives are taken captive. Time passes and Vijaymal grows up young. He attacks Bawangarh and, showing indomitable valour, frees his captive father and family members and brings along his wife. This saga is played throughout Bihar with Veer Rasa.

Salhais: This folktale is steeped in both Prem Rasa and Veer Rasa, which describes the heroine's courage and valour. Its protagonist is a young man named Salhais, who giantly loves a beautiful Malin girl named Dauna and this Malin girl too loves him very much. There is a triangle in the story, when another youth wants to marry Dauna, but Salhais becomes a hindrance, then that young man 'traps' Salhais on a false charge of theft and sends him to jail. After this, Dauna, with some tactic and courage, proves her lover Salhais innocent and gets him free. This is the underlying interest of this story. In this saga of love's victory, there is an emotional description too.

Hirni-Birni: This saga is of a person named Posan Singh, whose own character and his true love for his wife list the epic in the whole society. Two Natani sisters named Hirni-Birni try to assassinate Posan's character, but Posan Singh sticks to his character. Then both the sisters challenge his virility and Posan Singh defeats them by displaying his power and valour. Resultantly both the sisters become his maid servants. This song-saga hailing and praising character, dignity and courage is very famous in the whole of Bihar.

Kunwar Brajbhar (Prince): In Bihar it is also known as 'Sorthi Brajbhar'. This story is the story of the courage of a prince, who fights his feudal enemies in a tactful manner to get his rights and privileges and emerges victorious at the end. This saga is also sung in the frontier regions of Bihar.

King Vikramaditya: This is a dance sage, played on paklawaj musical instrument. Dancers dance on the instrument's music. This saga is related to King Vikramaditya of Kundilpur, in which there is a good blend of Vatsalya (Love), Karun (generosity) and Veer Rasa (melody).

Amar Singh Baria: This heroic saga is full of heroic rasa, whose hero named Amar Singh Baria is a brave and courageous warrior. He is a resident of Tirhut. The king of Tirhut persecutes the subjects, seeing the pathetic condition of the public, Baria revolts and fights with the king. Baria being the devotee and worshipper of Divine Goddess Kamala, Baria by Her blessings eliminates the trouble of people by defeating the king by the grace of Goddess.

Special Song: Peedia song, water demanding songs, lyrics chandelier-swing, Birha, Joga, Saprani etc. are sung. The culture of Bihar has a rich tradition of folk singing. Varied music include songs of Jhijhiya, songs of spring, songs of women's freedom, songs of social reform etc. Eastern songs of Bhojpur zone, Jhumar, Visriya, Badohiya, songs of fairs and Tirhuti of Mithilanchal, Batgamani, Nachari, Maheshvani, Sandesh songs, Mantra song, Andolan songs are the songs of this style.

The era of the great poet Maithil Kokil Vidyapati is called the 'golden age of folk songs'. Most of its songs have come under the category of folk songs due to historical tradition and folk behaviour. Its promotion is in every nook and corner of Mithila. Bhikhari Thakur of Chhapra, a Bhojpuri-speaking region, earned considerable fame as a folk lyricist and singer. Bharat Singh Bharti, Vishnu Prasad Sinha, Sharda Sinha, Dr. Shankar Prasad, Nandkishore Prasad, Shambhu Ram, Motilal Manjul, Vindhyavasini Devi, Lalita Jha, Renuka Sahai, Kavita Chaudhary, Grail Kujur, Umakant Kamal, Ajith Kumar, Akela and Kumud Albela etc. are popular to present these folk songs; harmonium, dholak, khadtal, manjira, bansuri, naal, ghada, khanjri, sitar, mridang, sarangi etc. are prominent in the presentation of these folk songs. According to the regional instruments and songs, instruments like dhol, dholak, dholki, tabla, nagara, manjira, shehnai, dafli, damru, dugdugi, conch, etc., are used. Jhal, kartal and conch are used in bhajans, kirtans, and religious songs. Folk dances are also imbibed in the folk songs in the state, in which the heart of the audience swells with the triveni of dance, songs and vocals. Besides, the state also has a rich tradition of folk dances along with folk songs.

FOLK DANCE

Folk dances have vital importance in Bihar. There is a bird's eye view of folk dances on all major occasions such as rites, festivals and entertainments. Dance creates a sense of mutual harmony and unity. In Bihar, men and women all together participate on these occasions. The following dances are notable among the major folk dances of the state:

Karma dance: This is primarily performed by the tribal populace of the state. A crowd of non-tribals also gather to see this. Along with the harvesting and sowing of crops, songs to appease 'Karam Devta' are played with dance. It is a group dance of men and women. Men and women put their hands on each other's waist and dance in a rhythm. It is mainly performed in Jharkhand.

Chhau dance: This dance primarily related to war and performed by male dancers. It has two categories. In the first category the dancer displays the spirit of heroic rasa with his expressions, energetic voice and rhythmic slow-fast movements of the feet. In the second category, Kalibhang is categorised, in which make-up Rasa predominates. This dance is quite popular in both Bihar and Jharkhand regions.

Jhijhiya dance: It is often performed at the occasion of Durga Puja, which is played in group by women. In this dance, women stand in a circle and hold one another's hands and dance. The main dancer holds a pitcher on her head, with a lamp burning on its lid. Songs based on the story of King Chitrasen and his queen are sung here. In this, the rhythm and tinkling of the feet of the dancers create an exuberating and attractive scene.

Vidyapat Dance: This is a group dance performed by the dancers singing the verses of the famous poet Vidyapati of Mithila. It is more prevalent in Mithila and Purnia.

Kathghodwa dance: This dance of Bihar is a very interesting folkdance, which is equally performed in Jharkhand with same fervour. In this dance, the dancer ties a horse-shaped structure made of bamboo splints to his back, which is decorated with colourful garments. The musicians play their instruments in sync with the rhythm and in the same rhythm the woodpecker (Kathghorwa) dancer dances. The main dancer and his companions also get due remuneration.

Dhobia dance: This is a caste dance of the Dhobi (washermen) society of Bihar, which is performed by them on their auspicious occasions. It is mostly prevalent in Bhojpur district. In this, the dancers recite songs enthused with make-up Rasa on the beat of instruments and perform a fascinating dance.

Pavadiya dance: This is a strange dance, performed by men, who are dressed as women. Wearing women's ghagra choli and adorning them, carrying drums and cymbals, manjiras in their hands, male dancers perform a charming dance by reciting songs like Sohar and Khelauna. This dance is performed at the birth of children.

Jogida dance: This dance is performed at Holi festival in countryside. In this, rural youth and girls paint one another, throwing Gulal and perfumes (abir) and dance while simultaneously singing Phag. There is a lot of joy, gaiety, glee, and youth in this dance.

Jharni dance: It is a famous folk dance of Muslim society of Bihar, which is performed in group at the occasion of Muharram. In this, dance is supported by reciting to express one's sorrow.

Karia Jhumar Dance: This is performed by women in groups at the fests and festivals. The performers walking around with arms in the back of one another and perform dance.

Khildin dance: This is played to entertain guests on auspicious occasions. Often, this dance is performed by skilled and professional women who accept award in lucrative manner by showing their charming performances.

Other dances

Gangia: In this women praise Ganga by performing Gangia.

Manjhi: The sailors in the rivers perform dance besides singing.

Gho-Gho Rani Dance: The dance by young children, in which one girl stays in the centre and other girls from all four sides make a circle and sing the song.

Godhin: In this the fish seller and the customers masquerade, while dancing.

Lodhiyari: In this, the farmer sings and dances with the animals at his house with gestures.

Money harvesting: After harvesting, the farmer family sings, rejoices and dances.

Bolbai: It is a dance of Bhagalpur and its surrounding areas, in which women depict the husband's going abroad scene.

Ghanto: This 'virah geet' is performed at the poor sister's in-law's house, by singing and dancing on receiving information of her brother's arrival at her house.

Inni-Binni: It is performed as the main dance of Angika region, in which women dance depicting husband-wife affairs.

Devhar: It is also called Bhagta dance. In this, the dancer dances as a representative of the gods and goddesses.

Bagulo: It is a dance of North Bihar, depicting quarrel of a woman with another woman on the way after leaving her in-laws' house in anguish.

Kajari: It is sung and danced in the months of Sawan (rainy season).

Basanti: It is often performed accompanied by singing by women on the arrival of Spring season.

Besides these, the Lagui dance style is also integrally associated with the folk culture of Bihar.

FOLK PLAYS

Bihar has a rich culture of folk plays along with folk songs and folk dances. These folk plays have great importance in the lives of the public. Acting, dialogue, plot, songs, dances etc. have great relevance in these plays. They are often presented in artificial light at night by skilled artists on cultural and auspicious occasions. Just as Ramlila, Krishna Leela, Swanga, etc. are staged in Uttar Pradesh, similarly folk plays are staged in Bihar. In all the plays, dance and songs accompany the dialogues. Sometimes large plays are staged, whose excellent performance keeps the audience hooked till the end. Simple, sweet and local language is used in these plays for easy understanding even by the illiterate audience. The description of folk plays prevalent in Bihar is as follows:

Drama Jat-Jatin: This folk play depicts all aspects of the married life of a Jat and his wife (Jatin) in a very entertaining and soulful manner. It is presented by women in the moonlit night of Shukla Paksha of Kartik month from Shravan month. Its spectators are also mostly women. Even men cannot stop themselves from enjoying it. There are two teams in this play. One team is of Jats and the other one is of Jatins. The girls of the Jat group wear the dress of the groom, while the girls of the Jatin group are decorated with lucrative saris and lilac flowers. Both the parties stand at a distance of five to six hands from each other. To start with there is group singing, followed by acting performance. The Jat group calls the groom behind him and the Jatin Dal follows the trend with the bride behind them. In the beginning, one group approaches the other group playing a song and takes a back turn. Then the Jatin crew goes ahead and sings in Cornish style. In this drama, with a glimpse of the rural environment of Bihar, all aspects of married life like love, anger, discord, honour, respect etc. are presented. It is a beautiful blend of both prose and poetry. This folk play is popular throughout Bihar.

Akuli-Bunk: This play is performed from the month of Shravan till the month of Kartik. At some places it is presented in Shukla Paksha any time limit. Its main characters are Anka, Banka, Tihuli etc. In the presentation of this play, a good vision of the rural environment and their lively performance by the stage actors are viewed and appreciated. In this play regional analogies are also used.

Sama-Chakeva: This play is organized in the month of Kartik on moonlit nights from Saptami to Poornima. Sama and Chakeva are siblings in this play. Among its other pots represent satmaiya, chugla, banattar, jhansikuta, vrindavan-muttedhi, atla-andli, batdekhni, gwalin, elephant, etc. are main tones. It is primarily presented by unmarried girls only. All the above pots are made of clay, which are placed around the flute-playing idol of Shri Krishna. Then the girls, dressed in colourful clothes, stand in a circle of these earthen pots, create Rasa like Radha-Krishna. This is a very popular play.

Kirtaniyan (Nardi): It is a devotional and religious play. Its main instruments are dholak, jhal and harmonium. In this play, the pastimes activities (Lilayen) of Shri Krishna are staged by the artists. In this, the actors perform kirtan along with acting. This theatrical performance gives a clear introduction of the devotional and rural faith.

Domakach: It would be more appropriate to call this play completely women-oriented because it is organized by the women of a family and those of its neighborhood in the absence of men. Also there is a reason behind this event that in the past, when all the men of the house or locality used to go away in a wedding ceremony, then the wrath of thieves had mounted. So women started this play with a view to staying united and awake all through the night, which has since been accepted in rural area.

No subject matter of this play is fixed. Hitherto it was presented only by the maid servants or maid attendants of the house, but now the women of the house have started playing it themselves. It also includes songs and dances supported by dialogues like humour, entertainments, jests, and wits. Only women perform the roles of male characters. These include characters like jalua, domin, daroga and anarkali. As a sequel to the presence of excessive obscenity in this play, it is not presented in the open stage. Mostly married women participate in it.

Foreigners (Videshiyan): The author of this play is Bhikhari Thakur, the famous folk poet of Bihar. He is accredited like Kalidas, in Bihar. The progress of this play is based on the folk play tradition and culture. Every artist is multidimensional in this play. Besides playing varied characters in the play, he also performs the role of a stage-inspector and stage-speaker. In this play, only men perform the role of women. There is also a clown or a jest, who is also an artist, to make the audience laugh. It also includes parbi, pavadia, nethua, gond, pachda, alha, barhamasa etc. This play is the most popular and famous folk stage drama of the theatrical genre of Bihar, which is also staged in national auditoriums.

The above description makes it clear that folk culture has occupied a great position in Bihar. The rural society here has played an important role in developing it at the state level. In Bihar, many theatrical organizations are working to develop theatrical arts further and to get national and global recognition from it. In these, many theatrical organizations and organizations like Bhojpur Manch, Yavanika, Darpan Kalakendra, Shivam Cultural Manch, Akshara Arts, Bihar Art Theatre, District Natya Parishad Abhinaya Kala Mandir and Nirala Club are engaged in their efforts in promoting tribal culture in almost all religions of Bihar.

TRIBAL CULTURE

People of all categories, castes and tribes reside in Bihar. The total populace of people belonging to Scheduled Castes and Scheduled Tribes in Bihar aggregates to 1,38,06,989. Of these, the Scheduled Caste population is 1,30,48,608, of which 68,84,676 are males and 62,63,932 are females. With the majority of Scheduled Tribes now moving to present-day Jharkhand, their total population in Bihar has been lowered to 7,58,38, of which 3,93,44 are males and 3,65,237 are females. The supremacy of the tribal society in the state may have been greatly reduced, but still tribal culture has its own importance.

Major tribes: Since the formation of Jharkhand state, in present Bihar, the number of tribes has reduced a lot, but some tribes are still there, which contribute to the rich social culture of Bihar through its ancient culture. Below given are the major tribes found in Bihar.

Gond: This tribe is found in Chhapra, Champaran and Rohtas districts of Bihar. Generally they do not have any settlement of their own, which is generally found among other tribes. These people settle along with non-tribals. Their language is Mundari, but now these people usually speak in the local dialect and language.

Khond: This tribe is engaged in farming activities and are residing in Shahabad region. Their language is local Sadani but now they mostly use Bhojpur .

Bedia: People of this tribe are often not mingling with one another, who reside mostly in Munger. They are also farmers and labourers and converse in the local language only.

Oraon: The people of the Oraon tribe, belonging to the Uran Proto-Australoid and Dravidian family, mainly reside in Jharkhand. After the bifurcation of Bihar and Jharkhand, they also live in small numbers in Bihar. Residing in the districts of Rohtas, Buxar, Darbhanga, Bhagalpur and Champaran, this tribe follows the mixed principles of Bongism, naturalism, Hinduism and Christianity. Their economic life philosophy depicts mixed composition.

Santhal: This tribe is the original tribe of Santhal Parganas (Jharkhand), who live in Purnia, Bhagalpur, Saharsa districts in Bihar. They are also assumed to belong to the Proto-Australoid family. Their language is Santhali, which belongs to the Austro-asiatic language family. Besides, these people also use Bengali and Hindi languages. Singbonga is their revered deity.

Khairwar: Primarily living in Jharkhand, this tribe is also found in Rohtasgarh region of Bihar state. In their tradition there is an accepted custom to worship Khair Ghas. That is why they are called Khairwar. The language of the people of this tribe is Mungri, but now these people have started using the local language of Bihar too.

Gorait: This tribe, living in Gaya and Bhojpur districts of Bihar, hail from Proto-Australoid group. Their family is considered the smallest unit in their social life. They follow the nuclear family system. They are married in intra-caste, but must be having different Gotras. Their main stay is farming and labour wages.

Chero: A few of Chero Tribe people primarily inhabited in Palamu village of Jharkhand people are found in Rohtas, Bhojpur and Munger districts of Bihar. The rigid, fearless and freedom loving Chero consider themselves to be Kshatriyas and Chauhan dynasty Rajputs. Some people have even started adopting Chandravanshiya as their surname. Their religious sect is influenced by the Hindus.

Kora: Kora tribe are residing in some parts of Jamui, Katihar, and Munger districts in Bihar. Their language is Mundari. These people also speak Sadani and Hindi. The people of this tribe make their homes in the mountains or plains for solitude. Their general occupation is agriculture, but these people are more dependent on forest produce and labour wages.

Korba: This tribe's population is now too small in India. Some people of this Scheduled Tribe in Bihar reside in Rohtas, Purnia, Munger and Katihar districts. There is a tradition of nuclear family adoption among them and inter-caste marriage in their social system. These people make a living from temporary and nomad agriculture and hunting.

Munda: Munda tribe reside in Buxar and Rohtas district of Bihar. Their language is Mundari, but now they have started conversing in Sadani too. They too are dependent on nomad agriculture. They worship Singbonga as their supreme deity, who is related to the earth.

Thus the social life of Bihar shows a mixed social structure. These tribes are extremely backward economically. The entire facilities of education and health have not yet reached to these people. Now there is an imperative need that the tribal culture should be protected by connecting them with the mainstream of development and progress.

Tribal inhabitants are actually an integral part of the cultural landscape of Bihar. They have a deep connection with literature and art. Now the tribal people have become completely localized in Bihar. Seized by mountains, forests and strange customs and traditions, their life has a long and glorious history of their experiences with nature. In them, there is a sense of freedom and exuberance in art and music.

Tribal art: The art of tribals is the result of their experiences of beautiful and lively depiction of nature with their happy mind. Though they may be surprised to see modern developments, yet the joy they get in their simplicity and fluidity is inexplicable. Their art is visible from the special artifacts made in their houses on the eves of festivals, fests, traditions, rites etc. These artifacts made of colours on their home's walls depicting beautiful trees, flowers and other natural shapes, carved mud on their domestic kitchenware, etc.

The efficiency and efficacy of aboriginal women to draw accurately parallel lines on their geometric drawings by hand stuns everyone. Most of the household decoration is performed by unmarried girls. The excellent piece of art and craft work carved on the mussels and pennies found nearby river by aboriginal tribals to make necklace sets are amazing examples of their art and philosophy.

Tribal Music and Songs: There is observed the natural glee in tribal music and songs. Most of their songs are dance based. The melody-colour of birds, sweet voice of river flow the bright colors of flowers and the deafening melodious flow of waterfalls form their inspirations. They have a rich store of music and songs to be played in each season.

The tribals have their own original musical instruments, which include mridang, cymbal, nagara, damru, dafali, etc. In their traditional style, their rhythm and cadence may not be understood, but the feeling comes fully alive. Songs like jadur, mage, karma, addandi, gemma etc. are sung abundantly at various occasions. At a wedding ceremony, the addandi dance sequence song display just rejoices all immensely and lively. On welcoming the Jadur season of spring, the harrow songs display richness of song and music of tribals at the time of paddy planting.

Tribal literature: The tribal literature related to folktales, folk phrases and the history of traditional generations gives a unique description of all the experiences of life. Their stories encompass feelings of mystery, adventure, gaiety, gratitude to god and great faith and belief in the characters of Tantra fables. It is their spontaneity and simplicity that they believe in the abode of gods, trees, stones, fields, barns, etc who protect them.

Modern society may call it superstition, but this faith is an integral part of their life. Efforts have been made to keep emphasizing this belief in their literature. The riddles of tribal literature are the subject of research. From the beginning of children's literature, these people have a tradition of making their children aware of all the experiences of life.

Fairs and Festivals

- **Major Fairs**
- **Major Festivals**
- **Fests**

MAJOR FAIRS

The grand tableau of the rural culture of Bihar is clearly visible in its fairs here. Some of its fairs here are famous all over the world. In the events related to religion and culture, not only the items and stuff made in the local markets are found there, but also local crafts are also seen there. The traders organise not only present their material and goods in regional fairs, haats and markets, but also exhibit the cultural life of that region. Some of the major fairs are described below:

Sonpur Fair: The world famous Sonpur fair is held on the banks of river Ganges in North Bihar in the month of Kartik. It is the largest cattle fair in Asia. Mythological beliefs are associated with this fair. There are famous temples of Hari (Vishnu) and Har (Shiva) at this centre. That is why that place is also called Harihar Kshetra (Region). It is believed that Hariharnath temple was built by Lord Rama with his own hands while attending Sita Swayamvar. It was repaired and renovated by Raja Mansingh. Raja Ramnarayan gave a comprehensive and fresh look to this temple in the Mughal period. These days, the Harihar Kshetra Mela is organized by the Chhapra District Administration with the help of the Government of Bihar, that starts from Kartik Purnima and lasts for a month. Preparations for the Sonpur fair culminate a month before Kartik Purnima. Major cattle traders of Pan India take their animals to the fair. Various exhibitions are also organized by the Government of Bihar. Through these fairs people are informed on health, education amenities etc. Besides, the work being done by the government for the welfare of farmers, state-of-the-art agricultural equipment and implements designed and manufactured by various organizations for the farmers are also displayed. Other useful information is also shared among the farmers.

Sonpur fair is the only fair in India wherein elephants were sold in large numbers. The sale of elephants has since been banned by the administration. The general public worships Lord Hariharnath by bathing at Konhara Ghat. Many types of cultural activities also run in the Sonpur fair.

Vaishali Fair: This fair is organized on the Trayodashi date of Chaitramas in Vaishali, the birthplace of Lord Mahavir, the 24th Tirthankar of Jainism. Jain followers from all over the country participate in this fair. Jain Acharyas organize polytheistic seminars and contemplate ceremonies here. In the fair, along with literature, pictures and sculptures related to Jainism, other items are also found.

Shravani Mela: It is organised in a periphery of 105 km from Sultanganj in Bhagalpur District Bihar to Deogarh (Jharkhand). In Shravan and Bhadrapada, Shiva devotees take water from Sultanganj to reach Deoghar on foot. The famous Ravanaeshwar Vaidyanath Jyotirlinga of Deoghar is one of the Druvadash Jyotirlingas. It is also called as

Kamna Linga. People also know him by the name of Vaidyanathdham or Babadham. Pilgrims from all corners of the country reach here all through the year.

Pitripaksha Mela: In Gaya, this fair is held fortnight before the Shardiya Navratri. In Pitripaksha, Hindus recall their ancestors and perform Shradh. It is their firm belief that the departed soul gets peace only when its Pind Daan is done in Gaya. Although Pind Daan is done throughout the year in Gaya, but Pind Daan done in Pitripaksha has special significance.

Fair of Baba Brahmeshwarnath: This fair is organized on Shivratri and Badi Ekadashi of Vaishakh month in a village named Brahmapur in Buxar district. This fair, held twice in a year, is also a big cattle fair. In this fair cows, bulls, buffaloes, horses, camels, etc. come from all over the country to purchase and sale. Many cultural programs are also organized in it. Devotees perform Jalabhishek in the temple of Bababrahmeshwar. This fair of religious, cultural and commercial Triveni is famous all over the country.

Malmas Mela: One month before Makar Sankranti (December 4 to January 4) Hindu society does not do any auspicious work. This contaminated month ends on the day of Makar Sankranti. On this occasion a grand fair is organized in Rajgir. It is believed that from this day the Sun enters Capricorn. Those who renounce mortal bodies on the day of Makar Sankranti do not have to take rebirth. On the day of Makar Sankranti, after taking a bath in the hot pool of Rajgir, aged people get fresh life.

Bettiah Fair: Every year on Dussehra eve, this fair is organized in Bettiah. In this cattle fair organized for about 15-20 days; thousands of people of the state come here to buy and sell their animals.

Saurath Fair: Every year in the month of Jeth-Ashadh, unmarried adult youths are presented for marriage in this fair running in 'Sabhagachi' (Madhubani district). This fair is famous for its amazing form in the world.

Simaria Fair: Every year in the month of Kartik when the Sun is in Uttarayan, this fair is organized around the "Rajendra Pul" in the far southeast, at 8.5km from the Barauni Junction. This fair has greater importance from the religious point of view. Every year in October-November, Simaria Mela (Kalpavas Mela) is organized at Simaria Ghat located on the bank of river Ganges. Thousands of devotees visit this fair not only from India, but also from Nepal and Bhutan. During this period the devotees live in thatched houses and take a dip in the Ganges. It is believed that bathing in the Ganges at this Ghat washes off all sins.

Kosi Fair: Every year on Paush Purnima near Katihar on the "Kosi River" devotees are showered with blessings. They also buy and sell wooden items.

Sabour Fair: This fair is organized for the development of agriculture in Sabour Agricultural University of Bhagalpur district. In this college under Rajendra Agricultural University, farmers are imparted information about the latest techniques, researches and discoveries of agriculture by agricultural scientists. New improved varieties of seeds are also propagated here.

Maghi Fair: This historical fair has been running 1888, which was hitherto known as the grand Chautwarni fair. People from the entire Koshi region and from the border areas of Nepal, Bhutan also come to take a dip in the holy Ganges river. Religiously, Ganga of the north channel of Manihari, has a different connotation, so people also come from across the river from Sahebganj, Pakur, Dumka (all in Jharkhand). Performing religious acts on this land of Manihari, the place of stay of Lord Shri Krishna during the historical Mahabharata period, provides a different holy blessing like a pilgrimage.

Lauria Nandan Garh Mela: This 15-day fair is organized every year in the month of December at 'Gulabbagh' of Purnia district.

Kakolat Fair: Every year at the occasion of Mesh Sankranti, this religious fair is organized for six days at a place called "Kakolat" in Nawada district. There is a waterfall in Kakolat. The height of this waterfall is 60 feet. Thousands of people from allwhere visit here every year to enjoy this fair.

Book Fair: Organized by the Center for Readership Development (CRD), Patna Book Fair is organized every year usually in the first week of November. It has been organized every year in Patna consistently since 1985. Major publishers from across the country display their books in this five-day fair. The book lovers and voracious readers of the state are benefitted by visiting it.

Papaharni Fair of Bhagalpur: On the day of Makar Sankranti, Papaharni pond situated at the foothills of Mandar mountain has great religious significance. Here, people take a bath and holy dip on the day of Makar Sankranti. It is a popular belief that by bathing in this pond, one gets reprieve from leprosy. They worship Lord Madhusudan. Dahi-chuda and sesame laddus are relished as a religious specialitly. Besides these fairs, Singheshwar fair, Bansi fair, Hardi fair, Kali Puja fair and Sahodara fair are also arranged in Bihar.

FESTS

Festivals are organized at the government and private levels in Bihar, which are delineated as follows:

Rajgir Mahotsav: Rajgir Mahotsav was celebrated with full grandeur, fervour and zeal from 27 December, 2019, to 29 December, 2019. This festival is arranged for three days. It was organized for the first time in 1986. Due to some reasons this festival could not be organized from 1989 to 1994, but it has resumed since 1995. Held in the historic Ajatashatru Fort Ground, this festival has become a symbol of the synthesis of historicity, antiquity, tradition and modernity.

Vikramshila Festival: In view of the historical, cultural and tourist relevance of Vikramshila University, which has had its global recognition in the education world since ancient times, the Government of Bihar started organizing a three-day Vikramshila Festival (28–29 and 30 January) in the year 2007. This festival is organized under the joint aegis of tourism department and district administration of Bhagalpur.

Vikramshila University established by Dharmapala (786 to 820 AD) was world class akin to Nalanda University. This university was the second residential university in the world. In Tibetan texts it is known as 'Srimadvikramashildev Mahavihara'. In 1203, Bakhtiyar Khilji demolished this university in the illusion of a fort.

Mandar Festival: Banka district, which is connected to the border of Bhagalpur, is famous for its Mandar mountain. The Mandar Festival is organized in its vicinity. This is an important fair of Bihar held on Makar Sankranti and this is the same area where Lord Vishnu was christened as Madhusudan after killing the demon Madhu-Kaitabha. According to the Puranas, this battle lasted for about 10 thousand years. On the other hand, it is mentioned in the Mahabharata that this fair is held every year on the occasion of Makar Sankranti as a symbol of the defeat of the gods and the demons in the churning of the ocean. It is known that Mandar was made Mathini during the churning of the ocean. Stone stairs have been carved to climb the Mandar mountain. Sitakund is found after climbing Mandar mountain. Padmashree Chitu Tudu says that the glory of Mandar is also described in Santhali songs. Simultaneously, Vasupujya, the 2nd Tirthankar of Jainism, had attained Kaivalya in Mandar. Nowadays, a five-day Mandar Festival is organized here on a large scale from the day of Makar Sankranti.

Champaran Festival: Champaran district has earned historical importance since ancient times. Here, there is evidence of Maharishi Valmiki's ashram being in the Ramayana period, then the Laat (inscription) of Emperor Ashoka still speaks volumes of its prosperity. Even at present, the followers of Buddhism visit from all over the country and abroad. Lord Buddha had stayed to in Kesariya enroute Kushinagar. Mahatma Gandhi started his first political Satyagraha in Champaran in 1917 regarding the crisis of indigo farmers. In view of the historical and mythological importance of Champaran, a three-day Champaran Festival is organized every year. This festival is organized every year next to Kesaria Bachha Singh College. The culture, art, traditions and historical tales of Champaran are organized on this occasion.

Vanavar Festival: Jehanabad district has a glorious past on the map of tourism. A two-day festival is organized every year at Vanavar (also known as Barabar in history), located about 25 km southeast of the district headquarters. The Vanavar hill group mainly includes the Vanavar and Nagarjuni hills. Although alluring specimens of sculpture, frescoes and fine arts are found in this hill group, yet the main attraction of this hill group is the caves here. Historical and archaeological heritage has got its fame through the festival. This hill is also called Gorkhagiri in an inscription inscribed in the famous Lomas Rishi Cave.

Tapovan Festival: This festival is organized at the occasion of Makar Sankranti (January 14), which is three-day long fair, as well as the Malmas fair is also arranged every three years, which continues for a month. It is said that the confluence place of all three, Dharma, Desire and Moksha is Tapovan. This place is near Tetaru village at a distance of about 18 kms from Rajgir. Covered with picturesque hills, Tapovan is the international centre.

The importance and antiquity of Tapovan have been detailed out by the well-known scientist Jagadish Chandra Bose, the Chinese traveller Fa-Hien and Hiuen Tsang. Mahakavi Bhasa has given an interesting description of Tapovan in his famous book "Swapnavasavadattam". In this pilgrimage centre Tapobhumi Tapovan was the ashram of Rishi Kashyap during the Bimbisara period. Buddha's son Rahul also did penance in Tapovan. Because of this underlying significance of Tapovan, since January 14, 2015, on the occasion of Makar Sankranti, the Tapovan festival is arranged every year.

Vaishali Mahotsav: Vaishali is famed as a historical city that simultaneously expresses the contemporary culture of both Mahavira and Buddha. The first republic was also sprouted in Vaishali. Nonetheless, the organization of Vaishali Mahotsav is especially focused solely on Mahavir, the originator of Jainism. Mahavir had spent 30 years of his incredible life in Vaishali.

Mithila Mahotsav: It is organized every year with a view to keeping alive the rich culture of Mithila and paintings of Madhubani. Mithila Mahotsav is organized by the Department of Tourism, Art, Culture and Youth Affairs. Mithila Painting Institute has also been established in Madhubani, which is the centre of attraction of the festival.

MAJOR FESTIVALS

The importance of folk culture songs, music and dance-plays of Bihar is also attributed to its fest and festivals. Apart from the national festivals in Bihar, there are also some local festivals, which provide enormous opportunities to its people to be ecstatic. There is a lot of fervour and glee on festivals here and hence children, youngsters and senior citizens participate in them. There are some festivals in Bihar, in which the presence of all the people of the family is mandatory. Biharis doing job or business in other states of North India definitely visit home on these festivals. In recent years, it has been observed that while in other states the festivals have become a mere holiday, ritual and formality, in Bihar they still carry the same importance as it was ever hitherto. Following are the festivals and festivities that impart a shared vision of folk culture and Indian culture.

Holi: This festival of the first day of the first month of the Hindu calendar, is celebrated with great fervor and enthusiasm in Bihar. The victory of good over evil, the victory of theism over atheism and the attack of devotion to God over the ego and arrogance are the basic concepts of this festival. Although it is a national festival and is celebrated with harmony all over the country, yet its pomp and show is visibly more pronounced in Bihar. On the full moon day of Falgun, the people of the village collect wood and straw etc. at one place and set it on fire in the night, where the raw grains of wheat are roasted and distributed among the people who attend it. In the early morning children come out of the house with pitchforks etc. and sprinkle colours on one another. Gradually, elders also join in and thus a wave of fagua songs starts to rise. Groups of Hurriyars play songs in the streets.

They bathe in the afternoon, after which a variety of the dishes are served and relished. People apply Abir-Gulal to one another. Elders are respected by touching their feet who give their blessings. Elders bless them. On this occasion any old differences, animosity, jealousy, ill wills and in-fights are all forgotten, all hug one another. In the evening, folk songs, folk dances and in some places folk plays are also performed. This festival, which provides an opportunity to enhance and enrich mutual brotherhood, fills life with colour and zeal.

Shivratri: This festival is celebrated on the Chaturdashi of the Krishna Paksha of the month of Shivaratri, Falgun. This festival is recognized as the marriage festival of Lord Shiva and Parvati. Men and women worship Lord Shiva by celebrating their wedding day and by observing fast.

Ramnavami This festival, celebrated as the birth anniversary of Lord Rama, is celebrated in Bihar since ancient times. This festival is celebrated on the Navami of Shukla Paksha of Chaitra month. Men and women keep busy till noon and celebrate the birth anniversary of Lord Rama. Kirtans, bhajans and Ramayana lessons are recited in the temples. The flag of Hanumanji is hoisted on houses and in temples. In some places, processions are also taken out with the flag marching on cart. The atmosphere remains gleeful and delighed till late night.

Makar Sankranti: This festival, also known as 'Til Sankranti' in Bihar, is celebrated with pomp and show in India on January 14. In Bihar, this festival is celebrated to welcome the arrival of a new crop of paddy. On this day all people bathe in rivers, water bodies and ponds. Chuda, Dahi and Tilkut are the main food items of this day which people enjoy. They also consume Khichadi as a custom on that day in the evening or the very next day.

Basant Panchami: It is celebrated in Bihar as a festival to worship and appease Saraswati, the goddess of learning and knowledge. The students' fraternity remains very excited and joyed on this day. Goddess Saraswati is established and worshiped on the fifth day of Shukla Paksha of Magha month. This festival is celebrated with great pomp throughout the day. Students greet one another and get blessings from elders. The next day the idol is immersed in a river or pond.

Durga Puja: This is one of the biggest festivals of Hindus, which is celebrated for ten days. From Sudi Pratipada to Navami of the month of Ashwin, nine forms of Maa Durga are worshipped. These are also called "Navratra" and many people keep fast on all these nine days. Every day Goddesses are worshipped at homes and in temples. Idol-immersion takes place on the day of Dashami and the festival of Dussehra is celebrated. During these ten days, the atmosphere of Bihar is visibly exuberant and religiously fervent.

Madhushravani: It is celebrated in Bihar by newly married girls from Badi Panchami to Sudi Tritiya of Shravan Paksha. This Madhushravani fast is observed by newlyweds in the first year of their marriage for the longevity of their husbands. Similar to Karva Chauth, this festival is also celebrated with great pomp in Bihar. At the end of the festival, there is a feast of Kheer-Puri and distribution of gram in the houses.

Diwali: It is celebrated on the new moon of Kartik month and is a symbol of light, enjoyment and prosperity. There is a belief that on this day Lord Rama returned to Ayodhya after conquering Lanka and in this happiness people started celebrating this festival. In Bihar, this festival is celebrated with great pomp and gaiety. Its preparations start a few days before the ultimate day. Houses, offices etc are cleansed painted and decorated with new pictures. The idols of Lakshmi and Ganesha are worshipped on this occasion. Fresh idols of Lakshmi and Ganesh are brought home on this day. There is a lot of brisk activity in the markets all these days. Earthen lamps, candles, fireworks, crackers, sweets, fruits etc. are bought hugely. In the evening, earthen lamps and candles are lit. Ganesh and Lakshmi are worshiped in the houses at night. The glee of this festival, filled with freshness and fervor is seen everywhere.

Govardhan Puja: Annakoot Puja or Govardhan Puja takes place on the next day of Deepawali. Poori and vegetables are made from Annakoot in temples, then it is distributed as Prasada. This festival is also called Godhan and special care of livestock is taken on this day. On this day all the animals are bathed and worshipped. The troughs of animals feed are is cleaned and the old ropes, chains are replaced. Godhan i.e. bullocks have special significance on this day.

Bhaiyaooj: It is a sentimental festival celebrated by girls and women on the day after Govardhan Puja. On this day, girls feed their brothers bajdi (five grains of gram or moong) and sweets, and then the brothers definitely gift them present. On this occasion, sisters wish their brothers a successful and long life.

Chitragupta Puja: This is a cherished festival of Kayastha society, also called 'Dawat Puja'. Chitragupta is worshiped on the next day of Bhaiyadooj. People have a tradition of worshipping their pen, ink pot, and stationery on this day.

Akshaya Navami: This is a religious festival celebrated on Kartik Sudi Navami in Mithilanchal region. On this day the village women cook food under the Amla tree. Subsequently, all the family members assemble there and worship the Amla tree. Then all together relish their meals. It is their firm belief that on this auspicious day God resides in the Amla tree.

Indra Puja: This festival celebrated from Shukla Paksha Ekadashi to Krishna Paksha Panchami of Bhadrapada month, is one of the major festivals of Bihar. In these nine days, the idol of Lord Indra is established and worshipped. On the concluding day this idol is immersed in the river or pond. They have their firm belief that on this day Lord Indra gets pleased with this worship and blesses and enriches his devotees by granting a rich harvest.

Kojagra: This is a caste based festival of the Brahmin community of Mithila. On this, eve Lakshmi and Ganesha are religiously worshipped. This festival has special relevance for newlyweds. The husband worships with full devotion and dedication on this day for the happiness of his married life, by chanting Mantras.

Chauth Chandra: This festival of Mithilanchal is celebrated on Shukla Paksh of Bhadrapada month. It is a female dominated festival. On this day women observe fast. It is a tradition to cook delicious dishes at home. In the evening, Puja-aarti is performed in the house and religious sermons and hymns are recited. After this, all the members of the house by placing fruits, curd, cream etc., in their hands worship the moon. The major dishes of this festival are Khajoor sweet (made from Maida flour); Pidkiya (delicious blend of semolina and curd) and it is a tradition to consume fruits and nuts according to one's full capacity.

Vatt Savitri: This is the regional festival of Mithila, celebrated by women on the new moon of Jyeshtha month. This is a form of Karva Chauth and Madhushravani fasts, where in women fast and worship the Banyan tree. They also dance and sing in groups. By reciting their songs, they worship banyan tree god for long life of their husbands. It is a mythological belief about Vatt Savitri that Sati Savitri, under banyan tree were showered with three blessings from Yamraj. Women worship this banyan tree, fan it with a hand-made fan and revolve around the tree by reciting songs.

Teej: This women-dominated festival is celebrated on the Shukla Paksha Tritiya of Bhadrapada month married women. It is also performed to wish for the long life of their husband, where in women fast all through the day and after seeing the first star in the evening, and touching the feet of the husband, praying God for husband's long life, conclude their fast.

Buddha Jayanti: Celebrated on the birth anniversary of Lord Buddha, is also rejuvenated with fervour and enthusiasm by Buddhists. Followers of both the branches of Buddhism celebrate this festival with gaiety on this day. A unique sense of faith and reverence is observed in this festival on the full moon day of Vaishakh month. All over Bihar, gatherings are organized by the Buddhist people to spread the message of religion and human ideals.

Mahavir Jayanti: Jains celebrate it as the birth anniversary of Lord Mahavir. All Jainism followers rejoice this festival with pomp and show on Sudi Trayodashi of Chait month. On this day the teachings and messages of Lord Mahavir are disseminated in a grand way.

Festival of Lights (Guru Gobind Singh Jayanti): Celebrated as Prakash Parv, this festival is celebrated with enthusiasm on Sudi Saptami of Paush month as the birth anniversary of the tenth Guru Gobind Singh of the Sikhs. A grand procession is taken out on this day, ahead of which 'Panch Pyare' (Five Disciples) walk reciting Sabad in the praise of the Guru. Prakashotsav is held every year on the birthday of Sri Guru Gobind Singh, the tenth and last Guru of the Sikhs. Shri Harimandirji Patna Sahib was got erected by Maharaja Ranjit Singh.

Muharram: It is the main festival of Islam, which is also the name of the first month of the Islamic calendar. This festival is celebrated on the 10th of this month to commemorate the martyrdom of Hazrat Hussain. A grand and religious procession of mourning is taken out in the Shia sect.

Bakrid: This is also the main festival of Islam, which is also known as 'Eid-ul-Azha'. It is a festival celebrated in the last month of the Islamic calendar. It is celebrated as the martyrdom day of Prophet Ibrahim. It is customary to offer animals sacrifices on this occasion. The end of the holy pilgrimage of Muslims also takes place at this time.

Eid: Eid is the most important festival of Muslim society. It is a month long festival. There is a strange blend of religious reverence and chastity. This is a month of Ramazan and all Muslims fast. There is a custom of praying five times. As the month of Ramazan comes to an end the festival of Eid is celebrated with great pomp. It is also called 'Eid-ul-Fitr'. There is a lot of activity on the day of Eid. Fairs are organized at various places. Dressed in new clothes, children, youngsters and old people hug each other. Eating and feeding vermicelli on this holy day has special significance.

Christmas: This is the most grandeur and important festival of Christianity, celebrated with great fervour on 25th December every year. This festival, commemorated in the memory of the birth of Lord Jesus Christ, is also celebrated with great enthusiasm in Bihar. On this day all christians visit church to pray god for peace and happiness in the world. On this occasion, people distribute gifts to children by disguising themselves as Santa Claus.

Nagpanchami: It is a major festival celebrated in Mithila and Anga regions, where in serpents are worshipped. Celebrated on Sudi Panchami of Shravan month, this festival is at times called 'Vishhara'. On this day, milk is offered to the snake god and women paint a symbolic snake god from the courtyard of the house to the entry door.

Chhath Puja: This is one of the major festivals of Bihar state, when even remotely working state residents visit home. It is a unique festival of devotion, reverence and gaiety. A day before this day, the fast begins, called "Kharna". This fast is a hard waterless fast of 36 hours. In this, the setting sun is offered Arghya by standing in a river or pond, placing the items of Arghya in a basket. People also follow the tradition of demanding alms with this basket. The same process is repeated at sunrise. The grandeur of this festival is sightful. Its greatness is that no differentiaion is noted between the rich and the poor, high and low in status.

Krishnashtami: This festival is celebrated with great enthusiasm in the whole country as well as in Bihar, on Krishna Paksha Ashtami of Bhadrapada month. People having faith in Lord Krishna fast all through the day and after seeing the moon at night, they break the fast by offering Argha. There are celebratory activities in hindu temples on this day. At night people also perform the play "Sama-Chakeva".

Rakshabandhan: This festival is celebrated with great gaiety pan India on the full moon day of Shravan month. This festival symbolises the affectionate bonding of brother and sister. Sisters tie rakhi on their brother's wrist and are promised protection by him. Most of the sisters visit their brother's home on this day.

Jeetiya: This fast is kept by ladies for the longevity of their sons on the Krishna Paksha Ashtami of the month of Jeetiya Ashwin. At a few places it is also kept by Angoothan Tradition. In this, women sit at the inner door of the house and consume chuda-dahi with their children in the last part of the night.

Many other regional festivals are celebrated in Bihar. Among these 'Sama-Chakeva' is based on brother-sister' mutual love, while in 'Jud-Sital' festival, people consume stale food and khichdi. Then mix mud and water and throw it on one another. Another "Mahalaya" festival lasts for 45 days in Pitri Paksha where in a huge fair is arranged in Gaya district. People from far and wide visit praying for peace of the souls of their departed ancestors. On Anant Chaturdashi, people worship Lord Vishnu with a string on their arm in aspiration to get His blessings. They tie "Anant Dora". Hence, festivals have great importance and relevance in the folk culture of Bihar.

Literature and Litterateur

- Language and Literature
- Prominent Litterateurs
- Journalism

LANGUAGE AND LITERATURE

Hindi is the main medium of expression in Bihar. It is the widest language of the linguist family. Regional variations are found in the Hindi language spoken in Bihar. Maithili in Northeast Bihar, Bhojpuri in Northwest and Southwest and Magahi in Southern Bihar are prominently spoken. All the languages spoken here are a mixed form of Hindi and Urdu. Dr. George Gierson is known as a dialect expert in Bihar. Brief introduction of the languages spoken in Bihar is as follows:

Hindi: The reputation of Hindi as an official language was maintained till the 25th year of Akbars rule. In the 26th year, due to Todarmal, the circulation of Hindi was stopped and Persian became the official language. On 4 September, 1937, a bill was introduced in the established assembly of the Viceroy, which started functioning in Bengali and Oriya in the courts of Bengal and Orissa. The language of Bihar was assumed to be Hindustani (Urdu), thereby the Urdu language and Persian script instead of the Hindi language and Devanagari script retained in the courts of Bihar. The newspapers were made accessible to the public as a medium of expression in the fifth and sixth decades of the 19th century, but all those newspapers were published in Urdu. The seventh decade of the nineteenth century is the period of renaissance in Bihar. Bihars first Hindi paper Bihar-Bandhu shifted to Patna. This gave the Hindi-speaking enlightened people of Bihar a medium of expression for the first time. In Bihar, a mass movement started for the recognition of the Nagari script in the courts, for the inclusion of Hindi in schools and for independent propagation of Hindi. The leaders of this movement were Govind Charan, Ramdin Singh, Keshavaram Bhatt, editor of Bihar Bandhu, Ayodhya Prasad Khatri and Ramkrishna Pandey. During the movement, the role of Peshkar Junglal of the District Magistrate of Arrah proved to be significant to set Hindi language in the courts. From 1 September, 1875, the public got the facility to lodge applications in Hindi language and Devanagari script along with Urdu in the courts of Bihar. The Calcutta High Court in its circular ordered the courts of Bihar state to work in Devanagari script and Hindi language. Along with Nagari, the Kaithi script was also prevalent in the courts. Kaithi was actually the script of the rural areas of Patna and Bhagalpur divisions of Bihar. With the use of Kaithi script, the prevalence of Nagari increased, because Hindi was the language of the people.

Khadgavilas Press was the first press in Bihar, to print the book in Kaithi. This press practically contributed the most in using Hindi in court. The first national language movement started in Bihar in 1860. The slogan of this movement was- Hindi should find a position in schools, Hindi should be introduced in courts. Resultantly Hindi was introduced in schools of Bihar in 1870. In those days, the education department of the United Provinces was under the influence of Raja Shiv Prasad. Hindi text books written by him came into circulation in almost all the schools of Hindi regions. Among his famous works were Vidyankur, Whip the lazy, Geography Hastamalak, Veer Singh-Vritant. Khadagvilas Press contributed immensely in the preparation of textbooks in Hindi. Babu Ramdin Singh, the founder of this press, composed Hindi Mathematics-Battisi. Khadgavilas Press got full support of Bhudev Mukhopadhyay, George Grierson, Munshi Radhalal Mathur, Munshi Ramprakash Lal and Mathura Nath Sinha in the production of independent and original text-books in Hindi. Chandiprasad Singh composed Varna-Vinod for the elementary classes. Ramdin Singh compiled Hindi literature (1st part).

Influenced by the literary practice of Ramdin Singh, it is stated that Bharatendu Harishchandra visited to Patna in the first week of March in 1884. Barring one or two books of Bhartenduji, the rest of his books had already been printed and published by other presses in Uttar Pradesh. Later, Khadgavilas Press started reprinting his works. Of these, the Satya Harishchandra Natak (Drama) had been in the curriculum for a long time in Bihar schools. A total of 129 of his texts were published in the form of Granthavali. In 1904, Babu Shivnandan Sahay compiled a book running in 500 pages titled Sachitra Harishchandra. Simultaneously, the book Biography of Harishchandra by Babu Radhakrishna Das was published.

A Hindi adaptation Kavi Vachan Sudha of Bankim Chandras Durgesh Nandini (Bengali novel) was published in Khadagvilas Press around 1870 to 1872. Later, Hindi translation of his major novels– Raj Singh, Radrani, Indira, Yuglanguriy, Kapalkundala, Krishnakants Daanpatr, Chandrashekhar, Devi Chaudharani and Rajni were published. Besides, Raja Rajeshwari Prasad Singh of Suryapura, Pt. Bhuvaneshwari Mishra of Darbhanga, Ayodhya Prasad Khatri of Muzaffarpur and Raja Jagannath Prasad Singh Kinkar of Dev etc. were great literary figures of that time.

The beginning of the golden age of Hindi literature is considered to be the beginning of the 19th century. Prominent litterateur of Bihar– Pt. Ramavatar Sharma, Pt. Chandrashekhar Shastri, Ram Lochan Sharan, Dr. Kashi Prasad Jaiswal etc. famed popular not only in Bihar but throughout the country with their works. Raja Radhika Raman Prasad Singh, Acharya Shivpujan Sahay, Awadh Narayan were prominent among the early novel writers. Prominent poets figured Ramdhari Singh Dinkar, R.C. Prasad Singh, Gopal Singh Nepali, Ram Gopal Rudra, Pt. Ramdayal Pandey, Collector Singh Kesari. National conscience was primarily inserted in the plays, novels, essays, poems of this time. Post Indias Independence, Hindi literature was prominently expressed about the creation of modern India. The contributions of Dr. Rajendra Prasad, Badrinath Verma, Pt. Chhavi Nath Pandey, Mathura Prasad Dixit were significant in these works. In present times, litterateurs like Nalin Vilochan Sharma, Kesari Kumar, Dr. Kumar Vimal, Alok Dhanwa, Dr. Vachandev Kumar, Dr. Kumar Vimal etc are contributing vitally in the promotion of Hindi in Bihar. Besides, Hindi Literature Conference, Rashtra Bhasha Parishad (National Languages Council) and Bihar Hindi Granth Academy have contributed significantly in the promotion of Hindi.

Urdu: With the forays made by Muslims in Bihar in the medieval period, Urdu has had a visible impact among its languages. The first book on the history of Bihar in Urdu language was authored by Ali Muhammad Shah Azimabadi. Dr. Azimuddin Ahmed adopted the English poetry style sonnet for the first time in Urdu language. Gul-e-Nagma is a compilation of his poems. Suhail Azimabadi is known in Bihar as the main propagator of the progressive Urdu ideology, while Qazi Abdul Wadeed is accredited with providing a scientific basis for research in Urdu literature.

The most important period to promote Urdu in Bihar was the late 19th century. Important contribution in this context was made by famous Urdu poets like Galib, Momin and Jock. Ali Muhammad Shahs collection of ghazals Maikhana-e-Ilham, Ajimoddin Ahmeds collection of poems Gule-Nagma became very popular. The influence of philosophy is clearly visible in the poems of Jimal Marjahari. Prof. Kalimuddin Ahmed comes out first in the category of critics in Urdu literature.

Qazi Abdul Wadood has been accredited with the scientific basis of research in Urdu. Noted poet Kaleem Aziz was bestowed the Padma Shri for revamping Urdu poetry. Abdul Shamads novel Do Gaj Zameen was conferred Sahitya Akademi. Besides, writers like Rizwan Ahmed, Shaukat Hayat, Safi Javed, poets Zahir Siddiqui, Sultan Akhtar, prose writers Lutfur Rahman, Bahav Asharfi etc also contributed immensely to promote Urdu literature. Urdu got the status of second official language in Bihar in 1984. The Government of Bihar has also made an important contribution in promoting Urdu by creating Urdu Academy.

Bhojpuri: The word Bhojpuri is famed on the basis of Bhojpur, the ancient district of Bihar. In the Buxar sub-division (which is now a separate district) of the erstwhile Arrah district, a large pargana named Bhojpur was settled by the Bhojvanshi Parmar kings who arrived from Ujjain, Madhya Pradesh. He named this capital after his ancestor Raja Bhoj as Bhojpur and the language often spoken was termed Bhojpuri. It is the language of an Aryan family.

Its history begins from the seventh century. It is majorly spoken in the regions of Western Bihar, Eastern Uttar Pradesh and Northern Jharkhand. Bhojpuri is mainly based on Sanskrit and Hindi for its vocabulary. Some of its words have been copied from Urdu. Bhojpurians having settled within and out of India in lacs in the past for employment, Bhojpuri has well spread all where. At present, Bhojpuri is the main spoken language in countries like Surinam, Guyana, Trinidad and Tobago, Fiji, Mauritius, etc. According to the 2001 census, Bhojpuri is spoken by about 3.3 crore people in India.

In Bihar, Bhojpuri is mainly spoken in Arrah, Chapra and Champaran. Dharti Das and Darya Das had played important roles in the promotion of Bhojpuri in the past. At present, Bhojpuri has got a new identity due to litterateurs like Mahendra Mishra, Bhikhari Thakur and Babu Raghuveer Nath.

Maithili: Maithili is the sub-national language of Nepal. It is mainly spoken in Northern Bihar in India and in the low land regions of Nepal. Hitherto, it was written in Mithilakshar or Kaithi script, which was similar to Bengali and Assamese scripts, but now it is written in Devanagari script. It is the language of an Aryan family.

The first evidence of Maithili stems from the Ramayana. In the past, Maithili was the official language of King Janak, the king of Mithila. Around 700, compositions were made in Maithili. Around the tenth century, Jyotishwar Thakur composed Varnaratnakar in Maithili. Vidyapati is the most famous poet of Maithili. At present, Maithili is spoken by around 7-8 crore people in India. Maithili has been included in the Eighth Schedule of the Indian Constitution by the Government of India on 22 December, 2003. Maithili has been accorded the status of literary language by the Sahitya Akademi of India since 1965.

Maithili is spoken in Bihar majorly in Darbhanga, Muzaffarpur, Purnia, Kosi, Bhagalpur divisions. After Vidyapati, Govind Das, Chanda Jha, Manbodh, Pt. Sitaram Jha, Jeevnath Jha etc. are considered to be the major writers of Maithili.

Magahi: The word Magahi is derived from Magadhi. Magahi was the language of the Magadha Empire in ancient times. Magahi is spoken in Bihar majorly in Patna, Gaya, Jehanabad and Aurangabad districts. Suresh Dubey is said to be the father of this dialect style. In modern times, as a result of study related to folk language and folk literature, collection of ancient traditional folk songs, folktales, folk dramas, idioms etc. of Magahi is being done very quickly. Yogeshwar Singh figures as the most famous litterateur in Magahi. Famous epics are Lalit Ramayana by Harinath Mishra, Lalit Bhagwat, Loha Marad by Ramprasad Singh, Gautam by Yogeshvar Prasad Singh Yogesh, Jarasandha by Yogesh Pathak. In Magahi novels, Sunita by Jayanathapati, Phool Bahadur, Gadhneet, Rajendra Prasad Choudheys Visesara, Chakradhar Sharmas Hi Re U Din, Sakalya, Babulal Madhukar's Ramatia, Ramanandans AAdmi Aur Devta etc. are prominent. The Do Phool by Chhotunarayan Sharma, Sona Ki Sita by Keshav Prasad Verma are famous playlet collections of Magahi. Gopal Rawat Pipashas Aadhi Raat Ke Baad, Raghuveer Prasad Samdarshis Bhasmasur, Baburam Singhs Lamgoda, Gandharis Sarap etc. are famous Magahi plays.

Angika: It is the vernacular language spoken in Bihar majorly in Bhagalpur and Munger districts. It is a dialect of Maithili. It is also known as Bhagalpuri. Since this language spoken in the ancient Anga region, this language was called Angika. It is written in Devanagari script. Dr. Tej Narayan Kushwaha has made his valuable contribution in popularizing this language by writing the history of Angika dialect. It is the language of an Aryan family.

JOURNALISM

Printing art had entered India towards the end of the 18th century. With the advent of Letters Press in India, journalism had made great forays. Prior to 1850, printing presses had been established in india at its major cities but Bihar was legged behind. Shah Kabiruddin Ahmed was the first in Bihar to establish the printing press in Sahasaram in 1850. This was named Mutahcobra. Urdu books were published from that press. The credit for the newspaper publishing in Bihar is conferred on William Taylor, who published the Urdu weekly Akhbar-e-Bihar on September 1856, to improve education in the state. The second attempt in this direction was made by sub-inspector Munshi Surajmal and the superintendent of Patna Normal School, Rai Sohna Lal, in 1860 to publish a newspaper called Akhbare-Akhiyar. They also published a newspaper named Chashm-e-Ilm in 1869.

Pt. Madan Mohan Bhatt was the originator of Hindi journalism in Bihar. In 1872 he started the publication of Hindi weekly edition of Bihar Bandhu from Calcutta (now Kolkata). It was printed from the Sripooran Prakash Press in Calcutta. With the publication started in Patna, Pt. Keshavram Bhatts Hindi Grammar, Foundation of Vidya and two plays Sajjad Sambal and Shamshad Shausan were published in Bihar. Subsequently, the second great effort in the field of Hindi journalism in Bihar was the establishment of Khadagvilas Press. This press was established in 1880 with the collaborative efforts of Ramdin Singh, Ramcharitra Singh and Sahab Prasad Singh. The compilation of all the works of Bhartendu Bhartendu Granthavali was published in 6 volumes from this press.

The first English newspaper The Bihar Herald was published in 1875 by Guru Prasad Sen. In 1881 the edition of the Indian Chronicle started in Patna. After this the editions of Bihar Times from Patna was started by Dr. Satchidanand Sinha, Mahesh Narayan, Nandkishore Lal and Shri Krishna Sahai in 1894. Simultaneously the publication of The Bihari was started by Maheshwar Prasad. From 1912 to 1927, The Bihari continued to be published as a daily newspaper. The publication of The Search Light was started in 1918 by Syed Haider Hussain. In 1985, this was dispensed with and replaced by the Patna edition of Hindustan Times. From 1914 to 1944, Patna Times was published by Yunus, the first Chief Minister of Bihar. The publication of The Indian Nation was started by Maharaja Kameshwar Singh of Darbhanga.

The Patna edition of The Times of India began its publication in May, 1986. The publication of Hindi version of The Indian Nation Aryavart started from Darbhanga in 1941, while the Hindi version of The Search Light started in 1947 under the name Pradeep. Pradeep in 1986, was substituted by publication of Hindustan from Patna. The Patna edition of Navbharat Times started in 1986, but this was closed in 1995.

PROMINENT LITTERATEURS

Sadal Mishra: He was the first prose writer of Hindi, whose prose style was later accepted in Hindi too. This great litterateur of Bihar was born in Arrah district in around 1767-1768. His compositions include Nasiketopakhyan or Chandravati, Ramcharitra, Phoolhan ke Bichhone, Sonam ke Thumb, Chahundisi, Barte Thein, Baajne Laga, Kaandti Hai, Gancho, etc. are prominent ones. The early Khari dialect of Sadal Mishra holds special importance among prose writers. He died in 1847.

Anil Kumar Mukherjee: Born on 14 January, 1916 in Bangladesh, Anil Kumar Mukherjee made an extraordinary effort to establish indigenous theatre as a theatre movement in Bihar. He also actively participated in the Quit India Movement. On 16 December, 1961 after staging the Palaki (palanquin) for the first time, his journey progressed at an uninterrupted pace. In the same year he founded the Bihar Art Theatre, which in later years became the centre of UNESCOs Jagrat Natya Sansthan. His play Viplavi became very popular. In 1970, he established the Bihar Natya Arts Training Centre. He composed more than 70 plays. His famous plays list Viplavi, Palanki, Another history in the dock, Trial of Sheikh Mujibur Rahman, Kathputli (Puppet), Akela (Alone), Kanchan Rang, Chindyon Ko Jhalar, Death of Salesmen, Goro Ke Intezaar Mein (Waiting for the Whites) etc. He died in Patna on 28 June, 1991.

Anoop Lal Mandal: The eminent author of about two dozen novels, Anoop Lal Mandal is called Premchand of Bihar. Among his famous works Abhiyan Ka Path, Aavaro Ki Duniya (The World of the Vagabonds), Uttar Pandulipi (The North Manuscript), Uttar Purush (North Purush), Kendra Aur Paridhi (Center and Perimeter), Jyotirmayi, Jawaala (Flame), Toofan Aur Tinke (Storm and Straws), Dard Ki Tasveere (Pictures of Pain), Das Bigha Zameen Ten Acres of Land), Nirwasita (Exile), Rakt Aur Rang (Blood and Colour), Bujhne Na Paaye (Not to be extinguished), Mimansa, Rooprekha (Outline), Weh Abhage (They are unfortunate), Samaj ki Vedi Par (At the altar of society), Sabita, Saki, etc. are prominent. This great litterateur, who started his career as a school teacher, was born in Sameli, Purnea district in September 1896. The memoirs written by him, Garibi Ke Din (Days of poverty) are the stories of his own lifes struggle. The film Bahurani was composed on the basis of his novel Mimansa. Her two stories Mann Ki Ganth (The knot of the mind) and Ek Prana Anek Uchhavas are famous. He died on 22 September, 1982 in his native village of Sameli.

Arun Kamal: Honored with Sahitya Akademi Award, Bharat Bhushan Agrawal Award, Soviet Bhoomi Nehru Award, Srikant Verma Memorial Award, Shamsher Samman and Nagarjuna Award, this great literateur of Bihar was born in Rohtas district on 15 February, 1954 in Nasriganj. In his poetry collection Apni Kewal Dhar, Saboot (Proofs), Naye Ilaake Mein (in Local area), Putli Mein Sansar, Main Woh Shankh Mahasankh, etc. are prominent among other works. His other works encompassing Kavita Aur Samay (Poetry and Time). Golmaje (Criticism), Kathopathan (interview) famed immensely.

R C Prasad Singh: Born in Airot village in 1911, Ramchandra Prasad Singh, at the age of 16, one of his poems Aam ka Ped (Mango tree) was published in a magazine Balak, which inspired him immensely. The poem Jeevan ka Jharna became very famous in Hindi literature. In 1938, a collection of his poetry Kalapi was published, which has all his poems written between 1930 and 1938. Ramchandra Shukla compiled Hindi literature history states Prasad Singhs poetry. In 1942, his poetry collection RC, two story collections Panchpallav and Khota Sikka were published. From 1948 to 1951. He worked as a Hindi professor in a college in Khagaria. He was awarded the Sahitya Akademi Award for Maithili literature. In his literature there is a glimpse of Uttar Chhayavad (post-shadowism) as well as on Prayogvad (experimentation). In 1996, he left his incredible works as an inspiration in this world.

Kashi Prasad Jaiswal: In 1924, Shri Kashi Prasad Jaiswalji, who created a revolution in Indian history with one of his compositions Hindu Polity, was originally born in Jhalda (West Bengal) on 27 November, 1881, but his working place (Karmabhoomi) was Patna. He authored another important book, History of India published in 1930. In this book, on the basis of Puranas, literature, inscriptions and coins, he described the Naga and Vakataka kingdoms since end of the Kushanas and the rise of the Gupta Empire. Later on, after the establishment of the Patna High Court in 1916, he took up the legal profession as advocate. He was well versed in archeology and ancient currency. He was one of the prominent founders of the Bihar and Orissa Research Society established in 1915. He prepared the outline of the present form of Patna Museum. In 1917, he edited Pataliputra from Patna. In 1934 and 1936, he was elected twice as the Chairman of the Indian Currency Committee. He was the first Indian invited to lecture at the Royal Asiatic Society in London on the subject of Mauryan coins.

Kumar Vimal: Dr. Kumar Vimal, famous as a poet, critic, literary-thinker in Hindi literature, was born on 2 October, 1931 in Kaluchak, Bhagalpur district. He was a lecturer for a major part of his career in DJ College, Munger, Har Prasad Das Jain College, Arrah and in Patna University. He had been associated with Bihar Public Service Commission for eleven years. Later on he worked as a Vice Chancellor of Nalanda University. In 1949, his poetry collection Angar was published. His poetry collections include Yeh Samput Sipi Ke (1972), Yeh Anant Anubhav Amrit (1975), Sarjana Ke Swar (1986), Yug Manav Bapu (1987), Ek Rashtra Hai – Ek Desh Hai (1988), Kavitayen Kumar Vimal Ki (1994) and Sagar Matha (2002) are prominent ones. His critical texts include Adhurdhanarishwar Dinkar, Mahadevi Varma: An Appraisal, Sahitya Vivek, Kavyanushilan Aadhunik-Atyaadunik, Chhayavaad Ka Saundriykaran Mulya Aur Mimamsa, Adhunik Hindi Kavya. Chintan, Manan, Vivechan, Alochana Anushilan, Mahadev ka Kavya Saushtvai, Teen Shikhar Kreetiyan are prominent. He died on 26 November, 2011.

Kedarnath Mishra Prabhat: Kedarnath Mishra Prabhat ji, the national level famed poet of the Hindi world, was born on 11 September, 1907, in Arrah. In 1933, he was appointed as a lecturer in the Police Training College, Hazaribagh. His major poetry collections are Taptagriha, Kaikeyi, Karn, Pravir, Sargat, Prabhas Krishna, Ritambara, etc. The Ritambara is basically the epic of the glory of humanity. Besides, he established himself as a skilled essayist through two prose collections namely Satyam Shivam Sundaram and Pahiye ki Dhuri. The Uttar Pradesh government honoured him for his two poetry collections Baitho Mere Paas and Setubandh, while in the Bihar Rashtrabhasha Parishad, he was awarded the Bihari Granth Lekhakaar Award and the Veteran Sahityakar Samman. He was also the editor of the weekly magazine Mahavir. He died on 2 April, 1984 in Patna.

Gopal Singh Nepali: The great poet Gopal Singh Nepali ji, who inspired the general public to actively participate in the Freedom Movement with his national songs during the Indian independence struggle, was born on August 11, 1911 in Bettiah. He started composing poetry at a young age of only 16. Ragini, Birdish, Umang, Nilima, Panchami and Naveen are some of his outstanding early works. The Himalaya Ne Pukara written by him during the Chinese invasion is a popular composition. At All India Hindi Conference (1931) Calcutta (now Kolkata), he met eminent personalities like Shivpujan Sahay, Ramdhari Singh Dinkar, Ramvriksha Benipuri, Banarasi Das Chaturvedi. On 7 April, 1963, he breathed his last.

Dr. Chaturbhuj: The author of nineteen historical and seven mythological plays, Dr. Chaturbhuj was born on 15 January, 1928 in Biharsharif. At 21, he wrote his first play Meghnath. In this very year his another play Sirajuddaula was published. His other plays are Pataliputra ka Rajkumar, Kalinga Vijay, Lord Buddha, Mir Kasim, Alexander Porus, Mudra Rakshas, Shivaji, Bahadurshah, Kansabadh, Jhansi Ki Rani, Bhishma Pratigya, Noor Jahan, Karn, Veer Abhimanyu, Aravalli ka Sher, Shri Krishna, Kunwar Singh, Peerali, Ravana, Morche Par, Babu Viranchi Lal, Nadi Ka Pani and Tipu Sultan. Two of his famous historical novels are Samudra Ka Panchhi and Rajdarshan. He was rewarded by the Government of Uttar Pradesh for the play Mir Qasim. He received citations from Buddhist countries for the plays Bhagwan Buddha and Kalinga Vijay. Besides, his three social plays, one comedy satirical drama, two solo collections, two story collections, two biographies and one article collection were published simultaneously in the name of Chaturbhuj Ratnavali. He died in 2009 in Patna.

Janaki Ballabh Shastri: The great poet of truth, modesty and beauty, Acharya Janaki Ballabh Shastri was born on 25 January, 1916 in Magra village of Gaya district. His first poem Roop-Arup was published in 1939. Carrying forward the tradition of Nirala in Hindi poetry, he beautifully delineated the consciousness and beauty of Indian culture with his creative writings. His major works are Kaanan, Aparna, Leela Kamal, Basanti (all story collections), Ek Kiran Sau Jhaeheyan, Do Tinko Ka Ghonsala, Ashwaghosha, Kalidas, Chanakya. (All Novels),

Smriti ke Vatayan, Hans Balaka, Karmakshetra-Kurukshetra, Neel Mohit, Roznamcha, Nirala Ke Patra, Ankaha Nirala (all memoirs), Chalantika (short story collection), Sune Kaun Nagma (Gazal Collection), Ajanta Ki Ore (travel-account) and Niralas contribution to Hindi literature are Mann Ki Baat, Manas-Chintan, Sahitya Darshan, Oriental Literature, Trayi (all essay collections), Kakali (Sanskrit Poetry Collection). He died on 7 April, 2011.

Devki Nandan Khatri: The great litterateur of Bihar, Devki Nandan Khatri was born on 8 June, 1861 in Pusa of Muzaffarpur district. Chandrakanta, Narendra Mohini, Kusum Kumari, Chandrakanta Santati, Bhootnath, Virendra Veer, Gupt Godan, Kajal ki Kothari, etc. are the major novels authored by him. A unique, interesting novel by him, Chandrakanta Santati, widely read by many people, motivated many to learn Hindi. In later days, he established Lahiri Press in Banaras. He died in 1913.

Devendra Nath Sharma: A scholar of Hindi literature who graced the post of Vice-Chancellor of Patna and Darbhanga University for years, was born on 7 July, 1918 in Kritpura village of Gopalganj district. He served Hindi by joining institutions like Bihar Independent Academy, Bihar Hindi Granth Academy, Bihar Inter University Board, University Grants Commission, Hindi Samiti of Uttar Pradesh, Bihar Rashtrabhasha Parishad and Bharatiya Hindi Parishad. His popular works include Rashtriya Bhasha Hindi, Samsyayeh aur Samadhan (reference texts), Sahitya Ki Nibandhwali, Brajbhasha ki Vibhutia, Chhayavad and Pragatiwad, Hindi Sahitya Ka Vrihad Itihas, Bhaktikaal, Amar Bharati. Upniyas Ka Shilp , Richards Ke Alochana Siddhant etc. He died on 17 January, 1919 in Patna.

Nalin Vilochan Sharma: A great story writer, editor, critic and poet Shri Nalin Vilochan Sharma was born on 8 February, 1916 in Patna City Bhadra Ghat locality. In 1942, he was appointed a lecturer of Sanskrit in the Department of Sanskrit in Jain College, Arrah. In September 1946, he was appointed as a lecturer in the Hindi department of Patna College. Among his famous stories are Vish ke Daant, Yeh Bimar Log, Pehli Ghanti, Barsane ki Radha, Ek Chaabok Pichhe, etc. Besides, Pidiyan, Dukaan Ki Raunak, Biscuits aur Papad, Lal Kothi, Mukhbir, Pados Ki Koyal etc. are his other prominent fables. With his work, he became a famed personality of Bihar as also of India.

Nagarjuna: A notable poet of independent India and great litterateur, who imparted a democratic voice to modern poetry, was born in 1911 in Tarouni village of Darbhanga district. He was progressive, rambunctious, frivolous in nature. Rebellion from tradition, rebellion against social, political system make his poems multifaceted. Besides Hindi, he also composed in Maithili. He used to write in Maithili as Yatri. His collection of Maithili poems Patraheen Nagan Gaach was awarded the Sahitya Akademi Award. His major works in Hindi literature include Yugdhara, Satrangi Pankhonwali, Pyasi Patharai Aankhen, Taalab ki Machhliyan, Chandana, Khichdi, Viplav Dekha Humne, Tumhe Kaha Tha, Purani Jutiyon Ka Koras, Hazar-Hazar Bahon Wali, Paka Hai Yeh Kathal, Apne Khet Mein, Main Military ka Budha Ghoda (poem collection), Bhasmasura Bhumija (Volume Poetry), Ratinath ki Chachi, Baba Batesarnath, Dukhmochan, Balchanma, Varuna ke Bete , Nai Paudh (novel). Paro (Maithili novel) are also his unique works.

Paresh Sinha: This great poet of Bihar, who played an important role in the J P movement, was born on 13 January, 1937 in Singriyawan village of Fatuha zone. In 1947, his first poem Sukhaad was published. His other major works are Jabron Ki Chhav Mein, Uttar do Yaksha, (poem collection), Teen terah Log and the Nagfani ke Phool (story collection), Gandhi Nahi Marega, Purusha Chhaya, Murde, Chehra Dar Chehra and Kate Hue Log (plays) are prominent. Andhere ke Virudh and Ek muhim Yeh Bhi were also produced as two tele films by him.

Poddar Ramavatar Arun: This great personality, decorated with the Padma Shri was born on 24 November, 1923 in Pethia Gachi locality of Samastipur. His first work Arunima (Epic) was Published in 1941. His other famous works are Shakuntala ki Bidhai, Vidyapati Sur Shyam, Vishva

Manav, Kosho, Kalidas, Videha Amrapali, Gohatya, Ashok Putra, Vananwari, Kaldarpan, Karl Marx, Kalchakra, Bhagwan Buddha ki Atamkatha, Guru Govind Singh ki Atam Katha, Nalanda ki Atam Katha, Bolti Rekhain, Arunayan, Ek Atamkatha etc. He was honored with Meera Samman, Kalidas Samman, Father Bulke Samman, Mahakavi Vyas, Sahitya Bhushan Samman, Vidyasagar Samman

Fanishwar Nath Renu: This great regional novelist of Bihar was born on 4 March, 1921 in the village of Aurahi Hingna in Araria district. Word of the story writer Phanishwar Nath Renu is one infested with mud and forest. He is one of the few eminent personalities through whom Bihar is known in the world of literature. He was also an ally in Jayaprakash Narayans entire revolution movement and was sentenced to prison in the emergency. He was gifted with Padma Shri by the Government of India for his literary contributions, but he returned the award against the atrocities done by the government. Among his early works Batbaba, Phalwan Ki Dholak, Gotranta are prominent. His initial ten stories were published in the weekly Vishvamitra published from Calcutta. In 1954, his famous work Maila Aanchal was published. His other famous works include Parati-Parikatha Rasapriya, Teesri Kasam (story), Deergtapa, Kalank mukti, Julles, Paltu Babu Road (Novel), Thumri, Agnikhor, Aadim Ratri ki Mahak, Ek Shravani, Dopahar ki Dhoop, Achhe Aadmi (story collection), Ren Jal dhan Jal, Van Tulsi Gandh, Shree-Ashrut Purva (memoirs), Nepali Karanti Katha (reportage) etc. are prominent. Lyricist Shailendra picturised a film on his story Teesri Kasam in 1966. He died on 11 April, 1977 in PMCH in the middle of his treatment.

Father Kamil Bulke: Father Kamil Bulke, an English citizen of the country of Belgium, who was decorated with Padma Bhushan for his contribution in the Hindi language and who made Bihar his work-land. He was born in Belgium on 1 September, 1909. In 1945, he scored an MA in Sanskrit from the University of Calcutta and MA in Hindi from Prayag University in 1947. In 1950, he started as a lecturer in the Department of Hindi in Saint Xavier College, Ranchi. His first composition English-Hindi Shabd Kosh was published in 1968, an eminent creation and literary work. His famous works include Ram Katha: Uttpatti Aur Vikas, Nil Pakshi (Translation from French), Bible (Translation of New Testament in Hindi), Manas Kaumudi, Prerit Charitra, Path Sangrah etc. He died on 17 August, 1982 during treatment at the All India Institute of Medical Sciences (AIIMS), Delhi.

Bhikhari Thakur: A popular poet, singer and playwright of social consciousness, Bhikhari Thakur was born in 1887 in Qutabpur village of Saran district. Without taking any formal education, he composed an unmatched literature. His plays Beti Beyog, Radhe-Shyam Bahar, Videshiya (Foreigner), Bhai Virodh (Brothers-Protest), Ganga-Snan, Widhwa-Wilap, Beti-Bechwa, Nanad-Bhojai, Kalyug Prem, Gabar-Ghichor, Putra-Vadhu present the teachings of morality to the society. In his poetry, Adoration (Shringar) is a captivating mixture of compassion, devotion and humour. He is also called Shakespeare of Bhojpuri.

Madhukar Singh: Born on 2 January, 1934 in Midnapore, West Bengal, Bhojpur was the work place of Madhukar Singh. He worked as a teacher for two and a half to three decades in Hari Prasad Jain School in Arrah for his livelihood. His major works are Bajat Anhad Dhol, Mayi, Sita-Ram Namaskar, Uttargatha, Arjun Jinda Hain, Jangli Sooarr, Sonbadhar ki Radha, Premchandra, Maxim Gorkki, Lok Kavi Bhikhari Thakur, etc. His short story collections are Bhai Ka Jakham, Agnu Kapar, Pehla Paath, Purna Sanaata, Michael Jackson ki Topi, etc. He was conferred the highest state award, Kathakar Samman, Phanishwar Nath Renu Samman and Nai Dhara Rachna Samman by the Government of Bihar.

Mohan Lal Mahato Viyogi: This timely creator of Bihar was born in Gaya on 1 November, 1899. Among his immortal works, Aryavarta, Nirman, Ek Tara, Nirmasya or Kalpana (all epics) are prominent ones. The epic Aryavarta, full of national sentiments, was written in Mitakshara verses. His first novel Bhai-Behan, published in 1932. He was also an eminent cartoonist. His famed cartoons were published in Madhuri, Manorama, Saraswati, and Sudha. From 1952 to 1962, he was a nominated member of the Bihar Legislative Council. He died on 7 February, 1990.

Raghuveer Narayan: Renowned Bhojpuri poetry Batohia writer Raghuveer Narayan and the author of Miya was born on 30 October, 1884 in Dahiyawan of Saran district. In 1905, he composed an English poem A Tale of Bihar. Besides Batohiya, he also got fame with another song Bharat Bhavani. His other poetic works are Raghuveer Patra Pushpa, Raghuveer Ras Rang, Nikunj Kala and Raghuveer Ras Ganga. He died in Chapra in January 1955.

Raja Radhika Raman Prasad Singh: Reputed story writer Raja Radhika Raman Prasad Singh was born on 10 September, 1890 in Bhojpur district. His famous works are Ram-Rahim, Purab or Paschim, Chumban or Chanta, Surdas, Sanskar, Purush or Nari, Apni-apni Nazar, Maya Mili Na Ram, Modern aur Sundar Kaun (novel). Among his stories Daridra Narayan, Dev Aur Rakshas, Mahal aur Jhompri, Toota hua Tara, Kusumanjali are most popular. In 1950, he started the publication of Nai Dhara magazine from Patna. He died on 24 March, 1971.

Ramji Mishra Manohar: This great litterateur was born in Patna in 1927. He started his journalistic life as a correspondent of Aryavart published from Patna in 1945. His major works are Dastan-e-Pataliputra, Bihar mein Hindi Patrakarita ka Vikas, Guru Gobind Singh aur Unke Paavan Astra and Guru Nanak. He died on 29 October, 1998 in Rajendra Nagar, Patna.

Ramdhari Singh Dinkar: A national poet and most widely renowned Ramdhari Singh Dinkar, who created a free poetic folk in the era of neoromantic poems, was born on 11 September, 1908 in Simaria village of Begusarai district. Through his poems, he capsized his ability to take poetry among the masses in the community and the society. His first book Pramaan-Patra was published immediately after he passed high school. He was the Head of Post-Graduation Hindi Department of Bihar University, Muzaffarpur. His immortal works include Rashmirathi, Urvashi, Kurukshetra, Sanskriti ke Char Adhyay (Four chapters of culture), Renuka, Indugeet, Hunkar, Samdheni, Nilkusum, Sipi aur Shankh, Parashurama Pratiksha and Hare Ko Harinam. In the poems of Dinkar ji, there was a unique blend of patriotism and Shringar (make-up). One side his compositions Kurukshetra and on other side is Urvashi. He preferred to use simplest words and vocabulary in his creations for easy grasping. He was a member of Rajya Sabha thrice. He died on 2 April, 1972.

Ramvriksha Benipuri: Ramvriksha Benipuri was born in 1899 in the village of Benipur in Muzaffarpur district. He was imprisoned twice in his freedom struggle participation between 1930 and 1945. He authored the renowned play Ambapali in Hazaribagh Central Jail. His popular works are Gehu Aur Gulab (Wheat and Rose), Mati Ki Moorte (Idols of the soil), Patito ke Desh Mein (In the country of fallen), Laltara, Chita Ke Phool, Kaidi Ki Patni (Prisoners Wife), Ambapali, Sita ki Ma (Sita Mother), Sanghamitra. , Amar Jyoti, Tathagat, Singhal-Vijay, Shakuntala, Ramrajya, Netradan (Eye Donation), Gaon Ke Devta (God of the Village), Naya Samaj (New Society) Vijeta (Victor) etc. As an editor, he edited weekly, monthly and part-time magazines like Tarun Bharat, Yuvak (Youth), Kisan Mitra (Farmer Mitra), Balak, Lok Sangrah, Karmaveer, Yogi, Janata, Himalaya, Nai Dhara, and Chunu-Munnu very eminently and successfully. In 1957, he was elected to the Bihar Legislative Assembly as an MLA.

Ramshobhit Prasad Singh: He was a well-known novelist, playwright, story writer and poet as well. Ramshobhit Prasad Singh was actually a librarian. He was born on 10 January, 1936 in Akhilpur village of Saran district. In 1960, he joined the Sinha Library. From 1974 to 1979, he edited the monthly magazine Pustkalya(Library). His major works Upnyas Sasmalochana Sandarbh (Novel Criticism Reference), Natak Samalochna Sandarbh (Drama Criticism Reference), Kavya Samalochna Sandarbh (Poetry Criticism Reference), Hindi Upnayas, Premchandotar Kaal, Rashtriya Ekta ke Prateek, Raghuveer Narayan, Batohiya ke Amar Gayak Library Organization and Administration and The Framework of Library Science are prominent.

Rameshwar Singh Kashyap (Loha Singh): He was born on 16 August, 1927 in Semra village of Rohtas district. He wrote compositions in both Hindi and Bhojpuri languages. His famous work is the play Loha Singh written in Bhojpuri language. His another comedy play Tasalwa Tod Ki Mod also became very famous. Both these plays had been telecasted by Akashvani Patna for a long time. He also composed the screenplays and songs for Bhojpuri films Kab Hoi Yeh Gabanma Hamar and Saiyan Se Bhaile Milanwa. In 1991, he was honoured with Padma Shri. In Hindi Aprajya Nirala, Neelkanth Nirala (poetry), Swarnarekha (novel) are his major works. He died on 20 October, 1992.

Lakshmi Narayan Sudhanshu: He was born on 15 December 1906 in Dhamdaha village of Purnia district. His first published novel was Matriprem. In 1962, he was elected unopposed as the Speaker of the Bihar Legislative Assembly. He died on 7 April, 1974.

Shivpujan Sahay: Shivpujan Sahay, an eminent litterateur who illuminated the name of Bihar in the field of literature and journalism, was born on 9 August, 1893. He was the editor of more than a dozen magazines. He was the Head of Department in Rajendra College, Chhapra for a few days. Subsequently he was promoted as the director of the well-known Sahitya Devi Sanstha, from where all his works were published in four volumes under the name of Shivpujan Granthavali. His major works include Dehati Duniya, Matwala Madhuri, Ganga, Jagran, Himalaya, Sahitya, Vahi Din Wahi Log, Mera Jeevan (My Life), Smriti Shesh and Hindi Bhasha Aur Sahitya (Hindi language and Literature), etc. He died on 23 January, 1963.

Vidyapati: He is reputed as one of the main pillars of Indian literary figures of devotional tradition and as the foremost poet of Maithili language, Vidyapati is well known to the masses. He was probably born in the village of Visfi in Darbhanga district in 1350. Among his major works in Maithili are Padmavali, Purusha Pariksha, Bhoo Parikrama, Kirtilata, Kirtipataka, Goraksha Vijay, Manimanjra. In the field of theology, his major works include Gangavakyavali, Daanvakyavali, Varsh Kritya, Durga Bhakti Tarangini, Shaivasarvasvasara, Gayapatalaka and Vibhagsar Purana All these compositions are in Sanskrit language.

Udayraj Singh: He was born on 5 November, 1921 in Suryapura, Rohtas. He edited the magazines Vikas and Saurabh. Among his major works are Navtara, Adhuri Nari, Rohini, Bhudani Sonia, Kuhasa Aur Aakritiyan etc. to commemorate his contribution in literature, the litterateurs are honored with the Udayraj Singh Memorial Awards every year.

Rajkamal Choudhary: He was born on 13 December, 1929 in his maternal grandmothers Rampur Haveli. The parental village of this great litterateur is Maheshi, Saharsa. His major works include Agni Snan in Hindi, Shahar Tha Shahar Nahi Tha, Nadi Behati Thee, Tash Ke Patto Ka Shahar, Machhli Mari Hui (novel), Bees Raniyon Ke Biscope, Ek Anar Ek Bimar (short novel), Mukti Prasanna, Kankavati, Is Akal Bela Mein (poem collection), Machhli Jaal, Samudri (story collection) etc. In Maithili, he wrote Adi Katha, Patharphool, Andolan (novel), Swargandha, Kavita Rajkamalak (poem collection), Ekta Champakali, Vishdhar, Kriti Rajkamalak (story collection).

Manager Pandey: Famous critic Manager Pandey was born in Lohti village of Gopalganj district on 23 September, 1941. His published books Shabd and Karma, Sahitya or Itihas-Drishti, Shitya ke Samajikshastra ki Mhoomika, Bhakti Andolan aur Surdas ka Kvay, Anabhai Sancha, Alochna ki Samajikta, Samkat ke Bavjood, Desh Ki Baat etc. are quite prominent. He was conferred by Hindi Academy, Delhis Literary Award, National Dinkar Samman, Ramchandra Shukla Shodh Sansthan Samman, etc.

Robin Shaw Puspha: His full name is Robin Shaw Pushp. He was born on 20 December, 1936 in Munger district of Bihar. He became famous as a storyteller, novelist, play writer and screenwriter. His major works Anyay ko Kshma, Dulhan Bazaar (novel), Agnikund, Ghar Kahan Bhag Gaya (story collection), Sone ki Kalamwala Hiraman (memoirs) are eminent ones. He died on 30 October, 2014 in Patna, the capital of Bihar.

Ravindra Prabhat: This great litterateur was born on 5 April, 1969 in Sitamarhi district of Bihar. His major works are Humsafar, Mat Rona Ramzani Chacha, Smriti Shesh Taki Bach Rahe Loktantra, Prem Na Haat Bikay, Hindi Blogging: Abhivyakti ki Nai Kranti, Hindi Blogging ka itihas, etc. He was awarded with Samvad Samman 2009, Srijanshree Samman 2011, Hindi Sahitya Shri Samman 2011, Baba Nagarjuna Janmashati Katha Samman 2012, Praless Chittaksrita Shikhar Samman, etc.

Saraswati Prasad: The creator of major compositions like Nadi Pukare Sagar and Ek Thi Taru, was born on 28 August, 1932 in Ara district of Bihar. She was the daughter of the late great poet Sumitranandan Pant. Kadambini, Saptahik Hindustan, Nancy, Moodhiwala, Prashno ke Aine Mein are also the major works written by her. This great litterateur of Bihar passed away on 9 September, 2013.

Rashmi Prabha: Rashmi Prabha, the daughter of late Mahakavi Sumitranandan Pant, was born on 13 February, 1958 in Sitamarhi district of Bihar. Shabdo ka Rishta of words, Anutarit, Anmol Sanchayan, Anugunj etc. are incredible works written by her. Besides, Satyarthi, Radha-Mira and Prem, Kavi Pant Ke Sath Kuch Doore, etc. are her major writings.

Ganga Nath Jha: This eminent writer, who compiled excellent works on philosophical subjects in Hindi, English and Maithili languages, was born in Bihar in 1872. He started teaching Sanskrit at Allahabad University by writing a dissertation on Prabhakars philosophy of Purva Mimamsa. After this he was promoted as the principal of Banaras Sanskrit College. In 1923, he was deputed as the Vice-Chancellor of Allahabad University. Vigyan Bhishvu ka Yogsar Sangrah, Bela Mahatyam, Bhakti Kallolini, Bhavabodhini, Prabhakar Pradeep in Sanskrit Nyayaprakash, Vaishesika Darpan, Kavi Rahasya in Hindi Vedanta Deepika in Maithili, Purvamamsa of Gemini in English, Philosophical Discipline, Shankaracharya and His Work for the Upliftment of the Country etc. are his major creations. He died on 17 November, 1941.

Harimohan Jha: He was born in 1908 in Bajitpur village of Vaishali district. He has hit hard with his writings against religious hypocrisy. Among his compositions Kanyadaan, Dwiragaman, Pranamya Devata, Rangshala, Babak Sanskar, Churchery Ekadashi, Khattar Kakak Tarang and Jeevan-Yatra are prominent works. His compositions are prominently in both Hindi and Maithili languages. He died in 1984.

Jagdishchandra Mathur: This cultural personality who gave multidimensional shape to Hindi theatre in Bihar was born on 16 July, 1917 in Shahjahanpur, Uttar Pradesh. His full-time plays include works such as Konark, Bindi, Shardiya, Pehla Raja, Dasaratha Nandan and Raghukul Reet, Bhor Ka Tara, O Mere Sapne evam Mere Srhishta Rang. Besides, while working as the Director General of All India Radio, he gave new impetus to various programs of Vividh Bharati.

Literature and Litterateur

Sr. No.	Litterateur	Famous compositions
1	Banbhatt	Kadambari, Harshacharitam
2	Vishnu Sharma	Panchtantra
3	Kautiliya	Arthashastra
4	Ashwaghosh	Mahayana Shraddhotpada Sangrah, Vajra Soochi
5	Aryabhata	Aryabhatiyam
6	Vatsyayan	Kamasutram

7	Madan Mishra	Bhav Vivek, Vidhhi Vivek
8	Vidyapathi	Padavalli, Kirtilata, Kirtipataka, Go-Raksha, Bho Parikrama
9	Mullah Dawood	Chandayan
10	Jyotishawar Thakur	Varn Ratnakar, Darshan Ratnakar
11	Phanishwar Nath Renu	Maulla Anchal, Juloos, Paltoo Babu Road, Dherag Taap
12	Ramdhari Singh Dinkar	Pranabhang, Urvashi, Renuka, Duandgeet, Hunkar, Raswanti, Chakarwal, Dhoop-chaon, Kuruskhetra
13	Baba Nagarjun	Baba Bateshwarbnath, Hazar Hazar Bahaonwali, Paro Kummbika, Tumne Kaha Tha
14	Devaki Nandan Khatri	Chandrakantah Santhati, Bhootnath, Kajar Ki Kothri, Naulakhahaar
15	Rahul Sankrutayan	Budacharya, Vinaypitika, Dhammpad, Darshan Digdarshan
16	Shah Azimabadi	Nakshopaydaar
17	Dr Rajendra Prasad	India divided, Champaran mein Satyagrah, Bapu Ke Kadamo Pe
18	Kedarnath Mishra (Prabhat)	Jwala, Kaikeyi, Ritu Vansh
19	Shivsagar Mishr	Doob Janam Chaiye
20	Ramvikrash Benipuri	Amrapali, Maati ke Moort, Chinta ke Phool, Sanghamitra
21	Vachaspati Mishr	Bhashya Mamti, Brahsiddhi ke Tikkakaar

❑❑❑

Bihar's Luminaries

From Aryabhatta of the ancient times to the Ananda of modern times, the mystics of Bihar have illuminated the whole world with their knowledge, know-how and experience. The famous personalities of Bihar are mentioned as follows:

Lord Buddha: Born in Lumbini, which is now part of Nepal, but the region is closely connected to Bihar and its teachings of the Middle Way and the Four Noble Truths had a profound impact on India and beyond.

Mahavira: The 24th Tirthankara in Jainism, Mahavira was also born in Bihar and his emphasis on non-violence (Ahimsa) and ethical conduct shaped the spiritual landscape of India.

Anugrah Narayan Singh: Anugrah Narayan Singh played an important role in the freedom struggle of India. In 1917, he carried forward the movement run by Mahatma Gandhi, against the exploitation of the farmers, during his visit to Champaran. He was made an active member of the reception committee in the session of the National Congress held in Gaya in 1922. In 1928 he was elected President of the Bihar State Congress Committee and was nominated Member of All India Congress Committee in 1935. In 1946 and 1952, took over the responsibility of department of Finance, Labour, Agriculture, etc., in the Government of Shri Krishna Singh.

Abdul Qayum Ansari: While maintaining Hindu-Muslim unity, in Bihar's freedom struggle, Abdul Qayoom Ansari, gave a befitting reply to the Britishers, by performing public service as Public Works Minister, Water Minister, Health Minister and Road Construction Minister in Bihar Government for about 17 years post independence. In 1946, he became the President of Bihar Pradesh Congress. He took keen interest in literature, published 'Maskhat' in 1934, 'Saathi' in 1948 along with Suhail Azimabadi and monthly magazine, 'Tehzeeb' in 1952. In July 2005, on his birth centenary, the Central Government issued a commemorative postage stamp.

Ali Imam: Ali Imam from Bengal, played an important role in the formation of the provinces of Bihar and Orissa. In 1910, he was nominated as a legal member of the Executive Council of the Governor General. In the same year, he was honoured with the title of 'Sir'. In 1917, he was nominated as a judge of the Patna High Court.

Anand Kumar: In order to extend academic support and financial aid to poor and talented children in Bihar for admission to IIT through competitive examination, Anand Kumar initiated the Super 30 institute to train them meticulously. Here even the children from the very low strata of the society are also trained to get into IIT every year. About 22 of 30 in 2004, 26 in 2005, 28 in 2006, and in 2007, 30 out of 30 children got success respectively. Apart from India, he is accredited now abroad in America, Japan, China, Germany, France, Singapore, etc.

R P Sharma: Under Patna University in TPS College served as a lecturer in Philosophy R.P. Sharma founded many latest institutions for the promotion of education in Bihar namely Naya Tola in Patna, as RPS Women's College, RPS Residential School in

Kadamkuan, in Bailey Road, Raghunath Girls High School and Ranka Devi Girls High School. He also authored books like 'Kaljayi Hanuman', 'Antaryatra', Jeewan ka Utkarsh', (Adhyan aur Chintan, Shiksha, Samasya aur Samadhan, etc.

Karpoori Thakur: Known as Chanakya of Bihar politics and immortal soldier of freedom struggle. Karpoori Thakur was the messiah of the poor and backwards in the true sense. He was elected an MLA for the first time in 1952 to the Bihar Assembly. In 1967, he was promoted to Deputy Chief Minister and Minister of Finance and Minister of Education in the Bihar cabinet. On 22 December, 1970, he was elected as the Chief Minister of the state for the first time. He had to resign from the post after six months. He again took oath as Chief Minister on 24 June, 1977. He again resigned from the post of Chief Minister on 24 April, 1978. His whole life was a symbol of the values of social justice, human rights, and secularism.

Kishor Kunal: Kishore Kunal was selected for the Indian Police Service in 1972. On 30 October, 1983, he started the restoration work of Mahavir temple and formed a trust for the maintenance of the temple. Presently, this trust namely Mahavir Mandir Trust runs K Mahaveer Health Institute, Mahaveer Cancer Sansthan, Mahaveer Netralaya and Mahavir Vatsalya Sansthan where complimentary services are provided to the public. The world's largest and gigantic temple is being constructed by this trust in East Champaran district. Many temples and monasteries of the state were freed from illegal seizure and renovated.

Kirti Azad: He had been a known and successful player of Bihar in the field of cricket. During the World Cup of 1983, being a member of the Indian team, he played an important role in India's victory over England in the semi-finals with his excellent bowling. Kirti Azad, son of former Bihar Chief Minister Bhagwat Jha Azad, has been active in politics.

KB Sahai: Shri Krishna Ballabh Sahai, who served as the third Chief Minister of Bihar, played an important role in India's freedom struggle. As a topper of Bihar-Orissa in English competition, he was selected in ICS. But on Gandhiji's call, he quit the ICS to join the freedom movement. From 1963 to 1967, he stayed as the Chief Minister of Bihar. He is considered as the father of land reforms in Bihar. In 1947, he brought a bill for the abolition of the Zamindari system in the assembly. With his efforts, the Bihar Land Reforms Act was implemented.

Khudabaksh Khan: The credit of establishing the Oriental Public Library in Bihar is accredited to Khudabaksh Khan. Because of his great efforts, presently this library is known as Khuda Bakhsh Library. This library is the pride of Patna city and is the identity of this city. The manuscripts of the ancient times are still preserved in this library.

Chitragupt Srivastava: Known as a music director in the Hindi film world, he directed music in about three dozen films. His filmy life started with the hit film "Bhabhi" of 1957. After this, his music famed in films like "Bada Aadmi", "Applam-Chaplam", "Jabak", "Ganga Maiya Tohe Pieri Chadhaibo", "Main Chup Rahungi", "Main Shaadi Karne Chala" etc.

Jagjivan Ram: Babu Jagjivan Ram, who struggled throughout his life for the respect of Dalits in Bihar and actively participated in the freedom struggle from Bihar, was born on 5 April, 1908, in Chandwa village of Shahabad district. In 1929, he founded the All India Ravidas Sansthan in Calcutta (now Kolkata): In 1937, he founded the Khatihar Mazdoor Sabha. On 2 September, 1946, he took oath as the Minister of Labour in the interim Union Cabinet. At the time of the declaration of emergency in 1977, he distanced himself from the Congress. In the new government, he was given the post of Deputy Prime Minister. At the last phase of his life, he rejoined the Congress.

Jaglal Choudhary: Jaglal Choudhary was a leading warrior in the freedom struggle. Despite of being a Doctor, he completely assimilated himself in the fight for freedom. In 1932, he joined the "Salt Satyagraha". In 1937, he was made the Health

Minister of Bihar. Immediately after getting health Ministry, he implemented prohibition on alcohol. In 1938, the Liquor Prohibition Bill was passed. In 1946, he was promoted as Health Minister in the Congress cabinet. In 1951, due to differences over the decision to release political prisoners, he quit the ministerial post.

Jaiprakash Narayan: This great personality of Bihar gave a new direction to politics in the whole of North India, including Bihar, born on 4 October, 1902 in Sitab Diara village of Saran district. From adolescence, he turned first towards Marxist ideology and then towards socialism. In 1930, he joined Congress and he was entrusted with the responsibility of the Labour-Farmer Department. In 1932, he was made the working general minister of Congress. After independence, he joined 'Bhoodan Movement' with Acharya Vinoba Bhave and devoted his life to Sarvodaya. In 1965, he got 'Magsaysay award'. In 1974, accepting the leadership of the students movement, announced a complete revolution. He was arrested after the declaration of emergency in 1975. A book based on his biography "Jai Prakash" was published by Ramvriksha Benipuri. In 1999, he was bestowed 'Bharat Ratna'. He is also known as 'JP' and 'Lok Nayak'. On October 8, 1999, he breathed his last.

Dashrath Manjhi: He built a 30-feet wide, 350-feet-long road by cutting a 360-feet high hill with his 22 years of long spell. This illuminary of Bihar soared his home, family, district, state and country in the world with his lofty spirits. As a result of his efforts, the distance from village to city reduced to 8 km from 50 km. A film based on his biography, Manjhi the Mountainman, was picturised in 2015 by director Ketan Mehta, in which Nawazuddin Siddiqui played the character of Dashrath Manjhi.

Dukhan Ram: Dukhan Ram was a great eye specialist by profession. In 1944, he was appointed as the Head of Eye Department in Patna Medical College. In 1945, he was honoured with the title of 'Rai Sahab'. Between 1953 and 1956, the post of Principal of Patna Medical College was modified. He was the honorary ophthalmologist of the first President of India, Dr. Rajendra Prasad and the fifth President, Fakhruddin Ali Ahmed. In 1962, he was awarded the title of "Padma Vibhushan". In 1988, he was honoured with 'Bihar Ratna'.

Pawan Kumar: Born on 14 September, 1978, Pawan Kumar is a popular cartoonist of India. In his career of 22 years, more than 5 thousand cartoons of his have been published in various publications. He got success by getting regular cartoon publications from Navbharat Times. The honors received by him are 'Shankar Dayal Singh Samman', 'Kalakriti Samman', "Kalashree Samman", "Rotary Award", "Sulabh International Award" and "Best Cartoonist of Bihar Award".

Prakash Jha: Prakash Jha is a well-known director in the Indian film industry. His important films directed are "Gangajal", "Apanaan", "Rajneeti", "Aarakshan", "Hip-Hip Huray", "Damul", "Katha Madhopur Ki", "Parineeti" and "Sonal", etc. Besides from this, he also directed Doordarshan's important serials 'Mungeri Lal Ke Haseen Sapne' and 'Rebellion'.

Batukeshwar Dutt: J.P. Batukeshwar Dutt was appointed along with Bhagat Singh to throw bomb in the Central Assembly. On 8 April, 1929, both of them bombed the Central Assembly. After this he remained active in the Indian freedom struggle for a long time. He was imprisoned repeatedly. This also includes the life sentence of Kalapani in the Central Assembly bomb case.

Babu Kunwar Singh: Babu Veer Kunwar Singh born on 23rd April, 1777 in Jagdishpur village of Bhojpur district, at the age of 49, he took over the zamindari of Jagdishpur. He vowed to oppose the British government from 1845. In this context, he associated with his brother Amar Singh, nephew Rathbhanjan Singh, Nishant Singh, Harikishun Singh and Jaikrishna Singh. In 1857, Mangal Pandey shot and killed an army officer in Barrackpore

Cantonment in Bengal. As a result, he was hanged. Due to this there was a rebellion among the soldiers. Veer Kunwar Singh had earlier contacted with the soldiers of Danapur Cantonment in Bihar who revolted under the leadership of Veer Kunwar Singh. At the age of 75, he successfully led this rebellion.

Bindeshwar Pathak: In the 1960s–70s decade, an active social effort was started to eliminate manual cleaning of toilets and scavenging practices. This program was associated with the cleanliness movement of Mahatma Gandhi. Due to this revolution, 0 to 65% in rural areas of the country and 15% to 83% of urban areas got success in creating clean toilets. This movement was started by Dr. Bindeshwar Pathak in the name of 'Sulabh Technique Movement'. So far, a total of 2 lakh accessible toilets have been constructed in India by them, while the Government of India has built about five crore forty lakh toilets by adopting accessible technology.

Bismillah Khan: The great shehnai player, who received the country's four prestigious civilian honours "Bharat Ratna", " Padam Bhushan", "Padam Vibhushan" and "Padamshree", was born on March 21, 1916 in Dumraon town of Buxar district. His good name was Kamaruddin Khan. At just 8, he was counted among India's famed musicians. In April 1956, he was awarded the Sangeet Natak Akademi Award, in 1964, "Padma Shri", in 1968 "Padambhushan", in 1980 "Padma Vibhushan", in 2007, he was awarded the Bharat Ratna. On August 5, 1947, he had the privilege to play shehnai at the Independence Day celebrations held at the Red Fort. He died on August, 21, 2006 at the age of 90.

B P Manda: In 1978, the then Prime Minister Morarji Desai constituted a five-member Civil Rights Commission under the chairmanship of B.P. Mandal. The commission, in its report in 1980, recommended reservation of seats in government and private educational institutions for other backward castes.

BS. Mukhopadhyay: One who showed his notable talent in the medical world, in the first attempt itself, Dr Mukhopadhyay completed MCH (Ortho) in December 1948. passed out with resounding score. From 1949 to 1961, he was an orthopaedic surgeon par excellence in Patna Medical College. His contribution in the field of bone TB treatment is unforgettable. He founded the Indian Orthopaedic Association in 1955.

Bhola Paswan Shastri: The first Dalit Chief Minister of Bihar, Bhola Paswan Shastri was called the saint of politics because of his simplicity and loyalty. From 22 March, 1968 to 29 June, 1968, from 22 June, 1969 to 4 July, 1969 and from 2 June, 1971 to 9 January, 1972, he served as the Chief Minister of Bihar. He was a great freedom fighter. During the freedom struggle, in Purnia he edited a weekly named "National Message".

Manoj Tiwari: He is a talented singer, film actor, TV actor from Bihar and now an MP. Manoj Tiwari brought laurels to Bihar at a very young age by gaining fame as an anchor and music director. His first film was 'Sasura Bada Paisawala' in Bhojpuri. Presently, he is the Lok Sabha member from Delhi.

Manoj Bajpayee: In the Indian film world, Manoj Bajpayee, the protagonist of successful films like 'Rajneeti', 'LOC'. "Kargil", "Road", "Pinjar", "Satya", "Shool", and "Aarakshan", is an evolving artist from Bihar. He first got national recognition in Doordarshan's serial 'Swabhimaan'. Besides, he also exhibited his talent in art films like 'Droha Kaal', 'Bandit Queen', 'Dastak', 'Zubaida' etc.

Mahesh Narayan: The credit for starting the separate Bihar province movement goes to Mahesh Narayan along with Satchidanand Sinha. In 1906, he co-authored the book 'Partition of Bengal' and 'Separation of Bihar' with Satchidanand Sinha. He also narrated articles for Bihar Separation through his magazine "The Bihar Times".

Rajendra Prasad: The first President of India, Deshratna Dr. Rajendra Prasad was born on 3 December, 1884 in village ziradei in Siwan district. He was the first Bihari to top in first division in University of Calcutta from City College, Calcutta (now Kolkata) and in G.V.V. College Muzaffarpur, he also worked there as a teacher. In 1910, meet Gopal

Krishna Gokhale, he meet to serve the country. After the establishment of Patna High Court in 1916, he started advocacy from there. He actively participated in "Champaran Satyagraha" with Gandhiji in 1917. He was jailed repeatedly in the freedom struggle. In 1934, he was made Congress President in the 48th session of Congress. Under his chairmanship, the Constitution of India was made by the Constituent Assembly. On 26 January, 1950, 10 May, 1950, 1952, and on 13 May, 1957, he was sworn in as the India's President three times. In 1962, he was awarded the 'Bharat Ratna'. He died on 28 February, 1963.

Ramchatur Malik: Ramchatur Malik finds an important position in taking the dhrupad-singing of classical music to a new height in Bihar. He used to recite the verses of Khayal, Thumri, Tappa, and Vidyapati along with Dhrupad very beautifully. The Bihar State Music Academy awarded him a 'fellowship' in 1953. He got 'Padma Shri' in 1970. The Government of Madhya Pradesh honoured him with the 'Tansen Award' in 1981.

Vindhyavasini Devi: Known as 'Bihar Nightingale,' Vindhyavasini Devi was a well-known artist who took folk songs to a very high level in Bihar. The first public performance of his singing took place in 1945. While teaching girls and imparting music education, she established the Vindhyakala Temple in 1949. She remained associated with All India Radio till 1979 when the Patna centre of Akashvani (All India Radio) was started in 1948. She composed many music texts, in which "Loksangeet Sagar", 'Sohar Episode', 'Vridha Kosh', "Lok Shabd Sagar" etc. are prominent. She also composed songs and did music direction work in some films. In 1974, she was awarded the "Padma Shri".

Virchand Patel: In the freedom struggle of India, Vircharan Patel is one of the prominent names of the freedom fighters of Bihar. With the Salt Satyagraha movement, he started taking active part in the freedom struggle. He was elected president in the Hajipur local body election in 1939. He resigned from the post of president in 1941 to participate in the 'Civil Disobedience Movement'. Hence, he was jailed repeatedly. In 1946, he was made Parliamentary Secretary in the Education Department of the Interim Government of Bihar. In 1952, he was upgraded to Deputy Minister of Agriculture Department. In 1957, he was handover the ministries of Agriculture, Health, and Food. Later on, he took oath as the Finance Minister in the Vinodanand Jha cabinet.

Shatrughan Sinha: Shatrughan Sinha, a great actor who impressed and convinced all with his talent in the Indian film world in the 1970-80s decade, was born on 5 July, 1946 in Patna. In his initial days, he acted as a villain in films. Later, he acted as a hero, then a politician. His major films are "Vishwanath", "Kalicharan", "Kala Patthar", "Dostana", "Khamosh", "Aan", "Shaan", etc.

Shanti Jain: Shanti Jain is a renowned singer, poet, writer and a notable example of women empowerment. Durga Saptsati, Sundarkand, Chhath marriage songs, bhajans etc. are prominently displayed in her singing, which has famed her from Bhojpuri folk songs. Besides, she has composed songs in many Bhojpuri films. She has been honoured with many awards including 'National Sangeet Natak Akademi Award'.

Kedarnath Prasad: A skilled academician, a great seer, an enlightened administrator and educationist, Dr. Prasad was born in Bahadwara (East Champaran) in 1926. His achievements were to become the Principal of Patna College, President of Economics and Vice Chancellor of Patna University. 'Strategy of Industrial Dispersal and Decentralized Development: A Case Study of Bihar', Economy of a Backward Region in a Backward Economy: A Case Study of Bihari Relation to Other States of India Vol-II, etc. are invaluable heritages written by him. Some of the other popular books of Dr. Prasad are 'India's Rural Problems', 'Lectures on Micro Economic Theory', 'Problems of Economic Development in the Third World', 'Technological Choice under Developmental Planning', etc.

Sharda Sinha: The idol of Bihar's culture, rites and tradition, Sharda Sinha is considered as an earthbound folk artist with his soil. Folk songs sung by him for marriage, Gauna, Chhath, etc. are definitely heard on special occasions of Bihar. Apart from this, he has also won the hearts ofpeople by singing songs in some Bhojpuri and Hindi films. She was honoured with 'Padm Bhusan', 'Padamsri' and 'Bihar Kokila' for folk song.

Shekhar Suman: Shekhar Suman is one of the prominent actors of Bihar, showing his talent 100% in the script full of humour, wits and satire. On television, 'Dekh Bhai Dekh', 'Reporter', 'One Hour Thrill', "T.V. Talk Show', 'Movers And Shakers', 'Pol-Khol', etc. are the major serials starring him.

Shrikant Thakur Vidyalankar: Pt. Shrikant Thakur Vidyalankar is a well-known name in the Hindi journalism field of India. In 1926, on the advice of Rajendra Prasad, he started journalism as an assistant editor of Hindi weekly "Mahavir". Later on, he started editing work in "Vishwamitra" published from Calcutta (now Kolkata) and Bombay (Now Mumbai). Started editing 'Pradeep' published from Patna in 1947, then he joined 'Aryavarta'.

Shri Krishna Singh: The architect of modern Bihar, Shri Krishna Singh was born on 2 October, 1887 in Khanwa village in Hisua block of Nawada district. He actively participated in the Lucknow Congress session of 1916. He actively participated in the 'Home Rule Movement' under the leadership of Tilak. In the "Champaran Satyagraha", he advocated the case on behalf of the farmers. In 1929, he formed the Kisan Sabha along with Swami Sahajanand Saraswati at the Sonepur fair. After the Bihar elections in 1937, the cabinet was formed under his leadership. In 1939, he resigned in protest against Britain's involving India in World War II. In 1946, he was re-elected he Chief Minister. From then till he died, he remained in the Chief Minister's post. He died on 3 January,1964.

Sanjay Upadhyay: Patna's Sanjay Upadhyay figures in the country's leading theatre workers and theatrical instructors. The plays "Bakri" and "Videshiya" directed by him came into prominence. He was the first Bihari to become the director of Shri Ram Centre, New Delhi. His famous plays are 'Jasma Odan', 'Nal-Daymanti', 'Khadia Ka Ghera', 'Rustom-Sohrab', 'Shri Penny Opera', 'Malvikamanimitram', 'Mati Gaadi', 'Kahan Gaye Mere Ugna', ' Dastan-e-Habba', etc.

Sachchidanand Sinha: Sachchidanand Sinha, who played an important role in the separation of Bihar from Bengal, was born on 10 November, 1871 in Arrah. He did his barrister education from London. After that he was made an active member of the British Committee of the Indian National Congress. In 1909, the second session of the Bihar Provincial Conference was convened in Bhagalpur under his chairmanship, in which he emphasised on the formation of a separate Bihar province. In 1924, he established the Smt. Radhika Sinha Institute and the Satchidanand Sinha Library in the memory of his wife. In 1936, he was appointed as the first non-official Vice Chancellor of Patna University.

Sir Ganesh Dutt: Sir Ganesh Dutt was born in 1868 in Nalanda district. After the establishment of the Calcutta High Court in 1904, he started legal practice advocacy from there. In 1921, he was elected to the Bihar, Orissa Legislative Council. In 1923, he was elected minister. While serving as a minister, he donated most of his salary for public welfare. Most of his income was spent on scholarships for poor and deserving students. He gave ₹4 lakh for the development of Patna University. Even at present, many educational institutions formed through his contribution are functioning in Bihar.

Siyaram Tiwari: He was a well-known artist of Dhurpad singing. He was a great scholar of Dhamar's rhythm of grih, ansh, matr, drut, laghu, plut and kak etc. He was a Ratna member of the Advisory Committee of Sangeet Natak Akademi, a member of Prayag Sangeet Samiti, a life member of the Audition Board of All India Radio Delhi and Patna. In 1955, he was awarded the 'Gold Medal' by the President. In 1971, he was awarded the "Padma Shri". In 1998, he was honoured with the "Tansen Award" by the Government of Madhya Pradesh.

Chandreshwar Prasad Thakur: CP Thakur, who fought successfully to get rid of Kaalajaar in Bihar, is a well-known politician and doctor of Bihar.

For his success, he was awarded the Padma Shri. Famous books compiled by him are 'Dynamics of Development', 'World Trade Organization', 'Glimpses of Indian Technology, 'Text Book of Medicine' and 'India under Atal Bihari Vajpayee' etc. From 1999 to 2004, he also handled the post of minister at the Centre.

Jagdev Prasad: Jagdev Prasad was born on 2 February, 1922 in Kurhari village of Kurtha block of Arwal district of Bihar. Coming in contact with Socialist Party leader Upendra Nath Verma, he got involved in editing the party's magazine 'Janata'. He started editing the weekly English paper 'Citizen' and Hindi weekly 'Uday' published from Hyderabad in 1955. In 1957, he contested the Lok Sabha elections for the first time from Sasaram Lok Sabha constituency, but he did not succeed. In 1962, he won the election from Kurtha assembly constituency. In 1968, he was made the Minister of Irrigation and Power". On 8 September, 1970, on public demand, he again became the Minister of Irrigation and Power. In 1974. He actively participated in the movement. With his hard labour force and art-skills, he always worked to enrich socialism. He died on 5 September, 1974 in Kurtha Block Complex.

Lalit Narayan Mishra: Lalit Narayan Mishra was born on 2 February, 1923 in Basau-Patuti in Saharsa district. He was elected to the 1st, 2nd and 5th Lok Sabha'. Besides, he was elected to the Rajya Sabha twice. In the central government, he served as the Minister of Planning, Labour and Training, Home, Finance, Defence Production, Foreign Trade and Railways. As the Minister of Trade, he did the work of taking India-Nepal relations to a new height. During this, Indo-Nepal agreement was signed with Nepal for flood control and construction of western canal in Kosi plan. His work of establishing Ashoka Paper Mill and Mithila University, bringing Mithila painting to the world, laying railway network in the Seemanchal areas of North Bihar is unforgettable. He died on 3 January , 1975 due to his injury in a bomb blast on 2 January, 1975 during the inauguration of a large railway line in Samastipur, Bihar, while being the Railway Minister.

Pir Ali: A prominent name of the freedom fighters who represented Bihar in the freedom struggle of 1857 was Pir Ali. The main centre of this movement which lasted from 1828 to 1888 was the city of Patna. Vilayat Ali and Inayat Ali of Patna were the main heroes of this movement. In 1857, this movement was led by Pir Ali. Later, they were hanged publicly by the Britishers from a tree in the Bankipur ground.

Pt. Ramanand Tiwari: He founded the "Bihar Policemen's Association", an organization of soldiers at the entire Bihar level, on 3 April, 1946. Pt. Ramanand Tiwari was a prominent fighter representing Bihar in the freedom struggle. Taking him as the leader of soldiers opposing the government, the English government became their enemy. Firing was carried out on them in Kadamkuan, which is famous as Kadamkuan shooting. On 29 March, 1947, his conversation with Gandhiji for about 18 hours is one of the major events of Bihar. In the memory of Pt. Ramanand Tiwari, a fierce freedom fighter, social worker and always agitating for legitimate demands, the state government organizes a state function every year on the occasion of his birth anniversary on 25 March at the statue site located at the northwest corner of Gandhi Maidan.

Suraj Narayan Singh: Suraj Narayan Singh was born on 7 May, 1906 in Narpati Nagar village of Darbhanga. At the age of 22, he became an active member of the Hindustan Socialist Republican Party. In 1938, he was imprisoned for 27 months for his active contribution to the 'Bakasht Movement' led by Swami Sahajanand Saraswati. During this, he fasted for 20 days in Hazaribagh Jail. JP at Deoli Camp The 33-day fast was broken with Gandhiji's intervention. It took only 6 minutes for Suraj Narayan Singh along with Jaiprakash Narayan, Yogendra Shukla, Gulabchandra Gupta, Ramnandan Mishra and Shaligram Singh to climb the wall of the Central Jail at 9:30 pm on the new moon night of Deepawali (November 8) in 1942. In 1962, he was elected MLA for the first time from Madhubani East assembly constituency. In 1969, he visited Moscow as the representative of India in the May Day celebrations. In connection with the Bangladesh liberation struggle, he travelled to Bangladesh in 1971 and 1972. Raising voice for the cause of labourers on 5 April, 1973 for his brutal injury at the hands of Ranchi Police, he martyred in April 1973.

Mandan Bharati: Mandan Mishra was a famous philosopher of Mithila and a disciple and follower of Kumaril Bhatt. His wife was Mandan Bharti. Supreme bluestocking Bharati, presided over the debate between Shankaracharya and her husband Mandan Mishra, she became a decision-maker and defeated Shankaracharya by arguing with him. This event dates back to 620-710 BC.

Kumaril Bhatt: Acharya Kumaril Bhatt is counted among the great scholars and wise man of Mithila. His period is believed to be between the sixth and ninth centuries. He propounded many sutras related to Nyaya, Mimamsa, Karma and Gyan. The ideas propounded by him on the religion and philosophy are relevant even today.

Udayanacharya: Udayanacharya was born in Kerijan village of Darbhanga district of Mithila region. He was the best and last representative scholar of the ancient tradition of Nyaya philosophy and Vaisheshik philosophy. Learners from far and wide used to visit to get education from Udayanacharya, rich in talent and knowledge. Seven texts composed by him: "Nyaya Appendix", "Kiranbali", "Tatparyaparishuddhi", "Atmatattva Vivek", "Nyayakusumanjali", "Lakshanavali", and "Kusumanjalikarika" have been written in the form of three commentaries and four essays.

Aryabhatt: The famous mathematician, astronomer and inventor of decimal and zero, Aryabhatta is believed to be born in Patna district in 476 AD. He is considered a scholar of Prakrit, Apabhramsa and Sanskrit languages along with Upanishads and philosophical texts. In his treatise 'Aryabhattiyam', he has detailed out the stability of the Sun and the circular earth revolving around it. In the scientific reason of solar eclipse and lunar eclipse, the eclipse isnot caused by the grasping of Sun or Moon by Rahu, but due to the shadows falling on Earth and Moon, the world got its knowledge from Aryabhatta. Information is also available from ancient literary sources about his being the Vice-Chancellor of Nalanda University. The method of writing large numbers in a nutshell with the help of vowels and consonants was propounded by him. For example, to write 432,00,00, he used the word rwyopt. He gave the value of pi to be about 3.1416. It was made known to the world by him that the composition of the earth is made of soil, water, fire and air. According to a mathematician like Smith, Aryabhata died in 550 AD at the age of 74.

Panini: An eminent scholar of grammar, Panini was born in Shalatula, now called Pakistan on the banks of the Indus river in 520 BC probably. With his famed composition 'Ashtadhyayi', he was known to be reputed master of grammar in the language world. The "Aashtadhyayi" is divided into eight parts. It explained nouns, verbs, vowels, consonants, structure of sentences, compound nouns, etc. Besides, due to the introduction of suffixes in words, the information about the creation of new words, from year to year, in which the suffix is added, were also first created to the world by him. Information about the Mauryan government system is also available from 'Aashtadhyayi'.

Yajnavalkya Maharishi: Yagyavalkya Videha was a contemporary of King Janak. In Ramayana, Mahabharata and many Puranas, authentic description is found in detail about him. He studied Rigveda from Bashkal sage, Samaveda from Jaimini sage, Yajurveda from Vaishampayana sage, and Atharvaveda from Aruni sage. One of his famed disciples is named Kanva Rishi, who rendered 'Kanvasangita' and 'Kanvashakha' on Shukla Yajurveda in the presence of Guru.

Guru Gobind Singh: Guru Gobind Singh was the tenth and last Guru of the Sikh Sect. He was born on 22 December, 1662 in Patna Sahib, Bihar. He is popularly known as 'Sarusyadani'. His childhood name was Govind Rai. In childhood he was also called Bala Pritam. He organized the Sikhs to protect the country, religion and freedom and moulded them in the military type environment. He made it mandatory for Sikhs to have "Punch Agreement"–Kesh, Kangha, Kada, Kirpan and Kachha. He resolved to protect his religion, his native land and himself. He was born to his father revered Shri Guru Teg Bahadur and mother Gujri Devi. He was installed as tenth Guru of Sikh Panth on 29 March, 1676. His slogan "Sat Sri Akal" is relevant even today. Khalsa Panth was started by him. After him, he abolished the Guru tradition in the Sikh sect and in its place talked about considering the "Granth Sahib" as the Guru of the Sikhs. He died on 7 October, 1708.

Mahesh Narayan: The contribution of Mahesh Narayan as a journalist in promoting Bihar is unforgettable. He was born in 1859. He started his career through journalism. By making the demand of 'Bihar for Biharis' a national issue, he reported for a magazine called 'Bihar Times', then started editing it. The famous book "Partition of Bengal" or "Separation of Bihar" was authored jointly by him and Satchidanand Sinha on the demand for the separation of Bihar from Bengal. He died in 1907 at a very young age.

Nandkishore Lal: Nandkishore Lal of Tekari of Gaya was born in 1866. Nandkishore Lal Tekari became the principal campaigner of the magazine “Bihar Times” in 1894 with the management of Tekari Raj. After Bihar got the status of a separate state, in 1915, he presided over the conference of Bihar Provincial Congress in Bankipur. He died in 1918.

Parmeshwar Lal: Nandkishore Lal's younger brother Parmeshwar Lal was born in 1874. He came in proximity with Dadabhai Naoroji while pursuing his legal education. With him, he toured the entire London. In the act of the president of the London Indian Society, Dadabhai Naoroji made him its vice-president. After his return to India, as association with the Congress, he participated actively in the promotion of nationalism among Indian masses. He also presided over the Bihari Students' Conference. He died in 1949.

Krishna Sahay: Krishna Sahay was born in 1866 in Sorampur village of Patna district. His elementary education took place at Patna Collegiate School. After advocating, in 1919, he fully supported the commissioner of Patna, Sir Ardle Earl, to establish Patna Law College. Besides advocacy, he pursued separation of Bihar from Bengal with Dr. Satchidanand Sinha. He was elected a member of the Biharotkal Legislative Council in 1913. Between 1919-21 he was nominated as a member of the Lieutenant Governor's Administrative Council. He died suddenly in 1902.

Maulana Mazharul Haque: Mazharul Haque was born on 22 December, 1866, in a village named Bahpura under Maner police station in Patna district. In 1888, he went to England and took Law Degree. There he formed 'Anjuman-e-Islamia' after returning. In 1891, after returning to India the was elected to the post of Munsif of Awadh in 1893. Relinquishing this post in 1896, he was elected as the Vice-Chairman of Chhapra Municipality. In 1906, he founded a party called All India Muslim League with the help of Hasan Imam. Under the Marle Minto Reforms in 1910, he was elected a member of the Central Legislative Council on a reserved seat for Muslims. He was instrumental to form an alliance between the Congress and the Muslim League in the Lucknow session of 1916. He made his major contribution in the "Champaran Satyagraha" of Mahatma Gandhi of 1917. He founded Bihar Vidyapeeth and Sadaqat Ashram. He died in 1930.

Kalavati Devi: "Padmashree" Kalavati Devi was born in Raniganj in Araria district in 1922. Through her hard work in extreme poverty, she created a girls' middle school in Raniganj in 1968 made people aware to educate women and prepared girls to send them school. Kalavati Devi received the honour of "Padma Shri" on 3 April, 1976. She herself gained her graduation at the age of 54 after getting "Padma Shri". She died on 23 November, 1988.

Nandalal Bose: Mahatma Gandhi once said about him, “He is a creative artist and I am not. God has given me the wisdom of art, but has not given me the means to shape it. He has the boon of both”. He was born on 3 December, 1882 in Haveli Kharagpur. With the desire of Jawaharlal Nehru, he got the opportunity to embellish the original copy of the Indian Constitution. He accomplished this distinguished work with the help of Vishwaroop, Gauri, Yamuna, Perumal, Kripal Singh and other students of Kala Bhavan. In the last years of his life, he received “Doctors of Letters”, “The Academy of Fine Arts Silver Jubilee Medal”, “Deshikottam”, “Padma Vibhushan”, “Dada Bhai Naoroji Memorial Prize”. He died on 6 April, 1966.

Laxminarayan Singh: The eminent musician of Panchgachia village under Saharsa district of Bihar, Laxminarayan Singh was a music institute in himself. He was born in 1882 to the landowner Priyatrat Narayan Singh. His paternal grandfather Rudra Narayan Singh was a contemporary of the great saint Laxminath Gosai of Mithilanchal. He was invited as the only member of the jury in the Lucknow music festival of 1928. On this occasion, he was bestowed with the titles of 'Sangeet-Martaad' and 'Sangeetarshi'.

Amarnath Jha: Official scholar of English language and literature, Dr. Jha was also a scholar of Hindi, Maithili, Sanskrit, Bengali and Urdu language literatures. He was born on 25 February, 1897 in Saribas Pahi village of Madhubani district. He passed out his graduation in Allahabad University and M.A. as a topper. Later he started working there as a tutor. At the age of 37, he became the chairman of the Faculty of Arts and was promoted as Vice-Chancellor at the age of 41. In 1953, he was promoted to the chairman of the Bihar Public Service Commission. He edited about two dozen books. His famous books are "Vichardhara" in Hindi, "Occasional Addresses" in English and "Shakespearean Comedy". He was awarded the civilian honour of “Padma Vibhushan". He passed away on 1 January, 1995.

Anandi Prasad Badal: Anandi Prasad Badal was born in 1939 in the village of Shripur in Purnia district. Since the beginning, his interest had been in theatrical acting as well as in preparing scenes and decorating make-ups. He founded the Hindi Natya Kala Parishad in his village. After completing his studies of fine arts in 1959, he started serving as an artist in the State Khadi Board. Till 1968, watercolour, poster colour, medium, tempra etc. were created in traditional painting patterns. Various aspects of women's life were prominently placed on their picture panels by him. 'Shantiprem', Beti Viddai, 'Pratiksha', 'Churiharin', 'Prakriti Kanya' and Blolapan, etc., were often imbibed in his art. In his paintings “Teen Roop Char Aankhen” famed immensely.

Pt. Indra Kishore Mishra 'Mallik': He was born in a famed musician 'Mallick' Bettiah Gharana. He was born on 1 January, 1956 in Chhapra village, Baju, Bettiah. Their family’s hard Riyaz (training) and creative talent have made a special contribution in making the singing pattern of the Bettiah Gharana a high place in the Indian Dhrupad tradition. For his remarkable contribution in the field of Dhrupad singing, he received "Swami Haridas Samman" (Bombay), "Champaran Vibhuti" (Motihari), "Kala Sanskriti Samman" Lucknow, "Charitr Mallick Award' (Govt of Bihar).

Ishwar Chandra Gupta: The birth of this great sculptor Ishwar Chandra Gupta, who illuminated Bihar at the global level in the field of visual arts, was born on 1 June, 1947 in Madhubani. In 1965, Lalit Kalakarini of Uttar Pradesh awarded to his sculpture 'Sita ki Khoj'. For art created out of terracotta medium full of religious narration, and beliefs. In 1967, he was awarded for the Indian Academy of Art, Amritsar and in 1969, the Indian Academy of Arts, New Delhi. In 1974, while honouring his talent, the British Council awarded him a Commonwealth Scholarship. He got fame all over the world due to his portrayal of the soulful folk tales of Mithila district through terracotta medium.

Ishwari Prasad Verma: Patna Kalam Chitra(Pen) pattern skilled painter Ishwari Prasad Verma was born in 1861 in Patna City. In his major works, the face made on ivory was prominent. This face shape made on one to two inch round ivory was especially admired by the English women. He was originally a painter of Patna Kalam style and was well versed in drawing silk ivory and paper.

Kumkum: The great actress Kumkum was born in 1940 in Sheikhpura district. To make her future in films, Zebunnisa went to Bombay in 1952 and became famous in the film city with her new name Kumkum. Her first film was "Mirza Ghalib" directed by Sohrab Modi. Her dance sequence in this film gave her an opportunity to dance in the lead song of the second film "Aarpaar", which pronounced and enhanced her recognition. Her most notable films were "Mr. And Mrs 55', 'Kaagaz Ke Phool', 'Pyaasa', 'Aankhen', 'Geet', 'Mother India' etc. Her last film "Jalte Badan" was released in 1973.

Upendra Maharathi: 'Padmashree' Upendra Maharathi was born in 1908 in Puri district of the state of Orissa. In 1931, he shifted to Bihar after getting a first class diploma in fine arts. In 1956, the Government of Bihar appointed him as 'Assistant Director, Industries'. During this, one of his books, Venushilp, was published. He imparted a new direction to folklore pattern and handicrafts. For his contribution in the upliftment of tribal art and folk art, the Government ofIndia honored him with "Padma Shri" in 1970. He died on 11 February, 1981.

Kumud Sharma: Kumud Sharma was born in 1926 in Patna. His art journey begins with the imitation of the paintings of Patna Kalam and Raja Ravi Varma. His first photo exhibition was held in 1966 at Sridharani Art Gallery, New Delhi. After this, his pictures exhibitions were exhibited in Delhi and Mumbai at every two to three years. He was appointed as the Principal of Ratnavali Vidya Mandir. He wrote children's theatre, radio plays and directed children's plays.

Krishna Kumar Kashyap: The commentator of the Devanagari geometric figure in Mithila painting, Shri Krishna Kumar Kashyap, is one of the personalities to enhance its fame in the world by running its training in the country and abroad. Under the banner of Bhartiya Vikas Manch, their training institutes besides Darbhanga, Samastipur, Madhubani and Sitamarhi, are in Italy, France and Geneva also. His five books on Mithila painting "Mithila Chitra Shiksha" Part-1, Part-2 and Part-3, 'Mithila Aripan' and "Akhar" were highly famed. Respecting his wish, the Government of Bihar has initiated the establishment of Mithila Painting University in Saurath (Madhubani).

Gajendra Narayan Singh: "Padmashree" Pt. Gajendra Narayan Singh was born on 10 September, 1939 on the holy land of Bihar. He authored several books related to the tradition of classical music, including 'Saptak', 'Swarganga', "Bihar Ki Sangeet Parampara" as major ones. In 2007, he was honored with "Padma Shri" and in 2008 "Bihar Ratna".

Jagdamba Devi: Jagdamba Devi was born on 25 February, 1901 in Madhubani district. The first exhibition of her paintings was held at 10 Janpath, New Delhi. The reason for her recognition is the creation of folk paintings with the help of natural colours in Mithila folk pattern. In 1970, she received the National Award for Handicrafts for Folk Painting. In 1975, she was decorated with "Padma Shri". He died on 8 July, 1984.

Jaikant Mishra: Despite being a teacher of English in Allahabad University by profession, Jaikant Mishra made his full contribution to Maithili literature. He has 6 original and 3 edited books in English related to Maithili language. The basis for the systematic study of Maithili literature, 'A History of Maithili Literature' was written by him in 1950. Sahitya Akademi honoured him with 'Bhasha Samman' in 2000.

Pyare Mohan Sahay: Pyare Mohar Sahai was born on 3 May, 1927 in Muzaffarpur. In Patna, he established the Pataliputra Kala Mandir institution. He acted in association with institutions like Delhi Art Theater and Little Theatre Group. He was awarded the 'Kirloskar Award' for his theatrical performance in the last session of the National School of Drama. He made his mark by working in Bhojpuri film 'Kab Hoihe Gabanma Hamar', Hindi film 'Damul'. Among the serials 'Pehla Part' and 'Maila Aanchal' are the major serials starring him.

Mahasundari Devi: One of the world famed people of Mithila folk painting, Mahasundari Devi was born on 6 April, 1922 in Madhubani district. By soaking the thread in black paint and making a blueprint on the paper and after the thread is dropped on the paper with the direct grip of the fingers, wonderful artwork is born. She was proficient in Kohbar writing. She created the Mithila Chitra pattern on the walls of Madhubani station, on the coaches of Jayanti Janata Express train, in the Rajya

Sabha complex of Delhi. In 1982, the Government of India honoured her with the National Award. In 2007, by the Government of Bihar, "Kala Vibhuti Samman" was awarded by the Government of India, "Guru Samman" in 2008 and "Padmashree" in 2011. She breathed her last on 4 July, 2013.

Prabhavati Devi: Known as the Ardhangini of Loknayak Jayaprakash Narayan, is also rich in her independent strong personality. After marriage, while Jayaprakash Narayan went to America for higher education, she came to Sabarmati Ashram in the presence of Gandhiji. In the freedom movement, by opposing illiteracy, child marriage and Purdah system, she did the work of awakening the women society by staying with Kasturba Gandhi. Taking an active part in the fight against dowry, she got more than 600 marriages done without dowry. She died on 5 April, 1973 due to cancer.

Yashoda Devi: Smt. Yashoda Devi, an eminent artist of Mithila folklore pattern, was born on 2 January, 1944 in Madhubani district. She received "State Award" in 1982-83, "Chitragupta Samman" in 1983 and "Vidyapati Award" in 1987. She was also a member of Bihar State Lalit Kala Akademi. She worked as a teacher in Madhubani painting, women's training camp organized by Bihar Education Project. She died of illness on 3 November, 2007.

Yogendra Mishra: Dr. Yogendra Mishra, born in Vaishali, the holy land of Bihar, is an unforgettable historian who has enhanced the identity of the state in Indian historiography. Dr. Mishra was an exceptional student, unique teacher and distinguished head of department of Patna University. About 30 books, 50 research papers, 27 biographies, about 400 radio talks and about 60 historical articles were published by him in various journals. Among his important books are "Ashoka", "The Hindushahis of Afghanistan and Punjab", "University of Odantpuri", "History of Videh", "Vaishali and its Remains", "Khoj of Shwetpur", etc.

Ram Sharan Sharma: A great historian was born in Barauni of Begusarai district on 26 November, 1919. In 1958, he became the chairman of the Department of History at Patna University. In 1973, he became the Professor and Head of the Department of History in the University of Delhi. Among his famous works 'Ancient History of Shudras', 'Role of World History', 'Introduction to Early India', "The Decline of Ancient Cities of India", "Political Ideas and Institutions in Ancient India", "Indian Feudalism" etc. are prominent. Their history writing was a wonderful combination of mythology, archaeology, anthropology, political science and economics. He died on 20 August, 2011.

Dr. Vashisht Narayan Singh: Dr. Vashisht Narayan Singh was born in Basantpur village of Bhojpur district on 2 April, 1942. In 1962, he studied in Netarhat Residential School and topped in the matriculation examination in Bihar. In order to graduate from Patna Science College, a stand alone special examination was organized for him in 1964, to test his talent, by the principal P. Nagendra there. He was awarded a bachelor's degree in mathematics in just 2 years. In those days the famed mathematician of the University of California, Prof. John L. Kelly visited to Patna to meet Narain Singh. Impressed by his talent, Prof. Kelly took him to America. In 1969, he completed his Ph.D. His research thesis are detailed out in Volume 52, Serial 2, of Year 1974 of the Pacific Journal of Mathematics. He also worked for NASA during the "Apollo Campaign". After his return, he worked at Indian Statistical Institute Calcutta (now Kolkata), IIT. Kanpur and Tata Institute of Fundamental Research, Bombay (now Mumbai). Subsequently, he suffered from psychosis and succumbed to it.

Vishwanath Prasad Shahabadi: Vishwanath Prasad Shahabadi was born on January 24, 1912 in Arrah district. He is known as the father of Bhojpuri cinema with the production of his first black-and-white Bhojpuri film "Ganga Maiya Tohe Piyari Chadhaibo" in 1962. His notable films are 'Solho Singaar Kare Dulhania' (Bhojpuri), 'Rutha Na Karo', 'Gangadham', "Geetganga", "Sasural" and "Tulsi Aur Ghar Jamai" (all Hindi). He died on 13 July, 2000.

Vishwabandhu: He was born on 23 November, 1930 in Danapur. He studied the folk dances, folk culture, folk tales and folk traditions of All-India provinces including Bihar. He was actively involved for some time as the main dancer of the Bharatiya Jana Natya Sangh (Ishta), Patna. Under IPTA, he directed folk dance for 17 song sequences on the topic of promotion of Bhojpuri civilization. The dance dramas created by him are 'Megh Malhar', 'Aghan Ke Bhor', 'Hir-Hirni', 'These Villages of India', 'Sama-Chakeva', etc.

Shah Azimabad: He illuminated the name of Bihar in Urdu poetry. He was born in 1846 in Patna. He started writing poetry at the age of 8. His poetry is kept in the list of Urdu poetry. Apart from compiling Ghazals, he was also active in Marsia Nigari, a special form of Urdu. He died in 1927.

Shobhana Narayan: Rewarded with many awards including "Sangeet Natak Akademi Award", "Padma Shri" and "Indira Priyadarshini Award", and "Rajeev Smriti Award", Shobhana Narayan is one of the talented artists of Bihar. During 1968 to 1974, she obtained his graduation and post graduation degrees in physics from Delhi University. After that she joined the civil service. She wrote dozens of books on the style of dance. She has always been projected in front of the world as a very successful administrator, a famous Kathak dancer, an ideal wife, and a loving mother.

Santosh Yadav: Primarily hailing from Haryana was married in Munger District of Bihar. She is the first woman who succeeded twice in mounting Himalayas' Mount Everest in 1992 and 1993. She was conferred Padma Shree in 2000. Bihar Election Commission projected her as Bihar icon in 2015 Bihar Assembly elections and in 2019 Parliament elections.

Sushant Singh Rajput: Basically hailing from Bihar, Sushant Singh registred a notable performance in Mumbai Film Industry. Born on 21 January, 1986, he was counted one among renowned actors. Stemming his career from a TV serial "Kis Desh mein hai Mera Dil", he got due recognition from acting in serial "Pavitra Rishta". He forayed into films with Abhshek Kapoor directed film "Kai Po Che" (2013) and marked a dent of his prowess in acting in his next notable movies like MS Dhoni, The Untold Story, PK, Kedarnath, Soan Chiraiya, Chhichhore. Unfortunatly, this budding actor committed suicide at his residence in Mumbai on 14 June, 2020.

Education, Health and Sports

- Education in Bihar
- Major Museums
- Health
- Sports
- Bihar State Sports Authority

EDUCATION IN BIHAR

Modern Education System

- Higher education in Bihar started with the establishment of Patna College in 1862.
- It was initially affiliated to the Calcutta University.
- Under the leadership of the then former Chief Minister Shri Krishna Singh (also known as Shri Babu), the Bihar government started educational development in the state under the National Education Policy.
- Prior to this, in 1937, the Bihar government headed by Shri Krishna Singh had started the illiteracy eradication program in Bihar.

Number of Higher Educational Institutions

Institute	Number
1. State Government Universities	17
2. Open University	1
3. Central University	4
4. Private State University	6
5. Research Institute	15
6. Institutions of National Importance	5
7. Government College	277
8. Local Government College	588
9. Post Graduate Centre	9
10. Teacher Training Centre	60
11. College of Engineering and Technology	55
12. Polytechnic	61
13. Recognized (college level) centre	28

Source: Education Department, Government of Bihar

- Prior to the year 1976, primary schools in urban areas of Bihar were under municipal corporations, municipalities and notified areas and primary schools in rural areas of Bihar were under Zilla Parishad.
- At present, the Department of Public Education handles the responsibility of education in the state, which is headed by the Principal Secretary.
- The control of both secondary and senior secondary level examinations in the state is under the Bihar School Examination Board (BSEB).
- Bihar Education Project Council was established in the year 1991 for the expansion and promotion of formal education. In this, UNICEF, the Central Government and the State Government had a share in the ratio of 3 : 2 : 1 respectively.
- In the year 1961, Bihar University Service Commission was formed, which is now called Bihar College Service Commission.
- The Bihar State University (Constituent) Service Commission was constituted in the year 1985.
- According to the 2011 census, Bihar ranks last among the states with a literacy rate of 61.8%.

- The male literacy rate in Bihar is 71.2% and the female literacy rate is 51.5%.

Provisional Annual Status of Education Report (ASER) 2024

The provisional Annual Status of Education Report (ASER) 2024, highlighted major trends in enrolment and learning outcomes in rural Bihar. The report showed an 11.9% increase in anganwadi enrolment for 5-year-olds, rising from 36.4% in 2018 to 48.3% in 2024. However, there was an 8.3% decline in govt school enrolment for the same age group. Pre-primary enrolment in govt schools dropped from 0.7% in 2018 to 0.4% in 2024 while private early childhood education (ECE) centres saw a modest increase from 17% to 18.4% over the same period.

The report also observed a decline in overall enrolment for 5-year-olds in both govt and private centres. Govt enrolment decreased from 27.4% in 2018 to 19.1% in 2024 and private enrolment fell from 6.3% to 4.2%. Despite these declines, the percentage of children aged five not enrolled anywhere reduced from 11.5% in 2018 to 8.8% in 2024. Meanwhile, the share of children in govt provisions (pre-school or school) increased from 64.4% in 2018 to 67.8% in 2024.

The findings are based on a survey of 22,778 households in 1,140 villages across Bihar's 38 districts. It covered 51,677 children aged 3-16, including 9,486 in the 3-5 age group, 37,247 in the 6-14 group and 4,944 in the 15-16 group. A total of 39,335 children aged 5-16 were tested for reading skills, 39,149 for arithmetic and 8,688 children aged 14-16 for digital skills.

The report revealed improvements in learning outcomes among children enrolled in govt schools. The percentage of Class III children who could read Class II-level text rose from 12.3% in 2018 to 20.1% in 2024. Similarly, 28.2% of Class III students could do subtraction in 2024, compared to 18% in 2018 and 21.2% in 2022. Among Class V students, 41.2% could read Class II-level text in 2024, up from 37.1% in 2022, and 32.5% could perform division, slightly better than 30% in 2022. For Class VIII students, 71.7% could read Class II-level text and 62% could perform division.

Institutes of National Importance Located in Bihar

Name	Place
Indian Institute of Technology	Patna
National Institute of Technology	Patna
All India Institute of Medical Sciences	Patna
Indian Institute of Management	Bodh Gaya
Bhagalpur Institute of Technology	Bhagalpur
Chanakya National Law University	Patna
Bihar Agricultural University	Bhagalpur

Central University Located in Bihar

Name	Place	Setup
Dr. Rajendra Prasad Central Agricultural University	Pusa Samastipur	1970
Nalanda International University	Nalanda	2013
Central University of South Bihar	Gaya	2015
Mahatma Gandhi Central University	Motihari	2015

State University Located in Bihar

Name	Place	Setup
Patna University	Patna	1917
B. R. Ambedkar Bihar University	Muzaffarpur	1952
Tilka Manjhi University	Bhagalpur	1960
Kameshwar Singh Darbhanga Sanskrit University	Darbhanga	1961
Magadh University	Bodh Gaya	1962
Veer Kunwar Singh University	Ara	1972
Lalit Narayan Mithila University	Darbhanga	1993
Bhupendra Narayan Mandal University	Madhepura	1994
Jaiprakash Narayan University	Chhapra	1995
Nalanda Open University	Bihar Sharif	1995

Maulana Mazharul Haq Arabic-Persian University	Patna	2004
Chanakya National Law University	Patna	2006
Aryabhatta Knowledge University	Patna	2008
Bihar Agricultural University	Bhagalpur	2010
Purnia University	Purnia	2016
Munger University	Munger	2017
Bihar Animal Science University	Patna	2018
Patliputra University	Patna	2018

Private University Located in Bihar

Name	Place	Setup
Amity University	Patna	2017
Sandeep University	Madhubani	2017
Central University	Nalanda	2017
Al-Karim University	Katihar	2018
Dr. C. V. Raman University	Vaishali	2018
Gopal Narayan Singh University	Sasaram	2018
Mata Gujri University	Kishanganj	2019

Centres of Education for Special Category

Education Centre	District
Madarsa Islami Shamshul Huda	Patna
Xavier's Fire Safety Academy	S.K. Puri, Patna
Deaf & Dumb School	Patna
Blind School	Kadamkuan, Patna
Girls School	Lakhisarai, Patna
Bhartiya Nritya Kala Mandir	Patna
Bihar National Language Council	Patna
School of Painting and Sculpture	Patna
Prakrit Jain Shashtra and Ahinsha Shodh Sansthan	Vaishali

Agriculture College in Bihar

Name	Place
Rajendra Agricultural University	Pusa (Samastipur)
Tirhut College of Agriculture	Dholi (Muzaffarpur)
College of Agricultural Engineering	Pusa (Samastipur)
College of Home Science	Pusa (Samastipur)
Basic Science and Humanities College	Pusa (Samastipur)
Bihar Agricultural University	Sebour Bhagalpur
Bihar Veterinary College	Patna
Sanjay Gandhi Institute of Dairy Technology	Patna
Horticulture College	Noorsarai (Nalanda)
Madan Bharati Agriculture College	Agwanpur (Saharsa)
Veer Kunwar Singh Agriculture College	Dumraon (Buxar)
Bhola Paswan Shastri College of Agriculture	Purnia
Dr. Kalam Agriculture College	Kishanganj
Fisheries College	Kishanganj

*Bihar Agricultural College itself is now known as Bihar Agricultural University.

College of Fine Arts

College	Location
Government College of Art and Craft	Patna
Faculty of Fine Art and Craft	Bhagalpur
Bhagalpur University	Bhagalpur

Bihar State Libraries

Name	Establishment Year
Khuda Baksh Library (The Patna Oriental Public Library) Patna	1938
Public Library Purnia	1952
Bhagwan Library, Bhagalpur	1913
Laxmeshwar Public Library, Darbhanga	1919

Srinandan Library, Chhapra	1935
Divisional Library Gaya	1955
Divisional Library, Saharsa	1954

State Specific Library

Name	Establishment Year
Gopal Narayan Library Patna	1912
Shree Sharda Sadan Library, Lalganj (Vaishali)	1914
Great Public Library, Patna	1916
Shree Hindi Library, Sohasarai, Nalanda	1924
Mahant Ramsharan Das Libraries, Samastipur	1939
Gyan Niketan Library, Sitamarhi	1946
Prabhavati Women's Library Patna	1973
Ghatapurak Subsidy Library (Sachchidanand Sinha Library) Patna	1924
Shree Krishna Sewa Sadan, Munger	–

MAJOR MUSEUMS

Museums are not only a repository of cultural heritage, but also perform the task of mental reconstruction. These are such a live centres from where after gaining cultural guidance, understanding their true meaning can be put to good use in new life. The museums in India started with the establishment of India Museum, Calcutta (now Kolkata) in 1814. The first museum in Bihar was established in 1855 with the establishment of the District Central Public Library of Gaya, whose purpose was to preserve the cultural heritage. Following are the major museums of Bihar:

Patna Museum: Patna Museum was duly established in 1917 in the northern part of the Patna High Court. Babu Sharadchandra Rai was appointed its first museum director. Relics and artifacts from antiquity to modern times are collected here. There is a huge storage of Prehistoric materials and pottery with stone, terracotta, metal statues from ancient times to the most modern coins, paintings and other artistic materials.

Chandradhari Museum: With the collection of personal valuable antiquities of Mr. Chandradhari Singh, a Zamindar of Madhubani, the Government of Bihar established a museum in Darbhanga in 1957, which was named as Chandradhari Museum. There are about 6 thousand antiquities and art materials in this museum, including artifacts, coins, paintings as well as metal, wood, clay, ivory objects, various types of beads, manuscripts, ancient weapons, furniture, precious stones, gold materials, Jewellery, clothes, instruments etc. are prominent.

Gaya Museum: Gaya Museum was established in 1952 with the personal collection of Gaya resident Shri Baldev Prasad, which was acquired by the Directorate of Archeology and Museums, Bihar on 4th February, 1970. This museum has an important collection of about 500 antiquities and art materials. Paleolithic antiquities are unique. The Gaya Museum is popular for its collection of Paleolithic and bronze sculptures and other art materials.

Narad Museum, Nawada: In 1974, the Collector of Nawada, Shri N.P Singh established Narada Museum. It was acquired by the Directorate of Archeology and Museums, Bihar on 15th August of the same year. Pala period stone crafts and manuscripts of the 8th to 9th century are stored here.

Babu Kunwar Singh Museum, Jagdishpur: In 1972, a museum was established in the memory of Babu Kunwar Singh by the Government of Bihar in his house. Some pictures, documents and idols made of plaster are stored here. Every year on 23rd April, Vijay Utsav is celebrated as a state festival in this museum.

Bhagalpur Museum: In 1976, the Government of Bihar, in view of the cultural wealth of the Bhagalpur region, established a multi-purpose museum in Bhagalpur. In this museum there is a collection of stone crafts and sculptures.

Maharaja Lakshmeshwar Singh Museum, Darbhanga: Darbhanga Rajdarbar requested the

Government of Bihar to open a museum in the name of Maharaja Laxmeshwar Singh by gifting about 1600 art objects. This museum was established by the Government of Bihar in May, 1989. Here, apart from small and big materials, rare ivory materials are also included.

Ramchandra Shahi Museum, Muzaffarpur: By collecting about 16,000 antiquities and art materials of Shri Vijay Kumar Shahi of Muzaffarpur, the state government established Ramchandra Shahi Museum in the name of his father in 1979. There is a collection of many types of rare art materials here.

Begusarai Museum was established in 1981 by the efforts of Dr. A. Kumar—Principle of G.D. College, and Dr. Piyush Gupta. This museum is known for the collection of Pala period crafts.

Mithila Lalit Sangrahalaya, Saurath (Madhubani): In 1981, this museum was established in 1981. The purpose of establishing this museum is to make Mithila painting and Mithila culture world famous. There are collection of paintings and manuscripts in the museum. Apart from this, Chapra Museum, Deep Narayan Singh Museum, Vaishali, Gandhi Smriti Museum, Bhitiharwa, Jannayak Karpoori Thakur Museum are also prominent in Bihar. Apart from the museums established by the state government, there are also central government museums located in Bihar. In 1917, the Archaeological Museum, Nalanda was established to preserve the material obtained from the excavation. The Bodh Gaya Archaeological Museum was built in the year 1956. Apart from these government museums, there are some non-government museums in Bihar, which are protected by the state government. Among them Gandhi Museum, Patna, Rajendra Smriti Sangrahalaya, Sadaqat Ashram, Patna, Swami Sahajanand Saraswati Museum, Jehanabad, Nagarjuna Museum, Jehanabad are prominent. Among the private museums, the Fort House of Patna City, the Folk Art Museum of Patna, the Art Gallery of Jain Siddhant Bhavan of Arrah, etc. are prominent.

HEALTH

Health is a major component of human development. Therefore, this is an area of priority for the government. For basic health service decentralized at the village level, good health infrastructure, drugs and equipment, skilled and trained medical personnel, there is a need to care and maintenance. In healthcare, besides medical needs, clean drinking water and nutritious food are also essential for a quality life. The healthcare system is divided into two broad categories–preventive and curative. Preventive service includes clean environment, nutritious food, sanitation, toilet facilities, and pure drinking water, while curative service covers all types of medical facilities.

There has been good progress in the health care sector in Bihar in recent years. Life expectancy, especially for women, has improved. Health Service is measured on the basis of several indicators, such as crude birth rate, infant mortality rate, child mortality rate, death rate within five years, neonatal mortality rate, total fertility rate, total fertility rate etc.

The basic healthcare facility in the state is divided into three levels. At the first level, there is an arrangement of Primary Health Centre (PHC), Sub Center and Additional Primary Health Center (APHC). At the second level, at the state level Hospital, and at the block level Community Health Centre (CHC) have been established, while at third level i.e. at top level, intensive care unit in which modern facilities, specialist doctors have been included.

At present, 36 district hospitals, 55 sub-divisional level hospitals, 70 referral hospitals, 533 primary health centers, 9729 sub centers and 350 additional primary health centers are established in the state in 2005 in Bihar. Nine hospitals in the state sub-divisionallevel have been upgraded into hospitals and 130 primary health centers into 30 bedded community health centres. Its main objective is to establish control over maternal and infant mortality. For the diseases prevention, vaccination program is being running in the state, under which T.T. (Anti-tetanus), BCG, OPV, DPT, Pinta and Measles etc. have been included.

Under the National Deworming Programme, Almendazole tablets were provided to 3 crore 46 lakh children of age group 1-19 years. Under the National Urban Health Mission, 73 urban PHC have been started. The Bill & Melinda Gates Foundation has partnered with the Bihar State government to improve health, focusing on maternal, newborn child health, family planning immunization and infections disease control. This collaboration aims to strengthen the state's public health system. Tapovardhan Naturopathy Centre, Bhagalpur Naturopathy has been developed as a Centre. Under the government's 'Saat Nishchay', the to start the Institute of General Nursing and Midwifery (509) in the next five years in 23 districts of the state target is. PPP Hospital, Patna by Global Health Private Limited (Medanta, Gurgaon) Jayaprabha Medanta Super Specialty Hospital has been established in the premises of Jayaprabha.

Integrated Child Development Scheme: This scheme was started in the state on 2 October, 1972, from 3 blocks. According to the 2011 census, the number of children under the age group of 0-6 years is 1.91 crore, that is 8.3 percent of the total population. In this service there is emphasis on the nutrition, immunization, health check-up, referral service, pre-school education and health education of children the age group of 3-6 years. Presently, 38 districts of Bihar a total of 544 ICDS programs are running in the state. A total of 91.6 thousand Anganwadi centers are functioning in the state under the 544 centers.

The Bihar government has launched several healthcare initiatives aimed at improving access to affordable and quality healthcare for its citizens, with a focus on maternal and child health, digital health, and addressing specific health needs. These initiatives include the Mukhyamantri Jan Arogya Yojana (CMJAY), which provides health insurance, and the Mukhya Mantri Digital Health Yojana (MMDHY), which aims to digitize the state's healthcare system. Additionally, the government supports free diagnostic services and free drug services through the National Health Mission (NHM).

Key Healthcare Initiatives:

- **Mukhyamantri Jan Arogya Yojana (CMJAY):** This scheme provides health insurance coverage of up to ₹ 5 lakh per family per year for secondary and tertiary care hospitalizations. It also covers empanelled private hospitals.
- **Mukhya Mantri Digital Health Yojana (MMDHY):** This initiative aims to digitize the state's health system, integrating 13,000+ patient health facilities and enhancing healthcare quality and transparency.
- **National Health Mission (NHM):** The NHM supports various health programs and strengthens the health delivery system, including free diagnostic services (pathology and radiology) and free drug services at hospitals and health centers.
- **Maternal and Child Health Programs:** The government supports programs like Pradhan Mantri Surakshit Matritva Aashwasan (PMSMA), LaQshya (labor room quality improvement), and Janani Suraksha Yojana (JSY) to improve maternal and child health outcomes.
- **Bal Hriday Yojana:** This scheme provides free treatment for children with congenital heart defects.
- **e-Sanjeevani telemedicine:** This initiative uses telemedicine to provide healthcare services, particularly in rural areas.
- **Chief Minister Medical Relief Fund:** This fund provides financial assistance to residents with incomes less than ₹ 2,50,000 for treatment of certain serious ailments in CGHS empanelled hospitals, including those outside Bihar.
- **Bihar Technical Support Program:** This program, a partnership with CARE and the Bill & Melinda Gates Foundation, focuses on reducing maternal, newborn, and child mortality and malnutrition, and improving immunization rates.

Rajiv Gandhi Kishori Sashaktikaran Yojana: (SABLA)

According to the census of 2011 in the state, the number of girls in the age group of 8–11 years is 83 lakhs, which is 16.7 percent of the total population of the state.This scheme was launched in November, 2010 with more focus on out of school girls. Improving the nutritional and health status of the girl child, home skills, life skills and promotion of vocational skills are the major priorities of this scheme. It is a centrally-sponsored scheme. It is being implemented in total 200 districts of the country, out of these, 12 districts of Bihar–Patna, Buxar, Gaya, Aurangabad, Sitamarhi, West Champaran, Vaishali, Saharsa, Kishanganj, Banka, Katihar and Munger districts this scheme implemented. Under this supplementary nutrition, there is a provision to provide (600 kcal) and 18–20 grams of protein daily additionally. In this scheme ratio of expenditure of the central and state governments is 60:40. This scheme for girls out-of-school between 11–14 years and girls between 14 and 18 years and school girls between 14 and 18 years was implemented for 300 days.

Indira Gandhi Matritva Sahyog Yojana (IGMSY)

According to Matritva Sahyog Yojana (NFHS-4), maternal malnutrition and anemia is a major challenge in Bihar. Among pregnant women in the state, 30.4% women suffer from Low Body Weight Index (LBWI) and 60.3% suffer from anaemia. Indira Gandhi Matritva Sahyog Yojana for pregnant and lactating women was launched in October 2010 as a fully centrally sponsored scheme. At present, this scheme is running in two districts of Bihar—Saharsa and Vaishali. Under this scheme, the beneficiaries are provided ₹6,000 per month in two instalment through a bank account.

Supply and Sanitation of Drinking Water

The main reason for the poor health condition in Bihar is the lack of basic facilities like cleanliness of drinking water. According to the 2011 census, only 4.4 percent of the households in the state use tap connection and their 89.6 percent of the households depend on hand pump/tube well/borewell water. A total of 76.9 percent in the state, 31.1 percent households in urban areas and 82.4 percent in rural areas there is a lack of toilets at home. Government of India on 2 October, 2014. The Swachh Bharat Mission (Rural) and the Swachh Bharat Mission (Urban) scheme, according to which the target to construct toilets in all households by the year 2019 has been set. Two major goals have been set by Bihar government in every house; tap water and construction of toilet in every house. There are seven schemes for clean water by the state government out of which three have been started for rural areas and one in urban areas. Under cleanliness programme the Lohia Swachh Bihar Abhiyan in rural areas and toilet construction scheme in urban areas were launched. Under the National Rural Drinking Water Supply Program (NRDWP) launched by the Central Government, by the end of 2022, there is a plan to provide 70 liters of water per family per day to all households in the country.

SPORTS

In 1961, the Bihar State Sports Council was formed for the development of sports in Bihar. Later, on the lines of Sports Authority of India, Bihar State Sports Authority was formed on 31 July, 1986. Cricket, Kabaddi, Football, Lawn Tennis and Hockey are mostly played in the state. Cricket with the Ranji Trophy became popular in Bihar. Football started in Bihar in 1897 with the English Shield. This shield belongs to Patna Athletic Association. Apart from this, chika, ice-paise, gulli-danda, langdi, denga-pani, bora-daga etc. are some regarded games.

Sr. No.	Sports Stadium	Location
1	Rajendra Stadium	Chhapra
2	Secretariat Indoor Stadium	Patna
3	Sanjay Gandhi Mini Stadium	Patna
4	Hazipur Stadium	Hazipur
5	Khudiram Bose Stadium	Muzaffarpur
6	Subramanmium Stadium	Gaya
7	Veer Kunwar Singh Police Stadium	Arrah
8	Moinul Haq Stadium	Patna
9	Jagjivan Ram Stadium	Khagaul
10	Indira Gandhi Stadium	Purnia
11	Mithilesh Stadium	Patna
12	Railway Stadium	Hazipur
13	Post Telegraph Entertainment and Indoor Stadium	Patna

Sports Trophy

Sports	Trophy
Hockey	Cousins Cup, Jaipal Singh Cup
Football	Moinul Haque Trophy, Governor Gold Cup, Ravi Neha Trophy, Anugraha Narayan Shield, Ravi Mehta Trophy, Republic Shield, President's Cup,
Cricket	Hemant Trophy, Randhir Verma Shield

Key Players

Sports	Players
Cricket	Saba Karim, Kirti Azad Tilak Raj, Subrata Banerjee, Ramesh Saxena, Shekhar Sinha, Kavita Rai, Hari Kidwagi, Keshav Prasad, Avinash, Rakesh Shukla, Daljit Singh, Baldev Gosai, Chir Singh, Samar Qadri, Rohit Raj, Vijay Bharti, Vikas Ranjan, Himanshu Hari Rajesh Chauhan
Football	Badri Prasad, P.K. Banerjee Vishaan Chandra Mishra, Awadhesh Kumar Sinha Subodh Kaziwal, Shatrughan Rai, Vijay Kumar, Chandrashekhar Azad, Mevalal, Shyam Sundar, Ravi Ranjan, Lalan Dubey, Rameshwar Lal, Abdul Samad, Abdul Latif, Chandeshar Prasad
Hockey	L. K Minz, James Kerketta, Helen Soya, Yasmani Sanga, Gopal Mangra Jaipal, Singh, Rashi Dulari, Amla Gudiya, Amrit Lakda, Pushpa Topno , Subare Sanga, Anmol Kide, S. Dungdung, Sushila Topno, Priyanka Kumari, Vishwasi, Ajitesh Roy, Anand Kumar Bara

Shooting	Jagarnath Mishra, Jaganath Singh, KK Jha, Pranav Sinha, Shekhar Bhagat, S K Rai Chaudhary
Chess	Anjana Jha Yogendra Prasad Srivastava, BK Srivastava, Barugiz Kasi Vishal Sarin Pathu Ramani, Divyendu Barua, Sanjeev Kumar, Dolan Bampa Bose, Saurabh Anand, Sanjeev Kumar Neha Singh
Tennis	Dinesh Mohan Chandrabhushan Bimude, Neesha Sen, Surendra Kumar, Khosu Sen, Shailya Kumar Upadhyay
Badminton	Ali Akbar, Sarojini, Kaveri Ghosh, Chittaranjan Sinha, Bagu Chatterjee, Raj Kumar Mishra, Mohan Ahuja
Baseball	Sunil Singh, Ajay Tiwari, Sudhanshu Shekhar, Smita Pal, Ehsan Ahmed
Taekwondo	Satyajit Shakta, Shalini Srivastava
Billiards	Kumar Adhanand Sinha, Kumar Taranand Sinha, Kumar Shyamanand Sinha
Carom	Rashmi Kumari, Bhajan Prakash, Neeraj Kumar, Mamta Kumari, Jai Prakash, Mo. Akib
Karate	Nand D. Prasad, Pinky Srivastava, Ananya Anand, Akash Kumar, Sudama Kumar Yadav Pooja Kumari, Saurabh
Athletics	Saroj Lakra, Jagraj Singh, Samitra Savaiya, Shivnath Singh, Jamil Ansari, Pushpa Ekka, Arvind Panna, Ompal Singh, Ajmer Singh, Iqbal Singh, Balwinder Singh, Bahadur Singh, Mercy Kuttan, Amitabh Rai, Shivnath Singh
Softball	Prachi Sharma, Vipin Kumar, Aditya Kumar, Akashdeep, Isha Archana, Farhad
Archery	Rajivar Guiyan, Purnima Mahato, Nirmal Kumar Singh, Pooja Kumari, Sapna Kumari
Pole Vault	Sundar Singh Tanwar, Chetna Solanki
Basketball	Rajesh Srivastava, Sunil Kumar Panda, Muskan Singh, G, Satya Saravati, Neeraj Kumar
Weightlifting	Budhva Urnva, Indrajit Singh, Ratan Kumar Basak
Table Tennis	Sanjeev Shankar, Anjali Jha Abhraneel Bhattacharya, Somnath Roy Shweta Kumari, Sagar Das, Ramneek Ratan, Pushkar Verma

BIHAR STATE SPORTS AUTHORITY

Bihar State Sports Authority has been established for the all-round development and propagation of sports under the state of Bihar state. It is headquartered in Patna. The Chief Minister of Bihar will be the ex-officio chairman of this authority. Besides, a Vice President, Commissioner-cum-Secretary, Department of Youth Affairs, Sports and Culture, Director, Students and Youth Welfare Department will be ex-officio members. Its members include 5 members of parliament/legislature members nominated by the state government (of which at least one shall be from the tribal areas), 7 sports promoters nominated by the state government/relating to sports development persons having knowledge of matters, representative of the Bihar Olympic Association and three outstanding sports persons (of which at least one shall be female) nominated by the State Government. The presidents of the Students Welfare Association of two universities of the state nominated by State Government on the rotation basic for one years. The principal of two Sports Training Centers nominated by state, two journalists nominated by the state government, seven representative of recognized state level sports federations nominated by the state government by rotation for one year will be included. The Secretary of this Authority shall be its ex-officio member.

Authority goals

1. To prepare and implement schemes for the development, promotion and progress of sports in the state in the light of the policy of the central government and the state government.
2. To continue and execution of plans handed over the for the improvement of sports, promotion and development by the Government of India, State Government, India Sports Authority and other bodies from time to time.
3. To establish new institutions and to run, manage and operate new and already existing institutions.
4. To advise the State Government in matters relating to the development of sports in the state.
5. To act as a medium between the state government and various state level sports institutions.
6. Organizing, sponsoring and sports competitions, training camps, exhibition matches and other sports activities by managing itself and to provide facilities and financial assistance to other institutions for such works.
7. To make arrangements for the promotion of sports activities in the rural areas of the state and to provide financial assistance and to organize competitions.
8. To make arrangements for education, training and facilities for attainment of higher level in various sports.
9. To plan, develop, construct, acquire and manage swimming pools, sports facilities, ancillary buildings, sports grounds, stadiums, sports infrastructure, etc. in the State, maintain and use, to provide other government and non-government organizations for achieving the corresponding objectives, facilities and financial assistance.
10. To control, develop and maintain Moinul Haque Stadium, Rajendranagar, Patna.
11. To implement the schemes when entrusted with the administration of the schemes, being run or proposed by the state government for the promotion and advancement of sports.
12. To establish sports centers in convenient places in the state for the development of sports.
13. To provide technical assistance to the organizers for the organization and conduct of International/National and state level tournaments, other assistance and to provide sports equipment, sports facilities and guidance from experts.
14. To take steps for the welfare of sportspersons, sports functionaries and such other persons and activate, prepare and implement schemes beneficial for retired sports persons and officials (including coaches).
15. To honour the sportspersons who have demonstrated exceptional talent in sports and to provide financial assistance and other facilities.
16. Organizing seminars/conferences etc. on sports and its related subjects.
17. To purchase or acquire ownership or lease or rent of movable and immovable assets and to sell, mortgage, transfer or other dispose of any such movable and immovable assets, provided that before every action is taken in such immovable assets it will be necessary to obtain the permission of the State Government.
18. To take all such actions and acts as which the authority consider necessary for attainment and for expansion any of the above objectives.

❑❑❑

Location and Relief

- **Geographical Location**
- **Geographical Structure and Relief**
- **Geographical Region**

GEOGRAPHICAL LOCATION

Bihar is a state of Eastern India located in the middle plains of the Ganges. The present form of Bihar came into existence after the separation of Jharkhand on 15 November, 2000. The area of present-day Bihar with a rectangular shape is 94,163 square kilometers (36,357 sq mi). It is 2.86 percent of the total area of India. Bihar is the 13th largest state of India in terms of area. According to the Census of 2011, the population of Bihar is 0,31,04,637. It is the third most populated state in the country. The geographical extent of Bihar lies between 24° 21' 10" to 27° 31' 15" north latitude and 83° 19' 50" to 88° 17' 40" east longitude. In this way, the latitudinal extension of Bihar is between about 30° and the longitudinal extent of about 5°. The length of Bihar from north to south is 345 km and width from east to west is 483 km.

Map: District Administrative Units of Bihar

Nepal is located on the northern border of Bihar, which determines the international border. The 7 districts of Bihar touching Nepal are West Champaran, East Champaran, Sitamarhi, Madhubani, Supaul, Araria, and Kishanganj. West Bengal is situated on the eastern border of Bihar, touching 3 districts of Bihar namely Kishanganj, Purnia, and Katihar. Jharkhand is situated on the southern border of Bihar, touching with 7 districts of Bihar are Bhagalpur, Banka, Jamui, Nawada, Gaya, Aurangabad, and Rohtas. Uttar Pradesh is situated on the western border of Bihar, touching with 8 districts of Bihar are Rohtas, Kaimur, Buxar, Bhojpur, Saran, Siwan, Gopalganj and West Champaran.

Bihar: The 13 districts of Bihar state neither determine the international border nor touch with any state. Out of all the 38 districts of Bihar, the largest district in terms of area is West Champaran and the smallest district is Sheikhpura. Gaya and Jamui districts are situated in the southernmost part of the state and West Champaran district is situated in the north. The border of Bihar starts from Kaimur district in the west and extends till Kishanganj in the east. The entire state is situated north of the Tropic of Cancer.

GEOGRAPHICAL STRUCTURE AND RELIEF

Structure

Rocks are found from a structural point in the state of precambrian aeon to quaternary. Rocks of the Precambrian era are found in the southern plateau of Bihar in the form of the Dharwar Formation and the Vindhyan Formation. The oldest rocks of the southern plateau are part of the Gondwana Land, the southern part of the Greater Pangea continent. The formation of the northern mountainous region has occurred in the last alpine rock formation. From the geological point of view, this time is the period of Mesozoic. The Intermediate Gangetic Plain was formed in the fourth epoch (Pleistocene). Its construction continues even today and this new structure is expanding on the largest area of the state. In this way, the massive impact of the structure on the relief of Bihar is visible.

On the basis of geological structure, four types of rocks are found in Bihar-

- Dharwad Rock
- Vindhya Rocks
- Tertiary Rocks
- Quaternary Rocks

1. Dharwad rock: The Dharwad rock of pre-Cambrian era is found in the Kharagpur Hills, Jamui, Bihar Sharif, Nawada, Rajgir, Bodh Gaya etc. areas of Munger district in the south-eastern part of Bihar. The hills found in these areas are part of the Chotanagpur plateau. At the time of the formation of the Himalaya Mountains, it was affected by the pressure force during the Mesozoic period, which led to the formation of many submerged valleys. Later, due to the deposition of alluvium, these hills got separated from the main plateau. Rocks like slate, quartzite and phyllite are found in the Dharwad rock sequence. These are basically igneous type of rocks, which have been transformed due to the effect of extreme pressure and heat over a long period of time. The deposits of mica are found in these rocks.

2. Vindhya Rock: The Vindhya Rock was formed in the Pre-Cambrian era. This rock is found in the south-western part of Bihar. It extends north of the Son River into Rohtas and Kaimur districts. Alluvial deposits are found on top of these rocks in the Son valley. Rocks of Kaimur order and Simri order are found in this. Pyrite mineral is found in these rocks, from which sulphur is released. These fossilized rocks include limestone, dolomite, sandstone and quartzite rocks. These rocks are almost horizontal. The abundance of fossils in the rocks proves that it has been an area of marine deposition in the past. Evidence of volcanic formation is also found in the Nabinagar area of Aurangabad district. The depth of the alluvium in this plain ranges from 00 m to 900 m and the maximum depth is up to 6000 m. The deepest alluvial deposits are found around Patna.

3. Tertiary rock: Tertiary rock is found in the Shivalik range in the southern range of the Himalayas. Its formation is related to the Miocene and Pliocene geological periods of the Mesozoic era, which are related to the second and third uplift of the Himalayan Mountains. Sandstone and boulder clay rocks are found in this range. Conglomerate rock predominates in the lower part. Because of the formation of the Tethys Sea depression, petroleum and natural gas are stored in it.

4. Quaternary rock: Quaternary rock is found in the form of a layered rock in the Gangetic plain, whose construction work is going on even today. The Gangetic plain is the remnant of the Tethys Sea formed by the deposition of sediments by the Ganges and its tributaries. The Himalaya Mountains have also been formed by the compression force on the debris of the Tethys Sea. At the time when the Himalayas were being formed by the force of compression, at the same time a huge trough was formed in the south of the Himalayas. In this trough, the deposition of sediments started from the plateau part of the Gondwana land and the rivers originating from the Himalayas, due to which the huge trough assumed the form of a plain.

The plain is made up of rocks made of alluvial, sand-gravel-stone and conglomerate. It is a very gently sloping plain, in which the depth of the alluvium is not the same everywhere. The depth of the alluvium this plain ranges from 100 m to 900 m and the maximum depth is up to 6000 m. The deepest alluvial deposits are found around Patna.

Relief (Physical Characteristics)

Various types of variations are found in the relief of Bihar. All types of landforms e.g., hills, plateaus and plains are found in Bihar. Although most of the terrain is plain, the Shivalik ranges in the north and the narrow plateau region in the south produce geomorphological diversity. The average elevation of Bihar is 473 ft (53 m) above sea level. On the basis of physical structure and study facilities, Bihar has been divided into three physical (natural) regions:

1. Shivalik Mountainous Region and Lowland Region of the North

- The **Shivalik mountainous region** of the north and the low land region of the north is an extension of the Shivalik range of the Himalaya Mountains on the northern boundary of West Champaran (Northwest Bihar). The Shivalik range covers an area of 932 square kilometres. The average height of this mountain range ranges from 80 m to 250 m. It has been eroded at many places by the rivers originating from the Himalayas. This Shivalik hill region has been divided into three sub-divisions:

1. Ramnagar Doon hill,
2. Harha Valley or Doon Valley,
3. Someshwar Range

(i) **Ramnagar Doon hills:** Ramnagar Doon located in the south of Someshwar range is 32 km long and 8 km wide. The highest part of this hill is Santpur, which has a height of 242 m.

(ii) **Harha Valley or Doon Valley:** Harha Valley or Doon Valley is a narrow longitudinal valley, between Ramnagar Doon and Someshwar Range. The length of this valley is 21 kilometers and the area is 214 square kilometres.

(iii) **Someshwar range:** The third part of the Someshwar range Shivalik hill is the Someshwar hill, which is spread over an area of about 784 square kilometers and whose top part separates Bihar from Nepal.

The length of this range extending from Triveni Canal to Bhikhna Thori Pass is 70 km. It is due to the fast flow of rivers, many passes have been formed in this range, in which Someshwara Pass, Bhikhna Thori Pass, Marwat Pass, etc. are prominent. These passes provide the route of traffic between Bihar and Nepal. The Someshwar range is the highest point of Bihar. Top peak is situated in Someshwar Fort, whose height is 880 meters.

- **Low land region:** Low land region is found in the northern part of the Ganges plain and in the southern part parallel to the Shivalik range. Low land region is found on the north-west and north-eastern border of the state. Due to high rainfall (from 50 cm to 200 cm) in this region, dense forest and marshy area has developed. The North-eastern Low land region is spread over Purnia, Araria, and Kishanganj districts. It is the highest rainfall receiving region of Bihar.

2. Gangetic Plain

The area of the Ganges Plain is 90,650 square kilometers, which is 96.27 percent of the total area of Bihar. This plain extends from the Shivalik range in the north to the Chotanagpur plateau in the south. From a geological point of view, this plain is Agragbhir (Foredeep). The average elevation of this plain ranges from 75 to 120 meters above sea level. The field is determined by the contour line of 150 meters. A contour line is a line drawn by joining places of equal elevation above sea level. The slope of this plain is from west to east. This gradient is very slow (5-6 cm per kilometer). This plain is wider in the west, while its width decreases towards the east. These passes provide the route of traffic between Bihar and Nepal. In the Someshwar range, the highest peak of Bihar, Someshwar Fort is situated, whose height is 880 meters. The plain of Bihar is divided into two parts by the Ganges river: (1) the northern Ganges plain, (2) the southern Ganges plain.

North Gangetic Plain: The area of the North Ganges Plain is 56,980 square kilometres. This plain is formed from the sediments deposited by the Ganges and its northern tributaries: Ghagara, Gandak, Budhi Gandak, Kosi, Mahananda, etc. The slope of this plain is from northwest to southeast. This plain is divided by rivers into several doab regions. The area situated between two rivers is called Doab region. The Ghaghra-Gandak Doab, Kosi-Gandak Doab, Kosi-Mahananda Doab are prominent regions. The northern Gangetic plain extends into West Champaran, East Champaran, Siwan, Gopalganj, Sitamarhi, Madhubani, Saran, Muzaffarpur, Darbhanga, Purnia, Saharsa, and Bhagalpur districts. In this plain, the abandoned and eroded Gokhur Lake and Chaur have been formed by the rivers. Regional variations are found in the northern Ganga plain due to the formation process. On the basis of this regional variation, the northern Gangetic plain has been divided into several sub-divisions.

(i) Sub-low land region (Bhabar region),

(ii) Bangar

(iii) Khadar

(iv) Chaur (Mann).

(i) Sub-low land region (Bhabar region): The sub- Low land or Bhabar region extends from west to east in the south of the Low land region. It is spread as a narrow belt of 40 km wide in 7 districts of North Bihar, West Champaran, East Champaran, Sitamarhi, Madhubani, Supaul, Araria and Kishanganj. In this, region. pebbles and sand are found.

(ii) Bangar: Bangar area is an area of old alluvial deposit, where flood water does not reach every year. This region is spread the south of the Bhabar region. Its expansion is mainly found in the north-western plains of Bihar.

(iii) Khadar: Khadar area is the deposition area of new alluvium, where flood waters spread every year. New soil is deposited every year due to floods, due to which the fertility of the soil is maintained. The Khadar region extends from the Gandak river in the west to the Kosi river in the east in the northern and north-eastern plains.

(iv) Chaur: Chaur (mana) is a naturally submerged lowland area in the northern Gangetic plain, which is called chaur or mana. The prime examples of Chaur are Lakhni chaur of West Champaran, Bahadurpur and Sunderpur Chaur of East Champaran, etc.

Chaur or Mana is basically Gokhur Lake, which has been formed due to the diversion of rivers. These are the main sources of fresh and deep water. Examples of prominent chaurs are Tetaria chaur of East Champaran, Madhopur chaur, Pipra chaur of West Champaran, Simri chaur, Saraiya chaur etc. The southern Gangetic plain is the extension of the southern Gangetic plain between the marginal plateau region to the south and the Ganges river. The total area of this plain is 33,670 square kilometer. The slope of the field is from south to north. This plain is formed by the deposits of rivers flowing through the plateau region.

Southern Gangetic plain: The extension of the Southern Ganges Plain lies between the marginal platean region to the south and the Ganges River. The total area of this ground is 33,670 sq. km. The slope of this plain is from south to north. This plain is formed by the deposits of rivers flowing through the plateau region. The width of the southern plain decreases from west to east. The reason for the decrease in width in the eastern part is the construction of a natural dam (dam) by the river Ganges. Patna metropolis is a city situated on the natural dam.Since the height of the natural dam (dam) is higher than the surrounding land, most of the rivers of southern Bihar flow parallel to the Ganges, not fall into the river directly. This type of flow system is called 'Pinet flow system'. Among these rivers are Punpun, Kiul, Phalgu etc. The Phalgu river terminates at the Tal region before it joins the Ganges. These rivers flow through the plateau region, hence the predominance of sand is found wetland. The submerged lowland area is found in the southern part of the natural dam, which is called Tala or Jalla area. This tala area is spread over a width of 25 km from Patna to Mokama. The examples of major wetlands are Barhiya Tala, Mokama Tala, Singhol Tala, Mor Tala, etc.

3. Southern Plateau Region: The southern plateau region is the frontier of the Chotanagpur plateau. Igneous and metamorphic rocks like granite and gneiss are found in abundance in this region. This plateau region extends from Kaimur in the west to Munger and Banka in the east. This is the oldest land area of Bihar, which includes the Kaimur or Rohtas plateau, the southern part of Gaya, the Giriyak hills, the hills of Nawada, Banka, and Munger, Kaimur or Rohtas Plateau.

(i) **The Kaimur or Rohtas plateau** is the eastern part of the Vindhya range. Its extension is 483 km in length and maximum 80 km in width starting from Jabalpur (Madhya Pradesh) to Rohtas (Bihar). The surface of the Kaimur plateau is eroded and rough. The average elevation of this plateau is between 300-450 meters. The highest part of this plateau is Rohtasgarh, whose height is 495 meters. This plateau is separated from the Chotanagpur plateau by the Son river. Sandstone is found in abundance in this plateau.

(ii) **The hilly region of Gaya** has several hill ranges found in Gaya, Aurangabad and Nawada districts. These hills are widespread in the plains. Among them the hills of Jethiyan, Hindaj, and the hills of Haldia are prominent. Ramshila, Pretshila, Bhutshila, Katari, Brahmayoni hills are situated in the vicinity of Gaya city. In this sequence, the hills of Barabar and Nagarjuni are situated on the border of Jehanabad and Gaya districts.

(iii) **Rajgir-Giriyak** Hill Area is mainly located in Nalanda district. It is basically an extension of the hill range of Gaya. Among these hills, Vaibhavgiri, Sonagiri, Vipulgiri, Ratnagiri, Udayagiri and Pir Ki Hills are prominent. The highest of these hills is Vaibhavgiri, whose height is 380 meters above sea level. The metamorphic rock in these hills is dominent in quartzite and slate.

(iv) **The Nawada-Munger** hill sequence starts from Nawada district in the south and extends to the Ganges river in the north, where many hill ranges are located, in which Kharagpur hill, Gidheshwar hill, Sat hill, Sheikhpura hill, Chakai Pahari, Bakia hill are the main ones. Kharagpur hill extends from Munger to Jamui. It is triangular in shape and has a predominance of quartzite rock.

GEOGRAPHICAL REGION

On the basis of the geographical area structure and the variation of relief, Bihar has been divided into three major physical divisions, (i) the Shivalik hill region, (ii) the Gangetic plain and (iii) the Chotanagpur marginal plateau region. Natural diversity, disparity in relief, heterogeneity of land, diversity of soil and vegetation is the basis of detailed field study of Bihar. Geographical region is determined by obtaining complete information of a wide area on the basis of homogeneity. In this direction, many scholars have tried to divide Bihar into many geographical regions. Geographical region is a region where there is uniformity in physical and socio-cultural elements like climate, soil, vegetation, land use pattern, cropping pattern, type of settlement etc. On the basis of equality of natural and socio-cultural elements, Prof. Inayat Ahmed and Prof. Ram Pravesh Singh has divided Bihar into 10 geographical regions:

1. Low land region
2. Ghaghra-Gandak doab

3. Gandak-Kosi doab
4. Kosi-Mahananda doab
5. Karmanasha-Son doab
6. Son-Kiul doab
7. East-central Bihar plain
8. Ganga Diara region
9. Kaimur plateau
10. Mica region

1. Low land region: This region is situated in the north-western and north-eastern part of the northern plain of the Ganges. The land is not cultivable due to annual rainfall of more than 40 cms on the Someshwar range of Shivalik and Ramnagar Doon hills in the northwest. Along with traditional methods, agriculture is done using new technology. Purnia, Araria, and Kishanganj are in the Northeastern low land region. This region is the rainiest region in Bihar. Annual rainfall is up to 200 cm here. There is good land for agriculture, in which good production of paddy, jute and sugarcane is done. As a result of excessive rainfall, this region is an area of marshy and dense forest. Due to the rough land, scattered settlements are found more in this region. The north-eastern low land region is in Purnia, Araria and Kishanganj. This region is the rainiest region in Bihar. Annual rainfall is up to 200 cm here.

2. Ghaghra-Gandak Doab: This region is a plain area with 20 cm annual rainfall. This region spread over Saran, Siwan and Gopalganj districts is a flat alluvial plain. Paddy, maize, wheat, sugarcane, oilseeds and pulses are grown here. This region, which is rich in agriculture, also has industries related to agriculture. Because of the high production of sugarcane, the sugar industry has developed more in this region. The main centers of sugar industry are Gopalganj, Chhapra, Siwan, Mirganj, Mehraura, etc.

3. Gandak-Kosi Doab: Districts in this region are East Champaran, West Champaran, Sitamarhi, Sheohar, Darbhanga, Muzaffarpur, Vaishali, Madhubani, Begusarai, etc. There is a plethora of industries in this region. Sugar industry and fruit processing industry are the major industries here. Darbhanga is famous for mango; Muzaffarpur for litchi; Hajipur for banana plantation. The main crops of this region are paddy, maize, sugarcane, wheat, barley, pulses, oilseeds, etc. Sugarcane, tobacco and red chillies are the main cash crops here. The centers of sugar industry are Chanpatia, Sugauli, Samastipur, Motihari, Bagaha, etc. Barauni is the most famous industrial town of this state. Fertilizer factory, oil refinery, and thermal power station are located here. Milk industry has developed in Barauni and Muzaffarpur.

4. The Kosi-Mahananda Doab: It consists of Purnia, Araria, Kishanganj, Madhepura, Khagaria and Saharsa districts. This state being a flood affected area, is a backward area from the point of view of agriculture, industry and transport etc. It receives excessive rainfall, due to which the Kosi and its tributaries bring floods every year. Although agriculture is done here, the future of agriculture is not certain due to the possibility of floods. The government has made efforts to control the flood situation through the Kosi project.

5. Karmanasha-Son Doab: Bhojpur, Rohtas, Kaimur and Buxar districts come in this region. It is an area with less rainfall from the climatic point of view, but a systematic canal system has been developed by making a barrage on the Son river. There is a good system of irrigation through canals in this region. Most of the rural population here is based on agriculture. Paddy is the main crop here. Other crops include wheat, pulses, oilseeds, and potatoes. The region has immense potential for agro-based industries. Rice mill has been the most developed in this state.

6. Son-Kiul Doab: This doab region, situated in the plain of South Bihar, is an area of low rainfall, where drought conditions often arise. Patna, Jehanabad, Gaya, Nalanda, Aurangabad, Arwal, Lakhisarai and Nawada districts come in this state. Arwal and Auringabad are irrigated by the Eastern Son canal system. Paddy, Wheat, Gram, Lentil, Khesari etc. are the major crops here. Silk textile industry has developed in Bihar Sharif and Obra in this region, handloom industry and rug industry has developed in Manpur of Gaya. Cement industry and edible oil industry have been established in Aurangabad.

7. The plain of east-central Bihar: It consists of Munger, Banka and Bhagalpur districts in this region. There has been little development in some of these areas. This region is backward in terms of agriculture and industry. Paddy, oilseeds and pulses are the main crops here. Proper irrigation facilities are not available in this region. Irrigation facility has been developed by constructing a reservoir on Chandan, Kiul and Barua rivers. Gun, tobacco and milk industries have developed in Munger and silk industry has developed in Bhagalpur.

8. Ganga Diara region: This area is affected by floods every year and the land which is visible after the flood is called Diara region. This is an area of new alluvium. Here the farmers cultivate with the help of temporary settlements (scattered settlements). Grass-'Houses made of thatch and bamboo are removed before the floods hit. The region is famous for the production of Rabi crops and vegetables. Every year a new diara area is created in floods.

9. Kaimur Plateau: Extends into the Kaimur and Rohtas districts of Southwest Bihar. This plateau is a part of Vindhya Mountains. This plateau region is about 350 meters high. Its area is 200 square kilometers. The main crops here are paddy, wheat, barley etc. Being a hilly area, stone-based industries have developed here. Pyrites and phosphates are found in the Kaimur plateau. Pyrite based sulphur industry is established in Amjhore, and limestone based cement industry in Banjari.

10. Mica region: This is mainly the mica belt of Koderma district of Jharkhand, which extends to the areas of the plateau regions of Bihar – Jhajha, Jamui, Gaya, and Nawada. Here mica is found in mixed form in Balthar soil. Wood, tasar (silk) and lacquer are produced in this region. Paddy, pulses and oilseeds are produced in agriculture. In this way the entire surface form of Bihar has been divided into the above ten parts. On the basis of homogeneity, some areas are clustered and developed while some areas are very backward. This is natural due to the variation of land, but this difference can be reduced to a great extent by human labour and technology.

Drainage System

- Rivers
- Waterfalls
- Wetland Area
- Hot Water Reservoirs (Springs)
- Lakes

RIVERS

The runoff system refers to a river system, which is formed by surface streams, rivers, lakes etc. by following a particular slope. The basis of the drainage system of Bihar is the river Ganges. The flow of the Ganges and its tributaries has played an important role in the development of the landform of Bihar. About 90 percent of the landform of Bihar has been developed by the drainage of rivers.

The average annual rainfall in Bihar is 1009 millimeters (109 cm), due to which the state has a network of rivers flowing throughout the year. On the basis of the flow system and origin, the rivers of Bihar have been divided into two categories:

(i) Rivers of Himalayan region,

(ii) Rivers of plateau or peninsular region.

The rivers of the above two categories join the main river Ganges. The rivers of the Himalayan region, which originate from the Himalayas and flow into the northern Bihar plain, form a parallel and circular flow system in the northern plain and changes its path. These rivers are moving from east to west. The root cause of this transfer is the rotational speed of the Earth, due to which erosion is more on the west coast. The most famous river for diversion is Kosi.

From the geographical point of view, the state has been divided into seven river zones:

1. Ghaghra-Gandak
2. Gandak-Bagmati
3. Bagmati-Kosi
4. Kosi-Mahananda
5. Karmanasha-Sone
6. Sone-Punpun
7. Punpun-Sakri

River Ganges: River Ganges of Bihar, in the central part flows from west to east. India's longest river Ganga has a total length of 2500 km, of which 445 km flows in Bihar. The flow area of this river in Bihar is 15165 square kilometers. Its origin is the Gomukh of the Gangotri glacier, located north of the Kedarnath peak of Uttarakhand. This river enters from Uttar Pradesh near Chausa in Buxar district of Bihar. The Ganges, Gandak, Saryu (Ghaghra) and Karmanasha rivers determine the boundary line of Bihar and Uttar Pradesh in this region. In this river from the north (on the left bank) the Ghaghra, Gandak, Bagmati, Balan, Budhi Gandak, Kosi, Mahananda and Kamala rivers meet from the south (on the right bank) the rivers Son, Karmanasha, Punpun, Kiul etc. First of the major rivers, Sone river in Bihar region, 10 km to west of Danapur near Maner meet in Ganga. The Ganges river enters Bengal forming a boundary line with the Sahebganj district of Bihar and Jharkhand. Ganga flows in the course of its journey in the districts of Buxar, Bhojpur, Saran, Patna, Vaishali, Samastipur, Begusarai, Khagaria, Munger, Bhagalpur, Katihar, etc.

Ghaghra (Saryu River): The origin of the Ghaghra River, which flows mainly in Uttar Pradesh, is Namya in Nepal. Its length is 83 kilometers in Bihar. It determines the boundary of Bihar and Uttar Pradesh. This river joins the Ganges near Chhapra in Saran district. It is also known as Lakhandei and Karnali in the upper reaches.

Gandak: The Gandak river is formed by the union of seven streams. Known by many names like Saptagandaki, Kaligandak, Narayani, Shaligrami, Sadanira etc., the river Gandak originated from the middle of Manangmot and Kutang (border of Nepal and Tibet) of Annapurna range of Nepal. Its total length in Bihar is 630 km. The Gandak crosses the Annapurna Range in Nepal to form a gorge. This river enters Bihar near Bhesalotan (West Champaran). Barrage has been constructed at Valmiki Nagar in West Champaran district. This river, setting the boundary of Saran and Muzaffarpur, passes between Sonpur and Hajipur and joins the Ganges in front of Patna. The world famous Harihar Kshetra fair (Sonpur cattle fair) is held every year at this confluence. This river is known as Gandak Narayani or Gandaki in Nepal.

The Burhi Gandak: This river divides the northern Bihar plain into two parts. It is the longest river of North Bihar originating from the Himalayas and flowing into North Bihar. It originated from Chatarwa Chaur near Vishambharpur of Someshwar range. It is the fastest river of North Bihar, whose flow is from northwest to southeast. It is an abandoned stream of the Gandak river, which has flown due to the westward displacement of the main river. The cities of Muzaffarpur, Samastipur, Khagaria, etc. are situated on the banks of Burhi Gandak. Other tributaries of Burhi Gandak are Danda, Pandai, Masan, Kohra, Balor, Sikta, Tiur, Tilawe, Dhanauti, Anjankote, etc.

Bagmati River: This is the major tributary of the Budhi Gandak. Bagmati originated from the Mahabharata range in Nepal. This river flows in Darbhanga, Muzaffarpur and Madhubani districts. The major tributaries of Bagmati are Lal Vakaiya, Murengi, Lakhandei, Adhbara, Sipridhar, Kola, Choti Bagmati, etc.

Kamala: This river originates from the Mahabharata range of Nepal and enters Jainagar (Madhubani district) in Bihar after being affected by the low land region. In the Mithila region it is considered as holy as the Ganges. Its major tributaries are Soni, Dhori, Bhoothi Balan, and so on. Balan river joins it near Pipraghat. The Kamala river, flowing 120 km in Bihar, splits into several streams. The name of many of them is Kamala. One of its major streams joins the Kosi, while one stream joins the Bagmati river in Khagaria district.

Kosi: Kosi originates from the Gosai place (Saptakushiki) in Nepal. Hence, the original name of Kosi is also Kaushiki. The Kosi river is formed by the union of seven streams. The names of these streams are Indravati, Sankosi, Tamrakosi, Lichhukosi, Dudhkosi, Arunkosi, and Tamurkosi. All these streams meet near Triveni, are called Kosi. The Kosi river is called the 'Sorrow of Bihar' due to the catastrophy of floods. This river flows in the districts of Supaul, Saharsa, Madhepura and Purnia etc. The Kosi river is famous for its diversion and has shifted 450 km from east to west in the last 200 years. The Kosi river forms a delta before joining the Ganges near Kursaila.

Mahananda: It is a river of the east flowing in the plain of northern Bihar. It determines the boundary line with Bihar and Bengal at many places. Emerging from the Himalayas, it joins the Ganges, flowing in Purnia and Katihar districts of Bihar. The main rivers of the plateau region are Son, Punpun, Phalgu, Karmanasha, North Koel, Ajay, Harohar, Chandan, Badhua etc. .

Son: Popularly known as Hiranyavah and Sonbhadra, the Son river is the most important river of South Bihar. Its place of origin is near Amarkantak (Madhya Pradesh) in Madhya Pradesh. The Narmada and Mahanadi also originate near the origin of Son, due to which the radial flow system is formed. This river flows through the rift valley. This river flows through Madhya Pradesh, Uttar Pradesh and Jharkhand and enters the Rohtas district of Bihar. It is the longest tributary of the Ganges flowing in South Bihar. The total length of Son is 784 km, of which 202 km flows through Bihar. The main tributaries of Son river are Gopad, Rihand, Kanhar and North Koel. The most important irrigation scheme of South-West Bihar is built on the Son river. The first dam on this river was built in 1873-74 at Dehri. Later the Indrapuri barrage was built on this river in 1968. A 1440 m long rail-cum-road bridge at Koilwar near Arrah was built in 1862 over the Son river, which is now popularly known as Abdul Bari Bridge. It is the longest rail bridge in India. Nehru Rail Bridge was constructed near Dehri on this river in 1900.

Phalgu: This river emerges in the form of several streams from the Chotanagpur plateau. Its main stream is called Niranjana. A river named Mohane joins it near Bodh Gaya. It is only after meeting the Mohane that it is known as the Phalgu River. All these rivers are seasonal rivers. It was on the banks of the Niranjana river that Gautam Buddha attained enlightenment. A Pitru Paksha fair is held on the banks of this river in Gaya, in which Pind Daan is performed for one's ancestors. This river is also known as Antasalila or Lilajan. This river splits into two branches near Barabar hill in Jehanabad district. Later on, the Phalgu River divides into many branches: Bhutahi, Karrua, Lokayana, Mahatvain, etc.

Punpun River: Punpun is a seasonal river, also known as Keekat and Bamagadhi. This river originates from the Chauraha hill area of Palamu district of Jharkhand. This river flows parallel to the Ganges in Aurangabad, Arwal and Patna districts of Bihar and joins the Ganges near Fatuha. Dardha, Yamuna, Madar, Bilaro, Ramrekha, Adri, Dhoba, and Morhar are the major tributaries of Punpun.

Ajay: Ajay River originates from Batbar, 5 km in the south of Jamui district. This river enters Deoghar district in Jharkhand from Bihar. It is also known by the name Ajayavati or Ajmati. This river flows in the east and south direction and enters Bengal and joins the Ganges. It was on the banks of the Niranjana river that Gautam Buddha attained enlightenment.

Sakri River: The origin of the Sakri river is the northern part of the Chotanagpur plateau (Hazaribagh plateau) in Jharkhand. This river flows in Gaya, Patna, Nawada and Munger districts of Bihar and joins the Ganges River. This river is also known as Sumagadhi.

Karmanasha: Karmanasha means the destroyer of karma. This river originates from Sarodag (Kaimur) in the Vindhyachal hills and joins the Ganges near Chausa. According to Hindu religious belief, this river is considered impure or inauspicious.

Chanan River: This river is also called Panchane. Its original name is Panchanan, which got disfigured and came to be called Chanan. This river has developed from the meeting of five streams, hence it is called Panchanan. The major streams of this river– Paimar, Tilaiya, Dharanje, Mahane etc. originate from the Chotanagpur plateau. All these streams flow together near Giriyak of Nalanda district due to the obstruction of Rajgir hill.

River Kiul: This river has its origin from the plateau of Hazaribagh. It enters Bihar near Satpahari in Jamui district. Its main tributaries are Burner, Anjan, Harohar (Halahal), etc. It joins river Ganga near Suryagarha in Lakhisarai district.

Length and Catchment Areas of Rivers of Bihar

Rivers	Total Length (in km)	Length in Bihar (in km)	Catchment area in Bihar (in sq.km)
Ganga	2510	445	15,165
Gandak	630	260	4,188
Ghaghra	1080	83	2,995
Burhi Gandak	320	320	9,601
Bagmati	597	394	6,500
Kamla	328	120	4,488
Kosi	720	260	11,410
Mahananda	360	376	6,150
Sone	780	202	15,820
Punpun	200	–	7,747
Karmanasha	192	–	–
Phalgu	235	–	–
Ajay	288	–	–

Rivers of Bihar—Their Place of Origin and Confluence/Estuary

River	Place of origin	Confluence/estuary
Ganga	Gangotri Glacier Gomukh (Uttarakhand)	Bay of Bengal
Gandak	Between Manangmot and Kutang in Annapurna Range	River Ganga (near Patna)
Ghaghra (Saryu)	Nampha (Nepal) near Gurla Mandhata peak	River Ganga (near Chhapra)
Burhi Gandak	Someshwar Range near Bishambharpur Chautarwa Chaur	River Ganga (near Khagaria)

Bagmati	Mahabharat Range (Nepal)	Burhi Gandak
Kamla	Mahabharat Range (Nepal)	Kosi
Kosi	Gosai Sthan (Saptkaushki, Nepal)	River Ganga (near Kursela)
Mahananda	Mahabharat Range (Nepal)	River Ganga (Manihari, near Katihar)
Sone	Amarkantak Peak (Madhya Pradesh)	River Ganga (between Danapur and Maner)
Punpun	Chhota Nagpur Plateau (Palamu)	River Ganga (near Fatuha)
Karmanasa	Sarodag (Kaimur)	River Ganga
Phalgu	Northern Chhota Nagpur Plateau (Hazaribagh)	Tala Region
Ajay	Batbarh (Jamui)	River Ganga (West Bengal)

HOT WATER RESERVOIRS (SPRINGS)

Hot Water Reservoirs or Springs: In addition to Sadawahi and seasonal rivers, other key sources of water in the state of Bihar are hot water basin, waterfall, lakes etc.

There are many basin of hot water in Gaya, Nalanda, and Munger regions. Such a place of natural water basin is called, where the water automatically comes out of the ground. It is geological hot water, which emerges from the earth's crust. The temperature of this water remains between 300 centigrade to 700 centigrade. The reason for the hot water is the mouth of the dead volcano and the radioactive minerals. Minerals, salts and sulphur etc are found in sufficient quantities in this water. The major centres of hot water in Bihar are Rajgir and Munger regions. A major feature of these water bodies is that the temperature of the water here remains almost the same throughout the year. The main hot water basin located in Rajgir are Saptadhara (Satdharva), Brahmakund, Suryakund, Makhdoomkund, Nanakkund, Gomukhund etc. The hottest water basin in these is Brahmakund, whose temperature is 870 centigrade, while the temperature of other water basin is 700 centigrade. The hot water basin located in Munger is basically situated in the hills of Kharagpur. The main water bodies here are Sitakund, Rameshwarkund, Lakshmankund, Rishikund, Janamkund, Laxmeshwarkund, Bhimabandh, Shringar Rishikund, Bhararikund and Panchtarkund etc. In this, the water of Lakshmankund is the hottest (620 centigrade). Apart from this, a hot water basin called Agnikund is found in Gaya.

Major Hot Springs of Bihar

Place	Name of Hot Spring
Rajgir	Brahma Kund, Saptdhara/ Sattadharwa Kund, Surya Kund, Makhdum Kund, Nanak Kund, Gomukh Kund
Munger	Lakshman Kund, Sita Kund, Rameshwar Kund, Rishi Kund, Janam Kund, Bhima Dam, Shrangar Rishi Kund, Bharari Kund, Panchtar Kund
Gaya	Agni Kund

WATERFALLS

Waterfall is the geographical position where the river descends on the hill or plateau area with the help of a steep slope. Where hard and soft rock lie horizontally, there is rapid erosion of soft rock, whereas hard rock remains in place. In the above situation water starts falling rapidly from top to bottom. In Bihar, waterfalls are basically found in the districts of Rohtas, Kaimur, Gaya, Nawada etc. in the marginal plateau areas. The most famous waterfall of Bihar, Kakolat Falls is located in Kakolat Hill (Nawada). It is located 16 km south of Nawada. Its height is 47 meters (160 ft), but the height of the main falls is 24 meters (80 ft). The Kakolat falls are formed by the meeting of seven streams descending from the Koderma plateau. Sukhladari falls are formed by the Kanhar River. It is situated on the border of Bihar and Uttar Pradesh. Dhuan Kund Falls are situated on the river Kao in Tarachandi hill, Rohtas. Durgavati Falls (Khadar Koh) is situated at a place called Chhanpapar in Rohtas district. Its height is 90 meters (300 ft). Among other waterfalls, Jiarkhund Falls on Phulwaria River in Bhojpur district is prominent.

Major Waterfalls in Bihar

Name of Waterfall	River	Place/District
Kakolat	Stream descending from Koderma Plateau	Kakolat (Nawada)
Sukhaldari	Kanhar	Rohtas
Dhua Kund (30 metres)	Kaav Dhoba, Bihar	Tarachandi (Rohtas)
Durgavati (Khadar Koh) (80 metres)	Durgavati	Chhanpapar (Rohtas)
Jiarkhund	Phulwaria	Jiarkhund (Bhojpur)
Tamasin	Mahane	–
Kuwari Dah (180 metres)	Asana	Rohtas
Rakim Kund	Gaighat	Rohtas
Okharin Kund (90 metres)	Gopath	Rohtas
Suara (120 metres)	East Suara	Rohtas
Devdari(58 metres)	Karmanasa	Rohtas Plateau (Rohtas)
Telhar Kund (80 metres)	West Suara	Rohtas Plateau (Rohtas)

LAKES

Many natural lakes are found in the plains of Bihar. Due to the low slope in the plain of North Bihar, the velocity of the river gets very slow. Hence, the river becomes unable to carry the depression brought with it. As a result, a circular flow begins to form. Gokhur Lake has been formed by rivers like Ganga, Budhi Gandak, Kosi, Mahananda etc. because of change in route by rivers and circular flow The main lakes found in the northern Bihar plain are Kanwar Lake or Kanwar Tal, Kusheshwar Asthan Lake, Ghogha Lake (Ghogha Chap), Simri-Bakhtiarpur Lake, Udaipur Lake etc. The lake-like watershed area is also known by the names of Tal, Chaur, Mana etc. in North Bihar. These watershed areas are called wetlands following are the major lakes:

Kanwar Lake: Kanwar Lake is located in Manjhol village of Begusarai. The area of this lake is 16 square kilometer. It is the largest Gokhur lake in Asia, which was formed by the digression of the Gandak river. Special types of vegetation are found in this lake, in which Hyda laricillata is Potomogentan, Welsneria, Leplerales, Nymphasa, Mympholodes, Sarpus Vetlveria etc. are prominent. The lake is visited by migratory birds from the Siberian region during the winter (November to January). Bird banding station has been established for research work near this lake. According to Ashok Ghosh, this lake was a great breeding ground for migratory birds till 1980, which is now decreasing continuously.

Kusheshwar Asthan Lake: This lake is located in Kusheshwar, Darbhanga. The area of this lake varies from 20 square kilometers to 50 square kilometers. During the rainy season, the lake expands immensely. Water supply in this lake is due to increase in the water level of the rivers Kamala and Kareh etc. during the rainy season. This lake is a major center of fish production. Here also migratory birds Pelican Dalmatia and Siberian Crane migrate during the winter season. In 1972, this lake was declared as a bird sanctuary.

Ghogha Lake: This lake is in Manihari of Katihar district. Its area is about 5 square kilometers. Many small lakes are situated around this lake. The source of water in the lake is monsoon rains as well as the water of Mahananda river.

Simri-Bakhtiarpur Lake: Situated in Simri-Bakhtiarpur of Saharsa district, this lake has been formed by the merger of many small lakes. There are major lakes like Jamuniya, Sardia, Kumibi, Gobra, etc.

WETLAND AREA

The land where the water table is usually at or near the surface of the ground, or where part of the land is covered by shallow water, is called a wetland. International Ramsar (Iran) Convention related to wetland was held in 1971. According to that wetland is an area which is a swamp, marshy landmass, land covered with vegetation material, natural or artificial, permanent or temporary. Fixed or flowing, sweet, areas of brackish or salt water and those areas of sea water, which are submerged in six meters of water in the tide, the land saturated with water is called wetland. This type of land remains wet either throughout the year or in a particular season.

The wetlands in the northern Bihar plain are basically found as fresh water sources in the form of lake, mana, chaur, diyar etc. In India 115 wetlands have been identified under the National Wetland Conservation Program. Under this program three wetland areas out of 115 have been protected in Bihar:

1. Kanwar, Begusarai,
2. Baraila, Vaishali,
3. Kusheshwar Asthom

In the Bihar State Irrigation Commission 1971, more than three lakh hectares of land in the state has been identified as wetland. Along with environmental and biodiversity, wetlands also have economic and resourceful importance, such as fisheries, production of makhana and water chestnut. Lowlands like Chaur, Mana, Diar, Jheel etc. are also useful in flood control, because the excess water of rivers gets stored in them during floods. Twenty-one percent of the total wetland lowlands of Bihar are privately owned and 79 percent under government ownership.

Bihar's Major Wetland (Lake, Chaur. Mana, Gokhur Lake) of Bihar

Water Submerged (Humid) land	Place	District
Kanwar Lake	Manjhaul	Begusarai
Kusheshwar Asthan Lake	Kusheshwar Asthan	Darbhanga
Ghoga Chap Lake	Manihari	Katihar

Simri-Bakhtiyarpur Lake	Simri-Bakhtiyarpur	Saharsa
Udaipur Lake	Udaipur	West Champaran
Bhusara Mann	Bhusara	Muzaffarpur
Brahmapura Mann	Muzaffarpur	Muzaffarpur
Kesariya Chaur	Motihari	East Champaran
Chaita Chaur	Pipra Pakri	West Champaran
Manasi Chaur	Phuliya Khar	Khagaria
Bharthua Chaur	Bharthua	Muzaffarpur
Bhagwa Chaur	Balua Bazar	Saharsa
Bora Chaur	Kharkata Tala	Saharsa
Parba Murli Chaur	Kumar Gej	Saharsa
Muradpur Chaur	Muradpur	Saharsa
Hariya Chaur	Akeelpur	Saran
Raghopur	Majipur, Mainaliya, Paitiya	Vaishali

❑❑❑

Climate and Soil

- Climate
- Soils
- Soils of South Bihar Plains
- Distribution of Rainfall
- Soils of North Bihar Plains
- Soils of Southern Frontier Plateau

CLIMATE

The state of Bihar is located in a subtropical zone. There is a great influence of monsoonal air on climate, therefore, it is a state of monsoon type of climate. The climate of Bihar is subtropical and humid. Latitude has the greatest influence on the climate of a place. Other factors include altitude, distance from sea, wind direction, forests, sea currents, amount of rainfall, direction of mountain etc. These factors are collectively called landforms. The factors affecting the climate of Bihar among these factors are latitude, altitude, distance from sea and amount of rainfall etc.

From the latitudinal point of view, Bihar is located in the north of the Tropic of Cancer. Therefore, the whole of Bihar falls in the subtropical zone. With high rainfall in the districts of Araria, Kishanganj, Katihar, Purnia, Saharsa, etc., in the eastern part of Bihar has humid climate; whereas in the north-western part, the semi-arid climate is found in Gopalganj, Siwan, Saran etc. There is an impact of the position of Himalayas in the northern part of the state. The streamy air coming from the Bay of Bengal collides with the Himalayan mountains and causes heavy rainfall. The amount of rainfall decreases from east to west. The cyclones arising from the Bay of Bengal in May-June and October-November also have an impact on the climate of the state. The temperate cyclonic rainfall also affects the state due to western disturbances in winters.

Although Bihar is a landlocked state, due to which continental climate should have influenced its climate, the state's climate remains moist for most of the year. Therefore, the climate of Bihar is called modified continental climate and not continental climate.

Different scholars have used different abbreviations for the climate of Bihar in their climate classifications. Köppen in his climate classification has classified Bihar in as Cwg (monsoon type and dry winter); Dudley Stamp, Kendrew, in the transition zone of subtropical climate. Trewartha in Caw (sub-tropical humid) and Thornthwaite in the (Caw) category.

Considering different climatic features, three types of seasons are found in Bihar:

1. Summer (mid-March to mid-June)
2. Rainy season (mid-June to mid-October)
3. Winter and autumn (mid-October to mid-March)

Summer Season: The summer season starts in the month of March. At this time, due to the Northern movement of the Sun, the temperature starts increasing. By the time of May, the temperature rises fast. The month of May is the hottest month. The average temperature of the state remains 35-45 degree centigrade in summer. With the increase in temperature, the plains become an area of low pressure. The dust storm begins to move at a high speed. Humidity decreases in this season. The winds are dry and hot, whose direction is from west to east. This hot and dry air is called 'Loo' (Hot waves). This hot air basically blows from a large low-pressure area formed due to excessive heating of the plains of Punjab and Rajasthan. Sometimes it rains in this season. A cyclonic storm occurs in the Bay of Bengal in May-June, causing rainfall in the eastern parts of the state. This type of cyclonic storm is called Nor'westers or Kaal Baisakhi. Gaya remains the hottest district of the state in summer.

Rainy Season: The rainy season starts from mid-June in Bihar and lasts till mid-October. By the end of the summer season, a low pressure area develops over the Bihar plain. This low pressure area acts as a monsoon trough which attracts monsoon air and brings rain.

Bihar receives most of its rainfall from the southwest monsoon or the summer monsoon. Monsoon arrives in Bihar by 10 June and spreads to the whole of Bihar by 15-20 June. The onset of monsoon first occurs in Kishanganj in the north-eastern part of Bihar by 10 June. Kishanganj is the most humid (rain receiving) district of Bihar. Patna receives 105 cm of rainfall only between June and September. As the monsoon wind moves to west, the amount of rainfall decreases. During this season, the humidity content in the air ranges from 80-90 percent. Because of the rising monsoonal air colliding with the Himalayan mountainous region, there is more rainfall in the Shivalik range, low land region and northern plains, while the southern Bihar plain receives less rainfall. A branch of monsoonal wind enters from the Chotanagpur plateau, causing rainfall in the marginal plateau areas. By mid-October, the monsoon starts to return from Bihar, the wind starts returning in the opposite direction, which is called the retreating of monsoon. The period between mid-October to November is of the autumn season. The main reason for the origin of the monsoon is the jet stream air which, starts assuming the form of the southern cold air of the Himalayas.

Winter Season: The winter season starts from the beginning of November. The main feature of this season is clean and cold air that starts flowing from the land towards the sea at a slow speed, and an anticyclonic situation arises. The average temperature in this season is 16 degree centigrade, while the minimum temperature in January is 4-10 degree centigrade. January is the coldest month in this season. There are light rains due to the Western Disturbance. Frost occurs due to increasing cold in January, which damages crops, especially potatoes. In January, due to the very low temperature, cold winds start running.

DISTRIBUTION OF RAINFALL

The distribution of rainfall in Bihar is uneven. The main reason for the unevenness is the variation in relief and the increasing distance from the sea. Bihar receives an average annual rainfall of 100.9 cm (1009 mm). The highest rainfall up to 180 cm occurs in Kishanganj. The northern Bihar plain receives rainfall ranging from 100 cm to 200 cm. In the northern plain, the amount of rainfall decreases from east to west. The amount of rainfall in Northeast Bihar and low land region is more than 200 cm.

The plains of South Bihar receive less rainfall than that of North Bihar. Nawada, Gaya, Aurangabad, Rohtas, and Kaimur districts of southern Bihar are the districts receiving less rainfall.

Apart from the summer monsoon rains, Bihar also receives rainfall in winters. Rainfall occurs in the plains in January-February due to 'Western Disturbance', which is beneficial for Rabi crops. This rainfall is caused by a temperate cyclone, which originates in the Mediterranean Sea. The cyclonic air moves forward and absorbs moisture in the Persian Gulf and enters Northwest India and causes rain, which affects Bihar.

SOILS

Soil is a layer of unorganized material on top of the solid crust, which is formed by the break-up of rocks. Rock particles, humus, water, air and micro-organisms are found in soil. In fact, soil is the result of the erosion of rocks and the physical and chemical changes that take place in them. Climatic factors like water, humidity, and temperature play a major role in soil formation. Climate is a dynamic factor that influences the process of soil formation through erosion, heat and rainfall.

About 90 percent of the surface of the state of Bihar is alluvial soil, which is made up of sediments brought by rivers in the alluvial plain to the north and south of the river Ganges. According to the Department of Agricultural Research of Government of Bihar, the soil classification of Bihar has been done. The basis of this classification is the parent rock, topography, physical and chemical composition. According to the Department of Agricultural Research, the soil of Bihar is mainly divided into three categories:

1. Soils of North Bihar Plain
2. Soils of South Bihar Plain
3. Soils of Southern Frontier Plateau

SOILS OF NORTH BIHAR PLAINS

Except the Shivalik range (the mountainous part of West Champaran) mainly alluvial soils are found in the North Bihar plains. This soil is formed by the Gandak, Budhi Gandak, Kosi, Mahananda, and its tributaries originating from the Himalayas. Forest or mountain soils have developed in the Shivalik hills. The soil of the plains of North Bihar has been divided into four sub-sections by the Department of Agricultural Research.

Sub-Himalayan mountainous soil: This soil is found in the north-western part of Champaran around the Someshwar range. With excessive rainfall on mountain slopes, the soil layer is thin. It is very fertile soil. It is clay soil, whose colour is light brown and yellow. Humidity (humidity) is found more in this area due to more rainfall and light formation of soil. This soil is rich in organic matter (humus). The main crops grown in this soil are paddy, maize, barley, etc.

Low land soil: In the southern parts of the sub-Himalayan mountainous soil, this soil extends in the form of thin soil of 3-8 km from West Champaran to Kishanganj. As a result of, to continuous seepage of water in the mountainous region, this soil gets sufficient moisture. Small particles of pebbles are also found in this soil and marshy land also developed in many places. The color of this soil is light brown or yellow. Sufficient amount of lime is found in this soil. This soil is suitable for cultivation of paddy, jute and sugarcane.

Old Jalor or Alluvial soil: This soil is also known as Balasundari soil. This soil is alkaline in nature, in which lime and potash are high. Old Alluvial or Bangar Soil is developed in areas where flood water does not reach every year. The extent of this soil is mainly in the western part of Ghaghra-Gandak Doab and Burhi Gandak. Lime content in this soil is more than 30 percent. It is deficient in phosphorus and nitrogen. This soil is suitable for sugarcane cultivation, as the soil has a comparatively high capacity to hold moisture due to the thickness of the soil. The color of this soil is brown and white. Other crops grown in this soil are maize, sugarcane, paddy, wheat and tobacco.

Khadar Soil: The soil formed from the sediments left after the flood every year by rivers is called new alluvial soil or Khadar soil. It contains many important mineral elements. The colour of this soil is dark brown. Chika (clay) is predominant in this. At some places sand is also found in abundance. The extent of this soil is found in the lower valley of the Ganges valley, Gandak, Budhi Gandak, Kosi and Mahananda.

This soil is best for paddy cultivation. Jute is cultivated in this soil due to high rainfall in Northeast Bihar. Nitrogen deficiency is found in this soil.

SOILS OF SOUTH BIHAR PLAINS

This soil is found in the southern plains of the Ganges. It extends between the Ganges River and the Chotanagpur Plateau. In South Bihar, alluvial soil is formed by the deposition of Son, Punpun, Phalgu and their tributaries. On the basis of the structural characteristics of the soil, the soils of the southern Bihar plain have been divided into four sub-classes:

Verdant soil or Kagaari Mitti: This soil is found in the form of embankments on the banks of rivers. This soil is developed in the form of thick tremors on the banks of rivers like Son, Kiul, Punpun, Phalgu, etc., on the southern bank of the Ganges river. This soil is lime predominant soil. Its formation is light and brown in colour. The main crops of this soil are corn, barley, mustard, chilli, etc.

Taal soil: Taal is an area of low land, which remains waterlogged during the rainy season. This soil is spread in a belt of 8 to 10 km wide from south Buxar to Bhagalpur of verdant soil. It is a brown coarse-grained soil. This soil is famous for the production of pulses.

Old alluvial/Karail-Kewal soil: The extension of this soil is found in the south of the Taal region in Buxar, Bhojpur, North Gaya, North Rohtas, Nalanda, Jehanabad, Munger, Patna, etc. Because of large area of this soil, regional variation is found in it. Its color ranges from dark brown to yellow. A mixture of sand, silt and teak is found in this soil. Alkaline and acidic properties are found in a fairly balanced form in this soil. It is highly fertile soil. The water holding capacity of this soil is high. The major crops grown in this soil are paddy, wheat, bajra, arhar, etc.

Balthar soil: This soil is found in the meeting area of the Chotanagpur plateau and the southern plain of the Ganges. The extent of this soil is found in the form of a narrow belt fro 5 to 5 km from Kaimur to Bhagalpur. It is also known as red-yellow soil. Light pebbles are found in this soil and there is an excess of red colour in it. The nature of this soil is acidic. This soil is capable of absorbing water. Iron is also found in this soil. As a result of, to excessive erosion, the possibility of agriculture in this soil is less. Crops of maize, jowar, bajra, potato, etc. are mainly grown in this soil.

SOILS OF SOUTHERN FRONTIER PLATEAU

Residual soils of red and yellow color are found mainly in the marginal plateau region of South Bihar. The soil of the marginal plateau region has been divided into two sub-classes:

Red sand soil of Kaimur mountain: This soil is found in the plateau areas of Kaimur and Rohtas. In this soil, traces of red sand and laterite are found along with sand. With abundance of natural vegetation in this area, more flora is found in this soil. It is a less fertile soil. The main crops grown in this soil are jowar, bajra, corn, pea, etc.

Red-yellow soil: This soil is found in Southeast Bihar's Jamui, Kharagpur hills of Munger, Banka, Nawada, Gaya, and Aurangabad plateau region. This soil is formed by the fragmentation of rocks like granite, neiss, schist, etc. The colour of this soil is red due to the presence of iron in the rock. Nutrient and humus deficiency is found in this soil. This is infertile soil. Mainly coarse cereals, pulses etc., are grown in this soil.

Forests and Wildlife

- Forests
- State Forest Development Agency
- Forest Policy
- Wildlife & Conservation

FORESTS

Bihar is a state with plain area. Natural vegetation is not environmentally friendly due to increasing population and pressure of agricultural practices on land. Bihar is a state with monsoon climate. Hence, the major factor for determining vegetation is the amount of rainfall. In the Shivalik range and in the mountainous region of Kaimur, the height also affects the vegetation. The total area of Bihar is 94163 square kilometres, of which the forest cover is of 7,532 square kilometres. This makes 8 percent of the total area of Bihar.

Depending on the amount of rainfall, the natural vegetation of Bihar can be divided into two classes:

1. Wet deciduous forest
2. Dry deciduous forest

Wet deciduous forest: Wet deciduous forests are found in an area with the annual rainfall of more than 120 cm. Wet deciduous forests are divided into 2 categories:

1. **Forests in Someshwar & Doon Category:** These forests are mainly found in Western Champaran. The amount of rainfall here is more than 160 cm. The major trees of these forests found on the high land and slopes of the hills are sal (Shorea Robusta), shisham, khair, semal, toon, etc. Savanna type of vegetation has also developed in these areas as a result of elevation.
2. **Lowland forest:** These forests are found in the northern-western and northern-eastern parts of the lowland region. These forests are found in the form of a narrow strip in Purnea, Saharsa, Araria, and Kishanganj districts. The main vegetation of these forests is bamboo, sawai, grass, reeds, shrub, elephant grass, etc. This type of vegetation is found in low marshland. A strip of Sal forest is found in the northern frontier areas of Saharsa and Purnea.

Dry deciduous forest: Dry deciduous forests are found in areas with annual rainfall of less than 120 cm. Shrubs, grass and small plants have grown in these forests. This type of vegetation has developed in the eastern, intermediate part of Bihar and the western part of the southern plateau. These types of forests are found in the dry plateau areas of Kaimur, Rohtas, Gaya, Aurangabad, Nawada, Jamui, Sheikhpura, and Banka districts. The major trees of these forests are rosewood, mahua, catechu, palash, asana, amla, amalatas, ebony, etc.

Keeping in mind the conservation and security of forests in Bihar, they have been divided into three classes:

1. Protected forests
2. Reserve forests
3. Unclassified forests

The protected forests are those forests where animals are not allowed to graze and wood is not allowed to be cut. They are under government protection. Reserved forests are those forests where the government gives permission for grazing animals, and cutting and picking wood in limited quantities. There is no restriction by the government for grazing animals and cutting wood in unclassified forests; however, a fee is charged for it.

Forests Cover of Bihar

Class	Area	% of Calculated Area by Sol (km^2)
Very dense forest	387	0.41
Medium dense forest	3284.21	3.49
Open forest	3861.24	4.10
Total	7532.45	8.00
Scrub	260.80	0.28

Status of Forest in Bihar - Forest Status Report-2023

- The total forest and tree cover of Bihar in the year 2023 was 7,299 sq km which includes natural forest and tree-rich vegetation areas of 12 districts which qualify for classification as forest.
- The area of forest cover and tree cover in Bihar was 9,309 sq km (9.9%) in 2019, which increased to 9,722 sq km (10.3%) in 2021.
- According to the Forest Status Report 2021, the forest cover of Bihar is 7,380.79 sq km which is 7.84% of the total geographical area of Bihar.
- As compared to State of Forest Report 2019, forest cover in Bihar has increased by 75 sq km which is 1.03% more than before, it has maximum 3,762 sq km open forest from 2021 followed by 3,286 sq km of medium dense forest.
- According to the India Forest Status Report 2021, Bihar has tree cover on an area of 2341 square kilometers, which is 2.48% of the total geographical area.
- Compared to the 2019 report, an increase of 338 square kilometers in tree cover has been recorded. Valmiki Nagar Tiger Reserve has forests in 796.12 sq km which is 85.71% of the total tiger reserve area (928.80 sq km).
- Bihar has one national park and 12 wildlife sanctuaries which cover 3.44% of the total geographical area of the state.
- On October 5, 2021, 'Kaimur Wildlife Sanctuary' was given in-principle approval as the second Tiger Reserve of the state.
- By 2021, the total number of tigers in Bihar has increased to 50.
- A resolution has been passed to set up a Zoo Safari at Rajgir.
- Sanjay Gandhi Biological Park has gained fame as Asia's largest center in rhino breeding center and second largest center in the world.
- Government Forest Training Center has been established in Gaya district.
- Overall, forestry and wood timber production contributed approximately 1.5 percent to the gross domestic product in Bihar in the last five years (2016–17 to 2020–21).
- During 2020–21, the share of forestry and wood production sector in agriculture-generated gross state domestic product was about 8.1% during the last five years.
- About 2.50 lakh saplings have been planted in the year 2021–22 in 8 forest divisions along the banks of Ganga and its tributaries.
- Under the Krishi Vaniki Yojana, bamboo plants are being planted on government land and in the nurseries of farmers.
- Under the Jal Jeevan Hariyali Mission, a target of planting 2.51 crore saplings was fixed for 2020-21. But exceeding the target, 3.92 crore plants were planted. Under this mission, a target was set to plant 5 crore saplings in 2021-22.
- The National Dolphin Research Center at Patna University was inaugurated by the Chief Minister of Bihar.
- Mahavir Biodiversity Park was inaugurated in Jamui district in 2020–21.

District-wise Forest Cover in Bihar

District	Calculated Area by SoI	2023 Assessment				% of Calculated Area by SoI	Change w.r.t. 2021 Roster based*	Scrub
		Very Dense Forest	Mod. Dense Forest	Open Forest	Total			
Araria	2,830	0.00	7.87	138.77	146.64	5.18	-1.64	0.40
Arwal	638	0.00	1.44	2.58	4.02	0.63	0.00	0.00
Aurangabad	3,305	0.00	65.56	92.22	157.78	4.77	3.97	14.01
Banka	3,020	0.09	100.62	194.81	295.52	9.79	19.16	32.45
Begusarai	1,918	0.00	28.03	51.47	79.50	4.14	-5.31	0.00
Bhagalpur	2,569	0.00	64.53	38.78	103.31	4.02	33.82	0.00
Bhojpur	2,395	0.00	19.23	12.34	31.57	1.32	-0.98	0.53
Buxar	1,703	0.00	3.04	2.97	6.01	0.35	-0.11	0.00
Darbhanga	2,279	0.00	44.17	100.06	144.23	6.33	6.69	0.00
East Champaran	3,968	0.00	66.48	120.94	187.42	4.72	19.44	0.00
Gaya	4,976	0.00	134.25	488.24	622.49	12.51	10.76	63.08
Gopalganj	2,033	0.00	4.68	6.62	11.30	0.56	2.64	0.00
Jamui	3,098	27.78	352.66	290.40	670.84	21.65	5.24	14.79
Jehanabad	931	0.00	0.06	6.04	6.10	0.66	1.30	3.07
Kaimur (Bhabua)	3,362	0.00	526.00	499.68	1,025.68	30.51	-35.35	38.50
Katihar	3,057	0.00	6.50	58.89	65.39	2.14	3.63	0.00
Khagaria	1,486	0.00	2.81	14.81	17.62	1.19	-0.50	0.00
Kishanganj	1,884	0.00	12.28	82.99	95.27	5.06	-7.56	0.00
Lakhisarai	1,228	16.16	126.61	26.77	169.54	13.81	1.38	4.18
Madhepura	1,788	0.00	1.38	58.63	60.01	3.36	6.17	0.00
Madhubani	3,501	0.00	42.19	189.99	232.18	6.63	25.71	0.00
Munger	1,419	39.19	240.65	26.17	306.01	21.57	3.30	9.04
Muzaffarpur	3,172	0.00	53.48	122.28	175.76	5.54	6.31	0.00
Nalanda	2,355	0.00	10.37	34.44	44.81	1.90	5.41	5.59
Nawada	2,494	0.00	199.53	306.77	506.30	20.30	-9.76	21.47
Patna	3,202	0.00	19.90	8.47	28.37	0.89	0.00	0.09
Purnia	3,229	0.00	5.34	55.34	60.68	1.88	5.09	0.00
Rohtas	3,851	0.00	350.25	317.81	668.06	17.35	1.66	43.42
Saharsa	1,687	0.00	3.98	31.85	35.83	2.12	2.86	0.00
Samastipur	2,904	0.00	101.81	47.43	149.24	5.14	-4.00	0.00
Saran	2,641	0.00	25.53	37.26	62.79	2.38	3.40	0.00
Sheikhpura	689	0.00	0.64	0.18	0.82	0.12	0.00	0.00
Sheohar	349	0.00	2.21	28.22	30.43	8.72	3.84	0.00

Sitamarhi	2,294	0.00	37.81	114.09	151.90	6.62	12.99	0.00
Siwan	2,219	0.00	2.51	6.90	9.41	0.42	2.00	0.00
Supaul	2,425	0.00	4.26	138.20	142.46	5.87	6.19	0.00
Vaishali	2,036	0.00	88.30	30.63	118.93	5.84	0.05	0.00
West Champaran	5,228	303.78	527.25	77.20	908.23	17.37	1.39	10.18
Grand Total	**94,163**	**387.00**	**3,284.21**	**3,861.24**	**7,532.45**	**8.00**	**129.19**	**260.80**

*Area figure calculated without normalization factor.

Division-wise Forest Cover in Bihar

Division	Digitized Division Boundary Area#	2023 Assessment				% of Digitized Division Boundary Area	Change w.r.t. 2021 Roster based*	Scrub
		Very Dense Forest	Mod. Dense Forest	Open Forest	Total			
Araria	4,779.62	0.00	19.15	221.04	240.19	5.03	-9.06	0.86
Aurangabad	3,947.40	0.00	66.91	95.04	161.95	4.10	3.95	12.89
Banka	3,026.70	0.09	100.59	195.82	296.50	9.80	18.90	26.51
Begusarai	3,411.95	0.00	30.66	65.96	96.62	2.83	-5.78	0.00
Bettiah	4,217.80	4.35	62.49	38.92	105.76	2.51	-1.07	2.36
Bhagalpur	2,551.31	0.00	66.75	39.75	106.50	4.17	33.45	0.00
Bhojpur	4,119.28	0.00	22.25	15.34	37.59	0.91	-1.09	0.46
Gaya	5,903.12	0.00	128.69	486.89	615.58	10.43	11.62	63.90
Gopalganj	4,292.59	0.00	7.16	13.37	20.53	0.48	4.55	0.00
Jamui	3,290.58	0.00	214.93	260.79	475.72	14.46	3.62	14.17
Kaimur (Bhabua)	3,353.17	0.00	518.10	493.55	1,011.65	30.17	-33.96	40.31
Mithila	6,016.19	0.00	88.01	298.94	386.95	6.43	31.70	0.00
Motihari	3,970.77	0.00	66.17	121.74	187.91	4.73	19.43	0.00
Munger	3,098.74	83.13	504.01	80.46	667.60	21.54	6.27	12.59
Nalanda	2,365.50	0.00	10.43	34.31	44.74	1.89	5.41	5.46
Nawada	2,484.75	0.00	189.72	300.42	490.14	19.73	-9.44	21.82
Patna	3,217.18	0.00	19.91	8.50	28.41	0.88	0.00	1.34
Purnia	6,267.56	0.00	11.78	112.21	123.99	1.98	8.72	0.00
Rohtas	3,848.97	0.00	355.18	318.03	673.21	17.49	1.66	41.91
Saharsa	3,464.26	0.00	5.34	90.16	95.50	2.76	8.95	0.00
Samastipur	2,681.62	0.00	102.15	47.77	149.92	5.59	-3.94	0.00
Saran	2,681.43	0.00	25.39	37.50	62.89	2.35	3.49	0.00
Sitamarhi	2,623.24	0.00	40.28	143.35	183.63	7.00	16.92	0.00
Supaul	2,417.75	0.00	4.29	138.30	142.59	5.90	6.21	0.00
Tirhut	3,177.05	0.00	53.26	122.62	175.88	5.54	6.25	0.00

Vaishali	1,989.48	0.00	88.09	30.45	118.54	5.96	0.04	0.00
VTR Ramnagar (VTP-1)	435.48	115.82	240.71	15.89	372.42	85.52	2.04	0.00
VTR Valmikinagar (VTP-2)	589.44	182.86	219.20	22.98	425.04	72.11	0.35	7.24
Area which does not fall in any division	368.41	0.75	22.61	11.14	34.50	9.36	0.00	8.98
Grand Total	**94,591.34**	**387.00**	**3,284.2**	**3,861.24**	**7,532.45**	**7.96**	**129.19**	**260.80**

#As per the division boundary shape file provided by State Forest Department.

*Area figure calculated without normalization factor.

Forest wealth

The produce obtained from forest is called forest wealth. Many types of major and minor products are obtained from the forests in the state of Bihar. The collection and marketing of forest products in the state is carried out by the Bihar State Forest Development Corporation.

Main products

The main product obtained from forests includes only wood. Following are the other major forest products found in Bihar:

Sal: This tree is found mainly in hilly slopes and lowland areas. Its wood which is hard and durable is previous. It is used in the construction of house, floor, furniture, train compartments and railway tracks, etc. Sal seeds are also used for extracting oil.

North Indian Rosewood (Shisham): This tree is mainly found in the south-eastern part of Bihar. Its wood is smooth and sharp. It is most commonly used in the furniture industry.

Semal/Silk Cotton Tree (Bombax Ceiba): Semal wood is light, soft, and white. It is most commonly used for making packaging boxes and in toy manufacturing. Semal tree is found in the lowland area of Northern Bihar. Its cotton is used for domestic needs and in medical field.

Toona (Red cedar): Toona trees are found on the hilly slopes of Bihar. Its strong wood is used in making furniture, household goods, toys, etc.

Apart from these, mango, peepal, neem, banyan, jackfruit, bamboo, etc. are also important trees. Mango trees are found mostly in the districts of Darbhanga, Bhagalpur, etc. of North Bihar. The mango tree produces fruit as well as wood for domestic use. Products from peepal and neem trees are used in pharmaceutical industry.

Secondary/minor products

The following are the secondary/minor products of the forests found in Bihar:

1. **Tussar/mulberry/silk:** Tussar is mainly produced in Bhagalpur, from silkworms grown on the Arjuna tree.
2. **Oil production:** Oil is obtained from the seeds of cotton, lacquer, mahua, etc. These oils are used as medicines.
3. **Lacquer production:** Lacquer is produced from Laccifer lacca or lacquer worms. Lacquer is produced in the border districts of Jharkhand. The laquer worm is reared on Kusum or Palash trees. It is used in the bangle and wood industries.

Other secondary products include tendu leaf, gum, tannin, herbs, bamboo, sawai grass, etc. The main areas of bamboo are the districts of Purnia, Kishanganj, Araria, etc. in the lowland areas. Sawai grass is produced in Bhagalpur district. Sawai grass is used for making ropes.

Forest products-based industry

Many industries based on forest products have developed in the state. The largest among them is the sawmill industry. Other major industries are as follows:

Industry	Centre
Seasoning & Cardboard Industries	Samastipur, Darbhanga
Plywood Industry	Hajipur, Bettiah, Patna, Muzaffarpur
Catechu Industry	Bettiah
Silk Industry	Bhagalpur

FOREST POLICY

The first forest policy of independent India was made in 1952. From 1952 till 1980s, there was so much destruction of forests in India that it became mandatory to formulate a new forest policy at the national level. Earlier policies were only intended to collect revenue. By 1980s, the impact of environmental problems was clearly visible. It was felt that conservation of forests was also necessary for other purposes besides revenue collection such as for soil and water conservation which is helpful in safeguarding ecosystem. These should also have the provision for the local residents to use the goods and services received from the forests. Keeping all these things in mind, a new forest policy was announced in 1988.

According to the National Forest Policy 1988, about 33.33 percent of the total area of a state should be covered by forest. Bihar is basically a state of plains; so, according to the National Forest Policy, forest cover on 22 percent of the total area of the state is mandatory for the protection of the environment. Only 7.27 percent of the total geographical area of Bihar is forest. From this point of view, Bihar is in a state of complete environmental imbalance. Therefore, keeping in mind the purpose of expansion of forest, many activities are being undertaken by the government.

Forestry program

The following objectives have been set under the forestry program:

1. Land 1000 square kilometres has been identified for forest development on wastelands.
2. Forest has to be developed on one-third of the total fallow land.
3. Government and private institutions have to plant trees on vacant land.
4. Trees are to be planted in public places, along paths, etc.
5. The emphasis has to be on social forestry.

Hariyali/Greenery mission

The Hariyali Mission is a component of the Agricultural Development Plan. Its purpose is to plant trees with the aim of forest cover in the state. The main objectives of the Hariyali Mission are:

1. Developing forest area up to 15 percent of the total geographical area of the state;
2. Soil and moisture conservation work in 2000 square kilometres of forest area under watershed development, in which rehabilitation work is to be done by planting trees in 1000 square kilometres of degraded (cut) forest area;
3. To increase the income of farmers through agroforestry;
4. Providing means of livelihood by giving strips of planted trees to the families living below poverty line and help in poverty alleviation;
5. Helping in meeting the domestic requirement by increasing the availability of forest produce in the state;
6. Strengthening the supply of raw materials to forest produce based industries and expanding them and promoting industrialization in the state;
7. Reducing the negative impact of climate change by establishing ecological balance in the state;
8. Plantation of trees, especially peepal, neem, sycamore, catechu, rosewood, banyan, teak and pakad trees on the embankments, banks of canals, schools, colleges, forests, and roadsides, and on agriculturally unusable land.

Green Cover Increasing through Jal Jeevan Hariyali Mission

The green cover in Bihar is increasing through Jal Jeevan Hariyali Mission and the environment and forest, forest and climate change department has been constantly developing the natural forest area by conserving soil and promoting eco-tourism. For this ₹ 517.28 crore was sanctioned to the department in the financial year 2024-25 and the fund will be utilised for increasing the green cover across the state.

Agricultural Forestry (Poplar E. T. P.) Scheme

The 'Agricultural Forestry (Poplar E.T.P.) Scheme' is for plantation of poplar by the entrepreneurs/ farmers/landowners on their land by the Department of Environment and Forests, Bihar.

Objectives

- Promoting poplar plantation in farmers' fields.
- Providing employment opportunities.
- Strengthening the financial situation of the farmers in the state.
- Promoting industrialization by providing raw materials to forest produce based industries.

Availability

Poplar plants are provided free of cost to the entrepreneurs/farmers/beneficiaries participating in this scheme from local nurseries of Environment and Forest Department. Plants of minimum 10 ft height and 2.5 inches girth are provided for planting poplar.

Benefits offered in the scheme

Technical information about planting and caring for poplar E.T.P. is given to the beneficiaries during training.

'Poplar Nursery Scheme' under the Chief Minister's Private Nursery Scheme

Under the Chief Minister's Private Plantation Scheme, the Poplar Nursery Establishment Scheme is being run by the Hariyali Mission for entrepreneurs/ farmers/landowners to set up Poplar nursery on their land. Free poplar cuttings are made available to the beneficiaries/farmers involved in this scheme. This produces poplar plants, which are bought back by the department at a predetermined rate.

The aim of the scheme

- To prepare more and more plants in less time.
- To promote poplar plantation in farmers' fields.
- To provide employment opportunities to the villagers.

Poplar cuttings are provided free of cost to the entrepreneurs/farmers/beneficiaries participating in this scheme, from the poplar nursery set up in the local office of the department. Beneficiaries are made available 10,000 (ten thousand) cuttings per acre.

Agroforestry Scheme in Bihar

The Agroforestry Scheme involves the provision of plants to farmers at a subsidized rate of ₹ 10 per plant from local nurseries. Farmers are given incentives for plant care, with an additional ₹ 60 per plant provided after three years if the survival rate exceeds 50 percent.

Chief Minister Private Nursery (for other species) Scheme

Large-scale tree plantation is required with the aim of increasing tree cover outside the forests. A large number of plants will be required for agroforestry in the state, for which a provision has been made to supply plants from private nurseries as well. Necessary support is provided to farmers for setting up the nursery. Different species of plants are developed in it.

The Chief Minister's Private Nursery Establishment Scheme offers financial support to farmers for preparing poplar and other species of plants, with predetermined rates of ₹ 30 per poplar plant and ₹ 24 per plant for other species.

The objective of this scheme is to prepare high-quality plants for maximum plantation and to provide employment opportunities to the villagers.

Tree Conservation Programme

Bihar has several tree conservation programs, including "Harit JEEVIKA Harit Bihar 5.0", which aims to plant 5 crore trees with the "One Didi-One Tree" model. The state also focuses on increasing forest cover, with the goal of reaching 17% of the total geographical area through afforestation and land use diversification. Initiatives like "Project Green Bihar" and "Jal Jeevan Hariyali Yojana" also contribute to these efforts.

Key Initiatives:

- **Harit JEEVIKA Harit Bihar 5.0:** This program involves self-help groups, particularly women, in planting trees, with the goal of planting 5 crore trees.
- **Project Green Bihar:** This project focuses on identifying suitable sites and engaging farmers to plant trees on their land, especially near forest areas, with expert guidance and monitoring.
- **Tree Plantation and Environmental Education in Bihar:** This project involves students and teachers in awareness programs, followed by tree planting and maintenance.
- **Hazard Mitigation:** Trees help prevent soil erosion, reduce flood risks, and improve overall ecological balance.

Chief Minister Student Plantation Scheme

In order to make the Environmental Protection Programme popular in schools, students studying in class 6 in all the recognized government and non-government schools in the state are included in this scheme.

Soil and Water Conservation Plan

Soil and water conservation works are being carried out in the state. Under this scheme, various structures are constructed to prevent soil erosion and to collect water on slopes of the hills. Nalanda, Munger, Gaya, Betiya, Banka, Jamui, Kaimur, Aurangabad and Rohtas forest divisions have been included in this scheme.

Under the Hariyali Mission in the state, there is a plan for forestry research such as seed collection, treatment, identification of good trees, establishment of tissue culture lab, construction of demonstration plot, soil testing, selection of suitable tree species for various agroclimatic areas, a plan for research on changes in the departmental programs and prevailing processes of forestry operations in view of climate change, etc. For this purpose, the state government has started research work in agreement with ICFRI on species of agroforestry such as poplar, rosewood, salix, melia and eucalyptus. At the initiative of the Department of Environment and Forests, Indian Council of Forestry Research and Education (ICFRE) imparts free training in Haldwani, Pantnagar and Jhansi. Farmers are provided with relevant training on different species of plants, to be planted under nursery and agroforestry.

Every Campus, Green Campus Programme

Under this scheme, various campuses in all the districts of the state such as schools, colleges, religious institutions, offices, clubs, committees and other government and non-government campuses have been included. A minimum of 50 and maximum of 1000 saplings are provided free of cost to an institution or campus. The selected institutions have complete authority over the plants distributed or planted.

STATE FOREST DEVELOPMENT AGENCY

According to the National Forest Policy, 1988, forests have to be expanded in the state for environmental balance, soil erosion, and flood control. With the usage by the rural people for the fulfillment of various needs, there is a plan to save the forests from decline and increase the forest resources. For the purpose of forest development and planning, the Government of India will implement all the schemes with its fund through the Village Forest Management and Safety Committee under joint forest management. The government has decided to develop, protect and enhance the state's natural forests through joint forest management system with the participation of common people. For this purpose, 10 forestry development agencies have been formed in the state under the Society Registration Act. Registration of village level joint forest management committees and development committees for eco-protected areas has been carried out by the forest development agencies. At present, the following programs and schemes are being implemented under the State Forest Development Agency:

1. **National Afforestation Programme (NAP):** Under this scheme, 100 percent funding is provided by the National Afforestation and Ecological Development Board of the Ministry of Environment, Forest and Climate Change, Government of India.

2. **Green India Mission (GIM):** In this plan, a multi-dimensional perspective plan has been prepared for the development of four selected areas of the state. These four areas are: 1. Ahaura, Kaimur; 2. Dharhara, Munger; 3. Banka; 4. Imamganj, Gaya.

3. **Tasar Food Plantation Program:** The Tasar Food Plantation Program is being conducted by the Industries Department of the Government of Bihar under the Chief Minister Tasar Development Project. Under this scheme, plantation of tasar food plant is to be done in 8030-hectare forest area.

It has been decided to organize 11 important forest days every year by the Publicity and Public Relations Division of the Department of Environment and Forests, Government of Bihar. These forest days are as follows:

Sr. No	Important Days	Date
1	World Wetland Day	2 February
2	World Forestry Day	21 March
3	World Migratory Birds Day	Second week of May
4	World Biodiversity Day	22 May
5	World Environment Day	5 June
6	Forest Festival Week	1-7 July
7	Bihar Earth Day	9 August
8	World Ozone Day	16 September
9	Wildlife Week	2-9 October
10	World Animal Welfare Day	4 October
11	Dolphin Day	5 October

WILDLIFE AND CONSERVATION

The top institute that executes and directs wildlife conservation schemes in India is the Wildlife Board of India. Its chairman is the Prime Minister. The Wildlife (Protection) Act, 1972 is applicable in other parts of the country except Jammu and Kashmir. In this Act, guidelines have been given for the conservation of wildlife and preservation of species that are getting extinct. Under this, the trade of rare and dying species has been banned.

Bihar currently boasts of the existence of one national park, one botanical garden and eleven wildlife sanctuaries, which is an incredible accomplishment. In order to prevent the territories of different animals from overlapping, the Bihar Wildlife Sanctuaries are not only endowed with an extremely large piece of land but are also equipped with rich medical facilities, which come in very helpful when it comes to caring for the animals.

Valmiki National Park offers a tranquil and lush environment for animals and birds and Valmiki National Park, Kaimur Wildlife Sanctuary, Gautam Budha Wildlife Sanctuary, Bhimbandh Sanctuary, Vikramshila Gangetic Dolphin Sanctuary, Udaypur Vanya Prani Sanctuary, Valmiki Wildlife Sanctuary are some prominent names of the list of Bihar Wildlife Sanctuaries.

Here is the overview of the bird and animal sanctuaries in the state of Bihar (2023-24):

Wildlife Sanctuaries in Bihar

Wildlife/Birds Sanctuaries	Place	Area Sq. km.	Species (Types and Numbers)
Valmiki Wildlife Sanctuary	Valmiki Reserve Division 1 and 2 Bethia & West Champaran	880.78	Mammal (58), Bird Species (261), Reptiles (26), Amphibians (13)

Valmiki Reserve Park	West Champaran	898.93	
Bhimbandh Wildlife Sanctuary	Munger	680.94	Trees (71), Shrubs (19), Herbaceous (42), Grass (33), Mammals (22), Birds (147), Reptiles (10).
Udaypur Wildlife Sanctuary	Betiah, West Champaran	8.87	Trees (53), Shrubs (13), Grass (8), Fauna (5), Butterflies (3), Dragonfly (4), Spiders (11)
Kaimur Wildlife Sanctuary	Kaimur and Rohtas	1784.73	Trees (40), Shrubs (45), Herbaceous (110), Grass (25), Animals (16), Birds (100)
Gautam Buddha Wildlife Sanctuary	Gaya	138.33	Mammals (11), Bird Species (100), Reptiles (10), Vegetation (255)
Rajgir Wildlife Sanctuary	Nalanda	35.84	Mammals (8), Bird Species (288), Reptiles (10), Vegetation (520)
Rajauli (Navada) Wildlife Sanctuary	Navada	21.27	Mammals (11), Bird Species (16), Reptiles (12), Vegetation (111)
Kusheshwar Bird Sanctuary	Darbhanga	29.21	Mammals (4), Bird Species (138), Reptiles (7), Vegetation (129)
Barela Jheel Bird Sanctuary	Vaishali	1.98	Mammals (4), Bird Species (117), Reptiles (8), Vegetation (179)
Nakti Dam Bird Sanctuary	Jamui	3.33	Mammals (4), Bird Species (199), Vegetation (15)
Nagi Dam Bird Sanctuary	Jamui	1.92	Mammals (4), Bird Species (199), Reptiles (8), Vegetation (15)
Vikramashila Gangetic Dolphin Sanctuary	Bhagalpur	63.11	Mammals (5), Bird Species (74), Fish (20), Vegetation (31)
Kanwar Jheel Birds Sanctuary	Begusarai	63.11	Mammals (5), Bird Species (244), Mammals (8), Vegetation (255)

The state government has earmarked 13 Eco-Sensitive Zones to conserve wildlife, waterfowl, and the environment. A forest area up to 2 km from the boundary of the wildlife sanctuary has been included under the eco-sensitive area. These eco-sensitive areas are as follows –

1. Nagi Dam Bird Sanctuary, Jamui
2. Nakti Dam Bird Sanctuary, Jamui
3. Valmiki Wildlife Sanctuary, West Champaran
4. Valmiki National Park, West Champaran
5. Valmiki Tiger Reserve, West Champaran
6. Kusheshwar Asthan Bird Sanctuary, Darbhanga
7. Gautam Budha Wildlife Sanctuary, Gaya
8. Bhimbandh Wildlife Sanctuary, Munger
9. Vikramshila Gangetic Dolphin Sanctuary, Bhagalpur
10. Udaipur Wildlife Sanctuary, West Champaran
11. Pant Wildlife Sanctuary, Rajgir, Nalanda
12. Barela Lake Bird Shelter, Vaishali
13. Kaimur Wildlife Shelter, Kaimur and Rohtas

Several other programmes have been launched to conserve the wildlife of the state. The total area of natural forests in Bihar is 6845 sq. km., out of which 3561 sq. km. of natural forests, 1 tiger reserve, 1 Gangetic Dolphin shelter, 5 wildlife shelters and 5 bird shelters are acquired for conservation and promotion of wildlife. Out of these, 3 shelters have been identified as Kanwar Lake Bird shelter (Kanwar Tal) Kusheshwar Asthan Bird shelter and Salim Ali Jubba Sahni Baraila Lake Bird shelter (Baraila Tal) as the main wetland.

There is a plan to establish a zoo safari in Rajgir, which has been approved by the National Wildlife Council. The final draft of the management plan of Bhim Dam Zoological Shelter, Munger has been prepared by the World Wildlife (WWF), which has been sent to the Government of India for approval. The work of preparing the management plan for Kusheshwar Asthan Bird shelter and Baraila lake Bird shelter has been done by the Wildlife Institute of India, Dehradun. The work of preparing the management plan for Pant Ashrayani, Rajgir is being done by TERI. The area declared under Kanwar lake bird shelter, Begusarai also includes the land of private ownership.

Valmiki Tiger Reserve is located in West Champaran, which is the only tiger reserve of the state, with a total area of 899.38 square kilometres. Besides tigers, there are other protected wild animals like leopards, bears, chital, and sambhar in this reserve. The Valmiki Tiger Reserve (VTR), the only national park in Bihar's West Champaran district, has recorded a 75 per cent increase in tiger count from 31 in 2018 to 54 in 2023. Enthused by the sharp increase of tiger population at VTR, the Bihar government has initiated the process of developing 'Kaimur Wildlife Sanctuary' (KWLS) measuring 1,504 sq km into another tiger reserve or 'tiger-bearing landscape' in the state.

Also the National Tiger Conservation Authority (NTCA), which is a statutory body under the Ministry of Environment, Forests and Climate Change, had officially announced the increase in tiger population in Valmiki Tiger Reserve (VTR) from 31 (2018) to 54 (2023).

Why has the Number of Tigers in VTR Increased?

1. A total ban on sand and stone mining inside VTR, and strict restrictions on mining in its eco-sensitive zone, helped increase grassland cover.
2. An increase in grassland cover thus helps in supporting the prey population, in turn increasing the chances of the carnivores' survival.
3. The reserve is dedicated to managing and sustaining the tiger population by raising awareness among local residents and monitoring mining activities in and around the area to minimize human-wildlife conflict.
4. The NTCA placed the reserve in the 'Very Good' category.

Sanjay Gandhi Biological Park, Patna is spread over 153.00 acres where 1180 wild animals of 100 species are being conserved and developed. Asia's largest and world's second largest centre for rhinoceros breeding is established in this park. This park has been declared at the first plastic-prohibited area of the state.

Compensation in lieu of loss of life and property by wildlife and control on wildlife

Lack of agricultural land in the state, the wildlife continues to come in conflict with the local residents. To manage this, a decision has been taken by the state government to give compensation for crop and house loss. Under this, the compensation for the loss of crop, loss of animal life, loss of house and loss of human life and disability is made by the revenue officers, and compensation is paid from the offices of Forest Divisional Officer. There is a provision of ₹2 lakh in case of death, ₹60 thousand for the seriously injured and ₹10 thousand for the general injury.

In various districts of the state, crops are being damaged by Nilgai. The District Officer and Sub-Divisional Officer have been authorized to grant permission to the farmers–whose crops are being damaged—to kill Nilgai. In case of damage to the crop by Nilgai, a provision has been made to give compensation to the farmers at the rate of ₹20 thousand per hectare.

NEW RAMSAR SITE DESIGNATED IN BIHAR

Kabar Taal wetland in Bihar has been declared the first Ramsar Site in the state. The area of the lake had reduced to 2,032 hectares in 2012 from 6,786 hectares in 1984, according to one study. The state government has identified a core zone to protect the wetland and minimise land conflicts in the area.

Kabar Taal is Asia's largest freshwater oxbow lake. According to the Ramsar Convention, it covers 2,620 hectares of the Indo-Gangetic plains in Bihar. "The Site is one of 18 wetlands within an extensive floodplain complex; it floods during the monsoon season to a depth of 1.5 metres. This absorption of floodwaters is a vital service in Bihar State where 70% of the land is vulnerable to inundation. During the dry season, areas of marshland dry out and are used for agriculture.

Many other programmes have been implemented for the protection of wild animals of the state.

- A Zoo Safari has been established in Rajgir, which has been approved by the National Council for Wildlife.
- The final draft of the Management Plan of Bhim Dam Zoological Sanctuary, Munger has been prepared by World Wildlife Fund (WWF), which has been sent to the Government of India for approval.
- The work of preparing the management plan for Kusheshwarsthan Bird Sanctuary and Barela Lake Bird Sanctuary has been done by the Wildlife Institute of India, Dehradun.
- Management plan of Pant Sanctuary Rajgir work is being done by TERI.
- Privately owned land is also included in the area declared under Kanwar Lake Bird Sanctuary, Begusarai.
- An amount of ₹1,916 lakh has been given for Ganga Dolphin Research Center in Patna, which includes 30 percent share of Government of India and 70 percent share of Bihar Government.
- Sanjay Gandhi Biological Park, Patna, which is spread over 153.00 acres, in which 1,180 wild animals of 100 species are being conserved and protected.
- Asia's largest and the world's second largest center of rhinoceros breeding is established in this park. This park is the first in the state to ban plastic when it comes to fighting plastic pollution.

Bhimbandh Wildlife Sanctuary

This wildlife sanctuary is located in Munger district.

- It was established in the year 1976.
- This sanctuary is spread over an area of about 682 sq km.
- Here leopard, bear, sambar, wild boar, wolf, monkey, langur, nilgai, crocodile, peacock etc. are found.
- Surrounded by picturesque hills, natural valleys and dense forests, Bhimbandh has limitless sources of hot water.
- It is famous as a great picnic spot for the youths during winter season.
- Barela Lake Salim Ali -Jubba Sahni Bird Wildlife Sanctuary
- This wildlife sanctuary is located in Vaishali district.
- This sanctuary was established in the year 1997.
- Cheetah, sambar, deer, bear, cuckoo, sparrow, parrot etc. are found here.
- Gogabil: Bihar's first community reserve is located in Katihar district of Bihar.
- 57 hectare area of the lake has been notified as Community Reserve and 30 hectare area has been notified as Conservation Reserve.
- One of the largest wetlands of Bihar.
- The Gogabil area was protected in 1990 as a 'protected area/safe zone'.
- In 2002, the concept of 'protected area/safe zone' was abolished.
- Since 2002, this area was declassified from the protected area category.
- It was given the status of Important (Special Bird Conservation Area) Area of India (IBA) in 2004.
- Gogabil has all the features to be included as a 'Ramsar Site of India'.

Kaimur Wildlife Sanctuary

- Located in Kaimur district. (Establishment Year -1979).
- It is spread in approximately 1,504.96 km^2 wide in area.
- Wildlife like wolf, black buck, chital, langur etc. are found here.
- It is situated on the banks of Sone river.

Pant (Rajgir) Wildlife Sanctuary

- This wildlife sanctuary is located in Nalanda district of Bihar.
- This wildlife sanctuary is spread across an area of 35.84 sq km.
- It was established in the year 1978.
- Animals like sheep, cow, bear, monkey etc. are found here.

Vikramshila Gangetic Dolphin Sanctuary

- This is an aquatic animal sanctuary which is related to the river Ganga. This aquatic life sanctuary is located in Bhagalpur.
- Vikramshila Gangetic Dolphin Sanctuary extends over a length of approximately 60 kms.
- It was established in 1990–91.
- Gangetic dolphins (sans) are specially protected under this sanctuary.
- Apart from this, this is also a habitat of fresh water fishes and turtles.

Nagi Dam Bird Sanctuary

- It is a bird sanctuary located in Jamui district of Bihar. It is 207 hectares (510 acres) area. It was established in 1984. The birds that are protected here includes cuckoo, sparrow, myna, parrot etc.

Nakti Dam Bird Sanctuary

- It is located near Nagi Dam Bird Sanctuary.
- It is located in Jamui district and was established in the year 1987.
- The area of the sanctuary is 3.33 sq km. Cuckoo, Myna, Sparrow, Parrot, Squirrel etc. are found here.

Udaipur Wildlife Sanctuary

- This wildlife sanctuary is located in West Champaran. Its area is 8.74 km^2. It was established in 1978. Cheetah, Sambhar, Deer, Bear etc. are found here.

Valmiki Wildlife Sanctuary

- This wildlife sanctuary is located in West Champaran district.
- This wildlife sanctuary is spread across an area of 898.45 km2.
- It was established in 1978.
- It is the habitat of the Indian tiger species (Panthera tigris).
- As per the estimates of the National Tiger Conservation Authority the number of tigers in Bihar increased from 8 (in 2010) to 31 in 2018. (As of 2023, the total number of tigers is estimated to be 54.) Bears, deer, chital, sambhar, cheetah etc. are found here.

  Note: It is a National Park (1990) and a Tiger Reserve.

Gautam Buddha Wildlife Sanctuary

- This sanctuary is located in Gaya district. It was established in 1976. Here leopard, cheetah, sambar, deer, chital etc. are found.

Kanwar Lake Bird Sanctuary

- This bird sanctuary was established in 1987. This bird sanctuary is located in Begusarai district of Bihar.
- This sanctuary is spread across an area of 67.5 sq kms. and is a centre of attraction for tourists because of the Siberian crane.
- Kanwar Lake has been declared as the 39th Ramsar site of the country. This is Bihar's first 'Ramsar' site.

Sanjay Gandhi Biological Park

- This is a zoo and biological park located in Patna. It was established in 1969.
- It is spread across an area of 153 sq km.
- Here, you can see rhinoceros, zebras, giraffes, tigers, crocodiles etc.
- This garden is the center of tourist attraction.

Agriculture

- **Land Use Model**
- **Agricultural Climate Region**
- **Horticulture in Bihar**
- **Bihar State Milk Co-Operative Federation**
- **Land Reforms**
- **Agricultural Region**
- **Major Crops**
- **Animal Husbandry and Fisheries**
- **Fourth Agriculture Roadmap (2023-28)**

Bihar is an agrarian state, where 86 percent of the population is dependent on agriculture. Plain fertile, alluvial loam soil, abundant water resources and plentiful human resources have made the agricultural sector an important part of the state's economy. It is because of scarcity of mineral resources that the possibility of development of basic industries is limited. Bihar produces 6.6 percent of India's total food grains. 18 percent of the total gross domestic production of the state comes from the agriculture sector. About 70 percent of the total working population in Bihar is engaged in agricultural work.

LAND USE MODEL

Agriculture is the foundation of Bihar's economy. The lifestyle of Biharis is related to agriculture. Therefore, the land use model has special significance in the state. Bihar is a state, prone to natural disasters like drought and floods every year. The population pressure is high in Bihar. Therefore, by increasing the agricultural production by the appropriate use of land resources, population can be sustained properly. Only by proper land management, proper development of barren land is possible along with control of floods and droughts.

Several factors have influenced the development of land use model in Bihar, which are as follows:

1. Relief
2. Climate
3. Rainfall
4. Human activity

Majority of Bihar is plain, which is under immense pressure of population. Traditional means have been used in agriculture. This has led to the development of subsistence agriculture in Bihar. It is because of the high rainfall in the plains of North Bihar and creation of alluvial plain by several perennial rivers like Ganga, Gandak, and Koshi that and the area of land under agriculture is more in Bihar than other states of the country. With population pressure, development work like rail, road, industry and residential areas have expanded. To meet the food requirement of the larger population, the agricultural land has been expanded by cutting forests. These reasons have caused deforestation to take place at a rapid pace. The area of land under forests is limited. Forests are found on only 7.21 percent of the total area of Bihar.

The plateau, hilly, rugged land, the expansion of agricultural land has been low in South Bihar, especially in low marginal plateau areas. There is more forest and pasture land in these areas. With less amount of rainfall, wasteland is more in the southern parts, especially Aurangabad, Gaya, and Nawada districts. The area under agricultural land has increased due to expansion of the Son Canal Irrigation Scheme in Southwest Bihar. There are a total of 1.61 crore holdings in Bihar, with an average size of about 0.4 hectares. Amongst them, 91 percent holdings are small and marginal in size.

The net sowing area of the state is 56.1 percent. The net sowing area is more than 60 percent in 5 districts of the state.

Crop Intensity

India is divided into 5 agricultural intensity zones. In this, Bihar is placed in high intensity zone (70–130%). This category also includes an area with 100–200 cm rainfall. It is basically a two-crop agricultural area. Presently, the agricultural intensity in Bihar is 146.3%. The main reason for the rise in the agricultural intensity is the expansion of irrigation facilities. The agriculture intensity is shown in the table below:

Sr. No.	Category	Area (in lakh hectares)
1	Gross crop area	78.82
2	Field sown more than once	21.70

The districts with the highest crop intensity are Saharsa, Sheohar, and Araria, while the districts with the lowest crop intensity are Sheikhpura, Arwal, and Munger.

Agricultural Crop Model

It is clear from the study of agricultural crop models in Bihar that there is a multiplicity of food crops. Bihar's agriculture is subsistence agriculture. Food grains are produced on 90 percent of the total agricultural area of the state. In recent years, the area of food grain crops has decreased. The area of pulses production has also decreased due to which the production of pulses has declined. The main reason for the decrease in the area of pulses production is the increase in the area of grain production and the area of cash crops due to the expansion of irrigation facilities. The development of agricultural crop models in Bihar has been done on the basis of agricultural sub-climatic zones. The following table shows the major crop models in different agro-climatic zones of Bihar:

Crop Model Zone

Agro Climate Zone	Crop	Main Districts
Zone – I	Paddy-wheat, paddy-rye, paddy-potato, paddy-maize, maize-wheat, maize-potato, maize-rye, paddy-lentil, paddy-linseed (Teesi)	West Champaran, East Champaran, Siwan, Saran, Sitamarhi, Sheohar, Muzaffarpur, Vaishali, Madhubani, Darbhanga, Samastipur, Gopalganj, Begusarai
Zone – II	Jute-wheat, jute-potato, jute-urad, jute-mustard, paddy-wheat-moong, paddy-rapeseed	Purnea, Katihar, Saharsa, Supaul, Madhepura, Khagaria, Araria, Kishanganj
Zone – III	Paddy-wheat, paddy-gram, paddy-lentils, paddy-rye	Sheikhpura, Munger, Jamui, Lakhisarai, Bhagalpur, Banka, Rohtas, Bhojpur, Buxar, Bhabhua, Arwal, Patna, Nalanda, Nawada, Jehanabad, Aurangabad, Gaya
Source: Agriculture Department, Government of Bihar		

Agricultural Composition Region

Agriculture or crop composition refers to the group of crops that are grown in a particular area in a particular year. The statistical method was first used by American scholar Weber in 1954 for determining the agricultural or crop composition region. Later on Doi used it in 1959. Both these scholars had determined the crop composition region based on the standard deviation method of statistics. In Bihar, the district has been considered as the unit of study of crop composition region. The crop composition region is determined by determining the order of the crops based on how much area is sown per year in each district. For this, the crop sown on at least one percent of the area is made the basis. At present, statistical method is used for its determination.

The crop composition region (crop association) in Bihar has been determined on the basis of 10 crops. There are 4 pulses crops such as Khesari, Masoor, Moong and Gram. There are three food crops such as paddy, wheat and maize; two cash crops are jute and sugarcane and one vegetable crop is potato.

In the Indian context, India is divided into 6 agricultural composition regions, in which most of Bihar comes under three-crop composition region. Under this, paddy, wheat and pulses are the main crops. Wheat is produced along with paddy in irrigated areas and pulses are produced in non-irrigated areas. Three-crop agricultural combination area of the state is densely populated region, due to which more emphasis is laid on the production of food grains.

AGRICULTURAL REGION

Determination of agricultural region is an important factor in terms of development and planning of agriculture. It is a geographical region, which is determined on the basis of similar types of climatic conditions, soil types, similarity in crop types and structural features. The determination of an agricultural region depends on the use of the sown land.

The classification of agricultural regions in Bihar has been done on the basis of experiential and statistical methods. Professor Parmeshwar Dayal and Ayodhya Prasad have used the experiential method to determine the agricultural regions. Professor Dayal divided the united Bihar into 57 agricultural regions on this basis, while Ayodhya Prasad divided Bihar into 5 agricultural regions.

In 1959, using the statistical method, Professor Inayat Ahmed divided Bihar into 12 agricultural regions and R.L. Singh divided it into 7 agricultural regions.

Agricultural scientists have divided Bihar into 4 agricultural regions based on the diversity of crops. Following are these 4 agricultural regions:

One-crop agriculture region: Those districts where only one crop (paddy) are produced is called one-crop agricultural region. Madhubani district of the state is placed in this category. Although pulses and oilseeds are also cultivated here, they are cultivated on less than one percent agricultural area of the district. Paddy is cultivated on most of the area of the district.

Two-crop agriculture region: Two major crops are grown in it. Under this, crop groups like paddy-wheat, paddy-maize, paddy-jute, or wheat-maize, etc. are grown. Plain agricultural areas come under these two-crop agricultural regions. Purnia district has been placed in the category of two-crop agricultural region.

Three-crop agriculture region: The agricultural areas in which three major crops are included are placed in the category of three-crop agriculture region. In this agricultural region in Bihar, two major crops are grown along with paddy out of wheat, maize, jute and khesari. These crops are sown on the basis of soil type and climatic characteristics of different regions.

Four-crop agricultural region: Four crops are sown in this agricultural region. Paddy is predominant in all areas of Bhagalpur, but it becomes four-crop agricultural region with maize, wheat and khesari. Paddy is also grown as the main crop in Saran and the other three crops are also grown on the basis of regional characteristics.

Production Level of Main Crops in Bihar (2020-21 to 2020-23)

Crops	2020-21	2021-22	2022-23	CAGR (%) in thousand tonnes
Foodgrains	17952.4	18486.9	19736.0	4.8
Cereals	17573.8	18099.0	19322.0	4.9
Rice	7392.7	7717.3	7872.9	3.2
Bodo Rice	657.0	709.9	725.7	5.1
Aghani Rice	6599.5	6862.9	6997.0	3.0
Garma Rice	136.2	144.5	150.2	5.0
Wheat	6635.0	6889.8	6600.0	-0.3
Maize	3521.4	3470.9	4829.4	17.1
Kharif Maize	225.1	235.0	445.1	40.6
Rabi Maize	2323.9	2325.1	3365.0	20.3
Garma Maize	972.4	910.9	1019.3	2.4
Total Coarse Grain	3546.1	3491.8	4849.0	19.9
Barley	14.4	12.4	12.4	-7.0
Sorghum	1.3	1.5	1.0	-13.5
Bajara	4.8	3.3	2.7	-25.1
Ragi	2.6	2.4	2.4	-4.4
Kodo-Sawa	1.6	1.3	1.2	-15.2
Total Pulses	378.6	387.9	414.0	4.6
Total Kharif Pulses	24.6	18.4	16.7	-17.6
Uradh	9.4	6.0	5.6	-23.61
Badai Moong	6.5	4.6	3.9	-22.1
Horse Gram	6.3	5.9	5.3	-8.8
Ghagra	0.4	0.4	0.4	-2.5
Other Kharif Pulses	1.9	1.6	1.5	-10.8
Total Rabi Pulses	354.0	369.5	397.3	5.9
Arhar Daal	23.4	20.9	24.3	1.8
Gram	54.5	54.4	57.2	2.5
Masoor Daal	124.6	124.2	131.7	2.8
Khesari	42.8	44.4	40.7	-2.5
Pea	19.4	15.7	16.6	-7.6
Garma Moong	88.3	109.0	125.8	19.3
Other Rabi Pulses	1.0	1.0	1.1	5.6

Total Oilseeds	124.2	121.5	139.6	6.0
Safflower	0.1	0.1	0.1	-3.4
Sunflower	9.9	9.0	9.0	-4.5
Mustard	95.5	88.4	106.8	5.7
Flaxseed	5.4	4.8	4.4	-9.3
Groundnut	0.8	0.7	0.7	-7.7
Total Fibrous Fruit	787.0	852.0	776.0	-0.7
Jute	618.0	713.0	630.0	1.0
Sugarcane (eekh)	12109.9	12025.6	14452.0	9.2

Cropping Pattern (2018-19 to 2022-23) in Percentage

Crop	2018-19	2019-20	2020-21	2021-22	2022-23
Foodgrains	87.1	87.1	87.4	87.6	87.9
Pulses	6.9	6.9	6.7	6.6	6.4
Oilseeds	1.5	1.5	1.7	1.7	1.7
Fibrous Fruits	1.2	1.2	0.9	0.8	0.9
Sugarcane (eekh)	3.3	3.3	3.3	3.3	3.1
Total	100.0	100.0	100.0	100.0	100.0

AGRICULTURAL CLIMATE REGION

The whole of India is divided into 15 different agro climatic zones. Bihar is in the agro-climate zone-IV of India. The region of the intermediate Ganges plain is included in this agro-climatic zone. The areas of Bihar and Eastern Uttar Pradesh are included in this region. Agro-climatic zone-IV is further divided into 6 sub-agro-climatic zones. There are three sub-agro-climatic zones in Bihar and three in Uttar Pradesh. The three sub-agro-climatic zones of Bihar are—

Northwest Alluvial Plain Region: About 13 districts of the state have been included in this area. This sub-agricultural climatic zone is located in the Himalayas. The amount of annual rainfall in this region is 1040–1450 millimeters. The climate here is dry and sub humid. Khadar, sandstone loam and alluvial soils are found in this area. These soils are of acidic nature. Agricultural work is done on 70 percent of the land of this state. About 42 percent of the land in this state is irrigated land.

Northeast Alluvial Plain Region: About 8 districts have been included in this area. This agro-climatic zone is a flood-prone region. The amount of annual rainfall in this region is 1200–1700 millimeters. The climate of this region is arid tropical climate. About 60 percent of the land in this region is agricultural. About 44 percent of this region is irrigated land.

Alluvial plain region of South Bihar: About 17 districts of the state have been included in this region. The amount of annual rainfall in this region is 990–1300 millimeters. Irrigation facility has developed the most in this area. About 75 percent of the land in this area is irrigated land. This area comes under the Son Canal Irrigation Area. This region is divided into two parts; first: the south-eastern alluvial plain, and second: the south-western alluvial plain. The table below shows the sub-agricultural climatic region and its related characteristics:

Important geographical features of the sub-agro-climatic zone of Bihar

	Sub-agro-climatic zone		
	Northwest Alluvial Plain Region	Northeast Alluvial Plain Region	Alluvial Plain Region of South Bihar
Districts	West Champaran, East Champaran, Siwan, Saran, Sitamarhi, Sheohar, Muzaffarpur, Vaishali, Madhubani, Darbhanga, Samastipur, Gopalganj, Begusarai (13 districts)	Purnia, Katihar, Saharsa, Supaul, Madhepura, Khagaria, Araria, Kishanganj (8 districts)	Sheikhpura, Munger, Jamui, Lakhisarai, Bhagalpur, Banka, Rohtas, Bhojpur, Buxar, Bhabua, Arwal, Patna, Nalanda, Nawada, Jehanabad, Aurangabad, Gaya (17 districts)

MAJOR CROPS

After the bifurcation of the state, due to the transfer of mineral resources and industries based on it to Jharkhand, agricultural produce and animal husbandry has become Bihar's main source of livelihood. The plains of Northern Bihar and the southern plains of the Ganges are favourable for agricultural work. Bihar is a region of intensive agriculture and due to the population pressure, agriculture is predominant for livelihood.

There are broadly 3 types of crops grown in the state: 1. Kharif, 2. Rabi, 3. Jayad

Kharif: There are mainly two types of crops—Bhadai and Agahan that are grown under the Kharif crop. The major kharif crops are paddy, maize, jowar, millet, and pulses such as arahar and moong. Kharif crops are sown in June-July and harvested in October-November. Some annual crops such as sugarcane and jute are also grown under the Kharif crop.

Rabi: Major crops under Rabi are wheat, barley, gram, pea, mustard, potatoes, etc. Rabi is sown in October-November and harvested in March-April. Under this, cash crops like tobacco, fruits, and vegetables are also grown.

Zaid: Zaid crop is grown in areas with regular irrigation between March-June. Corn, sorghum, green fodder, madua, etc. are grown under it.

The above mentioned Kharif, Rabi and Zaid crops are shown in the table below:

Types of Crops

Type of crop	Sowing time	Harvesting time	Main crops
Kharif i) Bhadai, ii) Agahani	June-July June-July	October-November August-November	Rice, maize, jowar, bajra, tur, moong paddy, maize, jowar, bajra, jute, paddy, sugarcane, and vegetable
Rabi	October-November	March-April	Barley, gram, peas, mustard, potatoes, lentils, and khesari
Zaid	April	June	Maize, sorghum, vegetable, green fodder, and madua

Main crop

The first major crop of the state is rice and the second major crop is wheat. Apart from these, maize, sorghum, millet, pulses, and oilseeds are produced. Among the cash crops, sugarcane, potato, tobacco, jute, red chilli etc., are the main crops of Bihar.

Food crops (grains)

Paddy: This is the main crop of Bihar, which is sown in most of the region. Paddy is a crop of hot and humid climate. All the geographical conditions required for paddy are present in Bihar, which are as follows:

- Minimum temperature 160 Celsius, maximum 270 Celsius and average temperature 240 Celsius.
- Average rainfall 100 cm to 200 cm
- Alluvial and loam soils
- Greater availability of labour

Two crops of rice are grown in the north-western part of Bihar and even three crops in the eastern part. Agahani paddy is sown in more than 80 percent of the region, while Garama paddy is grown in about 3 percent of the region. Boro paddy is grown in Purnia and in East and West Champaran. Boro paddy is sown in November-December and harvested in January-February. The major rice producing districts in Bihar are Rohtas, Aurangabad, West Champaran, Madhubani, Muzaffarpur, East Champaran, Sitamarhi, Darbhanga, Katihar, Purnia, Patna, Gaya, Jehanabad, Arwal, Bhojpur, Kaimur, etc. The major varieties of paddy such as Prabhat, Saket, Sita, Kanak, IR. 36, and Swarna Sub-1 are grown in Bihar. The major pests found in the paddy are stem borer, Madhua moth, milde moth, Babhani moth etc. Rohtas is the highest paddy growing district.

Wheat: It is the second major food crop of Bihar. Winter wheat is produced in Bihar. Since the winters in Bihar are dry, the crop requires irrigation. The suitable geographical conditions for wheat are as follows:

- Alluvial and loamy soils
- Temperature from 140 Celsius to 180 Celsius
- Rainfall 50 cm to 100 cm

Wheat is a rabi crop, which is sown in November-December and harvested in March-April. The major districts producing wheat are Rohtas, Bhabhua, Gaya, Darbhanga, Bhojpur, Siwan, Saran, Aurangabad, etc. Rohtas is the largest wheat producing district. Wheat is cultivated on 29 percent of the total agricultural land of Bihar. It is sown on about 22 lakh hectare area of Bihar. Bihar ranks seventh in the country in wheat production. Major varieties of wheat like C. 306, K. 9107, P.B.W. 343, H. D. 2824, etc. are sown in Bihar. The major pests and diseases infesting wheat are termites (Odontotermes obesus), mahoo (lahi), brown harada, yellow harada, scorching disease, bud disease, akdi disease, etc.

Maize: Maize is the third major food crop in Bihar after rice and wheat. Maize is cultivated in all seasons in Bihar. Suitable geographical conditions for maize are as follows:

- Temperature from 180 Celsius to 270 Celsius
- Rainfall 60 cm to 110 cm
- Heavy loamy and sandy, loamy soils

It is sown in June-July and harvested in September–October. The major areas producing maize are Katihar, Madhepura, Khagaria, Saran, Muzaffarpur, Champaran, Darbhanga, Saharsa, etc.

Maize seeds are sown 3-5 cm inside the soil, and they require irrigation 5-6 times. In many areas, mixed agriculture is practised, wherein potato or radish or pea is cultivated with maize during rabi season and urad, or cowpea, or tur is cultivated with maize during kharif season. At present, 'Shaktimaan', a seed of 'quality protein maize', has been prepared. Quality protein maize contains high amounts of lysine and tryptophan. The insects and diseases infesting in maize are kajra insect, torso borer, corn borer, sclerenchyma (scorching), harda (tanze) etc.

Barley: Barley is a rabi crop, which is mainly sown in non-irrigated areas. Barley is cultivated in regions with low rainfall and hot climate. The major districts producing barley are West Champaran, Bhabhua, Aurangabad, Muzaffarpur, Munger, Bhojpur, Saran, Darbhanga, Purnia, Gaya, etc. Barley is cultivated as a mixed crop with wheat, gram, mustard, etc. The major varieties of barley are Ratna, K.125, Azad, Jyoti, etc.

Madua (Ragi): It is a dry climate crop. Like jowar and bajra, madua (ragi) falls in the category of coarse grains. This crop is grown in sandy soil in the flood affected areas of Kosi. Bihar ranks first in India in the production of ragi. The largest producing district is Darbhanga. Apart from this, it is also produced in Supaul, Saran, Saharsa, Siwan, Madhepura and Gopalganj districts.

Food Crop (Pulses): Major pulses grown in Bihar are gram, arahar, khesari, lentil, moong, urad, etc.

Gram: Gram is a major rabi crop of Bihar. For, kewal and alluvial soils are suitable. Gram is produced in districts like Patna, Aurangabad, Nalanda, Bhojpur, Gaya, Lakhisarai, Bhagalpur, Rohtas and Jehanabad. Patna is the highest gram producing district. Like other pulse crops, gram increases the fertility of soil by fixing nitrogen through bacteria living in the knots formed in its roots. The major varieties of gram are Rajendra Chana, Pusa 256, R.A.U. 52, B.R. 72, etc. Mixed agriculture of rye, mustard, and chickpea is also carried out in the state. The major pests and diseases that occur in gram are pod borer, kajra insect, semilooper, ukhada disease, stemphylium blight, etc.

Arhar/Pigeon pea: Arhar is also called Tuar in Bihar. It is sown with the Kharif crop, but is harvested with the Rabi crop. It is the major pulse crop of Bihar. Its highest producing districts are Gaya, Aurangabad and Bhabua respectively. The districts with the largest area under Arhar are Bhabua, Gaya and East Champaran, respectively. It is grown in almost all the districts of Bihar.

Khesari: This is the major pulses rabi crop sown in Bihar. But it is a low-grade pulses crop. The districts producing it are Patna, Aurangabad and Jehanabad respectively. The largest area under Khesari is in Aurangabad, Patna and Jehanabad. Keval and loam soil are more suitable for its production.

Lentil: Lentil is the main rabi pulses crop of Bihar. The highest producing districts are Patna, Bhabua, etc. respectively. Apart from this, it is also grown in Gaya and Jehanabad.

Moong: Moong is a pulses crop which is sown after the harvesting of wheat. In many parts of the state, it is also sown in June-July at the time of sowing Kharif crop. The main districts producing it are Muzaffarpur, Saharsa, Darbhanga, Supaul, Katihar, Kishanganj, etc.

Oilseeds

Mustard and Rye: Mustard and rye are the major oilseed crops of Bihar. Their oil is mainly used in food. They are grown in the plains of Bihar. The districts with the most area under mustard are Samastipur, Begusarai, West Champaran, respectively. The highest mustard and rye producing districts are Begusarai, West Champaran, Patna, Samastipur, Muzaffarpur, Khagaria, etc.

Sesame: Black and white colored sesame is produced in Bihar. Sesame oil is used in food, cosmetics and as medicine. The highest sesame producing district is Supaul where sesame is cultivated on the largest area. Other sesame producing districts are Samastipur, Bhabua, Nawada, Kishanganj etc.

Castor: It is an oilseed crop, but its oil is not used as food. It is used in fire-burning, soap industry and as a lubricant. It is produced in all the districts of the state. Its plants are planted along the fields of the main crops. For this, any land, flat or uneven, is suitable.

Cash Crops: Cash crops have special importance in strengthening the economic condition of farmers in the state. These crops are usually sold from the fields, which directly benefits the farmers. Among these commercial crops, following are the major ones:

Sugarcane: It is the major cash crop of the state. Sugarcane is the basis of sugar industry, which is the main industry of Bihar. Sugarcane is mainly produced in the plains of North Bihar. Sugarcane is produced in the regions with high rainfall and irrigation. Ideal geographical conditions for sugarcane production are available in the state, which are as follows:

- Limestone loam soil
- Average temperature 260 Celsius
- An average rainfall of 140 cm

The major sugarcane producing districts in Bihar are East and West Champaran, Saran, Muzaffarpur, Darbhanga, Patna, Munger, Purnia, etc. Sugarcane is cultivated on 10 percent of the agricultural area in Gandak, Kosi Doab area. Sugarcane is cultivated on 3 lakh hectares (6%) of the total 76 lakh hectares of agricultural land in the state.

Jute: Jute is produced in areas with high rainfall, high temperature and fertile alluvial soil. It is cultivated in the north-eastern flood plains. After cutting, it is kept under water for some time. After that, the bark is removed from the stem, which later takes the form of fibre. Purnea and Katihar are the largest, producing districts in Bihar. Apart from them, it is also produced in districts like Saharsa, Muzaffarpur, Darbhanga, Madhubani, Kishanganj, etc. Jute is used in the packing industry as well as manufacturing of cloth, sack, rope, etc. Bihar is the second jute producing state in India after West Bengal.

Tobacco: Bihar is the sixth largest tobacco producing state in the country. Tobacco is produced mainly in the valley of the Gandak River in the state. The main tobacco producing districts are Vaishali, Sitamarhi, Begusarai, Purnia and Samastipur. The Virginian variety of tobacco is also grown in Purnea.

Chilli: It is the main cash crop of the state, which falls under the category of Agahani crop. Though it grown in all seasons, alluvial soil is most suitable for its production. The main chilli producing regions are Darbhanga, Samastipur, Vaishali, etc.

Tea: Tea is produced in Kishanganj and Purnea in Northeast Bihar. This region has suitable geographical location for tea production due to the highest rainfall and sloping land.

Mesta: This fibrous crop is similar to jute. This crop is produced in the plains of Bihar. The areas with high rainfall are suitable for its cultivation. This crop, which is grown in fertile land, is produced in the districts of Purnea, Saharsa, Patna, Darbhanga, etc.

Agriculture and Allied Sectors in Bihar

From 2018-19 to 2022-23, Bihar's agriculture and allied sectors contributed an average of about 20 per cent to the gross state value addition. During the same period, the crop sector contributed 9.9 per cent to the gross state value addition, followed by livestock at 6.6 per cent and aquaculture at 1.8 per cent. In the year 2022-23, the sugarcane production (eekh) of the state was 214.76 lakh tonnes and the average yield was 98.73 tonnes per hectare. In the year 2022-23, about ₹ 1275.62 lakh was distributed for seed production, distribution and training programs for farmers. In the year 2022-23, the total production of eggs was 327.43 crore tonnes, while that of fish was 8.46 lakh tonnes.

District wise trends of production and productivity of selected crops:

- **Rice:** Rohtas, Aurangabad and Kaimur together had the highest productivity of rice with 25.2 per cent share.
- **Wheat:** Wheat is a Rabi crop of Bihar. The highest productivity of wheat is in Khagaria (3960 kg per hectare) and the lowest productivity is in Jamui (1980 kg per hectare).
- **Maize:** The highest productivity of maize is in Araria (9872 kg per hectare).
- **Pulses:** The districts with highest productivity in terms of pulses are Begusarai (1324 kg per hectare), Nalanda (1283 kg per hectare) and Siwan (1280 kg per hectare).

Agricultural Innovation

In Bihar, due to structural facilities like irrigation facilities, improved seeds, more use of chemical fertilizers, mechanization in agriculture, etc., there has been diffusion of crops and diversification of production. Advanced/improved seeds, food and water are called green revolution techniques.

The Bihar government emphasized on the creation of irrigation capacity and increase in crop density with its technology in Agricultural Road Map-III (2017-22). In the Agricultural Road Map-II (2012-17), emphasis was on the development of high yielding seeds. To distribute this seed variety to farmers, agricultural extension services like 'Kisan Vikas Shibir' and 'Agricultural Advisor' are being used. Among them artemisia annua, dhaincha, herbal and medicinal plants, organic farming, honey production, fisheries, etc., are important.

In order to promote organic farming in the state and to limit the use of chemical fertilizers, cultivation of dhaincha is being encouraged. Dhaincha plant is the main source of green manure. The green manure produced from it produces large amounts of organic acids, which increase the quality and productivity of sterile, saline, and alkaline soil. Green manure made from dhaincha is more useful for paddy cultivation because it increases the amount of vitamin A and protein in rice. Dhaincha is sown after wheat, which is ready in 50-55 days. The dhaincha crop is buried inside the soil, which then takes the form of green manure. "National Mission on Medicinal Plant Year" is celebrated annually since 2008-09 to promote medicine agriculture in the state. Under this, emphasis is laid on the production and use of medicinal plants. In addition, vermi-compost production has been made demand based.

Fruit production

The agro-climatic conditions and alluvial soils of Bihar are suitable for the production of fruits. The main fruits produced in Bihar are litchi, mango, banana, guava, lemon, pineapple, papaya, amla, etc.

Bihar accounts for more than half of the total production of litchi in India. Litchi is a horticultural crop for which humid climate is suitable. In Bihar, litchi is mainly produced in the plains of Northern Bihar in Muzaffarpur, Vaishali, Champaran, Samastipur, Bhagalpur. The amount of sugar in litchi is 10-15 percent and the amount of protein is 1.1 percent. The main varieties of litchi are indigenous, arlibedana, shahi, mandaraji (china), kaswa, etc. The royal litchi is most famous of all.

Fruit Production in Bihar

- Banana: 20.04 lakh ton
- Mango: 17.56 lakh ton
- Guava: 4.36 lakh ton
- Litchi: 3.09 lakh ton

Vegetable production

Potato is cultivated during autumn in Rabi season. It is sown from October to December. The major varieties of potato sown in Bihar are Rajendra Aloo-3, Kufri Jyoti, Kufri Badshah, Kufri Pokhraj, Kufri Sutlej, Kufri Bahar etc. Potato is the main vegetable crop of the state. Loam soil and sandy soil are suitable for it. Nalanda is the largest potato producing district. Patna and Saran occupy the second and third place. Nalanda, Patna, and Katihar are the leading districts in onion production.

Main Crops of Bihar and the Regions of Production

Crop	Regions of Production
Rice	Rohtas, West Champaran, East Champaran, Arwal, Buxar
Wheat	Rohtas, Gaya, Darbhanga
Maize	Saran, Muzaffarpur, Khagariya, Begusarai, Munger
Barley	West Champaran, Saharasa, Purnia
Madua/ragi	Saharasa, Muzaffarpur, Saran
Millet	Patna, Munger, Gaya
Linseed	Patna, Bhojpur, Gaya
Mustard/rye	Patna, Muzaffarpur, Darbhanga
Sesame	West Champaran, Shahabad
Pigeon pea	Darbhanga, Muzaffarpur, Munger
Gram	Bhojpur, Buxar
Lentil	Patna, Champaran, Gaya
Khesari	Patna, Gaya, Bhojpur
Sugarcane	Champaran, Saran, Muzaffarpur
Jute	Purnia, Katihar
Tobacco	Darbhanga, Muzaffarpur, Munger, Samastipur, Saharsa
Potato	Patna, Nalanda, Saran, Samastipur

HORTICULTURE IN BIHAR

Horticulture is a sunrise sector, which has potential to promote economy. Horticulture is the branch of plant agriculture which deal with garden products normally fruits and vegetables and also ornamental plants. This term covers all format of garden management, but in general words it refers to use of commercial production. Broadly speaking horticulture comes between domestic gardening and field agriculture by all formats of crops have close relation with agriculture. At the outset it is important to go through floriculture deals with the production of flowers (Ornamental cut flowers, pot plants, and generics). Further horticulture is a broad class which includes shrubs, trees, and vines having commercial importance. The success of horticulture crops are influenced by various factors. Among these forces the main are climate, terrain, and so many other variations and changes.

The state of Bihar is located in the Ganges basin's plains. It has large groundwater resources and alluvial soil. The state agriculture is rich and also diverse. The main cereal crops of the state are wheat, maize, and rice. Pulses like arhar, gram urad, moong, pea, are grown in the state include potatoes, onions, and cauliflowers. In fruit production, it is 3rd largest producer of pineapple, the largest producer of lychee, and a significant producer of mango, and guava. Jute and sugarcane are two income crops in the state. The state vegetable production is increasing day by day. Near about 12 percent of the state gross area is presently covered by vegetables farming, and its percentage is increasing. Potato, tomato onion, cauliflower and brinjal are the main vegetable crops. In yesteryears we have seen an early variety of cauliflower arrive on the market in Hajipur, Sonepur and Vaishali. Vegetable production is properly distributed among different districts. Sitamarhi, Vaishali, Muzaffarpur, West Champaran, Samastipur, Katihar, and Begusarai are the districts having proper shares in total vegetable output, in addition to Patna and Jehanabad, where vegetable production is top in the state. In the district of Bihar, rice is grown. All three different types of rice are grown at three different times in the year like autumn rice, aghani rice, and summer rice. Near about 6 million tonnes of rice are produced every year in the state. Wheat cultivation is largely confined to western Bihar.

Growth of Horticulture in Bihar: In yesteryears, Bihar has witnessed a proper increase in the production and also export of horticultural produces. Horticulture industry is growing slowly in Bihar over the last decades. The Bihar's agro-climatic conditions and fertile soil make it suitable for growing wide range of horticultural products. The state initiatives to promote horticulture related activities have also contributed to much to the growth of the horticulture. However this sector faces challenges that need to be located like inadequate infrastructure, lack of market connectivity and limited access of credit to the producers. Horticulture has been important sector in the state to the state economy. The Bihar favorable agro-climatic conditions and fertile land make it productive for a wide range of horticultural produces. The state is known for its production of fruits like to litchi mango, guava, and banana, as well as vegetables such as cauliflower, cabbage, tomato, and brinjal. The state is also a good producer of flowers like marigold, rose, and jasmine. Further horticulture has a good potential in Bihar and has right policies and investments it may contine to grow and contribute to the state economy.

The government of Bihar has implemented several schemes and initiatives to promote horticulture and address the challenges faced by farmers. Government of Bihar launched Various Schemes in this Regard which are follows:

- **Bihar Horticulture Development Society:** It works towards developing and promoting horticulture and enhancing the livelihoods of produce.
- **Horticulture Mission:** This initiative aims to promote holistic growth of the horticulture in the state.
- **Krishi Vigyan Kendras:** These centers provide technical support to farmers for improving horticultural practices. KVKs promotes horticulture in the state.

This state also has a small scale industrial sector. As of 2022 agriculture accounts for 28% industry 17% and service 62% of the economy of the state. Bihar is located in the eastern part of the country having very good benefits for its location and proximity of market. It is also connectivity to culcutta and haldia ports. It has availability of raw materials like iron and coal from neighbouring state. The economy of the state is fastest growing, which is mainly service based. Apart from this agriculture and industrial sectors are also promoting economy of the state.

Impact of Horticulture on Socio Economic Development: In Bihar the impact of horticulture on socio-economic conditions has been multifaceted which requires a comprehensive analysis. In yesteryears horticulture has emerged as an important sector in the economy of Bihar contributing to agricultural growth and socio-economic development. Bihar located in the eastern part of India, is predominantly an agrarian state when agriculture become the primary source of livelihood for most of the population. Horticulture, which includes the cultivation of fruits, flowers vegetables, and medicinal plants has gained important in the resources. The state ecological zones provide proper conditions for the cultivation of horticultural crops, making it one of the leading producers of fruits and vegetables. The significant impacts of horticulture and its product on socio-economic conditions in Bihar is its role in enhancing agricultural productivity. Horticultural crops have higher value addition potential and have less price fluctuations. By diversifying cropping patterns and practicing latest horticultural system farmers have become able to get more yields and better returns on investments. Further the cultivation of high-value horticultural crops like vegetable and fruits has enabled farmers to get higher prices in the market therefore by improving their income levels and standard of living.

Horticulture has became a major source of income generation and employment provider in the state mainly in rural part where agriculture is the main occupation. The harvesting, processing and cultivation of horticultural products require a proper amount of manpower by creating employment opportunities for a great number of people, including farmers. Horticulture has emerged as a key driver of socio-economic condition in Bihar with its significant contributions to agricultural production income generation employment creation poverty reduction and also food security. By promoting the potential of horticulture and addressing the challenges, the state can achieve growth, improve the livelihoods and contribute to the overall development of Bihar.

ANIMAL HUSBANDRY AND FISHERIES

Under agriculture, animal husbandry, fisheries, fruits production, and floriculture are also included with crop production. Animals, sheep, poultry, pig, goat, etc. are reared in Bihar under animal husbandry. Animal husbandry is the main source of income and employment for the rural population in the state. This sector contributes approximately one-fifth of the total rural income. It provides employment opportunities on a large scale to marginal farmers, workers, and women.

In Bihar, animal husbandry work is carried out with the following objectives:

- For the use of animals in agricultural work
- For obtaining milk and milk related products
- To obtain meat and leather

Milk and dairy products, poultry, meat, fish etc. are among the products obtained from the animal husbandry sector. The Bihar State Cooperative Milk Producers Federation (COMFED) was established in 1983 to increase milk production in Bihar. It is the agency that implements Operation Flood (White Revolution) programme in the state. COMFED has adopted a three-tier model for the establishment of milk cooperatives, which has three levels as follows:

1. Cooperative committees of milk producers at village level
2. Milk associations at district level
3. Milk federation at the state level

COMFED also markets milk products by the name of 'Sudha Dairy' in Bihar, which is based on the pattern of Gujrat based Anand Dairy.

BIHAR STATE MILK CO-OPERATIVE FEDERATION

The Bihar State Milk Co-Operative Federation Ltd is a state government cooperative under the ownership of Ministry of Cooperation, Government of Bihar, India. It was established in 1983 as a state government cooperative of the Government of Bihar. It markets its products under the label "Sudha Dairy". The co-operative facilitates the procurement, processing, and marketing of dairy products. It provides education to the unions on efficient dairy processing, and assists them with animal care including artificial insemination, vaccination, and feeding.

The Dairy co-operative was founded in 1983 to coordinate the work of various local milk unions. The government opened Nalanda dairy in 2013 which is the Largest Automation based Dairy Plant in Eastern India. The establishment of Sudha was a result of White Revolution. In January 2021, the organisation had decided to make two new dairy plants in Bhagalpur and Purnia districts.

Eight district level Milk Producers' Cooperative Unions are affiliated to the Federation. These unions cover 38 districts. In addition, rest of areas are covered directly by the Federation. They are:

- **Magadh Milk Union, Gaya:** Covering Gaya, Aurangabad, Jehanabad, Arwal and Nawada Districts.
- **Vaishali Patliputra Milk Union, Patna:** Covering Patna, Vaishali, Nalanda, Saran and Sheikhpura districts.
- **DR Milk Union (DRMU), Barauni:** Covering Begusarai, Khagaria, Lakhisarai, and part of Patna Districts.
- **Tirhut Milk Union (TIMUL), Muzaffarpur:** Covering Muzaffarpur, Sitamarhi, Sheohar, East Champaran (Motihari), Chakia, West Champaran, Siwan, and Gopalganj.
- **Mithila Milk Union, Samastipur:** Covering Samastipur, Darbhanga & Madhubani districts.
- **Shahabad Milk Union, Ara:** Covering Bhojpur, Buxar, Kaimur & Rohtas districts.
- **Vikramshila Milk Union (VIMUL), Bhagalpur:** Covering Bhagalpur, Munger, Banka and Jamui Districts.
- **Kosi Milk Union, Purnia:** Covering Purnia, Katihar, Araria, Kishanganj, Supaul, Saharsa and Madhepura Districts.

Cows and buffaloes are prominent among milch animals. The best breeds of cows in the state are Jersey, Australian, Dogli, Sahiwal, Punjabi, Gir, Sindhi, Tharparkar, Devni, etc. The main breeds of buffaloes are Mathurahi, Murra, Bhadavari, Jaffarabadi, Surti, Mehsana, Nagpuri, Rohtak, etc.

Meat is the main source of protein in food. Meat is obtained from goats, sheep, poultry and pigs. In Bihar, goat is reared mainly in Araria, East Champaran, Bhagalpur, Katihar, Purnia, Kishanganj, Banka, Gopalganj, etc. Along with meat, sheep are also a major source of wool production. Sheep farming in Bihar is mainly carried out in the plateaus. The maximum numbers of sheep in the state are in Kaimur, Aurangabad, Bhojpur, Supaul, Gaya, Jehanabad, West Champaran, Munger, Nalanda, etc. districts. Bihar occupies second position in India in poultry farming. Poultry farming is mainly practised in the districts of Muzaffarpur, Kishanganj, Purnia, Araria, Katihar, Saran, Gaya in the north-eastern parts of Bihar.

Livestock and Fish Production in Bihar (2018-19 to 2022-23)

Year	Milk (lakh tonnes)	Egg (crores)	Wool (lakh kgs)	Meat (lakh tonnes)	Fish (lakh tonnes)
2018-19	98.18	176.33	3.12	3.64	6.02
2019-20	105.00	274.00	3.10	3.83	6.4

2020-21	115.00	301.32	1.70	3.85	6.83
2021-22	122.00	306.00	1.72	3.92	7.62
2022-23	125.00	327.00	1.73	3.96	8.46
CAGR (%)	6.49	14.46	16.02	1.94	8.91

Source: Department of Animal Husbandry and Dairying, GoB

Fisheries

In Bihar, fish production has increased to 8.73 lakh metric tonnes in 2023-24 from 4.79 lakh metric tonnes in 2014-15. This represents an 81.98% growth and has positioned Bihar as the fourth-largest inland fish-producing state in India, up from the ninth position in 2014-15.

Moreover to promote community fisheries in the state, Government of Bihar has also taken several initiatives under State Plan Scheme which inter-alia includes Fisheries Training Scheme, Fisheries Exposure Visit Scheme, Input for Fish Farming Scheme, installation of Aerators in Fish Ponds Scheme, installation of Tubewell and Pumpset Scheme, Hatchery Development Scheme, Renovation of Old Pond, Quality Fish Fingerling Production Scheme, Wetland Development Scheme, River Ranching Scheme, Construction of Fish Ponds in Plateau Region, Diversification of Fish Species Scheme.

Besides, the projects with a total outlay of ₹ 522.41 crore including central share of 158.82 crore have been sanctioned under Pradhan Mantri Matsya Sampada Yojana (PMMSY) with release of central fund of ₹79.84 crores during last four years (2020-21 to 2023-24) and current Financial Year (2024-25). The major approved fisheries activities under the aforesaid scheme include finfish hatcheries, brood banks, expansion of aquaculture area through rearing and grow-out ponds, Stocking of Fingerling (FL) in Wetlands and Reservoirs, development of ornamental fish rearing and breeding units, promotion of recreational fisheries, establishment of RAS and biofloc units, installation of cages in reservoirs, establishment of cold storages, feed mills, fish kiosks and Post-harvest transport vehicles, etc.

In addition, a total of 1290 nos of Kisan Credit Cards (KCC) have been sanctioned to fishers and fish farmers in Bihar to help them to meet their working capital requirements.

FOURTH AGRICULTURE ROADMAP (2023-28)

On October 18, 2023, President Droupadi Murmu inaugurated the Fourth Agriculture Roadmap of Bihar (2023-28) by unveiling the stone slab through remote at the Bapu Auditorium of the Samrat Ashoka Convention Centre.

Key Points:

- Addressing the program organized on this occasion, Chief Minister Nitish Kumar said that the first agricultural roadmap of the state was started in the year 2008. The second agricultural roadmap was launched by the then President Pranab Mukherjee and the third agricultural road map was launched by President Ramnath Kovind.
- Farmers have benefited a lot from the agricultural roadmap in Bihar. The production and productivity of paddy, maize, wheat and potatoes has increased. From 2008 to 2012, work was done under the first agricultural roadmap. In the year 2011-12, a farmer from Nalanda left China behind by producing the highest amount of paddy per hectare. Earlier the record per hectare was in the name of China. A village in Nalanda district also made a world record in the production of potatoes.
- From 2012 to 2017, work was done under the second agricultural roadmap, as a result of which the production of fruits, vegetables, milk, eggs and fish has increased significantly. Farmers have benefited greatly from increased productivity.
- Work was scheduled under the third agricultural roadmap from 2017 to 2022, but its tenure was

extended by one year to 2023. Fourth agricultural roadmap has been started for the remaining work and further work and expansion. Under this, work will be done quickly, so that farmers can get more benefits.

- Fish production in Bihar has increased two and a half times. Now Bihar has become self-sufficient in fish production. Bihar has received Krishi Karman Awards for the production of rice, wheat and maize. The production of potato, cabbage, brinjal and tomato has also increased significantly. The production of Makhana has also increased significantly in Bihar.
- The Chief Minister said that in the Fourth Agricultural Roadmap, along with agriculture, arrangements have also been made for proper care of animals. Animal hospitals are being opened in every 8 to 10 panchayats, so that animals can be properly cared for and treated. A large part of North Bihar is the Chaur region. There is water there for 9 months in a year. There is 9 lakh hectare land area. Under the agricultural roadmap, a scheme has been started for 6 such districts.
- To meet the goals of the Fourth Agriculture Roadmap, the Cabinet approved ₹ 1 lakh 62 thousand crore. Agriculture is the basis of the livelihood of 75 percent people in the state. The Fourth Agriculture Roadmap has taken all things into consideration and has been made very comprehensive. This will not only increase production and productivity, but will also increase the income of farmers. The state will also benefit from this.

LAND REFORMS

Land reform is a major factor in agricultural development. Other inputs such as irrigation, fertilizers, pesticides, mechanization, etc. depend on the success of the land reform programme. Bihar is the first state in the country to enact the Land Reform Act. Inequality in land distribution is the main problem of agriculture in Bihar. More than 80 percent of Bihar's holding units are less than 1 hectare. Most of the farmers in the state are in the category of marginal farmers or landless labourers. The history of Land Reform Programme in Bihar is very old. In 1793, Lord Cornwallis implemented the Zamindari system under permanent settlement in the Bihar-Bengal region. The system implemented by Cornwallis established the temporary land management and full government control over some land which was also known as Khasmahal. In 1938, the Agricultural Income Tax Act was enacted in Bihar. After independence, many acts and laws have been enacted to remove the inequality of land distribution in Bihar, major amongst which are as follows:

- The Land Reforms Act, 1950, in which legislation related to the abolition of zamindari and abolition of middlemen was made.
- In 1953, government ownership was established over all the land of Bihar.
- The Shareholders Act, 1957 was enacted. It is also called the 'Princely Tenancy Act', in which a law was made to give permanent tenancy rights to the tenants with less than 1 acre of ownership.
- In 1961, the Land Ceiling Act was enacted, in which the maximum extent of land was determined. Under this act, an arrangement was made for holding a maximum of 20 acres of irrigated land or 60 acres of unirrigated land by one person. This act was amended in 1973, 1976 and 1982.
- The Tenancy Act was enacted in 1986.

With lack of proper implementation of these laws, there is inequality in the distribution of land even today, which has adversely affected the agricultural production. In 2006, the Land Reform Commission was constituted by the state government under the chairmanship of D. Bandopadhyay, whose task was to determine the boundary of the land and discuss the implementation of the settlement system in rural areas. This commission submitted its report related to Bhoodan to the government in 2006-07. Nonupdating of land records is also a major problem in the state although the pilot project for digitalization of the land records has started in Musahari circle of Muzaffarpur district. The land records are being computerized in all the districts in collaboration with the National Informatics Center (NIC).

The sharecropper system of the Bihar Tenancy Act of 1885 has also had an impact on the land reform work of Bihar. In 1885, it was arranged that if a sharecropper has been holding/tilling a land continuously for 12 years, then the sharecropper will have occupancy rights on that land. The Sharecropper Law was amended by the Government of Bihar in 1970, according to which no sharecropper will have any right over the land where the landlord holds 5 acres of irrigated or 10 acres of unirrigated land or if the landlord is blind, leper, paralyzed, insane, widowed, or a soldier.

❑❑❑

Means of Irrigation

- **Major Means of Irrigation**
- **Kosi Project**
- **Gandak Project**
- **Son Project**
- **Accelerated Irrigation Benefit Program**
- **Rainbow Revolution**
- **ICAR Research Complex for Eastern Region, Patna**

Bihar's agriculture is monsoon-based. About 56.4 percent of the state's agricultural land is irrigated. The main feature of the rainfall during monsoon is its uncertainty and inequality in distribution. The average annual rainfall in the state is 1009 millimetres, but most of this rainfall is approximately 85 percent between the southwest monsoon and June-September. In this way, dry weather prevails in the state for a long period. The dry season irrigation makes it necessary for crops and other agricultural activities.

Irrigation provides basic infrastructure to the agrarian economy. It is an extremely important tool to increase the productivity of agriculture. Other inputs of agriculture such as fertilizer, improved seeds, mechanization, use of pesticides and the success of new and modern techniques to increase agricultural production also depend on the development of the means of irrigation. The state has abundant water resources, but the distribution of rainfall is uneven and for proper use of water resources, artificial irrigation is required. In Bihar, agriculture has been in the regressive state due to the inadequate availability of irrigation and inefficient utilization of water resources. Therefore, at present, a positive effort has been made by the government towards the development of irrigation facilities, due to which the means of irrigation have increased rapidly.

MAJOR MEANS OF IRRIGATION

There are four major means of irrigation in Bihar:

1. Canal
2. Well
3. Tube well
4. Pond

Apart from these, ahar and pine are other means of irrigation, especially in the plains of South Bihar, which is the major medium of participatory irrigation management. At the time of independence, the irrigation through wells, ponds, canals, tube wells and other means was 14.65 percent, 11.05 percent, 40 percent, 19.58 percent and 14.72 percent, respectively. But gradually, this trend changed.

Canal is the major source of irrigation in Bihar. There are 11 major canals and their branches in Bihar which are spread in different districts. There are two types of canals in Bihar:

1. **Continuous canals:** They store water throughout the year. Most of the canals of North Bihar are continuous rivers, which have

been created either directly from rivers or from the artificial reservoirs in the dams built on them.

2. **Seasonal canals or inconstant canals:** They are drawn directly from the rivers, but excess water from the rivers flows in the rainy season in them. Continuous canals are more beneficial for agriculture than seasonal canals.

The second major source of irrigation is tube wells, which are powered by diesel engines or electric power. The geographical structure of the Gangetic plain in Bihar is similar to that of the Artigian well in which underground water is found at low depths. This generates ideal conditions for tube well irrigation. In the tube wells, which are called wells of the modern era, water is drawn by the pump by inserting hollow pipes in depth ranging from 15 to 100 meters in wells. Presently, diesel engines have been replaced by machines powered by electricity. With increase in power generation in the state, tube well irrigation has expanded rapidly.

There is an old method of irrigation by ponds, which is adopted in almost all the districts in the state. Gopalganj district in the state practices irrigation by ponds more than others.

Apart from this, wells have been a means of irrigation in the state since ancient times. The ground water level in the Ganges Plain is at a sufficient height. Sometimes, the source of water is even found just after digging 10 feet. Both raw and pucca wells are found in the state. Dhenkuli and rahat are used to extract water from them, which reaches the fields by drains. Maximum irrigation is done through wells in the districts of Saran, Siwan, Gopalganj, etc. in the state.

Mode of irrigation	Percentage of irrigated area	Most irrigated districts
Tube wells	53.46	Patna, Kishanganj
Canal	28.41	Rohtas, West Champaran, Aurangabad
Pond	3.22	Madhubani, Gopalganj
Well	0.54	Saran, Siwan, Gopalganj
Others	4.37	--

The most irrigated districts in the state are Arwal, Rohtas, Jamui, Buxar, Bhojpur, Gopalganj, Siwan, etc. The districts in medium category irrigation are Patna, Kaimur, Gaya, Aurangabad, Banka, Munger, Lakhisarai, Begusarai, Sheohar, etc. Districts with less than 50 percent irrigation are Supaul, Saharsa, Araria, Katihar, Kishanganj, Purnia, Samastipur, Madhubani, etc.

Area of the Most Irrigated Districts (in percentage)

Districts	Irrigated area	Districts	Irrigated area
Arwal	86.85	Rohtas	83.07
Jamui	75.09	Buxar	74.44
Bhojpur	74.14	Gopalganj	71.65
Siwan	70.87		

Canal Irrigation

Canals are a major source of irrigation in Bihar. About 28.41 percent of the total area of the state is irrigated by canals. In the state, two types of canals are used for irrigation: Continuous canals and seasonal canals. For the proper use of water resources in the state, two types of policies have been adopted for canal irrigation:

- Canals in Multipurpose River Valley Project
- Irrigation Canal (Command Area Irrigation Scheme)

Following are the major Multipurpose River Valley Projects in Bihar: 1. Kosi Project 2. Gandak Project 3. Son Valley Project

KOSI PROJECT

It is a joint project of India and Nepal. In 1954, an agreement was signed with Nepal for the formulation of this scheme, which was amended in 1961. Its construction work was started in 1955 and it was completed in 1963. The main objective of the construction of this project is controlling floods, irrigation, hydroelectricity production, malaria eradication, land conservation, etc. The Kosi river cuts the mountain near Chatra Garj and enters the field. Many dams and embankments have been built on this river, from which many canals have been drawn. Concrete dam has been constructed in Hanuman Nagar (Nepal) which is located on the border of Bihar. The length of this dam is 1140 meters.

Two major canal systems have been developed from the Kosi Canal:

1. Eastern Kosi Canal System
2. Western Kosi Canal System

1. Eastern Kosi Canal System: The main canal is 44 km in length. It has 4 branches:

(i) Murliganj Canal, Length – 64 kilometres
(ii) Janakinagar Canal, Length – 82 kilometres
(iii) Purnia (Banmankhi) Canal, Length – 64 kilometres
(iv) Araria Canal, Length – 52 kilometres

Nepal and districts like Madhepura, Saharsa, Purnia, Katihar, etc. in Bihar are irrigated by these branches of Eastern Kosi canal system. A 20 MW power generation centre has been set up at Kataiya on the East Kosi Canal. The eastern canal system irrigates 5 lakh hectares of land.

Western Kosi Canal System: The length of this canal is 115 km. From this canal, irrigation is provided to the districts of Madhubani, Darbhanga, Muzaffarpur, etc. About 3.25 lakh hectares of land is irrigated through this canal system.

GANDAK PROJECT

The Gandak River Project is a joint project of Bihar and Uttar Pradesh in collaboration with the Government of India. Based on the agreement of 1959, Nepal is also being given its benefit. Under this project, a dam was constructed at a location called Triveni Ghat in Valmiki Nagar (Bihar) in 1969-70. Half of the dam is in Bihar and half of it is in Nepal. Therefore, it is also called 'Triveni Canal System'. Two main canals have been constructed under this project:

1. Eastern Triveni Canal
2. Western Triveni Canal

1. Eastern Triveni Canal: It is also called Tirhut Canal. Its total length is 293 kilometres. About 6.6 lakh hectares of land is irrigated through this system. The districts of East Champaran, West Champaran, Muzaffarpur, Vaishali, Samastipur etc are irrigated through this canal. The district that gets benefitted the most from this canal is Western Champaran.

2. Western Triveni Canal: Its total length is 200 km, of which 19 km is in Nepal, 112 km is in Uttar Pradesh and 69 km is in Bihar. This canal is also called 'Saran Canal' as it provides irrigation to Gopalganj, Saran and Siwan districts of Saran division. About 4.84 lakh hectares of land is irrigated through this canal system.

Under the Gandak Project, there are two more canals—the Eastern Nepal Canal and the Western Nepal Canal. Both these canals are located in Nepal. On the Western Nepal Canal, the hydroelectricity station is set up at Surajpura, while on the Eastern Nepal Canal, hydroelectricity station is set up at Valmiki Nagar. The production capacity of both these hydroelectricity stations is 15 MW each.

SON PROJECT

The first major irrigation project of Bihar, the Sone Project, was constructed in 1874 by building a dam at a place called Barun near Dehri. The length of this dam is 3801 meters and height is 2.44 meters. This irrigation project was created to irrigate the most drought-prone area of Bihar, South-western Bihar, which has also benefited. At present, this area has become a granary of Bihar. In 1968, a 14,010-metre-long barrage was constructed at Indrapuri. Two canals have been drawn from Son River near Dehri:

1. Eastern Son Canal
2. Western Son Canal

1. Eastern Son Canal: Its total length is 130 kilometres. It originates from Baroon and reaches Patna. This canal irrigates about 2.5 lakh hectares of land. It irrigates Aurangabad, Gaya, Jehanabad, Arwal, and Patna districts.

2. Western Son Canal: It originates near Dehri. This canal provides irrigation in the districts of Rohtas, Kaimur, Buxar, Bhojpur, etc. Over 3 lakh hectares of land is irrigated by the Western Canal. Two hydroelectric stations have been established on the Sone Canal System:

1. Dehri Hydropower Station - 6.6 MW
2. Baroon Hydropower Station - 3.3 MW

Bansagar Water Dispute Agreement

The Bansagar water dispute is between Bihar and Uttar Pradesh. During the Rabi season, there is a shortage of water in the districts which are dependent on Son canal irrigation such as Kaimur, Rohtas, Buxar, Bhojpur, Arwal, Aurangabad and Gaya. These districts require 6000 to 8000 cusecs of water, while only 3000 to 4000 cusecs of water is released by Uttar Pradesh into the Son River. The problem has arisen due to the construction of a dam on the Rihand river, a tributary of the Son, by Uttar Pradesh. Uttar Pradesh has to release 5000 cusecs of water per day as per the agreement with Bihar, on the basis of which the Indrapuri barrage was constructed in Bihar in 1967 on the Son river near Dehri along with two canals. But after 1975, the water flow from Son started to decrease and the problem of irrigation started to arise in Bihar. In Madhya Pradesh too, there was a proposal for building a dam for hydroelectricity generation in Shahdol District on the Son River.

Therefore, in order to solve this problem, a water sharing agreement related to Son River was signed between Madhya Pradesh, Bihar and Uttar Pradesh in 1973. The Bansagar reservoir has been built by constructing a dam on the Son River in Shahdol District of Madhya Pradesh. It is named after the famous Sanskrit scholar Banabhatta. The construction work of this dam started in 1978 and was completed in 2006. According to this agreement, the total annual water flow of the Son River and her tributaries is expected to be 14,250 lakh acres, of which Bihar has been allocated 7,750 lakh acre feet, Uttar Pradesh has been allocated 1,250 lakh acre feet and Madhya Pradesh has been allocated 5,250 lakh acre feet. Out of 7,750 lakh acre feet water in Bihar, 50 lakh acre feet water was kept safe for the Son canals. The agreement also had a provision that in case there was less water availability in the Son region, then the cuts in the three states would not affect the allocation of 50 lakh acre feet of water kept safely for the Son canals. The Bansagar reservoir has a capacity of 40 lakh acre feet; so, water was allocated in the ratio of 2:1:1 to Madhya Pradesh, Bihar and Uttar Pradesh, and its construction cost was also distributed in the same proportion. In Bihar, this project helps irrigate an area of 940 square kilometres. Under this project, 425 MW of power is produced, which is used by Madhya Pradesh.

Apart from this, there was a provision to provide 250 lakh acre feet of water from Kanahar, a tributary of Son River, to Uttar Pradesh. Despite the Bansagar agreement, Bihar is not receiving adequate water supply. Uttar Pradesh and Madhya Pradesh provide water to their hydroelectricity projects by stopping Bihar's share of water. The Son River Commission was formed in 1980 to deal with this problem, but due to differences among the states and apathy of the centre, it was dissolved in 1987.

In addition to the multipurpose project, some other canals have also been developed which are as follows:

1. Dhaka Canal: East Champaran
2. Teur Canal: On the Teur River in East Champaran
3. Kamla Canal: On the Kamala River, in Darbhanga and Madhubani districts
4. Sakri Canal: On the Sakri River, in Gaya and Munger districts
5. Yamuna Canal: To the left of the Yamuna River, in Jehanabad.

Tube well

Tube well irrigation began in the 1930s in the plains of Bihar. Its maximum development has been seen in districts such as Araria, Gaya, Samastipur,

Begusarai, Kishanganj, Shivhar, Nalanda, Jehanabad, etc. The highest amount of irrigation by tube wells is done in Araria. The least amount of irrigation by tube wells is done in Rohtas District, which is due to lack of canal irrigation in this area.

A subsidy-based scheme called 'Bihar Centenary Private Tube Well Scheme' has been started by the state government. Under this scheme, two types of tube wells are being installed:

1. Shallow tube wells (70 m deep)
2. Tube wells with medium depth (70–100 m deep)

A subsidy of maximum 15,000 rupees is being given for shallow tube wells and a subsidy of 35,000 rupees is being given for deep tube wells. To encourage installation of private tube wells, two schemes—Million Shallow Tube Well Programme and Bihar Ground Water Irrigation Scheme (BIGWIS) have been launched.

Other sources of irrigation in Bihar are wells, ponds, puddles, ahars, pines, squares, etc. Irrigation through pond is mainly done in Siwan, Bhagalpur, Saharsa, Muzaffarpur and Gaya districts, while irrigation sources like ahar and pine are most commonly used in Patna, Munger, Darbhanga, and Bhojpur districts. In the state, 80 percent of the irrigation potential is used for agriculture of paddy and wheat.

Apart from these, there are several irrigation projects, among which Durgavati reservoir scheme, Upper Kiul Reservoir Project, Bagmati Project, Barnal Reservoir Project are prominent. Durgavati Reservoir Scheme is an irrigation scheme for Kaimur and Rohtas districts. The Durgavati River originates from the Kaimur Hill and joins the Karmnasha River. The Upper Kiul Reservoir Project has been built by constructing a dam in the Gahri village on the River Kiul. Through this, irrigation is done in Lakhisarai and Munger districts. Under the Bagmati Project, a canal has been created by constructing a dam at Ramnagar near Dong in Sitamarhi. The Barnal Reservoir Scheme is built on the Barnal River in Jamui District.

Many dams have been constructed for the purpose of irrigation. Among these dams, the Chandan Reservoir Dam was built on the Chandan River in Bhagalpur in 1972 and the Barhua Reservoir Dam was built on the Barhua River in Bhagalpur in 1965.

Major irrigation projects of Bihar

Sr. No.	Type of Project	Name of the Project	River	District/State
1	Multipurpose scheme	i. Son Valley Project	Son	Rohtas, Bihar
		ii. Gandak Valley Project	Gandak	Bihar, Uttar Pradesh
		iii. Kosi Valley Project	Kosi	Bihar, Nepal
2	Irrigation project	i. Durgavati Reservoir Scheme	Durgawati	Kaimur and Rohtas
		ii. Upper Kiul Reservoir Scheme	Kiul	Lakhisarai and Munger
		iii. Bagmati Project	Bagmati	Sitamarhi
		iv. Barnal Reservoir Project	Barnal	Jamui
		v. Teur Canal Scheme	Teur	Eastern Champaran
		vi. Kamala Canal Scheme	Kamal	Darbhanga, Madhubani
		vii. Sakri Canal Scheme	Sakari	Gaya, Munger
		viii. Chandan Reservoir Scheme	Chandan	Bhagalpur
		ix. Batua reservoir scheme	Batua	Bhagalpur

3	Schemes of minor irrigation	i. Jamania Pump Canal Scheme	—	—
		ii. Sammat Bigha Morhar Scheme	Morhar	Jehanabad
		iii. Kachnama Weir Scheme		Jehanabad
		iv. Mor Weir Scheme	—	—
		v. Solhanda Weir Scheme	Yamuna	Jehanabad
		vi. Sugarave Weir Scheme	—	—
		vii. Lavaich Rampur Barrage	Dardha	—
		viii. Nawagarh Scheme	—	Jehanabad
		ix. Sesamba Weir Scheme	—	Jehanabad
		x. Isarawe Check Dam	—	Gaya
		xi. Bhaitaura Dam	—	Gaya
		xii. Kadahar Weir Scheme	—	Gaya
		xiii. Bachhraja Weir Scheme	—	Madhubani

Despite the multiplicity of water resources in Bihar, drought conditions continue to arise. Therefore, emphasis is being laid on interconnection of rivers for optimum utilization of water resources. The major river interconnection scheme is shown in the table below:

River Interconnection Scheme in Bihar

Names of Rivers	Beneficiary Districts	Achievement/Availability
Budhi Gandak-Noon-Waya-Ganga	Samastipur, Begusarai, Khagaria	1.26 lakh hectare irrigation potential created
Sakari-Nata River	Nawada, Nalanda, Sheikhpura	About 68 thousand hectare irrigation potential created
Kosi-Mechi	Araria, Saharsa, Supaul, Kishanganj, Purnia	About 2.11 lakh hectare irrigation potential created

Out of the above mentioned schemes, approval has been received from the Central Water Commission for linking the Sakri-Nata River, while the Budhi Gandak-Ganga Link Scheme and the Kosi-Mechi Link Scheme have been sent by the National Water Development Authority (NWDA) to the Central Water Commission for approval.

There are 9 schemes operating under the Command Area Development and Water Management programme (CADWM) under the irrigation programme in the state. The Water Regulatory Authority has been established by the Water Resources Department under the Bihar State Water Policy, 2015.

ACCELERATED IRRIGATION BENEFIT PROGRAM (AIBP)

Under the Accelerated Irrigation Benefit Programme, the Central Government provides assistance in two ways to Bihar. About 90 percent central assistance is provided for the schemes in North Bihar and 75 percent for the remaining state schemes. The schemes covered under this programme include the work of repair and restoration of West Kosi Canal Scheme, Kosi Barrage Scheme, Durgavati Reservoir Scheme, Punpun Barrage Scheme, etc.

RAINBOW REVOLUTION

The Rainbow Revolution has been started under the Agricultural Road Map for agricultural development in Bihar. For this, electricity is being supplied for agricultural use by dedicated agriculture feeders. In Bihar, electricity is unavailable in all areas due to less production as compared to its consumption. Electricity is needed for domestic use, commercial use and agricultural irrigation in rural areas. At present, only 5.83 percent of the total energy consumption is used for agricultural irrigation, which is much less than the 38 percent used by the state of Haryana, which is the highest. The national average is also 20.3 percent, which is much higher than Bihar. The per capita electricity consumption in Bihar is 122.11 units, which is far behind the national average of 778.71 units. Keeping in view the above circumstances, the work of separation of agricultural and non-agricultural feeders is being carried out; its main objective is to provide assured power for agricultural use within a specified period by dedicated agricultural feeder and to provide electricity for other activities in rural areas in addition to agriculture.

The table below shows the estimated need and availability of energy for the agricultural sector in Bihar.

Year	Estimated demand for power for agriculture sector (in MW)	Total estimated demand for power (in MW)	Estimated availability of power (in MW)
2015-16	995	5957	5314
2016-17	1476	6750	8032
2017-18	1855	7597	8935
2018-19	2191	8385	9314
2019-20	2637	9181	9314
2020-21	3190	9982	9314
2021-22	3852	10760	9314
Source: 17th Report of E.P.S.			

The goal of this Rainbow Revolution is to promote the anticipated development in agriculture and agro-based industries by providing energy to irrigation pump sets and ensuring the availability of energy for other works in the agricultural sector, in a time bound manner. Currently, rural feeders are of mixed nature providing electricity for rural usages other than agriculture, which creates obstacles in agricultural irrigation. That is why, a dedicated feeder is needed. This provision will enable power supply to irrigation pumps within a set period of time, and rural and domestic consumers will also get supply of electricity by rotation. According to the form "Faster, Sustainable and More Inclusive Growth: An approach to the 12th Five Year Plan" issued by the Planning Commission, three-phase power can also be supplied 24 x 7 for rural needs in the country by separating agricultural feeders.

Salient features of the scheme

The plan has three main components:

1. Separation of feeders;
2. Installation of distribution transformers of suitable capacity near irrigation pump sets;
3. Asset mapping, related GPS survey and consolidated improvement and strengthening of distribution network;

Under the Dedicated Agricultural Feeder Programme, the Government of Bihar plans to construct 968 (11 kv) new feeders in the 55,925 km line by the financial year 2021-22 and to install 1,46,269 distribution transformers for power supply to 19,29,000 pump sets. Following are the major benefits of this scheme—

- Dedicated agricultural feeders will provide uninterrupted power supply to the agriculture sector;
- The overall development of the rural economy will improve the standard of living and socio-economic conditions of the people;
- Energy purchase costs will come down;
- Better energy accounting for agricultural consumption will be ensured;
- Distribution subsystem will be strengthened;
- A. T. (Average Transmission and Consumption) survey will decrease;
- The system will be strengthened by developing infrastructure;
- Voltage profile will be better for rural consumers;
- Illegal power connections and the possibility of power theft will decrease.

For implementation of the Dedicated Feeder Scheme for Agriculture, a roadmap has been prepared at three levels–current status, plan format and execution.

Current Status	Plan Format	Execution
Assessment of existing basic rural power network	Study of methods adopted by various states	Selection of Patna District for pilot project
Identification and drawing of existing tube wells and agricultural fields	Designing a techno-economic network format of dedicated agricultural feeder	Preparation of a framework for monitoring and evaluation for the implementation of the scheme
Estimation of current and proposed power load of pump sets for irrigation	Strengthening of related power sub-stations, 33 kV lines and grid sub-stations.	Implementation of the plan in a phased manner
	Preparation of BOQ and DPR	
	Identifying the difficulties arising for the simple implementation of the plan and a strategy for their diagnosis	
	Selection of agency for execution of plan on turn-key basis	

ICAR RESEARCH COMPLEX FOR EASTERN REGION, PATNA

In the 11th Five Year Plan, on 22 February, 2001, the Research Complex of the Indian Council of Agricultural Research for the Eastern Region (ICAR-RCER) was established in Patna. Its two research centres are located in Darbhanga and Ranchi. The Makhana Research Centre in Darbhanga also works under it.

The eastern region of India is rich in natural resources and agro-friendly water and soil resources. But this capability has not been developed towards poverty alleviation, development and raising the standard of living.

Therefore, this campus was established for the agricultural development of the eastern regions, for the management of land and water resources, crops, horticulture, aquatic crops, fisheries, animals, and poultry, the establishment of agricultural processing, etc.

❑❑❑

Minerals and Industries

- Mineral Wealth
- Businesses and Industries
- Agro-based Industries
- Mineral-based Industries
- Forest-based Industries
- Food Processing Industries
- Udyog Mitra
- Industrial Zones of Bihar
- Bihar Industrial Area Development Authority (BIADA)
- Decentralized Biomedical Waste Incinerator Inaugurated in Buxar

MINERAL WEALTH

Minerals play an important role in the development of any state. Prior to the partition of the state (2000), Bihar had a majority of metallic and non-metallic minerals. But after partition, most of these resources went to Jharkhand. Among the currently available mineral materials are pyrite, porcelain, agnes soil, limestone, manganese, mica, asbestos, saltpetre, etc. In the south-western and south-eastern regions of Bihar, rocks of Archean Age are found in Gaya, Nawada, Nalanda, Munger, Jamui, Bhagalpur and Banka districts. The Vindhyan rock formations are found in the southwestern parts of the state. Basically, the metallic minerals are found in the rocks of the Archaean Era.

Deposits of non-metallic minerals have occurred in the rocks of the Vindhyan group. The following are the main mineral resources found in Bihar.

Manganese: It is a metallic mineral found in sedimentary rocks of Dharwadi rocks in the form of a dark-coloured natural ash. Silomoulin and Bronite are its major ores. It is mixed with copper to make turbine blades in the steel industry. This metal is found in Gaya, Munger, and Patna districts of the state.

Mica: The mica belt, spread over an area of about 3400 square kilometres in the state, extends from the eastern part of Nawada District to Jharkhand. Its thickness has been found to be up to 30 metres. Asbestos, in its large size with orthoclase and tourmaline, is found as large grains in the districts of Munger, Gaya, and Bhagalpur in Bihar. It is used in electrical and heat conductor devices. It is used in rubber industry, paint industry, and electronic industry.

Pyrite: According to the Indian Bureau of Minerals about 95 percent of the country's pyrite reserves and production are found in Bihar. The mineral is found mainly in the upper Vindhya rock group of Rohtas District in the state. Iron pyrite is found in the area of 109 square kilometers in Amzor of Rohtas. There is a deposit of about 400 million tonnes of pyrite in Manda, Kuriyari and Kararia. It is a source of mineral sulphur. It is used in making super phosphate, sulfur acid, rayon, petroleum refining, solid rubber, and sugar. Pyrite Phosphate and Chemicals Limited (PPCL) is a public sector enterprise established by the Central Government in Amzor.

Porcelain: Porcelain is formed due to the loss of granite's felspar mineral. The lack of potash and soda in this soil, make it fire-retardant. It is used in the production of ceramic items, heat-proof furnaces, textile industry, fertilizer industry, medicine, paint, pesticide and cement industries. It is found in Bhagalpur, Vaishali, and Munger districts of the state.

Agnisah/fire-proof soil: This type of soil produced from sedimentary rocks is resistant to high temperature. It is used in manufacturing high heat furnaces, boilers, fire-fighting equipment. It is mostly found in Munger, Bhagalpur and Purnia districts in the state.

Limestone: This stone obtained from Vindhya rocks, is found in the form of heavy deposits of pebbles. Being a chemical organizer, this multi-use mineral is a major raw material for cement and iron steel. In the sugar industry, it is needed in the purification of sugar. The best quality limestone in the state is obtained from the hills of Rohtas, the Kaimur Plateau and Munger. Cement is manufactured from this category of limestone. The medium and low-grade limestone is used in steel industry, sugar industry and building materials. Most of its mines in the state are in Ramdihara, Baulia, and Banjari regions of Rohtas.

Asbestos: This fibrous mineral is formed by the combination of magnesium, silica and water. Chrysotile and amphibole are its main varieties. As it is electricity resistant and has high heat tolerance, it is used in the manufacture of equipment exposed to fire and electricity. It is used in railway coaches, ships, boilers, etc. Clothes made from it are used in fire-fighting work. Its mines are found in Munger District of the state.

Saltpetre: This mineral is found in the form of sodium nitrate and potassium. Approximately 20,000 tons of this mineral is produced in the state every year. It is used in explosive manufacturing, glass industry and to make steel flexible. This mineral is found in Muzaffarpur, Saran, Darbhanga, Gaya, and Munger districts of the state.

Monazite: This mineral derived from pegmatite rocks is a mixture of thorium, uranium, cerium and tantalum. It is found in Gaya and Munger districts of the state.

Beryllium: This mineral is used in the manufacture of mixed metals. It is obtained from igneous rocks. It is used in spring industry, manufacture of valves, carburetors in ships, chlorocent lamps, neon signs, cyclotron and explosive materials. It is found in Gaya District.

Uranium: This nuclear mineral is obtained from igneous rocks. It is found in the compound form of pegmatite, pitchblende, and uranium. Uranium of the pegmatite variety is found in the asbestos mines of Akbari mountain in Gaya District and in the pegmatite forages in Nawada District. There is a very large mine in Sungri of Dhalbhum. It has been known to have a huge reserve in the Boundary Fault in the Magadha division.

Gold: This precious mineral found in Jamui District of the state. Karmatia, Rani Pahari, Vadmaria, Marahi Pahadi, etc. have the accumulated reserves of gold in the Sone block of Jamui District. The Bihar State Geological Survey Department has sought permission from the Geological Survey of India (GSI) for gold mining. G.S.I. has confirmed that there are gold reserves in Rajgir's Kabootara and Nakia mountain regions.

Coal: This mineral is found in the Bhagalpur and Munger districts near the Rajmahal region. The state of Bihar is home to 160 million tonnes of coal resources according to the Geological Survey of India (GSI).

Quartz and silica sand: This mineral is found in Bhagalpur, Jamui, Munger, and Nawada districts of the state.

Quartzite: This mineral is found in Lakhisarai, Munger, and Nalanda districts of the state.

Lead and zinc: This is a very useful mineral, which is obtained from the galena mineral bed. It is found in small quantity in Bhagalpur.

Granite: This mineral is found in Bhagalpur, Gaya, Jehanabad, and Jamui districts of the state.

Iron-ore: This mineral is found in Bhagalpur, Gaya and Jamui districts of the state. Hematite variety of iron ore is found in Bhagalpur, and magnetite variety of iron ore is found in Gaya and Jamui.

Talc or soap stone: This mineral is found in Munger District.

Bauxite: This mineral is found in Munger and Rohtas districts of the state.

Felspar: This mineral is found in Gaya, Jamui and Munger districts of the state.

Major Minerals of Bihar

Mineral	Region
Pyrite	Amjhore and Banjari (Rohtas)
Bauxite	Kharagpur (Munger), Banjari (Rohtas)
Tin	Devraj and Kurkkhạnd (Gaya)
Graphite	Simultala (Jamui)
Asbestos	Gaya, Nawada, Jamui, Banka
Talc	Gaya, Munger, Nawada
Porcelain	Munger, Bhagalpur
Granite, Asbestos, Slate, Silica, Gold	Munger
Dolomite	Rohtas
Uranium	Gaya, Nawada
Saltpetre	Saran, Gopalganj, Siwan, Vaishali, Muzaffarpur
Fire clay	Bhagalpur
Beryllium	Nawada
Petroleum	Western Champaran, Saharsa, Purnia, Kishanganj

BUSINESSES AND INDUSTRIES

The process in which the nature of raw materials is changed and they are made more useful is called industry. Industry is called the secondary sector of the economy. Bihar lacks industrial infrastructure. With the lack of raw material and power resources, and excess of arable land, Bihar is basically a state with agro-based economy. Bihar has agriculturally suitable geographical conditions, but in the absence of industrial infrastructure, the agro-based industry has also not developed.

In Bihar, on the basis of agro-based resources, rice mills, sugar industries, food processing industries, pulses mill industries, jute and its industries and forest-based industries have been established in limited numbers. But there is immense potential for their development. There is limited availability of mineral resources like limestone, sandstone, pyrites, etc. in the southern plateau of Bihar, on the basis of which the cement industry has developed. Thus, Bihar is in a state of imbalance from the point of view of industrial development. From the point of view of industrial workers, Bihar's share at the all-India level is just 5.2 percent.

The industrial units in Bihar are not evenly distributed in all the districts. Most of the large and medium-sized industrial units are located in Patna, while there is not even a single industrial unit in the Kosi division. At present, out of 38 districts, there are 10 such districts in the state where no industrial unit has been established.

Large and Medium Industries Unit (in percentage)

Name of the Division	Industrial Units	Name of the Division	Industrial Units
Patna	38.2	Purnia	6.9
Tirhut	21.6	Saran	5.4
Magadh	7.9	Bhagalpur	3.9
Darbhanga	7.3	Kosi	0.0
Munger	6.9		

The industrial units of Bihar can be divided into large, medium and small categories on the basis of size.

Large industries

After the bifurcation of the state, most of the big industries moved to Jharkhand and due to lack of industrial infrastructure in Bihar, the establishment of new industrial units was also very slow. Bihar's big industries, such as cement, sugar, jute, etc. are plagued with problems.

Micro, small and medium scale industries

In present-day Bihar, there is a greater potential for the development of small and cottage industries. Large industries are capital intensive and provide less employment opportunities, while small and cottage industries are labor intensive. The latter provide more employment opportunities in less capital. The District Industries Center has been established with the aim of developing small industries.

AGRO-BASED INDUSTRIES

The major agro-based industries in Bihar are sugar industry, rice mill industry, textile industry, food processing industry, pulses mill industry, jute-based industries.

Sugar industry

Sugar industry has been the most important industry of Bihar. It is a weight degeneration industry based on impure raw material. In Bihar, about 10 tonnes of sugar is produced from 100 tonnes of sugarcane. Sugarcane, which is the raw material of the sugar industry, is grown in large quantities in the north-western part of Bihar and the northern Gangetic plains. Sugarcane is cultivated on an area of about 3 lakh hectares in the state, which is 6 percent of the total agricultural area. There are 28 sugar mills in Bihar, out of which only 9 sugar mills are currently operational. The remaining 19 mills are closed.

The attempt to establish the first sugar mill in Bihar was made by the Dutch company in 1841, which was unsuccessful. Hence, the first successful sugar mill was established in 1903 in Madhaura (Saran). Major centres of sugar industry are Madhaura, Chanpatia, Sugauli, Sakri, Bihta, Goraul, Motipur, Warisaliganj, etc. At the time of independence in 1947, Bihar was second in sugar production in the country. Bihar used to produce 22.7 percent of the sugar in India, which has now come down to a meagre 2 percent. At the time of independence, there were 66 sugar mill units in the country, out of which 33 were in Bihar, while at present, there are 386 sugar mill units in the country, out of which only 29 are in Bihar. Most of them are in a sick state. In 1974, Bihar State Sugar Corporation was established as a government company for the development of units of the ailing sugar industry. In 1976, 7 sick sugar mills were nationalized, which included Banmankhi, Goraul, Rayam, Warisaliganj, Samastipur, and Guraru. Thereafter, in 1977, Lohat and Sakri in 1979, New Siwan, and in 1980, Motipur Sugar Mill were nationalized.

Sugar mills in Bihar

Northwest Bihar

Despite the emphasis on industrialization and production of agriculture based products, sugar mills of North Bihar are closing one by one. There were 16 sugar mills here once, out of which nine have been closed. Only seven are operational. The closure of mills not only affected employment, but lakhs of farmers were separated from cash crop farming.

There are a total of six sugar mills in West Champaran in Narkatiaganj, Lauriya, Majhaulia, Chanpatia, Bagaha and Ramnagar. Chanpatia sugar mill is closed since 1994. The only Riga sugar mill in Sitamarhi was running well, but due to the tussle between the workers and the management, the crushing season could not start this time. Lohat sugar mill of Madhubani is also closed since 1996 due to systemic flaws. Production has been stalled in Motipur sugar mill of Muzaffarpur since 1997. Hasanpur mill is operational in Samastipur, while the mill located in the district headquarters has been closed since 1985. Darbhanga is in the worst condition. Once upon a time, Sakri and Rayam sugar mills were named here. Sakri was closed in 1993 and Rayam was closed a year later in 1994. The same was seen in East Champaran. Chakia sugar mill here has been closed since 1994 and Motihari sugar mill since 2009.

Southwest Bihar

It includes Rohtas, Bhojpur, Gaya, Nawada, and Patna districts. They have 8 sugar mill units. Following are the major factors or causes for setting up of sugar mills in Bihar:

- Warm humid climate, which is conducive for sugarcane cultivation
- More than 100 centimeters of rain and irrigation facilities from canals and watercourses
- Renewed fertile and alluvial plains due to floods
- The only major cash crop of sugarcane in the state
- Wide market and availability of intense labour
- Connectivity with other parts of the country by road and rail

Major problems of sugar industry of Bihar

Bihar, which was the second largest sugar producing state of the country at the time of independence, is currently producing only 3 lakh tonnes of sugar. Most of the sugar mill units are sick. Following are the major problems of sugar industry in Bihar:

- Most of the units are old, whose parts have been worn out. Consequently, the cost is high and low-quality sugar is produced. Hence, the demand is less due to which profit and savings are less. Hence, they need modernization.
- There is a shortage of capital. In Bihar, the problem of capital arises due to low savings rate, low capital formation rate and high interest rate, etc. There is a shortage of infrastructure such as electricity, roads, rail wagons, communication, etc.
- Production of low-quality reed, which reduces the yield of sugar.
- Adverse government policies, such as the dual price system, are applicable to sugar marketing due to which, since 1967, sugar mills have to give 30-60 percent sugar to the government for public distribution system at a lower price.
- Sugar mill units are facing losses due to the high minimum support price of reed.
- Adverse license policy prevails.
- There is competition between sugar and jaggery units. Cheap reed and labour supply and high cash profit of the cottage jaggery industry, causes 40 percent of the reed is being consumed in jaggery manufacture, which is causing a loss to the sugar industry.

For the development of sugar industry in Bihar, it is necessary to make the following efforts:

- Encouraging reed growth of improved species is needed.

- There is a need for modernization of machines and components.
- The cooperative unit of farmers will have to be emphasized upon.
- Farmers need to be paid in cash.
- There is a need to develop infrastructure for both sugarcane production and sugar mills in rural areas.
- There is a need to promote other industries based on sugar industry such as paper, ethyl alcohol, medicine, etc.

Many activities are also being undertaken by the government for the development of sugar industry, such as the process of privatization has been started by removing the restrictions on Bihar State Sugar Corporation. About 15 closed mills and 2 distillery units are being rebuilt at private cost. An Investment Promotion Board has been formed in the state, under which proposals related to construction and restoration of 37 sugar mills have been passed. Among these 37 units, 27 new sugar mills, 8 old sugar mills, and 2 ethanol producing units are to be built.

Textile industry

Handloom, silk, and jute are the main industries under the textile industry in Bihar. There has been very little development of cotton textile in the state as there is no production of cotton which is the raw material for cotton textile industry. Mainly handloom sector has developed in Bihar. More than 1.32 lakh weavers are working in the handloom sector. There are 1089 Primary Weaver Cooperation Committees functioning in the state, under which 15 thousand handlooms are operational. There are 2 marketing organizations acting as the apex organization in the state —

1. Bihar Handloom Cooperative Union
2. Bihar State Wool and Sheep Association

Under these, there are six regional handloom associations that are located in Nalanda, Sitamarhi, Siwan, Madhubani, Purnia, and Bhagalpur. According to a survey, 54 percent weavers had their own handlooms, and 46 percent weavers had rented handlooms. The main source of income of about 62 percent of the weavers is from weaving. About 8 institutions have been set up by the government in the state to train the handloom weavers and for their capacity building. The institutes are located in Chakand (Gaya), Amarpur (Banka), Obra (Aurangabad), Patna City (Patna), Baran (Bhagalpur), Kako (Jehanabad), Zhonganagar (Nalanda) and Purnia City (Purnia). At present, the handloom industry is grappling with a variety of problems, such as lack of raw materials, lack of training using new technology, lack of rational pricing, lack of credit facilities, marketing problems etc.

Several efforts have been made by the government to promote the handloom industry. Handloom Mahasankul has been established in Bhagalpur. A programme called Chief Minister Integrated Handloom Development Scheme has been started in 2012-13. Under this scheme, weavers are provided ₹15.000 for purchasing new looms, ₹5,000 for purchasing goods and ₹40,000 for building work sheds per weaver.

There are 14,000 power looms operating in Bhagalpur, Gaya, and Banka districts in the state. These power loom units produce staple bed sheets and ornamental clothing, etc. A training centre has been set up by the Ministry of Textiles, Government of India, at Nathnagar in Bhagalpur in which 120 power loom weavers are trained every year.

Handloom Concentration Districts in Bihar

Districts	Products
Bhagalpur	Silk, cotton, decorative fabrics, staple bed sheets, export quality silk, and cotton clothes
Banka	Tassar silk, export quality silk clothes and seti towels
Gaya	Cotton clothes, bed sheets, and towels
Nalanda	Decorative curtains, bed shells, interior decorating materials, and decorative clothes

Nawada	Tassar silk and women's dress accessories
Madhubani	Fine cotton clothes, dhoti clothes
Aurangabad, Rohtas	Woolen blankets, woolen carpets and saris
Kaimur	Woolen carpets, Banarasi saris
Patna, Siwan	Cotton clothes, decorative clothes
Purnia, Katihar	Jute bags, jute composite materials, interior decoration materials
Source: Department of Industries, Government of Bihar	

Silk Industry

The major area of silk production in Bihar is Bhagalpur and its surrounding areas. Bhagalpur is an important centre of silk textile production in the state. In Bihar, 11 mulberry, 6 tassar and 1 castor centre have been established for textile development. To encourage the silk industry in the entire state, 4 regional offices have been set up in Bhagalpur, Muzaffarpur, Gaya, and Darbhanga districts. Bihar Silk and Textile Institute is being established in Bhagalpur. The state government has implemented 'Mukhyamantri Tassar Vikas Yojana' to increase silk production and employment in rural areas. Under this scheme, there are plans to plant Arjuna and Asan trees in Banka, Munger, Nawada, Kaimur, Jamui, and Gaya and in the waterlogged areas of North Bihar. Arjuna and Tassar trees are suitable for silk worm rearing. The following programs are included under the 'Mukhyamantri Tassar Vikas Yojana':

i. Plantation in 10,200 hectares for rearing of tassar insect, and formation of 408 self-help groups under the leadership of Resham Mitra

ii. Formation of 55 self-help groups for silk thread production

iii. Establishment of Cocoon Bank

Begusarai is the only district in the state where castor silk is produced. The Bihar Silk and Textile Institute was established in 1922 in Nathanagar, Bhagalpur to promote silk production and for training. A computer-based design (CAD) unit is being set up in this institute. Mulberry reeling centers are established in Kishanganj and Bhagalpur, in which training on mulberry silk reeling and spinning is imparted.

Cotton Clothes

The production and export of clothes in Bihar has been in place since ancient times. But Bihar has remained decentralized and unorganized. Two factories were established in the organized area at Dumraon and Phulwari Sharif, but, at present, they are closed. The Bihar State Textile Corporation was established in 1970, with the aim of nationalizing private units. The cotton textile industry in Bihar is mainly established as a handloom industry. Bhagalpur and Gaya are the major centers of cotton clothing production. Manpur of Gaya City is a major center of cotton textile industry where about 1000 power looms are installed. Here bedsheets, gamchhas, dhotis, saris etc. are produced.

Jute Industry

Jute is the main agro-based industry of Bihar, which is based on the fibrous crop jute. Jute is produced in the north-eastern districts of Bihar such as Purnia, Katihar, Kishanganj, Araria, etc. At the time of independence, jute factories were established in Katihar, Samastipur and Purnia in Bihar. But after the partition of the country, most of the jute producing area went to Bangladesh and due to the modernization of factories and lack of capital, the jute industry became sick. The state of jute industry also became miserable due to increasing demand for synthetic fibres. However, due to the increasing demand for jute and goods manufactured from it, emphasis is being laid on the development of this industry.

At present, three jute industries are functioning in the state. These factories are established in Katihar, Purnia, and Darbhanga. Presently, to promote the jute industry, a jute park is being established in Maranga, Purnia under public and private partnership.

MINERAL-BASED INDUSTRIES

Cement Industry

The availability of limestone in the mountainous region of Kaimur, in the south-western part of Bihar, brings immense potential for the development of the cement industry. Depending upon the availability of raw materials, the cement industry has been established in Banjari and Dalmia Nagar in Rohtas. Kalyanpur Cement Limited (KC) was established in Banjari in 1937. 'Shree Cement' has been established in Aurangabad. At present, the Dalmia Nagar factory is closed. Financial and managerial problems are the root cause of its closure. 'Eco Cement' has been established in Bhabhua. Lack of power/energy is the reason for the non-development of the cement industry in this region even after the availability of raw materials.

Crusher industry

The mountainous plateau border region of South Bihar is rich in rocks like granite, gneiss, cysts, etc. Based on this, the crusher industry (stone cutting industry) has developed on a large scale in the districts of Kaimur, Rohtas, Aurangabad, Gaya, Nawada, Jamui, Munger, etc.

Chemical industry

Despite the scarcity of minerals in Bihar, Barauni has developed into a mineral based industrial complex. Oil refineries, thermal power plants, fertilizer plants and many small industrial centres have been developed in Barauni. The Barauni oil refinery was established in July 1964 with the cooperation of the Soviet Union and Romania. The cost of setting up this factory was ₹49.4 crores. The initial production capacity of this factory was 1 million metric tons per year, which increased to 3 million metric tons per year in 1969. Here, the crude oil comes from Assam, Nigeria, Iraq and Malaysia. Barauni is connected to Haldia and Paradip ports by oil pipeline. The Barauni Thermal Power Station was established in 1962 with a production capacity of 320 MW. A nitrogen fertilizer-based factory—Hindustan Fertilizer Industries—is established in Barauni. Here, ammonia sulfate and super phosphate are produced using naphtha and gypsum as raw materials. A pyrite-based 'Pyrites Phosphate and Chemical Limited' (PPCL) factory is established at Amazor in Rohtas District. In this factory, sulphur and phosphate fertilizer are manufactured from pyrites. 'Bihar Insecticide Limited' was established on 27 February, 1982, as a state government-public undertaking in Purnia. Basic chemicals were produced by this company; it is currently in a sick condition.

Railway factory

Railway related industries were already established in Mokama (Patna) and Jamalpur (Munger) in Bihar. 'Bharat Wagon and Engineering Company Limited' is in Mokama and railway workshop is in Jamalpur. Bharat Wagon and Engineering Company Limited (BWEL) is a public sector undertaking of the Government of India. It is an ISO 9001:2008 certified company. Until 2008, this venture was under the Department of Heavy Industries and Public. It is under the Ministry of Railways since August 13, 2008. Bharat Wagon and Engineering Company Limited was established in December 1978 with the merger of two sick private companies—Arthur Butler Company Limited, Muzaffarpur and Britannia Engineering Company Limited, Mokama. In 1983-84, a company manufacturing LPG cylinders at Bela, Muzaffarpur was merged with them. Since 1986, subsidy is given by 'Bharat Heavy Industries Corporation Limited', Calcutta, which works under the Department of Heavy Industries. The wagons are manufactured by its unit set up in Muzaffarpur and Mokama. The Jamalpur Locomotive Workshop was established on

8 February, 1862. It was the first full facility-based workshop in India that set up under the East Indian Railway Company.

The construction of the Ordnance Factory at Rajgir, Nalanda was approved in 2001. Rajgir Ordnance Factory is the first modern factory in Asia manufacturing the state-of-the-art BMCS (Bi-Modular Charge System). BMCS increases the firepower of cannon shells. It is being used in Bofors cannon. New railway factories are being set up at Harnaut (Nalanda), Bela (Saran), Madhaura (Saran) and Madhepura. Rail wheel factory was set up in Bela (Dariyapur block of Saran District) in 2004. Its headquarters is in New Delhi. The production in this factory started in 2014. The electric locomotive factory is being set up in Madhepura as a joint venture of French company Alstom S. A. and Indian Railways. In this factory, 800 high-capacity locomotives will be manufactured in a period of 11 years. The carriage repair rail workshop at Harnaut (Nalanda) was established in 2003. A diesel engine factory is being set up at Madhaura in Saran district.

Glass industry

The glass industry has developed in Bihar on the basis of the availability of raw materials like sand, silica, limestone, sodium sulfate, potassium carbonate, borium oxide obtained from the plateau of southern Bihar and plateaus of Jharkhand. The major centres of glass industry are located in Patna, Darbhanga and Bhagalpur.

Cigarette and Beedi Industry

There is enough raw material available in the state for the manufacture of cigarettes and beedis. Tobacco is produced in the plains of North Bihar. Bihar itself is a large market for manufactured goods. This industry has developed in Begusarai, Jamui, Biharsharif, Ara, Buxar, Darbhanga, etc. ITC's tobacco-based cigarette factory is set up in Munger. India's oldest tobacco manufacturing unit in Munger was founded in 1905 by Raj Enterprises, which was later acquired by the Indian Tobacco Company. The Indian Tobacco Company is a private sector consumer goods company that was established in 1910 and it is headquartered in Kolkata.

The ITC Munger Dairy Plant has been set-up and is operational with a capacity of 2 lakh liters of milk per day. The plant is expected to be expanded to 4 lakh liters per day. In addition to progressing milk, the plant also produces value-added products like ghee, milk powder and milk in pouches.

FOREST-BASED INDUSTRIES

There is a shortage of forest resources in Bihar yet, many medium and small industries have developed on the basis of forest resources obtained. Among them, saw industry, paper and cardboard, kattha, bamboo and cane-based industries have developed.

The saw mills have developed in the northern parts of Bihar, especially in the lowland region. The saw mills have developed in East Champaran, West Champaran, Araria, Kishanganj, and Bhagalpur; Gaya, Nawada, Rohtas, etc. districts in South Bihar. The policy of banning the saw mills has been made due to decline in forests and the need for maintaining the balance in the environment, due to which their number is coming down. Bamboo is the main vegetation found in the lowland region of North Bihar and in the northern parts of Gaya. Its wood is strong. Therefore, a wood-based small and cottage industry has developed due to it. Bamboo is known as the 'wood of the poor'.

Bamboo and Sawai grass are the main raw materials for the paper industry in the state. Therefore, some factories based on these have been developed in the state. With the abundance of forests in the Kaimur hill region in the southwestern part of the state, the paper industry in Dalmia Nagar, Rohtas was established in the private sector, but, at present, it is closed due to financial and management problems. In addition, paper factories–'Thakur Paper Mill' in Samastipur and 'Ashok Paper Mill' were established in Darbhanga.

These paper factories were supplied raw material by the Bihar Forest Development

Corporation, but due to non-availability of raw materials on time, labour management problem, financial problem, modernization of machines, etc., these factories are closed at present. In the Shivalik mountain region, catechu is produced as there is abundance of Khair trees. Catechu based industrial units are established in Betiya and Gaya.

FOOD PROCESSING INDUSTRIES

Bihar is a state with an agrarian economy. Therefore, the food processing industry has immense potential for development in the state. The food processing industries are mainly based on rice, wheat, maize, dairy products, edible oil, fox nut and fruits. About 45,000 people are employed in these units.

Fox nut is cultivated commercially in the state in wetlands (submerged area) in Darbhanga, Madhubani, Sitamarhi, etc. districts of North Bihar. Fox nut is an important source of protein and carbohydrates. Fox Nut Research Institute is established in Darbhanga. There is immense potential for the development of food processing industry in Muzaffarpur and Vaishali based on Litchi, on banana in Vaishali, on mango in Darbhanga and Bhagalpur, on guava in Rohtas and Kaimur. In this direction, several schemes are also being run by the State Food Processing Directorate, which are as follows –

i. **Integrated Development Project:** Through this project, up to 40 percent subsidy is given by the government.

ii. **Food Park Scheme:** JVL company is building a mega food park in Rohtas on an area of 85 acres at the cost of ₹117.2 crores. About 2000 megatons of raw materials, 15,000 megatons of grains and 2,000 megatons of processed food products will be kept here after the starts of the project. There will be a deep fridge facility for storing 500 megatons of food products. Apart from this, the Pristine Company in Mansi, Khagaria, and the Amrapali Group in Buxar are in the process of setting up food parks, while Ruchi Soya, Parle and Vitamin Group are already operating in the state. Under this, the limit of interest subsidy on setting up a food park is 35 percent of the project cost.

iii. **Modernization scheme for rice mills:** The Government of India has given 25 percent subsidy for the modernization of rice mills set up under the National Food Processing Mission.

iv. **Cold Storage Scheme:** Under this scheme, 30 percent subsidy is given to cold storages with 5-10 thousand tonnes capacity and 35 percent subsidy to cold storages with capacity of more than 10 thousand tonnes. The subsidy amount is fixed up to ₹5 crores.

Tea industry

At present, tea is cultivated on about 50 thousand acres of land in Bihar. Therefore, the tea industry is expanding at a rapid pace. The highest production of tea is from Kishanganj District. Pothia, Tehkurganj and Kishanganj areas of Kishanganj are the major tea growing regions. More than 40 thousand tons of tea is produced in Bihar every year. There are 7 tea processing centres in Kishanganj. Due to excess raw material, more centres are likely to be set up.

Leather industry

Bihar accounts for 8 percent of India's cattle, 12.1 percent of goats, 4.2 percent of buffaloes and 1.9 percent of sheep. According to the Central Leather Research Institute (CLRI), Chennai, there is annual production of 26.4 lakh skins and 50.9 lakh leather from cattle in Bihar. The main centres of skin and leather in the state are located in Patna, Ara, Aurangabad, Munger, Muzaffarpur, Pawai of Katihar, and of Purnia.

Khadi and Rural Industries

The Khadi and Rural Industries Commission (KVIC) has been constituted as a statutory body under the Ministry of Micro, Small and Medium Enterprises, which is the national nodal agency for khadi and its related products. To promote the rural industry, the 'Prime Minister Employment Generation Program' (PMEGP) has been implemented. The Khadi and Rural Industries Commission acts as the nodal agency under the 'Traditional Industry Rejuvenation Kos Scheme' (SFRTI).

UDYOG MITRA

'Udyog Mitra' was established in 2004 under the Societies Act, 1860. It was established by merging two existing societies, viz, 'Industrial Data Bank' and 'Single Window System'. The Industrial Data Bank was established in 1986 to provide data and information related to industries. The Single Window System was also established in 1986, as a koshang of the Department of Industries, whose main task was to help investors in the industrial sector overcome the problems.

The main objectives of the formation of Udyog Mitra are as follows:

- Providing all types of facilities to entrepreneurs under Single Window System for setting up industries.
- Assisting in the preparation of projects for large, medium and small-scale industries.
- Providing land through BIADA for setting up industries, and resolving problems related to various departments such as Bihar State Electricity Board, Bihar State Pollution Control Board, Central Excise and Sales Tax Department, etc.
- Providing industrial information and data to entrepreneurs, consultancy planners, etc.
- Providing infrastructure facilities to the entrepreneurs, such as energy, water, land, sheds, transport and communication facilities, and facilities for taking the products to market.

BIHAR INDUSTRIAL AREA DEVELOPMENT AUTHORITY (BIADA)

To promote industrialization in Bihar, the Bihar Industrial Area Development Authority (BIADA) has been established under the statutory provisions of the Bihar Industrial Area Development Act, 1974. The basic objectives of the formation of this authority are as follows –

- Providing infrastructure for industries, such as roads, water, energy, etc., within the industrial sector.
- To assist and encourage entrepreneurs to set up industries in accordance with the industrial policies implemented in the state.
- To create a conducive environment for investors for the establishment of industries in the state and to provide information about the provisions related to industrial policy.

The head office of BIADA is located in Patna, while 4 regional offices are functioning in the following cities—

1. Patna
2. Bhagalpur
3. Muzaffarpur
4. Darbhanga

Prior to the bifurcation of Jharkhand, 6 Industrial Zone Development Authorities were established in Adityapur, Bokaro, Ranchi, Patna, Darbhanga, and Muzaffarpur. Bihar's Industrial Commissioner office is in Patna.

Under the 4 regional offices of BIADA, 50 Industrial Areas (IA), Industrial Estates (IE), Large Industrial Areas (LIA), Growth Centres (GC) and Mega Industrial Parks (MIP) are included.

The industrial Areas (IA), Industrial Estates (IE), Large Industrial Areas (LIA), Growth Centres (GC) and Mega Industrial Parks (MIP) under the four Industrial Development Authorities regional offices of the state are shown in the table:

Regional authority		
Patna	IA	Pataliputra, Fatuha, Hajipur, Nawada, Gaya, Jehanabad, Baroon, Aurangabad, Dehari, Vikramganj, Bihiya, Bihta
	EPIP	Hajipur
	IE	Biharsharif, Kopakala, Barauni
	GC	Aurangabad, Buxar
	MIP	Giddha
Darbhanga	IA	Bela, Khagaria, Samastipur
	IE	Sahrasa, Udakishanganj, Pandaul, Muraliganj, Jhanjharpur, Dharampur
	GC	Chhonar
Muzaffarpur	IA	Muzaffarpur, Kumarbagh, Ramnagar, Sitamarhi, Raxaul
	IE	Betiya, Siwan
Bhagalpur	IA	Barari, Munger, Lakhisarai, Purniya city, Forbesganj, Katihar, Khagara
	IE	Maranga, Kahalgaon, Bhediyadangi
	GC	Sitakund, Jamalpur

PSUs in Bihar Controlled by Central Government

Location	Name of the Industry
Barauni	Fertilizer Corporation of India Limited
Barauni	Indian Oil Corporation Limited
Mokama	Bharat Wagon and Engineering Company Limited
Bela, Chhapara	Rail Wheel Factory
Madhaura, Chhapara	Diesel & Electric Engine Factory (under construction)
Madhepura	Railway Electric Locomotive Factory (under construction)
Harnaut	Carriage Repair Rail Workshop

INDUSTRIAL ZONES OF BIHAR

When many types of industrial activities become centralized in a particular region, then that region is called as industrial zone. The development of an industrial zone depends on the availability of raw materials, means of transport, capital, skilled labour, etc. In Bihar, industries that are based mainly on agriculture and forest have developed. These industrial centres are so scattered that they cannot be called industrial zones. Yet, they are similar to industrial zones. Keeping in mind the industrial development of Bihar, it can be divided into 6 industrial zones –

Gaya-Guraru Industrial Region: This is basically an agro-based industrial region, where cotton textile industries are established in Gaya, sugar mills are established in Gurura etc. Manpur of Gaya is the centre of handloom industry. Guraru's sugar mill is currently closed. The stone crushing industry has developed due to the availability of hills around Gaya.

Industrial Area of Southeast Bihar Plain: It is spread in the districts of Lakhisarai, Munger, Bhagalpur etc. in the eastern part of the Gangetic southern plain. The gun and cigarette industry in Munger, the railway workshop in Jamalpur, the silk industry in Bhagalpur and Nathnagar have been developed.

Industrial Zone of Southwest Bihar Plain: This industrial region has developed in the districts of Patna, Buxar, Bhojpur, etc. in the western part of the southern plain of the Ganges. Leather industry in Mokama, railway coaches, small iron unit, sugar industry in Bihta, leather industry in Digha (Patna), textile industry in Phulwari Sharif (Patna) and textile industry in Buxar have been developed.

Barauni Industrial Area: It is the most prosperous industrial region of Bihar, where many modern industries are established. Oil refineries, chemical fertilizers and thermal power bodies are set up in Barauni. The raw material for the oil refinery is obtained from the oil field of Assam. The crude oil comes from Haldia port and Assam oil fields by a pipeline. A chemical fertilizer factory based on naphtha, a by-product of the oil refinery, is established here. In addition, petrochemicals and dairy industries are established in Barauni.

Sugar Industrial Zone of Northwestern Ganges Plain

This region is a major sector of agro-based sugar industry. In this region, favourable geographical conditions are available for sugarcane production. Several sugar mills are established in the districts of East Champaran, West Champaran, Siwan, Gopalganj, Saran etc., whose main centres are Madhaura, Chanpatia, Maharajganj, Gopalganj, Pachrukhi, Hathua, etc.

Additionally, rice mills have developed in the lowland area. The main centres of rice mill are Narkatiaganj, Raxaul, Bairgania, Sitamarhi, Jainagar, Jhanjharpur, Jogbani, Forbesganj, etc.

DECENTRALIZED BIOMEDICAL WASTE INCINERATOR INAUGURATED IN BUXAR

Decentralized Biomedical Waste Incinerator inaugurated in Buxar, Bihar by the office of the Principal Scientific Advisor to Government of India and Buxar District Administration. This technology was developed by Ganesh Engineering Works. It was selected through Biomedical Waste Treatment Innovation Challenge that was launched in June 2020. It was developed under the Innovation challenge organised under Waste to Wealth Mission.

The Decentralized Biomedical Waste Incinerator is a portable, forced draft incinerator which has the capability to handle 50 kg of biomedical waste made of cotton, plastic, or similar materials per hour. Thus, it can handle 5 kg waste per batch. Waste heat recovery will be undertaken from hot gas for any productive application located near the site of installation. Different waste heat end products will be tested during the pilot at different sites such as distilled water, steam, gas burning, hot water etc. Efforts will be taken to utilize technology in residential or public places to ensure zero smoke, chimney usages, compact system, waste heat recovery, etc. This mission is one among nine scientific missions of Science, Technology, and Innovation Advisory Council (PM-STIAC) of Prime Minister. It is spearheaded by the Office of Principal Scientific Advisor to Government of India.

❑❑❑

Basic Infrastructure

- **Transportation**
- **Communication System**
- **Energy**
- **Bihar Renewable Energy Development Agency (BREDA)**
- **Bihar State Hydroelectric Power Corporation Limited**

TRANSPORTATION

Transportation is called the artery of economy. For the rapid development of any economy, the development of infrastructure is mandatory. There are 3 major components of infrastructure—transport, communication and energy. In Bihar, the pace of development of the major elements of infrastructure, such as roads, railways, civil aviation, postal facilities, energy sector etc. has been slow.

Road Transport: At the time of independence, the total length of paved roads in Bihar was 2104 km. Based on the width, 4 types of highways have developed in the state–

i. One-lane road — width 3.75 m
ii. Intermediate-lane road — width 5.50 m
iii. Two-lane road — width 7 m
iv. Roads with more two lanes — width more than 7 m

In Bihar, the expansion of the national state highways, district highways and rural highways has been made.

National Highway

National Highways are important in terms of connecting important cities, national capital, state capitals, ports, etc. via road network. The responsibility of construction and maintenance of national highways is with the National Highways Authority of India (NHAI).

In the State of Bihar, a popular destination for spiritual tourists from all over the world, the length of National Highways has been doubled in the past four years. Till 2014, the length of National Highways was 4,447 km a doubling of the highway network within a few years.

Here's a breakdown of some specific national highways in Bihar:

1. NH 27EW: 487 km (302.6 mi)
2. NH 31: 415 km (257.9 mi)
3. NH 33: 332 km (206.3 mi)
4. NH 119: 93 km (57.8 mi)

The number of National Highways have been increased to 102. Road development works worth ₹ 20,000 Cr. are progressing rapidly. In the next few years, investments worth ₹ 60,000 Cr. will be made towards transforming the road sector in Bihar, and creating new socio-economic opportunities for the people.

Buddhist Circuit: The Buddhist Circuits include all the places of high significance that are

Holy Sites of Buddhism; where Lord Buddha was born, attained Enlightenment, preached his first Sermon and attained Nirvana. Lumbini, Bodhgaya, Sarnath and Kushinagar are the primary pilgrimage destinations along Buddhist Circuits associated with the life and teachings of Lord Buddha. Apart from these, there are numerous other sites where Buddha and the Bhikshus travelled during his life after his transformation, which are held in deep veneration.

Visitors from all over the world can travel through the Buddhist Circuit today.

Buddhist Circuit: Bodhgaya- Nalanda-Rajgir-Vaishali-Kahalgaon-Patna. Dharmayatra Circuit: Bodh Gaya-Sarnath-Kushinagar-Piparvah. Extended Dharmayatra Circuit: Bodh Gaya-Vikramshila-Sarnath- KushinagarKapilvastu-Sankisa–Piparvah.

Bihar has national highways with total length of 5,358 km (3,329 mi) and state highways with total length of 4,006 km (2,489 mi). Also. Bihar has 921 km (572 mi) of proposed Expressways.

The state is being equipped with more sustainable energy sources, CNG filling stations are being put up in different cities.

To manage overall road transport facilities in the state, Bihar State Road Transport Corporation (BSRTC) was set up in 1959 under the provisions of Road Transport Corporation Act, 1950.

BSRTC operates and maintains a fleet of more than 300 buses connecting all cities and towns within state of Bihar and neighboring states too. BSRTC not only connects every nook and corner of the state but also links this state with other surrounding regions including Uttar Pradesh, Jharkhand, Chhattisgarh, West Bengal and Odisha. However, contract for operation and maintenance of the buses has been given to two private companies viz. GIPL and Royal Cruiser. This contract is based upon public-private partnership.

National Highways in Bihar

Number	Length (km)	Length (mi)	Southern or Western Terminus	Northern or Eastern Terminus
NH 922	138.0	85.7	The highway starting from its junction with NH-22 near Patna connecting Ara, Bhojpur and terminating near Buxar in the State of Bihar.	
NH 727AA	13.0	8.1	The highway starting from its junction with NH-727 near Manuapul connecting Patzirwa, Paknaha in the state of Bihar, Pipraghat and terminating at its junction with NH-730 near Sevrahi in the state of Uttar Pradesh.	
NH 727A	4.5	2.8	Uttar Pradesh and terminating at its junction with NH 227A near Mairwa	
NH 727	112.0	69.6	The highway starting from its junction with NH-27 near Kushinagar in the State of Uttar Pradesh connecting Chhitanuni Rail-cum-Road Bridge, Bagaha, Lauriya, Bettiah and terminating at its junction with NH-527 D near Chhapwa in the State of Bihar.	
NH 722	75.0	46.6	The highway starting from its junction with NH-22 near Muzaffarpur connecting Rewaghat and terminating at its junction with NH-31 near Chhapra in the State of Bihar.	
NH 531	95.0	59.0	The highway starting from its junction with NH-31 near Chhapra, Siwan and terminating at its junction with NH-27 near Gopalganj in the State of Bihar.	
NH 527D	67.2	41.8	The highway starting from its junction with NH-27 near Piprakothi connecting Sagauli, Raxaul, in the State of Bihar and terminating at Indo/Nepal Border.	
NH 527C	64.2	39.9	The highway starting from Majhauli on NH-27 connecting Katra, Jajuar, Pupri and terminating at Charout on NH-227 in the state of Bihar.	

NH 527B	53.8	33.4	The highway starting from its junction with NH-27 near Darbhanga connecting Aunsi and terminating at its junction with NH-227 near Jaynagar in the State of Bihar.
NH 527A	75.3	46.8	The highway starting from its junction with new NH No. 527 B near Pokhrauni Chowk connecting Madhubani, Rampatti, Jhanjharpur, Samey Chowk, Awam, Laufa, Bheja, Bakaur and terminating at its junction with NH No. 327 near Parsarma in the State of Bihar.
NH 527	9.3	5.8	The highway starting from its junction with NH-27 near Forbesganj and terminating at Jogbani in the State of Bihar.
NH 431	69.0	42.9	The highway starting from its junction with NH-31 near Phatuha connecting Chandi, Harnaut and terminating at its junction with NH-31 near Barh in the State of Bihar.
NH 333B	17.7	11.0	The highway starting from its junction with NH-33 at Munger and terminating at its junction with NH No-31 at Khagaria in the state of Bihar.
NH 333A	198.9	123.6	The highway starting from its junction with NH-33 near Bar Bigha connecting Shekhpura, Sikandra, Jamui, Jha-Jha, Banka in the State of Bihar and terminating at its junction with NH-133 near Godda in the State of Jharkhand.
NH 333	141.2	87.7	The highway starting from Bariyarpur on NH-33 connecting Kharagpur, Laxmipur, Jamui, Chakai in the state of Bihar-Jharkhand
NH 331	65.0	40.4	The highway starting from its junction with NH-31 near Chhapra connecting Baniapur, and terminating at its junction with NH-27 near Muhumadpur the State of Bihar.
NH 327A	25.0	15.5	The highway starting from Supaul on NH-327 and terminating at Bhaptiahi on NH-27 in the state of Bihar.
NH 327	233.5	145.1	The highway starting from Galgalia on N.H-327 (W.B/Bihar) Thakurganj, Raniganj, Bahadurganj, Araria, Bhargama, Tribeniganj, Pipra, Supaul, (Bariyahi Bazar) Bangaon and terminating at Maheshi (Tarapeeth) in the state of Bihar.
NH 322	58.0	36.0	The highway starting from its junction with NH-22 near Hazipur and terminating at its junction with NH-122 near Mushrigharari in the State of Bihar.
NH 319	125.0	77.7	Junction with NH-19 near Mohania - Dinara, Charpokhari, a junction with NH-922 near Ara
NH 231	209.0	129.9	The highway starting from its junction with NH-31 near Maheshkund in the State of Bihar connecting Sonbarsa Raj, Simri Bakhtiyarpur, Saharsa, Madhepura, Sarsi, Purnia and terminating at its junction with NH-31 near Kora in the State of Bihar.
NH 227L	20.4	12.7	The highway starting from its junction with NH- 227 near Umagaon connecting Basopatti and terminating at its junction with NH- 527B near Kalnahi in the state of Bihar.
NH 227J	30.0	18.6	The highway starting from its junction with NH- 227 near Saharghat connecting Uchhait, Benipatti and terminating at its junction with NH- 527B near Rahika in the state of Bihar
NH 227F	36.3	22.6	The highway starting from its junction with NH- 227 near Chakia (Chorma chowk) connecting Pakridayal, Dhaka, Phulwaria Ghat and terminating at Bairgania in the state of Bihar near Indo / Nepal Border.
NH 227A	137.0	85.1	Up / Bihar Border - Siwan - Mashrakh - Chakia

NH 227	215.0	133.6	The highway starting from its junction with NH-27 near Chakia connecting Narhar, Pakri Bridge, Madhuban, Shivhar, Sitamarhi, Harlakhi, Umgaon, Jaynagar, Laukaha, Laukahi and terminating at its junction with NH-27 near Narahia in the State of Bihar.
NH 219	46.8	29.1	The highway starting from its junction with new NH No. 19 near Mohania connecting Bhabhua, Chainpur, Chand in the State of Bihar and terminating at its junction with NH-19 near Chandauli in the state of Uttar Pradesh
NH 139	153.6	95.4	The highway starting from its junction with NH-39 near Rajhara connecting Chhatarpur, Hariharganj in the State of Jharkhand, Aurangabad, Daudnagar, Arwal, Naubatpur and terminating at its junction with NH-31 near Patna in the State of Bihar.
NH 133B	5.0	3.1	Jharkhand Border- Manihar (NH-31)
NH 133	10.9	6.8	The highway starting from its junction with NH-33 in the state of Bihar connecting Godda and terminating at Choupa More on NH-114A in the state of Jharkhand.
NH 131A	81.2	50.5	West Bengal- Ahmedabad, Manihari, Katihar on NH-31 - Purnia on NH-27
NH 131	136.0	84.5	The highway starting from its junction with NH-31 near Bihpur connecting Kishanganj, Madhepura and terminating at Birpur in the State of Bihar near Indo/Nepal Border.
NH 122A	31.8	19.8	Vishwanathpur Chowk on NH-22 - Koili, a- Nanpur on NH-527C
NH 122	110.0	68.4	Junction with NH-22 near Muzaffarpur - Dholi, Mushrigharari - junction with NH-31 near Barauni
NH 120	244.0	151.6	Junction with NH-20 near Bihar Sharif connecting Nalanda, Rajgir, Hisua, Gaya, Daudnagar, Nasriganj, Karakat, dawath, Nawanagar, and terminating at its junction with NH-922 near Dumraon
NH 119	93.0	57.8	The highway starting from its junction with NH-19 near Dehri connecting Akbarpur, Jadunathpur and terminating at Bihar/UP Border near Jadunathpur in the State of Bihar.
NH 33	332.0	206.3	The highway starting from its junction with NH-139 from Arwal connecting Jahanabad, Bandhuganj, Ekangarsarai, Biharsharif, Mokama, Luckeesarai, Munger, Bhagalpur, Kahalgaon in the State of Bihar, Sahibganj, Rajmahal, Barharwa in the State of Jharkhand and terminating at its junction with NH-12 near Farakka in the State of West Bengal.
NH 31	415.0	257.9	The highway starting from its junction with NH-27 near Unnao connecting Lalganj, Raebareli, Salon, Pratapgarh, Machhlishahr, Jaunpur, Varanasi, Ghazipur, Ballia in the State of Uttar Pradesh Chhapra, Hajipur, Bakhtiyarpur, Mokama, Begusarai, Khagaria, Bihpur, Kora, Katihar in the State of Bihar, Harishchanderpur and terminating at its junction with NH-12 near Pandua in the State of West Bengal.
NH 27EW	487.0	302.6	Uttar Pradesh Gopalganj, Pipra Kothi, Muzaffarpur, Darbhanga, Forbesganj, Araria, Purnia, in the State of BiharWest Bengal
NH 22	282.3	175.4	Sonbarsa (Indo/Nepal Border), Sitamarhi, Muzaffarpur, Hajipur, Patna, Punpun, Gaya, Bodh Gaya, Dobhi - Jharkhand.
NH 20	107.7	66.9	Junction with NH-31 near Bakhtiyarpur - Bihar Sharif, Nawada, Rajauli -Jharkhand
NH 19GQ	206.0	128.0	Uttar Pradesh, Mohania, Aurangabad, Dobhi-Jharkhand

State Highways

Bihar has many state highways, including SH 2, SH 4, SH 5, SH 6, and SH 69. SH 69 is one of the longest in Bihar. Some other notable highways include SH 1, SH 15, SH 16, SH 17, SH 18, SH 23, SH 48, SH 49, SH 50, SH 56, SH 63, SH 64, SH 68, SH 70, SH 73, SH 74, SH 76, SH 77, SH 78, and SH 81.

Here's a more detailed look at some of these state highways:

- **SH 2:** Connects Bihta to Arwal, passing through Bikram and Paliganj.
- **SH 4:** Connects Fatuha to Gaya, passing through Daniawan, Hilsa, Ekangarsarai, and other towns.
- **SH 5:** Connects Biharsharif to Arwal Road, passing through Jehanabad and Telhara Road.
- **SH 6:** Connects Biharsharif to Kharagpur Road, passing through Shekhpura, Jamui, and Sikandara.
- **SH 69:** A long route from Dumaria to Talab.
- **SH 81:** Connects Sakaddi near Arrah to Nasriganj near Dehri-on-Sone.
- **SH 17:** Connects Chausa to Sasaram.

Main District Road Network

The main district roads are important roads within the districts which connect the less developed areas to district headquarters, nearest state highways, national highways, railways, and cities. These roads collect traffic from rural roads at the lowest level of the road classification system.

The total length of major district roads in the state is 14,886 km. The three districts that got the maximum expansion in the main district road are: Patna (434 km), Darbhanga (410 km), and Jamui (344 km). At the same time, the least beneficiary districts are Bhojpur (4 km), Jehanabad (7 km), and Khagaria (13 km).

Rural road network

Rural road connectivity is a natural way to improve the survival of rural areas. Rural roads make a substantial contribution in enabling the socio-economic development of villages and towns. The length of rural roads is 96,833 km. The top three districts in terms of rural road network are Madhubani (6360 km), Muzaffarpur (5797 km), and East Champaran (5795 km).

Indo-Nepal Border Road Project

The Central Government has approved the construction and upgradation of 1377 km of roads along Indo-Nepal border, under Border Road Management-5 (VRM-5), at an estimated cost of ₹3853.00 crores. States of Bihar, Uttar Pradesh, and Uttarakhand will be benefited by this project.

The part of the road passing parallel to the border of Nepal will go from Madanpur in Uttar Pradesh to Galgalia in West Bengal and will pass through 7 districts of Bihar – West Champaran, East Champaran, Sitamarhi, Madhubani, Supaul, Araria, and Kishanganj.

Road transport

In a developing state like Bihar, road transport is a more useful medium than other modes of transport. The Bihar State Road Transport Corporation was established in 1959 to provide adequate bus facility in the state. The Public-Private Partnership (PPP mode) scheme was launched by this corporation to strengthen its financial position.

Rail Transport

Rail transport is crucial for Bihar's economy and development, serving as a vital link for freight and passenger movement, both within the state and to other parts of India and even neighboring countries like Nepal. It facilitates trade, connects rural areas, and contributes to overall socio-economic growth.

Key aspects of rail transport's importance in Bihar:

- **Freight Movement:** Railways play a major role in transporting goods from Bihar to other states and vice versa, with a significant volume of cargo moved annually.

- **Connectivity:** Bihar has several railway lines connecting it to Nepal, facilitating trade and travel across borders. The Raxaul rail link is particularly important for transporting goods to and from Nepal through Kolkata/Haldia ports.
- **Economic Growth:** Rail transport supports economic activities by providing efficient and cost-effective means of moving goods, which is crucial for industries and businesses in Bihar.
- **Rural Connectivity:** Railways provide a vital link to rural areas, facilitating access to markets and other essential services, which is important for the state's development.
- **Tourism:** Railways also play a role in promoting tourism, with various trains connecting tourist destinations within Bihar and beyond.
- **Energy Efficiency:** Rail transport is generally more energy-efficient than road transport, contributing to sustainability and reducing carbon emissions.
- **Electrification:** The electrification of rail tracks in Bihar has improved efficiency and sustainability, enabling the use of electric locomotives.

Challenges and Future Development:

- **Infrastructure:** While rail transport is important, there are some challenges related to infrastructure, operational efficiency, and connectivity.
- **Improved Efficiency:** Efforts are being made to improve rail efficiency, including modernizing existing infrastructure, increasing the use of electric locomotives, and improving connectivity.
- **Multimodal Integration:** Integrating rail transport with other modes of transport, such as roads and waterways, is crucial for a more efficient and effective logistics system.

The whole of India is divided into 18 railway zones from an administrative point of view. The only railway zone in Bihar is the headquarters of the Middle Eastern Railway located at Hajipur. This zone was build in 2002. Following are the four railway divisions in Bihar:

1. Sonpur Division, Middle Eastern Railway, Hajipur
2. Danapur Division, Middle Eastern Railway, Hajipur
3. Samastipur Division, Middle Eastern Railway, Hajipur
4. Katihar Division, Northeast Frontier Railway, Gauhati

Apart from this, the area of Bhagalpur, Jamalpur in Bihar comes under the Malda Division of Northeast Railway Calcutta. Under North Eastern Railway Gorakhpur, Varanasi Railway Division includes areas of Bihar such as Chhapra, Siwan and Gopalganj.

The Calcutta-Mughalsarai railroad passing through Bihar, construct in 1860-62, goes through Patna. This is the first railway line of Bihar. The railway lines of Bihar are located in four zones—

1. Middle East Railway, Hajipur
2. Northeast Frontier Railway, Guwahati
3. Northeast Railway, Calcutta
4. Northeastern Railway, Gorakhpur

The Northeast Frontier Railway has Purnia area under it, the Northeast Railway has Bhagalpur area under it, Northeastern Railway has Chhapra area under it, while most of Bihar's Central East Railway falls under Hajipur.

Air Transportation

Compared to other states in the country, the development of air transport has been less in Bihar. The reason for this is economic backwardness, under-development of industrialization and urbanization, etc., although in the state, airports of national level are established in Patna and Gaya. An international airport has been built at Bodh Gaya. Air services are available from Bodh Gaya to Sri Lanka and Bangkok. Air services are available from the state capital of Patna to Kathmandu, Kolkata, Mumbai, Ahmedabad, Lucknow, Ranchi, and Delhi.

The airport in Patna has been named Jayaprakash Narayan Airport. Airports have also been built at Muzaffarpur, Jogbani, Raxaul, Bhagalpur and Bihta. The major airlines that provide services in Bihar are Jet Airways, IndiGo, Indian Airlines, etc.

The airways flying from Patna include IndiGo, Jet Airways, Air Asia and Air India. Currently, the maximum number of flights are by IndiGo. Air Asia is a Malaysian aviation company. Following are the major airports located in Bihar –

Sr. No.	Name	Location	Type
1	Jaiprakash Narayan International Airport	Patna	International
2	Gaya International Airport	Bodh Gaya	International
3	Bhagalpur Airport	Bhagalpur	Domestic
4	Darbhanga Airport	Darbhanga	Defence
5	Jogbani Airport	Jogbani	Domestic
6	Chunapur Airport	Purnia	Defence

Water Transport

Water transport is the cheapest and pollution free mode of transport. It is the most suitable means for transporting heavy goods. In Bihar, rivers like Ganga, Ghaghra, Gandak, Budhi Gandak, Bagmati, Kosi, Son etc. are available for water transport. The National Waterway Transport Number 1 on the Ganges River, which is from Allahabad to Haldia, passes through Bihar. It was established in October 1986. Its length is 1620 kilometers; a permanent terminal is also set up in Patna while Floating terminal is in Bhagalpur. The regional office is established at Gaighat in Patna on the Ganges River. Indian Inland Waterways Transport was established on 27 October, 1986, which is headquartered in Noida, Uttar Pradesh. It works under the Ministry of Waterways and Surface Transport, Government of India. Its regional offices are located in Patna, Calcutta, Guwahati and Kochi.

The canals drawn from the Kosi, Gandak and Son Rivers have been made navigable. Buxar Canal and Arrah Canal are also navigable. In Bihar, boating is done for about 100 km in Ghaghra, 200 km in Kosi, 240 km in Gandak, and 195 km in Son.

Rope Way

Bihar has two main ropeways: the Rajgir Ropeway and the Mandar Hill Ropeway. The Rajgir Ropeway is particularly known for its scenic views of the Vishwa Shanti Stupa on Ratnagiri Hill. The Mandar Hill Ropeway, located in Banka district, provides access to historical and religious sites on Mandar Hill.

COMMUNICATION SYSTEM

Bihar has a two-tier communication system: intra-district and inter-district. Intra-district communication uses wireless technology to connect police stations and district headquarters, while inter-district communication utilizes HF and satellite-based networks like POLNET. The state also has a well-established telecommunications infrastructure with various mobile service providers.

Intra-District Communication:

Wireless technology connects police stations (PSs) and police outposts (OPs) to the district headquarters and vice versa within each district.

Inter-District Communication:

- **HF Communication Network:** For wireless communication between district headquarters.
- **POLNET (Satellite-based Network):** Provides wireless communication between district headquarters.

- **Telecommunications:** India primarily uses the GSM mobile system, with 900 MHz and 1800 MHz bands.
- Major mobile service providers in Bihar include VI, Airtel, Jio, and BSNL/MTNL.
- International roaming agreements exist with many foreign carriers.
- **Other Considerations:** The Bihar government has approved a Road Development Vision-2020 for expanding road infrastructure and connectivity.
- There are also communication plans for various assembly constituencies in the state.
- Bihar is well-connected to other Indian cities through its airports, with Patna airport being a restricted international airport.

Postal system

The postal system in Bihar, like the rest of India, is managed by India Post. It operates within the Bihar Postal Circle, headed by the Chief Postmaster General. The postal system relies on a network of post offices, including Head, Sub, and Branch Post Offices, as well as Gramin Dak Sewa Post Offices in rural areas. Bihar is also introducing a new system to expedite letter and parcel delivery within two days, using dedicated postal vehicles.

Bihar is set to revolutionize its postal services with a new system ensuring that letters and parcels will be delivered within just two days. This game-changing plan, starting this financial year, promises to significantly reduce delivery times, moving away from the previous system that took over a week. Dedicated postal vehicles will transport letters and parcels across districts, ensuring faster and more efficient delivery across the state.

Under the ambitious plan, a network of dedicated postal vehicles will transport letters and parcels between districts, ensuring that items reach the main post office of another district within just 24 hours. From there, they will be swiftly routed to local sub-post offices and delivered to recipients the following day. This shift to a more efficient road-based system will significantly reduce delays traditionally caused by rail transport.

ENERGY

Energy Department

Energy Department, Bihar, is a State Government Department, assigned to carry out all the activities of Power Sector, enforced upon the relevant Acts and Rules of Electricity, Power & Energy, co-ordinate among all the power utilities and stakeholders operating in the state and advice the State Government on all matters relating to Power, Electricity & Energy.

Bihar has adopted a long-term approach for energy sector to fulfill its vision to provide "Har Ghar Bijli" as outlined in 7 Nischay. The vision roadmap supports low carbon pathway to sustain the economic growth. The vision focus on increasing the number of state-owned power generation plants, with increased share of renewable energy, separate feeder for agricultural purpose, demand-side management by improving the overall efficiency in distribution system and strengthening the distribution companies.

The highest recorded power demand in Bihar was 8,005 MW. The Central Electricity Authority (CEA) also notes that the electricity demand for Bihar is increasing, with a forecast for a 7.51% annual increase in demand from 2024-25 to 2033-34. In 2023, the demand was reported to be 9002 MW.

Per capita energy consumption to increase from 134 kilowatt-hours (2012–13) to 363 kilowatt-hours (2023–24).

The top five districts in electricity consumption are Patna, Gaya, Muzaffarpur, Rohtas and Nalanda.

Bihar Aims to be in India's Top 10 Green Energy States by 2030

Bihar is lagging far behind other states of the country in terms of green energy, but it has recently taken serious steps in this direction. According to the guidelines of the government of India, the Bihar government has decided that by March 2030 approximately 44% of the total electricity supplied in Bihar will be from green energy. At present this share is less than 15%.

While the total electricity consumption in the state has reached 6,500 megawatts, production from green energy is only 6%. Every day, Bihar produces 415 megawatts of non-conventional energy. In this, the share of solar is 218 megawatts (141 megawatts from on-grid, ground-mounted projects, 56 megawatts from rooftop, and 21 megawatts from off-grid solar power plants), biofuels is 126 megawatts and small hydro power is 71 megawatts . These have been installed on government and private buildings. There is not a single wind or geothermal project in Bihar.

Bihar Electricity Regulatory Commission has set different targets to obtain electricity from solar, wind and water sources and has assigned the responsibility of compliance to the power company. The target is to achieve at least 24.81% solar energy in 2023-24, and by almost one and a half times to 33.57% by 2030. Similarly, the electricity produced from wind and water sources will have to be increased by 850 times. This will be the biggest challenge for power companies. Power companies will have to submit status reports to the commission twice every year on how much electricity they have obtained against the annual target from various sources of renewable energy.

Solar is the biggest energy production tool for Bihar in green energy. But the big problem has been intermittency: the production of solar energy is possible only when there is sunlight during the day and comes to a halt at night.

In such a situation, pump and battery storage systems can prove to be a game changer for the solar mission. Power companies have committed to include this in the projects at Kajra and Kaimur. According to BREDA, 20% of the total electricity generated in Kajra Solar Project will be stored in batteries so that the grid continues to get continuous electricity. While, at the hydro-solar project at Kaimur, there will be a system of pump-based electricity storage to be set up in the hills. For this, two reservoirs will be created, one on the top of the hill, and another below. The elevation is kept such that the water flowing towards the lower reservoir passes through the turbine and generates electricity. However, electricity is also required to transport water from the lower reservoir to the upper level for which solar energy can be used for this. Hence, solar electricity will be produced during the day which will pump the water to the upper reservoir, and hydroelectric power will be produced at night which can be added to the grid.

Presently there are about 1.78 crore electricity consumers in Bihar consuming 37,331 million units of electricity. By the financial year 2024-25, the number of these consumers is expected to increase to 1.90 crore and electricity consumption is estimated to be 45.5 million units. There will be more than 68 lakh electricity consumers under South Bihar Electricity Company and more than 1.20 crore electricity consumers under North Bihar Electricity Company.

To meet the surge in power requirements, a total of 450 megawatts of solar energy projects are under process, these include:

1. 200 megawatts at Kajra in Lakhisarai and 250 megawatts at Peerpainti in Bhagalpur. For this, 2,225 acres of land has been given to Bihar Power Generation Company. With the detailed project report (DPR) ready, the project awaits cabinet approval. According to the plan, 80% of the budget will be availed through a loan from financial institutions, while 20% will be received from the state government as equity as capital investment. The target is to start production in 2024.
2. Sutlej Jal Vidyut Nigam (SJVN) is setting up a solar generation unit of 125-megawatt capacity in Jamui and 75-megawatt capacity in Banka. For this, the land for both projects is being marked and the registration process is nearing completion. The tender has been invited for Jamui solar unit. After the work order, the work will be completed in one and a half years.

3. An effort to produce solar energy and hydroelectric power simultaneously has been started in the hills of Kaimur. The power company has expressed the possibility of producing 1,000 to 1,500 megawatts of electricity based on pumped storage here. The responsibility of the study for this has been given to the professional organization WAPCOS Limited. This organization will submit its report to the nodal agency SJVN within three months, after which the work will start.
4. BREDA has started setting up solar power plants on the banks of canals. In the first phase, Son Canal near Bikram in Patna district and Phulwaria reservoir, 30 kilometers away from Nawada, have been selected; 2- and 10-megawatt solar power plants will be installed there respectively. For this, the process of obtaining a No Objection Certificate (NOC) from the Water Resources Department is underway. A target has been set to produce electricity in 1.5 years after completing the tender process. The power company, BREDA, has set a target of obtaining 760 megawatts of electricity from renewable energy sources by March 2024. In this, 300 megawatts of power will be obtained from the fifth phase of Solar Energy Corporation of India while 210 megawatts of power will be obtained from the hybrid project by 2023 only.
5. Grid-connected rooftop solar power plants are being installed in government buildings. There is a plan to add 150 to 200 megawatts of solar energy to this. Of these, 20 megawatts are operational, while work orders have been made for 65 megawatts.
6. The state government is giving 45% to 65% subsidies to private houses to equip them with solar power and connect them to the grid.
7. Solar streetlights are being installed in the Panchayati Raj bodies also. Instructions have been given to install at least 10 solar lights in all wards.
8. The target is to provide the benefit of solar irrigation pumps to 10,000 farmers by 2025.
9. According to the company, about 100 megawatts of electricity is being received from the bagasse-based co-generating units of the sugar mills of the state.
10. There is also a plan to establish a floating solar power plant near the canal at Uderashthan Barrage in Jehanabad district. However, on visiting the site it was learned that despite a site inspection for a floating solar power plant conducted three years ago, there is still no sign of implementation. The barrage's Junior Engineer Rakesh Kumar said that he has no information about the work done after the site inspection.

Recent projects

A floating solar power plant of 2.4-megawatt capacity has been established in Rajapokhar of Sakhua village located in Deenapatti Panchayat of Pipra, Supaul and 1.6-megawatt floating solar power plant has been established in the pond located in Kadirabad locality of Darbhanga city. The specialty of this power plant floating in the pond is that fish are being reared below it, while electricity is being produced from the solar power plate installed above. These plants keep floating in the pond with the help of drums. At present, electricity is being produced from both these plants.

Preparations for the future: Green energy in parts of Patna, Rajgir and Bodhgaya

The state-owned electricity company has decided to replace thermal energy with solar energy in two big cities of the state, Rajgir and Bodhgaya, as well as in some parts of the state capital, Patna city. For this, the power company has signed an agreement with Solar Corporation of India, a government of India undertaking, for the purchase of 480 megawatts of power for 25 years. This electricity will be available at 2.5 to 3 rupees per unit, which will be cheaper than the present thermal power units.

Bihar's Institutional Structure in Power Sector

The Bihar State Electricity Board was constituted in April 1958 under Article 5 of the Electricity (Supply) Act, 1948, for the management of power generation, transmission, distribution and other activities in Bihar. In order to improve the power system, the Bihar State Electricity Board was divided into 5 companies in November 2012 under the new Bihar State Electricity Reform Transfer Scheme, 2012, which are as follows –

1. Bihar State Electricity (Holding) Company Limited (BSPHCL)
2. Bihar State Electricity Generation Company Limited (BSPGCL)
3. Bihar State Power Transmission Company Limited (BSPTCL)
4. South Bihar Power Distribution Company Limited (NBPDCL)
5. North Bihar Power Distribution Company Limited (SBPDCL)

BSPHCL has been assigned the responsibility of the shares of the other 4 companies and has been given ownership of the assets of the erstwhile Bihar State Electricity Board. It primarily functions as an investment company. It serves to coordinate the activities of other companies and settle disputes.

BSPGCL coordinates between subsidiaries engaged in power generation. This task includes all the matters relating to the construction, operation, and maintenance of production centres and related facilities in the roles of coordination and suggestion.

BSPTCL is responsible for power transmission and has been given the ownership of the transmission assets of the erstwhile Bihar State Electricity Board.

Both NBPDCL and SBPDCL distribute electricity to all consumers and implement rural electrification schemes under Rajiv Gandhi Rural Electrification Scheme, Special Backward Region Grant Fund, Restructured Accelerated Power Development and Reforms Programme, State Plan and schemes funded by Asian Development Bank.

Electrification Program in the State

In order to increase power distribution and supply, the central government runs 3 important schemes in the state—

1. Integrated Power Development Plan
2. Deendayal Upadhyaya Gram Jyoti Yojana
3. Special Scheme (Backward Region Grant Fund)

The 'Integrated Power Development Scheme' was launched in December 2014. It was launched in the 12th Five-year Plan. It included the restructured Accelerated Power Development and Reforms Programme.

'Deendayal Upadhyaya Gram Jyoti Yojana' was launched by the Central Government in December 2014. The Rajiv Gandhi Rural Electrification Scheme, which was already operational, was also included in this scheme. Under this scheme, electrification is being done in all 38 districts of the state.

To improve power generation and distribution in the state, a document titled '24 Hour Electricity for All' has been issued. As on March, 2020, the total power generation capacity in the state was 6073 MW, of which the share of thermal power was 70.27 percent. Electricity generation is carried out in both public and private sectors in Bihar.

Energy production centres in Bihar

Kahalgaon Super Thermal Power Station: Kahalgaon Super Thermal Power Station is an NTPC controlled thermal power generation unit located in Bhagalpur District. It was established in 1992. Its total installed generation capacity is 4 x 210 MW and 3 x 500 MW, i.e., 2,340 MW. Coal is supplied to this power station by the Rajmahal coal mine of Eastern Coal Fields Limited and the source of water supply is the Ganges River.

Barh Super Thermal Power Station: It is located in Barh, in the Patna District. Its construction started in 1999, and production started from 2013. It has a total installed capacity of 3,300 MW, i.e., 5 × 660 MW. It is under the control of NTPC. The first phase (3 × 660 MW) of the Barh Super Thermal Power Station was built by the Russian company called Technopromexport (TPE), and the second phase (2 × 660 MW) was built by Bharat Heavy Electricals Limited (BHEL). Bihar gets 26 percent (1183 MW) of its total production in the first phase and 50 percent of the total production in the second phase. Sikkim and West Bengal have also been given a stake in the second phase production by NTPC. It is connected to the Haldia Port by the National Waterway No.1 through the Ganges River.

Barauni Thermal Power Station (BTPS): The Barauni Thermal Power Station earlier had 7 separate units, out of which now units 1 to 5 have exhausted their working life and are not available for production. After restoration work, the production in the seventh unit of 110 MW has started. At the same time, the work of restoration of the sixth unit of 110 MW is in progress. In addition, the work on two new units of 250 MW each is also underway. The Commercial Operation Date (COD) of the eighth unit has been announced by the National Thermal Power Corporation. Furthermore, the capacity enhancement of the ninth unit has been achieved in March 2018 itself, and the work of starting its commercial production is in progress. In order to reduce the cost of electricity generated by these units, the state government, along with the expertise of the Thermal Power Corporation, has transferred the ownership of Baroni Thermal Power Station to National Thermal Power Corporation.

Kanti Bijli Utpadan Nigam Limited (KBUNL): Located in Muzaffarpur, it is a joint venture of National Thermal Power Corporation and Bihar State Power Generation Company Limited. In this, the shareholding of both the parties in its equity is in the ratio of 65 : 35. Here two units (units 3 and 4) of 110 MW each have also been completed and the production has started. Also, as per the decision of the state government, its 100% equity share has been transferred to National Thermal Power Corporation.

Kosi Hydroelectricy Centre: About 4 units of 4.8 MW each were constructed between 1970–78 at Kosi Hydroelectric Power Station (Kataiya), Birpur. In 2003, this project was included under Bihar State Hydroelectric Corporation.

In addtion to the above-mentioned 3 power generating units, the following power generation units are being constructed at present:

Nabinagar Plant (Phase I): This project is located in Aurangabad district of Bihar. Nabinagar Power Generation Company Pvt. Ltd. (NPGCL) is a joint venture between National Thermal Power Corporation and Bihar State Electricity Generation Company Ltd., with 50:50 share in its equity. Later, the state government transferred its entire ownership to the National Thermal Power Corporation. The construction work of the first 660 MW (total of 1320 MW) was completed in July 2019. The construction of the other two units, that is unit 2 was completed in March 2021 and unit 3 was completed in May 2022.

Power Project at Buxar: Satluj Hydroelectric Corporation is the implementing agency for construction of 2 units of greenfield power project of 660 MW at Chausa. Its detailed project report was updated in January 2018. Investment approval has also been given by the central government in March 2019. Its foundation stone has been laid by the Hon'ble Prime Minister in March, 2019. Consultancy service has been entrusted to National Thermal Power Corporation for main plant and RITES for railway infrastructure. Topographical survey of the project area, construction of boundary wall pillars and barbed-wire fencing has been completed. At present, construction of foundation of pillars, excavation and many other works at site are in progress.

Ultra Mega Power Project (UMPP): A proposal has been prepared to set up a power project of about 4000 MW in Banka, for which 2,500 acres of land has been marked. The Central Water Commission has given approval for 120 cusecs of water to be drawn from the Ganga river. The project would be executed through a two Special Purpose Vehicle (SPV) structure which is incorporated by the Power Finance Corporation. The Ministry of Power has approved Barahat (Pirpainti) coal block allotment for this project. By this project, Bihar will receive 2000 MW electricity.

Details of Existing and Planned Generation Units

KANTI TPP (2 × 110 MW) and (2 × 195 MW)	
2016-17	Units 1 & 2 – (110 MW each)
2017-18	195 MW Unit 3
2018-19	195 MW Unit 4 completed
BARAUNI TPP (2 × 110 MW) and (2 × 250 MW)	
2016-17	110 MW Unit 7: Nov. 16
2019-20	Unit 8 (250 MW) – COD on 01.03.2020
2021-21	Unit 9 (250 MW) – COD in Feb. 2021 Unit 6 (110 MW) – COD in Oct. 2021
NABINAGAR (NPGCL) (3 × 660 MW) 1980 MW	
2019-20	Unit 1 (660 MW) – COD on 06.09.19 (Share of BSPHCL - 517 MW)
2021-21	Unit 2 (660 MW) – COD in March 2021 (Share of BSPHCL - 517 MW)
2021-22	Unit 3 (660 MW) – COD in June' 2021 (Share of BSPHCL - 517 MW)
NABINGAR (BRBCL) (4 × 250 MW) 1000 MW	
2021-22	Unit 4 (250 MW) – COD in Aug 2021 (Share of BSPHCL - 25 MW)
NORTH KARANPURA TPP (3 × 660 MW) 1980 MW	
2021-22	Unit 1 (660 MW) – COD in June 2021 (Share of BSPHCL - 230 MW) Unit 2 (660 MW) – COD in Nov 2021 (Share of BSPHCL - 230 MW)
2022-23	Unit 3 (660 MW) – COD in May 2022 (Share of BSPHCL - 230 MW)
DARIPALI STPS (2 × 800 MW) 1600 MW	
2019-20	Unit 1 (8000 MW) – COD in March 2021 (Share of BSPHCL - 80 MW)
2020-21	Unit 2 (8000 MW) – COD in May, 2021 (Share of BSPHCL - 80 MW)
Barh TPP Stage-I (3 × 660 MW) 1980 MW	
2021-22	Unit 1 (660 MW) – COD in March 2021 (Share of BSPHCL - 342 MW) Unit 2 (660 MW) – COD in September 2021 (Share of BSPHCL - 342 MW)

2022-23	Unit 3 (660 MW) – COD in April 2022 (Share of BSPHCL - 342 MW)
BUXAR TPP (2 × 660 MW) (1320 MW)	
Beyond 2023	Unit 1 & 2 ((1320 MW) – COD in FY 2023-24
BANKA UMPP (4000 MW)	
Beyond 2023	4000 MW
Source: Department of Energy, GoB	

BIHAR RENEWABLE ENERGY DEVELOPMENT AGENCY (BREDA)

Most of the electricity in Bihar is produced in the form of thermal power. This accounts for only 2.3 percent of the total production. Therefore, to reduce the ratio of thermal power generation and increase renewable energy generation, the Government of Bihar has constituted BREDA which is responsible for developing and using non-conventional sources for power generation in the state.

BIHAR STATE HYDROELECTRIC POWER CORPORATION LIMITED

Bihar State Hydroelectric Power Corporation Limited is a state government company which was established on 31 March 1982. Apart from thermal power, hydropower is also generated from water resources in Bihar and it is currently being exploited through several hydroelectric projects. Bihar State Hydroelectric Corporation Ltd. was established to oversee the expansion of hydroelectric projects in the state. During the Tenth Plan, the Corporation, in addition to its earlier mandate for small hydel projects, also began to explore the possibilities of large hydel projects. Presently 13 small hydroelectric projects are operational in the state with a total installed capacity of 54.3 MW.

1. **Koshi Hydroelectric Station (KHPS):** Four units of 4.8 each at Koshi Hydroelectric Station (Kataiya), Birpur were constructed between 1970 and 1978. The project was transferred to Bihar State Hydroelectric Corporation (BSHPC) in November 2003. Renovation work of 3 out of 4 units has been completed and work of power generation has started.
2. **Eastern Gandak Canal Hydroelectric Project:** The Eastern Gandak Canal Hydroelectric Project at Valmikinagar in West Champaran was started in 1996-97. It has 3 units of 5 MW each.
3. **Sone Western Link Canal Hydroelectric Project:** The Sone Western Link Canal Hydroelectric Project, located at Dehri-on-Sone in Rohtas, consists of 4 units of 1.65 MW each, which was commissioned in 1991-92.
4. **Sone Eastern Link Canal Hydroelectric Project:** This hydroelectric project at Barun in Aurangabad has 2 units of 1.65 MW each which was started in 1996-97.
5. **Agnoor Hydroelectric Project:** The Agnoor Hydroelectric Project in Arwal consists of 3 units of 0.5 MW which was commissioned in 2004-05.
6. **Dhelabagh Hydroelectric Project:** There are 2 units of 0.5 MW in Dhelabagh Hydroelectric Project located in Rohtas; it was commissioned in 2006-07.
7. **Triveni Link Canal Hydroelectric Project:** This hydroelectric project in West Champaran has 2 units of 1.5 MW each which was started in 2007-08.
8. **Nasriganj Hydroelectric Project:** The Nasriganj Hydroelectric Project in Rohtas has 2

units of 0.5 MW each which was commissioned in 2007-08.

9. **Sebari Hydroelectric Project:** There are 2 units of 0.5-0.5 MW in Sebari Hydroelectric Project in Rohtas which was started in 2007-08.
10. **Jainagara Hydroelectric Project:** The Jainagara Hydroelectric Project in Rohtas has 2 units of 0.5 MW each which was commissioned in 2008-09.
11. **Shrikhinda Hydroelectric Project:** Shrikhinda Hydroelectric Project in Rohtas consists of 2 units of 0.35 MW which was commissioned in 2009-10.
12. **Belsar Hydroelectric Project:** There are 2 units of 0.5 MW in Belsar Hydroelectric Project in Arwal which was started in 2011-12.
13. **Arwal Hydroelectric Project:** There is 1 unit of 0.5 MW in Belsar Hydroelectric Project in Arwal which was started in 2011-12.

Population and Domicile

- Population
- Population Policy
- Population Density and Distribution
- Rural and Urban Domicile

POPULATION

According to Zimmermann, the father of resource geography, human resources are the best resources. The development of a country or state depends on the development of human resources. The state of Bihar is the richest state in terms of human resources.

The area of Bihar is 94,163 square kilometers, which is 2.86 percent of the total area of India. According to the 2011 census, the total population of Bihar is 10,40,99,452, which makes 8.58 percent of the total population of India, that is, there is more population pressure on the area. Bihar is the third most populous state in India after Uttar Pradesh and Maharashtra, while Bihar ranks first in terms of population density. The population density of Bihar is 1106 persons per sq. km. There are currently 38 districts in Bihar. The population of the most populous district of Patna is 5838465. The least populous district is Sheikhpura, which has a population of 6,36,342. The district with highest density in the state is Sheohar where it is 1,880 persons per sq. km. while the lowest population density is of Kaimur which is 848. The district with highest sex ratio in the state is Gopalganj, where the sex ratio is 1021, while the district with lowest sex ratio is Munger, where it is 876. From the literacy point of view, Rohtas is the most literate district with the literacy rate of 73.37, while the least literate district Purnia has the literacy rate of 51.08 percent.

Population growth

The census in India started in 1872 during the era of Lord Mayo. But 10-year and systematic census began in 1881 during Lord Ripon's time. The Census Act was enacted in 1848 to carry out the census work after independence. According to this Act, the authority related to census in India is with the Registrar General. According to the 2011 Census, Bihar's decadal growth rate has been 25.07 percent. The table below shows the comparative situation of Bihar and other states as per the 2011 census.

Population as per Census 2011

Sr. No.	State	Population	Rank
1	Uttar Pradesh	199812341	1
2	Maharashtra	112374333	2

3	Bihar	104099452	3
4	West Bengal	91276115	4
5	Andhra Pradesh	84580777	5
6	Madhya Pradesh	72626809	6
7	Tamil Nadu	72147030	7
8	Rajasthan	68548437	8
9	Karnataka	61095297	9
10	Gujarat	60439692	10
11	Odisha	41974218	11
12	Kerala	33406061	12
13	Jharkhand	32988134	13
14	Assam	31205576	14
15	Punjab	27743338	15
16	Chhattisgarh	25545198	16
17	Haryana	23351462	17
18	Jammu-Kashmir	12541302	18
19	Uttarakhand	10086292	19
20	Himachal Pradesh	6864602	20
21	Tripura	3673917	21
22	Meghalaya	2966889	22
23	Manipur	2570390	23
24	Nagaland	1978502	24
25	Goa	1458545	25
26	Arunachal Pradesh	1383727	26
27	Mizoram	1097206	27
28	Sikkim	610577	28
Source: Census 2011			

The trend of population growth in Bihar has been changing. Between 1901 and 1921, population growth took place at a very slow pace. The population growth was negative (–0.97 percent) in the decade of 1911 to 1921 as a result of the effects of epidemics and famines. The growth rate between 1921 and 1951 was 10.58 percent. The population growth rate has increased rapidly since 1951 and the growth rate was the fastest (28.62 percent) between 1991 and 2001. The main reason for this increase is due to the improvement in health services resulting in control of death rate, while the birth rate could not be controlled due to economic backwardness and lack of improvement in education.

Between 2001 and 2011, there was a trend of decrease in population growth rate, and the decadal growth rate was 25.07 percent. The comparative growth rate of decadal population growth of Bihar and India from 1901 to 2011 is shown in the table below –

Comparison of the Trend of Population Growth in Bihar and India (Decadal growth rate in percent)

Year	Growth rate of Bihar	Growth rate of India
1901-1911	1.52	5.75
1911-1921	–0.97	–0.31
1921-1931	9.74	11.00
1931-1941	12.22	14.22
1941-1951	10.58	13.31
1951-1961	19.79	21.64
1961-1971	20.91	24.80
1971-1981	24.16	24.66
1981-1991	23.38	23.87
1991-2001	28.62	21.54
2001-2011	25.07	17.7
Source: Census 2011		

The trend of population growth rate in Bihar has been different in different decades. Regional variation in growth rate is also found within the state for various reasons. The growth rate in some districts has been rapid, while in some districts it has been low. Between 1901 and 2011, the growth rate in the districts of Araria, Kishanganj, Purnia, Katihar, etc. in Northeast Bihar was 7.46, while it was negative in other districts like Nalanda, Patna, etc. In the decade of 1911 to 1921, when negative growth was recorded in the entire country, in many districts of Bihar like Araria, Kishanganj, Purnia and Katihar, there was a growth rate of 6.78 percent, while the increase in Bhagalpur and Banka districts was 6.70 percent. In districts like Munger, Khagaria, and Lakhisarai, the growth rate was 4.91 percent. After independence, the average growth rate in Bihar in the decade of 1951 to 1961 was 19.79 percent, with the highest growth rate being 50.53 percent in Supaul and 45.01 percent in Araria. The reasons for the rapid growth in these areas were improvement in health services, control of floods in Koshi areas and the resettlement of Bangladeshi refugees. The population grew at a rapid rate of 28.62 percent in the state from 1991 to 2001. The highest growth rate in this decade was 36.61 percent in Shivhar and 35.40 percent in Purnia, while the lowest growth rate was 18.94 percent in Sheikhpura and 18.75 percent in Nalanda.

The average decadal population growth rate in Bihar in the decade 2001 to 2011 is 25.07 percent. The district with the highest growth rate is Madhepura, where the growth rate is 30.65 percent, while the district with the lowest growth rate is Gopalganj, which has a growth rate of 18.83 percent. The table below shows the districts with the highest and lowest decadal growth in the state from 2001 to 2011.

Districts with decadal growth rate of 2001-2011 (Decadal growth rate in percentage)

Districts	Highest growth rate	Districts	Lowest growth rate
Madhepura	30-65	Gopalganj	18-83
Kishanganj	30-44	Darbhanga	19-00
Araria	30-00	Arwal	19-01
Khagaria	29-46	Munger	19-45
East Champaran	28-89	Rohtas	20-22
Source: Census 2011			

POPULATION DENSITY AND DISTRIBUTION

Like India, imbalance in population distribution is also found in Bihar. The major factors behind disproportionate distribution are topographical diversity, climate, availability of water, soil type and economic activities like development of agriculture, industry, transport, etc. The pressure of population is high in some districts in Bihar, while in some districts the population is found to be sparse. Patna district has 3.40 percent of the total geographical area of the state while the population is 5.56 percent of the total population of the state. According to the 2011 Census, more population than the area is found in the districts of Patna, East Champaran, Muzaffarpur, Darbhanga, etc. while the ratio of area and population is almost equal in the districts of Bhojpur, Gopalganj, Madhepura, Saharsa, etc. In some districts of South Bihar like Gaya, Rohtas, Kaimur, the pressure of population is less than the land. The main reason for the low population is the presence of hilly, plateau region on most of the terrain of these districts, which makes unfavourable for human habitation.

On the basis of population density, Bihar can be divided into 3 parts –

Districts with highest population density

This includes 20 districts of Sheohar, Patna, Darbhanga, Vaishali, Begusarai, Muzaffarpur, Siwan, Sitamarhi, Saran, Samastipur, East Champaran, Madhubani, Gopalganj, Nalanda, Jehanabad, Bhagalpur, Bhojpur, Saharsa, Madhepura and Khagaria, whose density is higher than the average population density of 1106 in Bihar. The district with the highest population density is Sheohar, whose population density is 1182 per person per square kilometer. The primary reason for the high density of these districts is the availability of fertile alluvial plains and adequate water facilities, which are favourable for agriculture.

Districts with moderate population density

This includes 20 districts of Arwal, Purnia, Katihar, Buxar, Araria, Munger, Sheikhpura, Supaul, Kishanganj, Nawada, Gaya, Lakhisarai, etc. The density of these districts is between 800 and 1100.

Districts with low population density

It includes 6 districts with a density of less than 800, which are Rohtas, Aurangabad, West Champaran, Banka, Jamui, and Kaimur. Kaimur district has the lowest population density of 488 persons per square kilometer.

The table below shows the districts of high and low population density in the state as per the 2011 Census.

Districts with High and Low Population Density

Districts	Maximum density	Districts	Minimum Density
Sheohar	1882	Kaimur	488
Patna	1803	Jamui	567
Darbhanga	1721	Banka	672
Vaishali	1717	West Chamaparan	750
Begusarai	1540	Aurangabad	760
Source: Census 2011			

Sex ratio

The ratio of the number of females per thousand males in a country or state is called the sex ratio. During the census from 1901 to 2011, the sex ratio has been changing. The sex ratio in Bihar was 1061 in the year, 1901, 1051 in 1911, and 1020 in 1921. Till 1921, the number of females was more than that of males, but in 1931 it was reduced to 995. After 1971, the situation started deteriorating, and in 2011 the sex ratio in Bihar becomes 916, which is less than the national average of 940. The main reason for low sex ratio is foeticide, socio-religious superstition, illiteracy, etc. However, at present, ban on foeticide, ban on child marriage, anti-dowry and other laws have been enacted. The district with highest sex ratio in Bihar is Gopalganj (1015), while the one with the lowest sex ratio is Munger (879).

Disparity is found in the sex ratio both in rural and urban areas. In Bihar, in rural areas, the sex ratio is 927 and in urban areas, it is 869. In India, the sex ratio in the rural area is 946 while the sex ratio in the urban area is 900.

Districts with high and low sex ratio

Districts	High sex ratio	Districts	Low sex ratio
Gopalganj	1015	Munger	876
Siwan	984	Bhagalpur	879
Saran	949	Khagaria	883
Kishanganj	946	Sheohar	890
Source: Census 2011			

Literacy

According to the Census Department of the Government of India, a person above the age of 7 years, who knows how to read, write, and understand any one language is called literate. Till 1971 Census, this standard was fixed at 4 years instead of seven years. According to the 2011 Census, Bihar's literacy rate is 63.82 percent while the national average is 74.04 percent. Bihar has a male literacy rate of 73.39 percent and female literacy rate of 53.33 percent. The district with the highest literacy rate in Bihar is Rohtas (75.59 percent), while the lowest literacy rate is in Purnia (52.49 percent). The rural literacy rate in the state is 61.83 percent, and the urban literacy rate is 78.75 percent. The table below shows the districts with higher literacy and lower literacy.

Districts with high and low literacy

Districts	High literacy	Districts	Low literacy
Rohtas	75-59	Purnia	52-49
Munger	73-30	Sitamarhi	53-53
Bhojpur	72-79	Katihar	53-56
Aurangabad	72-77	Madhepura	5378
Patna	72-47	Saharasa	54-57
Source: Census 2011			

Rural and urban population

Agriculture is the main source of livelihood of the people of Bihar. Hence, majority of the population lives in villages. According to the 2011 Census, 11.30 percent of Bihar's population lives in cities, while 88.70 percent lives in villages. The district with the highest rural population is Samastipur (96.54 percent), while the district with the lowest rural population is Patna (56.52 percent). More than 95 percent of the population lives in villages in the districts of Banka, Sitamarhi, Kaimur, Shivhar, Supaul, Madhepura, etc. Patna, Munger, Bhagalpur, Begusarai, Sheikhpura, Nalanda, Rohtas, Bhojpur, Lakhisarai, and Gaya have a rural population below 88.70, which is below the state average.

In Bihar, the growth rate of urbanization has been low due to its agrarian economy. After the bifurcation of the state in 2000, the level of urbanization has reduced further. The highest urban population in the state is found in Patna (43.48 percent) and the lowest is found in Munger (28.30 percent).

The following table shows the districts with more urban and rural population:

Districts with More Urban and Rural Population

Districts	Rural	Districts	Urban
Samastipur	96-54	Patna	43-48
Banka	96-48	Munger	28-30
Kaimur	95-98	Bhagalpur	19-97
Sheohar	95-72	Begusarai	19-19
Supaul	95-26	Sheikhpura	17-14
Source: Census 2011			

According to the definition of census department, there were 271 cities in the state as per 2001 census. Census cities have been divided into 6 classes on the basis of population by the Census Department. Census cities are displayed in the table:

Type of city	Population	Number	Percentage of total urban population
First class	More than 1 lakh	20	52-62
Second class	50000-99999	17	17-58
Third class	20000-49999	79	24-49
Fourth class	10000-19999	53	7-03
Fifth class	5000-9999	29	1-79
Sixth class	Less than 500	05	0-18
Total	–	**211**	**100**

Age structure

In Bihar, the percentage of the number of children in the age group of 0 to 14 years is 13.24. According to the 2011 Census, the number of children under 6 years of age is 17.90 percent, which is higher than the national average of 13.12 percent. In the age group of 0 to 6 years, the share of boys is 17.74 percent and that of girls is 18.07 percent. The sex ratio in the age group of 0 to 6 years was 942 in 2001, which has come down to 935 in 2011. The highest sex ratio in this category is 971 in Kishanganj, while the lowest sex ratio is 904 in Vaishali. The district with the highest population in the age group of 0 to 6 is Khagaria (21.33 percent) followed by Kishanganj and Araria. The highest number of boys in this age group is 20.63 percent in Khagaria and 15.63 percent in Patna. The highest number of girls is 23.4 percent in Supaul District, while their lowest number is 15.75 percent in Patna.

The percentage of rural population in the age group of 0 to 6 years is 18.55 while the percentage of urban population is 14.35. In this age group, the district with the highest rural population is Khagaria, while the district with the highest urban population is Sheohar.

Population of Scheduled Castes and Tribes

The number of scheduled castes in Bihar is 14.56 percent. The district with the highest scheduled caste population is Gaya (29.6 percent), while the district with the lowest population is Kishanganj (6.6 percent). The sex ratio in the scheduled tribes is 923 and the literacy rate is 28.5 percent. Among the scheduled castes, Siwan is the district with the highest sex ratio while the district with the lowest sex ratio is Bhagalpur. In terms of literacy, Munger has the highest literacy rate of 42.6 percent, while Sheohar has the lowest rate of 16.9 percent.

According to the 2011 census, the scheduled tribe population in Bihar is 0.9 percent. The district with the highest scheduled tribe is Katihar (5.9 percent). 4.8 percent in Jamui, 4.7 percent in Banka, 4.4 percent in Purnia are scheduled tribes. The scheduled tribes are not found in Sheohar, Darbhanga, Khagaria, Sheikhpura, and Nalanda districts. The sex ratio of scheduled tribes is 929 in the state and the literacy rate is 28.2 percent. The district with the highest sex ratio is Gopalganj (1063) and one with the lowest sex ratio is Patna (726). The highest literacy rate is 78.6 percent in Begusarai while the lowest literacy rate is 12.9 percent in Lakhisarai.

Religious structure

Many religious groups are found in Bihar. Among them are Hindus, Muslims, Christians, Sikhs, Jains and Buddhists. Hindus are 83.2 percent, Muslims are 16.5 percent and Christians are 0.1 percent of Bihar's total population.

Problems and solutions related to population

According to the 2011 census, the total population of Bihar is 10,40,99,452 which is 8.58 percent of the total population of the country. The population density is 1106 which is the highest in the country. The annual growth rate is 2.57 percent and the decadal growth rate is 25.07 percent. The reasons for the rapid growth in the population are the control over mortality rate due to the availability of health facilities and the increase in food production, while on the other hand, the birth rate has not been controlled. The growth rate is rapid due to the gap in the birth rate and the death rate.

It is because of rapid growth rate and increasing population, various that problems have arisen, such as food problem, problem of malnutrition, problem of poverty and unemployment, problem of environmental degradation, low standard of living, low income per person, low productivity, etc.

POPULATION POLICY

Population growth is a serious problem for Bihar as much as it is for India. Many commissions, programs and policies have been implemented to control the population. In 1948, the family planning program was implemented. In 1978, the National Population Commission was formed. In 1984, the Swaminathan Committee was formed. Through the above policies and programs, attempts were made to control the population. The National Population Policy was announced in 1999. The following objectives have been set in this policy:

- Providing population stability by 2045;
- Improving the quality of health and family welfare programs;
- Ensuring greater participation of women in programs related to population control.

In the light of the National Population Policy, several actions are being taken to control the population in Bihar, such as bringing the Total Fertility Rate (TFR) to 2.1 level to stabilize the population by 2045. Special emphasis has been laid on family planning program measures such as sterilization, supply and promotion of contraceptive devices, financial assistance, making rural healthcare more effective, etc.

Demographic Details and Administrative Set-up of India and Bihar (2001 and 2011)

Indicator	Bihar		Indi	
	2001	2011	2001	2011
Population (in crores)				
Total	8.29	10.41	102.87	121.06
Rural	7.43	7.23	74.25	83.37
Urban	0.87	1.18	28.61	37.71
Sex ratio (females per thousand males)	919	918	933	943
Density (persons pr sq. km)	880	1106	325	382
Decadal growth rate (percentage)	28.6	25.1	21.5	17.6
Administrative set-up				
Number of districts	37	38	593	640
Number of development blocks	533	534	5463	5924
Statutory/census (number of citires)	130	199	5161	7935
Number of villages	45098	39073	638596	597369
Source: Census of India, 2001 and 2011				

RURAL AND URBAN DOMICILE

The history of human settlements starts from the pre-Neolithic era when the introduction of agricultural work brought stability to human life. An evidence of Neolithic settlements in Bihar has been found in Chirand in Saran District. Most of the land of Bihar is situated in the fertile plain of the Ganges valley, due to which the development of agro-based economy has taken place. The predominance of rural population is found as it is an agriculture dominated area. The total population of Bihar is 10,40,99,452. According to the 2011 Census, 89.53 percent of this population lives in villages. Rural settlements are spread over an area of 92,358.40 square kilometers in a total area of 94,163 square kilometers in Bihar.

The development of human settlement depends on the economic activity and on the basis of human activity. Two types of settlements have developed on these grounds:

1. Rural Settlements
2. Urban Settlements

According to the Census Department of India, rural and urban settlements are divided on the following basis:

(i) Population: A settlement with a population less than 5000 is called a rural settlement, and a settlement with a population of more than 5000 is called an urban settlement.

(ii) Working Population: A settlement with 75 percent of the working population engaged in agricultural work is called rural settlement, while it is called an urban settlement if more than 75 percent of the working population is engaged in non-agricultural work.

Population above 14 years and up to 60 years is called working population. Population under 14 years and above 60 years of age is called dependent population.

(iii) Density: A human habitation with more than 400 persons per square kilometer is called urban settlement, while a human habitation with less than 400 persons per square kilometer is called a rural settlement.

Rural settlements

Bihar is a state dominated by agricultural work, due to which there is an abundance of rural slums and rural population. In rural settlements, dense and sparse settlements are the two types of settlements that have developed.

Factors affecting the development of dense rural settlements

Natural factors

The distribution of topography has had the greatest impact on the development of dense settlements in Bihar. These types of settlements are found in the alluvial plains. In flood-affected areas, dense settlements have developed on high embankments due to protection from flood.

Economic factors

Economic factors include the main ones like production capacity of the land, transport facilities, farming system, zamindari system, etc. Intensive settlements have developed in areas where rice production is high.

Social and political factors

Among social factors, caste system, caste sentiment, religious beliefs and social traditions influence the development of the settlement.

Major factors affecting sparse settlements

Natural factors

Natural factors include the heterogeneous topographic distribution, which leads to the lack of suitable land for settlement and lack of arable land.

Economic factors

Among economic factors, consolidation, demarcation, modernization of agriculture, etc., have led to the development of scattered settlements.

Social and political factors

In a state like Bihar, scattered settlements have developed due to the predominance of conservative social and religious beliefs. With presence of strong tendency of caste system, fragmented settlements have developed in the form of caste groups.

Rural Settlement Distribution Format

In Bihar, there is a difference in the characteristics of rural settlements based on topographical variation and social and economic conditions. Depending on the development of colony, type, internal structure, etc., many types of rural settlements have developed.

Types of Rural Settlements

1. Compact Settlement
2. Dispersed Settlement

On the basis of density, the compact settlement is further divided into the following parts:

Compact Settlement

Compact settlements develop at sites where there is only one central settlement in the village around which the settlement develops. The houses are adjacent to each other, the streets are crooked and narrow. These types of settlements have developed in Bihar on the high mounds or edges in the flood plains of North Bihar. Such settlements are mainly found in flooded areas of Kosi, Kamla, Gandak, Ganga, etc.

Semi-Compact Settlements

In semi-compact settlements, one main settlement and several hamlets develop independently. Social life and zamindari system have had a greater impact on the development of such settlements. These types of settlements are found in the northern and southern plains of Bihar.

Elongated or Linear Compact Settlement

The linear compact settlements have developed on roads, and banks of canals and rivers. These types of settlements have developed mainly in the flood plains of northern Bihar along the river banks and canals, whereas they are also found in the plateau areas of southern Bihar along the roads.

Dispersed settlements have developed in different formats in different parts of the state. These are of the following types:

Fragmented or Hamletted Settlement

A fragmented settlement implies that a village consists of many small compact settlements, that is, many settlement centres have developed there. As a result of the influence of caste system in Bihar, tolls have developed with the names of castes. They are mainly found in the districts of Purnia, Katihar, Saharsa, Darbhanga, Samastipur, Muzaffarpur, etc.

Semi-sprinkled Settlement

Semi-sprinkled settlements are found in the form of small tolls and scattered houses. In this type of settlement, the power of decentralization works. Most of the houses are built on footpaths or narrow streets. This type of settlement is found in the heterogeneous topographic regions of southern Bihar.

Dispersed settlement

In scattered settlements, houses are built separately and far apart. Such settlements are found in areas with limited arable land and rugged terrain. This type of settlement has developed in the Diara region of the Ganges River.

Linear Dispersed Settlement

Linear Dispersed Settlements have developed along sidewalks in asymmetrical plateau and on the banks of trails in wooded areas.

Urban Domicile

Evidence of urbanization in Bihar is available from the Later Vedic period and Mahajanapada period when cities like Pataliputra, Anga, Rajgriha, etc. were developed. Ajatashatru's son Udayan founded Pataliputra on the banks of the Ganges. The development of cities like Pataliputra, Gaya, Bhagalpur and Buxar on the banks of various rivers like Ganga, Phalgu, Saryu, Son, Gandak, etc. started during ancient times in Bihar. In the medieval period, especially during the Afghan rule, urbanization was made more effective. Sher Shah founded Patna. Later, Mughal ruler Aurangzeb established a new city called Azimabad in Patna. Planned cities were developed during the British period, for instance, Western Patna was planned from an administrative point of view.

According to the 2011 Census, only 11.30 percent of Bihar's population lives in cities. The main reason for the low level of urbanization is that most of the land is plains due to which majority of the population is dependent on agriculture. Another reason for the low level of urbanization in Bihar is low level of education, high level of poverty-unemployment and lack of mineral resources. As a result of lack of minerals, the rate of industrialization is quite low, whereas industrialization accelerates urbanization. In 1901, Bihar had only 4.70 percent urban population, which has increased to 11.30 percent in 2011. The following table shows the growth of urban population in different decades:

Urbanization Trend in Bihar (1901-2011)

Year	In percentage	Decadal growth rate
1901	4-70	-
1911	4-72	1-74
1921	4-60	8-17
1931	4-80	22-00
1941	5-40	33-66
1951	6-80	38-14
1961	8-40	49-03
1971	10-00	43-44
1981	12-72	53-63
1991	13-17	30-69
2001	10-47	22-49
2011	11-30	35-11

Source: Census Department, Government of India

By 1921, the urban growth rate in Bihar was only 8.17 percent per decade, which was very low. The reasons for its decline were famines and epidemics that occurred between 1911–1921. After 1921, the growth rate was very rapid. It was 22 percent in the decade of 1921–1931. After independence, the growth rate reached 49.03 percent between 1951-1961. The growth rate was fastest between 1971–1981, which was 53.63. In 1981, the ratio of urban population in Bihar was 12.72, and the ratio of urban population to rural-urban population in Bihar was highest in 1991 census, which was 13.17 percent. After 1991, this ratio declined and in 2011 Census, the urban population is 11.30 percent. The growth rate of urban population in the decade 2001 to 2011 was 35.11 percent. Begusarai district saw the highest increase in urban population in the state, which is 426.89 percent. The reason for this rapid growth is the establishment of many industries in this district. After Begusarai, there was an increase in urban population of 58.93 percent in East Champaran, 56.46 percent in Kaimur and 55.68 percent in Nawada in the last decade.

According to the 2011 census, the district with the largest urban population is Patna and the largest city is also Patna. The major cities of the state and their population are shown in the table below –

Major/Large Cities as per 2011 Census

Rank	City	Population
1	Patna	2046652
2	Gaya	470839
3	Bhagalpur	410210
4	Muzaffarpur	393724
5	Purnia	310817
6	Darbhanga	306089
7	Bihar Sharif	296889
8	Arrah	261099
9	Begusarai	251136
10	Katihar	240565

Source: Census 2011

❑❑❑

Tourism and Tourist Destinations

- Tourism
- Tourist Destinations
- Tourism Policy

TOURISM

The word 'tourism' is devived from Latin word Tornos. The term was first used in 1643 to refer to travel. Tourism is a journey, the aim of which is to experience pleasure with entertainment, health benefits, education, religion, etc.

Bihar is a suitable state from the point of view of tourism industry. The land of Bihar has been attracting scholars, tourists, and foreign travelers since ancient times. From the point of view of tourism, the glorious traditions, rich culture and fair and festivals of Bihar are important. The state government earns income from the tourism industry and people also get employment. Despite the potential of this industry in Bihar, proper development has not taken place. International, national and local level tourist places are in abundance in the state.

The international-level tourist destinations include places like Vaishali, Bodh Gaya, Patna, Rajgir, Nalanda, and Vikramshila. The national-level tourist destinations in the state include places like Rohtas, Munger, Sitamarhi, Pavapuri, Buxar, Sasaram, Madhubani, Hajipur, and Sultanganj, while local-level tourist destinations include picnic spots, natural lakes, waterfalls, shrines, etc. Janaki Circuit, Gandhi Circuit, and Sufi Circuit have been constructed for the development of cultural heritage. Extensive arrangements have been made to provide security to all tourist destinations and tourists. It is because of these arrangements, an increase in the number of tourists has also been observed in the state. Bihar which is the land of confluence of all the religions along with Buddhism and Jainism, is immensely revered by people of all religions.

TOURISM POLICY

The Bihar Government has formulated the Bihar Tourism Policy to promote the tourism sector. Under this policy, special emphasis has been laid on guides, travel planning, hotel management, food management, etc. A tourism security force is being formed to make tourism safe and friendly. The symbol of Bihar tourism is 'Peepal tree' and the tagline is 'Blissful-Bihar'. With an aim to develop the sites of archaeological and historical importance as tourist centres, the state government has entered into an agreement with the Archaeological Survey of India in which the Kesariya, Maner and mausoleum of Sher Shah will be developed in the first phase. In order to promote tourism, a tourism map has been prepared, which has been titled 'A Journey through Bihar'. A website called www.bihartourism.gov.in has been launched for the purpose of giving information about various places and facilities of Bihar tourism.

Eight Tourism Circuits have been identified by the Department of Tourism of Bihar. These eight circuits are:

1. **Buddhist Circuit:** Bodhgaya (Gaya), Rajgir (Nalanda), Nalanda, Vaishali, Lauria Nandangarh (East Champaran), Lauria Areraj (East Champaran), Kesariya (East Champaran), Vikramshila (Bhagalpur) and Jehanabad.
2. **Sufi Circuit:** Manersharif (Patna), Khanqah Mujivia (Patna), Mittan Ghat (Patna), Hajipur Karbala (Vaishali), Hasanpur (Nalanda), Bibi Kamal Sahib (Jehanabad), Badi Dargah (Nalanda) and Chhoti Dargah (Nalanda).
3. **Jain Circuit:** Vaishali, Rajgir (Nalanda), Pavapuri (Nalanda), Nathnagar (Bhagalpur), Mandar Hill (Banka), Champanagar (Bhagalpur), Kundalgram (Nalanda), Samosaran (Nalanda), and Lachhaur (Jamui).
4. **Ramayana Circuit:** Valmiki Nagar (West Champaran), Pretashila (Gaya), Ahilya Sthan (Darbhanga), Kako (Jehanabad), Sitakund (Sitamarhi), Sinheshwar (Madhepura), Ramshila (Gaya), Buxar and Giddheshwar (Jamui).
5. **Shiv Shakti Circuit:** Shiv Shakti Circuit includes Mundeshwari Sthan (Kaimur), Chandi Sthan (Munger), Ugratara Sthan (Mahishi, Saharsa), Aami (Saran), Thawe (Gopalganj), Tarachandi Sthan (Rohtas), Bakhorapur (Bhojpur) and Shyamakali (Darbhanga). The Shiva circuit includes Guptadham (Kaimur), Baijudham (Gaya), Koteshwar Dham (Gaya), Sinheshwar Dham (Madhepura), Kusheshwar Sthan (Darbhanga), Sinheshwar Sthan (Jehanabad), Ajgaibinath (Sultanganj, Bhagalpur), Ashok Dham (Lakhisarai), Garibnath (Muzaffarpur), Mahendranath (Saran) and Brahmeshwarnath (Buxar) are included.
6. **Sikh Circuit:** Patna Sahib (Patna City, Patna), Balaleela Sahab (Patna), Guru Tegh Bahadur Gurdwara (Gaya Ghat, Patna), Guru Nanak Kund (Rajgir Nalanda), Arrah, Katihar, Gaya and Sasaram, Bhagalpur, Guru's Baug (Patna City, Patna), Gurdwara Pakki Sangat (Munger) and Gurdwara Hindi Saheb (Danapur, Patna).
7. **Gandhi Circuit:** Motihari (East Champaran), Bettiah (West Champaran), Bhitiharwa Ashram (West Champaran), Vrindavan (West Champaran), Sadakat Ashram (Patna) and Gandhi Museum (Patna).
8. **Natural and Wildlife Circuit:** Major natural beauty spots of the state have been included in it.

A Land of Possibilities in Tourism

The list of extensively protected monuments in Bihar is long. The World Heritage Sites and many sites like the ruins of Nalanda and Vikramashila have the potential to be the World Heritage Sites. The historical buildings can be developed as special heritage zones. In order to promote the cultural heritage of Bihar, museums are being upgraded and developed in coordination with the Archaeological Survey of India and other state governments; the newly inaugurated Bihar Museum in Patna is a prominent example of this. For the purpose of development of handloom and handicrafts of Bihar, Shilpagram (Craft Village) and handicraft market are being encouraged near the tourist places.

The aim is to promote the social and economic benefits of tourism in rural areas as well as develop and promote rural tourism around the arts and crafts of Bihar. For example, working villages like Tehta (Jehanabad), Nepura (Nalanda), Ranti and Jitavpur (Madhubani), Patharkatti (Gaya), Nathanagar (Bhagalpur), etc. can be targeted for the development of rural tourism. The sulphuric hot springs of Rajgir and Munger can be developed for aquatherapy-based wellness tourism. It can develop into the most unique tourism form of Bihar.

Ecological and Wildlife Tourism

Eco-tourism can be encouraged by integrating wildlife sanctuaries to develop potential tourist destinations. Marked tourist places like Rajgir (Nalanda) Bhimbandh Sanctuary (Munger), Kaimur Sanctuary (Kaimur), Gautam Budha Sanctuary (Gaya), Naktidham (Jamui), Gogalbil Sanctuary (Bhagalpur), Kanwar Lake (Begusarai), Ghorakatora Lake (Nalanda), Ka Kakolat Falls

(Nawada), Telhar Falls (Rohtas), Gangetic Dolphin Sanctuary (Bhagalpur) and Valmiki National Park (Western Champaran) can be developed as eco-tourism circuits. The entire Ganges River can be developed as a tourist area to develop historical sites along the water route along the banks of Buxar, Patna, Munger, Bhagalpur, etc. The dolphins swimming in the Ganges river attract tourists. Various types of aquatic sports, such as river rafting, parasailing, etc. can also be provided as an attractive form of tourism.

TOURIST DESTINATIONS

Nalanda: One of the ancient knowledge centres of the world, Nalanda is located at a distance of about 90 km from the state capital of Patna. The Nalanda University has been a distinguished centre of Buddhist education. This university was founded by Emperor Kumaragupta of the Gupta dynasty. Its downfall was caused due to the conflict between the Pala dynasty and the Sena dynasty. Currently, it is being renovated with the cooperation from China. Lakhs of travelers from abroad visit Bihar to see this historic tourist place which is connected by road, rail, and airways.

Rajgir (Rajgriha) is a historical site located in Nalanda. It is situated between five hills. It was established by Bimbisara and Ajatshatru as the capital of the Harayak dynasty of the Magadha Empire. The evidence of the oldest architecture of India is found in Rajgriha. After the death of Mahatma Buddha, the first Buddhist Sangeeti was organized in the Saptaparni cave of Rajgriha. The highest World Peace Stupa in the world has been constructed by the Government of Japan on the Ratnagiri hill of Rajgriha. The ropeway has been constructed to reach the Shanti Stupa. Livelihood excursions, Son Bhandar, Amravan, Venuvan, Makhdoom Saheb's Hujra and many hot water pools are located in Rajgriha. The Rajgir Mahotsav is organized by the State Tourism Department.

Pavapuri located in Nalanda is the nirvana site of Lord Mahavira. A lotus shaped pond has been constructed at his cremation site. There is a Jain monument in its centre which is famous as the Jal Mandir. The ancient name of Pavapuri was Apapuri.

Badi Dargah, Nalanda: There is a large dargah of Hazrat Malik and Sheikh Makhdoom Shah Sharfuddin on the Pir Hill located in Nalanda. Along with this, the small dargah of Hazrat Badruddin and Jama Masjid are also the centres of faith for the devotees of the country and abroad.

Makhdoom Kund, Rajgir: Makhdoom Kund in Rajgir is a very sacred religious place for Muslims. It has the residence of Saint Makhdoom Shah Sheikh Sharfuddin. There is a pool of hot water which is made of natural waterfalls. Muslims visit this place from all over the country and abroad to bathe in the Makhdoom Kund and worship God.

Bihar Sharif: Bihar Sharif is currently the headquarters of Nalanda. Makhdoom Saheb's Dargah is located here, where Ursa (fair) is held every year. Malik Ibrahim Bayan's tomb is also located in Bihar Sharif.

Vishwa Shanti Stupa: In 1969, with the cooperation between India and Japan, a grand and huge World Shanti Stupa was built on the Ratnagiri mountain peak in Rajgir to spread the teachings of Buddha. Buddhist devotees from India and abroad visit here in large numbers on the anniversary of this stupa and receive the teachings of Lord Buddha.

Additionally, Venuvan Vihar located in Rajgir gifted to Buddha by Bimbisara, Saptaparni Caves, Jeevak-Amravan, and Stupa built after Buddha's Nirvana at Vaishali to preserve his relics are also major religious sites in Bihar. It is a reflection of the rich and advanced state of the Buddhist tradition.

Kundagram: This birth place of Bhagwan Mahavira is known as the holy place of Jain religion. This holy place is located in Vaishali District which is about 54 kilometers north of Patna.

Pavapuri: Bhagwan Mahavir attained nirvana at this place. Lord Mahavira, who gave the message of equality, peace and non-violence to the world, gave up his bodily existence in 468 BC. This place is located in Nalanda District which is about 92 km from Patna.

Rajgir: Located at a distance of 102 km from Patna, Rajgir has many sacred temples of Jainism, among which are the Maniar Math, the Son Bhandar and the holy temple of the Jains located on the top of the mountains.

Gaya: Gaya holds a very important place among religious tourist spots. A grand and huge fair is organized in Pitrupaksha, in which Hindu pilgrims from all over the world participate to offer prayers for their ancestors. This famous religious tourism centre situated on the banks of the River Phalgu, houses the revered Vishnupad Temple of Hindus. This temple was renovated by Maharani Ahalyabai Holkar of Indore. There are many more tourist places around Gaya. Thousands of travelers visit to see the beautiful view of the city by climbing the Bramhayoni Hill and Ramshila Hill. Mangalagouri Temple is also the main Shaktipeeth Temmple of Hindus. Gaya is connected by rail, road, and airways.

Bodhgaya Mahabodhi Temple: This famous temple is located 14 km from the city of Gaya. This place had a stupa built by Emperor Ashoka in the third century, which was later built by the Kushan ruler Huvishka as a grand and huge temple. In this temple, a very big idol of Buddha in the posture of Padmasana is installed.

Bodhivriksha: There is a huge peepal tree near the Mahabodhi temple. It is located behind the temple. It is said that Buddha attained enlightenment under this tree. The present Bodhi tree is the fifth generation of that Bodhi tree.

Vajrasana: This is a place in the shape of a platform where Lord Buddha was seated for meditation. Buddhist followers have a deep reverence for this platform.

Lord Buddha attained supreme knowledge at Bodh Gaya in Gaya. Nestled on the banks of the River Phalgu (Niranjana), 12 kilometres south of Gaya, this town is considered to be a revered pilgrimage centre by Buddhists around the world. This Bodhi tree in the courtyard of the grand and huge temple of Mahabodhi has developed into its fourth generation, under which Lord Buddha had attained enlightenment. This Mahabodhi tree, which was demolished by Shaivite ruler Shashank and Ashoka the Great's queen Tishyarakshita, is flourishing today. Nearby is the scenic Tibetan monastery where the Buddhist cycle continues uninterruptedly. There are grand temples built by Sri Lanka, Japan, Thailand, China and Burma, which display mixed architecture. Most foreign tourists visit here.

The Vishnupad Temple located in Gaya District is the centre of the Vaishnavaites' supreme faith. According to mythological belief, the footprints of Lord Vishnu are here. This temple is 30 metres tall and has 8 pillars. Silver sheets have been mounted on these pillars. In the sanctum sanctorum of the temple, there are traces of 40 cm long feet of Lord Vishnu.

Chovar's Shiv Mandir: This temple, which is located about 25 km east of Gaya, is a famous temple of Lord Shiva at a place called Chovar in Tanakuppa block. Excavations in this village have led to the discovery of the ancient Ashtadhatu sculptures and silver coins.

Brahmayoni Hill: On the Brahmayoni Hill located in Gaya District, there is a temple of Lord Shiva under a huge banyan tree; one has to climb 440 stairs to reach it. According to legends, earlier the River Phalgu used to flow over it, but due to the curse of Goddess Sita, now it flows at the bottom of the hill. A temple of Maa Gauri is also situated on this hill.

Sun Temple, Aurangabad: This 500-year-old temple near Aurangabad city is famous for its architectural style. This temple is 100 feet high and unlike other sun temples, it is west-facing. This temple was built by Chandravanshi King Bhairavendra Singh of Umga. On Chhath festival, devotees come from far and wide to offer prayers to God.

Vaishali: The history of Vaishali, which has been the centre of politics since ancient times, has been splendid. It is a very famous religious place due to being the birthplace of Bhagwan Mahavir.

Vaishali became the city of the first republic of the world twenty-five hundred years ago. The republic was established by the Lichchavi rulers. The great emperor Ashoka had installed a lion-pillar here. The world's highest World Peace Stupa (125 m), which is famous in the world, is a major centre of tourism. Vaishali has a long history of architecture, literature and emperors and is a centre of tourist attraction. The importance of Vaishali for tourism is enhanced by the ancient ponds, the Bawan Pokhar Temple, the Buddhist Stupa, the green bowl temple, the Ashoka ki Lat and many discourse sites of Lord Buddha.

Chaumukhi Mahadev Temple, Vaishali: Located 54 km from Patna, this temple is situated in Vaishali District. An ancient Shivling is found here. There are doors around this temples hence, it is called Chaumukhi Mahadev Temple.

Harihar Kshetra Mandir, Hajipur: Located on the banks of the Gandak river about 36 km north of Patna city, this temple is very ancient. According to the mythological beliefs, Lord Vishnu had cut the head of an elephant with his charka upon hearing the call of the suffering elephant. Thousands of devotees come here. The famous Sonepur fair of Kartik month takes place in this area.

Nepali Temple, Hajipur: Situated at the holy confluence of the Ganges and Gandak rivers, this temple is an excellent example of art. Its wooden columns are very attractive; they have the figures of many deities engraved on them.

Chechar: Shwetpur, Kotigram, Kushpallava, Vishalanagari, etc. are also the names of Chechar. It is a Stone Age site located 14 km away from Hajipur. It was discovered in 1978 by Dr. Yogendra Mishra.

Patna: Patna, which has been famous by the names of Pataliputra and Pushpapur in the ancient times, Azimabad in the medieval period, is the capital of the state of Bihar at the present time. Pataliputra was founded by Udayan, the son of Ajatashatru, ruler of the Haryanka dynasty, in a village called Patali. Greek traveler Megasthenes in his book 'Indica' called Pataliputra as 'Palibothra'. Medieval Afghan ruler Sher Shah Suri changed it from Pataliputra to Patna. The 10th and last Sikh Guru Gobind Singh was born in 1666 in Patna Sahib where the present-day Srihar Mandir Sahib Gurdwara is located. Among other historical and notable sites in Patna, the remains of the ancient Pataliputra are located in Kumhrar. The remains of Mauryan palace have been found in Kumhrar. This palace was built in red sandstone which was brought from the Chunar region of Uttar Pradesh. It consisted of 80 wooden poles. There is Agam Kuaan 3 kilometres west of Kumhrar that was built during the Mauryan period. Before becoming the ruler, Ashoka is said to have killed his 99 brothers and thrown them into this well. There is a temple of Sheetala Devi here. In Dhawalpura, Patna, the remains of the mosque built by Sher Shah, the mosque built by Saif Khan and madrasa have been found. The Pastor's Mansion is located in Patna City. It is a testimony to Roman Catholic art, which was built in 1751 by the Capuchin Fathers.

Khudabaksh Library is located on Ashok Rajpath. It is an example of Rajput and Mughal architecture. In addition to the main building of the library, there is a Curzon Reading Room. This library was established in 1891 by Khudabaksh. A stone mosque is located on Ashok Rajpath, which was built in 1621 by Parvez Shah, son of Jahangir. Here, manuscripts, books related to Arabic, Persian, Urdu, and other languages, medieval paintings and Quran Sharif are kept safely. The martyr's memorial is located in the secretariat complex in Patna, where there is a memorial of 7 revolutionaries who were martyred in the 'Quit India Movement' of 1942. The Patna Museum was established in 1917. It is a beautiful example of Mughal and Rajput architecture. In it, the famous Yakshini idol and many Pala Ashtadhatu idols are stored.

Golghar is located near Patna's historic Gandhi Maidan, which was built by Captain John Garstin as a granary in 1786 during the time of Warren Hastings. This Golghar is 29 meters tall with a circumference of 125 metres. Other prominent places for sightseeing in Patna include '40-feet bronze statue of Mahatma

Gandhi built in Gandhi Maidan, Sanjay Gandhi Udyan, Pir Ali Park, Patandevi Temple, Kachchi Dargah, Kali Mandir, Buddha Smriti Park, Eco Park, Planetarium, Shri Krishna Science Centre, Chhajjubagh Kothi, Kargil Chowk, Kamaldah, etc.

Patna College, situated on the banks of the river Ganges at Ashok Rajpath, was founded in 1853. The building was constructed as a warehouse by the Dutch East India Company. It is the oldest college in Bihar and the fifth oldest college in India.

In Patna District, 30 kilometers away from Patna, the site related to 'Maner Firdausi Sufi Silsila' is located. Here, the dargah of Sufi saint Pir Hazrat Sharfuddin Shah Makhdoom Yahya Maneri is located. His mausoleum is famous as 'Badi Dargah'. Shah Daulat's tomb is also built near his mausoleum which is known as 'Chhoti Dargah'. Shah Daulat was the disciple of Yahya Maneri.

There are two ancient temples of Rambhakta Hanuman in Patna. An ancient temple adjacent to Patna Junction was rebuilt a few years ago. Thousands of Hanuman devotees arrive here every day to offer worship. The second temple is located in the Jala area of Begumpur, which is close to Patna Sahib railway station. This temple was built in the 16th century. It became famous by the name 'Jalla ka Mahaveer Mandir'. Sheetala Mata Temple is located behind an ancient well near Gulzar Bagh station. Thousands of devotees arrive here to worship Shitala Maa during Navratri.

Chaitanya Mahaprabhu Temple is located in the Gaighat area in Patna City. This temple is about 400 years old. Along with worshiping here, devotees get acquainted with rare literary texts, works, manuscripts and paintings of innumerable historical significance. Annapurna Temple is located in the Macchharatta lane adjacent to Ashok Rajpath in Patna City. It is an ancient temple of Goddess Durga, also known as Annapurna Temple.

Kalisthan Temple is dedicated to Mata Kali, which is located in Patna near Mangal Talab in Chowk area. This temple is very ancient and is famous for its place of worship.

Badi Pattandevi Temple, Patna: One of the 51 Shakti Peeths, this famous temple of Maa Durga is located in Maharajganj area in Patna District. Devotees come here throughout the year to pay their respects.

Chhoti Pattadevi Temple, Patna: This temple is dedicated to Mata Bhagwati Durga. It is a very ancient temple in Patna. Devotees worship in large numbers here.

Shiva Temple, Baikathpur: This ancient temple dedicated to Lord Shiva is located on the banks of the Ganges in Baikathpur (Patna). This temple was built by King Mansingh. A huge fair is organized here on the day of Shivratri.

Birla Mandir, Patna: This temple, built by the honourable Rajabaldevdas ji Birla of India, is located in the Sabzibagh area, about one kilometer from Gandhi Maidan in Patna. It was constructed in 1942.

Patthar Ki Masjid, Patna: Located in the Sultanganj area of Patna, this mosque was built by Shahzada Parvez, son of the Mughal Emperor Jahangir. Therefore, it is also called 'Sangi Masjid'. It is an excellent example of Mughal architecture. There is a mosque built during the reign of Sher Shah Suri in Hajiganj area in Patna, where there is a tomb of Hazrat Muhammad Shah Sufi.

Temple of Umanath: There is an 800-year-old famous temple of Lord Shiva located in Badh in Patna district, which is popularly known as Umanath.

Khanqah, Phulwari Sharif: It was established by Hazrat Makhdoom Shah in the 13th century. It has been an important centre of Islam. In the month of Rabiul-Awwal, an Urs Sharif is celebrated in memory of Prophet Muhammad, which is held for three days. Followers of Islam from India and abroad come here and see the holy hair of Prophet Muhammad.

Imambara, Patna City: Imambara, built near Bulandibagh, is a holy place for Muslim devotees. Apart from this, there is also a grand mausoleum of Shah Arjani near Gunsar Lake.

Takht Shri Harminder Sahib, Patna: Takht Shri Harminder Sahib located in Patna City is a historical and scenic place associated with the Sikh faith. It is the birthplace of Govind Singh, the 10th Guru of the Sikhs. Guru Gobind Singh was born on 26 December, 1666. The pugura related to the childhood of Guru Gobind Singh ji, four iron arrows, sword, paduka and many items have been kept here safely. This place is a centre of faith for Sikh people. Prakash Parv is celebrated every year in Patna Sahib on the birthday of Guru Gobind Singh.

Gurudwara Gaighat, Patna: This place is located 8 kilometers from Patna Junction. It is a famous pilgrimage of Sikhs located in Alamganj area of Gaighat. Guru Nanak stayed here in 1509. In 1666, Tegh Bahadur, the Guru of Sikhs, stayed here along with the family.

Gurudwara Handri Sahib, Danapur: This gurudwara located in Danapur is a wonderful confluence of grandeur and religiosity. Guru Gobind Singh stayed here for some time while travelling from Patna to Punjab.

Guru ka Bagh, Patna: It is located 3 kilometers east of Patna's Harminder Sahib on Patna-Fatuha road. Guru Tegh Bahadur met his son Govind Rai here while returning from Bengal.

Gurudwara Govind Ghat, Patna City: This place is related to Guru Govind Singh Ji. It is about 200 metres away from Harminder Sahib and is situated on the banks of the Ganges River. Apart from this, Guru Singh Sabha Gurdwara of Purnia and Gurdwara of Gaya and Munger are the pride of Sikhism.

Kamaldah, Patna: The ancient and famous temple of Jainism is located near Kamaldah, which is near the Gulzar Bagh railway station. Jains throng this place for worship.

St. Joseph's Church, Bankipur: This church is famous for its exquisite artifacts. It is located in Bankipur, Patna. On the occasion of Christmas, the excitement of the followers of Christianity can be seen here.

Bhagalpur: It is famous as the Silk City of Bihar. Bhagalpur is famous for Tasar silk. The ancient Vikramashila University was located in Bhagalpur District, which is being renovated. The capital of the ancient Anga Mahajanapada was located in Bhagalpur. The temple of Ajgaibinath is located in Sultanganj, on the banks of river Ganges.

Mandargiri, Bhagalpur: It has the idol of Goddess Bhagwati Durga made of granite rock. It is located in Mandargiri, Bhagalpur. This temple is situated at an altitude of about 800 feet. This mountain has mythological significance, and it is believed that Mandaragiri mountain was used during Samudramanthan.

Temple of Ajgaibinath: This ancient temple of Lord Shiva is located on the banks of River Ganges in Sultanganj. During the month of Shravan, a large number of people visit here to worship.

Champa: This capital of ancient Anga Mahajanapada was included in 6 major Buddhist cities. It was built by Mahagovind. This city is named after Champa, the son of Prithulaksha. According to the stories in Mahajataka, Mahatma Buddha visited Champa many times. Chinese travellers Fa-Hien and Hiuen Tsang had also travelled to Champa.

Munger: Munger, situated on the banks of River Ganges, was the centre of Anga Mahajanapada in ancient times. At the beginning of the modern era, Mir Qasim, the Nawab of Bengal, developed it as the capital.

Bihar Yoga Bharti, Ganga Darshan is located in the World Yogpeeth Campus in Munger. This place was earlier known as 'Karna Chaura'. Yoga education based on Gurukul system is imparted here. This type of Yoga institution was first established by Swami Shivanand Saraswati in Rishikesh, which was called 'Yoga Vedanta Forest Academy'. Inspired by him, Swami Satyanand Saraswati established the 'Bihar School of Yoga' in Munger in 1963. Later in 1994, Niranjanananda Saraswati established Bihar Yoga Bharati in the premises of Gangadarshan Vishwa Yogpeeth.

Chandika Devi Temple, Munger: The temple of Maa Chandika Devi, situated on the banks of the Ganges in Munger district, is a famous Shaktipeeth. Mother Sati's right eye fell on this site. The golden eye is installed in the main temple.

Shringa Rishi: Named after Shringamuni during the Ramayana Age, this mountain is located 32 km southwest of Munger District, where a fair is held on the day of Shivaratri. In 1766, British troops revolted against the British Governor Clive in the same area; it is termed as White Mutiny.

Bhulani Dham, Rohtas: This temple is located in a village called Bhulani near Vikramganj in Rohtas district. It is near the ancient temple of Mata Parvati, where a grand and huge fair is held every year in April and October.

Guptdham, Rohtas: Located in Rohtas, this temple has a natural Shiva lingam, which is worshiped as Gupteshwar Nath. A huge and grand fair is organized here on the day of Basant Panchami and Shivaratri.

Maa Tarachandi: There is a temple of Maa Tarachandi in the cave of Kaimur Hill, which is 6 kilometers from Sasaram. It is also one of the 51 Shakti Peeths of Maa Durga.

Sasaram: Sasaram is famous for the mausoleum of the famous Afghan ruler Sher Shah Suri and his father Hasan Khan Sur. This mausoleum is the best example of the octagonal style (Afghan style) in the middle of a pond.

Mundeshwari Temple, Kaimur: The ancient temple of Goddess Mundeshwari Devi is situated at an altitude of 608 feet on the Pavara Hill in Bhagwan block near Bhabhua in Kaimur District. There is a Panchmukhi Shivling of Lord Shiva in this temple, whose form appears different in the morning, afternoon and evening.

Girija Sthan, Madhubani: This ancient temple is located in a place called Faluhar in Madhubani district. Unmarried girls worship Goddess Parvati and ask for suitable groom.

Somnath Temple: A big fair is held every year in this temple which is located in Madhubani District. The marriages of Maithil Brahmins are decided upon here.

Chinnamastika Mandir, Ucchaith, Madhubani: The famous and ancient temple of Maa Durga is located here. In this temple, Mahakavi Kalidas used to worship Mother Kali.

Ram Janaki Temple, Sitamarhi: According to mythology, in this land of Bihar, Mithila King Janak was advised by the sages to perform a Haleshti Yajna and plow the fields with his hands. While using the plow, a gem in the form of a girl was discovered in a pitcher that was broken due to the plow. The girl was named Sita because of the plough. Sitamarhi district was named after the daughter of the land–Sita. Later, a grand temple of Ram Janaki was built here. Today, this temple is the main centre of faith for hundreds of Ram devotees.

Ahirauli Temple, Buxar: This temple is located 5 kilometres northeast of the district headquarters in Buxar District. It is named after Ahilya, the wife of the sage Gautama. Khichdi fair is organized here every year on the day of Makar-Sankranti.

Ugratara Temple, Saharsa: The ancient Ugratara Temple is located at Mahishi which is 16 km west of Saharsa City. It is believed that in the 8 century, Adi Shankaracharya defeated the scholar Mandan Mishra in a debate here. After that, Shankaracharya was defeated by Bharati Devi, wife of Mandan Mishra. The famous Tara Peetha is also located here where Sati's left eye had fallen.

Kapileshwar Sthan: This place is located on a mound between Baruari and Jagatpur villages on the banks of Kheradahra, a branch of the Kosi River in Supaul District. A Shiva temple is located here.

Sinheshwar Sthan, Madhepur: It is believed that this Shiva temple was established by Shringi Rishi. It is located 8 km north of Madhepura. It is about 200 years old.

Areraj's Shiva Temple, Motihari: This ancient temple dedicated to Lord Shiva is located in the south-western part of Motihari District headquarters. Devotees come here in large numbers in the month of Shravan to worship.

Kesariya: Kesariya is located in East Champaran. A stupa of Lord Buddha was found during the excavations in this place. The height of the Buddhist Stupa in Kesariya is 1042 feet. It is also known as 'King Ben's Devra'. Chinese traveler Fa-Hien had visited this place.

Rampura: An Ashokan era pillar with scripture was found in Rampura located in West Champaran. A top pillar are the figures of Lion and Bull. This place was first discovered by Clile in 1899.

Thawe, Gopalganj: There is an ancient temple near Thawe village, which is dedicated to Goddess Durga. It is also recognized as a Siddhapeeth. A big fair is held here in the month of Chaitra, in which people participate in large numbers.

Ambika Temple, Aami: A grand and ancient temple of Maa Ambika Bhavani is situated at a place called Ami in Chhapra District. It is believed that after Sati's self-immolation, when Lord Vishnu cut off the organs of Sati with his chakra, a limb was also dropped here. Hence, it is called Shaktipeeth.

Kusheshwar Sthan, Samastipur: A very old and magnificent temple of Lord Shiva is located at Kusheshwar Sthan, Samastipur. A grand fair is held here on the day of Shivratri.

Ahilya Sthan, Darbhanga: The village of Ahiyari under Darbhanga District Sadar Subdivision is known as Ahilya Sthan. It is said that Rama saved Ahilya at this place at the order of Sage Vishwamitra. A historical temple is located here. This place hosts a large fair twice a year.

Dekuli Dham, Darbhanga: A huge temple of Lord Shiva is located in Biraul block of Darbhanga District. A grand fair is held here every year on the occasion of Shivaratri.

Koteshwarnath Temple, Jehanabad: This is a very ancient Shiva temple. It is located in the main village on the banks of the River Mohar. A huge fair is organized here on Shivratri.

Chamunda Temple: Chamunda Temple is a famous Shaktipeeth situated in Rupo village on Nawada-Roh-Kawakole road. It is believed that the head of Goddess Sati fell here after it was cut. According to Markandeya Purana, Goddess Durga became famous as Chamunda after Chand and Mund were killed.

Dhimeshwar Sthan: An ancient temple of Chinnamastika Devi is located in Dhimeshwar Sthan of Banmakhi block, which is West of Purnia. It is believed that the heart of Mother Sati fell here.

Navlakha Temple: This temple, known as Ram Janaki Thakurwadi, is located in Vishnupur, Begusarai. It was built in 1953 by Mahant Mahavir Das Ji. The construction of this temple took about 10 years and costed ₹9 nine lakh; hence it was named Navlakha Temple.

Apart from this, St. Thomas Catholic Church in Gaya, St. Francis Cathedral in Muzaffarpur, Our Lady of Sorrows Church, Ara, etc. are notable.

Monuments Declared Protected in Bihar by Archaeological Survey of India

Sr. no.	Protected Monument	Village/Location	District
1	Patalpuri Caves	Patharghatta Hill	Bhagalpur
2	Shilamurti Samuh	Patharghatta Hill	Bhagalpur
3	Remains of Vikramshila Mahavihar	Antichak, Oriyap	Bhagalpur
4	Shila Mandir	Kahalgaaon, next to Vikramshila Mahavihar	Bhagalpur

5	Ashokan era stone pillar	Lauriya, Areraj	East Champaran
6	Ashokan era stone pillar with the head of Lion	Lauriya, Nandangarh	West Champaran
7	Remains of two Ashokan era stone pillars	Rampurwa	West Champaran
8	Mound at the site of Vedic burial	Marhiya	West Champaran
9	Buddhist Stupa	Tajpur (Kesariya)	East Champaran
10	Remains of fort, remains of lake	Sagardih	East Champaran
11	Remains of fort	Chaan fort	West Champaran
12	Remains of fort and stupa	Marhiya	West Champaran
13	Vedic berial mounds	Lauriya, Nandangarh	West Champaran
14	Vedic berial mounds	Pakri	West Champaran
15	Remains of an ancient fort or castle	Balirajgarh	Madhubani
16	Ancient hill of Shobhanath Pahadi	Hasra, Jagdishpur	Gaya
17	A cluster of ancient Buddhist statues	Ghejan	Jehanabad
18	A cluster of ancient Buddhist statues and figures	Guneri village	Gaya
19	Satgharva (A group of seven caves)	Barabar-Nagarjuha Hill	Jehanabad
20	Shamsher Khan's Tomb	Shamshernagar	Aurangabad
21	Ancient Fort	Kurklhar	Gaya
22	King Vishal's Fort	Basarh	Vaishali
23	Jama Masjid	Hajipur	Patna
24	Archaeological site	Kumhrar	Patna
25	Archaeological site	Bulandi Bagh	Patna
26	Excavated archaeological site (with Stupa)	Harpur Basant	Vaishali
27	Choti Pahadi ka Tila	Chhoti Pahari	Patna
28	A Group of Seven Mounds	Pahadidih	Patna
29	A Group of Sculptures	Datiyana	Patna
30	Walls of a Fort	Rajgruha	Nalanda
31	All archaeological sites, monuments and sculptures of Rajgruha	Rajgruha	Nalanda

32	Excavated remains	Nalanda Village	Nalanda
33	The Tomb of Malik Ibrahim Bayan	Bihar Sharif	Nalanda
34	Statue of Buddha	Jagdishpur	Nalanda
35	Tombs of Makhdum Shah Daulat Maneri and Ibrahim Khan	Maner	Patna
36	Remains of ancient Mauryan wall made of wood	Sandalpur	Patna
37	Jama Masjid built by Mir Ashraf	Patna City	Patna
38	Ancient remains	Ghora Katora	Nalanda
39	Ancient lake	Maner	Patna
40	Ancient cities, ancient ruins and all other ancient sites	Manjhi	Saran
41	Tomb of Hasan Shah	Sasaram nagar	Rohtas
42	Tomb of Sher Shah Suri	Sasaram nagar	Rohtas
43	Ashoka's inscription	Ashikpur Chandan Shahid Hill	Rohtas
44	Ancient fort	Rohtas Hill	Rohtas
45	Tomb of Bakhtiyar Khan	Malik Sarai (Chainpur)	Bhabua
46	Ancient Temple of Mundeshwari	Pawara (Ramgarh)	Bhabua
47	Ashok Pillar and Stupa	Kolhua	Muzaffarpur
48	Shiv Mandir	Konch	Gaya
49	Ekashm Stambh	Lat	Jehanabad
50	Eksahm Pillar	Near Tarachandi temple in Sasaram nagar	Rohtas
51	Ancient mound	Buxar nagar	Buxar
52	Ancient ruins and sculptures	Kuadol near Kazisarai	Jehanabad
53	AncestralhomeofDr.RajendraPrasad	Ziradei	Siwan

Monument Declared Protected by Directorate of Archaeology, Government of Bihar

Sr. no.	Protected Monument	Village/Location	District
1	Golghar	Patna	Patna
2	Agamkuan	Gulzarbag	Patna
3	Begu Hajjam's Mosque	Patna City	Patna

4	Jain Temple	Kamladah, Gulzarbag	Patna
5	Dorukhi Pratima	Kankadbag	Patna
6	Chhoti Patan Devi	Patna City	Patna
7	Shergarh Fort	Sabji Bazar, Sasaram	Rohtas
8	Alawal Khans' Mausoleum	Sasaram	Rohtas
9	Sun Temple, Kandaha	Mahwara, Mahishi	Saharsa
10	Katara Fort	Muzaffarpur	Muzzafarpur
11	Nepalese Temple	Hajipur	Vaishali
12	Kheri (Archaeological site)	Shahkund	Bhagalpur
13	Jalalgarh Fort	Kasba	Purnia
14	Arrah House	Arrah	Bhojpur
15	Chausagarh	Narvatpur	Buxar
16	Dawood Khan's Fort	Dawoodnagar	Aurangabad
17	Ramshila Hill	Gaya nagar	Gaya
18	Vishnupad Temple	Gaya nagar	Gaya
19	Pretshila Hill	Bahadur Vigaha, Pahad Shrinkhala	Gaya
20	Bramhyoni Hill	Gaya	Gaya
21	Hazarimal Old Dharamshala	Betia	Bettiah

❑❑❑

Disaster Management

- Flood
- Earthquake
- Disaster Management
- State Disaster Management Plan
- Drought
- Cyclone
- The Disaster Management (Amendment) Bill, 2024
- Bihar Disaster Risk Reduction Roadmap 2015-30

Accidents that occur suddenly and cause substantial damage or harm to life and property are known as calamities. The term calamity can be used for such perilous, accidental, undesirable or grave incidents that are either man-made or natural, and can cause serious damage to the affected community.

Floods, droughts, earthquakes, tsunamis, volcanic eruptions, hurricanes, storms, cyclones, etc. are some major natural calamities. Whereas wars, deforestation, ecological balance disturbances, pollution, etc., are some salient man-made calamities. A natural calamity is a spontaneous occurence that has a great impact on human lives, for example volcanic eruptions, floods, droughts, and earthquakes. Man-made calamities are results of carelessness, mistakes, and mismanagement. Man-made calamities are also known as technological or social calamities.

Bihar's geographical location, landscape and human activities are major reasons for different types of calamities faced by the state. The entire Bihar State is prone to one calamity or the other. As far as earthquakes are concerned the entire state is prone to it. More than 70 percent of the region is prone to floods, and more than 30 percent of the state is affected by droughts. Natural fire and lightning as well as cyclones also affect many parts of the state. Some of the major calamities faced by Bihar are floods, droughts, cyclones, lightning, etc.

FLOOD

Its geographical features and location, make Bihar one of the most severely flood-hit state of the country. The entire region of North Bihar and some parts of South Bihar are prone to floods. When the water in river goes above the danger mark or when a large part of landscape gets submerged in water due to natural or man-made reasons, then that situation is known as Flood. Bihar is such a state that faces the problems of flood and drought at the same time. Some parts of North Bihar experience floods whereas South Bihar battles with droughts. The region between Gandak and Budhi Gandak faces the problem of irregular monsoons that causes the situation of drought. According to National Flood Commission (1986), almost 65.5 lakh hectare land (which is almost 37 percent of entire area of the state and includes 39 out of 46 districts of undivided state) of Bihar was affected by floods. According to a report by Agriculture Ministry of Government of India, published in 1986, almost 20 lakh hectares land in Bihar was affected by droughts and that was almost 12 percent of the entire area of the state.

According to National Flood Commission 2006, almost 400 lakh hectares land in the entire country is affected by floods, and out of this, 16.5 percent area falls under Bihar itself.

Flood Situation In Bihar

North Bihar experienced a major flood event in late September and early October 2024, affecting over 1.5 million people and 429 villages across 17 districts. The situation worsened as floodwaters spread to new areas, with thousands of displaced residents facing shortages of relief materials. Rivers like the Kosi, Gandak, Bagmati, and Mahananda threatened embankments, and the release of 6.6 lakh cusec of water from the Birpur barrage on the Kosi River in Nepal contributed to the severity of the flooding. The floods in North Bihar were particularly severe, with the Kosi river's embankment breaching in several locations. The combination of heavy rainfall, the release of water from barrages, and the nature of the rivers carrying large amounts of sediment contributed to the floods. The floods affected a large number of people, displaced residents, and damaged infrastructure.

Flood Affected Districts

Flood (28)	High Flood Consequence Region (15)	East Champaran, Sitamarhi, Katihar, Sheohar, Madhubani, Vaishali, Muzaffarpur, Darbhanga, Samastipur, Madhepura, Saharsa, Supaul, Khagaria, Begusarai, Bhagalpur,
	Low Flood Consequence Region (13)	East Champaran, Gopalganj, Siwan, Saran, Buxar, Bhojpur, Patna, Nalanda, Lakhisarai, Sheikhpura, Purnia, Araria, Kishanganj
Source: Disaster Management Department, Government of Bihar.		

The catastrophe of flood in Bihar lasts for almost 4 to 6 weeks (one and half months). Bihar is the second largest flood-affected state of the country, after Assam. The main reason for floods in Bihar is the irregularity in monsoon. Monsoon rains can fall up to 60 percent more or less than usual, or in other words, the irregularity in monsoon is up to 60 percent. Thus, more than average heavy rainfall can result in floods. Apart from irregularity in monsoon, other factors responsible for floods in the state are as follows:

1. Extensive cutting of forests is a major reason for floods. It is the main reason for floods in plateau region of Bihar and waterlogged areas of Himalayan region. Majority of rivers flowing through Bihar originate from the Himalayas. Deforestation in the Himalayan region is also a reason for the floods.
2. Heavy rainfall in Himalayan region naturally results in flood-like situations in the rivers flowing through this region.
3. The landscape of plains of Bihar is also a major reason for floods. River water spreads very fast in smooth and flat land, which causes flood-like situation.
4. Drainage of a river on low sloping land causes surface deposit that results in flood-like situation. Rivers that are visceral increase the catastrophe of floods.
5. Kosi is considered as the 'Sorrow of Bihar', but many rivers apart from Kosi also cause sudden floods. Rivers in South Bihar often cause sudden flood in the region. It is because of rampant cutting down of forests, and extensive cattle grazing, that the volume of rain water flowing in rivers in south, has increased from 13 to 14 percent from its normal volume of 7 percent.
6. North Bihar as well as South Bihar witness floods due to sudden release of water from reservoirs. These waters are mainly released into canals. The surface of canals has risen due

to regular silt deposition over a period of time. Hence, the water, released into it submerge the adjoining land areas. In 1995-96 Banka, Jamui, and Bhagalpur were affected by sudden flood because water was released in Morahni, a tributary of River Chanan.

7. Development of cracks or damage in weak dams cause the water from river transform into sudden flood.
8. Plains of South-eastern Bihar are full of anikats (small dams) which are not easily visible because they are filled by sand. As a result, flood water submerges a large area very quickly.
9. Regions of source of water like canals and drains are shrinking continuously due to extensive urbanization. As a result, rain water causes flood-like situation in urban areas.

Steps taken towards rescue and safety

After independence multipurpose river valley projects were given priority. These projects were given top priority in first three Five-year Plans. Embankments were given priority in the Fourth Five-year Plan. Sixth Five-year Plan focused on water removal system. It was in this plan that programs were started to save the hutments. In this program, the level of embankments and lands near rivers were risen. In the Sixth Five-year Plan, 80 percent of grant approved for flood control was spent on management of pre-existing embankments, and remaining 20 percent was used to start new programs. About 3600 km of embankments were made, and the figure was only 160 km in 1954. There are 7 flood broadcast centers across India, and Patna is one of them. Danger marks have been assigned to all the rivers. Central government has made plans to establish flood broadcast centers at 100 centers across the country. These programs have declared 20 lakh hectares land free from floods. Flood relief kit has been provided in flood affected districts. NDRF is setting up 200 safe locations in flood-hit districts. A position of emergency manager has been created in 10 flood-affected districts.

Many embankments have been built in order to prevent floods. Some of them are as follows:

- Koilwar–Buxar embankment near River Ganga.
- Badlaghat–Nagarpara embankment in Khagaria District.
- Tinmohani–Kursela–Khagaria embankment on River Kosi.
- Bhutahi Balan embankment in Darbhanga District.
- Hajipur–Bajipur embankment in Vaishali District.

Measures and Advisory

Flood control programs in Bihar require a new approach. In order to achieve this, following measures are advised:

1. Cutting down plants and tree is the primary reason for floods. Successful implementation of forestation programs is an effective way to control floods. Therefore, it is necessary to stop deforestation and plant trees in areas that have waterlogging problem.
2. Contour farming is required in the irregular plateau lands and Shivalik region in South Bihar. As a result the water flows into the rivers at regular intervals, which helps in controlling floods in the area.
3. Programs that help in building anikats and removal of silts from the surface of canals should be started. This measure will help in control of sudden floods that are caused by canals.
4. Credible and widespread information about floods is need of the hour. Effective information network can help in reducing the loss to life and property caused by floods in the area.
5. The clay houses in flood-affected areas in Bihar should immediately be replaced by brick houses. Bricks are more resistant to water as compared to clay.
6. Cultivation of waterborne crops like fox nuts or lotus seeds (Makhana) and water chestnut,

(Singhara) as well as pisciculture should be encouraged. This step can help transform loss incurred due to floods into profit-making projects. Low wetlands in this region are ripe for these products.

7. Cultivation of new varieties of paddy that are more resistant to floods should be tried.
8. Open bridges and culverts should be built so that floods do not impact the traffic movement.
9. Fast and effective ways to supply flood relief materials in flood-affected areas should be sought. Disaster management camps should be set up at places that face the danger of floods.

DROUGHT

If the average rainfall for continuous 4 weeks, during the month of monsoon i.e., from June to mid-October is 5 cm or less, then such condition is known as Drought.

Bihar is not a drought prone area from the geological perspective because in geography, geologists consider those places to be acute drought prone area that receive less than 50 cm rainfall. Every region of Bihar receives more than 50 cm rainfall but even those regions that receive around 50 to 150 cm rainfall are prone to drought. All the regions of Bihar (except central western region of Gopalganj and Siwan) receive more than 150 cm rainfall, and although the recurrence of drought is low, the probability still remains. According to experience-based studies, the situation of drought in Bihar occurs once every four years. Bihar is a state that faces the dichotomy of floods and droughts at the same time. In 1987, when northern part of Bihar was submerged in floods, South Bihar was battling the situation of drought. In 1966–67, entire Bihar was hit by famine. In year 2013, 33 out of 38 districts of the state were declared drought-affected owing to low or no rainfall. According to a report by Disaster Management Department of the Government of Bihar, 13 out of 38 districts of the state are affected by droughts. Out of these, 5 districts are acute drought prone area, 3 districts are declared to be drought prone and 5 districts are partially drought prone areas.

Drought-Prone Districts:

- Munger, Nawada, Rohtas, Bhojpur, Aurangabad, and Gaya: are specifically mentioned as drought-prone areas.
- Sheikhpura, Jamui, Lakhisarai, Bhagalpur, and Banka: are part of Agro-Climatic Zone III (A), which also includes some drought-prone areas.
- Arwal, Patna, Nalanda, Jehanabad, and some parts of Buxar: are in Agro-Climatic Zone III (B), which is also prone to droughts.

Factors Contributing to Droughts

- **Inadequate Rainfall:** Lack of sufficient rainfall is a major factor in drought conditions, affecting both North and South Bihar.
- **Monsoon Variations:** The south-west monsoons bring less rain to the southern districts compared to the northern regions, leading to water scarcity.
- **Uneven Rainfall Distribution:** Uneven distribution of rainfall across different regions within Bihar, particularly in the south, contributes to drought vulnerability.
- **Climate Change:** Weather irregularities, including changes in monsoon patterns, are expected to become more common, increasing the risk of droughts in Bihar.

According to the book Regional Planning in India Volume – I, authored by Prof. Inayat Ahmed and D K Singh, there is a constant probability of droughts across 45 percent area of Bihar. There are two main reasons behind droughts in Bihar – first reason is scarce rainfall in the region due to adverse impact of continental weather, as Bihar is situated far from seas and the second reason is unpredictability of monsoons in the region. It is a special characteristic of monsoon that as the amount of rainfall decreases, the probability of drought increases. The effect of El Nino also results in monsoon drought. The unpredictability in monsoon is up to 60 percent. Rampant deforestation is another major reason for droughts in Bihar. The total forest area in Bihar is only 7.21 percent, whereas it should be 33 percent from the ecological point of view. Deforestation has caused a reduction in amount of average rainfall which has had an adverse impact on both surface and underground water. Cutting down of forests has also caused a decrease in moisture retaining capacity. Rocks get overheated due to large-scale soil erosion, and this causes scarcity in relative humidity of lower atmosphere. With all these factors, around 20 percent region of Bihar is affected by droughts. Kaimur, Rohtas, Aurangabad, Gaya, Nawada, with Lakhisarai, Munger, Jamui, Sheikhpura, Bhagalpur, Patna, Nalanda, Jehanabad, etc. are drought prone districts of Bihar. Drought increases the risk of other huge problems like food scarcity, fodder scarcity, and drinking water scarcity. It has an adverse effect on the economy of the state. Droughts have also caused a decrease in availability of per capita drinking water in the state.

Measures taken to curb the problem of drought

Multipurpose river valley projects is the first step towards curbing drought problem. Son Command Area Project is the oldest project of this state. The project was built in 1874. It has helped in improving the irrigation system of Rohtas, Kaimur, Arwal, Bhojpur, and other districts. It is an irrigation system built in the most dry areas of Bihar, and due to this projects, this region has now become the grain store of Bihar. Gandak Project has had a positive impact on those parts of state that were frequently hit by droughts. Kosi Irrigation Project has also helped in prevention of droughts. Koyalkaro Project in Jharkhand is under contruction, which will benefit Aurangabad District. Chanan–Barua–Kiul Command Area Project is very important as it benefits Jamui, South Munger, Banka and Sheikhpura districts. This project is aimed to safeguard standing crops.

Minor irrigation projects are being developed very quickly in order to tackle droughts. Irrigation projects that aim to covers lands below 2000 hectares fall under this category. Bihar has developed many minor irrigation projects after the drought of 1967. In order to ensure proper development of such projects, Government of Bihar formed minor irrigation department in year 1967 itself. National Water Policy was adopted in 1987 which aimed to save standing crops in the field by using the water stored in ditches along the roads and railway tracks as well as by using the water in ponds. Silts have been removed from anikats. Diesel pump sets and bamboo boring are given priority in Kosi region. Under the IRDP scheme, peasants are given subsidy if they purchase boring and pump sets or its accessories. In order to control the menace of natural calamities like floods and droughts, many steps have been taken towards water management:

1. Embankments along the eastern and western coast of Kosi are being repaired and reinforced. Reinforcement of Sanjay Current, Haiya Current and Bochaha Current are being reinforced under Kosi Flood Recovery Project (Kosi-I) in Bihar. An 8-km-long road has been constructed under Bihar Kosi Basin Development Project (Kosi-II)
2. About 57 km long new embankments have been built in the second phase of Bagmati Food Management Project.
3. Under Bagmati Flood Management Project, raising height and reinforcement of two sections of length 105 km and 50 km have been completed.
4. About 8 irrigation projects have been completed in order to curb the problem of drought. The names of these projects are: Bachhraja Biyar Project, Kachnama Vier Project, Navagarh Project, Sammat Project, Bigha Biyar Project, Sesanba Viyar Project, Isarve Check Dam, Bhetoura Dam, and Kadhar Viyar Project.

EARTHQUAKE

As far as earthquakes are concerned, entire Bihar falls under earthquake affected region. Bihar is situated on two tectonic plates, viz., Indian Plate and Chinese Plate and thus, chances of seismic disturbances are always present. According to Disaster Management Department of the Government of Bihar, 15.2 percent part of the state falls in Zone-V, 63.7 percent part falls in Zone-IV, while 21 percent part comes under Zone-III.

Zone-V is the most sensitive one in context of earthquakes whereas Zone-IV and Zone-III come under the category of normal earthquake affected areas. The table below explains the spread of earthquake prone zones in Bihar according to Disaster Management Department of the Government of Bihar.

Zone	Intensity of earthquake (MSK scale)	Name of districts
Zone-V	IX	Purnia, Araria, Kishanganj, Sitamarhi, Darbhanga, Saharsa, Madhepura, Supaul, Madhubani, and Sheohar
Zone-IV	VIII	East Champaran, West Champaran, Gopalganj, Siwan, Saran, Muzaffarpur, Vaishali, Samastipur, Begusarai, Khagaria, Munger, Sheikhpura, Lakhisarai, Katihar, Bhagalpur, Patna, and Nalanda
Zone-III	VII	Gaya, Aurangabad, Rohtas, Kaimur, Buxar, Bhojpur, Jehanabad, Arwal, Nawada, Jamui, and partially southern part of Banka

Tectonic plates are the main reason behind earthquakes in Bihar. The table shows the major earthquakes that ocured in Bihar till date.

Date	Magnitude	Notes
1934	8.4	The 1934 Nepal-India Earthquake also known as the Bihar Earthquake was one of the most destructive earthquakes. It caused over 15,000 fatalities.
1988	6.2	A major earthquake occurred in Bihar.
2015 (Apr.)	4.3	A magnitude of 4.3 earthquake occurred near Patna.
2015 (May)	4.6	A magnitude of 4.6 earthquake occurred near Patna.
2017 (June)	4.5	A magnitude of 4.5 earthquake occurred near Patna.
2022 (Jan.)	4.2	A magnitude of 4.2 earthquake occurred near Patna.

CYCLONE

Cyclones, especially tropical cyclones affect the north-eastern and some parts of south-werstern region of Bihar. Purnia and Kishanganj are chief districts among those affected by cyclones. Tropical cyclones originate in the form of storm in the Bay of Bengal during the month of May–June and October–November. October–November is the time when the chief kharif crop of Bihar, paddy, is ready to be cultivated. Thus, a cyclone at this time has a major impact on the crop of paddy and thousands of acres of crop is destroyed, which life gives rise to a situation of calamity. In May 2016, a cyclone in the north-eastern part of Bihar caused huge loss of life and property. About 18 districts of the state were hit by this cyclone. Out of these 18 districts, Madhubani, Kishanganj, Sitamarhi, Purnia, Darbhanga, and Bhagalpur were most severly hit. About 42 people of the state lost their lives in this cyclone and more than 100 were injured in it.

Other Calamities

Other calamities include hailstorms, thunderbolt, cold waves and man-made accidents. The state encounters hilly, cold waves during the months of December and January, which causes death of many people due to extreme cold, and it also causes damage to the rabi crops. During the season of festivals and celebrations, people gather in huge numbers in fairs and often, accidents like stampedes and boat overturning happen that cause loss of life and property.

DISASTER MANAGEMENT

Disaster management comprises perpetual and continuous process of measures taken to make, regulate, coordinate and implement the programs. They are mentioned as follows:

1. Taking steps to prevent the probability and dangers of any calamity;
2. Reducing the impact or intensity or risks of the calalmity;
3. Adopting capacity-building measures through knowledge and research-based management programs;
4. Making preparations to tackle the calamity
5. Taking immediate steps in case of any disaster or any disaster like situation;
6. Analysing the intensity or impact of the calamity beforehand;
7. Taking steps to rescue the stranded people and work for their treatment and relief;
8. Taking measures for rehabilitation and reconstruction after the calamity has passed.

The continuous process of disaster management is made up of 6 elements. These include prevention measures before the calamity strikes, steps, and actions like rehabilitation, reconstruction, and normal life resumption after the calamity has passed.

There are three major stages in disaster management:

1. Pre-calamity stage
2. Calamity stage
3. Post-calamity stage

Pre-calamity stage comprises preparation for the calamity, redressal of the calamity and prevention of the calamity. Preparation for the calamity includes identifying the nature and readiness for it, research about the calamity, forecast about the calamity, calamity warning mechanism, education about the calamity, etc.

Carrying out rescue works on war footing, shifting the affected people from the calamity-affected area to safe places or rescue camps, and make arrangements for the availability and regular supply of food, water, medicine and other necessary items are included in the calamity stage.

Post calamity stage includes relief works, steps for rehabilitation and reconstruction of property and steps for bringing life back to normalcy.

THE DISASTER MANAGEMENT (AMENDMENT) BILL, 2024

The Disaster Management (Amendment) Bill, 2024 was introduced in Lok Sabha on August 1, 2024. The Bill amends the Disaster Management Act, 2005. The Act establishes: (i) National Disaster Management Authority (NDMA), (ii) State Disaster Management Authority (SDMA), and (iii) District Disaster Management Authority. These authorities are responsible for disaster management at the national, state, and district level, respectively.

- **Preparation of disaster management plans:** The Act provides for constitution of a National Executive Committee and a State Executive Committee to assist NDMA and SDMA in performing their functions. A key function of these Committees is preparing national and state disaster management plans, respectively. NDMA and SDMA approve the respective plans and coordinate their implementation. The Bill instead provides that NDMA and SDMA will prepare disaster management plans.
- **Functions of NDMA and SDMA:** Under the Act, key functions of NDMA and SDMA at their respective levels include: (i) reviewing the disaster management plans of government departments, (ii) setting guidelines for preparation of disaster management plans for authorities below them, and (iii) recommending

provision of funds for disaster mitigation. The Bill adds certain functions for these authorities at their respective levels. These include: (i) taking periodic stock of disaster risks, including emerging risks from extreme climate events, (ii) providing technical assistance to authorities below them, (iii) recommending guidelines for minimum standards of relief, and (iv) preparing national and state disaster databases, respectively. The databases will contain information on: (i) the type and severity of disaster risks, (ii) allocation of funds and expenditure, and (iii) disaster preparedness and mitigation plans. Functions of NDMA will also include: (i) assessing disaster preparedness of states, and (ii) undertaking post-disaster audit of preparedness and response.

- The Bill also empowers NDMA to make regulations under the Act with prior approval of the central government.
- **Urban Disaster Management Authorities:** The Bill empowers the state government to constitute a separate Urban Disaster Management Authority for state capitals and cities with a municipal corporation. The Urban Authority will comprise the Municipal Commissioner as the chairperson, the District Collector as the vice chairperson, and other members specified by the state government. It will prepare and implement the disaster management plan for the area under it.
- **Formation of State Disaster Response Force:** The Act provides for constitution of a National Disaster Response Force for specialist response to disaster situations. The Bill empowers the state government to constitute a State Disaster Response Force (SDRF). The state government will define the functions of SDRF and prescribe the terms of service for its members.
- **Statutory status to existing committees:** The Bill provides statutory status to existing bodies such as the National Crisis Management Committee (NCMC) and the High Level Committee (HLC). The NCMC will function as the nodal body for dealing with major disasters with serious or national ramifications. The HLC will provide financial assistance to state governments during disasters. It will approve financial assistance from the National Disaster Mitigation Fund. The Cabinet Secretary will serve as the chairperson of NCMC. Minister of the department with administrative control over disaster management will serve as chairperson of the HLC.
- **Appointments to NDMA:** The Act provides that the central government will provide NDMA with officers, consultants, and employees, as it considers necessary. The Bill instead empowers NDMA to specify the number and category of officers and employees, with previous approval of the central government. NDMA may also appoint experts and consultants as necessary.

Local disaster management

Local authority of disaster management includes panchayati raj institutions, municipalities, district and cantonment boards and town planning authority which are used to control and direct public services during the time of disaster. These local bodies ensure capacity-building among their own employees, staffs and officers as well as locals in order to tackle any upcoming disaster. In addition to this local authorities along with National Disaster Management Authority, State Disaster Management Authority and District Disaster Authority prepares disaster prevention and control plans.

STATE DISASTER MANAGEMENT PLAN

Section 23(1) of the National Disaster Management Act, (NDMA) states the provisions for preparation of State Disaster Management Plan. The responsibility of disaster management plan lies with the State Executive Committee. The Government of Bihar has set up SDMP in 2014 under the provisions of this Act.

State Disaster Management Plan can be divided into two parts:

1. Disaster Risk Management
2. Disaster Crisis Management

Disaster risk management includes prevention of disaster, reduction of intensity of disaster and preparations for the eventuality. Disaster crisis management includes response and relief, rehabilitation and reconstruction and includes the concept of 'Build Back Better'.

BIHAR DISASTER RISK REDUCTION ROADMAP 2015-30

The Government of Bihar has prepared roadmap 2015–30 to minimize the risks arising due to disasters and calamities. The third edition of World Congress on Disaster Risk Reduction was organized from 14 to 18 March, 2015, in Sendai City in Japan, which was attended by representatives from 190 countries. The conferences have been held in Japan, with the first in Yokohama (1994), the second in Hyogo (2005), and the third in Sendai (2015). In order to reduce the risk of disasters between 2015–30, 4 priorities and 7 goals were agreed upon in this congress.

Priorities

1. Understanding disaster risk;
2. Strengthening disaster risk governance to manage disaster risk;
3. Investing in disaster risk reduction for resilience;
4. Enhancing disaster preparedness for effective response and to 'Build Back Better' in recovery, rehabilitation and reconstruction.

Seven goals agreed upon in the roadmap 2015-30 are as follows:

1. Substantially reduce global disaster mortality by 2030.
2. Substantially reduce the number of affected people globally by 2030.
3. Reduce direct disaster economic loss in relation to global gross domestic product (GDP) by 2030.
4. Substantially reduce disaster damage to critical infrastructure and disruption of basic services.
5. Substantially increase the number of countries with national and local disaster risk reduction strategies.
6. Substantially enhance international cooperation to developing countries, through adequate and sustainable support to complement their national actions.
7. Substantially increase the availability of and access to multi-hazard early warning systems and disaster risk information and assessments to people.

Keeping the priorities and goals agreed upon in World Congress for Disaster Risk Reduction held in Sedai in mind, Bihar Disaster Risk Reduction Roadmap 2015–30 has been framed. For this, different departments of Bihar, partners in disaster risk reduction, experts and the society involved came together with the government to organize the first Bihar Disaster Reduction Conference in May 2015. In the concluding session of this event, Bihar Disaster Risk Reduction Structure was adopted in the form of Patna Declaration–2015 to make the state more secure and Bihar Disaster Risk Reduction Roadmap, 2015–30 has been framed on the same lines.

Some of the salient features of Bihar Disaster Risk Reduction Roadmap, 2015–30 are as follows:

1. Road map 2015–30 has set four goals that are as stated under:
   (a) Reduce the standard loss occurred due to natural calamities up to 75 percent as compared to the statistics of baseline till 2030.
   (b) Reduce lives lost due to transportation related disasters in Bihar, substantially over baseline level by 2030.
   (c) Reduce people affected by disasters in Bihar by 50% of over baseline level by 2030.
   (d) Reduce economic loss due to disasters in Bihar by 50% over baseline level by 2030.
2. Roadmap 2015–30 has been divided into 9 sections. In order to achieve its target, short-term goals to be achieved by 2020, medium-term goals to be have achieved by 2025 and long-term goals to be achieved by 2030 have been included. The actions included in this program have been divided into 5 sections like resilient villages, resilient cities, resilient

livelihoods, resilient basic services and resilient critical infrastructure.

3. Resilient villages imply the inclusion of the concept of disaster risk reduction in the programs that are being run for the development of villages, enhancement and capacity-building of community institutions in the villages and analysis of disaster risk, imparting knowledge about information planning and its usage, pre disaster warning and ensuring the reach of emergency services and developing L1 (small scale) disaster counter capability in the villagers through these activities.
4. Resilient cities mean the inclusion of the concept of disaster risk reduction in the programs run for the development of the cities, capacity-building of community institutions of the cities and through them induce the analysis of disaster risk, information and usage about communication network in the people living in the cities, ensure early warning and unhindered supply of essential services and develop disaster countering mechanism in the people to combat a disaster of L1 (small scale) level.
5. Resilient basic services mean health and medicine, education, habitation, drinking water, sanitation, etc should be made counter disaster effective and take measures to ensure the unhindered supply of all these services even in the times of disaster. In order to achieve task, this it is important to strengthen the concerned departments so that they can identify the risks and prepare counter measures and make flexible, yet effective, counter plans.
6. Roadmap 2015–30 mentions the formation of Roadmap Implementation Support Unit (RISU) in the Disaster Management Department. A statewide task force under the leadership of the minister of Disaster Management Department has also been proposed. Roadmap 2015–30 is effective for 15 years.

Governance Structure

- Political System
- Governor
- State Legislature
- Chief Minister and the Council of Ministers in the State
- Advocate General
- Lokayukta
- Important Commissions

POLITICAL SYSTEM

A new state by the name of Bihar and Orissa came into existence on 22 March, 1912, through an official proclamation. The provisions of Government of India Act 1920 were enacted in Bihar on 29 October, 1920 and Satyendra Prasanna Sinha took charge as the first governor of the state. Through the provisions of Government of India Act 1935, it was decided to implement bicameral legislature in center and allow provincial autonomy to the states or provinces. On 1 April, 1936, Bihar and Orissa were divided into 2 separate states by the same names. The Act of 1935 assigned 152 and 30 seats, respectively to the Vidhan Sabha and Vidhan Parishad of Bihar. Elections for the first Vidhan Sabha in Bihar were held under the provisions of this act in 1937. Out of 152, 70 seats were reserved for general people, 15 seats for scheduled castes, 7 seats for the scheduled tribes, 39 seats for Muslims, 4 seats for women, 2 seats for Anglo Indians, 2 seats for the European community and 13 seats were reserved for people from the elite community like business, industry, landlords, teachers and Christians of Indian origin. Congress won 98 seats, while Muslim League won 20 seats in this election. Shri Krishna Singh was elected as the leader of the Congress Party. On the directions from the central leadership of the congress party, Shri Krishna Singh put forward a demand for political autonomy before the governor. Expressing his angst after the governor refused to entertain his demand, Shri Krishna Singh refused to form his council of ministers. In the meantime, an acting government under the leadership of Md. Yunus of the Independent Party was formed in Bihar in March 1937, but Md Yunus' council of ministers could neither call a meeting of the Vidhan Sabha nor could it decide a date for oath taking of its members. Amidst all this, central leadership of the Congress Party and the Governor General reached an agreement, after which first Congress Government was formed in Bihar under the leadership of Shri Krishna Singh on 20 July, 1937. Dr Sachchidanand Sinha was elected as the pro tem speaker of Bihar Vidhan Sabha. On 23 July, 1937, Shri Ramdayalu was elected as the speaker while Shri Abdul Bari was elected as the deputy speaker. On 23 July, 1939, the Government of Bihar resigned in protest of including India in the Second World War without her consent and thus, the Vidhan Sabha was dissolved.

Elections were held again in 1946 and in April 1946, Shri Krishna Singh assumed the charge of the chief minister of the state. About 39 members from this Vidhan Sabha were elected for the constituent assembly. Some of the prominent names included Dr. Sarojini Naidu, Dr. Sachchidanand Sinha, Dr.

Rajendra Prasad, Shri Jagjivan Rama and Tajajhul Hussein. First general election of Bihar as per the provisions of constitution of independent India were held in 1952. At that time, total number of members in the Bihar state assembly was demarcated as 331 (330 elected and 1 nominated). Dr Shri Krishna Singh assumed the position of Chief minister of Bihar even after the first general elections of independent India. On 15 November, 2000, Bihar was bifurcated. New state of Jharkhand was formed with 18 out of 56 districts of erstwhile Bihar. After the bifurcation total number of districts in Bihar remained 38. In undivided Bihar, the total number of members of Lok Sabha was 54, total number of members of Rajya Sabha was 22, total number of members of legislative assembly was 324, total number of members of Vidhan Parishad was 96. After the division, total number of members of Lok Sabha reduced to 40, total number of members of Rajya Sabha became 16, total number of members of Vidhan Sabha became 243, and total strength of Vidhan Parishad was reduced to 75.

GOVERNOR

Executive, judiciary and legislature are the three pillars of the state government. Governor is the constitutional head as well the head of executive in the state. The powers and rights of governor have been mentioned in Articles 153 to 162 of the Constitution of India. Entire administration is run in the name of governor. He enjoys some privileges but still he is bound by the advice of the council of ministers. In India, it is a normal practice to appoint only one person as the governor of a state but an amendment in 1953 in Article 153 of the Constitution of India empowers the president to appoint a person as the governor of two or more states.

Eligibility

Article 157 of the constitution lays down the following conditions for a person to be appointed as the governor of any state:

1. He should be a citizen of India.
2. He must be at least 35 years of age.
3. He should not hold any office of profit in the central or state or both governments.
4. He should not be a member of any house of the parliament of India or state legislature of any state. If the president appoints a person who is a member of parliament or any state legislature as the governor of a state, then that person must resign from his membership immediately after his appointment.

Appointment of Governor

The governor is appointed by the president on the advice of the Prime Minister of India for a period of 5 years. But according to the provisions of Article 156 of the Constitution of India, the governor shall remain in the office till the pleasure of president. The salary of the governor is drawn on the Consolidated Fund of She state. He is allowed an official residence which is free of rent, allowances and other perks. According to the provisions of Article 158 of the Constitution of India, the salary, allowances and privileges of governor shall not be changed to his disadvantage during his tenure.

Powers of Governor

Various articles of the Constitution of India give legislative, statutory, financial, and judicial powers to the governor. He also enjoys discretionary powers in special situations.

(a) Legislative powers

The chief minister of a state is appointed by the governor. The council of ministers is also appointed by the governor on the advice of chief minister.

While appointing the judges of state high court, the president seeks advice from the governor of the state.

The nominated members of state legislature are nominated by the governor.

About 1/6 members of total members of Vidhan Parishad are appointed by the governor. They are appointed from the field of arts, literature, science and social services.

Appointment of the advocate general of the state and the members of State Public Service Commission is also done by the governor.

(b) Statutory powers

The power to summon the session of state legislature, prorogue of the state legislature and dissolve the Vidhan Sabha lies with the governor of the state.

The annual finance report is tabled in the state legislature after the consent of governor.

The governor makes recommendation to introduce money bill and finance bill in the state legislature.

The governor has the power to send urgent messages to the legislature, and he also enjoys the power to address the state legislature.

Any bill passed by the state legislature comes into effect only after the governor gives his consent.

According to the provisions of article 213 of the Constitution of India, the governor has the right to issue ordinance, and this right can not be challenged in any court of India. Such ordinances remain in effect only for 6 months. If the session of state legislature resumes before completion of 6 months of ordinance, then it is mandatory to get it passed from the Vidhan Sabha.

State Public Service Commission and accountant general present their annual report to the governor and the governor tables it in the state legislature.

The decision of governor in disputes regarding the eligibility of any member of the state legislature is final, but he is bound to consult the Election Commission before arriving at any conclusion.

If the office of chairman or deputy chairman of Vidhan Parishad falls vacant then the governor passes an order allowing a member of the house to act as the chairman and preside over the meeting of the house.

According to article 352(1) of the Constitution of India, governor does not have power to declare emergency in the state in case of external aggression or armed rebellion. Under the provisions of Article 356, the governor can recommend to the president to impose President's rule in the state under special circumstances.

(c) Financial powers

Money bill can be introduced in the state legislative assembly only after the recommendation from the governor.

No expenditure can be incurred on the Contingency Fund of the State without the consent from the governor.

The governor, through the finance minister of the state, introduces the annual budget of the state in the Vidhan Sabha.

Governor presents the annual financial report of the state legislature.

The governor also enjoys the power to make recommendations to seek grants.

(d) Judicial powers

Appointments and promotions of district judges are done by the governor.

The governor can reduce the sentence or grant pardon to any person of the state.

The governor has no right in appointments of judges of high court, but under the provisions of Article 217(1) the president is bound to seek his advice in their appointments.

(e) Discretionary powers

If any party fails to secure clear majority after legislative elections, then the governor can exercise his discretionary powers to summon the leader of any party and ask them to form the government.

The messages sent to the president by the governor are done at his discretion.

STATE LEGISLATURE

Article 168 of the Constitution of India states that there shall be a legislature (Vidhan mandal) for each state that shall comprise the governor, legislative assembly and legislative council (if there is legislative council in the state). Article 169 states that the parliament of India has the power to frame rules for the creation or abolishment of Vidhan Parishad in any state but for any such provision, the concerned state legislative assembly should pass a resolution by not less than two-thirds majority. At present, 6 states have functional legislative council– Uttar Pradesh, Bihar, Karnataka, Maharashtra, Telangana and Andhra Pradesh. In 2019, the Vidhan Parishad of Jammu and Kashmir was abolished through the Jammu Kashmir Reorganisation Act, 2019. This reorganization transformed the state into 2 Union Territories Jammu & Kashmir and Laddakh. Bihar state legislature comprises two houses—legislative assembly (lower house) and legislative council (upper house).

Legislative Council

Orissa–Bihar state legislative council came into existence on 7 February, 1921. Sir Walter Mande became its first chairman. Legislative council for Bihar, after its separation from Orissa, wads formed on 28 March, 1936. Article 169 of the constitution of India contains provisions for the formation of legislative council in any state. As per the constitution the total number of members of legislative council cannot exceed one-third of the total number of members of the legislative assembly of that state. Before the separation of Jharkhand from Bihar, the total number of members of legislative council was 96, but at present, it is reduced to 75. It is a permanent house and can never be dissolved. The membership of its members is valid for six years. One-third members of the house retire in every two years.

One-third members of legislative council are elected by the members of local bodies, municipalities, district councils, etc. One-third members are elected by the members of legislative assembly. About One-twelfth members are elected by such teachers of higher secondary schools and colleges who have atleast 3 years of teaching experience. About one-twelfth are elected by such residents of Bihar who are graduates from esteemed universities in India and have acquired their graduation atleast 3 years prior to the election. Remaining one-sixth members are nominated by the governor of the state from the field of arts, literature, science, cooperatives, and social services.

In order to convene a session of the legislative council, it is mandatory that at least 10 or 1/10 of its total members, whichever is larger, should be present in the House. The members of the legislative council have full rights to express themselves in the House, and their statement can not be challenged on any grounds in any court of India. Members of the legislative council cannot be arrested in case of civil matters 40 days prior to and 40 days after the completion of session of legislature. The session of legislative council is called by the governor. It is mandatory to call at least two sessions of the house in a year, and the duration between the last day of a session and first day of the next session should not be more than six months.

Qualifications to become a member of legislative council

1. He should be a citizen of India and should at least be 30 years of age.
2. His name should be registerd in the electoral roll of the region from where he wishes to contest.
3. He should not hold any office of profit in the Government of India or the state government.
4. He should be mentally sound and not insolvent.
5. He should not have been declared unfit to contest elections on grounds of any criminal activities by the Election Commission.

Proceeding of Legislative Council

Financial proceeding

Real power in financial matters of the state lies with its legislative assembly. A money bill is introduced only in the state legislative assembly. After the money bill is passed from the legislative assembly, it is tabled in the legislative council. Legislative council can withhold this bill for a maximum period of fourteen days. If the legislative council fails to pass the bill within 14 days or suggests any amendments to the bill, then it is the prerogative of the legislative assembly to either accept or reject the amendments, and the bill is considered to be passed from both the houses.

Legislative proceeding

General bills can be introduced in the legislative council, but before the bill is sent to the Governor for consent, it is mandatory to get it passed from the legislative assembly. If a bill is passed in the legislative assembly, but is stuck in the legislative council, then the legislative council can either reject it completely, make amendments, or keep it with itself for a maximum period of three months. After, this is if the legislative assembly passes the bill again with or without the suggestions made by the legislative council, it is again tabled in the legislative council. If the bill is not passed again by the legislative council or is blocked for a period of one month, the bill is considered to be passed from both the houses.

Constitutional proceedings

If a constitutional amendment bill is sent to a state legislature for recommendations, then the legislative council is an equal partner in the process of constitutional amendment. The council of ministers is responsible only to the legislative assembly. Legislative council cannot bring a no confidence motion to remove the council of ministers.

Chairman and deputy chairman of the legislative council

The chairman and deputy chairman of the legislative council are elected by the members of the house. The chairman or deputy chairman can be removed from their office only after serving a 14-day notice. Their salaries are drawn on the Consolidated Fund of the State.

Legislative Assembly

Article 170 of the Constitution of India states that there shall be a legislative assembly in every state of India whose members shall be directly elected by the people of the legislative constituencies of the state. It also states that the total number of members in a legislative assembly can be maximum 500 and minimum 60. But Sikkim with 32 members, Goa with 40 members, Mizoram with 40 members and Arunachal Pradesh with 40 members are exceptions to this rule. The delimitation recognition of a constituency of state legislative assembly is decided by the Election Commission of India. Prior to the formation of Jharkhand, total number of members of Bihar legislative assembly was 324 that was reduced to 243 after the partion of the state. Out of this, 242 members are required to be elected by direct election, and the governor shall recommends the name of one Anglo-Indian as a representative of that community for the remaining one seat but the reservation for people from the Anglo-Indian community in the state legislative assemblies have been abrogated by 104th constitutional amendment in December 2019.

The tenure of a legislative assembly is 5 years, but in case of proclamation of emergency, it can be increased by 6 months. Its tenure can be increased maximum by 1 year at a time. This provision is stated in a Article 172(1) of the Constitution of India. The proceedings of legislative assembly can be terminated earlier in case no party is able to win majority or if the present government loses its confidence. The session of legislative assembly is called by the governor, and the maximum gap between two sessions of legislative assembly can be 6 months. Out of total 243 seats in Bihar legislative assembly, 38 seats are reserved for the scheduled castes and 2 seats are reserved for the scheduled tribes.

Qualifications to become a member of legislative assembly

1. He should be a citizen of India and at least 25 years of age.
2. He should not be holding any office of profit in the Government of India or in any state government.
3. He should be mentally sound and not insolvent.

Speaker and deputy speaker of legislative assembly

The provision of one speaker and one deputy speaker has been assigened to legislative assembly of every state through Article 178 of the Constitution of India. They are elected by the members of the legislative assembly. The speaker of the state legislative assembly is the presiding officer of the house in the same way as the speaker of the Lok Sabha. In the absence of the speaker, deputy speaker presides over the proceedings of house. The speaker and deputy speaker can be removed from the position only by a no confidence motion after serving a 14-day notice to them.

Powers of the speaker of legislative assembly

1. He/she delivers the governor's message to the legislative assembly and informs the governor about the decisions of the assembly.
2. If the number of votes in favour and against any motion introduced in the assembly are not equal, then the speaker does not take part in the process of vote division, but if the votes are equal then he is allowed to cast his decisive vote for or against the motion.
3. After a bill is passed by both the Houses, peaker of the legislative assembly puts his signature on it.
4. Speaker is neutral to any party in the legislative assembly.

Rights of members of legislative assembly

According to Article 194 of the Constitution of India, a member of a state legislative assembly has the right to express himself in the house with act prior permission from the speaker of the house. Statements made by a member on the floor of the house can not be challenged in any court of India on any grounds. The members of legislative assemblies cannot be arrested 40 days prior to or after the session of legislature of civil matters.

Proceedings of Legislative Assembly

Legislative proceedings

State legislative assembly has the power to frame laws on subjects mentioned in the State list as well as Concurrent list. Any bill that has been passed by the legislative assembly is tabled in the legislative council. Legislative council can either give its consent or make some amendments to it or it can withhold it for a maximum period of three months. After the bill is passed again in the legislative assembly it is again sent to legislative council to get it passed. This time, the legislative council can again make amendments to it or it can withhold it for maximum period of one month. After this, the bill is considered to be passed from both the houses with or without amendments.

Financial proceedings

Money bill can be introduced in the state legislative assembly only. Once a money bill is passed from the legislative assembly, it is sent to the legislative council. The legislative council is bound to act on it within a period of 14 days. After this, the legislative assembly is not bound to accept the amendments proposed by the legislative council. Legislative council can pass it with or without amending. Afterwards, it is sent to the governor for his/her consent. The governor is bound to give his/her consent to a money bill.

Constitutional proceedings

The Parliament of India needs the approval of at least half state legislative assemblies of India in order to amend some articles of the Constitution of India. The members of legislative assemblies have a right to participate in the process of election of the President of India. Members of the legislative council do not enjoy this right. Members of the legislative assembly elect one-third members of the legislative council. The members of legislative assembly participate in election of the representatives of their state in Rajya Sabha. Legislative assembly has full control over the council of ministers. Council of ministers of the state is responsible to the legislative assembly. No confidence motion against the Council of ministers can only be brought in the legislative assembly. A resolution passed by two-thirds majority in the legislative assembly can be sent to the Parliament of India for consideration to create or abrogate legislative council in the state. Legislative assembly of a state can penalize any person for breach of privilege of the house.

CHIEF MINISTER AND THE COUNCIL OF MINISTERS IN THE STATE

According to the provisions of Article 163 of the Constitution of India, there shall be a council of ministers to advices and assist the governor in discharging his/her duties and that council of ministers shall be headed by the chief minister of the state. The executive power of the state rests with the governor, but in reality, this power is enjoyed by the chief minister along with his council of ministers.

Formation of council of ministers

According to Article 164 of the Constitution of India, the governor appoints the chief minister of a state. It is a common practice to appoint the leader of the party or alliance that has secured majority in the elections as the chief minister of the state. But if any party or alliance fails to get majority, then the Governor can use his discretionary power to appoint the chief minister of the state. If a person who is not a member of any house is elected as the leader of majority party or alliance then it is mandatory for him or her to become a member of either house within a time span of 6 months from the day that person assumes the office. Remaining members of the council of ministers are appointed by the governor on the advice of the chief minister. If a person who is not a member of any house of state legislature is appointed as a minister then it is mandatory for him to become a member of either house within 6 months from his date of appointment in order to remain a minister.

After the 91st constitutional amendment, 2003 came into effect, the total number of ministers including the chief minister cannot exceed 15 percent of the total strength of state legislative assembly, but this number cannot be less than 12. The council of ministers is collectively responsible to the legislative assembly, and personally they are responsible to the governor. Monthly salaries and allowances of the ministers are decided by the legislative bodies of the state. Every minister takes the oath of office and confidentiality in front of the governor before assuming his/her charges as a minister.

Functions of council of ministers

The state legislature carries out the administrative, legislative and financial activities in the state just like the Parliament of India. The council of ministers acts as the torch bearer of legislature as well as the center of administration of state. The council of ministers acts as a bridge between the legislature and the executive. All the programs related to the proceedings of legislative assembly are prepared by the council of ministers prior to the start of session. Any decision regarding introduction of any bill in the house is done through this process. Members of the council of ministers take part in all the meetings of the state legislature because they are a member of the legislature. Any question asked on the floor of house has to be answered by the minister of the concerned department. Prior to introduction of budget in the legislative assembly, it is approved by the council of ministers. Approval of expenditures from different heads, imposition of any new tax on the people of the state, issue of grants to local bodies, etc. are some important tasks of the council of ministers. It is the responsibility of the council of ministers to ensure that the laws made by the legislature are implemented on ground. All the important appointments of the state made by the governor are done on the advice of the council of ministers.

Tenure

According to the provisions of article 164(1) of the Constitution of India, the tenure of the state council of ministers is of 5 years. All the members of council of ministers remain in their office till the pleasure of the governor. In order to remove any minister from the council of ministers, the government has to act according to the advice of the chief minister. Normally the council of ministers remains in existence till the time the government enjoys majority in the house. If the chief minister resigns from his office, the council of ministers is assumed to be dissolved. In case the constitutional machinery in the state fails, then through the provisions of Article 356 of the Indian constitution, the council of ministers can be dissolved before expiry of the term. The council of ministers dissolves as soon as the tenure of legislative assembly ends.

Functions of the chief minister

Chief minister is the head of the cabinet. The administration of the state is entirely under the control of the chief minister. The cabinet of state is formed by the governor on the advice of the chief minister. The ranks of cabinet minister, minister of state, independent charge and minister of state are assigned by the chief minister. The distribution of department to different ministers is done by the governor at the advice of the chief minister. The council of ministers can be reshuffled from time-to-time at the advice of the chief minister. The chief minister acts as a bridge between the governor and the council of ministers. The chief minister delivers the governor's message to the council of ministers, and he also informs the governor about the decisions of the council of ministers. Chief minister is considered to be the leader of the state legislature.

ADVOCATE GENERAL

There is an Advocate General in every state who shall be an officer of the state just like the Attorney General in the center (Article 165). The Advocate General is the law officer of the state. He is appointed by the governor. The eligibility for a person to be appointed as the Advocate Genereal is the same as the eligibility to become a judge in the High Courts but there are no specific qualifications regarding his age that is required for this position. The tenure of the Advocate General depends upon the pleasure of the governor. Some of his important duties are–advicing the state government on issues related to law and rules, discharging the legal obligations that have been assigned to him by the governor, discharging any legal duty assigned to him by the constitution or any other act, etc. The Advocate General is allowed to take part in proceedings of the state legislature or any committee which he is a member of, besides being allowed to speak in the same. He is not allowed to vote in any HGouse of the state legislature.

LOKAYUKTA

Lokayukta is an anti-corruption organization that established by the states of India. It established on the lines of 'ombudsman', popular in the Scandenavian countries. Justice Sridhar Basudeva Sohni became the first Lokayukta of Bihar, and his tenure was from 28 May, 1971, to 25 May, 1978. Till date 8 Lokayukts have served in Bihar. President of India gave his consent to the Lokpal and Lokayukt Act 2013, on 1 January, 2014 according to which the functions of a Lokayukta are as follows:

1. Investigate the complaints of citizens related to justice and harassment that arise due to bad governance;
2. Provide for investigation into complaints of corruption, misuse of powers and dishonesty against public servants; information regarding such kinds of auxiliary works towards eradication of corruption and redressal of complaints can be provided by a notification from the office of the governor;
3. Supervision of investigations of anti-corruption agencies, officers and proposals;
4. Investigate any action on the orders of governor.

Lokayukt a submits annual report on the work undataken to the governor. In order to investigate the chief minister, ministers, members of legislative assembly and legislative council and officials of the state government it is mandatory to get approval from the state government. The tenure of Lokayukta is 5 years.

IMPORTANT COMMISSIONS

State Election Commission

The State Election Commission mentioned in Article 243(T) of the Constitution of India is an organization that is responsible for successful completion of panchayat elections in the state. A state election commissioner comes under this institution who is appointed by the governor. Responsibilities of preparation of electoral roll for the panchayat elections and successful operation, direction and completion of election rests solely with the state election commissioner. The conditions required to remove a judge of high court from his office applies to the process of removal of state election commissioner.

Bihar Human Rights Commission

In order to safeguard human rights in the State of Bihar, a Human Rights Commission was established on 3 January, 2000. It was reconstructed on 26 June, 2008. Former Chief Justice of Jammu and Kashmir High Court and Rajasthan High Court, Mr. S N Jha was appointed as the first chairman of Bihar Human Rights Commission. This commission draws its rights and powers from the Human Rights Protection Act, 2003. Apart form other factors its autonomy is guaranteed by the appointment process of its members, their fixed tenure, legal guarantee drawn from Section 23 and financial independence provided by Section 33 of the Act. Only a retired judge of a High Court of India can be appointed as its chairman.

The commission takes cognizance of matters related to human rights violation, harassment by police, custodial deaths, death in police encounters, harassment at the hands of any other public servant, etc. The commission expresses its views on those matters that have the possibilities of human rights violation.

State Women Commission

State Women Commission has been established in order to safeguard the rights of women and their welfare, and to keep a vigil on all state-run programs. Apart from a chairman of the commission 7 non-government members are nominated in the commission by the state government on the basis of their ability. Out of these 7 members, there is a provision to nominate one member each from the scheduled castes, scheduled tribes, minorities, backward castes, one member from among the persons having experience in the field of law, experience of self-service organizations and one experienced in the field of social welfare. All these members are women. The tenure of State Women Commission is decided by the government or it can be maximum 3 years. Some of their important functions are as follows:

1. Investigate and enquire all the facts related to women safety in the existing legal structure.
2. Send an annual report about the work of the commission towards improving women safety, to the government.
3. Sub-mitting recommendations regarding the efficient steps taken for improving women's safety in the state in its annual report.
4. To bring the matters of oppression against women in the state as well as the violation of laws related to women in the notice of concerned authorities.
5. Take note of complaints or take self-cognizance of irregularities in the laws framed for providing full rights to women, safeguarding the existing rights, women equality, and their development.

Bihar Public Service Commission

The provision of Union Public Service Commision for the Union of India and State Public Service Commission for the state has been mentioned in Article 315 of the Constitution of India. Bihar Public Service Commision became functional on 1 April, 1949. Its members are appointed for a period of 6 years, or till they attain the age of 65 years, whichever is earlier. The chairman as well as the members of the commission are appointed by the governor. Shri Rajdhari Sinha was the first chairman of Bihar Public Service Commission.

State Information Commission

The Right to Information Act has come into force in the whole of India (except than Jammu and Kashmir) from October 12, 2005. The basic duty under this Act is that in a democratic regime, the government and the government machinery should be accountable to the public and there should be transparency in the activities of the government machinery. According to Section 15 of the Act, the State Information Commission has been constructed for each state government by notification of the state government on August 22, 2005. The number of State Information Commissioners in the State Information Commission will not exceed 10, can be kept as per the requirement. The headquarter of the commission is in Patna.

Bihar Staff Selection Commission

Bihar Staff Selection Commission was established on 4 November 1975 and has been established for the appointment of non-gazetted class 3 officials below 6,500 to 10,500 pay grade (Fifth Pay Commission) through the Act number 7/2002 of the Bihar Government. With its formation School Services Board was merged with it. Position for one chairman and two members were created for the Commission. The state government nominates secretary level class 1 officers from the Indian Administrative Services, from various departments as the members of the commission.

❑❑❑

Administrative System

- Divisional Administration
- Sub-divisional Administration
- District Administration
- Block Administration

An independent administrative set up was established in the state after the formation of the separate state of Bihar in the year 1912. The administrative structure of Bihar emerged in a new shape after the creation separation of separate states of Odisha in 1936 and Jharkhand in 2000. At present there are 44 different departments in Bihar secretariat. Businesses in all these departments are transacted by the governor. A minister is the head of his/her department. He/she can appoint one government and one private secretary to assist him/her with his/her works. His/her other associates include staffs like personal assistant and typist, etc. Other than the secretaries, his associates also include special secretary, additional secretary, joint secretary, deputy secretary and director. Number of posts in a department can be increased by the approval from finance department.

In order to assist the chief minister oversee the function of all these departments, and discharge his/her other duties, there is a secretariat. In general, a senior official from the Indian Administrative services is appointed as the chief of the chief minister's secretariat and additional secretaries, deputy secretaries and other secretaries are appointed as his/her associates. The chief secretary of the secretariat is also the chairman of the public services. He/she is the focal point of coordination and cooperation among all the departments. Since the chief secretary is the chief advisor of the cabinet, he is also the head of government machinery. It is the chief secretary who presents documented list of secretaries of all the departments to the chief minister and as the chief public relations officer he/she also acts as the bridge in the negotiations between his/her state and the central government as well as other states. Providing secretarial assistance to the Chief Minister and the council of ministers, obtaining required information from the office of governor and chief minister and forwarding it in official capacity, giving advice in the matters of formation and implementation of departmental policies, preparing the drafts of urgent ordinance, preparing the messages and speeches to be read out by the Governor, taking requisite and necessary action on the advices from different ministries, preparing of budget on the advice from the finance ministry, giving advice on the suggestions that come during the days of financial emergencies, framing rules regarding salaries, appointments and promotions in the state, taking necessary actions regarding transfer and postings, etc., preparing the annual report about functions of different departments, etc., are some of the main works of the secretariat.

In addition to this, ensuring the collection of public revenue, framing the polices and directions in order to ensure the smooth functioning of departmental affairs, selecting candidates for training and framing training policies, forming different committees as per the requirement and ensuring timely and appropriate disbursement of grants coming from the central and state government are other chief functions of the secretariat.

In order to run the administration, the administrative structure has been divided into five levels that carry out the functions of framing government policies, rules and programs. Divisional administration, district administration, sub-divisional administration, block level administration and Gram Panchayat level of administration are included in the five-layered structure of administration in state.

DIVISIONAL ADMINISTRATION

There are nine divisions in the state, and they are headed by Divisional Commissioners. These commissioners are senior and seasoned officers of the Indian Administrative Services. The work profile of a commissioner includes supervising the legislative and development related works of district magistrate, and some duties related to court proceedings. In addition to a secretary, equivalent to the rank of additional district magistrate, the associates of a commissioner include a deputy director (food), deputy director (panchayati raj) and additional district magistrate (flying squad).

DISTRICT ADMINISTRATION

The state is divided into 38 districts. District magistrate is the chief of administration in a district. He/she discharges his/her duties in various roles. Collection of land revenue, collection of canal and other duties, collection of state loans, evaluation of different national calamities and extending government help for the same, effective implementation of stamp act, works related to general and special land acquisition, payments against jamindari bonds, proper maintenance of all land records, works related to land registration, maintaining the statistical records, etc. are the duties of a district magistrate.

Execution of government orders, making arrangements for district treasury, training administrative services officers, issuing citizenship certificates and character certificates, making arrangements for and settlement of Scheduled Casts, backward classes, army personnel and landless persons, making deputations of magistrates in district collectorate, taking appropriate decisions on pension-related matters of officers and staffs of state government, arranging for regular meetings of district level committees and chairing the same, making apt security arrangements in case of visits by ministers from center and state, regulating budgets of all district level personnel, making necessary security arrangements during visits by the president, vice president or the prime minister in the district are some of the chief functions of a district magistrate. Some other important works of a district magistrate include taking note of complaints of common people along with the necessary actions on them, supervising the district education officers in order to ensure the quality of education in the district, supervising on matters related to ensuring the supply of items of basic necessity in the district, keeping a check on officers of sub-divisional level/ village level as well as granting leaves to them.

Appointments of magistrate during festivals and VIP visits in the district issuing caste certificates to people belonging to scheduled castes and scheduled tribes ensuring flag march by the army and security personnel in affected areas during the times of violence, riots and arson taking necessary steps if there seems a failure of rule of law in the district like imposing curfew, etc., appointing of acting magistrates; making pre-scheduled, scheduled or unscheduled visits to district prison, assigning categories to the prisoners on the grounds of their behaviour and releasing them on parole; presenting the annual crime records of the district to the state government; annual inspections of all the police stations falling within the purview of district; payment of grants to the victims of violence, calamities, accidents and extremism; ensuring peaceful completion of all the district level elections;

ensuring levy and collection of entertainment tax on associated institutions; ensuring that voter list is up-to-date; performing the delimitation of all Lok Sabha and Vidhan Sabha constituencies; ensuring successful completion of all works related to census, etc., are some of duties that fall within the magisterial purview of district magistrate.

Some of the primary duties of a district magistrate are to ensure proper coordination with the superintendent of police in the police department, forest officer in the forest department, assistant registrar from the cooperative department, district agriculture officer in the agriculture department, assistant mining officer in the mining ministry, civil surgeon from the health department, assistant registrar in the department of registration, district industry officer in the department of industries, superintendent in the manufacturing department and district supply officer in the supplies department. Thus, a district magistrate is the chief of a district who, in his/her full authority and capacity acts as a bridge between the residents of his/her districts and the state government.

SUB-DIVISIONAL ADMINISTRATION

There are 101 sub-divisions in Bihar. Sub-divisional administration falls below the divisional and district administration, and it is headed by sub-divisional magistrate (SDM). This position is given to an officer either from the Indian Administrative Services or the State Administrative Services. Bihar employs officers from both the services in its sub-divisional administration. These officers discharge various duties in their region just like a district magistrate in his/her district. They play an important role in disposing off matters related to revenue, law and order, and justice. In addition to this, they also supervise the development programs in their sub-division. These officers are also responsible for collection of agricultural and land revenue, and they conduct hearings for appeals against the orders by circle officers. They appoint officers and staffs to work as their subordinates. They keep a check on police and pass necessary orders in order to maintain law and order in their region. They also give recommendations on requests for issue of arms and carry out annual inspection for the same. Apart from these tasks, they also makes necessary security arrangements for VIPs visiting their region.

BLOCK ADMINISTRATION

There are 534 blocks in Bihar. Block administration is the second level in district administration that includes circle officer, block development officer, block agriculture officer, animal husbandry officer, block supplies officer, block welfare officer and other designated officers. Out of these, the work of circle officer and bloc development officer are very important.

Circle Officer and his duties

The position of circle officer is often given to officers promoted from state administrative services and other services. Maintenance and upkeep of land revenue, land records, law and order, election, census and agricultural statistics; issuance of income certificate and caste certificate; residential certificate; maintenance of law and order; along with peace and harmony among various groups during festivals and making necessary security arrangements for VIP visits; preserving land-related rights of people from tribal communities; completion of all work related to public welfare; calculation and issuance of compensation to the victims of calamities, riots, violence and accidents in their region are some of the works carried out by them in their circle and village areas.

Block Development Officer and his works

This position is given to officers from the Indian Administration Services and State Administrative Services. The officer acts as a coordinator and associate to officer in every department in the block. Implementation of schemes by the central government, giving his/her recommendation to applications regarding self-employment in village areas, and implementing developmental works in village areas are some of his/her main duties.

Divisions, Districts and Sub-divisions in Bihar

Division	District	Sub-division
1. Patna	1. Patna	1. Patna Sadar, 2. Danapur, 3. Barh, 4. Patna City, 5. Masaurhi
	2. Nalanda	1. Bihar Sharif Sadar, 2. Hilsa, 3. Rajgir
	3. Rohtas	1. Sasaram Sadar, 2. Bikramganj, 3. Dehri
	4. Bhabua (Kaimur)	1. Bhabua Sadar, 2. Mohania
	5. Bhojpur (Arrah)	1. Arrah Sadar, 2. Jagdishpur, 3. Piro
	6. Buxar	1. Buxar Sadar, 2. Dumraon
2. Magadh	1. Gaya	1. Gaya Sadar, 2. Sherghati, 3. Tekari, 4. Nimchak, 5. Bathani
	2. Jehanabad	1. Jehanabad Sadar
	3. Arwal	1. Arwal Sadar
	4. Nawada	1. Nawada Sadar, 2. Rajauli
	5. Aurangabad	1. Aurangabad Sadar, 2. Daudnagar
3. Saran (Chhapra)	1. Saran (Chhapra)	1. Chhapra Sadar, 2.Marhaura, 3. Sonpur
	2. Siwan	1. Siwan Sadar, 2. Maharajganj
	3. Gopalganj	1. Gopalganj Sadar, 2. Hathua
4. Tirhut (Muzaffarpur)	1. Muzaffarpur	1. Muzaffarpur East, 2. Muzaffarpur West
	2. Sitamarhi	1. Sitamarhi Sadar, 2. Pupri, 3. Belsand
	3. Sheohar	1. Sheohar Sadar
	4. West Champaran (Betia)	1. Bettiah, 2. Bagaha, 3. Narkatiaganj
	5. East Champaran	1. Motihari Sadar, 2. Areraj, 3. Chakia, 4. Pakdidayal, 5. Raxaul, 6. Sikaharna
	6. Vaishali	1. Hajipur, 2. Mahua, 3. Mahnar

5. Darbhanga	1. Darbhanga	1. Darbhanga Sadar, 2. Benipur, 3. Biraul
	2. Madhubani	1. Madhubani Sadar, 2. Benipatti, 3. Jainagar, 4. Jhanjharpur, 5. Phulparas
	3. Samastipur	1. Samastipur Sadar, 2. Dalsingh Sarai, 3. Patori, 4. Rosara
6. Kosi (Saharsa)	1. Saharsa	1. Saharsa, 2. Simri, 3. Bakhtiyarpur
	2. Supaul	1. Birpur, 2. Triveniganj, 3. Nirmali, 4. Supaul
	3. Madhepura	1. Madhepura, 2. Udakishunganj
7. Purnea Division	1. Purnea	1. Purnea Sadar, 2. Banmankhi, 3. Bayasi, 4 Dhamdaha
	2. Araria	1. Araria Sadar, 2. Forbesganj
	3. Kishanganj	1. Kishanganj
	4. Katihar	1. Katihar Sadar, 2. Barsoi, 3. Manihari
8. Bhagalpur	1. Bhagalpur	1. Bhagalpur Sadar, 2. Kahalgaon, 3. Naugachia
	2. Banka	1. Banka Sadar
9. Munger	1. Munger	1. Munger, 2. Haveli Khadagpur, 3. Tarapur
	2. Lakhisarai	1. Lakhisarai
	3. Jamui	1. Jamui
	4. Khagaria	1. Khagaria, 2. Gogri
	5. Sheikhpura	1. Sheikhpura
	6. Begusarai	1. Begusarai, 2. Teghra, 3. Balia, 4. Majhauli, 5. Bakhri

DETAILS OF DISTRICTS

The details of 38 districts are as follows:

1. Patna

Established	It is an ancient city
Borders	North – Saran South – Jehanabad East – Begusarai, Munger West – Bhojpur
Area	3202 sq km
Main rivers	Ganga, Son, Punpun, etc.

Administrative distribution

Headquarters	Patna
Division	Patna
Sub-division (6)	Patna Sadar, Patna City, Danapur, Barh, Masaurhi, Paliganj
Panchayat	327
Rajaswa Gram	1157

Constituencies

Lok Sabha constituencies: 2 (Patna Sahib and Patliputra)

Vidhan Sabha constituencies: 4 (Mokama, Badh, Bakhtiarpur, Digha, Bankipur, Kumhrar, Patna Sahib, Fatuha, Danapur, Maner, Phulwari, Masaurhi, Paliganj, Bikram)

Blocks (23)

1. Patna Sadar	2. Phulwari Sharif
3. Sampatchak	4. Fatuha
5. Khusrupur	6. Dhaniyawan
7. Bakhtiyarpur	8. Barh
9. Belchhi	10. Atmalgola
11. Mokama	12. Pandarak
13. Ghosvari	14. Bihta
15. Maner	16. Danapur
17. Naubatganj	18. Masaurhi
19. Dhanaura	20. Punpun
21. Paliganj	22. Bikram
23. Dulhin Bazar	

Geographical location

Latitudinal expanse	25°37'N
Longitudinal expanse	85°12'E
Temperature	46.6° C (max) 1.1° C (min)
Average rainfall	1052.6 mm
Height above sea level	53 m
Soil	Ancient tal soil

Demographic details (2011)

Total population	58,38,465
Population density	1823 persons per sq km
Decadal growth rate	23.7 percent (2001 - 2011)
Gender ratio	897 females per 1000 males
Literacy rate	70.7 percent
Male literacy rate	78.5 percent
Female literacy rate	62.0 percent
Languages	Magahi, Bhojpuri, Maithili, Hindi and Urdu

Primary industries: Sugar (Bihta), biscuit, bulb, tractor, sindur, gulal, crackers (Patna City), shoes (Digha and Mokama), freight rail wagons (Mokama), bronze industry, paper industry (Patna), alcohol, leather (Digha, Patna), tobacco, cotton garment industry, etc.

Chief crops: Flax seed, potato, millet, masur, rye, mustard, wheat, maize etc.

Tourist sites: Agam Kuan, Kamaldah, Mahavir Mandir, Jain Mandir, Darakhi Devi Mandir, Chhoti Patan Devi, Datiyana, Kumhrar, Panch Pahadi, Chhoti Pahadi, Maner Sharif, Gol Ghar, Shahid Smarak, etc.

2. Nalanda

Established	9 November, 1875
Border	North – Patna South – Nawada, Gaya East – Sheikhpura, Lakhisarai West – Jehanabad, Patna
Area	2,355 sq. km

Main rivers	Phalgu, Mohania

Administrative distribution

Headquarters	Bihar Sharif
Division	Patna
Sub Division (3)	Nalanda district, Bihar Sharif, Rajgir, and Hilsa

Constituencies

Lok Sabha constituencies: 1 (Nalanda)

Vidhan Sabha Constituencies: 7 (Bihar Sharif, Rajgir, Islampur – Nalanda, Haranaut, Nalanda, Asthawan, Hilsa)

Blocks (20)

1. Sarmera	2. Asthawan
3. Bihar Sharif	4. Rahui
5. Ajaypur Noorsarai	6. Tharthari
7. Islampur	8. Karai Parsarai
9. Nagarnausa	10. Bind
11. Hilsa	12. Ekangarsarai
13. Parvalpur	14. Harnaut
15. Chandi	16. Bena
17.Katrisarai	18. Rajgir
19.Silao	20 Giriyak

Geographical location

Latitudinal expanse	24°- 25°7' N
Longitudinal expanse	85° 18' - 85° 65 E
Temperature	40° C (max) 6° C (min)
Average rainfall	858.11 mm
Height above sea level	67 m
Soil	Red soil, bangar soil

Demographic details (2011)

Total population	28,77,653
Population density	1222 persons per sq km
Decadal growth rate	21.4 percent (2001-2011)
Gender ratio	922 females per 1000 males
Literacy rate	64.4 percent
Male literacy rate	74.9 percent
Female literacy rate	53.1 percent
Languages	Magahi and Hindi

Primary industries: Bidi industry and armament industry.

Chief crops: Paddy, maize, gram, onion, potato, etc.

Tourist sites: Buddhist era Nalanda, remains of the Nalanda University, Pawapuri, Rajgir, hot spring, Venu Van, Maniyar Math, Japanese temple, Shanti Stupa, Ghora Katora, Bargaon, Jagdishpur, etc.

3. Rohtas

Established	9 November, 1972
Border	North – Buxar and Bhojpur South – Kaimur hills East – Aurangabad West – Kaimur (Bhabhua)
Area	3881 sq km
Main rivers	Son, Kaav

Administrative distribution

Headquarters	Sasaram
Division	Patna
Sub-division (3)	Sasaram, Bikramganj, Dehri
Panchayat	246
Rajaswa Gram	2088

Constituencies

Lok Sabha constituencies: 2 (Sasaram, Karakat)

Vidhan Sabha constituencies: 7 (Karakat, Nokha, Dinara, Karaghar, Chenari, Dehri, Sasaram)

Blocks (19)

1. Karaghar	2. Kochas
3. Dinara	4. Dawath
5. Suryapura	6. Bikramganj
7. Karakat	8. Nokha
9. Sanjhauli	10. Rajpur
11. Nasriganj	12. Tilouthu
13. Akodhigola	14. Dehri
15. Sasaram	16. Shivsagar
17. Chenari	18. Rohtas
19. Nauhatta	

Geographical location

Latitudinal expanse	24° 30'- 25° 20' N

Longitudinal expanse	83° 14' - 85° 20 E
Temperature	45° C (max) 10° C (min)
Average rainfall	952 mm
Height above sea level	107.78 meters
Soil	Bangar soil, balthar soil

Demographic details (2011)

Total population	29,59,918
Population density	763 persons per sq km
Decadal growth rate	20.8 percent (2001 - 2011)
Gender ratio	918 females per 1000 males
Literacy rate	73.4 percent
Male literacy rate	82.9 percent
Female literacy rate	63 per cent
Languages	Bhojpuri and Hindi

Primary industries: Sugar, paper, soda, vegetable, casting industries in Dalmianagar, cement factories in Dalmianagar and Banjari, quilt and carpet, etc. are manufactured in Darihatt and Kabdih. Leather industry, oil mills, chemical fertilizer industries are located in Dalmianagar.

Chief crops: Paddy, wheat, etc.

Tourist sites: Shershah's tomb in Sasaram, Rohtas Fort, Indrapuri Dam (Dehri), Aashik, Tarachandi Mandir, etc.

4 Kaimur (Bhabua)

Established	1991
Border	North – Buxar and Uttar Pradesh South – Kaimur Hills East – Rohtas West – Uttar Pradesh and River Karmanasha
Area	3,332 sq km
Main rivers	Son, Karmanasha, Durgavati

Administrative distribution

Headquarters	Bhabua
Division	Patna
Sub-division (2)	Bhabua, Mohania

Constituencies

Lok Sabha constituencies: 1 (Sasaram)

Vidhan Sabha constituencies: 4 (Ramgarh – Kaimur, Chainpur, Bhabhua, Mohania)

Blocks (11)

1. Bhabhua	2. Ramgarh
3. Mohania	4. Durgawati
5. Adhuara	6. Bhagwanpur
7. Chand	8. Chainpur
9. Kudra	10. Rampur
11. Nuaon	

Geographical location

Latitudinal expanse	25° 02' N
Longitudinal expanse	83° 33 E
Temperature	45° C (max) 4° C (min)
Average rainfall	777 mm
Height above sea level	76 m
Soil	Bangar soil and balthar soil

Demographic details (2011)

Total population	16,26,384
Population density	488 persons per sq km
Decadal growth rate	26.2 percent (2001 - 2011)
Gender ratio	920 females per 1000 males
Literacy rate	69.3 percent
Male literacy rate	79.4 percent
Female literacy rate	58 percent
Languages	Bhojpuri, Hindi, English, Oraon, Urdu

Primary industries: Rice mill, oil mills, etc

Chief crops: Paddy, wheat, etc.

Tourist sites: Adhura, (Masahi on Kaimur Hills, Mandeshwari Devi Temple) etc.

5. Bhojpur

Bhojpur is a district located in western part of Bihar. Earlier it was a part of Shahabad. Shahabad district was established in 1972. In 1992, Shahabad district was divided and Bhojpur, Buxar, and Rohtas districts were formed.

Established	1992
Border	North – Uttar Pradesh and Saran District of Bihar South – Rohtas and Arwal East – Patna West – Buxar
Area	2,474 sq km
Main rivers	Son and Ganga

Administrative distribution

Headquarters	Arrah
Division	Patna
Sub-division (3)	Arrah-sardar, Jagdishpur and Piro

Constituencies

Lok Sabha constituencies: 1 (Arrah)

Vidhan Sabha Constituencies: 7 (Arrah, Jagdishpur, Barhara, Tarari, Sandesh, Agiaon and Shahpur)

Blocks (14)

1. Sandesh	2. Sahar
3. Agiaon	4. Piro
5. Udwantnagar	6. Garhani
7. Koilwar	8. Jagdishpur
9. Charpokhari	10. Shahpur
11. Bihiya	12. Arrah
13. Barhara	14. Tarari

Geographical location

Latitudinal expanse	25° 10'- 25° 40' N
Longitudinal expanse	83° 45' - 84° 45' E
Temperature	38° C (max) 11° C (min)
Average rainfall	1166.2 mm
Height above sea level	193 m
Soil	Bangar soil

Demographic details (2011)

Total population	27,28,407
Population density	1139 persons per sq km
Decadal growth rate	21.6 percent (2001 - 2011)
Gender ratio	907 females per 1000 males
Literacy rate	70.5 percent
Male literacy rate	81.7 percent
Female literacy rate	58 percent
Languages	Bhojpuri, Hindi and Urdu

Primary industries: Rice mill, small-scale industries of leather, oil mills, jaggery manufacturing mills, tobacco industry, garment industry, etc.

Chief crops: Paddy, wheat, and sugarcane

Tourist sites: Jagdishpur (birthplace of Babu Kunwar Singh), Aranyadevi Temple, Kunwar Singh Museum (Arrah), Koilwar Bridge (officially Abdul Bari Bridge), etc.

6. Buxar

Buxar is located in the western part of Bihar. Earlier it was a part of Shahabad district. In 1992, Shahabad district was divided into three separate districts—Rohtas, Bhojpur and Buxar.

Established	17 March, 1992
Border	North – Uttar Pradesh and River Ganga South – Kaimur (Bhabhua), Rohtas East – Bhojpur West – Uttar Pradesh and river Karmanasha
Area	1,703 sq km
Main rivers	Son, Karmanasha and Ganga

Administrative distribution

Headquarter	Buxar
Division	Patna
Sub-division (2)	Buxar, Dumraon
Panchayat	142
Rajasva Gram	1134

Constituencies

Lok Sabha Constituency: 1 (Buxar)

Vidhan Sabha Constituency: 4 (Buxar, Brahampur, Rajpur and Dumraon)

Blocks (11)

1. Chausa	2. Rajpur
3. Itarhi	4. Buxar
5. Dumraon	6. Nawanagar
7. Kesath	8. Chougain
9. Simri	10. Brahampur
11. Chakki	

Geographical location

Latitudinal expanse	25° 33' N
Longitudinal expanse	83° 58' E
Temperature	42° C (max) 10° C (min)
Average rainfall	774.82 mm
Height above sea level	55 m
Soil	Bangar soil

Demographic details (2011)

Total population	17,06,352
Population density	1002 persons per sq km
Decadal growth rate	21.7 percent (2001 - 2011)
Gender ratio	922 females per 1000 males
Literacy rate	70.1 percent
Male literacy rate	80.7 percent
Female literacy rate	58.6 percent
Languages	Bhojpuri and Hindi

Primary industries: Cotton yarns, garment and lantern industry, quilt and carpet industry, tobacco industry, etc.

Chief crops: Paddy and wheat

Tourist sites: Battlefield of Chausa, fort of Mir Qasim, Tadka Vadh Sthal, abode of Maharshi Vishvamitra, Naulakha Temle, etc. are some main tourist spots.

7 Gaya

Established	1865
Border	North – Jehanabad South – Jharkhand East – Nawada West – Aurangabad
Area	4976 sq km
Main rivers	Phalgu

Administrative distribution

Headquarters	Gaya
Division	Magadh
Sub-divisions (2)	Gaya Sadar, Neemchak, Bathani, Sherghati, Tekari

Constituencies

Lok Sabha constituencies: 1 (Gaya)

Vidhan Sabha constituencies: 10 (Gaya Sadar, Belaganj, Atri, Tekari, Sherghati, Gurua, Bodh Gaya, Wazirganj, Barachatti)

Blocks (24)

1. Dobhi	2. Mohanpur
3. Barachatti	4. Imamganj
5. Sherghati	6. Dumariya
7. Banke Bazaar	8. Amas
9. Gurua	10. Konch
11. Tekari	12. Guraru
13. Paraiya	14. Belaganj
15. Fatehpur	16. Tankuppa
17.Khizarsarai	18. Neemchak Bathani
19. Atri	20. Muhra
21. Manpur	22. Bodh Gaya
21.Wazirganj	24. Gaya Sadar
25. Amas	

Geographical location

Latitudinal expanse	24° 5'- 24° 10' N
Longitudinal expanse	84° 4' - 84° 5' E
Temperature	49° C (max) 2° C (min)
Average rainfall	1242 mm
Height above sea level	111 m
Soil	Bangar soil

Demographic details (2011)

Total population	4391418
Population density	883 persons per sq km
Decadal growth rate	26.4 percent (2001 - 2011)
Gender ratio	937 females per 1000 males
Literacy rate	63.7 percent
Male literacy rate	73.3 percent

Female literacy rate	53.3 percent
Languages	Magahi and Hindi

Primary industries: Cotton garments (Gaya), sugar, lac industry, oil mills, etc.

Chief crops: Paddy, wheat, maize, sugarcane, flaxseed, millet, etc.

Tourist sites: Bodh Gaya, Vishnupad Temple, Buddhist Temple, Sujata Garh, Ramshila Hills, Pretshila Hills, Guneri, Brahmayoni Hills, Taradih, Hekari Fort, Kurisarai, Hasra Kol, Shobhnath, Great Buddha Statue, Surya Kund, Chinese Temple, Mangla Gauri Temple, Tibetan Monastry, Jama Masjid, Indosan Nippon Japanese Temple, etc.

8 Jehanabad

The district of Jehanabad was carved out from Gaya. Prior to this, it was a sub-division of Gaya.

Established	1 August, 1986
Border	North – Patna South – Gaya and Aurangabad East – Nalanda West – Bhojpur and Arwal
Area	931 sq km
Main rivers	Phalgu

Administrative distribution

Headquarters	Jehanabad
Division	Magadh
Sub-divisions (1)	Jehanabad
Panchayat	93
Rajaswa Gram	611

Constituencies

Lok Sabha constituencies: 1 (Jehanabad)

Vidhan Sabha Constituencies: 3 (Jehanabad, Makhdumpur, Ghosi)

Blocks (7)

1. Jehanabad	2. Makhdumpur
3. Kako	4. Ghosi
5. Ratni Faridpur	6. Hulasganj
7. Modanganj	

Geographical location

Latitudinal expanse	25° 0'- 25° 15' N
Longitudinal expanse	84° 31' - 85° 15' E
Temperature	45° C (max) 0.8° C (min)
Average rainfall	1074.5 mm
Height above sea level	113 m
Soil	Balthar soil and ancient soil

Demographic details (2011)

Total population	11,25,313
Population density	1209 persons per sq km
Decadal growth rate	N A
Gender ratio	922 females per 1000 males
Literacy rate	66.8 percent
Male literacy rate	77.7 percent
Female literacy rate	55.0 percent
Languages	Magahi and Hindi

Primary industries: No major industry is present in the district

Chief crops: Paddy, wheat, maize, khesari, etc

Tourist sites: Nagarjun Museum, Baba Siddhnath Temple, Sapt gufa (seven caves), Mirabigaha, Lomas Rishi cave, Karn gufa, Ghejan Gopi gufa, Vishva jhopdi, Sudama gufa, Nagarjun gufa, tomb of Hazrat Kamal Bibi, cave of Barabar, etc.

9 Arwal

The district of Arwal was carved out from Jehanabad. Arwal is situated on the banks of River Son.

Established	September 2001
Border	North – Bhojpur South –Aurangabad East – Jehanabad West – Rohtas
Area	638 sq km
Main rivers	Son

Administrative distribution

Headquarters	Arwal
Division	Magadh
Sub-divisions (1)	Arwal Sadar
Panchayat	65

Rajaswa Gram	335

Constituencies

Lok Sabha constituencies: 1 (Arwal)

Vidhan Sabha Constituencies : 2 (Arwal and Kurtha)

Blocks (5)

1. Arwal	2. Kurtha
2. Kaler	4. Sonbhadra Banshi Suryapur
5. Karpi	

Geographical location

Latitudinal expanse	25° 0'- 25° 15' N
Longitudinal expanse	84° 7' - 85° 15' E
Temperature	42° C (max) 14° C (min)
Average rainfall	817 mm
Height above sea level	67.9 m
Soil	Ancient soil

Demographic details (2011)

Total population	7,00,843
Population density	1099 persons per sq km
Decadal growth rate	19 percent
Gender ratio	928 females per 1000 males
Literacy rate	67.4 percent
Male literacy rate	79.1 percent
Female literacy rate	54.9 percent
Languages	Magahi and Hindi

Primary industries: Total number of industrial units in the district is 850. Out of these, the number of registered industrial units is 169. Industries based on agriculture are in abundance. Timber and metal based industries are functional in the district.

Chief crops: Paddy, wheat, maize and gram are the chief crops of the district.

Tourist sites: None

10. Nawada

Border	North – Nalanda South–Hazaribagh (Jharkhand) East – Sheikhpura and Jamui West – Gaya
Area	2494 sq km
Main rivers	Sakri

Administrative distribution

Headquarters	Nawada
Division	Magadh
Sub-divisions (2)	Nawada, Rajauli
Panchayat	187
Rajaswa Gram	1081

Constituencies

Lok Sabha constituencies: 1 (Nawada)

Vidhan Sabha Constituencies: 5 (Nawada, Warisaliganj, Rajauli, Hisua, Govindpur)

Blocks (14)

1.Warisaliganj	2. Kashichak
3. Pakribarawan	4. Kawakole
5. Hisua	6. Narhat
7.Meskaur	8. Sirdala
9. Rajauli	10. Akbarpur
11. Govindpur	12. Nawada
13.Roh	14. Nardiganj

Geographical location

Latitudinal expanse	25° 31'- 25° 08' N
Longitudinal expanse	84° 00' - 86° 30' E
Temperature	46° C (max) 4° C (min)
Average rainfall	1037 mm
Height above sea level	80 m
Soil	Bangar soil

Demographic details (2011)

Total population	22,19,146
Population density	890 persons per sq km
Decadal growth rate	22.6 percent
Gender ratio	939 females per 1000 males
Literacy rate	59.8 percent
Male literacy rate	70.0 percent
Female literacy rate	48.9 percent
Languages	Bhojpuri, Hindi, and Urdu

Primary industries: Asbestos, sugar, etc.

Chief crops: Paddy, wheat, lentils, oilseeds, etc.

Tourist sites: Kakolat Waterfalls, Sekhodevra Ashram, Kawakole Hills, Apsadh Garh, Parvati Hills, Baba Ki Mazar, Narad Museum, Guniyaji Teerth (pilgrimage), Hanuman Temple, Prajatantra Dwar, etc.

11. Aurangabad

Aurangabad district was carved out from Gaya. Prior to this, it was a sub-division of Gaya district.

Established	19 November, 1973
Border	North – Arwal and Jehanabad South –Palamu (Jharkhand) East – Gaya West – Rohtas
Area	3305 sq km
Main rivers	Son, Punpun, Auranga, Batane, Morhar, and Adari

Administrative distribution

Headquarters	Aurangabad
Division	Magadh
Sub-divisions (2)	Aurangabad, Daudnagar

Constituencies

Lok Sabha constituencies: 1 (Aurangabad)

Vidhan Sabha Constituencies : 6 (Aurangabad, Nabinagar, Rafiganj, Kutumba, Obra, and Goh)

Blocks (11)

1. Barun	2. Kutumba
3. Aurangabad	3. Rafiganj
4. Madanpur	6. Deo
7. Goh	8. Haspura
9. Obra	10. Daudnagar
11. Nabinagar	

Geographical location

Latitudinal expanse	24° 19'- 26° 10' N
Longitudinal expanse	84° 00' - 84° 55' E
Temperature	40° C (max) 5° C (min)
Average rainfall	1231 mm
Height above sea level	30 to 65 m
Soil	Residual soil

Demographic details (2011)

Total population	25,40,073
Population density	769 persons per sq km
Decadal growth rate	26.2 percent
Gender ratio	926 females per 1000 males
Literacy rate	70.3 percent
Male literacy rate	80.1 percent
Female literacy rate	59.7 percent
Languages	Magahi and Hindi

Primary industries: Quilt, cloth, carpet, paan (beetle leaves), etc. Quilt is manufactured in Tandva, and carpet and cloth are manufactured in Obra.

Chief crops: Paddy, wheat and maize are chief crops of this district.

Tourist sites: Sun Temple in Dev, Fort of Daudnagar, Tomb of Shamsher Khan in Shamsher Nagar, Mausoleum of Raja Narayan Singh in Pawai, Jhunjhunwa Hills, etc.

12. Saran

Established	1981
Border	North – Gopalganj, East Champaran South – Bhojpur, Patna East – Vaishali, Muzaffarpur West – Siwan, Uttar Pradesh
Area	2641 sq km
Main rivers	Ganga, Ghaghra, and Gandak

Administrative distribution

Headquarters	Saran
Division	Saran
Sub-divisions (3)	Chhapra, Marhaura and Sonpur

Constituencies

Lok Sabha constituencies: 1 (Chhapra)

Vidhan Sabha Constituencies: 6 (Chhapra, Ekma, Manji, Baniyapur, Marhaura, Sonpur, Taraiya, Garcha, Parsa, and Amnaur)

Blocks (20)

1. Rivilganj	2. Manjhi
3. Ekma	4. Lahladpur
5. Nagra	6. Baniapur
7. Eisuapur	8. Chhapra Sadar
9. Jalalpur	10. Garkha
11. Taraiya	12. Masrakh
13. Panapur	14. Marhaura
15. Amnaur	16. Maker
17. Parsa	18. Sonpur
19. Dariyapur	20 Dighwara

Geographical location

Latitudinal expanse	25° 36'- 26° 13' N
Longitudinal expanse	84° 24' - 85° 15' E
Temperature	42° C (max) 10° C (min)
Average rainfall	818.87 mm
Height above sea level	36 m
Soil	Residual soil, alluvial soil, loam soil

Demographic details (2011)

Total population	39,51,862
Population density	1469 persons per sq km
Decadal growth rate	26.2 percent
Gender ratio	954 females per 1000 males
Literacy rate	66 percent
Male literacy rate	77 percent
Female literacy rate	54.4 percent
Languages	Bhojpuri, Hindi, Urdu, and Maithili

Primary industries: Sugar mills, brass industry and handicraft industry, chocolate industry, etc.

Chief crops: Paddy, wheat, barley, and maize are chief crops of this district.

Tourist sites: Sonpur Mela, Harihar pilgrimage site, Kali Temple in Ami, Abode of rishi Gautam in Rivilganj, Chirand, Dodh Ashram, birth place of Bharat Ratna Lok Nayak Jai Prakash Narayan in Sitabdiara, etc.

13. Siwan

Established	11 December, 1972
Border	North – Gopalganj South – Saran, Uttar Pradesh East – Gopalganj, Saran West – Uttar Pradesh
Area	2219 sq km
Main rivers	Daha, Jharhi

Administrative distribution

Headquarter	Siwan
Division	Saran
Sub-divisions (2)	Siwan Sadar and Maharajganj
Panchayat	293
Rajaswa Gram	1530

Constituencies

Lok Sabha Constituencies: 2 (Siwan, Maharajganj)

Vidhan Sabha Constituencies: 8 (Siwan, Barharia, Raghunathpur, Ziradei, Goriakothi, Daraundha, Maharajganj, and Darauli)

Blocks (19)

1. Pachrukhi	2. Daraundha
3. Maharajganj	4. Barharia
5. Goriakothi	6. Raghunathpur
7. Siswan	8. Andar
9. Darauli	10. Mairwa
11. Guthani	12. Siswan
13. Hussainganj	14. Bhagwanpur Hat
15. Lakri Nabiganj	16. Basantpur
17. Hasan Pura	18. Nautan
19. Ziradei	

Geographical location

Latitudinal expanse	25° 53'- 26° 23' N
Longitudinal expanse	84° 01' - 85° 47' E
Temperature	44° C (max) 10° C (min)
Average rainfall	1200 mm
Height above sea level	77 m
Soil	Alluvial soil, loamy soil

Demographic details (2011)

Total population	33,30,464

Population density	1501 persons per sq km
Decadal growth rate	27.2 percent
Gender ratio	988 females per 1000 males
Literacy rate	69.5 percent
Male literacy rate	80.2 percent
Female literacy rate	58.7 percent
Languages	Bhojpuri, Hindi, Urdu, and Maithili

Primary industries: Sugar mills, brass industry, and handicraft industry, clay and pottery industry, etc.

Chief crops: Paddy, wheat, and sugarcane

Tourist sites: Ziradei (birth place of Dr. Rajendra Prasad), Baba Mahendranath Temple.

14. Gopalganj

Established	12 October, 1973
Border	North – West Champaran South – Siwan East – East Champaran West – Uttar Pradesh
Area	2033 sq km
Main rivers	Gandak

Administrative distribution

Headquarter	Gopalganj
Division	Saran
Sub-division (2)	Gopalganj and Hathua
Panchayat	234
Rajaswa Gram	1530

Constituencies

Lok Sabha Constituencies: 1 (Gopalganj)

Vidhan Sabha constituencies: 6 (Gopalganj, Kuchaikot, Hathua, Barauli, Bhorey, and Baikunthpur)

Blocks (14)

1. Bhorey	2. Vijaipur
3. Uchkagaon	4. Kateya
5. Phulwariya	6. Panchdewari
7. Hathua	8. Thawe
9. Gopalganj	10. Kuchaikote
11. Manjha	12. Barauli
13. Baikunthpur	14. Sidhwaliya

Geographical location

Latitudinal expanse	26° 12' 26° 39' N
Longitudinal expanse	83° 54' 84° 55' E
Temperature	45° C (max) 10° C (min)
Average rainfall	290 mm
Height above sea level	65 m
Soil	Tarai soil

Demographic details (2011)

Total population	2562012
Population density	1260 persons per sq km
Decadal growth rate	19 percent (2001-2011)
Gender ratio	1021 females per 1000 males
Literacy rate	65.5 percent
Male literacy rate	76.5 percent
Female literacy rate	54.8 percent
Languages	Bhojpuri, Hindi, and Urdu

Primary industries: Sugar mills, oil mills (Hathua)

Chief crops: Paddy, wheat, sugarcane, maize and arhar

Tourist sites: Temple of Maa Durga in Thawe, Dighva Dubouli, Lakdi Dargah, fort in Husepur built by Hathua Maharaj, Ramgarhwa Dih.

15 Muzaffarpur

Established	1875
Border	North – East Champaran, Sheohar and Sitamarhi South – Vaishali East – Darbhanga, Samastipur West – Saran, Gopalganj
Area	3172 sq km
Main rivers	Burhi Gandak and Bagmati

Administrative distribution

Headquarter	Muzaffarpur
Division	Tirhut
Sub-divisions (2)	East Champaran and West Champaran

Constituencies

Lok Sabha Constituencies: 1 (Muzaffarpur)

Vidhan Sabha constituencies: 11 (Muzaffarpur, Sahebganj, Aurai, Kanti, Bochahan, Minapur, Gaighat, Paroo, Sakra, Baruraj and Kurhani)

Blocks (16)

1. Kurhani	2. Muraul
3. Bandra	4. Aurai
5. Katra	6. Mushahari
7. Kanti	8. Marwan
9. Motipur	10. Paroo
11. Saraiya	12. Bochahan
13. Minapur	14. Gaighat
15. Sahebganj	16. Sakra

Geographical location

Latitudinal expanse	25° 54'- 26° 23' N
Longitudinal expanse	84° 53' - 85° 45' E
Temperature	44° C (max) 5° C (min)
Average rainfall	118.7 mm
Height above sea level	170 m
Soil	Balsundari soil and new alluvial soil.

Demographic details (2011)

Total population	48,01,062
Population density	1514 persons per sq km
Decadal growth rate	28.1 percent (2001 - 2011)
Gender ratio	900 females per 1000 males
Literacy rate	63.4 percent
Male literacy rate	71.3 percent
Female literacy rate	54.7 percent
Languages	Bajjika and Hindi

Primary industries: Sugar mills, medicine industry, leather industry, petroleum industry, gas cylinder refill industry, thermoelectric power plant, engineering industry, rail wagon and coaches, garment manufacturing industry, etc.

Chief crops: Paddy, wheat, sugarcane, maize, etc.

Tourist sites: Raman Devi Temple, Kali Temple in Raman, Dargah of Kamal Shah, Sahid Khudiram Bose Memorial, Katragarh Kolhua Hills, Baba Garib Nath Temple, Litchi Gardens in Bochahan, Jhaphan and Mushahari, Jubba Sahani Park, Ram Chandra Sahi Museum, Chaturbhuj Sthan Temple, Shri Ram Temple, etc.

16 Sitamarhi

Established	11 December, 1972
Border	North – Nepal South – Muzaffarpur, Darbhanga East – Madhubani West – Sheohar, East Champaran
Area	2294 sq km
Main rivers	Bagmati

Administrative distribution

Headquarter	Sitamarhi
Division	Tirhut
Sub Divisions (2)	Sitamarahi Sadar, Belsand and Pupri

Constituencies

Lok Sabha constituencies: 1 (Sitamarhi)

Vidhan Sabha constituencies: 8 (Sitamarhi, Parihar, Riga, Runni Saidpur, Belsand, Bathnaha, Bajpatti and Sursand)

Blocks (17)

1. Runni Saidpur	2. Belsand
3. Parsauni	4. Nanpur
5. Pupri	6. Bokhra
7. Choraut	8. Parihar
9. Sonbarsa	10. Bathnaha
11. Sursand	12. Riga
13. Suppi	14. Majorganj
15.Bairgania	16. Dumra
17. Bajpatti	

Geographical location

Latitudinal expanse	25° 36'- 26° 6' N
Longitudinal expanse	85° 29' - 85° 48' E
Temperature	44° C (max) 5° C (min)
Average rainfall	1200 mm
Height above sea level	56 m

Soil	Aluvial soil and loamy soil

Demographic details (2011)

Total population	34,23,574
Population density	1492 persons per sq km
Decadal growth rate	27.6 percent (2001 - 2011)
Gender ratio	899 females per 1000 males
Literacy rate	52.1 percent
Male literacy rate	60.6 percent
Female literacy rate	42.4 percent
Languages	Bajjika, Maithili and Hindi

Primary industries: Sugar mills in Riga, rice, oil, tobacco, etc.

Chief crops: Paddy, wheat, khesari and maize, etc.

Tourist sites: Punaura Haleshwar Temple, birth place of mata sita, Janki Temple, Punaura Urvija kund, Kapraul (it is assocated with sage Kapil), Parsaui (it is associated to saint Parshuram), Sun Remple, Goraul sharif (holy place for Muslims), Sita Kund, Bagahi Math, Panth Pakar, Damami Math, Baba Nageshwar Nath Temple, Rani temple, etc.

17 Sheohar

Established	6 October, 1994
Border	North – Sitamarhi South – Muzaffarpur East – Madhubani West – East Champaran
Area	349 sq km
Main rivers	Bagmat, Burhi Gandak, and Lalkiya

Administrative distribution

Headquarters	Sheohar
Division	Tirhut
Sub-divisions (1)	Sheohar

Constitucncics

Lok Sabha constituencies: 1 (Sheohar)

Vidhan Sabha constituencies: 1 (Sheohar)

Blocks (5)

1.Purnahiya	2. Piprarhi
3. Tariyani	4. Sheohar
5. Dumri Katsari	
Panchayat	53
Rajaswa Gram	207

Geographical location

Latitudinal expanse	25° 24’- 26° 18' N
Longitudinal expanse	85° 12’ - 85° 30’ E
Temperature	42° C (max) 10° C (min)
Average rainfall	956 mm
Height above sea level	80 m
Soil	Alluvial soil, residual soil, and loamy soil

Demographic details (2011)

Total population	6,56,246
Population density	1800 persons per sq km
Decadal growth rate	27.2 percent (2001 - 2011)
Gender ratio	893 females per 1000 males
Literacy rate	53.8 percent
Male literacy rate	61.3 percent
Female literacy rate	45.3 percent
Languages	Hindi, Maithili and Urdu

Primary industries: No major industry is functional in Sheohar

Chief crops: Paddy, wheat, maize, oilseeds, tobacco, red chilies, etc.

Tourist sites: Shiva Temple of Devikuli.

18 West Champaran

Established	1971
Border	North – Nepal South – Gopalganj East – East Champaran West – West Champaran
Area	5228 sq km
Main rivers	Gandak

Administrative distribution

Headquarters	Bettiah

Division	Tirhut
Sub-divisions (3)	Bettiah, Bagaha, Narkatiyaganj
Panchayat	315
Rajaswagram	1483

Constituencies

Lok Sabha constituencies: 1 (West Champaran, Valmiki Nagar)

Vidhan Sabha constituencies: 9 (Narkatiyaganj, Bettiah, Ramnagar, Lauriya, Bagaha, Chanpatia, Sikta, Nautan and Valmiki Nagar)

Blocks (18)

1. Narkatiyaganj	2. Gaunaha
3. Sikta	4. Mainatand
5. Majhaulia	6. Chanpatia
7. Lauriya	8. Bettiah
9. Bairiya	10. Nautan
11.Yogapatti	12. Bagaha-1
13. Bagaha – 2	14. Ramnagar
15.Jhakaraha	16. Bhitaha
17. Madhubani	18. Piprasi

Geographical location

Latitudinal expanse	26° 16'- 27° 31' N
Longitudinal expanse	83° 50' - 85° 18' E
Temperature	43° C (max) 8° C (min)
Average rainfall	1422 mm
Height above sea level	113 m
Soil	Alluvial soil and residual soil

Demographic details (2011)

Total population	39,35,042
Population density	753 persons per sq km
Decadal growth rate	29.3 percent (2001 - 2011)
Gender ratio	909 females per 1000 males
Literacy rate	55.7 percent
Male literacy rate	65.6 percent
Female literacy rate	44.7 percent
Languages	Hindi and Bhojpuri

Primary industries: Sugar mills, paper mills and raw leather industry, milk and dairy products

Chief crops: Paddy, wheat, sugar cane, maize millets, etc.

Tourist sites: Valmiki Nagar, Gandhi Ashram in Bhitiharwa, pillar of Ashoka in Lauriagarh Panchmandir in Ramnagar, Hazarimal Dharmashala Stupa in Maharia, birth place of renowned British author George Orwell in Motihari, etc.

19 East Champaran

Established	1971
Border	North – Nepal South – Gopalganj and Muzaffarpur East – Sheohar and Sitamarhi West – West Champaran and Gopalganj
Area	3968 sq km
Main rivers	Gandak, Burhi Gandak

Administrative distribution

Headquarters	Motihari
Division	Tirhut
Sub-divisions (5)	Motihari Sadar, Chakia, Areraj, Raxaul, Sihrahana, and Pakridayal
Panchayat	405
Rajaswa Gram	1345

Constituencies

Lok Sabha Constituencies: 1 (East Champaran)

Vidhan Sabha constituencies: 12 (Motihari, Dhaka, Pipra, Govindganj, Raxaul, Harisiddhi, Sugauli, Chiraiya, Narkatia, Kesariya, Madhuban, and Kalyanpur)

Blocks (27)

1. Areraj	2. Harisiddhi
3. Paharpur	4. Sangrampur
5. Raxaul	6. Ramgarhwa
7. Adapur	8. Chauradano
9. Motihari	10. Sugauli
11. Turkaulia	12 Banjaria
13. Kotowa	14. Piprakothi
15. Dhaka	16. Chiraiya
17. Ghorasahan	18. Bankatwa

19. Chakia	20. Mehsi
21. Kalyanpur	22. Kesaria
23. Pakaridayal	24. Madhuban
25.Tetaria	26 Phenhara
27. Patahi	

Geographical location

Latitudinal expanse	26° 16'- 27° 1' N
Longitudinal expanse	84° 30' - 85° 16' E
Temperature	46° C (max) 5° C (min)
Average rainfall	1242 mm
Height above sea level	113 m
Soil	Alluvial soil and lowland soil

Demographic details (2011)

Total population	50,99,371
Population density	1285 persons per sq km
Decadal growth rate	29.4 percent (2001 - 2011)
Gender ratio	902 females per 1000 males
Literacy rate	55.84 percent
Male literacy rate	65.3 percent
Female literacy rate	45.1 percent
Languages	Hindi and Bhojpuri

Primary industries: Sugar mills in Chakia, Sugauli and Motihari, cottage industry for buttons in Mehsi

Chief crops: Paddy, wheat, maize, khesari, jute, arhar, millet, etc.

Tourist sites: In order to find solution to the tyranny faced by poor indigo peasants at the hands of zamindars, Mahatma Gandhi visited Motihari in 1917. Ashram in Motihari, pillar of Emperor Ashoka near Areraj, pillar of Emperor Ashoka in Amgarh, Lauriya, Areraj, Kesaria, Sagardih, etc. are chief attractions.

20 Vaishali

Established	12 October, 1972
Border	North – Muzaffarpur South –Patna and River Ganga East – Samastipur West – Saran, River Gandak
Area	2036 sq km
Main rivers	Gandak and Ganga

Administrative distribution

Headquarter	Hazipur
Division	Tirhut
Sub-divisions (3)	Hazipur, Mahua, Mahnar
Panchayat	290
Rajaswa Gram	1638

Constituencies

Lok Sabha Constituencies: 2 (Vaishali, Hazipur)
Vidhan Sabha constituencies: 8 (Hazipur, Mahua, Mahnar, Raja Pakar, Raghopur, Patepur, Lalganj, and Vaishali)

Blocks (16)

1. Hazipur	2. Lalganj
3. Vaishali	4. Patehri Belsar
5. Bhagwanpur	6. Raghopur
7.Bidupur	8. Mahua
9. Raja Pakar	10. Jandaha
11. Patepur	12. Goraul
13.Chehar Kalan	14. Mahnar
15. Sahdai	16. Desri

Geographical location

Latitudinal expanse	25° 0'- 25° 301' N
Longitudinal expanse	84° 0' - 85° 0' E
Temperature	44.5° C (max) 6° C (min)
Average rainfall	1168 mm
Height above sea level	52 m
Soil	Loamy soil

Demographic details (2011)

Total population	3495021
Population density	1717 persons per sq km
Decadal growth rate	28.6 percent (2001-2011)
Gender ratio	895 females per 1000 males
Literacy rate	66.66 percent
Male literacy rate	75.4 percent

Female literacy rate	56.7 percent
Languages	Hindi, Maithili, and Urdu

Primary industries: Sugar mills in Chakia, woolen yarn industry, Jarda industry, etc.

Chief crops: Paddy, wheat, banana, litchi, mango, tobacco, maize, etc.

Tourist sites: Capital of ancient republic of Vaishali near Lalganj, center for Buddhism, Chechra (Shwetpur), Buddhist stupa in Madhupur built during the era of Emperor Ashoka, ancient Buddhist and Jain sites in Hazipur, Ram Chaura Nepali Temple, fort of king of Vaishali, Bavan Pokhar temple (temple of 52 ponds) Abhishek Pushkarni, Vishva Shanti Stupa, Kundalpur, fort of King Vishal

21. Darbhanga

Established	1875
Border	North – Madhubani South – Samastipur East – Saharsa West – Muzaffarpur
Area	2279 sq km
Main rivers	Kamla Balan

Administrative distribution

Headquarters	Darbhanga
Division	Darbhanga
Sub-divisions (3)	Darbhanga Sadar, Benipur, and Biraul
Panchayat	324
Rajaswa Gram	1269

Constituencies

Lok Sabha Constituencies: 1 (Darbhanga)

Vidhan sabha constituencies: 10 (Darbhanga Urban, Darbhanga Rural, Keoti, Alinagar, Jale, Kusheshwar Asthan, Hayaghat, Gaura Bauram, Benipur and Bahadurpur)

Blocks (18)

1. Baheri	2. Hayaghat
3. Hanuman Nagar	4. Darbhanga
5. Bahadurpur	6. Singhwara
7. Jale	8. Keoti
9. Tardih	10. Manigachhi
11. Alinagar	12. Benipur
13. Ghanshyampur	14. Kiratpur
15. Kusheshwar Asthan	
16. Kusheshwar Asthan (East)	
17. Biraul	
18. Gaura Bauram	

Geographical location

Latitudinal expanse	25° 53'- 26° 27' N
Longitudinal expanse	85° 45' - 86° 25' E
Temperature	43° C (max) 9° C (min)
Average rainfall	1143 mm
Height above sea level	52 m
Soil	Alluvial soil

Demographic details (2011)

Total population	3495021
Population density	1717 persons per sq km
Decadal growth rate	19.5 percent (2001 - 2011)
Gender ratio	911 females per 1000 males
Literacy rate	56.6 percent
Male literacy rate	66.8 percent
Female literacy rate	45.2 percent
Languages	Hindi, Maithili, and Urdu

Primary industries: Sugar mills in Raiyam, jute industry, paper industry, cotton yarn industry in Pandaul, bidi industry, etc. are some of the primary industries of the district.

Chief crops: Paddy, wheat, makhana, mango, jute, tobacco, maize etc.

Tourist sites: Fort of Darbhanga Maharaj, Ahilya Sthan, Gautam Kund, Bahera, Dekulidham, Kusheshwar Sthan, jarhatia, akashvani and doordarshan broadcast center in Ahiriya are major tourist attractions.

22. Madhubani

Established	1972
Border	North – Nepal South – Darbhanga East – Supaul West – Sitamarhi

Area	3501 sq km
Main rivers	Kamla, Balan, Bhutsi

Administrative distribution

Headquarter	Madhubani
Division	Darbhanga
Sub Divisions (3)	Madhubani, Jainagar, Benipatti, Jhanjharpur, Phulparas
Panchayat	399
Rajaswa Gram	1111

Constituencies

Lok Sabha constituencies: 2 (Madhubani, Jhanjharpur)

Vidhan Sabha constituencies: 10 (Madhubani, Khajauli, Bisfi, Jhanjharpur, Harlakhi, Benipatti, Rajnagar, Babubarhi and Phulparas)

Blocks (21)

1. Ladaniya	2. Jainagar
3. Basopatti	4. Harlakhi
5. Madhwapur	6. Bisfi
7. Benipatti	8. Rahika
9. Pandaul	10. Khajauli
11.Kahuahi	12. Rajnagar
13. Babubarhi	14. Khutauna
15. Laukahi	16. Ghoghardiha
17. Phulparas	18. Andhrathadi
19. Jhanjharpur	20 Lakhnaur
21. Madhepur	

Geographical location

Latitudinal expanse	25° 59'- 26° 39' N
Longitudinal expanse	85° 43' - 86° 42' E
Temperature	42° C (max) 5° C (min)
Average rainfall	1273.2 mm
Height above sea level	80 m
Soil	Alluvial soil

Demographic details (2011)

Total population	44,87,379
Population density	1282 persons per sq km
Decadal growth rate	25.5 percent (2001-2011)
Gender ratio	926 females per 1000 males
Literacy rate	58.6 percent
Male literacy rate	70.1 percent
Female literacy rate	46.2 percent
Languages	Hindi and Maithili

Primary industries: Sugar mills in Sakri and Lohar, Khadi industry in Loha Kapasia, makhana industry etc.

Chief crops: Paddy, wheat, makhana, khesari, maize, etc.

Tourist sites: Remains of royal palace of Darbhanga Maharaj in Rajnagar, Madhubani paintings, fort of Rajawali, Baliraj Fort, Bhagwati Sthan Uchhaith, Koilakh, Saurath Mela (It is a fair of grooms from the Maithil Brahman community where fathers gather to select suitable husbands for their daughters).

23. Samastipur

Established	14 November, 1972
Border	North – Darbhanga, Muzaffarpur South – Begusarai East – Saharsa West – Vaishali
Area	2904 sq km
Main rivers	Burhi Gandak, Kosi and Balan

Administrative distribution

Headquarters	Samastipur
Division	Darbhanga
Sub-divisions (4)	Samastipur Sadar, Dalsingh Sarai, Patori, and Rosera

Constituencies

Lok Sabha constituencies: 2 (Ujiyarpur, Samastipur)

Vidhan Sabha constituencies: 10 (Samastipur, Rosera, Kalyanpur, Morwa, Rairanjan, Ujiryarpur, Bidhutpur, Warisnagar, Mohiuddin Nagar and Hasanpur)

Blocks (20)

1. Sarairanjan	2. Patori
3. Mohanpur	4. Mohiuddinnagar
5. Kalyanpur	6. Warisnagar

7. Khanpur	8. Samastipur
9. Pusa	10. Tajpur
11. Morwa	12. Hasanpur
13. Bithan	14.Bibhutpur
15. Singhia	16. Rosera
17. Shivaji Nagar	18. Dalsingh Sarai
19.Ujiyarpur	20. Vidyapati Nagar

Geographical location

Latitudinal expanse	25° 51' 39" N
Longitudinal expanse	85° 46' 45"' E
Temperature	32.43° C (max) 8° C (min)
Average rainfall	926.36 mm
Height above sea level	35 m
Soil	Alluvial soil

Demographic details (2011)

Total population	4261566
Population density	1467 persons per sq km
Decadal growth rate	25.5 percent (2001-2011)
Gender ratio	911 females per 1000 males
Literacy rate	61.9 percent
Male literacy rate	71.3 percent
Female literacy rate	51.5 percent
Languages	Hindi and Maithili

Primary industries: Sugar mills in Hasanpur, jute industry in Muktapur, paper industry in Samastipur

Chief crops: Paddy, wheat, red chillies, tobacco, maize etc.

Tourist sites: Pusa Agricultural University, Panda village, rural institutions of Vaishali, Manipur Temple, Vidyapati Temple, etc.

24. Saharsa

Established	1 April, 1954
Border	North – Supaul South – Khagaria East – Madhepura West – Darbhanga
Area	1687 sq km
Main rivers	Koshi and Kamla

Administrative distribution

Headquarters	Saharsa
Division	Kosi
Sub-divisions (4)	Saharsa Sadar, Simri Bakhtiarpur

Constituencies

Lok Sabha constituencies: 1 (Madhepura)
Vidhan Sabha constituencies: 4 (Saharsa, Mahishi, Sonbarsa, Bakhtiarpur)

Blocks (10)

1. Nauhatta	2. Mahishi
3. Banma Itrahi	3. Sattar Kataiya
5. Kahara	6. Salkhua
7. Simri Bakhpur	8. Patarghat
9. Saur Bazar	10. Sonbarsa

Geographical location

Latitudinal expanse	25° 53'- 25° 88' N
Longitudinal expanse	86° 06' - 86° 36' E
Temperature	31.05° C (max) 16.67° C (min)
Average rainfall	948.48 mm
Height above sea level	1661.30 m
Soil	Alluvial soil and balsundari soil

Demographic details (2011)

Total population	19,00,661
Population density	1127 persons per sq km
Decadal growth rate	26 percent (2001-2011)
Gender ratio	906 females per 1000 males
Literacy rate	53.2 percent
Male literacy rate	63.6 percent
Female literacy rate	41.7 percent
Languages	Hindi, Maithili, Angika, Bangla, and Urdu

Primary industries: Jute industry, bidi industry, and soap industry in Saharsa

Chief crops: Paddy, wheat, Madua (ragi), jute, barley, maize, etc.

Tourist sites: Bangaon, Saur Bazar, Sonbarsa forests in Harsiddhi, Kandaha Sun Temple, Matasyagandha Raktkali Temple, Ugratara Peeth.

25. Supaul

Established	14 January, 1991
Border	North – Nepal South – Madhepura, Saharsa East – Araria West – Madhubani
Area	2425 sq km
Main rivers	Kosi

Administrative distribution

Headquarter	Supaul
Division	Kosi
Sub-divisions (4)	Supaul, Virpur, Nirmali, and Triveniganj

Constituencies

Lok Sabha constituencies 1 (Supaul)
Vidhan Sabha constituencies: 5 (Nirmali, Triveniganj, Supaul, Chhatapur and Pipra)

Blocks (11)

1. Supaul	2. Pipra
3. Basantpur	4. Chhatapur
5. Raghopur	6. Pratapganj
7.Triveniganj	8. Saraigarh-Bhaptiyahi
9. Kishanpur	10. Nirmali
11. Marauna	

Geographical location

Latitudinal expanse	25° 37'- 26° 0' N
Longitudinal expanse	86° 22' - 87° 10' E
Temperature	36° C (max) 10° C (min)
Average rainfall	1084 mm
Height above sea level	34 m
Soil	Khadar soil

Demographic details (2011)

Total population	22,29,076
Population density	919 persons per sq km
Decadal growth rate	28.7 percent (2001 - 2011)
Gender ratio	929 females per 1000 males
Literacy rate	57.7 percent
Male literacy rate	69.9 percent
Female literacy rate	44.8 percent
Languages	Hindi and Maithili

Primary industries: Rice industries

Chief crops: Paddy, wheat, jute, moong, maize, etc.

Tourist sites: Remains of king's fort in Ganpatganj, Varadraj Perumal Dev Sthanam, Mazarat Pirganj, Das Mahavidya Temple, Navgrah Temple, Bhim Shankar Mahadev, Van Durga Temple, Kosi Barrage, Tilheshwar Mahadev, etc.

26. Madhepura

Established	19 May, 1981
Border	North – Supaul South – Bhagalpur East – Purnea West – Sahaharsa
Area	1788 sq km
Main rivers	Kosi

Administrative distribution

Headquarter	Madhepura
Division	Kosi
Sub-divisions (2)	Madhepura, Udakishunganj

Constituencies

Lok Sabha constituencies: 1 (Madhepura)
Vidhan Sabha constituencies: 4 (Alamnagar, Bihariganj, Singheshwar and Madhepura)

Blocks (13)

1. Chousa	2. Alamnagar
3. Puraini	4. Udakishunganj
5. Gwalpara	6. Bihariganj
7. Shankarpur	8. Kumarkhand
9. Madhepura	10. Ghelardh
11. Gamhariya	12. Singheshwar
13. Murliganj	

Geographical location

Latitudinal expanse	25° 31'- 26° 20' N
Longitudinal expanse	86° 36' - 87° 07' E
Temperature	40° C (max) 7° C (min)

Average rainfall	1300 mm
Height above sea level	43 m
Soil	Alluvial soil

Demographic details (2011)

Total population	20,01,762
Population density	1120 persons per sq km
Decadal growth rate	31.1 percent (2001 - 2011)
Gender ratio	911 females per 1000 males
Literacy rate	52.3 percent
Male literacy rate	61.8 percent
Female literacy rate	41.7 percent
Languages	Hindi and Maithili

Primary industries: Rice mills, jute industry, electric engine manufacturing factories for railways

Chief crops: Paddy, jute, maize, etc

Tourist sites: Shiv Temple in Singheshwar sthan and the fair held at this place, Udakishunganj community Durga Mandir, Maharashi Mehi Avataran Temple in Majhua, Ram Nagar Kali Temple, fort of Srinagar, Baba Vishu Raut Pachrasi Dhaam, Chandika Temple in Viratpur, etc.

27. Purnea (Purnia)

Established	Not available
Border	North – Araria South – Bhagalpur East – Kishanganj, Katihar West – Madhepura
Area	3229 sq km
Main rivers	Kosi, Parna, Mahananda, Suvara, Kali and Koli

Administrative distribution

Headquarters	Purnea
Division	Purnea
Sub-divisions (4)	Purnea, Banmankhi, Dhamdaha and Baisi
Panchayat	246
Rajaswa Gram	1296

Constituencies

Lok Sabha constituencies: 1 (Purnea)

Vidhan Sabha constituencies: 7 (Purnea, Rupauli, Dhamdaha, Banmankhi, Kasba, Amour, Baisi)

Blocks (14)

1. Rupauli	2. Bhawanipur
3. Barhara	4. Dhamdaha
5. Banmankhi	6. Baisa
7. Amour	8. Baisi
9. Dagarua	10. Purnea East
11. Krityanand Nagar	12. Kasba
13. Srinagar	14. Jalalgarh

Geographical location

Latitudinal expanse	25° 13'-80" N – 27° 07'-59"N
Longitudinal expanse	86°59'-06" E – 87°52'-35"E
Temperature	48° C (max) 3° C (min)
Average rainfall	1470 mm
Height above sea level	171 m
Soil	Alluvial soil

Demographic details (2011)

Total population	32,64,619
Population density	1011 persons per sq km
Decadal growth rate	28.3 percent (2001 - 2011)
Gender ratio	921 females per 1000 males
Literacy rate	51.1 percent
Male literacy rate	59.1 percent
Female literacy rate	42.3 percent
Languages	Hindi, Maithili, Bangla, Surjapuri, Polia, Angika, and Santhali

Primary industries: Rice mills

Chief crops: Paddy, jute, wheat, barley, banana, maize, etc.

Tourist sites: Temple of Maa Puran Devi, Kali Temple in Purnea City, Dhimeshwar (Mahadev) Temple in Banmankhi, Narsingh Avatar (incarnation of Lord Vishnu) stambh, fort of Jallgarh, Bayasi Dargaah, Chunapur Mata sthan, Varuneshwar sthan, Dhimeshawar sthan, etc.

28. Araria

Araria district was carved out of Purnea district. Earlier, it was a sub-division of Purnea district.

Established	14 January, 1990
Border	North – Nepal South – Supaul East – Kishanganj West – Purnea
Area	2830 sq km
Main rivers	Kosi, Suvara, Kali and Koli

Administrative distribution

Headquarters	Araria
Division	Purnea
Sub-divisions (2)	Araria and Forbesganj
Panchayat	218
Rajaswa Gram	742

Constituencies

Lok Sabha constituencies: 1 (Araria)

Vidhan Sabha constituencies: 6 (Narpatganj, Raniganj, Forbesganj, Araria, Jokihat and Sikti)

Blocks (9)

1. Raniganj	2. Bhargawa
3. Araria	4. Kursakanta
5. Palasi	6. Sikti
7. Forbesganj	8. Narpatganj
9. Jokihat	

Geographical location

Latitudinal expanse	25° 46' N
Longitudinal expanse	86° 28' E
Temperature	41° C (max) 5° C (min)
Average rainfall	1195 mm
Height above sea level	47 m
Soil	Balsundari soil

Demographic details (2011)

Total population	28,11,569
Population density	993 persons per sq km
Decadal growth rate	30.3 percent (2001 - 2011)
Gender ratio	921 females per 1000 males
Literacy rate	53.53 percent
Male literacy rate	62.30 percent
Female literacy rate	43.93 percent
Languages	Hindi Maithili, Bhojpuri and Urdu

Primary industries: Jute industry (There are a lot of jute industries in the region.)

Chief crops: Paddy, jute, wheat, maize, etc. are the chief crops of the region.

Tourist sites: Khadgeshwari Kali Temple, Raniganj Vriksh Vatika, Biodiversity Park, Pratikriti stupa, Sultan Pokhar, and Baba Sundar Nath Dhaam

29 Kishanganj

Established	14 January, 1990
Border	North – Nepal South – Purnea East – West Bengal West – Araria
Area	1884 sq km
Main rivers	River Mahananda

Administrative distribution

Headquarters	Kishanganj
Division	Purnea
Sub-divisions (1)	Kishanganj
Panchayat	126
Rajaswa Gram	802

Constituencies

Lok Sabha constituencies: 1 (Kishanganj)

Vidhan Sabha constituencies: 6 (Kishanganj, Bahadurganj, Thakurganj and Konchadhaman)

Blocks (7)

1. Dighalbank	2. Bahadurganj
3. Terhagachh	4. Kishanganj
5. Kochadhaman	8. Thakurganj
7. Pothia	

Geographical location

Latitudinal expanse	25° 20 - 26° 30" N

Longitudinal expanse	87° 07' - 88° 19' E
Temperature	41° C (max) 5° C (min)
Average rainfall	2250 mm
Height above sea level	173 m
Soil	Lowland soil

Demographic details (2011)

Total population	1690400
Population density	897 persons per sq km
Decadal growth rate	30.4 percent (2001-2011)
Gender ratio	950 females per 1000 males
Literacy rate	55.5 percent
Male literacy rate	63.7 percent
Female literacy rate	46.8 percent
Languages	Hindi Surjapuri, Urdu, and Bangla

Primary industries: There are a lot of jute industries in the region.

Chief crops: Paddy, jute, wheat, etc.

Tourist sites: Hargauri Temple in Thakurganj, Khagra Mela, Nehru Shanti Park, fort of Churli, residence of Nawab of Khagra, River Mahananda, etc.

30. Katihar

Established	2 October, 1973
Border	North – Purnea South – River Ganga, Jharkhand East – West Bengal West – Purnea
Area	3057 sq km
Main rivers	River Mahananda, Ganga, Kamla

Administrative distribution

Headquarters	Katihar
Division	Purnea
Sub-divisions (3)	Katihar Sadar, Barsoi, and Manihari
Panchayat	238
Rajaswa Gram	1250

Constituencies

Lok Sabha Constituencies: 1 (Katihar)

Vidhan Sabha constituencies: 6 (Katihar, Kadwa, Balrampur, Pranpur, Manihari, Barai and Korha)

Blocks (16)

1. Barari	2. Kursela
3. Sameli	4. Korha
5. Falka	6. Katihar
7. Dandkhora	8. Hasanganj
9. Pranpur	10. Mansahi
11. Manihari	12 Amdabad
13 Kadwa	14. Azamnagar
15. Barsoi	16. Balrampur

Geographical location

Latitudinal expanse	25° 42' – 26° 22' N
Longitudinal expanse	87° 10' – 88° 05' E
Temperature	29.86° C (max) 16.39° C (min)
Average rainfall	1032 mm
Height above sea level	31 m
Soil	Alluvial soil

Demographic details (2011)

Total population	3071029
Population density	1005 persons per sq km
Decadal growth rate	28.4 percent (2001 - 2011)
Gender ratio	919 females per 1000 males
Literacy rate	52.2 percent
Male literacy rate	59.4 percent
Female literacy rate	44.4 percent
Languages	Hindi, Surjapuri, Maithili, Marwadi, Polia, Angika, Urdu, and Bangla

Primary industries: Jute industry and paper industry etc.

Chief crops: Paddy, jute, wheat, maize, etc.

Tourist sites: Goga Lake, ancient fort of Nawabganj, Manihari, Shiva Statue made of black stones in Rajvirat, Gorakh Nath Temple, Bagi Math, Kali Maa Temple, Ramkrishna Ashram

31. Bhagalpur

Established	Not available
Border	North – Madhepur, Purnea, Katihar South –Banka East – Jharkhand West – Munger
Area	2569 sq km
Main rivers	River Ganga and Chandan

Administrative distribution

Headquarters	Bhagalpur
Division	Bhagalpur
Sub-divisions (3)	Bhagalpur, Kahalgaon, and Naugachhiya
Panchayat	242
Rajaswa Gram	1535

Constituencies

Lok Sabha constituencies: 1 (Bhagalpur)

Vidhan Sabha constituencies: 7 (Nathnagar, Sultanganj, Kahalgaon, Pirpainti, Bihpur, Bhagalpur, and Gopalpur)

Blocks (16)

1. Bihpur	2. Narayanpur
3. Kharik	4. Naugachhiya
5. Ismailpur	6. Gopalpur
7. Rangra Chowk	8. Sultanganj
9. Shahkund	10. Nathnagar
11. Jagdishpur	12. Sabour
13.Goradih	14. Kahalgaon
15.Pirpainti	16. Sanhaula

Geographical location

Latitudinal expanse	25° 7' - 25° 30' N
Longitudinal expanse	86° 37' - 87° 30' E
Temperature	44.5° C (max) 8° C (min)
Average rainfall	1166.2 mm
Height above sea level	43 m
Soil	Alluvial soil, tal soil

Demographic details (2011)

Total population	30,37,766
Population density	1182 persons per sq km
Decadal growth rate	25.4 percent (2001 - 2011)
Gender ratio	880 females per 1000 males
Literacy rate	63.1 percent
Male literacy rate	70.3 percent
Female literacy rate	54.9 percent
Languages	Hindi, Maithili, Khadi boli, Pratyushni, and Urdu

Primary industries: Tassar (silk) industry, handicraft industry, sugar industry, alcohol industry (Sultanganj), cotton cloths industry, etc.

Chief crops: Paddy, jute, wheat, gram, sugar cane, etc.

Tourist sites: Baba Ajgaibinath Temple in Sultanganj, remains of ancient Vikaramshila University of the Buddhist era, Kheri Hills, ancient Champa nagri, Jai Prakash Biological Park, central jail, clock tower, Stone Temple in Kahalgaon, Patalpuri Cave, Pattharghatta Doodheshwar Temple, Manaskamna Temple (Nathnagar) and Buddhanath Temple, etc.

32. Banka

The district of Banka was carved out from Bhagalpur. Prior to this, it was a sub-division of Bhagalpur District.

Established	21 February, 2001
Border	North – Bhagalpur South – Jharkhand East – West Bengal West – Jamui
Area	3019 sq km
Main rivers	River Chandan, Chir, Orhani, Belharni, and Barua

Administrative distribution

Headquarters	Banka
Division	Bhagalpur
Sub-divisions (1)	Banka
Panchayat	185
Rajaswa Gram	2110

Constituencies

Lok Sabha constituencies: 1 (Banka)

Vidhan Sabha constituencies: 6 (Banka, Katoriya, Belhar, Amarpur, and Dhraiya)

Blocks (11)

1. Rajaun	2. Dhraiya
3. Bounsi	4. Barahat
5. Bnka	6. Fullidumar
7. Amarpur	8. Shambhuganj
9. Chandan	10. Katoriya
11. Belhar	

Geographical location

Latitudinal expanse	22° 30' – 25° 09' N
Longitudinal expanse	84° 30' – 87° 12' E
Temperature	45° C (max) 15° C (min)
Average rainfall	1200 mm
Height above sea level	79 m
Soil	Alluvial soil

Demographic details (2011)

Total population	20,34,763
Population density	674 persons per sq km
Decadal growth rate	26.5 percent (2001-2011)
Gender ratio	907 females per 1000 males
Literacy rate	58.2 percent
Male literacy rate	67.6 percent
Female literacy rate	47.7 percent
Languages	Hindi and Angika

Primary industries: Paddy crusher, oil milling, cloth weaving, etc.

Chief crops: Paddy, maize, potato, khesari, wheat, gram, sugar cane, etc.

Tourist sites: Baunsi Mandaar Hills, Paapharni Temple, Jethornath Temple, Bhuteshwar nath Temple.

33. Munger

Established	1832
Border	North – Khagaria South – Jamui East – Bhagalpur West – Lakhisarai
Area	1419 sq km
Main rivers	River Ganga

Administrative distribution

Headquarters	Munger
Division	Munger
Sub-divisions (3)	Munger Sadar, Haveli Kharagpur and Tarapur
Panchayat	101
Rajaswa Gram	866

Constituencies

Lok Sabha constituencies: 1 (Munger)

Vidhan Sabha constituencies: 3 (Munger, Jamalpur, and Tarapur)

Blocks (9)

1. Munger Sadar	2. Haveli Kharagpur
3. Sangrampur	4. Tetiyabambar
5. Tarapur	6. Asarganj
7. Dharhara	8. Bariyarpur
9. Jamalpur	

Geographical location

Latitudinal expanse	25° 45' – 25° 15' N
Longitudinal expanse	85° 45' – 86° 45' E
Temperature	45° C (max) 3.5° C (min)
Average rainfall	1273.2 mm
Height above sea level	52 m

Soil	Alluvial soil that is smooth and light red in colour.

Demographic details (2011)

Total population	1,36,775
Population density	964 persons per sq km
Decadal growth rate	20.2 percent (2001 - 2011)
Gender ratio	876 females per 1000 males
Literacy rate	70.5 percent
Male literacy rate	77.7 percent
Female literacy rate	62.1 percent
Languages	Hindi and Angika

Primary industries: Rail engine, gun, cigarette, slate stone, tobacco, alcohol, handloom, etc.

Chief crops: Paddy, maize, barley, millet, wheat, gram, arhar, etc.

Tourist sites: Gomukh kund, Lakshaman kund, Rameshwar kund, Sita kund, Bhimbandh wildlife reserve, fort of Mir Qasim, Kashtharni ghat, International Yoga University, etc.

34. Lakhisarai

Established	3 July, 1994
Border	North – Begusarai South – Jamui East – Munger West – Patna, Nalanda
Area	1228 sq km
Main rivers	River Ganga, Mohane, Kiul, and Haruhar

Administrative distribution

Headquarters	Lakhisarai
Division	Munger
Sub-divisions (1)	Lakhisarai
Panchayat	80
Rajaswa Gram	1250

Constituencies

Lok Sabha constituencies: 1 (Lakhisarai and it falls under Munger Lok Sabha constituency)

Vidhan Sabha constituencies: 3 (Lakhisarai, Surajgarha)

Blocks (7)

1. Sadar Lakhisarai	2. Barahiya
3. Pipariya	4. Surajgarha
5. Chanan	6. Halsi
7. Ramgarh Chowk	

Geographical location

Latitudinal expanse	25° 00' – 25° 20' N
Longitudinal expanse	84° 55' – 86° 25' E
Temperature	45° C (max) 4° C (min)
Average rainfall	858 mm
Height above sea level	53 m
Soil	Khadar soil

Demographic details (2011)

Total population	10,00,912
Population density	815 persons per sq km
Decadal growth rate	24.8 percent (2001 - 2011)
Gender ratio	902 females per 1000 males
Literacy rate	62.4 percent
Male literacy rate	71.3 percent
Female literacy rate	52.6 percent
Languages	Hindi, Maithili, and Angika

Primary industries: Vermilion, gulal, tobacco, etc.

Chief crops: Paddy, maize, wheat, gram, masur, etc.

Tourist sites: Ashok Dham Temple, Krishi Hills, Jalappa Sthan, and Pokhrama

35. Sheikhpura

Established	31 July, 1994

Border	North – Lakhisarai South – Nawada East – Jamui West – Nalanda
Area	689 sq km
Main rivers	Ganga, Mohane, Haruhar, Kiul, and Tahi Sakro

Administrative distribution

Headquarters	Sheikhpura
Division	Munger
Sub-divisions (1)	Sheikhpura
Panchayat	54
Rajaswa Gram	310

Blocks (6)

1. Sheikhpura	2. Barbigha
3. Sheikhpura Sarai	3. Ghat Kusumba
5. Chewara	6. Ariyari

Constituencies

Lok Sabha constituencies: Sheikhpura Vidhan Sabha constituency 40 of Sheikhpura falls under Jamui Lok Sabha constituency, whereas Barbigha Vidhan Sabha constituency 39 of Sheikhpura falls under Lok Sabha constituency of Nawada.

Vidhan Sabha constituencies: 2 (Sheikhpura and Barbigha)

Geographical location

Latitudinal expanse	24° 45' - 25° N
Longitudinal expanse	84° 45' - 86° 45' E
Temperature	45° C (max) 16° C (min)
Average rainfall	1200 mm
Height above sea level	47 to 69 m
Soil	Alluvial soil and loamy soil

Demographic details (2011)

Total population	636342
Population density	924 persons per sq km
Decadal growth rate	21.1 percent (2001-2011)
Gender ratio	930 females per 1000 males
Literacy rate	63.9 percent
Male literacy rate	73.6 percent
Female literacy rate	53.4 percent
Languages	Hindi, Magahi and Urdu

Primary industries: Gun, cigarette, cotton cloths etc.

Chief crops: Paddy, gram, wheat, maize, masur, etc.

Tourist sites: Hills of Sheikhpura, Maadar village (birth place of Dr Shri Krishna Singh, first Chief Minister of Bihar), Shri Vishnu Dham Barbigha, etc.

36. Jamui

Established	21 October, 1991
Border	North – Lakhisarai and Munger South – Giridih East – Banka West – Nawada and Sheikhpura
Area	3098 sq km
Main rivers	Ajay, Mohane, Haruhar, Kiul, and Batua

Administrative distribution

Headquarters	Jamui
Division	Munger
Sub-divisions (1)	Jamui
Panchayat	153
Rajaswa Gram	1506

Constituencies

Lok Sabha constituencies: 1 (Jamui)

Vidhan Sabha constituencies: 3 (Jhajha, Jamui, Sikandara and Chakai)

Blocks (10)

1. Chakai	2. Sono
3. Gidhour	4. Jhajha
5. Barhat	6. Khaira
7. Jamui	8. Laxmipur
9. Sikandra	10.Islamnagar–Aliganj

Geographical location

Latitudinal expanse	24° 55' N
Longitudinal expanse	86° 13' E
Temperature	42° C (max) 5° C (min)
Average rainfall	1102 mm
Height above sea level	1000 m
Soil	Lowland soil

Demographic details (2011)

Total population	17,60,405
Population density	568 persons per sq km
Decadal growth rate	25.8 percent (2001-2011)
Gender ratio	922 females per 1000 males
Literacy rate	59.8 percent
Male literacy rate	71.2 percent
Female literacy rate	47.3 percent
Languages	Angika

Primary industries: Slate, asbestos, colour, etc.

Chief crops: Paddy, gram, wheat, barley, etc.

Tourist sites: Minto Tower (Gidhour), Panchpahadi, Giddheshwar Temple in Khaira, Simultala, Kali Temple, Chandrashekhar Museum, Kakan Temple, etc.

37. Khagaria

Established	1980
Border	North – Saharsa South – Munger and Bhagalpur East – Madhepura and Bhagalpur West – Begusarai and Samastipur
Area	1486 sq km
Main rivers	Phalgu

Administrative distribution

Headquarters	Khagaria
Division	Munger
Sub-divisions (2)	Khagaria and Gogri
Panchayat	129
Rajaswa Gram	306

Constituencies

Lok Sabha Constituencies: 1 (Khagaria)

Vidhan Sabha constituencies: 4 (Khagaria, Alauli, Parbatta, and Beldaur)

Blocks (7)

1. Beldaur	2. Chautham
3. Mansi	4. Gogri
5. Parbatta	6. Khagaria
7. Alauli	

Geographical location

Latitudinal expanse	25° 15' – 25° 44' N
Longitudinal expanse	86° 17' – 86° 52' E
Temperature	45° C (max) 10° C (min)
Average rainfall	1056 mm
Height above sea level	36 m
Soil	Khadar soil and red soil

Demographic details (2011)

Total population	1,66,686 (2011)
Population density	1122 persons per sq km
Decadal growth rate	Not available
Gender ratio	866 females per 1000 males
Literacy rate	57.9 percent
Male literacy rate	65.3 percent
Female literacy rate	49.6 percent
Languages	Angika, Maithili, Hindi, and Urdu

Primary industries: Slate, asbestos, colour, etc.

Chief crops: Paddy, jute, maize, banana, wheat, chilies, etc

Tourist sites: Maa Katyani Sthan, Shyamlal National High School, Ajgaibinath Mahadev Temple, Sanhauli Durga Sthan, Badla Ghat, etc.

38. Begusarai

Established	2 October, 1972
Border	North – Samastipur South – Lakhisarai East – Khagaria and Munger West – Samastipur and Patna
Area	1918 sq km
Main rivers	Ganga, Kamla, Budhi Gandak

Administrative distribution

Headquarters	Begusarai
Division	Munger
Sub-divisions (5)	Begusarai, Manjhaul, Balia, Bakhri, and Teghra
Panchayat	231
Rajaswa Gram	1229

Constituencies

Lok Sabha constituencies: 1 (Begusarai)

Vidhan Sabha constituencies: 7 (Cheriya – Bariyarpur, Bachhwara, Teghra, Matihani, Sahebpur Kamal, Begusarai, Bakheri)

Blocks (18)

1. Balia	2. Sahebpur Kamal
2. Dandari	4. Bachhwara
5. Mansoorchak	6. Bhagwanpur
7.Cheriya Bariyarpur	8. Teghra
9. Bakhari	10. Garhpura
11. Nawkothi	12. Chhorahi
13.Matihani	14. Barauni
15. Samho Akha Kurha	16. Khudabandpur
17. Begusarai	18. Birpur

Geographical location

Latitudinal expanse	25° 15' – 25° 45' N
Longitudinal expanse	86° 45' – 86° 36' E
Temperature	23° C (max) 8° C (min)
Average rainfall	1384 mm
Height above sea level	41 m
Soil	Alluvial soil

Demographic details (2011)

Total population	2970541
Population density	1549 persons per sq km
Decadal growth rate	26.4 percent (2001 – 2011)
Gender ratio	895 females per 1000 males
Literacy rate	63.9 percent
Male literacy rate	71.6 percent
Female literacy rate	55.2 percent
Languages	Maithili and Hindi

Primary industries: Oil refinery, fertilizer factory, petrochemical industry, wax industry, glass industry, thermal power plant

Chief crops: Paddy, maize, wheat, sugarcane, red chilies, etc.

Tourist sites: Kanwar Lake Bird Sanctuary, Naulakha Temple, Fort of Ajatshatru, Jaimangla Garh Temple, Begusarai Museum, Rajendrapur Simaria Ghaat, etc.

❑❑❑

Chapter 26

Judiciary

- **Jurisdiction of High Court**
- **Subordinate Courts**

Article 214 of the Constitution of India contains the provisions for Constitution of one High Court in every state of India, but to assign one High Court to two or more states or Constitution of more than one High Court for a state having huge population is the prerogative of the Parliament of India. High Court is the apex institution of judiciary in a state. District and sessions court, city civil and sessions court, chief judicial magistrate, chief metropolitan magistrate, munsif and other magistrates come under the High Court. The High Court of a state is comprised of one chief justice and other judges who are appointed at regular intervals by the President of India. In terms of number of Judges in the High Court, Allahabad High Court has the highest number of judges (160 approved). At present, the total number of judges in High Court of Bihar is 30. It was established on 3 February, 1916, in Patna.

Eligibility

In order to become a judge in High Court, one should have following eligibility criteria:

1. He shoud be a citizen of India.
2. He should have held a judicial office in India for 10 years.
3. He should have served as an advocate of a High Court or more than one High Court for 10 years.

Judges of High Courts remain in their office till they attain 62 years of age. The office of a High Court judge can fall vacant, if he submits his resignation or if an impeachment motion on grounds of misconduct is passed by two-thirds majority of members present and voting and by a majority of total strength of both the houses separately, or if he is transferred to High Court of another state by the President, or if he is promoted as a judge in the Supreme Court of India by the President. The salaries and other allowances of a High Court judge is drawn from the Consolidated fund of the State. Before entering their office, they take oath of office and secrecy in front of the Governor.

JURISDICTION OF HIGH COURT

According to provisions of Article 226 of the Constitution of India, any matter related to fundamental rights can be directly brought to the notice of High Court. The High Court has a right to issue five kinds of writs in order to safeguard the fundamental rights: (a) Habeas Corpus, (b) Mandamus, (c) Prohibition, (d) Certiorari, and (e) Quo-Warranto.

Matters related to divorce, inheritance, water, armed departments, contempt of court, company acts, etc. also fall under the primary jurisdiction of the High Court.

High Court can hear appeals against the order of subordinate courts in such civil matters where the amount involved is ₹5000 or more.

High Court can hear appeals against the order of subordinate court in such criminal matters, in which the convict has been awarded a sentence of 4 years or more.

Capital punishment awarded by a district and sessions court in case of murder is not executed, until it is validated by the High Court.

Any matter that requires interpretation of the Constitution of India can be brought directly before the High Court.

Just like the Supreme Court of India, the High Courts also have the right of judicial reviews of laws. High Court can pronounce any act passed by the Parliament of India or any legislative assembly as unconstitutional if it feels that the said act is discordant to any article in the Constitution of India, but such orders by High Court can be challenged in Supreme Court of India.

Orders by a High Court can be challenged in the Supreme Court of India but in order to do so permission of the High Court is necessary. Supreme Court can take suo moto cognizance of any orders by a High Court.

High Court can ask its subordinate court about, the details of proccedings in that court. It can transfer any case from one subordinate court to another. It can frame rules regarding salaries, allowances, and services of employees of its subordinate court. It can appoint staffs in its subordinate courts.

SUBORDINATE COURTS

Several different categories of courts function under the High Court. These courts are known as subordinate courts. Special provisions regarding the subordinate courts are mentioned in Articles 233 to 236 of the Constitution of India. There is a court in every district of the state. All the matters and appeals related to that district fall under the jurisdiction of that court. Additional district court, munsif magistrate courts, second class special judicial magistrate court, special judicial magistrate courts for railways, etc. function under the district court. Court of district judge and court of munsif magistrate come under the category of subordinate courts. The court of district judge comprises courts of additional judge, joint judge and assistant judge. Courts of second class subordinate courts are also known as munsif judges or civil judges, and they are formed at the district level. The appointment of district judges are done by the governor at the advice of High Court. In order to be appointed as a district judge, the person concerned should hold an experience of at least 7 years in central or state judicial services.

❑❑❑

Local Self Governance

- Gram Panchayat
- District Council
- Panchayat Samiti
- Urban Self-government

Self-governance at Village Level

The system of Panchayati Raj in India started on 2 October, 1959, in Nagaur District of Rajasthan as a part of a three-tier governance on the recommendations by Balwant Rai Mehta Committee constituted by the central government in 1957. In the three-tier system of governance, there is a provision for Gram Panchayat at the village level, Panchayat samiti (council) at the block level, and district council at the district level. Ashok Mehta Committee which was related to Panchayati Raj, studied the results of this system and gave its report in 1978. The most important recommendation by this committee was to make a two-tier structure for Panchayati Raj. In 1985, Planning Commission set up the G V K Rao Committee which was aimed to review to the programs run for eradication of poverty and rural development. This committee made recommendations to strengthen the Panchayati system. A year later, in 1986, a committee was formed under Lakshmi Mall Singhvi which made recommendations to revive the Panchayati Raj system. In 1988, a sub-committee of parliamentary advisory committee headed by P K Thungan made recommendations to grant constitutional status to Panchayats.

Bihar government passed the Bihar Panchayat samiti and District Council Act, 1961, for the first time which became a law on 17 February, 1962. Three units for local bodies, Gram Panchayat, Panchayat samiti and district council were established through this act. Panchayat elections for years 1952, 1955, 1958, 1965, 1972 and 1978 were held in accordance with this act but due to lack of legal support, those elected gram Panchayats failed from the perspective of autonomy.

The present Panchayati Raj System has been implemented through the addition of 11 Schedule in the Constitution of India by 73rd constitutional amendment. Through this amendment the three tier system of panchayati raj administration has been adopted which is comprised of gram panchayat, panchayat samiti and district council. In 2018, there were 38 district councils, 534 panchayat samiti and 8,391 gram panchayats in Bihar.

GRAM PANCHAYAT

Gram Panchayat is the smallest unit of administration. After the Parliament of India passed the 73rd constitutional amendment act, 1992, the Bihar Government enacted the Bihar State Panchayati Raj Act, in year 2006. Gram sabha, working committee, Mukhiya, gram sevak, gram raksha dal and gram cutcherry (court) are the 6 parts of gram panchayat in Bihar. Every panchayat functions for a duration of 5 years from the date of its first meeting. If the panchayat is dissolved earlier, then there is a provision to conduct elections within six months from the date of its dissolution. If a dissolved panchayat is reconstituted after re-lection, the tenure of this Panchayat is valid for the remaining time for the earlier Panchayat. If the remaining time is less than 6 months, then it is not mandatory to conduct elections. According to the provisions of Article 243 (f) of the Constitution of India, any person who is eligible to be a member of the state legislature shall be eligible to become a member of the panchayat. Only conditions that he or she should have attained the age of 21 years. Article 243 (d) contains the provisions for reservation of seats for the representation of Scheduled Castes and Scheduled Tribes in proportion to the population of these communities in the village. There is a provision for 50 percent reservation for women in every department including those with 1 seat in the panchayat. Total number of gram courts in all panchayats of Bihar is 8474.

Gram sabha is the legislature of the gram panchayat. All the citizens who live in that village and are of 18 years of age or above, are its members. It is mandatory to convene two meetings of gram sabha in a year. Approval of works related to administration, approval of annual budget and statement of account, pondering upon the matters related to tax, etc. are some of its chief functions.

There is a working committee in every gram Panchayat which is headed by the Mukhiya. Other than the Mukhiya, there are eight members in the working committee. Mukhiya is the head of the executive of the gram panchayat. He calls and presides over the meeting of the working committee. Control on government employees of rural level, imposition of penalties on the advice of working committee, and imposition of taxes in some new fields, are some of the main functions of Mukhiya. The election of Mukhiya is conducted through elections by direct represention system by the members of the gram sabha. The members of the working committee nominate one person from among themselves as the Deputy Mukhiya. Deputy Mukhiya discharges the duty of Mukhiya in his absence, but a Deputy Mukhiya cannot work as the Mukhiya continuously for more than 6 months.

There is an office for every gram panchayat in which a government employee works as the panchayat sevak. Panchayat sachiv functions in the capacity of the secretary of Mukhiya.

The judiciary of gram panchayat is known as gram cutcherry or court. Among all the bodies of self-governance, gram Panchayat is the only institution that enjoys judicial powers. In order to ensure smooth functioning of gram panchayat, Sarpanch along with five members (panchs) are elected through election. Their tenure is of 5 years as well. Mukhiya, or a member of working committee cannot become a member of gram court.

Details of Panchayati Raj Institution in Bihar

Details	Number	Details	Number
District council	38	Gram Panchayat Sachiv	8387
Panchayat samiti	534	Nyay Mitra	6947
Gram Panchayat	8471	Gram Cutcherry Sachiv	7474
Members of Gram Panchayat	1,14,691	District Panchayati Raj officer	38
Members of the Panchayat samiti	11,497	Block Panchayati Raj officer	716
Members of the district council	1,161	Members of Gram Cutcherry	114691
Source: Panchayati Raj Department, Government Bihar			

Every five years, the state government constitutes a finance commission, known as Panchayat Finance Commission to inspect the financial situation of the gram panchayats. Panchayat Finance Commission advices the government on matters like distribution of taxes levied by the state government among the gram panchayats, kind of taxes and fees, toll tax, etc. that would be completely directed towards the gram panchayat, grants to the panchayats, any other advice regarding improvement of financial condition of the gram panchayat etc.

PANCHAYAT SAMITI

Panchayat Samiti is the self-governance body at the block level. Panchayati Samiti Pramukh, uppramukh, standing committee, and block development officer are the four important parts of panchayat samiti. The members of panchayat samiti are elected at the time of panchayat elections itself. One member is elected for a population of 5000. Apart form this, the Mukhiya, the MLA under whose constituency that gram panchayat comes, and the Lok Sabha MP of that constituency are also the members of panchayat samiti. There is a provision of reservation for the representation of people from Scheduled Castes, Scheduled Tribes and other backward classes in proportion to their population in the village. Other than this, there is a provision for 50 percent reservation for women in all categories. Elected members elect a pramukh and one uppramukh for a period of 5 years. The state government appoints one block development officer in every block on the recommendation made by the state public service commission. He acts as the executive officer and the secretary of the panchayat samiti. There is a provision for constitution of three committees on various subjects within the panchayat samiti. At present, there are 534 panchayat samitis functional in Bihar.

The panchayat samiti gets its income from the grants given by the state government or local authorities or district councils, loans approved by the government, toll taxes levied by the panchayat samiti and other taxes imposed by the panchayat samiti. Some of the important functions of panchayat samiti are: consideration of the annual plans of all the gram panchayats, and present it before the district council, preparation of annual budget of the samiti, implementation and completion of works delegated by the government or the district council, extension relief works at the time of disaster, etc.

DISTRICT COUNCIL

District council is the apex body in the Panchayati Raj system. All the panchayat committees of a district come under the district council. Chairman, deputy chairman, standing committee, and district development officer are four main parts of a district council. The members of a district are: all the chieftans of all the panchayat samiti of that district; all the members of legislative assemblies; and all the members of Lok Sabha whose constituency comes wholly or partly in district; all those members of state legislative council and Rajya Sabha who belong to that district; and one elected member for a population of every 50,000. All the district councils have one chairman and one deputy chairman who are elected by the members of the council from among themselves for a tenure of five years. There are 38 district councils functional in all the districts of Bihar.

District councils act as a bridge between the state government, and the district for all the development works. Some of the main functions of chairman of district council are – sending a report about the works of secretary of district council to the district magistrate and keeping a vigil on the works of blocks and panchayat samitis of that district. District development commissioner works as the secretary of the district council. Secretary of the district council acts as the chief advisor of the council as well as the coordinating officer between all the committees.

Some of the important functions of district council are: acquisition and preservation of local markets and haats in villages; assurance of grants to panchayat samiti or gram panchayat; providing relief works in times of calamities or disaster; coordination of development programs decided at the district level; coordination of development works ongoing in more than one block, etc. Bank tax as approved by the state government, electricity fee, fee on boat and passenger registration, cess on cleanliness management during pilgrimage and fairs, cess on other kinds of fairs, water cess, grants received from the governments etc. are some of the source of incomes for the district council.

URBAN SELF-GOVERNMENT

Through 74th Amendment Act Part 8 (A) has been added to make a provision in the Constitution of India regarding establishment of self-governing bodies for urban India. Municipal corporation and municipal council existed prior to this. Article 243Q provides for establishment of 3 kinds of municipalities of every state:

1. A Nagar Panchayat is for those areas which are transitional areas i.e. transiting from Rural Area to Urban areas.
2. A Municipal Council is for smaller urban area.
3. A Municipal Corporation is for larger urban areas.

Besides, an urban local self-governing body can be created for any such region, which is aimed to be declared an industrial town area, or has already been declared industrial town area.

The number of members in a municipal corporation is in accordance with the number of wards, assigned to that town on the basis of its population. All the members other than the councillor, representatives of the members of parliament and representatives of members of legislative assemblies are directly elected by the citizens of that town. There is provison of reservation by the government for the people from Scheduled Castes, Scheduled Tribes and other backward classes in this corporation. Reserved seats keep changing serially with every election. A municipal corporation is functional for a duration of 5 years if it is not dissolved before that for any reason.

Every municipality is divided into several wards on the basis of the population of that town. For municipal corporation the maximum number of wards a town with population of more than 10 lakh is 75 and the minimum number is 67, for a town with a population of more than 5 lakhs but less than 10 maximum number of wards is 67, and minimum is 57 and for a town with population more than 2 lakhs, but less than 5 lakhs the maximum number of wards is 57 while the minimum number is 45. For municipal council in a town with a population of more than 1. 5 lakh but less than 2 lakh, the maximum number of wards assigned is 45, and the minimum number of wards is 42, for a town with population more than 1 lakh, but less than 1 lakh the maximum and minimum number of wards are 42 and 37, and for the town with a population more than 40 thousand but less than 1 lakh the maximum number of wards is 37 and minimum is 25. For Nagar Panchayat, the maximum number of wards assigned is 25 and the minimum number of wards assigned is 10.

Following qualifications are required to become a member of municipality:

- He/she must be a citizen of India.
- He/she must have attained the age of 21 years.
- He/she should be eligible to be elected as a member of the state legislative assembly.
- He/she should not have any pending dues of municipality.
- The person should have two or less offsprings.

The Patna Municipality was renamed Patna City Municipality in 1917 after it was founded on November 2 1864. The Patna Municipal Corporation (PMC) established on August 15, 1952 in accordance with the Patna Municipal Act, 1951, replaced these as well as the Patna Administrative Committee and the Patna-Bankipur Joint Water Works Committee.

Bihar has 19 municipal corporations, 88 nagar parishads (city councils) and 154 nagar panchayats (town councils) for the management of its urban regions.

Bihar has 19 municipal corporations that administer urban areas. These are:

1. Arrah
2. Begusarai
3. Bhagalpur
4. Chhapra
5. Darbhanga
6. Gaya
7. Katihar
8. Madhubani
9. Munger
10. Muzaffarpur
11. Patna
12. Purnia
13. Sitamarhi
14. Aurangabad
15. Araria
16. Buxar
17. Nawada
18. Bettiah
19. Samastipur

Municipality, standing mayor, mayor, deputy mayor and town commissioner are 4 parts of a municipal corporation. As per the provisions of Article 29 of Bihar Municipal Corporation Act 2007, State Election Commission of Bihar has notified for reservations for the seat of chairman of municipal corporation on around a dozen of municipal corporations. According to this notice, 5 seats have been reserved for women. This includes municipal corporations of Patna, Arrah, Bihar Sharif, Bhagalpur (backward class), and Darbhanga. Whereas seats for 5 municipal corporations, viz., Munger, Begusarai, Purnea, Katihar and Chhapra have been kept unreserved, Muzaffarpur Municipal Corporation has been reserved for backward classes, and Gaya Municipal Corporation has been reserved for Scheduled Castes. Mayor, deputy mayor and other members form a standing committee of municipal corporation. Town commissioner acts as the principal secretary to the mayor of municipal corporation. An officer from Bihar Administration Services or Indian Administration Services becomes the town commissioner. Apart from them, town finance and accounts controller, a senior officer of auditor general, or an officer of Bihar Account Services, inter town auditor, chief town engineer, chief town medical officer, town planner, town law officer, town secretary, three additional town commissioners and other officers also work for the municipal corporation. Patna Municipal Corporation was established in 1952.

In their first meeting after the elections of municipal corporation, municipal council and nagar panchayats are conducted the councillors elect a chief councillor and a deputy chief councillor from among themselves. Chief commissioner can resign from his post by tendering his resignation letter under his signature to the commissioner. The chief councillor and deputy chief councillor can also be removed from their post, if at least one-third members make a request for the same and a resolution to this effect is passed by a majority of members of the council. City executive officer, city finance officer, town engineer, town medical officer, town secretary, internal auditor etc. are the officers of municipal council and Nagar Panchayat. The chief councilor of municipal corporation is known as mayor while the deputy chief councilor is known as deputy mayor. The chief councillor of municipal council is known as town chairman and the deputy chief councilor is known as deputy town chairman. Chief councilor of nagar panchayat is known as town chief and the deputy chief councilor is known as deputy town head. City executive officer acts as the secretary to the town chairman and town head.

Some important works of municipal council are: ensuring proper water supply to the town, water removal, proper disposal of solid waste, upliftment of poor colonies and hutments, construction and maintenance of bridges, forestation, transport system, making remedies to keep environment pollution free etc. Apart from these works assigned by the central or state government other tasks are also listed in the workbook of municipality.

Rurban Mission in Bihar

Districts	Phases
Patna	Bairiya (phase - 1), Saksohra (phase - 3)
Gaya	Nauranga (phase - 1), Tankuppa (phase - 3)
Saharsa	Sonbarsa (phase -1)
Rohtas	Kuchila (phase - 1)
Samastipur	Kariyan (phase - 1)
Purnea	Khokha (phase -2)
West Champaran	Barwat Parsian (phase-2)
Kaimur	Tori (phase - 3)
Lakhisarai	Pipariya (phase - 1)

Source: Rural Development Department, Government of Bihar

Important Economic Indices

- Demography
- Economic Backwardness in Bihar
- Poverty in Bihar
- Human Development Index
- Potential of Growth
- Unemployment in Bihar

Economy of Bihar in the present time can be analysed in light of the following economic indices

DEMOGRAPHY

According to 2011 Census data, population of Bihar is 10.41 crore, which is 8.6 percent of total population of the country. The decadal growth rate in Bihar during 2001–2011 was 25.1 percent whereas the decadal rate for the country in the same period was 17.6 percent.

Looking at this decadal growth data, it can be safely assumed the demography in Bihar is going through a phase of transition. While on one hand population density in Bihar is 1,102 persons per square km, for India it is 382 persons per sq km. Rate of urbanization in Bihar is only 13.2 percent which is quite low compared to the national average, which is 31.2 percent. What is more worrisome is the fact that during 2001 to 2011 rate of urbanization in Bihar grew only by 0.8 percent, while in the same period the countries rate of growth of urbanization was recorded 3.4 percent.

Gender ratio in Bihar is 918, while the national gender ratio is 943. It is encouraging for Bihar that child gender ratio for India is 919, while for Bihar it is 942. This shows that in future the gender ratio will get better. There is a huge difference in gender ratio in different districts. On one hand, the gender ratio in Gopalganj is 1,021, on the other hand it is lowest with 876 in Munger. Out of 38 districts, population density in 10 districts is more than 1,400 persons per sq km, which reflects the immense pressure of population in the state.

HUMAN DEVELOPMENT INDEX

Human development index displays the health development of any country or state. Human development index (HDI) is a mixture of statistics based on life expectancy, education and per capita income. The concept of human development index was put forward by, Mahboob Ul Haque an economist of Pakistani origin in United Nations Development Program in 1990. Three indices are used to establish the human development index and they are as follows:

1. Life Expectancy Index (LEI)
2. Education Index (EI)
3. Per Capita Income (II)

The HDI is a summary measure for assessing average achievement in three basic dimensions of human development: a long and healthy life, access to knowledge and a decent standard of living. India's HDI value for 2022 is 0.644— which put the country in the Medium human development category—positioning it at 134 out of 193 countries and territories.

On the basis of United Nations Development Program, Indian Government also publishes Human Development Index Report for all its states.

List of Indian States and Union Territories by Human Development Index

The following values are estimates from 2022 calculated by Global Data Lab, using the same method of calculation as UNDP.

Rank	State/Union Territory	HDI (2022)
1	Goa	0.760
2	Kerala	0.758
3	Chandigarh	0.751
4	Puducherry	0.741
5	Delhi	0.734
6	Jammu and Kashmir	0.720
7	Lakshadweep	0.719
8	Himachal Pradesh	0.715
9	Sikkim	0.712
10	Mizoram	0.709
11	Andaman and Nicobar Islands	0.706
12	Punjab	0.698
13	Haryana	0.696
14	Maharashtra	0.695
15	Tamil Nadu	0.692
16	Arunachal Pradesh	0.683
17	Manipur	0.683
18	Uttarakhand	0.681
19	Nagaland	0.679
20	Daman and Diu	0.674
21	Karnataka	0.673
22	Telangana	0.660
23	Rajasthan	0.652
24	Meghalaya	0.650
25	Gujarat	0.646
–	**India (average)**	**0.644**
26	Andhra Pradesh	0.642
27	West Bengal	0.635
28	Chhattisgarh	0.625
29	Dadra and Nagar Haveli	0.624
30	Tripura	0.624
31	Assam	0.615
32	Madhya Pradesh	0.611
33	Odisha	0.610
34	Uttar Pradesh	0.609
35	Jharkhand	0.600
36	Bihar	0.577

Index for Goa is 0.760 while for Bihar it is 0.577. Thus Bihar is at quite low position when it comes to human development index. Lack of education, poverty, bad health, infrastructure and malnutrition are some of the major reasons for low human development index in the state.

ECONOMIC BACKWARDNESS IN BIHAR

Bihar is a low-income, developing state. The state is rich in natural resources, but conventional and ancient ways of production are still in use in Bihar due to poverty. One of the major indicators of economy of Bihar is that a large part of its working population is still engaged in primary activity, i.e., agriculture. Agriculture contributes to a large part in the economy of Bihar. Labour is available in abundance in Bihar, but it is very difficult to provide remunerative employment to entire working population. There is a shortage of capital in the economy of state. Therefore, the capital required to expand the industries to employ the labour of state is difficult.

The number of labours indulged in agricultural produce is very large than what is actually required. Thus the marginal produce of labour in subsistence field, that is, agriculture, is negligible or zero or negative. Therefore, disguised employment is still prevalent in agriculture. Some important characteristics of economy of Bihar are as follows:

1. **Low per capita income:** Low per capita income of the state displays its backwardness. The per capita income of Bihar is very low as compared to other states. Bihar has a low per capita income compared to other states in India. In 2023-24, Bihar's per capita income was estimated at around ₹60,000, significantly lower than the national average. This means the average income per person in Bihar is considerably less than the average income across the country.
2. **Use of conventional methods in production:** In Bihar, while modernization efforts are underway, conventional farming methods remain prevalent, particularly among smaller farmers. These methods, including traditional

crop rotations, manual labor, and less intensive irrigation, are often used due to factors like limited access to resources and a strong cultural connection to farming practices. However, there's also a growing awareness and adoption of modern techniques, like the System of Rice Intensification (SRI), which are proving more efficient.

3. **Low productivity rate in agricultural sector:** Agricultural productivity rate is at a very low mark in Bihar due to lack of land reforms and distance from the effects of green revolution. Most of the farmers in Bihar come under the category of marginal farmers. About 21 percent of total cultivable land of Bihar is under the possession of only 2 percent people. Productivity in Bihar is 2,779 kilogram per hectare, whereas in Punjab, it is 3,483 kilogram. Only 56.4 percent land in Bihar is irrigated and due to this, agriculture in Bihar is in a very bad state.

4. **Menace of flood:** About 73.06 percent land of Bihar or in other words almost two-thirds land of Bihar is suffering from floods. Total of 28 districts are affected by floods and 2.5 lakh hectares land is affected from the problem of waterlogging. About 17.2 percent part of total flood-affected area of the country lies in Bihar. Out of total damage caused due to floods in India, Bihar's contribution is around 12 percent. Almost 21 percent of total population affected by floods reside in Bihar.

5. **Lack of Energy:** Energy is the base of development. In Bihar the established capacity of electricity production is minimal. Government data reveals that in 2022, Bihar required 36,635 million units of electricity but received only 35,873 million units, falling short by 762 million units, nearly two percent of the total demand.

6. **Industrial backwardness:** Bihar's industrial backwardness is a multifaceted issue rooted in weak infrastructure, limited resources and governance challenges, hindering its ability to attract investment and foster economic growth. With lack of mineral resources in Bihar, the development of mineral-based industry has been very low. Agriculture based industrial resources are present in the state, but due to lack of fundamental facilities, the development of industries has been very slow. The following facts indicate the low level Industrial backwardness in Bihar:
   - 75 to 77% of the total workforce of Bihr is still involved in agricultural activities.
   - The share of agriculture sectors in GDP is also high, about 25%, which is higher than the national average (16.38% at a constant price of 2011–12).
   - Lack of mineral resources.
   - Lack of skilled laborers.
   - Lack of capital and investment.
   - Unfavorable governance environment.

7. **Poor quality of fundamental infrastructure:** The economic growth of Bihar has been slow because there is a lack of fundamental infrastructure like transport, communication, energy, etc. Road, rail and air transport facility in Bihar is in a poor state.

8. **Less number of financial institutions:** While Bihar has seen an increase in commercial bank branches, the number of financial institutions per capita is still lower compared to other states in India, particularly in rural areas. Despite an increase in the number of commercial bank branches (7485 in 2022-23), the banking density (branches per lakh population) is 6.1, slightly lower than the previous year. This means that for every 1 lakh people, there are only 6.1 branches, indicating a lower level of banking infrastructure compared to other states. The ATM density is 5.8 per lakh persons, which is also lower than the national average. Bihar's Credit Deposit (CD) ratio is 47.6% (2022-23), which is among the lowest in India. This means that only about 47.6% of the deposits are being converted into loans, indicating limited credit penetration and a potential gap in financial inclusion, particularly in rural areas.

POTENTIAL OF GROWTH

There is ample water, soil and human resource available in the state. Efficient usage of these resources can put Bihar in the category of developed states. Universal development programs are is being run by the state government to eradicate backwardness. Indradhanush Kranti and Bihar Industrial Encouragement Policy, were announced by the Bihar Government to avoid the plight of agriculture and industrial backwardness, respectively.

Despite a lack of mineral resources, the availability of water resources, soil resources, and human resource in abundance in Bihar, makes it a state with one of the highest potential. World's most fertile land, the alluvial plains of Ganga cover a large part of Bihar, where the large network of perennial rivers present the most favourable geographical conditions for the development of agriculture. Judicious and maximum use of all kind of resources to increase the rate of growth is only possible through human resource, and Bihar is a rich state in this resource as well.

At present Bihar, government is trying to different ways to remove problems of Bihar, to eradicate economic backwardness, poverty, unemployment, illiteracy and to improve the standard of life of people of state. For this, government has framed different strategies on the basis if regional resources for the development of the state. Many steps in direction of administrative reforms and law and order reforms have been brought in to encourage capital investment, the most important condition for the growth of state. E-administration, fast track court for control on crime and corruption, STF and SAF have been established for this. A new policy was framed in 2016 to encourage investment and industrial development so that a favourable environment for investors can be created in the state. Even during the present times, implementation of new methods in the field of agriculture and development of agriculture is being stressed upon.

Many steps that were taken by the government has brought a change in conditions. Law and order and administrative reforms have been stressed. Policy framing, implementation, and evaluation needs to be stressed upon. State Administrative Reforms Commission was set up to bring reforms in administration, and it recommended lessening the number of departments.

E–Administration is being stressed upon in the state and administrative structure based on information and science and technology is also being strengthened. In order to encourage better communication system in the state, Bihar State Wide Area Network Project has been started under public private partnership model and all the district and block offices have been added to this project. Every panchayat and person should have access to E–administration, and to achieve this, Vasudha centers have been established. A Special Court Act was founded in the year 2009 to curb the corruption in the state. Under this Act, actions have been taken on people having direction proportionate assets and their properties have been seized. In year 2011, MLA local region development fund was abolished because it was being misused and it was replaced by Chief Minister Regional Development Program. Right to Service Act 2011 has been implemented so that common people can have easy access to the administration and all the services are delivered in a time-bound manner.

The possibility of agricultural development in Bihar is immense. Therefore, it is the need of the hour that agriculture is given due importance while prioritizing the development of state and policies should be framed accordingly. Bihar is a leading producer of fruits and vegetables. Mango, banana, litchi, makhana, papaya, Guava etc. are some of the major fruit produces of the state. Food processing industry, based on fruits can be established to increase the cost value of these fruits. This will help not only in increasing the per capita income, but will also help in raising the standard of living of people; moreover, it will also create more job opportunities for the people of state. It is necessary to establish mango and makhana based industries in Darbhanga, litchi based industry in Muzaffarpur and banana based industry in Hazipur. Similarly, small-scale and cottage industry like stone crushing industry can be set up for local resources on Rohtas, Aurangabad, Gaya, Nawada, Jamui etc., districts of Southern Bihar. There are many (submerged) wetland areas in Northern Bihar which can be developed for pisciculture, aquaponics, tourism etc., which will not only increase the income of people but will also create more job opportunities for local people.

Human resource is available in excess in Bihar. It is necessary to develop skills in them and make them employable. For this, it is necessary to develop Bihar as a hub of education. With technical institutions in Bihar, thousands of students are forced to go to other states to receive education, and spend crores of rupees in those states. Therefore, development of good quality higher education institutions in the state will not only stop this heavy outflow of money from the state, but will also attract students from other states to come to Bihar for education.

Tourism sector in Bihar also shows immense possibilities. The state is enriched with historic, cultural, religious, and natural tourist spots. Places of Buddhist relevance are being connected to form Buddhist circuit and places of Jain relevance are being connected to form Jain circuit for the development of tourism in the state. Many tourist places of international relevance like Bodh Gaya, Rajgir, Vaishali, and Valmiki Nagar are situated in Bihar.

POVERTY IN BIHAR

Poverty is a major problem in Bihar. Most people in Bihar are poor because they are unable to provide for basic necessities of life – food and clothes. Poverty in Bihar can be seen in two ways – relative poverty and absolute poverty. Relative poverty shows the level of difference in different income groups. Income of different age groups of population are considered in relative poverty and the income group with lowest 5 percent and 10 percent is compared with income group of top 5 percent and 10 percent. Results, thus, derived display relative poverty.

In India, the standards and point of view of Planning Commission is accepted in demarking the poverty line and poverty ratio. More than two-thirds population does not have access to clean nutritional food and clean drinking water. Even those who are placed above the poverty line fear that if any disaster or difficult situation arises, they too might go below the poverty line.

The impact of poverty is visible in all the sectors of Bihar, be it per capita gross domestic product or the situation of per capita consumption. Underweight new born babies, infant mortality rate, literacy rate, gender biased distribution system indicate towards the grave poverty and economic imbalance in the social sector in the state. Rising population, low economic growth rate, minimal opportunities of employment and low gross state domestic product, minimal opportunities of production and low quality of natural resources have risen the poverty line of the state. In the year 1983–84, 62.5 percent people of Bihar came below the poverty line. The Bihar Economic Survey 2024-25 reports a population below the poverty line of 15.17%. This figure represents the percentage of people in Bihar living below the poverty line during the period 2024-25.

First official attempt to demarcate the poverty line in India was done by Planning Commission in July 1962. During the Fifth Five-year Plan, Planning Commission established a task force. In July 1958, on the basis of minimum nutrition intake, this task force recommended 2,435 calories (around 2,400) intake per day per person or income of ₹20 per month for rural population and 2,095 calories (around 2,100) intake per day per person, or an income of ₹25 for urban population. This method of measuring poverty is known as food entry method.

Seventh Finance Commission put forward the concept of augumented poverty lines in which per capita monthly expenditure and public expenditure like expense on education, etc. were joined together. A committee was set up under Prof D T Lakdawala in 1989. The recommendations of the committee regarding measurement of poverty were accepted in Ninth Five-year Plan. According to this team of experts, in every state, different poverty lines have been demarcated on the basis of cost level. Further, poverty line in every state will be different. This way, at present, there are 35 different poverty lines in India which was earlier 28. The committee recommended different cost indices for rural and urban population which are as follows:

Poverty line in rural areas: For this the Lakdawala expert team recommended consumer price index (CPI for industrial workers) for agricultural workers.

Poverty line in urban areas: Lakdawala committee has recommended consumer price index for (CPI for Industrial workers) and for different urban workers.

According to report of Tendulkar committee apart from food being consumed, poverty line should be determined on the basis of 6 fundamental necessities: education, health, fundamental infrastructure, clean environment, and work and benefits for women. On the basis of this report, the determination of poverty shall be done on the basis of deprivation of things of basic necessities.

Determination of poverty line on the basis of concept recommended by the Tendulkar Committee, formed by the Planning Commission was done for entire nation as well Bihar in year 2004 and 2011–2012. Tendulkar Committee determined ₹816 per capita income per month for rural areas and an income of ₹1000 per person per month for urban areas. A committee was set up by the Planning Commission under C Rangarajan which presented an estimate in 2013, which is based on the data received from Family Consumer Expenditure Survey 2011–2012 from the 68th round of J N S . According to this the new poverty line shall be expressed as the expenditure of ₹33.33 and ₹27.20 per person per day for urban and rural areas respectively. Approved poverty rate is 21.82 percent. Out of which poverty in rural areas is 25.70 percent and that for urban areas is 70 percent.

Bihar's contribution in population of India is 8.6 percent, but in population below poverty line it is 13.3 percent. Bihar government calculated the poverty line on the basis of Tendulkar Committee set-up by the Planning Commission and it was determined as ₹778 per person per month for rural areas and ₹923 per person per month for urban areas.

Average monthly per capita expenditure as collected by National Sample Survey, is another indicator of poverty.

In.case of fast growth rate and buying capacity of poors, Bihar Government has made tremendous progress. But still, poverty rate is very high in urban areas. Despite a rise in gross state domestic product and adding the factors of primary sector, poverty in urban areas is rising continuously. A major outcome of poverty is growth of dirty colonies. According to census 2011, the population of people living in dirty colonies in Bihar is 12.4 lakhs which is 10.5 percent of total population of the state. Maximum number of dirty colonies in Bihar are found in cities with a population between 20 thousand and 1 lakh.

Rural poverty is the main reason for poverty in Bihar. The poverty in urban areas is an expansion of rural poverty. Almost 60 percent of rural population in Bihar is living below the poverty line. From a class point of view, almost 50 percent of landless people live in rural areas. Almost 77 percent of population working in agricultural sector and 42 percent landowners are living below the poverty line. These numbers are very high as compared to national average. If a caste based analysis of poverty in Bihar is done, then it is found that 79 percent people from scheduled castes and 73 percent people from scheduled tribes are living below the poverty line.

UNEMPLOYMENT IN BIHAR

Unemployment is a major problem in Bihar. Economist Keynes gave the theory of employment in his book 'General Theory of Employment: Interest and Money', published in 1936. The problem of unemployment in developed countries are demand-generated, but in developing countries like India, the problem of unemployment is supply-generated. Problem of unemployment means that a person is ready to work on wage prevalent in market, but he/she is not able to find any work. If all those people who are looking for work get work on current regular wage, then the economy will be in a stage of full employment. According to this assumption, if a person is working 8 hours a day for 273 days, then it is considered as a standard year. This concept was first used in the Sixth Plan to measure employment.

As per to this theory, if a person is employed for 273 days and is working for 8 hours, then we shall refer to it as full employment. Seasonal unemployment and disguised employment are prevalent in Bihar.

1. This unemployment is found mainly in the agricultural sector. In agriculture, employment is generated during the time of tilling the fields, sowing of seeds, crop cultivation etc.
2. Disguised unemployment is also found mainly in rural areas. In this case, more people than required are working in order to receive maximum level of agricultural produce. If such people are removed from agricultural works, even then there will be no impact on agricultural produce. Such people are known to in disguised unemployment. The concept of disguised unemployment was mentioned for the first time by Mrs. Joan Robinson in 1936. Amartya Sen has defined human labour in terms of excess of hours. Vakil and Brahmananda have studied on the product use of this excess labour in Wage Goods Model:

The Planning commission has set up Bhagwati Commission in 1973 which propagated three concepts for the measurement of unemployment and they are as follows:

1. **Usual Status:** As per usual status, if a person is unable to find employment for 183 days, then it is known as usual status of unemployment. Rate of usual unemployment is also known as chronic unemployment rate.
2. **Current Weekly Status:** Current weekly status implies the presentation of employment status of a person, a week or 7 days prior to the date of review. If anybody has not worked even for an hour in current week, then that status is known as current weekly unemployment.
3. **Current Daily Status:** It shows the everyday work status of a person for seven days prior to the date of review. If a person is employed for less than 1 hour in a day, then it is known as current daily unemployment. If he is employed for more than 1 hour but less than 4 hours, then it will be considered as employment for half a day.

While usual status umnemployment rate and weekly status unemployment rate are personal rates, the current daily status unemployment rate shows the rate of time. In the Eleventh Five-year Plan, current daily status unemployment has been used to calculate the estimates of employment and unemployment in the country. To sort out this problem, many programs like IRDP, NREP, TRYSEM, RLEGP were implemented in the Sixth Plan. After the Sixth Plan, unemployment and poverty were kept at priority in almost all the plans. Mahatma Gandhi National Rural Employment Guarantee Act was put in force in year 2011 to provide guaranteed employment.

The unemployment rate in Bihar is currently at 3.4%, slightly higher than the national average of 3.2%. Youth unemployment in urban areas of Bihar is 10.8%.

While some sources indicate a higher unemployment rate of 11.4% based on CMIE data, other sources, like the Economic Survey 2024-25, report a lower rate of 3.2% in 2023-24. These discrepancies might be due to different data sources and methodologies used to calculate unemployment.

Youth unemployment group (15-29 years) is 10.8% in urban Bihar.

- **Labour Force Participation Rate (LFPR):** Bihar's LFPR is 43.4%, lower than the national average of 56.0%.
- **Economic Survey:** The Economic Survey 2024-25 reports a 3.2% unemployment rate in 2023-24.

In order to curb the problem of unemployment, labour-oriented manufacturing and service sector were recognized as high employment possibility sectors, and skill development was stressed upon. The government is implementing various schemes to address unemployment, including MGNREGA but more needs to be done to create sustainable employment. Solutions include promoting entrepreneurship, diversifying industries, improving education quality, establishing job matching centres and expanding government schemes.

In order to help skillful and eligible candidates get job in foreign countries, Bihar government has set up Overseas Planning Bureau.

Disguised unemployment is the major problem of unemployment in Bihar, and there is only one way to overcome this problem. Non-agricultural sector should be developed, and in some important sectors in agriculture like agriculture based industries, dairy sector, pisciculture etc. are promoted and developed accordingly. Likewise, cottage industries should also be promoted so that maximum number of rural population can get proper employment. Poverty eradication programs can be joined to reduce the problem of unemployment.

Union and State Sponsored Programs

- Union Government Sponsored Programs
- State Government Sponsored Programs

UNION GOVERNMENT SPONSORED PROGRAMS

Pradhan Mantri Suraksha Bima Yojana

This program was inaugurated on 9 May, 2015. The aim of this program is to build a universal social security system for all Indians, especially those who belong to poor and weaker section and labours of the unorganized sector.

All the Indians falling in the age bracket of 18-70 are eligible for benefits under this scheme. As per the provisions of this scheme, the premium amount has been decided at ₹12 per person, per year. It will be joined with automatic payment method. In case of death due to accident or complete disability, payment of a sum of ₹2 lakh, and in case of partial disability a sum of ₹1 lakh has been decided, as per the provisions of this scheme.

Pradhan Mantri Jivan Jyoti Bima Yojana

This scheme is applicable in cases of both natural or accidental death. Under the provisions of this scheme, the sum receivable will be ₹2 lakh. The premium amount will be ₹330 per annum, that will be applicable to all the citizens between 18-50 years.

Rashtriya Swasthya Bima Yojana

This scheme was launched on 2 October, 2007, for the families of unorganized sector living below the poverty line and it was implemented on 1 April, 2008. Under this scheme, the total value of insured amount is ₹30,000 per family. The amount of premium is borne by, both the union as well as the state government in a ratio of 75 : 25. In north-eastern states and Jammu and Kashmir, this ratio is 90 : 10.

Sampoorna Bima Gram Yojana

This scheme was launched on 13 October, 2017, by the then Minister of State for Telecommunications, Mr. Manoj Sinha. Under this scheme, in every district of the country, at least one village with minimum 100 families will be identified and all the families in that village will be covered with at least one Gramin Dak Jivan Bima Policy. All the Sansad Adarsh Village have been included in this scheme.

Skill Development Programs

India comes in the category of countries that have abundant human resource. Therefore, if such a huge human resource is connected with skill development then it will give new wings to the development of the nation. Keeping these goals in the backdrop, in the Eleventh Five-year Plan, the government included as much human resource as possible and launched a comprehensive skill development program. In the coordinated action program of skill development, the government has set a goal to develop 500 million skilled personnel so that the nation gets the assistance and guidance of skilled people from different fields.

A three-tier institutional infrastructure has already been prepared in this matter which will help in taking the skill development forward. These are Pradhan Mantri National Skill Development Council, National Skill Development Corporation and National Skill Development Coordination Board. The National Skill Development Coordination Board has worked on five major subjects related to skill development.

- Works related to apprenticeship training;
- Works related to change in syllabus on a continuous basis;
- Works related to business education;
- Works related to accreditation and certification; and
- Works related to determination of conditions because of lack of skills.

The establishment of National Skill Development Corporation is an institutional arrangement of a non-profit corporation by finance ministry to encourage the efforts of private sector in the field of skill development. The corporation will determine the syllabus and parameters in skill training in different fields. A National Skill Development Fund has also been set up to meet the financial needs of National Skill Development Corporation which will function as a trust. The corporation can give training about the structure of the syllabus and parameters. In addition to this, after the completion of training and exam conducted by an authorized institute there is an arrangement to issue certificate and award of ₹1000.

National Skill Development Fund has been established as a trust to collect funds for National Skill Development Corporation.

Pradhan Mantri Kisan Samman Nidhi Yojana

The aim of this scheme is to provide a guaranteed supplementary income to small and marginal farmers to meet their investment and other needs as well as to help in providing for emergency requirements prior to and during the harvest season.

This scheme was officially launched by Prime Minister Narendra Modi on 24 February, 2019, from Gorakhpur, Uttar Pradesh. Earlier it was mandatory for the beneficiary families to have the joint ownership of maximum 2 hectares of cultivable land, in the records of state and union territories. But after a decision taken by the union cabinet on 31 May, 2019, the mandatory condition of ownership of maximum 2 hectares land has been removed. After inception of these reforms, now almost 14.5 crore beneficieries have come under the Pradhan Mantri Kisan Yojana. As per this scheme, an annual sum of ₹6000, in three quarterly instalments (₹2000 in each instalment) will be directly transferred to aadhar-linked bank accounts of eligible farmers (small and marginal). This scheme has been mandated effective from 1 December, 2018 and benefits of this scheme to the eligible farmer families will be payable after this date.

Pradhan Mantri Kisan Pension Yojana

Pradhan Mantri Kisan Pension Yojana was approved in the first cabinet meeting of second term of Prime Minister Narendra Modi on 31 May, 2019. As per the provisions of this scheme, any farmer in the age group of 18 to 40 years can be a part of it. Under this scheme, there is a provision of giving ₹3,000 per month as pension to the farmers when they attain 60 years of age. In this scheme, the union government will match the sum deposited by the eligible farmers in the pension fund.

Pradhan Mantri Ji - Van Yojana

On 28 February, 2019, Cabinet Committee on Economic Affairs (CCEA) under the chairmanship of Prime Minister Narendra Modi approved Pradhan Mantri Ji-Van: Jaiv Indhan-Vatavaran Anukool Fasal Awashesh Nivaran Yojana. Under this scheme, outlay of a sum of ₹1969.50 crores between the year 2018–19 to 2023–24 has been approved. As per the provisions of this scheme, funds have been allocated for two phases for supporting 12 commercial projects for the first phase and 10 demonstration projects.

National Nutrition Mission

To find the solutions for malnutrition based problems and raise the level of nutrition in the country. The union cabinet approved the National Nutrion Mission on 30 November, 2017. The aim of this mission is to reduce stunting, undernutrition and low birth weight by 2% per annum. Under this mission, it has been aimed to reduce anaemia by 3 percent.

There is provision of implementing this mission in entire country through a phased manner and for that, 315 districts in year 2017-18, 235 districts in year 2018-19 and all the remaing districts in year 2019-20 will be included. Starting from year 2018-19 and for a period of 3 years, a budget of almost 9 and half thousand crores have been allocated for this mission. For the allocated budget, 50 percent will be granted Government of India and remaining 50 percent will collected from IVRD or multilateral development banks.

Pradhan Mantri Vaya Vandan Yojana

Pradhan Mantri Vaya Vandan Yojana was launched by the then Union Finance Minister Shri Arun Jaitley on 21 July, 2017, in New Delhi. The aim of this scheme is to provide social security to senior citizens during old age and for the protection of citizens older than 60 years against a fall in the interest income due to unfavourable market conditions in the future. This scheme is being regulated by the Life Insurance Corporation of India. The sum insured under this scheme is ₹5 lakh and the duration is ten years. The annual rate of interest on this amount is 8 percent per annum which is payable on a monthly basis. In case of untimely death of insured, the sum will be given to the nominee.

Pradhan Mantri Matri Vandana Yojana

This scheme is effective from 1 January, 2017. Pradhan Mantri Matri Vandana Yojana is being implemented by Women and Child Development Ministry under the provisions of National Food Security Act 2013. Under the provisions of this scheme, a cash sum of ₹5000 will be granted to pregnant and lactating mothers on the birth of their first child. There is a provision of disbursing this sum in three instalments. First installment of ₹1000 will be given at the time of registration of pregnancy. Second instalment of ₹2000 will be given after six months of pregnancy on receiving at least one ante-natal check-up. Third instalment of ₹2000 will be given after child birth is registered and the child has received the first cycle of vaccines.

The pregnant women who are a regular employee of central or state government, or those who are receiving similar benefits under some other law will not be eligible for benefits under this scheme.

Mission Rainbow (Indradhanush)

This mission was launched by the Government of India in December 2014. This mission is functioning under the health and family welfare ministry. The main aim of this mission is to provide complete vaccination at a fast rate to all the infants and pregnant women. Under this scheme full vacination has to be provided to all the infants below two years and seven vaccines to pregnant women. Diseases like tetanus, polio, diphtheria, TB, hepatitis B, Japanese encephalitis, etc. have been included under this scheme. Pneumonia was added in this list in 2017.

Ayushman Bharat

Ayushman Bharat was announced by Prime Minister Narendra Modi on 23 December, 2018. The main aim of this scheme is to provide high quality health services to poor and marginalized people and provide health insurance to those who are unable to do it for themselves.

Characteristics of Ayushman Bharat

- More than 10 crore families and 50 crore people will be covered in this ambitious scheme. Thus, it will be the biggest program in the world in health sector.

- Two types of heath services have been adopted in Ayushman Bharat. First is the establishment of health and welfare centers so that people can avail good healthcare facilities near their homes and second is Pradhan Mantri Arogya Yojana that has been launched which includes poor and economically weaker people. Thus, it is an important step in the direction of universal health coverage and continuous growth target 2030.
- This scheme is also unique because of the fact that health services in India is not as good as compared to international standards, and every year, more than 6 crore people fall below the poverty line in search of good quality healthcare services. Thus, this scheme will be beneficial not only in providing better health facilities but will also function as an important instrument towards the goal of poverty eradication programs.
- About 40 percent population has been targeted in this scheme and because of that 8.30 crore rural families and 2.33 crore urban families will benefit from it.
- Health insurance of up to ₹5 lakhs will be provided under this scheme.
- This scheme covers different types of diseases. There are 1,350 medical packages in this scheme and it covers 23 serious diseases as well as mental illnesses.
- Secondary and tertiary healthcare services have been completely covered under this scheme.
- Both public as well as private hospitals have been included under this scheme.
- One of the major benefits of this scheme is that a beneficiary can avail its benefits anywhere in India, which means this scheme is portable all across the country.

Eligibility condition for the scheme

The selection of candidates for this scheme will be done on the basis of census of 2011.

Those who are homeless or live in huts or shanties or are cleaners will be the main eligible candidates for this scheme. In other words, the most marginalized section of society is the biggest beneficiary of this scheme.

According to the conditions of this scheme, those who have a credit card with a limit of more than fifty thousand, or those who themselves or whose family member(s) is/are government servant(s) or those who own a two-wheeler, three-wheeler, or four-wheeler, or fishing boat, or the family that pays income tax or owns a house of 3, or more rooms made up of bricks, or own 2.5 hectares irrigated land and has at least on irrigation tool etc. have not been included in this scheme.

Electoral Bond Scheme

Electoral Bond Scheme, 2018 was notified by the Ministry of Finance on 2 February, 2018. According to the eligibility conditions of this scheme, all Indian citizens, any institution regularized in India and a union of Indian citizens will be eligible to buy this scheme. Those political parties who are registered under section 29(a) of the Public Representative Act, 1951 and have secured at least 1 percent of total vote cast in the last elections held for the Lok Sabha or Vidhan Sabha will be able to encash these bonds.

As per the provisions of this scheme the electoral bonds will be issued in value of ₹1 thousand, 10 thousand, 1 lakhs, 10 lakhs and 1 crore. These bonds will be valid for a period of 15 days from the date of their purchase, and if they are not encashed within that duration, then that that amount is deposited in Prime Minister's Relief Fund.

Beti Bachao Beti Padhao Yojana

This scheme was lauched from Panipat District of Haryana on 22 January, 2015. This scheme is a joint effort of 3 ministries—women and child development ministry, health and family welfare ministry and human resource ministry.

The aim of this scheme is to reduce gender-based discrimination and increase the gender ratio. It is also aimed to improve the gravely deteriorating infant gender ratio by multidimensional intervention in infant gender ratio through inclusion of enforcement of education in girls and their universal empowerment.

Initially, this scheme was implemented in 100 districts with worst gender ratio, under which a goal to increase the gender ratio by 10 points in a year was set up. At present, this scheme is functional all across the country.

Pradhan Mantri Ujjwala Yojana

With a motto of Clean Fuel, Better Life, Prime Minister Narendra Modi inaugurated the Pradhan Mantri Ujjawala Yojana on 1 May, 2016 from Balia in Uttar Pradesh. The aim of this scheme is to provide clean fuel (LPG) to all the poor families who live below the poverty line.

As per the provisions of this scheme, the goal of free distribution of cooking gas to women from 5 crore families living below the poverty line within next three years was set up, which was later revised to 8 crore in 2018-19. This scheme provides a financial aid of ₹1600 for every LPG connection to the families living below the poverty line. Under this scheme, the senior women of the family, identified through the data of census 2011, will be given a LPG connection without any security deposit. This scheme is managed by the petroleum and natural gas ministry of the Government of India.

Deendayal Antyodaya Yojana – National Urban Livelihood Mission

Golden Jubilee Urban Employment Mission, which was launched in December 1997, was restructured in September 2013 and relaunched by the title – National Urban Employment Mission. It was once again restructured in July 2015 and renamed as Deendayal Antyodaya Yojana – National Urban Livelihood Mission. The aim of this mission is to reduce poverty and vulnerability of the urban poor households, by enabling them to access gainful self-employment and skilled wage employment opportunities, resulting in an appreciable improvement in their livelihoods on a sustainable basis, through building strong grassroots level and to provide shelters equipped with all basic necessities to the urban homeless people. On 20 February, 2016, government has included all the constitutional local urban bodies of the country in this scheme.

In this mission, up to ₹15000 is spent on employment training of every urban poor through skill development and placement. In addition to this up to ₹18,000 is spent on every urban poor in Northeast and Jammu and Kashmir. This mission is functioning under Ministry of Housing and Urban Poverty Alleviation.

Deen Dayal Antyodaya Yojana – National Rural Livelihood Mission

This scheme is subsequent to Golden Jubilee Rural Self Employment Scheme, launched in 1997 which was renamed to National Rural Livelihood Mission on 3 June, 2011. At present, its name has been changed to Deen Dayal Antyodaya Yojana – National Rural Livelihood Mission. The aim of this mission is to reduce poverty by enabling the poor households to access gainful self-employment and skilled wage employment opportunities, resulting in appreciable improvement in their livelihoods on a sustainable basis. At least, one female member from each identified rural poor household is to be brought under the Self-Help Group (SHG) network in a time-bound manner. This mission aims to improve the livelihood of around 7 crore rural people.

Pradhan Mantri Awas Yojana (Urban)

This scheme was launched on 25 June, 2015 under the flagship of Ministry of Housing and Urban Poverty Alleviation. As per the provisions of this scheme, it shall be worked upon from 2015 to 2022. The aim of this scheme is to provide houses to all the poor people living in cities. This scheme aims to build 1.20 crore houses till year 2022. This scheme will cover all declared 4041 constitutional towns based on census data of 2011. The scheme shall be implemented in three phases:

- For 100 cities in between April 2015 till March 2017;
- For 200 cities in between April 2017 till March 2019;

- For all the remaining cities in between April 2019 till March 2022.

Under the provisions of this scheme, such house building technology will be stressed upon, which will provides affordable housing and not take more than 3 months for construction.

Pradhan Mantri Awas Yojana (Rural)

Implemented by the Ministry of Rural Development, this scheme was launched by 20 November, 2016. The aim of this scheme has been set up to provide house to everybody. In the first phase of this scheme, a goal to build 1 crore houses till 2019 has been set up. Moreover, a financial aid of ₹1.20 lakh per unit for plain areas and ₹1.30 lakh per unit for hilly areas will be provided.

The beneficiaries of this scheme will be identified on the basis of socio-economic census of 2011. This scheme also contains a provision that if a beneficiary wishes he or she can get a loan of ₹70,000 from the bank. This scheme will be funded by both the union as well as state government in a ratio of 60 : 40 for plain areas and 90 : 10 in hilly areas. Under the provisions of this scheme the women in the family will be given priority in handing over the ownership of the house.

Bharat Nirman Yojana

This scheme was launched in December 2005 to build the infrastructure and basic facilities in rural areas. There are 6 components of this scheme– road, irrigation, water supply, rural electrification, construction of buildings and rural telecom connectivity. By providing these fundamental facilities, an attempt has been made to bring city-like basic necessities up to a level in villages as well. Thus, it is a scheme which can curb the difference between urban and rural areas and also which can bring a substantial change in the lifestyle of those lives in villages.

Rural housing schemes like Indira Awas Yojana, Rajiv Gandhi Rural Electrification Scheme related to electrification of villages, Pradhan Mantri Gram Sadak Yojana related to road building, etc. have also been included in this scheme.

Major Goals of Bharat Nirman Yojana

- Construction of 60 lakh additional houses for the marginalized to double the preset aim of houses;
- To complete rural water supply scheme till year 2011;
- To ensure irrigation for additional one crore hectare of land;
- To link all villages of 1,000 population with roads and also to link all ST and hilly villages up to 500 population with roads;
- To supply electricity to all remaining 1,25,000 villages and to provide electricity connection to 2.3 crore houses;
- To provide telephone facility to all remaining 66,822 villages.

The importance of this scheme can also be understood by the fact that building infrastructure in rural areas will also help in growth of the village and creation of jobs, which will also play an important role in curbing the problem of unemployment.

Indira Awas Yojana

Launched in 1985-86 and restructured in 1999-2000, this is a scheme aims to build houses free of cost for poor people living in villages. This scheme is sponsored by the union government which contained provisions to be financed by the union as well state government in a ratio of 75 : 25 but since 1 April, 2013, this ratio was made be 50 : 50.

Pradhan Mantri Gramoday Yojana

This aim of this scheme relates to reconstruction of rural roads and connectivity of villages. As per the provisions of this scheme, the union government will provide financial aid to state governments to implement the specific schemes related to this field. The union government will frame the guidelines in this scheme and will also frame the rules for implementation of this scheme. Minimum Service Scheme, functional prior to the launch of this scheme has also been included.

Ganga Gram Pariyojana

Ganga Gram Scheme was launched on 23 December, 2017, in Vigyan Bhawan in New Delhi in Ganga Gram Swachchhata Conference. Functioning under the Namami Gange Project, this scheme is associated with complete cleanliness of the villages situated across the banks of River Ganga. The aim of this scheme is to develop the villages situated across the banks into Adarsh villages. This project will be implemented under Ministry of Jalshakti / Department of Drinking Water & Sanitation.

Under this scheme, almost 4,470 villages situated at the banks of River Ganga will be developed in an integrated manner on the basis of cleanliness in which amount of ₹829 crores has been granted to 1674 gram panchayats to build toilets. This scheme stresses on the following:

- Solid and liquid waste management;
- Refurbishing of ponds and other water resources;
- Water conservation project;
- Promotion of organic farming and cultivation of medicinal herbs.

Pradhan Mantri Sahaj Bijli Har Ghar Yojana (Saubhagya Yojana)

This scheme was launched in September 2017. This scheme has been launched under the power ministry. In this scheme, there is a provision of providing free electricity connection to all the APL and BPL families living in the rural areas and all the BPL families in the urban areas. The primary aim of this scheme is universal electrification for all the families across the country. Rural electricity board has been nominated as the nodal agency for the implementation of this scheme. The beneficiaries of this scheme will be identified on the basis of data from census 2011.

Samarth Yojana

A new scheme was approved by the Cabinet Committee on Economic Affairs on 20 September, 2017, for capacity building in the textile sector. In the backdrop of this, the Ministry of Textile issued guidelines for Samarth Yojana on 23 April, 2018. The duration of this scheme is three years from year 2017-18 to 2019-20 and the total budget expenditure for this is 1,300 crore rupees. Under the provisions of this Act, a goal to provide training to around 10 lakh people in the textile sector has been set up so that they can look for better opportunities for their livelihood. Under the provisions of Samarth Yojana, in August 2019, the union ministry of textile has signed Memorandum of Understanding with 16 states which will provide skills to around 4 lakh people.

Saathi Pahal

Saathi (Sustainable and Accelerated Adoption of efficient Textile technologies to Help Small Industries Initiative) is a joint initiative of Ministry of Textiles and Ministry of Electricity. An agreement was signed, 24 October, 2017, for the implementation of this initiative.

Under this initiative, Energy Efficiency Services Limited (EESL), a public sector entity under the administrative control of Ministry of Power, would procure energy efficient powerlooms and provide them to the small and medium powerloom units at no upfront cost. The powerloom owners can repay for these machines in instalments over 4 to 5 years to Energy Efficiency Services Limited. This process will help in improving both the production as well as energy efficiency of powerloom industry.

Pradhan Mantri Krishi Sinchayee Yojana

This scheme was launched on 1 July, 2015. Accelerated Irrigation Benefit Programme, Integrated Watershed Management Programme and the On Farm Water Management Program have been amalgamated in this scheme.

The major objective of this scheme is to achieve convergence of investments in irrigation at the field level, improve efficient use of water through high technology, techniques and methods.

The programme will be supervised and monitored by an Inter-Ministerial National Steering

Committee constituted under the chairmanship of Prime Minister with union ministers from concerned ministries.

A budget allocation of 50 thousand crores has been done for a period of 5 years from 2015-16 to 2019-20 for this scheme. The state agricultural ministries will act as nodal office for the implementation of this scheme.

Pradhan Mantri Fasal Bima Yojana

This scheme was launched on 13 January, 2016. It is effective since kharif crops of 2016. The objective of this scheme is to provide financial assistance to farmers in case of loss of produce due to natural calamities, insects and diseases. Rabi, kharif, commercial and horticulture crops have been included in this scheme.

The premium payable under this scheme is 2.0 percent for kharif crops, 1.5 percent for rabi crops and 5 percent for commercial and horticulture crops. As per the provisions of this scheme, the amount of premium will be the specified percentage of sum insured or estimated loss, whichever is lower.

Soil Health Card Scheme

This scheme was launched by Prime Minister Narendra Modi in Suratgarh in Rajasthan on 19 February, 2015. The prime minister launched this scheme with the motto of "Swasth Dharaa. Khet Haraa" (Healthy Earth, Green Farm).

The objective of this scheme is to let the farmers know about real health of their farms and suggest ways to improve the same so that sustenance farming can be encouraged. Under the provisions of this scheme soil heath cards have to be distributed to 14 crore farmers in the next 3 years. These cards will be issued once in a cycle of 3 years.

This scheme is being implemented under the observation of Agriculture and Cooperative Minsitry in all the states and union territories of India.

Smart City Mission

This mission was launched on 25 June, 2015. The objective of this mission is to develop basic facilities in cities to provide a civilized, good quality life style to the people as well as to build a clean and enduring environment. Under this mission, it is aimed to develop a total of 100 smart cities across all the states and union territories of India for which more than 100 cities have been selected so far.

For the financing part of this scheme, it has been decided that ₹100 crores per city per annum will be granted by the union government and the same amount shall be granted by the state governments.

Shyama Prasad Mukherjee Rurban Mission

This schem was launched on 21 February, 2016. This mission is implemented under the Ministry of Rural Development. The objective of this mission is to provide urban facilities which include skill development and economic growth for the rural areas. This scheme has been launched with an objective to bring fast economic growth to rural areas. Under this mission, a provision to develop rural clusters of 300 villages has been set up named Rurban clusters.

The state government will select such villages that have a population of 25-50 thousand in plains and coastal areas and 5-15 thousand in desert, hilly tribal areas and islands.

Under this mission a budget expenditure of 5142.08 crores has been allocated for a period of 5 years from 2015-16 to 2019-20.

Atal Pension Yojana

This scheme was launched on 1 June, 2015 to merge the already functional self-reliance scheme. This scheme was announced by the Finance Minister in his budget speech of year 2015-16. It is a pension scheme functional under Ministry of Financial Affairs.

The objective of this scheme is to provide social security to unorganized poor labours employed in the private sector. This scheme will be applicable to all those citizens employed in the private sector who are not a member of any statutory social security scheme. Under this scheme, there is a provision of giving a pension between ₹1,000 and ₹5,000 to the subscribers when they attain the age of 60 years on the basis of the premium paid. As per the eligibility conditions for this scheme all the Indian citizens between the age group of 18 to 40 years and having a valid bank acoount will be eligible for the benefits. Minimum duration for payment of premium by the subscriber is 20 years. There is also a provision that the government will pay 50 percent of premium for 5 years or ₹100 rupees per month, whichever is lower.

Balika Samriddhi Yojana

This scheme was launched in year 1997 with an objective to change the society's point of view towards girls. It was restructured in 1999. Prior to 1999, a grant of ₹500 was given to the mother of a girl child, born in a family that lived in rural area and being below the poverty line. In the restructured scheme, the grant of ₹500 that was paid cash is now deposited in a bank account that pays interest in the name of new born girl child.

Kishori Shakti Yojana

This scheme is launched considering the girls of adolescent age. It is a special scheme for the girls between the age of 14-18 years which aims to use the ICDCS infrastructure for versatile development of girls including nutrition, literacy, and commercial efficiency.

Mother's Absolute Affection (Maa) Program

This program was launched on 5 August, 2016. This scheme is functioning under the Union Health and Family Welfare Ministry.

The main objective of this scheme is to spread awareness about breastfeeding among the people. The scheme emphasizes on making mother, aware about the benefits of breastfeeding so that the act is encouraged. For the implementation of this program, Union Health and Family Welfare Ministry has granted a sum of ₹30 crores out of which ₹4.3 lakhs have been granted to each district.

Jal Shakti Mission

This mission was launched on 1 July, 2019. The main objective of this scheme is to work on initiaves for water conservation, water storage and water management in such areas where there is scarcity of water.

This mission has been launched amidst continuously falling water level, shortage of water and the conditions arisen in 2019 due to less than expected monsoon. The objective of government under this scheme is to provide clean drinking water to every household of the country on a sustained basis.

About 1592 development blocks from 256 districts have been included in this mission. Some of the salient features of Jal Shakti Mission are as follows:

- Water conservation and storage of rain water;
- Re-use of water;
- Rejuvenation of old and conventional water sources;
- Creation of drainage fields;
- Forestation.

Pradhan Mantri Jan Dhan Yojana

This scheme was launched on 28 August, 2014, with the motto of "Mera khata bhagya vidhata" ("My account, fate restorer").

The primary objective of this scheme is the financial inclusion of poor and marginalized people and to make them economically stronger. Some of the major components of this scheme are provision of fine financial services to marginalized and poor people such as savings bank account credit insurance pension, etc. Under the provisions of this scheme, major goal is to promote financial awareness and connect them with direct benefit transfer. A rupay debit card along with an accidental insurance of ₹1 lakh is another major characteristic of this scheme.

A major achievement of this scheme is that total ₹31.42 crore bank accounts have been opened till 4 April, 2018.

Pradhan Mantri Mudra Yojana

This scheme was launched on 8 April, 2015. Mudra: Micro unit development and refinance agency was established under the the the Companies Act 2013 as an ancillary unit of Indian Small Industries Development Bank.

The primary objective of Pradhanmantri Mudra Yojana is to provide finance to the poor people. As per the provisions of this scheme, the goal is to provide best and world class level of single window financial services for the comprehensive economic and social development of those who are at the lowest level of the pyramid. Micro institutions have been divided into three categories under this scheme:

Shishu Udyog – up to 50 thousand

Kishor Udyog – 50 thousand to 5 lakh

Tarun Udyog – 50 thousand to 10 lakh

Swachh Bharat Abhiyan Clean India Mission

Launched on 2 October, 2014 on the occasion of birth anniversary of Mahatma Gandhi the objective of Swachh Bharat Abhiyan is to make India open defecation free till the year 2019.

The aim of this mission is to be achieved through the construction of personal mass and community toilets so that India can be the occasion of 150th birth anniversary of Mahatma Gandhi on 2 October, 2019.

There is a plan to keep the villages clean using solid and liquid waste management with the help of gram panchayats. In order to ensure the proper implementation of the schemes an expert committee comprising 19 members has also been formed. Under this mission, total estimated cost of program in 4041 statutory cities for a period of 5 years will be around 6400 crore rupees.

There are two subsidiary missions of swachh Bharat Mission first Swachh Bharat Rural Mission and second Swachh Bharat Urban Mission.

Startup India

Startup India was announced on 15 August, 2015 and this scheme was inaugurated on 16 January, 2016.

Primary objective of the scheme is to encourage entrepreneurship and to build a favourable environment for startup businesses. As per the eligibility for the scheme, it is mandatory that the establishment of company and its registration should be in India. Also, the annual turnover of the company in a financial year should not be above 25 crore. The startup should be working towards innovation/improvement of existing products services and processes, and should have the potential to generate employment or create wealth. A fund of 10,000 crores has been set up for financial assistance of entrepreneurship based startups. This fund be managed by SIDBI.

Stand-up India

Stand-up India was announced on 15 August, 2014 whereas it was inaugurated on 5 April, 2015 in Noida, Uttar Pradesh.

The objective of this scheme is to make the reach of women and entrepreneurs from Schedule Caste and Tribe Institutional Financial Infrastructures easy and accessible. Under this scheme every branch of all the commercial banks must provide a loan of ₹ 10 lakhs to 1 crore to at least one borrower from Schedule Caste and new tribe and women for a new business. SIDBI will provide a refinance window of ₹10,000 crore under this scheme. Also, there is a provision in this scheme that National Credit Guarantee Trust Company Limited will create a guarantee system through a fund of ₹5000 crores.

Make In India

Make In India Scheme was launched on 25 September, 2014. The objective of the initiative is to showcase India as the most preferred global manufacturing investment, and new application destination for better promotion of the manufacturing sector, so that India can be established as a major hub in this sector.

About 25 special industrial fields have been identified for Make in India scheme so that a better promotion for them can be done. A goal of increasing the contribution of manufacturing sector in gross domestic product of India to 25 percent from 16 percent and creation of 100 million jobs in this sector.

Sangam Project

This project was launched in March 2019. To train functionaries and officers across India on Swachh Bharat e-Learning Portal, this scheme is implemented as a joint project of Microsoft and the Ministry of Housing and Urban Affairs.

Sangam, actually is a cloud hosted mobile first community platform through which the officers of municipality will be trained for Swachh Bharat e-Learning portal.

Pravasi Teerth Darshan Yojana

On 22 January, 2019, Prime Minister Narendra Modi announced the preparations regarding the Pravasi Teerth Darshan Yojana during the inaugural ceremony of 15 Pravasi Bharatiya Divas.

Under this scheme the Government of India will facilitate pilgrimage (teerth yatra) to various holy places for a selected group of non-resident Indians twice a year. The overseas Indians living in Mauritius, Surinam, Guyana, Fiji, Trinidad and Tobago, and the girmitiyas (descendents of Indian labourers) in Jamaica will be given preference in the selection of intended non-resident Indians.

Swadesh Darshan Scheme

This scheme was launched in January 2015. It is a scheme launched by the Ministry of Tourism in India. It is a completely center-backed scheme. The main objective of this scheme is to develop specific theme-based tourism circuit in the country. These tourist circuits will be developed on the principles of high tourist value, competitiveness and sustainability in an integrated manner. Five theme-based tourist circuits that will be developed in the first leg of this scheme are: Buddhist circuit, Himalayan circuit, Krishna circuit, Northeastern circuit and Coastal circuit. Many other circuits like wildlife circuit, tribal circuit, desert circuit, sufi circuit, tirthankar circuit, heritage circuit, eco circuit etc., will also be included in this scheme in the later phases. At present, total number of such circuits is 15.

Udaan Yojana

Launched with a tagline of 'Ude Desh Ka Aam Nagarik' (Udan) or let the common citizen of India fly, functioning under the Civil Aviations Ministry of India since 27 April, 2017, is associated with the projects to strengthen the regional aviation market in India. It is a scheme of Government of India which is related to development of airports and regional air connectivity as well as ease of flying for the common man in India.

The primary objective of this scheme is to create affordable, economically viable and profitable aviation at a regional level so that flying can be made affordable and accessible to common man in small and medium cities. This scheme will be applicable for flights operating for a distance of 200 to 800 kms. Airport Authority of India has been made the implementation agency of this scheme. There is also a provision to grant subsidy by the estate government to cover the economic losses to the airlines.

Deen Dayal Sparsh Yojana

Deen Dayal Sparsh Yojana was launched on 3 November, 2017, by the then Minister of State for Telecommunications, Shri Manoj Sinha.

It is a scholarship scheme which aims at promoting zest for postal tickets and also at promoting research in this field. Its full form is SPARSH – Scholarship for Promotion of Aptitude & Research in Stamps as a Hobby. This scheme is applicable to students of standards 6 to 9. Under this scheme, 920 scholarships (₹ 500 per month) will be awarded.

SANKALP and STRIVE Schemes

Cabinet Committee on Economic Affairs approved the SANKALP and STRIVE schemes on

11 October, 2017. Both these schemes are related to skill developments as per the requirement of the market.

SANKALP is the short form for Skills Acquisition and Knowledge Awareness for Livelihood Promotion.

STRIVE is the short form for Skill Strengthening for Industrial Value Enhancement.

Atal Bhujal Yojana

In order to encourage groundwater conservation in regions with low groundwater reserve, Prime Minister Narendra Modi launched the Atal Bhujal (groundwater) Yojana on 25 December, 2019. The structure of this scheme has been framed with an objective to bring a behaviuorial change, in the management of groundwater resources, at the community level in selected water stressed areas in identified states viz., Gujarat, Haryana, Karnataka, Madhya Pradesh, Maharashtra, Rajasthan and Uttar Pradesh.

Under the provisions of this scheme out of the total budget expenditure of ₹6,000 crores, 50 percent will come as loan from the World Bank which will be repayed by the central government and remaining 50 percent will be sponsored by the central government through regular budget allocation in the form of grants.

This scheme is expected to benefit almost 8350 gram panchayats across 78 districts in these states. Under this, a provision has also been made to connect the youth with opportunities of job creation through pisciculture.

Pradhan Mantri Matsya Sampada Yojana

On 20 May, 2020, union cabinet under the chairmanship of Prime Minister Narendra Modi approved the implementation of Pradhan Mantri Matsya Sampada Yojana. The primary objective of this scheme is to achieve sustainable and accountable growth in the field of fish rearing through 'blue revolution'.

This scheme will be implemented for a period of five years starting from financial year 2020-21 to 2024-25. With an estimated budget of 20,050 crores, this scheme will be implemented as a center sponsored and central government scheme. In this the share of central government will be 9,407 crores, state government will be 4,880 crores and the share of beneficiaries will be 5,763 crores. There will be two componenets of Pradhan Mantri Matsya Sampada Yojana—first, central scheme and second, center-sponsored scheme. Center-sponsored scheme has been divided into 3 categories and these are—encourangement to produce and productivity, infrastructure and post production management and fish rearing management and regulatory framework.

GOAL Scheme

Union Tribal Affairs Minister Shri Arjun Munda launched the GOAL program (Going Online As Leaders) for tribal affairs ministry in partnership with Facebook. The program has been designed with a long-term vision to develop the potential of tribal youth and women to help them acquire skills and knowledge through mentorship in various sectors. The GOAL programme is designed to provide mentorship to tribal youths through digital mode.

The program intends to upskill and empower 5,000 tribal youths in the current phase to harness the full potential of digital platforms and tools to learn new ways of doing business, explore and connect with domestic and international markets. One of the major characteristics of the program is that it will enable tribal women in remote areas to use digital platforms for sharing their aspirations, dreams and talent and will create an environment for their empowerment.

Deen Dayal Upadhyay Shramev Jayate Scheme

This scheme was launched on 16 October, 2014. It will be implemented by the Ministry of Labour and Employment.

The objective of this scheme is to build a favouarable environment for industrial development through transparency and efficiency in the field of labour. Five ongoing schemes—dedicated labour facility portal, new system of ad hoc inspection, universal account number training encouragement scheme and restructures of national health insurance scheme have been included in this scheme. In order to provide online registration facility to the labours in Shram Suvidha Portal, there is a provision to grant Unique Identification Number as well.

Atal Bhashanter Yojana

This program was inaugurated in December 2018. This scheme has been implemented by the Ministry of Foreign Affairs with the primary objective of providing training to linguists.

Under the provisions of this scheme linguists will be trained and a group of interpreters shall be formed for translation of Arabic, Japanese, Russian, French, Mandarin, and Spanish languages to Hindi language and vice versa.

Agnipath Scheme

Agnipath Scheme is a tour of duty style scheme approved by the Government of India on 14 June 2022 and implemented in the country a few months later in September 2022, for recruitment of soldiers below the rank of commissioned officers into the three services of the armed forces. All recruits will be hired only for a four year period. Personnel recruited under this system are to be called Agniveers, which will be a new military rank.

PM e-Bus Seva

Launched in 2023 PM-eBus Sewa supports public transport by deploying 10,000 electric buses under a PPP model. It aids in reducing greenhouse gas emissions and includes urban mobility projects like the National Common Mobility Card for seamless travel in urban areas.

Amrit Bharat Station Scheme

Amrit Bharat Station Scheme is an ongoing Indian Railways mission launched in February 2023 by the Ministry of Railways to redevelop 1275 stations nationwide. It is both enabler and beneficiary of other key Government of India schemes, such as BharatNet, One Station One Product, Make in India, Startup India, Standup India, industrial corridors, Bharatmala, Dedicated Freight Corridor Corporation of India and Sagarmala.

PM Vishwakarma

Launched in 2023, it aims at improving the quality as well as the reach of products and services of artisans and craftspeople and to ensure that they are integrated into the domestic and global value chains.

One Nation One Subscription

Launched on 1st January 2025, One Nation One Subscription (ONOS) is a one-stop digital library in India with institutional access to global research in various academic disciplines. The project is sponsored by the Government of India after the approval of One Nation One Subscription (ONOS) bill by the cabinet.

This will enable users to access paywalled articles for free. ONOS is expected to host 13000 journals.

The Government of India allocated Rs 6,000 crore for three years until 2027 to build this digital library. The government's autonomous university libraries' database called Information and Library Network Centre (INFLIBNET), which is a project by the University Grants Commission (UGC) is to host the ONOS database.

STATE GOVERNMENT SPONSORED PROGRAMS

Alpasankhyak Kalyan Chhatravas

The Alpasankhyak Kalyan Chhatravas is a govt scheme that provides financial assistance to children studying between the classes of 11th and 12th and who come from marginalised communities. Under the Sarkari Yojana, the Bihar government deposits ₹ 1000 per month to youngsters so that they can use that money to buy whatever they need. Along with the monetary support, 9 kg of rice and 6 kg of wheat are also given to students every month so that they consume nutritious food.

Awsar Badhe Aage Badhe

The Awsar Badhe Aage Badhe is a state government scheme that aims to help youngsters grow and build their personal and professional lives. The Yojana was designed to build and improve infrastructure concerning educational institutions offering various disciplines in every district of Bihar so that the youth can have as many options as possible.

Bihar Anganwadi Beneficiary Scheme

The Bihar Anganwadi Beneficiary Scheme is a scheme that aims to deliver essential services to children and expecting and new mothers so that they stay healthy in such sensitive times of their lives. The scheme works through Anganwadi centres and aims to reduce mortality rates and malnutrition.

Bihar Diesel Grant Scheme

The state govt of Bihar launched the Bihar Diesel Grant Scheme to provide subsidies on diesel to farmers of the state. The scheme provides a subsidy of ₹ 750 per acre per irrigation for Kharif crops at the rate of ₹ 75 per litre. To avail the benefits of the subsidy scheme, the farmers should have a land of at least 8 acres. This Sarkari scheme is an exceptional initiative aimed at reducing the financial burden of farmers.

Bihar Mukhyamantri Vridhajan Pension Yojana (MVPY)

The Bihar Mukhyamantri Vridhajan Pension Yojana (MVPY) is a pension scheme that provides pensions to senior citizens above the age of 60 years residing in the state. Under the scheme, ₹ 400 is given to senior citizens between the ages of 60-79 years and ₹ 500 to senior citizens above 80 years per month. The pension is deposited directly into the bank accounts of beneficiaries and helps them in leading a healthy independent life.

Patrakar Pension Samman Yojana

The Patrakar Pension Samman Yojana is a govt pension scheme that provides monthly financial aid to the journalists of the state who are now retired. According to the scheme, retired journalists above the age of 60 years are entitled to receive ₹ 6000 per month for at least the next 20 years. The scheme recognises the work of journalists and provides them with financial security as a token of appreciation for their work.

Bihar Rajya Fasal Sahayata Yojana

The Bihar Rajya Fasal Sahayata Yojana is an agriculture scheme that aims to compensate the farmers who have suffered financial loss of crops. As per the Yojana, if a farmer's crop is destroyed up to 20% then they are entitled to receive ₹ 7500 as compensation and if the damage is more than 20% then they are entitled to receive ₹ 10,000.

Bihar Saur Kranti Sinchai Yojana

The state govt launched the Bihar Saur Kranti Sinchai Yojana to promote and encourage farmers to use sustainable farming measures. As a start, the scheme provides a subsidy of 75% to the farmers so that they can purchase solar pumps for irrigation. Farmers must have at least an acre of land to a maximum of 5 acres to avail the benefits of the subsidy scheme.

Ghar Tak Pakki Gali-Naliyan

The Ghar Tak Pakki Gali-Naliyan is an exceptional govt initiative that aims to construct proper roads and drainage facilities across the whole state. The scheme represents the state's commitment to improving the infrastructural facilities to make it an ideal state for the people.

Mukhya Mantri Kanya Utthan Yojana

For the empowerment of girls, Mukhya Mantri Kanya Utthan Yojana was launched by Chief Minister Nitish Kumar. Under this scheme expenditures is incurred on education, health and social welfare. The girl students are given ₹ 54,100 from their birth till graduation. Amount of ₹2,000 is given at the time of birth. Under the provisions of this scheme, unmarried girls are given ₹10,000 and girls who complete their graduation are given a reward of ₹25,000.

Mukhya Mantri Anusuchit Jaati evam Anusuchit Janjati Udyami Yojana

Mukhya Mantri Anusuchit Jaati evam Anusuchit Janjati Udyami Yojana was launched in Bihar on 4 August, 2018.

Mukhya Mantri Vridha Pension Yojana (MMVPY)

Mukhya Mantri Vridha Pension Yojana was launched by Government of Bihar. Under the provisions of this scheme, pension of ₹400 per month is given to people over 60 years of age, and ₹500 monthly pension is given to people over 79 years of age. This pension is given to such people who do not receive pension from any other mode. This scheme is effective since 1 April, 2019.

Bihar Student Credit Card Scheme

This scheme was launched on 2 October, 2016. Under the provisions of Bihar Student Credit Card Scheme, assistance is provided to those students who have completed their intermediate level education and wish to take admission in higher education, or commercial courses, or technical courses like B.A, B.Sc, engineering, MBBS, management, law, etc. Under this scheme, apart from the college fee, hostel fee, and in case hostel is not allotted, then the cost of living, study materials etc. is borne by the government. A nominal goal to provide education loans to five lakh students has been set up under this scheme. This scheme will be helpful for those students who are economically incapable. Moreover, it will help in increasing the admission rate in higher education. Under the provisions of this scheme, students can take a loan of up to ₹4 lakhs from banks. The unique characteristic of this scheme is that government comes as a guarantor for the loans taken under the scheme.

Mukhya Mantri Nishchay Swayam Sahayata Bhatta Yojana

Mukhya Mantri Nishchay Swayam Sahayata Bhatta Yojana was launched on 2 October, 2016. Under the provisions of this scheme, a monthly allowance of ₹1000 will be given for two years to unemployed youths, between the age of 20 to 25 years, so that they can look for better job opportunities. This scheme has been implemented by the Planning and Development Department of the Government of Bihar. The students who receive allowance under this scheme are given a mandatory training of language (Hindi/English) and communication skills, basic computer knowledge and behaviourial skills.

Kushal Yuva Karyakram

Kushal Yuva Karyakram was launched on 2 October, 2016. Under this scheme those students who have completed matriculation and intermediate are given training of language (Hindi/English) and communication skills, basic computer knowledge and behavioural skills. This training will be of 80 hours for language (Hindi or English) and communication skills, 120 hours for basic computer knowledge, and 40 hours for behavioural skills. This scheme will be implemented by the Labour Department of Government of Bihar. A skill training center has been established in every block of the state under the provisions of this scheme where training for Hindi and English language art of communication, basic computer knowledge and behavioural skills are imparted. To provide training to the students of the state, Labour Department has tied up with Maharashtra Knowledge Corporation Limited (MKCL), a Maharashtra based company.

Mukhya Mantri Vidyut Sambaddh Nishchay Yojana

This scheme was launched on 15 November. It was launched with the slogan – 'Har Ghar Bijli Lagatar' (Uninterrupted power supply to every household). Under the provisions of this scheme, the state government ensures electricity connection along with meter to every household in rural region by the help of its resources.

Mukhyamantri Gramin Peyjal Nishchay Yojana

In order to ensure the supply of drinking water to rural areas, this scheme was launched on 27 September, 2016. It was implemented in those areas which have high concentration of iron, fluoride or arsenic. Clean drinking water was supplied to the families of all 22,261 quality affected regions in 2,411 Gram panchayats in the state through pipes. This scheme was implemented by public health mechanism department.

Mukhyamantri Rural Drinking Water (non quality affected region) Nishchay Yojana

Mukhyamantri Rural Drinking Water (non quality affected region) Nishchay Yojana was launched on 27 September, 2016. This scheme was launched in those regions where drinking water is free from concentration of fluoride and arsenic. This scheme was implemented by public health mechanism department.

Mukhya Mantri Shahri Peyjal Nishchay Yojana

In order to ensure clean drinking water to every house in cities, Mukhya Mantri Urban Drinking Water Nishchay Yojana was launched on 27 September, 2016. This scheme was implemented by Urban Development and Housing Department. The objective of this scheme is to ensure supply of clean drinking water through taps to 140 urban local bodies in the state. This scheme will start from local bodies with low population and then spread out to all the local bodies in a phased manner.

Gramin Tola Sampark Nishchay Yojana

Government of Bihar had decided to construct and connect every house with paved roads and paved drainage. For achieving this objective Gramin Tola Sampark Yojana was launched. This scheme was launched on 28 October, 2016. Single all weather connectivity is being built across all the districts, villages with population of 500 or more, and villages with a population of 250 or more in 11 districts have been covered under the Pradhan Mantri Gram Sadak Yojana. This scheme was launched to provide road connectivity to villages with a population less than 500 but more than 250 in remaining 27 districts. The objective under this scheme is to connect the economically and socially backward districts, as well as districts with majority tribal population. State government has identified 33,461 habitations with no connectivity.

Mukhyamantri Gramin Gali-Nali Pakkikaran Nishchay Yojana

In order to provide clean surroundings to people living in rural areas Government of Bihar has decided for pavement of streets and drains in this area. This scheme was launched on 28 October, 2016. The objective of this scheme is to provide all the people with paved streets and drainages by year 2019-20, through community participation.

Mukhyamantri Shahri Nali-Gali Pakkikaran Nishchay Yojana

Mukhyamantri Shahri Nali-Gali Pakkikaran Nishchay Yojana was launched on 28 October, 2016 to ensure pavement of all the streets and drains in the cities. The implemention of this scheme is carried out by Urban Development and Housing Department.

Urban Infrastructure and Governance Program

There are two programs functioning under this scheme–Patna City phase (Patna, Danapur, Khagaul, Phulwari Sharif) and Bodh Gaya. A total amount of ₹75.608 lakhs were approved for water supply and solid waste management projects in Patna, Danapur, Khagaul and Phulwari Sharif and water supply and sewage management projects in Bodh Gaya. Out of these projects, Khagaul water supply project has been completed and Phulwari Sharif Project is in its last stage.

Nagar Sudhar Samarthan Program

To bring reforms in 28 largest urban local bodies of Bihar, International Development Deartment of United Kingdom is assisting in Nagar Sudhar Samarthan Program. Under this project, there is a provision to develop basic infrastructure in 1402 dirty colonies in these cities. With an expected expenditure budget of ₹402 crores, the infrastructure under this project includes paved roads, drainages, personal toilets, hand pumps and solar street lights, etc. Out of the total expenditure, 90 crores will be borne by the International Development Department of United Kingdom and the rest will be borne by the state government.

Mukhya Mantri Bhikshavriti Nivaran Yojana

Primary objective of Mukhya Mantri Bhikshavriti Nivaran Yojana is to wear away detach the beggars from their occupation. Disabled people have also been included in this scheme. Under the provisions of this scheme, beggars and disabled people are provided with facilities like shelter, medicines, and others. For the implementation of this scheme, State Society for Rehabilitation of Ultra Poor has also been set up. This institution works for the upliftment of extremely poor, disabled people and beggars. A non-government organization, Medha is already working to carry out a survey of beggars. District level screening committee inspects the survey carried out by Medha and takes further course of action. Representatives of non-government organizations, disabled persons, and district magistrate are members of this committee.

A 3-step model has been decided for rehabilitation of disabled and beggars – advice and rehabilitation, skill development, and self employment.

To provide medical facilities to disabled, beggars and the ultra poor, a hospital in Patna has been identified to be the nodal hospital where these people can get all kinds of medical attention. It is planned to start such hospitals in other districts of the state as well.

Child Marriage Prohibition Scheme

Child Marriage Prohibition Scheme has been launched to stop child marriages in the state. Primary objective of this scheme is to stop child marriages and provide opportunities of education, physical, mental and comprehensive development of adolescent boys and girls. Child Marriage Prohibition Act, 2008 does not give legal recognition to any such marriage which is conducted prior to the legal age of marriage. The prescribed legal age for marriage for girls is 18 years and for boys it is 21 years. State government is running many programs to stop child marriages, and Bihar Women Development Corporation is playing an important role in it.

Kabir Antyeshti Anudan Yojana

Kabir Antyeshti Anudan Yojana was launched by the state government in year 2007. Under this scheme, in case of death of a family member, the dependents are given a grant of ₹1500 to conduct the last rites of the deceased. The dependent in the rural area can apply to the Mukhiya and in urban areas, the person can apply to the ward commissioner. After this, they are given a grant of ₹1500 in cash.

Mukhya Mantri Gram Sadak Yojana

Mukhya Mantri Gram Sadak Yojana is an ambitious project of the state government of Bihar. Primary objective of this project is to connect all the unconnected villages and colonies with a population 500 and 999 with all weather roads in a phased manner on account of the data available through the Census of 2001. The implementation of this program will be done by a working division of the Rural Works Department through to the process of e-tender. The Rural Department shall be allotted the budget from the treasury of the state government. The Rural Works Department will provide this amount in the form of grants to already established rural road development agencies that will implement this scheme with the help of the working division of Rural Works Department. The sites will be identified on the basis of priority. Under the provisions of this scheme, there is an arrangement for construction of single roads only. If a road has already been constructed, then the construction of new road cannot be done under this scheme. For the annual maintenance of roads built under this scheme village engineering organisation is given excess funds.

Mukhyamantri Setu Nirman Yojana

In Bihar Mukhyamantri Setu Nirman Yojana is implemented to build new bridges on all the roads in the state. Under the provisions of this scheme reconstruction of old and damaged bridges, widening of narrow bridges, refurbishing of already constructed bridges and construction of such roads is done which have not yet been notified but are very important for connectivity with Gram Panchayat. Under the provisions of this scheme renovation and construction of such bridges the cost between 10 lakhs and 10 crores will be allocated. The operational committee for this project includes a chairman, nominated by the Chief Minister, Chairman of District Council as a member and District Officer as the secretary. In this scheme, the implementation of 33 percent or up to 25 lakhs, whichever is less, shall be issued by the District Magistrate and the remaining 67 percent or for more than 25 lakhs projects, the issue of funds will be done by the Bihar State Bridge Construction Corporation.

Mukhyamantri Region Development Scheme

This scheme was launched by the state government in 2011-12. This scheme is operated by Planning and Development Department, Bihar Government. The primary objective of this scheme is to build basic infrastructure in all the rural and urban regions of every district of the state in order to bring balanced regional development among them.

Shatabdi Ann Kalash Yojana

Shatabdi Ann Kalash Yojana has been launched to help the people suffering from hunger and starvation. If an adult person is starving, then there is a provision for him to get 10 kg food grains, and in case of adolescents, 7 kg food grains from public distribution system shops free of cost. The responsibility of food grain distribution has been given to Mukhiya, Sarpanch, Panch, and Ward Members. On the recommendations of District Magistrate, the entitled person can get food grains for more than a week.

Mukhya Mantri Teevra Beej Yojana

Mukhya Mantri Teevra Beej Yojana was launched by the Government of Bihar in the year 2008-09. The objective of this scheme was to deliver new varieties of seeds to farmers in all the villages at the same time. In every revenue village, following a base of two farmers, per farmer—6 kg paddy, 20 kg wheat, 8 kg grams, and 4 kg masur is distributed, in a function organized, by the public representatives at 90 percent grant. Bio fertilizers are also distribute free of cost along with this. The selection of farmers is done at the panchayat level by the farmer advisors.

Beej Gram Yojana

Beej Gram Yojana was launched by the Government of Bihar in year 2008-09. The objective of this scheme was to make better quality seeds in the village itself with the help of farmers. Under this scheme, one village is selected from every block. All the farmers of the selected villages are provided with high quality seeds of paddy, wheat or pulses at 50 percent subsidy. Selection of farmers is done by the district agriculture officer. It is mandatory to have 25 acres land in the selected village otherwise the neighbouring village is selected.

Mukhyamantri Niji Poudhshala Yojana (Hariyali Mission)

Mukhyamantri Niji Poudhshala Yojana was launched by the Government of Bihar in year 2013. This is also known as Hariyali Misson. This scheme is operated by the Environment and Forest Department of the state government. The objective of this scheme is to prepare nursery of different hybrid varieties of plants at a large scale with assistance of entrepreneurs and farmers so that the goals of plantation can be achieved. Apart from creating an opportunity for creating wealth for the entrepreneurs and farmers, this scheme will also create job opportunities. Plants and trees like sagwan, semal, gamhar, mahogany, amaltas, mahua, neem, sheesham, and bamboo are planted under this scheme. In order to reap benefits of this project, the applicant should have land in his or her name.

Ganna Vikas Karyakram

Ganna Vikas Karyakram was launched by the Government of Bihar in 2012-13. A framework was built for development of sugarcane with the help of agriculture roadmap. Under this scheme, sugarcane farmers are given different kinds of facilities.

Seeds are made available at a subsidized rate. Those farmers that produce seeds of sugarcane are given a promotion rate of ₹50 per quintal on sugar cane by the sugar mills. The sugar mills that produce seeds of sugar cane are given an encouragement amount of ₹15,000 per hectare, but to avail this amount it is mandatory that the seed management is done by Bihar State Seeds Certification Agency. An encouragement amount of ₹25,000 per hectare will be given to seeds produced by Sugarcane Research Center, Lucknow. Apart from this, facilities like training before sowing and guaranteed availability of harvesters is also ensured.

Mission Indradhanush

Mission Indradhanush was launched in the 20 most backward districts of Bihar on 7 April, 2015. Under the provisions of this scheme, on the seventh day of every month, vaccination drive is organized for 7 kinds of diseases for children.

Yukti Yojana

Yukti Yojana was launched by the Government of Bihar on 23 April, 2011. Under the provisions of this scheme, all pregnant women can avail services related to abortion in all the government and non-government institutes. This scheme is being operated by Bihar State Health Committee.

Jayaprabha Janani Shishu Arogya Express Yojana

This scheme was launched by the Government of Bihar on 1 May, 2012. The responsibility of operation of this scheme has been given to New Delhi based organization – Studio On Wheel. This air conditioned express train aims to provide free medical and health services to pregnant women, children, senior citizens and those injured in road accidents. The toll free number for this scheme is 102.

Parwarish Yojana

Parwarish Yojana was launched by the Government of Bihar in the year 2014. The objective of this scheme is to ensure the upbringing of orphans and marginalized children at a community level. Children suffering from HIV and leprosy or the children whose parents are suffering from HIV or leprosy have also been included in this scheme.

Mukhyamantri Kanya Suraksha Yojana

This scheme was launched in Bihar with an aim to increase gender ratio, encourage birth registration and stop female foeticide. This scheme is effective from 7 July, 2008. The benefits of this scheme are availed by female child born in BPL families after 22 November, 2007 whose birth have been registered within a span of one year. The benefits are provided in form of ₹2000 cash deposited in Children's Care Fund in UTI MF. After year 2014, this amount is being deposited in IDBI and UCO banks as fixed deposit. The benefit of this scheme is limited to only two girl children in family. The benefits of this scheme can be availed by submitting an application in the nearest Anganbari center.

Mukhyamantri Kanya Vivah Yojana

This scheme was launched by the Government of Bihar on 22 November, 2007. Under the provisions of this scheme, married women are given a sum of ₹10,000 by cheque or demand draft after the registration of marriage between a girl of over 18 years and boy of over 21 years age in the rural or urban area. The benefits of this scheme can be availed by only those family whose annual income is less than ₹60,000.

Swayam Sakshasm Yojana

This scheme has been launched by the Government of Bihar for unemployed students from the backward classes. If any unemployed youth has completed his higher studies or training in the field of audit rail, fashion designing, coaching center, handcraft, printing press, engineering, law, architecture, hotel management etc., then the government will provide a loan of up to ₹5 lakhs at an interest rate of 5 percent. This loan is available for youth between the age group of 15 to 35 years. In order to avail the benefits of this scheme, it is mandatory that the annual income of the applicant is not more than 40 thousand per annum in rural areas, and not more than ₹55,000 per annum in urban areas. The time period for repayment of loan is maximum 10 years.

Tharu Scheduled Tribe Development Scheme

This scheme was launched for the development of Tharu Scheduled Tribe. Tharu Tribe was included in the list of Scheduled Tribe in Bihar in the year, 2003. A committee has been set up under the chairmanship of Chief Secretary which works special for the upliftment of Tharu Tribe. Under this, 5 girls and 5 boys residential high schools have been built for people from Scheduled Tribe, especially in the West Champaran District. Apart from this, Consolidated Tharuhat Development has also been set up in West Champaran (Bettiah).

Student's Guidance Center Scheme

This scheme was launched by the state government in year 2009-10. This scheme is operated by Chanakya Management Institute, Patna for which the financial assistance is provided by Scheduled Castes, Scheduled Tribes Welfare Department, Government of Bihar. The objective of this scheme is to provide long-term free coaching for CAT and other competitive exams to such graduate students, residing in Bihar who belong to scheduled castes or scheduled tribes and whose family income is less than 2,50,000 per annum. These students are given a scholarship or ₹1000 for 75 percent attendance. For this scheme, 100 students are elected from Scheduled Castes and 20 students are selected form Scheduled Tribes.

Mukhyamantri Mahadalit Rojgar Yojana

This scheme was launched by the state government in year 2012-13. The primary objective of this scheme is to bring the direct benefits of MGNREGA to 22 lakh mahadalit families of the state. Under this scheme a special camp is being organized for preparation of job card for the mahadalit families. Further, those who are looking for jobs, are given employment under MGNREGA within 15 days. Those who get jobs under this scheme are made swift payment as well.

Mukhyamantri Mahadalit Poshak Yojana

This scheme was launched in year 2009-10 for all the mahadalit students of classes 1 to 5 enrolled in government schools. Under the provisions of this scheme ₹500 is given for buying uniforms, shoes etc. Its distribution among students is done by public representative in a camp organized at the panchayat level.

Dashrath Manjhi Skill Development Program

Dashrath Manjhi Skill Development Program was launched by Bihar Mahadalit Development

Mission. The objective of this scheme is to provide free commercial training to mahadalit young men and women. This scheme was launched in June 2013. Under this scheme, training is imparted in various courses and trades like computer accounting tally, mobile repairing, computer hardware and networking, nursing, security guard, etc.

Mukhymantri Shram Shakti Yojana

This scheme was launched by the Government of Bihar in financial year 2008-09. Its objective was to provide special training to minority workers free of cost. After the training is complete, the trainees are given a loan of minimum ₹50,000 at simple interest. Through Bihar State Minority Financial Corporation, this training is being given by the Institute of Plastic Engineering and Technology, Hazipur and Raymond, Patna.

Bihar Grihstha Yojana

Bihar Grihstha Yojana was launched by the Government of Bihar in year 2010-11. Under the provisions of this scheme, landless families from Scheduled Castes, Scheduled Tribes, extremely backward classes backward classes are given ₹20,000 to buy 3 dismil land.

Bihar Kerosene Oil Coupon Scheme

Bihar Kerosene Oil Coupon Scheme was launched in Bihar in June 2008. There have always been complaints about black marketing of kerosene oil and that poor people are unable to get kerosene in the state. Under the provisions of this scheme all the families from all the classes are issued 12 blue coloured coupons that last for a year to buy kerosene at the rate of ₹2.75 per liter in urban areas and ₹2.25 per liter for families in the rural areas. The allotted amount of kerosene oil is being provided by the shopkeeper, by showing the ration card and coupon, similar to ration coupon.

Aao Bihar Yojana (Come to Bihar Scheme)

This scheme has been launched for people of the state. If someone is the owner of 2 acres or more land and wants to sell his property for purpose of setting up industry or institution, then he/she can get his/her property listed along with all the requisite details in the office of District Magistrate. For this, the seller will have to disclose the selling price of his/her land. The selling price will be determined by the landowner at his/her own will, and the individual will have to give a undertaking stating that the sale price will be valid from the date of registration up to a fixed date in future. This scheme has been launched to curb the problems arising in land acquisition by the state, and also to encourage investment in new industries and technologies, thus been aptly named Aao Bihar (Come to Bihar).

The district administration will enlist the land after checking the legal ownership and that the land is free of disputes. In the first phase the information will be sent to BIADA, which will upload this information on its website. After the information is uploaded, state government, through advertisements, will inform all the potential clients that at various places, dispute-free registered land is available for sale. Thus, the role of the government will be of a contact point, so that there is no problem in sale and purchase of land and also the landowner gets his desired price. By enlisting in this scheme, all the landowners from Bihar can make their contribution in the growth of the state.

Samarthya Yojana for Public Distribution Scheme

Samarthya Scheme has been launched to provide financial assistance to sellers involved in public distribution system so that they too can become financially able. At present, the public distribution sellers have to pay for 2 to 3 months of food grain stocks in advance. Even if their limit has reached maximum, then also they have to make advance payment for at least two months worth of stock of food grains. There are many public distribution sellers who are weak economically. As a result, they face many financial problems, they have to take loans to make the advance payment, which in return causes loss on their actual profit. In absence of finance, it becomes difficult to pay for food grains in advance and 100 percent amount is never deposited. In such a scenario, the public distributors are entrapped in the web of shopkeepers, middlemen and brokers. All these condition lead to either shortage of food grains or their black marketing increases. In order to find a solution to this problem, negotiations were held with Bihar Gramin Bank and a coordination was established to provide a cash credit of ₹50,000 to these sellers so that immediate financial assistance is possible. Madhya Bihar Gramin Bank organized a campaign and provided the public distribution sellers with ₹2,89,00,000 cash credit.

Mukhyamantri Nischay Swayam Sahayata Bhatta Yojna

Allowance is provided by the Government of Bihar to the educated unemployed citizens under the Chief Minister Self Help Allowance Scheme, so that the citizens of the state do not have to face financial crisis.

The amount of self-help allowance will be paid to the eligible applicant at the rate of ₹1000 per month for a maximum period of two years.

From the age group of 20 to 25 years, unemployed young men/women who are not studying and are looking for employment and whose educational qualification is inter (12th) passed from a government-recognized institution located in the state but Have not received higher education.

The applicant should be a permanent resident of the district of Bihar state, where he is submitting the application in the district registration centre.

Mukhyamantri Vridhjan Pension Yojna

The scheme "Mukhyamantri Vridhjan Pension Yojna" is an old-age pension scheme implemented by the Department of Social Welfare, Government of Bihar to provide financial assistance to elderly citizens. Under the scheme, a monthly pension

- The applicant should be a permanent resident of Bihar.
- The age of the applicant should be 60 years or above.
- The applicant should not be a retired government employee, in order to avail of the benefits of the scheme.
- The applicant should not be receiving any pension from government service, family pension or social security pension any other source for this purpose.
- A monthly pension of ₹400 will be provided to individuals who are in the age group of 60-79 years.
- A monthly pension of ₹500 will be provided to the individuals whose age is 80 years and above.

Note: The pension amount is transferred directly to the beneficiary bank account using the Direct Benefit Transfer (DBT) method.

Old Age Home (Sahara)

Under this scheme construction and operation of the old age home "Sahara" will be included in which destitute Housing, clothes, food, medical facilities, etc. are made available for qualitative improvement in the standard of living of poor and poor elders, for cooperation and proper care.

- Applicants should come under the below poverty line (BPL) category (or)
- Annual Income should be below ₹ 60,000.

Bihar State Journalist Insurance Scheme

The "Bihar State Journalist Insurance Scheme, 2014" was launched by the Information and Public Relations Department, Government of Bihar. The scheme aims to provide financial benefits of ₹5,00,000 and facilities under a group mediclaim & personal accident insurance scheme to working media representatives. Under this scheme, spouse and two dependent children of the media representative will be included in this Insurance Scheme.

This insurance is valid for one year with provisions for annual renewal.

Niji Talabon Ka Jirnoddhar Ki Yojana

The "Niji Talabon Ka Jirnoddhar Ki Yojana" was launched by the Animal and Fisheries Resources Department, Government of Bihar. The scheme specifically allocates resources for extremely backward castes, scheduled castes, and scheduled tribes, ensuring inclusive growth and support for marginalized communities. Under the scheme, the target is to renovate 150.00 hectares of private ponds.

Increase Water Holding Capacity: Enhance the water holding capacity of private ponds to boost fish productivity and production.

Economic Benefits for Fish Farmers: Provide benefits to private fish farmers through the expansion/renovation of their ponds.

Non-residential sports training scheme of Bihar

On October 17, 2023, Bihar's Art and Culture Ministry has launched the 'Non-Residential Sports Training Scheme' to enhance the talent of the players.

With the help of this scheme, modern training facilities will be provided to the players of Bihar. The players registered in the non-residential sports training scheme will attend the training venue at the scheduled time of sports training and receive training. This scheme will be operated in every district. Under this scheme, trainee players aged between 8 to 14 years will be given training in sports. Players will be provided modern training facilities so that their performance can be improved.

Mukhyamantri Alpasankhyak Udyami Yojana

The "Mukhyamantri Alpasankhyak Udyami Yojana" launched in September 2023 is a component of the umbrella scheme "Mukhyamantri Udyami Yojana", launched by the Department of Industries, Bihar. The main objective of the scheme is to promote entrepreneurship and self-employment among individuals from all categories in the state.

Under this component, financial assistance of up to ₹10,00,000 is provided to applicants from Minority communities for establishing and operating business ventures, thereby fostering economic growth and empowerment in the state.

- The applicant must be a permanent resident of Bihar.
- The applicant must belong to the Minority community.
- The applicant should have passed at least 10+2, Intermediate, ITI, Polytechnic Diploma, or equivalent.
- The applicant must be aged between 18 and 50 years.
- The business unit must be a proprietorship or partnership firm.

Center and State Sponsored Schemes

Schemes / Programs	Date / year	Objective
First Five Year Plan	1952	Stress on agricultural development
Small Scale Industries Development Organiation (SIDO)	1954	For the development of new industries
Intense Agriculture District Program (IADP)	1960-61	Ensure availability of seeds, fertilizers, tools and loans to farmers
Intense Agriculture Area Program (IAAP)	1964-65	Development of specific crops
Rural Electrification Board	1969	Electric supply for agriculture and industrial sector

Vibhedikaran Byaj Dar Yojana	1972	Provide loan at subsidized rate of 4 percent to the weaker sections of society
Control Area Development Program	1974-75	Irrigation facility for small and large projects
20-point Programme	1975	Poverty eradication and improvement of standard of living
Desert Development Program	1977-78	Control of rise in desert area and environmental balance
Food grains for Work Program	1977-78	Providing food grains for developmental programs
Training to Rural Youth for Self Employment (TRYSEM)	15 August, 1979	Training program to curb the problem of unemployment in rural youth
Integrated Rural Development Program (IRDP)	2 October, 1980	Provide loan to poor families for self employment
National Rural Employment Program	1980	Provide beneficial employment to poor people
Development of Women and Children in Rural Areas (DWCRA)	1982	Provide employment opportunities to rural women from BPL families
Rural Landless Employment Guarantee Program (RLEGP)	15 August, 1983	Provide employment to landless farmers and labourers
Council for Advancement of People's Action and Rural Technology (CAPART)	1 September, 1986	Rural property this scheme has been named Gangotri on 28 December, 2004
Self Employment Program for Urban Poor	1986	Financial and technical support for self-employment
Nehru Rojgar Yojana (NRY)	October, 1989	Provide employment to urban poor
Jawahar Rojgar Yojana (JRY)	April, 1989	Provide employment to rural people
Employment Guarantee Program	2 October, 1993	Provide employment
Pradhan Mantri Rojgar Yojana (PMRY)	2 October, 1993	Provide employment to educated youth
Rashtriya Matritva Labh Yojana	1995	Financial support of ₹300 to pregnant women of 19 years or above, from BPL families
Vridhavastha Pension Yojana	1995	Provide monthly pension of ₹200 to helpless old people of 65 years or above
Sangam Yojana	1996	For the welfare of disabled

Kasturba Gandhi Shiksha Yojana	15 August, 1997	Establishment of girl school in districts with low female literacy rate
Ganaga Kalyan Yojana	1997-98	Provide financial support to farmers for removal and maintenance of surface and underground water
Swarn Jayanati Shahri Rojagar Yojana (SJSRY)	1 December, 1997	Provide profitable employment opportunities in urban areas. Eradication of urban poverty; basic urban facilities for poors
Jawahar Gram Siddhi Yojana	1 April, 1999	Improve the life of rural poor and provide profitable employment
Annapurna Yojana	19 March, 1999	Free food grains to elder people
Swaranjayanti Gram Swarojgar Yojana (SJGSY)	1999	Bring the beneficiary above the poverty line within three years. Six programs have been included in this scheme - (i) IRDP, (ii) TRYSEM, (iii) DWCRA, (iv) SITRA, (v) MWS, (vi) GKY
Janshri Bima	10 August, 2000	Provide insurance cover to people below the poverty line
Pradhan Mantri Gramoday Yojana	2000	Comprehensive development of villages
Antyoday Yojana	2000	Provide grains at ₹2 per kilo and rice at ₹3 per kilo to the most poor among the BPL families
Ashrya Bima Yojana	June, 2013	Provide insurance cover to those who are left unemployed
Sampoorna Gramin Rojagar Yojana (SGRY)	25 December, 2001	Job creation in rural areas
Valmiki Ambedkar Avas Yojana	2001, December	Provide clean homes to urban slum population
Sarva Shiksha Abhiyan	2000-01	Provide free and good quality education up to standard 8 to all the children between 6 to 14 years
Khaddyan Bank Karyakram	2001	Establishment of food grain bank at the panchayat level
Mahila Swayam Siddhi Yojana	12 July, 2001	Socio-economic empowerment of women/ merger of Indira Mahila Yojana and Mahila Samriddhi Yojana

Swajal Dhara Yojana	25 December, 2002	Provide handpumps, well and ponds with the help of Gram Panchayats
Nirmal Bharat Yojana	1 August, 2002	Expansion of facility of public toilet in slum areas
Pradhan Mantri Gram Sadak Yojana	25 December, 2000	100 percent central scheme, to connect the villages with a population of more than 500
Janraksha Bima Yojana	2002-03	Treatment of up to ₹30000 of selected people in select hospital at payment of ₹1 per day
Jai Prakash Narayan Rojgar Guarantee Yojana	2002-03	Provide employment to needy and poor people in backward rural areas of the country
Provision of Urban Amenities to Rural Areas (PURA)	15 August, 2003	Provide high-class facilities in villages
Jawahar Lal Nehru National Urban Renewal Mission	3 December, 2005	Development of urban infrastructure
National Rural Health Mission	12 April, 2005	Strengthen the primary health structure
Bharat Nirman Yojana	16 December, 2005	Rural infrastructure, all round and comprehensive development program
Aam Admi Bima Yojana	2 October, 2007	Insurance benefits to the head or sole earner of land-less rural families
Naional Health Insurance Scheme	1 October, 2007	Scheme for personal insurance, to provide insurance cover to every member of BPL families working in the unorganized sector
Sabla Yojana	19 November, 2010	Central scheme for empowerment of adolescent girls
Swavalamban	27 September, 2010	New pension scheme for unorganized sector
Rajiv Gandhi Scheme for Adolescent Girls	1 April, 2010	Operated by ICDS
Mahila Krishi Sashaktikaran Yojana	1 April, 2010	A subsidiary of National Livelihood Mission
National Rural Livelihood Mission	2009-10	New name for SGSY
Rajiv Avas Yojana	2009-10	Related to freedom from slums
Pradhan Mantri Adarsh Gram Yojana	2009-10	Scheduled castes majority village development program

Mahila Kisan Sashaktikaran Yojana	2010-2011	Provide for specific necessities of rural farmer women
Mahatma Gandhi National Rural Employment Guarantee Act	2006	To give right to employment in rural areas
PGSY - II	2013	NREGA, started with a new name MGNREGA on 2 October, 2009
Nirbhaya Fund	2013	To provide safety to women in selected states and safeguard their dignity
Mission Indradhanush	25 December, 2014	To provide 7 different vaccines to children who are deprived of vaccination
Swachchch Bharat Mission	2 October, 2014	To make all villages open defecation free by 2 October, 2019
PAHAL	15 November, 2016	Direct benefit transfer scheme for LPG. The subsidy given through this scheme will be deposited in the linked bank account
Beti Bachao, Beti Padhao Program (BBBP)	22 January, 2015	For survival and safety of girl child, to control the infant gender ratio
Pradhan Mantri Jan Dhan Yojana (PMJDY)	28 August, 2014	Revised target to open 10 crore bank accounts till 25 January, 2015. 1 lakh accidental insurance cover to the account holder and life insurance cover of ₹30,000 will be available automatically
National Health Mission	2013	To provide cheap and quality health services. N.R.S.M and N.U.H.M are its two sub-missions. Cities with a population of more than 50,000 and district headquarters with population more than 30,000 are included in NUHM, and less populous areas are included in NRHM
Nayi Manjil	2014 -15	Educational and skill development scheme for minorities who were forced to leave their studies
MANAS and Cyber Gram		Entrepreneurship and skill development in minority students
Pradhan Mantri Swasthya Suraksha Yojana (PMSSY)	March, 2016	To remove the imbalance in health services; to remove the lack of medical studies in the statcs

National Livelihood Mission		To organize all rural families, poverty eradication
Nayi Roshni	2014-15	Leadership quality development training in women
Matritva Shayog Yojana	2014	Restructured form of earlier Indira Gandhi Matritva Sahyog Yojana
Janbandhu Kalyan Yojana	2014-15	Central scheme for scheduled tribes. Initiated with a budget allocation of 100 crores
E-Visa	2014-1 5 (proposed in the budget)	Proposal for electronic travel authorization insurance for tourism
Shyama Prasad Mukherji Urban Mission	2014-15	Operational from 21 February, 2016, to provide urban facilities in rural areas
Deen Dayal Upadhyay Gram Jyoti Yojana	2014-15	To provide 24 hour electricity to all the rural household
Varishtha Pension BimaYojana (VPBY)	15 August, 2014	This was a pension scheme which was implemented only for a year from 15 August, 2014 to 14 August, 2015
Pradhan Mantri Gram Sadak Yojana	2014-15, restarted	This scheme was launched during the tenure of NDA; this scheme has been reintroduced in a more effective manner in the budget
Pradhan Mantri Suraksha Bima Yojana	9 May, 2016	Annual premium of ₹12. aoutomatic deduction from Jan Dhan account; in case of death, the dependents will receive a sum of ₹2 lakh
Atal Pension Yojana	9 May, 2016	The amount of pension is subject to the premium deposited by the insurance holder; for five years the central government will pay 50 percent of monthly premium or ₹1000, whichever is lower.
Pradhan Mantri Jivan Jyoti Bima Yojana	9 May, 2016	Premium amount of ₹330 per annum for life insurance. Valid for those between 18 and 50 years of age, in case of death ₹2 lakh will be given to nominee
Stand Up India	5 April, 2016	Scheme related to encourage new emerging entrepreneurs
Gram Uday se Bharat Uday Abhiyan	14 April, 2016	Scheme to strengthen the Panchayati raj system, social homogeneity, rural development and growth of farmers

Pradhan Mantri Avas Yojana (Rural)	25 April, 2016	Scheme to strengthen the Panchayati raj system, social homogeneity, rural development and growth of farmers
Stand India Loan Scheme	5 April, 2016	Scheme to encourage entrepreneurship among the Scheduled Castes, Scheduled Tribes and women
Pradhan Mantri Ujjwala Yojana	1 May, 2016	Scheme to provide gas connection to BPL families
National Health Policy	15 March, 2017	Health related reforms in all the sectors
UDAN Yojana	17 April, 2017	To encourage the regional aviation market
Pradhan Mantri Matritva Vandana Yojana	17 May, 2017	Safeguarding motherhood
Pradhan mantri Vay Vandana Yojana	21 July, 2017	Pension for people more than 60 years old
Pradhan Mantri Jan Arogya Kendra	25 September, 2018	To provide free medical and health services of up to ₹5 lakh to poor people
One Nation, One Card	4 March, 2019	To enable people to pay for metro services and other transport fee including the toll tax all across the country
One Nation One Ration Card Scheme	2019	To provide cheap food grains to poor people
UDAN Yojana	7 March, 2019	To develop idle and less developed air strips
Kisan Samman Nidhi Yojana	2019-20	This scheme was launched with an objective to support the farmers
Atal Bhujal Yojana	25 December, 2019	Reforms in ground water management
Pradhan Mantri Kalyan Yojana	March, 2020	For the welfare of poor people
Mission Sagar	May, 2020	To deliver COVID-19 related assistance to the countries in the Indian Ocean Littoral States. The countries included were Maldives, Mauritius, Madagascar, Comoros and Seychelles.
National Technical Textile Mission	26 February, 2020	To position India in technical textile as a global leader.
Mission COVID Suraksha	29 November, 2020	To enable the development of indigenous, affordable and accessible vaccines for the country and will complement the ongoing mission of Atmanirbhar Bharat.

Prime Minister Street Vendor's Atmanirbhar Nidhi (PM SVANidhi)	1 June, 2020	To facilitate collateral free working capital loans of up to INR 10,000/- of one year tenure, to approximately 50 lakh street vendors to help resume their business in the urban areas.
Mission Karamyogi	2 September, 2020	To prepare the Indian Civil Servant for the future by making him more creative, constructive, imaginative, innovative, proactive, professional, progressive, energetic and technology-enabled.
National Digital Health Mission	15 August, 2020	To develop the backbone necessary to support the integrated digital health infrastructure of the country.
Mukhyamantri Alpasankhyak Udyami Yojna	September, 2023	To promote enterpreneurship and self-employment to all categories.
Non-residential Sports Training Scheme	October, 2023	To enhance the talent of the players.

❑❑❑

Financial System

- Components of the Indian Financial System
- Banking Sector in Bihar

COMPONENTS OF THE INDIAN FINANCIAL SYSTEM

Capital Markets: The capital market refers to the market where financial instruments are bought and sold.

Money Markets: Money market is the market where short-term monetary assets or securities (typically with a duration of less than one year) are traded. These assets are close substitutes for money. The money market is divided into two parts: the organized money market and the unorganized money market.

The organized money market is systematically operated and regulated by the Reserve Bank of India (RBI). The RBI sits at the top of the organized money market and controls liquidity within it. The primary components of the money market include the Reserve Bank, commercial banks, and cooperative banks.

Alongside the organized sector, the unorganized money market also exists, commonly referred to as indigenous bankers. Despite the rapid expansion of the banking sector, moneylenders still play a significant role in rural areas. To reduce rural dependency on these moneylenders, the development of Self-Help Groups (SHGs) is being promoted.

Reserve Bank of India

Reserve Bank of India is at the apex of organized money market which controls the liquidity in money market. Reserve Bank of India, commercial banks and cooperative banks are three main components of money market. Apart from organized money market, the unorganized money market also has its expansion, which is also known as indigenous banker. Despite a fast-paced growth in the financial sector, the role of money lenders (sahookars) is very important in the rural areas. In order to reduce the dependence of villagers on money lenders, self-help groups are being developed. The beginning of banking in India can be considered from 1786 when General Bank of India was established. East India Company established bank of Bengal in 1809, Bank of Bombay in 1840 and Bank of Madras in 1843, which were collectively known as the Bank of Presidency. In the same way, Bank of Hindustan in 1870, Allahabad Bank in 1865 and Punjab National Bank in 1894 were also established. In 1921, all the Presidency Banks were merged; thus, Imperial Bank of India was established which was governed by European shareholders. Reserve Bank of India was established in year, 1935. The headquarters of Punjab National Bank at that time, was situated in Lahore.

BANKING SECTOR IN BIHAR

The number of internet banking users increased rapidly from 7.28 million as of 31 March 2021 to 11.89 million as of 31 March 2023.

Out of the 7,883 bank branches in Bihar as of 31 March 2023:

- 48% were in rural areas,
- 31% in semi-urban areas, and
- 21% in urban areas.

The largest network of 3,956 branches belonged to public sector banks, followed by 2,110 branches of regional rural banks, and 1,230 branches of private sector banks. As of 31 March 2023, cooperative banks had 294 branches and microfinance banks had 293 branches in the state.

In the financial year 2022–23, banks in Bihar achieved an annual credit plan of ₹2,20,520 crore, which was 37.1% higher than the previous year and 108% of the target set for the year.

In 2022–23, the achievement rate for non-priority sectors was 151.1%, which was significantly higher than the 94.0% for priority sectors. Among priority sectors, the achievement rate was 101.4% for agriculture and 78.7% for small and medium enterprises.

The Credit-Deposit (CD) ratio of banks in Bihar has improved significantly in recent years, rising from 53% on 31 March 2022 to 55.6% on 31 March 2023.

The proportion of Non-Performing Assets (NPAs) in the total outstanding loans of banks in the state has steadily declined. It was 11.3% in 2021–22, which dropped to 9.3% in 2022–23. The total NPAs of banks in Bihar were ₹23,870 crore in 2021–22, which reduced to ₹22,944 crore in 2022–23.

Kisan Credit Card Scheme (KCC)

The scheme was launched in the year 1998–99 with the objective of providing flexible and cost-effective crop loans to farmers.

It is implemented by all commercial banks, regional rural banks, state cooperative banks, central cooperative banks, and Primary Agricultural Credit Societies (PACS).

Under the Kisan Credit Card scheme, every beneficiary is provided with a credit card and a passbook that mentions the loan limit and validity period.

In 2019–20, a total of 1,66,434 Kisan Credit Cards were issued, out of which the maximum, i.e., 1.33 lakh cards, were issued by commercial banks.

Pradhan Mantri MUDRA Yojana (PMMY)

To provide refinancing to the last-mile financiers, the Micro Units Development and Refinance Agency (MUDRA) was established under the Union Budget (2015–16), and the Pradhan Mantri MUDRA Yojana (PMMY) was launched on 8 April 2015.

Under this MUDRA scheme, refinancing is provided for products requiring loans up to ₹10 lakh, and the scheme supports microfinance institutions through refinancing.

Under PMMY, MUDRA offers three products based on the stage of growth and funding needs of micro-enterprises:

- Shishu – loans up to ₹50,000
- Kishore – loans from ₹50,000 to ₹5 lakh
- Tarun – loans from ₹5 lakh to ₹10 lakh

Approximately, 60% of the funds are allocated to the Shishu category.

The aim of the Pradhan Mantri MUDRA Yojana is to provide formal bank credit to more than 5.7 crore informal sector micro-entrepreneurs and other aspiring small entrepreneurs.

Performance of Pradhan Mantri Mudra Yojana in Bihar (2019–20)

Category	Number of Loans (in lakhs)	Targeted Amount (in ₹ crore)	Disbursed Amount (in ₹ crore)	Achievement (in %)
Shishu	14.94	4393.08	4350.11	99.0
Kishore	2.70	3450.32	2858.06	82.8
Tarun	0.22	1687.72	1490.72	88.3
Total	**17.86**	**9531.12**	**8698.89**	**91.3**

Source: State-Level Bankers Committee Report

Under the Mudra scheme, unincorporated small businesses with individual or partnership ownership are eligible for assistance. These enterprises include small manufacturing units in rural and urban areas, service sector units, shopkeepers, food service units, repair shops, machine operators, small industries, and others.

Investment plus Credit-Deposit Ratio

Banks support the economy not only by giving credit but also by investing in state government securities and shares and bonds of state undertakings, semi-government bodies, and joint venture companies. Therefore, the total involvement of banks in a state's economic activities is better represented by the Investment plus Credit-Deposit Ratio (ICD Ratio) rather than just the Credit-Deposit Ratio.

Credit-Deposit Ratio of Regional Rural Banks in Bihar

Bihar has three Regional Rural Banks:

- Madhya Bihar Gramin Bank (sponsored by Punjab National Bank)
- Uttar Bihar Gramin Bank (sponsored by Central Bank of India)
- Bihar Gramin Bank (sponsored by United Commercial Bank)

Each bank serves specific regions. As of September 2018:

- Bihar Gramin Bank had the highest ICD ratio of 73.6%
- Madhya Bihar Gramin Bank had the lowest ICD ratio of 46.8%
- The overall ICD ratio for Regional Rural Banks in Bihar was 54.3%

Share of Advances to Priority Sectors by Region

In Bihar, the share of advances provided by banks to priority sectors was:

- 75% in 2016–17
- 71.8% in 2017–18

National Bank for Agriculture and Rural Development (NABARD)

NABARD was established on 12 July 1982, based on recommendations of a committee chaired by B. Shivaraman. It was formed to provide loans for:

- Agriculture
- Agro-based industries
- Rural and cottage industries
- Handicrafts and other rural crafts

NABARD manages the Rural Infrastructure Development Fund (RIDF), created to compensate for the shortfall in credit provided by commercial banks. It also provides loans to state governments for irrigation, soil conservation, watershed management, drinking water supply, cold storage, and other rural infrastructure projects.

Rural Infrastructure Development Fund (RIDF)

Established in 1995–96 by the Central Government to expedite the completion of projects by state governments and government-owned corporations. It provides low-interest assistance for financing rural infrastructure projects. NABARD manages this fund.

The RIDF was created to address the following goals:

1. Make previously unsuccessful state investments productive.
2. Create additional irrigation capacity.
3. Generate employment for rural populations.
4. Boost the state's economic assets.
5. Improve road connectivity between villages and market centers.
6. Enhance the quality of life through education, health, and clean drinking water facilities.

Currently, around 36 activities are covered under RIDF, grouped into three categories:

1. Agriculture and allied sectors
2. Social sector
3. Rural road connectivity

Micro Finance in Bihar

Microfinance institutions play a crucial role in providing credit to low-income families, supporting:

- Employment generation
- Economic development
- Overall empowerment

Microfinance opens the credit market for poor families, even without collateral, ensuring capital through small loans to boost productivity. These institutions are vital in improving financial inclusion in Bihar. However, the interest rates on loans provided by these institutions are generally higher than those of scheduled commercial banks, making borrowing costlier.

Bihar has a large number of Self-Help Groups (SHGs). SHG–Bank Linkage Programs implemented by scheduled commercial banks, Regional Rural Banks, and cooperative banks have become major microfinance programs in the country.

Thanks to initiatives by Bihar's Rural Livelihood Mission 'Jeevika', the state has made remarkable progress in promoting financial inclusion through SHGs.

The State Level Bankers Committee also identified key factors responsible for the success of SHGs in other states, which are lacking in Bihar, such as:

- The attitude and education of rural people
- Availability of professionally run microfinance institutions
- Easy regulatory framework
- Government support
- Channeling government assistance through SHGs

Rural Self Employment Training Institutes (RSETIs in the Districts of Bihar)

S. No.	District	Sponsor Bank
1	Bhojpur	Punjab National Bank
2	Buxar	
3	Kaimur (Bhabhua)	
4	Lakhisarai	
5	Nalanda	
6	Nawada	
7	Patna (Danapur)	
8	Rohtas	
9	Gaya	
10	Jehanabad	
11	Arwal	
12	Aurangabad	
13	Sheikhpura	Canara Bank
14	East Champaran (Motihari)	
15	Gopalganj	
16	Saran (Chhapra)	
17	Siwan	
18	West Champaran (Bettiah)	
19	Darbhanga (Bahadurpur)	
20	Katihar	
21	Madhubani	
22	Muzaffarpur	
23	Vaishali (Hajipur)	RUDSETI
24	Sheohar	Bank of Baroda
25	Sitamarhi	
26	Jamui	State Bank of India
27	Araria	
28	Kishanganj	
29	Madhepura	
30	Purnia	
31	Saharsa	
32	Supaul	
33	Begusarai	UCO Bank
34	Bhagalpur	
35	Munger	
36	Banka	
37	Khagaria	Union Bank of India
38	Samastipur	

Source: Department of Labour Resources, Government of Bihar

❑❑❑

State Policies

- Industrial Policy Overview
- Bihar Industrial Development Scenario
- Bihar IT Promotion Policy, 2024
- Bihar Biofuels Production Promotion Policy, 2023
- Bihar Electric Vehicle Policy, 2023
- Bihar Logistics Policy, 2023
- Bihar Prohibition and Excise (Amendment) Bill, 2022
- Bihar Textile and Leather Policy, 2022
- Bihar Startup Policy, 2022
- Bihar Industrial Investment Promotion Policy (Textiles & Leather), 2022
- Bihar Ethanol Production Promotion Policy, 2021
- Bihar Oxygen Production Promotion Policy 2021
- Bihar Oxygen Production Incentive Policy 2021
- Industrial Investment Promotion Policy, 2016
- Bihar Prohibition and Excise Act, 2016 (Implemented from 2nd October 2016)
- Bihar Public Grievances Redressal Act, 2015
- Priority Sectors
- Information Technology Policy
- Bihar Right to Public Services Act, 2011
- Bihar Agricultural Land (Conversion for Non-Agricultural Purposes) Act, 2010

INDUSTRIAL POLICY OVERVIEW

Industrialization and Industrial Development are often considered as the indicators and engines of economic growth. The development of the agriculture and service sectors also depends on the growth of the industrial sector. On one hand, industrial development generates demand in the economy by creating employment and income, and on the other, it lays the foundation for rapid and self-reliant economic development of the country.

BIHAR INDUSTRIAL DEVELOPMENT SCENARIO

Bihar Industrial Area Development Authority (BIADA): The Bihar Industrial Area Development Authority (BIADA) was established to implement the Bihar Industrial Investment Promotion Policy, 2016 effectively. A key mandate of BIADA is to develop land and other logistics for enterprises. BIADA has developed nine clusters comprising 75 Industrial Areas (IA), Industrial Estates (IE), Growth Centers (GC), and Mega Industrial Parks (MIP). These nine clusters are:

1. Begusarai

2. Bhagalpur, Saharsa, and Purnia
3. Gaya
4. Patna
5. Darbhanga
6. Hajipur
7. Muzaffarpur
8. Bihta
9. Motipur

As of 30th September 2023, BIADA had acquired 7,347.53 acres of land and constructed 711 sheds. About 14% of the acquired land is used for infrastructure, administrative blocks, roads, etc. Of the total acquired land, 47% lies in two clusters—Bihta and Motipur. According to the Bihar Economic Survey 2023–24, 51% of the allocable acquired land has been allotted to industrial units. Specifically, 70% of land in the Bihta cluster and 69% in the Muzaffarpur cluster has been allotted to industries.

There has been significant improvement regarding land under litigation. As of 30th September 2023, only 540.67 acres (7%) of the total acquired land was under litigation, compared to 13% as of 30th September 2022. This indicates a remarkable improvement in the land acquisition process for industrialization in Bihar.

BIHAR IT PROMOTION POLICY, 2024

To promote investment and employment in the Information Technology (IT), IT-enabled Services (ITES), and Electronics System Design & Manufacturing (ESDM) sectors, the Bihar government has proposed the Information Technology Policy, 2024.

The policy focuses on various segments, including core technology/ITES/ESDM areas as well as auxiliary sectors such as:

- Data centers
- AVGC (Animation, Visual Effects, Gaming, and Comics)
- IT platforms
- Big Data and Analytics
- Smart technologies
- Drone manufacturing

Under this policy, investors are offered several incentives, including:

- **Capital Subsidy**: 30% capital investment subsidy up to ₹30 crore, or
- **Interest Subsidy**: 10% interest subsidy for five years up to ₹40 crore.
- **Lease Rent Subsidy**: 50% subsidy on lease rent for five years for IT/ITES/ESDM units operating from leased offices or commercial spaces.
- **Energy Subsidy**: 25% reimbursement of fixed, energy, and electricity charges.
- **Employment Generation Subsidy:** 100% reimbursement (up to ₹5000 per employee) on employer contribution towards EPF and ESI for five years.

Additionally, "Mega Units" with investment over ₹100 crore or direct employment to over 1000 people in IT will be provided with customized incentive packages.

BIHAR BIOFUELS PRODUCTION PROMOTION POLICY, 2023

With the objective of promoting renewable energy, the Bihar Biofuels Production Promotion Policy, 2023 has been approved. It provides incentives for:

- New greenfield standalone units producing 100% ethanol
- Units producing compressed biogas or bio-CNG

For FY 2024–25, a total budget of ₹1,833.09 crore is proposed:

- ₹1,732 crore under scheme head
- ₹101.09 crore under establishment and committed expenditure

Under the Bihar Clean Fuel (City Bus Promotion) Scheme, 2023, private diesel city buses in Patna will be replaced with CNG buses. The vehicle owners will be given an incentive of 30% of the ex-showroom price (including all taxes) or up to ₹7.5 lakh, whichever is lower.

BIHAR ELECTRIC VEHICLE POLICY, 2023

Taking a significant step toward environmental protection, the Bihar government has launched the Electric Vehicle Policy, 2023 with the goal of establishing Bihar as a model state in the EV transport ecosystem.

Under this policy:

- For the first 10,000 two-wheelers, a purchase subsidy of ₹5000 per kWh (maximum ₹10,000) will be provided.
- For the first 1000 four-wheelers, a subsidy of ₹10,000 per kWh will be provided, up to ₹1.25 lakh for general category and ₹1.50 lakh for SC/ST buyers.
- Additionally, the government offers a 75% tax exemption on two-, four-, passenger, and heavy motor vehicles and 50% exemption for other vehicle categories.
- The government will also provide purchase incentives for EV charging equipment.

BIHAR LOGISTICS POLICY, 2023

To encourage investment in the logistics sector, the Bihar Logistics Policy–2023 has been implemented. It aims to expand infrastructure such as warehousing, shipping, rail, road, air freight, express cargo, and other logistics facilities. The goal is to ensure the people of Bihar have access to essential commodities at relatively lower costs.

BIHAR PROHIBITION AND EXCISE (AMENDMENT) BILL, 2022

Through the Bihar Prohibition and Excise (Amendment) Bill, 2022, the state government introduced new provisions to effectively implement the prohibition on alcohol in Bihar:

- A person caught consuming alcohol for the first time will now be released after paying a fine.
- From the second offense onwards, imprisonment will be applicable, and those involved in running liquor rackets will be punished promptly.
- This amendment aims to reduce the backlog of alcohol-related cases in courts and relieve the government from repeated criticism by the judiciary.
- Now, based on the report of the arresting officer, a magistrate will decide whether to release the accused or not.
- Vehicles seized with alcohol can now be released by the District Magistrate after collecting a fine. Previously, only courts had the authority to release such vehicles.
- Illegal alcohol trade is now categorized under organized crime, and there are provisions for confiscation of property of those involved in such activities.

BIHAR TEXTILE AND LEATHER POLICY, 2022

On June 8, 2022, Bihar's Chief Minister Nitish Kumar launched the Investor Meet cum Bihar Textile and Leather Policy, 2022 at the Convention Hall in Patna.

Key highlights of the new policy include:

- A capital investment subsidy of 15% on plant and machinery, with a maximum limit of ₹10 crore.
- A subsidy of ₹2 per unit on electricity charges.
- Workers employed in the industry will receive a monthly subsidy of ₹5,000 for five years.
- Units involved in exports will receive 30% transport subsidy.
- A freight subsidy of ₹10 lakh per annum will be provided for five years.
- For patent registration, 50% of the registration cost will be subsidized, up to a maximum of ₹10 lakh.

BIHAR STARTUP POLICY, 2022

On June 17, 2022, the Bihar government approved the Bihar Startup Policy, 2022. Under this new policy, an institutional framework will be established through the Bihar Startup Fund Trust, Startup Policy Monitoring and Implementation Committee, Initial Screening Committee, and Startup Support Unit. The Development Commissioner of Bihar will be the chairman of the Bihar Startup Fund Trust, and the Principal Secretary of the Department of Industries will be the chairman of the Monitoring and Implementation Committee. The policy's implementation will be carried out through the designated Directorate.

Under this policy, a third-party agency will design a rating system, approve the portal according to the rating system, recommend startup certification, and suggest seed/funding/matching grants based on the startup rating. The entire application process and certification will be conducted online through the portal. Provisions for the establishment and strengthening of incubation centers to promote startups will be made, and online portals will provide 1:1 matching grants from the state government, central government, and multi-lateral data agencies. Basic infrastructure such as shared software, hardware, and workplaces will be provided for startups.

Additionally, extra grants, rebates, and subsidies will be available for entrepreneurs from Scheduled Castes, Scheduled Tribes, women, and persons with disabilities. This policy will be effective from the date of notification and will remain in force for five years. The activities under the Bihar Startup Policy, 2017 will be considered covered under this new policy.

BIHAR INDUSTRIAL INVESTMENT PROMOTION POLICY (TEXTILES & LEATHER), 2022

On May 26, 2022, the Bihar government approved the Bihar Industrial Investment Promotion Policy (Textiles & Leather), 2022. This policy aims to promote development and investment in the textile, garment, silk charkha, leather, and all types of shoe industries at the state level. It will be effective from the date of notification and will remain in force for five years.

Under this policy, entrepreneurs and investors interested in investing in the textile and leather industries will be provided with capital grants up to ₹ 10 crore by the state government. A discount of ₹ 2 per unit on electricity bills will be provided for five years from the start of commercial production. The state government will also contribute ₹ 3,000 to ₹ 5,000 per month towards the wages of workers employed in the industries. To speed up industrialization in the state, the policy includes provisions for a freight subsidy of ₹ 10 lakh per year and a patent subsidy of ₹ 10 lakh per patent.

Additionally, the policy provides 100% exemption on SGST, skill development grants of ₹ 20,000 per employee per year for all eligible units, 100% exemption on stamp duty/registration fees, and 100% exemption on agricultural land conversion fees.

This policy will provide various benefits like electricity charges exemption, employment subsidy, capital grants, freight subsidy, patent subsidies, and other benefits for eligible industrial units.

On March 19, 2021, the then State Industry Minister, Syed Shahnawaz Hussain, launched the Ethanol Production Promotion Policy, 2021. After the approval of this policy by the State Cabinet, Bihar became the first state in India to implement the Ethanol Promotion Policy under the National Biofuel Policy, 2018. There is a significant potential for increasing ethanol production in the state by using sugarcane juice, corn, and broken rice as feedstock. The National Biofuel Policy, 2018, and subsequent announcements by the Government of India provide a favorable regulatory and institutional environment for increasing ethanol production in states like Bihar, where abundant raw materials such as sugarcane, corn, and rice are available. This policy has been introduced to leverage the opportunities in ethanol production, which will provide a sustainable source of income for farmers, entrepreneurs, and workers employed in ethanol units.

BIHAR ETHANOL PRODUCTION PROMOTION POLICY, 2021

In addition to the incentives provided under the Bihar Industrial Investment Promotion Policy, 2016, the following special incentives are provided under the Ethanol Production Promotion Policy, 2021:

- Permission is granted for ethanol production from all feedstocks approved under the National Biofuel Policy, 2018 and by the National Biofuel Coordination Committee.
- The policy aims to promote investment in new/greenfield ethanol manufacturing units producing fuel-grade ethanol in Bihar by creating an enabling environment and offering financial incentives.
- It seeks to support and incentivize such investments.

- The objective is to increase the income of farmers by encouraging the production of feedstock/raw materials used in ethanol manufacturing.
- The policy also aims to generate employment opportunities at the local level through the promotion of new ethanol industries.
- A capital subsidy amounting to 15% of the expenditure on plant and machinery is provided, with a maximum cap of ₹5 crore.

BIHAR OXYGEN PRODUCTION PROMOTION POLICY 2021

The COVID-19 crisis placed immense pressure on the existing healthcare infrastructure of the state, including its medical facilities. A large number of infected patients required continuous oxygen support both in hospitals and at home. The existing oxygen production capacity was insufficient to meet the increased demand.

To fulfill the sudden surge in demand for medical oxygen, both the central and state governments decided to divert industrial oxygen for medical purposes. However, this was only a temporary measure.

To enhance oxygen production for medical purposes in Bihar, the Oxygen Production Promotion Policy 2021 was adopted by the Bihar Government. The objectives of this policy are:

- To increase oxygen production in Bihar as part of efforts to combat the health crisis caused by the COVID-19 pandemic.
- To promote and facilitate investment in medical and industrial oxygen manufacturing units in Bihar by creating an enabling environment and providing financial incentives.
- To build sufficient local capacity for oxygen production in the state, thereby reducing dependence on other states.
- To generate local employment opportunities and skilled manpower in the oxygen manufacturing sector.
- Under this policy, incentives will be provided for:
  - Liquid medical oxygen
  - Medical oxygen manufacturing
  - Storage tanks
  - Cylinder manufacturing
  - Oxygen concentrators
  - Related equipment and oxygen logistics units

BIHAR OXYGEN PRODUCTION INCENTIVE POLICY 2021

The COVID-19 crisis has placed significant pressure on the state's healthcare infrastructure, including its medical system.

A large number of infected patients required continuous oxygen support in hospitals and at home.

The existing production of oxygen was not sufficient to meet the increased demand.

To fulfill the sudden surge in demand for oxygen for medical purposes, both the central and state governments decided to use industrial-grade oxygen for medical purposes.

However, this was certainly a temporary measure. With the aim of increasing medical oxygen production in Bihar, the state government adopted the "Oxygen Production Incentive Policy 2021."

The objectives of this policy are as follows:

- To increase oxygen production in Bihar to support the ongoing efforts to combat the health crisis caused by the COVID-19 pandemic.
- To encourage, facilitate, and provide financial incentives for investment in medical and industrial oxygen manufacturing units in Bihar by creating an enabling environment and providing grants.
- To develop sufficient local capacity for oxygen production in the state to reduce dependency on other states.
- To create skilled workforce and employment opportunities locally in the oxygen manufacturing sector.

Under this policy, units involved in the production of liquid medical oxygen, medical oxygen manufacturing, storage tanks, cylinder manufacturing, oxygen concentrators and accessories, and oxygen-related logistics will be incentivized. Oxygen production is prioritized as a high-priority sector under the Bihar Industrial Investment Promotion Policy 2016. Therefore, in addition to a 30% capital grant, these units are eligible for all the benefits offered to high-priority sectors under this policy.

INDUSTRIAL INVESTMENT PROMOTION POLICY, 2016

After a comprehensive review of the Industrial Policy, 2011, the Industrial Investment Promotion Policy – 2016 was formulated. The policy focuses on:

- Strengthening infrastructure,
- Prioritizing progressive technology and future growth sectors,
- Promoting skill development, and
- Ensuring balanced regional development across all geographical regions of the state.

Bihar is among the fastest-developing states in India. The state has witnessed notable improvements in:

- Public finance management,
- Infrastructure development,
- Law and order mechanisms,
- Government expenditure, and

Under the Industrial Investment Promotion Policy 2016, the Bihar Government received 1,603 investment proposals amounting to ₹19,348.87 crore between 2016 and December 2020. Out of these, 262 units started operations by December 2020, with actual investments totaling ₹1,886.42 crore, generating employment for around 7,100 individuals.

Subsidies amounting to ₹170.87 crore were disbursed to industrial units between 2017–18 and December 2020.

Objectives of Industrial Investment Promotion Policy, 2016

1. Achieve a 15% annual industrial growth rate.
2. Increase the contribution of the secondary sector to more than 25% of the Gross State Domestic Product (GSDP) under the National Productivity Policy and Make in India initiative.
3. Create 5 lakh direct employment opportunities across all economic sectors.
4. Attract ₹15,000 crore of actual investment.
5. Develop high-quality infrastructure to attract investment.
6. Ensure equitable distribution of investment benefits across all regions to address industrial imbalances.
7. Provide special economic benefits to:
   - o Scheduled Castes (SCs),
   - o Scheduled Tribes (STs),
   - o Women,
   - o Persons with disabilities,
   - o Elderly,
   - o Widows, and
   - o Acid attack victims.
8. Promote skill development of locals, targeting 1.5 crore skilled youth under the state's 'Saat Nischay' (Seven Resolves).
9. Enhance competitiveness of Micro, Small & Medium Enterprises (MSMEs) and promote zero-effect manufacturing practices.

Strategies Under the Industrial Promotion Policy, 2016

1. Encourage investors engaged in value addition to agricultural products (fruits, vegetables, and crops), and help enhance farmer income through food processing and preservation.
2. Promote traditional skills of artisans by seeking larger markets for handloom and handicraft products.
3. Invest in skill development and technical education to establish Bihar as a source of skilled labor—forecasted to be in high demand domestically and internationally.
4. Provide preference to MSMEs based on:
   - o Low land requirement,
   - o High labor intensity,
   - o Low capital and energy use.
5. Promote cluster development in the MSME sector.
6. Focus on industries based on local products, skills, and consumption.
7. Give preference to low-energy consumption and low-pollution industries.

8. Promote large-scale units under the proposed Amritsar-Kolkata Industrial Corridor (AKIC) through integrated production clusters. The government will assist investors in land acquisition within these designated zones; outside them, investors are expected to arrange land themselves.
9. Encourage new investments in heritage tourism, for which the state offers substantial opportunities.
10. Promote investment in Development and management of new/existing facilities through Public-Private Partnerships (PPP).
11. Develop ancillary units to support investments in both public and private sectors.
12. Set up an 'Industry Dialogue Portal' to resolve project implementation issues for investors through a single platform.

Limitations of the Policy

The Industrial Promotion Policy shall apply to all new units across the state, subject to the following conditions:

1. Any unit engaged in the production of goods that does not result in value addition through production activities shall not be considered under this policy. Units engaged solely in trading activities shall not be covered under the ambit of this policy.
2. Units promoted by individuals, firms, or companies that have ever been blacklisted by the State or Central Government shall not be eligible to avail benefits under this policy.
3. Units promoted by individuals, firms, or companies that have previously been declared defaulters by any bank or financial institution or have outstanding dues to the State Government shall not be eligible for the benefits of this policy.
4. No claims for incentives under this policy shall be entertained as compensation for losses incurred due to natural disasters or business-related losses.
5. This policy shall be applicable to private investment including foreign investment but shall not be admissible to public sector investments made solely by the Central or State Government or in partnership with private entities.

BIHAR PROHIBITION AND EXCISE ACT, 2016 (IMPLEMENTED FROM 2ND OCTOBER 2016)

The Bihar Prohibition and Excise Act, 2016, was implemented on 2nd October 2016 to enforce, implement, and promote complete prohibition of alcohol and intoxicants within the jurisdiction of Bihar state, and for matters connected therewith or incidental thereto.

According to this Act, the state government may, through a notification, declare substances, goods, or chemical components that can be used as an alternative to alcohol, as intoxicants. The notification issued by the state government will enable the appointment of an Excise Commissioner who will be responsible for the implementation of this Act. The District Collector will be responsible for ensuring the complete prohibition and enforcement of the provisions of this Act within their jurisdiction. The District Superintendent of Police will assist the Collector in ensuring complete prohibition.

No individual shall manufacture, bottle, distribute, transport, store, possess, purchase, sell, or consume any intoxicants or alcohol. However, the state government, under the provisions of this Act, may, through a notification, renew existing licenses for the production, mixing, bottling, storage, import, and export of alcoholic beverages or intoxicants.

The state government may impose appropriate restrictions on vehicles carrying exciseable intoxicants or final products.

Any person found violating the provisions of this Act by using intoxicants or alcohol in a public place, or found drunk or under the influence, shall be punishable with a minimum imprisonment of five years, which may be extended up to seven years, along with a fine of at least one lakh rupees, which may be increased up to ten lakh rupees.

If someone creates a disturbance under the influence of alcohol or intoxicants, including within their own home or premises, or allows others to do so, or allows addicts to gather in their premises, they shall be punishable with imprisonment of at least 10 years, which may extend to life imprisonment, along with a fine of at least one lakh rupees, which may be increased to ten lakh rupees.

If a chemist, medicine seller, or pharmacist allows the consumption of intoxicants declared by the state government for medicinal purposes, which are not authentically medicinal, in their business premises, they shall be punishable with a minimum imprisonment of eight years, which may extend to ten years, and a fine of at least one lakh rupees, which may be increased up to ten lakh rupees.

Any media, including films and television, or any individual directly or indirectly promoting or publishing any advertisement of alcohol or intoxicants shall be punishable with imprisonment of at least three years, which may extend to five years, or a fine, which may be increased up to ten lakh rupees, or both.

If the District Magistrate finds that any person's death or injury was caused by the consumption of alcohol sold in violation of this Act, the manufacturer or seller, whether convicted of an offence or not, shall be ordered to pay compensation of at least four lakh rupees to the legal representatives of the deceased, two lakh rupees to seriously injured individuals, and 20 thousand rupees to individuals suffering from minor injuries.

If a holder of an authorized license or permit fails to present their permit when requested by an excise officer, or violates the terms of the permit, they shall be punishable with a fine of at least one lakh rupees, which may be increased to ten lakh rupees.

If the holder of a permit fails to cooperate during an inspection or fails to submit required documents, they shall be fined at least one lakh rupees, which may be increased to ten lakh rupees. If they fail to pay the fine, an additional fine of ten thousand rupees per day of delay shall be levied.

Any individual who attacks, threatens, or obstructs an excise officer, police officer, or any other officer performing their duties, shall be punishable with imprisonment of at least eight years, which may be extended to ten years, along with a fine of at least one lakh rupees, which may be increased up to ten lakh rupees.

If an excise officer, police officer, or any other person enters or conducts a search in a private place under the guise of this Act without proper grounds or with the intent to harass, they shall be liable for imprisonment for up to three years or a fine, which may be up to one lakh rupees, or both.

If the District Magistrate is satisfied based on reports from excise or police officers that any specific village, town, or community in an area has repeatedly violated the provisions of this Act, they may impose a collective fine on such group or community.

All crimes punishable under this Act shall be tried in the Sessions Court. The state government, if necessary in public interest, may establish special courts in each district, in consultation with the Chief Justice of the High Court, to handle cases under this Act.

If difficulties arise in the enforcement of this Act, the state government may issue notifications to make provisions it deems necessary to remove the difficulty. Each notification issued under this section will be presented before the State Legislature as soon as possible.

BIHAR PUBLIC GRIEVANCES REDRESSAL ACT, 2015

The Bihar Public Grievances Redressal Act, 2015 was implemented across the state on June 5, 2016, to grant the public the right to resolve grievances within a defined time frame and to make provisions for related matters. Under this Act, the state government can periodically notify the appointment of public grievance officers, first appellate authorities, second appellate authorities, review authorities, state authorities, and the prescribed time limits.

Public grievance officers will provide a hearing to the parties involved in any complaint filed under this Act within the prescribed time limits. To effectively address public grievances, the state government will establish information and related centers. Public grievance officers' posts have been created in all 101 sub-divisions, 38 districts, and 44 departments of the state.

Any person who has not been provided an opportunity to be heard within the prescribed time frame, or who is aggrieved by the decision of the public grievance officer, can file an appeal before the first appellate authority within 30 days from the expiry of the time limit or the decision date. The first appellate authority can accept appeals within a maximum of 60 days and may provide a hearing to the complainant and either issue an order or reject the appeal.

An appeal against the decision of the first appellate authority can be filed before the second appellate authority within 30 days, but the second appellate authority will only accept appeals within a maximum of 45 days. If the public grievance officer fails to comply with the order within the prescribed time limit, a person can file an appeal directly with the second appellate authority. The second appellate authority will provide a hearing and issue an order or reject the appeal within a specified time (no more than 30 days).

An application for the revision of an order made by the second appellate authority can be filed before a designated authority appointed by the state government within 60 days of the decision, but the designated authority will only accept applications within a maximum of 75 days.

The state government can issue rules through notifications for the implementation of this Act. If difficulties arise in giving effect to any provision of this Act, the state government may take appropriate action, but no such action will be taken more than two years after the commencement of this Act. Any order issued under this Act will be placed before the state legislative assembly as soon as possible after its issue.

PRIORITY SECTORS

Bihar has natural advantages in certain sectors such as food processing, leather, and tourism. To ensure maximum employment generation and improve the living standards of people, the State Government intends to focus on these benefits. The priority sectors include:

1. **Food Processing Sector:** Bihar, being an agriculture-based economy, has a vast base for agricultural and animal produce, which ensures sufficient supply of raw materials for food processing. Despite natural resources, the level of food processing is low. There is immense potential for development to meet the needs of the growing population, offering a sustainable consumer market. This sector can play a leading role in the state's industrialization. Key products include food grains (cereals and pulses), oilseeds, fruits (mango, guava, litchi, banana), vegetables (potato, cabbage, cauliflower, okra), makhana/groundnut, animal products (milk, meat, fish, eggs, honey), etc.
2. **Tourism Sector:** The policy envisions promotion of spiritual tourism through circuits such as the Buddha Circuit, Sufi Circuit, Jain Circuit, Ramayana Circuit, Shakti Circuit, Sikh Circuit, Gandhi Circuit, Shiva Circuit, Mandar and Ang Circuits, and Kanwar Yatra Route. Additionally, focus is given to cultural and heritage sites, ecological and wildlife sanctuaries. Investment opportunities include: taxi services, luxury car and coach buses, air taxis and helicopters, special tourist trains, boats, hotels, motels, resorts, and guest houses.
3. **Small Equipment Manufacturing Sector:** Under Bihar's Agricultural Roadmap, mechanization of agriculture is an essential component. The State Government offers additional incentives for equipment such as power tillers, tractors, sowing machines, and power threshers. Electrification has increased the usage of agricultural pumps. The agricultural machinery market is growing rapidly, leading the government to prioritize small manufacturing units related to agriculture.
4. **Information Technology, IT-Enabled Services, and Electronics Hardware Manufacturing Sector:** Globally, IT and IT-enabled services, along with hardware industries, are among the fastest-growing sectors, expected to reach approximately USD 2.4 trillion by 2020. These services are vital across sectors including agriculture, education, healthcare, energy, telecommunication, and rural development. The sector holds immense

potential for startups and enterprises. Bihar offers advantages such as a young educated workforce and low-cost labor. The government has planned to set up IT parks in Bihta (Patna) and Rajgir.

5. **Textile Sector:** This sector contributes 14% to industrial production, 4% to GDP, and 13% to export earnings of India. It provides direct employment to 4.5 crore people. In Bihar, silk is a key product, with Bhagalpur known as a silk hub. Tasar silk is a unique product of Bihar. In 2014-15, Bihar produced approximately 60 tonnes of silk and 1420 thousand tonnes of jute. About 14,000 power looms exist mainly in Bhagalpur, Gaya, and Banka districts, producing cotton sheets and bedsheets. A Ministry of Textiles training center in Nathnagar (Bhagalpur) trains 120 power loom weavers annually. Bihar has about 1 lakh weavers. Development goals include boosting fiber production (cotton, jute, silk, banana), garment and home textiles, and technical textiles in segments like Agrotech, Buildtech, Clothtech, Geotech, Hometech, Indutech, Meditech, Mobiltech, Oekotech, Packtech, Protech, and Sporttech.
6. **Plastic and Rubber Sector:** Plastic is widely used in packaging, preserving the shelf life and quality of food items. Due to increasing demand, this sector offers substantial growth opportunities. Government programs such as household water supply require plastic pipes. Priority sub-sectors include irrigation products, packaging, food storage items, water supply pipes, electrical fittings, automobile products, medical supplies, construction materials, sports and leisure products, and plastic testing services.
7. **Renewable Energy Sector:** Currently, the state relies mainly on conventional energy sources. Per capita electricity consumption in Bihar is 322 kWh. The potential for rural energy is about 12.559 GW. Priority areas include solar power, biomass, and hydropower.
8. **Healthcare Sector:** With a population density of 1,106 persons per square km, Bihar's health indicators show the infant mortality rate in 2018 was 32 per 1,000 live births, same as the national average. However, Bihar's Total Fertility Rate (TFR) was 3.2 compared to India's 2.2. The policy includes provisions for investment in manufacturing of healthcare diagnostic equipment.
9. **Leather Sector:** Leather is a major foreign exchange earner for India and offers vast employment opportunities. Bihar has the availability of raw hides, labor, and domestic markets, indicating immense potential for growth in this sector.
10. **Technical Education Sector:** This sector offers vast investment opportunities. Potential areas include the establishment of engineering colleges, polytechnic institutes, and skill development centers with advanced equipment for high-quality training.
11. **Ease of Doing Business Reforms:** To attract investment and provide large-scale employment, the State Government is committed to creating a favorable investment environment. For easy access to information, the Government has established the "Udyog Samvad Portal" a single-window platform for investors. It provides access to acts, rules, circulars, notifications, application procedures for approvals, and a grievance redressal mechanism, allowing direct communication with the Principal Secretary of the Department of Industries.

Tax-Related Reforms

Various tax reforms have been adopted to simplify doing business, which are as follows:

1. Online application facility for Value Added Tax (VAT), Professional Tax, Entry Tax, Entertainment Tax, and Luxury Tax.
2. Mandatory clear timeframes for application tracking and issuance of registration certificates.
3. Online facility for obtaining registration certificates and inspection reports.
4. Online verification facility for registered and rejected vendors.

Environmental Reforms

The State Government has taken several corrective steps to improve the environment, which are as follows:

1. Online consent management system for obtaining "Consent to Establish" and "Consent to Operate" under the Air and Water Acts, as well as under the Hazardous Waste Rules.
2. Exemption for Green Category industries from obtaining "Consent to Establish" and "Consent to Operate" certificates.
3. Validity of Consent to Operate (CTO) extended from 3 years to 5 years.

Way Forward (Future Directions)

To facilitate easier business operations in Bihar, the following initiatives are planned:

1. **Single Window Clearance System** – A new and simplified process will be introduced by making necessary legal changes.
2. **Standardized Application Form** – A uniform application form will be introduced for coordination among all no-objection certificate (NOC) issuing agencies.
3. **Provision of a Program Management Agency** – The Department of Industries will empanel a Program Management Agency to provide technical support and secretarial services to the competent committee for approving investment proposals and monitoring progress.
4. **Amendment in BIADA Act** – The Bihar government will review the current Bihar Industrial Area Development Authority Act, 1974, and amend its legal framework to strengthen planning and development of industrial areas.
5. **Inclusion under the Bihar Right to Public Services Act, 2011** – Additional investor-related services will be brought under the Bihar Right to Public Services Act, 2011 to ensure time-bound delivery and accountability.
6. **Provision for Self-Certification** – Self-certification will be allowed under the Single Window System. Authorized authorities may conduct random inspections after the start of production.
7. **Rationalization of Laws and Provisions** – Although labor laws have already been made more practical in the state, further simplification will be reviewed in consultation with industry representatives.

Strengthening Infrastructure for Industrial Investment

Bihar is one of the larger states in India in terms of geographical area, with a total area of approximately 9.36 million hectares. Around 57% of the total land is used for agriculture. BIADA is the main agency for allotting land/industrial plots to units in Bihar. BIADA has regional offices in Patna, Darbhanga, Muzaffarpur, and Bhagalpur. BIADA develops infrastructure in industrial areas, such as roads, electricity, water, and drainage, and then allots the plots.

The state government has allotted land for the following major parks and clusters:

- Pristine Mega Food Park (Khagaria)
- Purnasar Jute Park (Purnia)
- IT City and Electronic Manufacturing Parks (Rajgir and Bihta)
- Leather Cluster (Muzaffarpur)

Promotion of Micro, Small, and Medium Enterprise (MSME) Clusters (Establishment of Common Facility Centers)

There are several active and potential MSME clusters in Bihar, which are listed below:

1. Brass and Bronze Utensil Industry Cluster, Parev (Patna)
2. CFL and LED Bulbs, Patna City (Patna)
3. Leather Footwear, Patna City (Patna)
4. Makhana Cluster in four districts (Darbhanga as the main center)
5. Leather Products Cluster, Saran (Chhapra)
6. Incense Stick Manufacturing Cluster, Gaya
7. Lac Bangles Cluster, Muzaffarpur
8. Leather Shoes and Slippers Cluster, Muzaffarpur
9. Brass and German Silver Utensils Cluster, West Champaran
10. Rice Milling Cluster, East Champaran
11. Rice Milling Cluster, Lakhisarai
12. Brass Alloy Utensils Cluster, Vaishali
13. Leather Shoes and Slippers Cluster, Nalanda
14. Readymade Garments Cluster, Patna City (Patna)

15. Silao Khaja Cluster, Nalanda
16. Sweet and Savory Khaja Cluster, Madhepura
17. Bamboo-Based Products Cluster, Madhepura
18. Handloom and Khadi (Post-Processing) Cluster
19. Handicrafts Cluster
20. Small Machinery and Equipment Manufacturing Cluster, Aurangabad and Raxaul (East Champaran)

All of the above clusters lack adequate facilities and are technically underdeveloped. These issues can be addressed through technical and skill upgradation. Keeping this need in mind, the "Chief Minister MSME Cluster Development Scheme" was launched in 2013.

Incentive for Private Industrial Parks

The Bihar Government introduced the 'Private Industrial Park Policy' in 2013 with the aim of encouraging private participation. Any individual, partnership firm, company registered under the Company Act or Society Act can establish a private industrial park. The park must arrange for the land independently; the state government will not have any involvement. The minimum area for the park will be 25 acres, while for an IT park, the proposed land area must be 3 acres, and the land should be entirely owned by the promoter without any encumbrances or liabilities. The land should not be taken on lease.

The state government is committed to providing an enabling environment and economic incentive packages to entrepreneurs for industrial encouragement. There will be no stamp duty payable by IDA/BIADA for land allocation. The land conversion fee for agricultural land to industrial land will be reimbursed 100% after the unit starts commercial production. New units will receive tax relief up to 70% of the approved project cost for non-priority areas and 100% for priority areas.

Special Incentives for Scheduled Caste/ Scheduled Tribe Entrepreneurs

Special incentives are provided under the Industrial Investment and Promotion Policy for entrepreneurs from Scheduled Castes and Scheduled Tribes. These entrepreneurs will receive interest subsidy at a rate of 11.5% or the actual interest rate of the term loan, whichever is lower. The total interest subsidy amount will be 34.5% of the approved project cost for priority areas and 17.25% for non-priority areas. The maximum limit of interest subsidy will be ₹ 11.5 crore. VAT, CST, and entry tax will be reimbursed up to 92%, with a maximum of 80.5% for non-priority areas and 11.5% for priority areas. These entrepreneurs will also be provided with Project Management Consultancy.

Industrial Rehabilitation Fund

A corpus fund will be established with the cooperation of commercial banks, state government, industry associations, and others to revive sick industries. This fund will provide financial assistance to sick, small, and medium industrial units whose rehabilitation packages have been approved, as quickly as possible.

This policy will be effective for five years from the date of issuance. In case of any disputes or issues regarding the interpretation of any terms, the decision will be taken by the Industrial Development Commissioner or the Principal Secretary of the Department of Industries. This decision will be final and binding for all concerned departments.

INFORMATION TECHNOLOGY POLICY

In recent years, the development of Information Technology (IT) software and related services has been progressing rapidly worldwide. India's success in the export of IT software and related services is well-known. Currently, India dominates the global market, controlling about 65% of the offshore IT sector and 46% of the IT-related services market. There are immense growth prospects in this sector, and it can play a significant role in job creation in India.

However, the development of information technology has largely been concentrated in a few states, leaving much of the country, including Bihar, underserved. The state government has a strong ambition to promote rapid development in the IT sector and the associated services by encouraging investment, enabling the people of Bihar to benefit from better civic amenities and economic growth right at their doorstep.

The policy outlines the following approaches to ensure the development of better civic services along with growth in IT software and related service exports:

1. Efforts to develop and disseminate a knowledge-based economy in the state.
2. Development of IT infrastructure in the state to ensure access to all citizens and reduce the digital divide between rural and urban populations.
3. Making Bihar an attractive hub for investment in the IT and IT-related service industries.
4. Making Bihar a leading state in IT facilities.

Objectives

To fulfill the vision of the state's IT vision for 2015, the following objectives need to be adopted:

1. Developing human and intellectual capital resources by promoting computer literacy at the school level and training youth for employability in IT.
2. Attracting capital investment in IT and related services to create local employment.
3. Investing in IT infrastructure to develop world-class facilities.
4. Promoting e-Governance through the National e-Governance Plan, bringing maximum government departments and citizen services online.
5. Encouraging investment in the state's IT infrastructure by private industries.
6. Creating an environment conducive to business for IT and related service industries by increasing government opportunities.
7. Establishing a legal framework to regulate IT industries, protect intellectual property rights, patents, and trademarks, and prevent the misuse of technology.

Classification of Information and Communication Technology Policy

To achieve rapid development and simplification, the Information and Communication Technology Policy has been classified into the following categories:

1. IT policy for industries
2. IT policy for education
3. IT policy for government
4. IT policy for citizens

IT Policy for Industries

All IT, ITES (Information Technology Enabled Services), and electronic hardware manufacturing units will be eligible for the incentives provided under the Industrial Incentive Policy of 2011.

1. **Pre-production facilities:** IT, ITES, and EHM units established in industrial areas, sheds, IT parks, or outside them will be granted a 100% exemption on stamp duty and registration fees for land lease, sale, and transfer. This exemption will only apply to new units, and existing units expanding production by over 50% (and those that have not previously received this exemption) will be eligible for it on the land used for expansion.
2. **Post-production facilities:** After production begins, units will be eligible for reimbursements up to ₹6,00,000 for expenses such as project reports, land purchase, technical knowledge, capital subsidy, etc. Additionally, 50% of the costs incurred in preparing project reports (up to ₹2,00,000) will be reimbursed, provided the reports are validated by an IT department-approved company. For project reports related to carbon credits, 50% of the cost (up to ₹50,00,000) will be reimbursed if carbon credits are obtained.
3. **Financial Assistance for Technology Acquisition:** Industry players who obtain technical knowledge from recognized national research centers, laboratories, or institutions will be reimbursed 30% of the costs incurred, up to a maximum of ₹15,00,000.
4. **Quality Certification Incentives:** Units obtaining national or international quality certifications (e.g., ISO, SEI, CMM level 2) will be reimbursed 75% of the certification fee, provided the software company meets the prescribed quality standards.

5. **Land Incentives:** IT, ITES, and EHM units allocated land in Bihar Industrial Area Development Authority (BIADA), Export Promotion Industrial Parks, Food Parks, or IT Parks will receive incentives on land prices. Small and medium units will receive a 50% or up to ₹15,00,000 grant, while large and mega units will receive 25% or up to ₹30,00,000 grant. The Bihar government will also identify and reserve suitable government land for these units wherever possible.

This translation covers the key components of the policy initiatives and incentives aimed at promoting ethanol production, IT development, and infrastructure improvements in Bihar.

This text outlines various incentives and schemes for promoting Information Technology (IT) and related sectors in Bihar. Here are the key points summarized:

1. **Captive Power Generation Incentives:**
   - A 50% subsidy will be provided for plant and machinery installation for captive power generation, with no maximum limit. Existing units are also eligible.
   - 60% subsidy for setting up plants and machinery for non-traditional energy sources.
2. **Capital Investment Subsidy:**
   - 20% capital investment subsidy (up to ₹75 lakh) for IT hardware, IT equipment, and software network ventures.
3. **Entry Tax Benefits:**
   - For new IT and IT-enabled services units, 80% of VAT will be refunded as entry tax benefits.
4. **VAT Refund:**
   - New industries will be entitled to a refund of 80% VAT for up to 10 years, with a maximum limit of 300% of capital investment.
5. **Exemptions:**
   - Full exemptions for the first 7 years in luxury tax, electricity charges, and land conversion fees for new IT, IT-enabled services, and EHM units.
6. **Employment Creation Grants:**
   - IT, IT-enabled services, and EHM units creating 100 jobs will be eligible for a grant equivalent to one year's EPF contribution.
7. **Single Window System:**
   - A single window agency will help process approvals for new IT units and assist entrepreneurs in post-approval activities.
8. **Special Provisions for Legal Compliance:**
   - IT and IT-enabled service units can self-certify compliance with various labor and environmental laws.
9. **Cyber Crime and Security:**
   - A Cyber Crime Cell will be set up in Patna for handling data security breaches and other IT-related crimes.
10. **IT Policy for Education:**
    - Efforts will be made to introduce IT training in schools, with the goal of expanding computer literacy across 1000 schools.
11. **Bihar Knowledge Society:**
    - This initiative will create new IT training institutes to offer short-term IT courses to unemployed youth.
12. **Promotion of Foreign Language Training:**
    - Programs will be introduced to teach foreign languages like German, French, and Arabic to improve employment opportunities abroad.
13. **E-Governance:**
    - A focus on improving e-governance by creating digital infrastructure such as data centers and web portals, and ensuring efficient connectivity between government departments.
14. **Green IT Initiatives:**
    - Encouragement for recycling IT hardware and using renewable energy sources like solar and wind to reduce the state's electricity crisis.
15. **E-Government Development:**
    - The state will create a comprehensive e-governance framework, linking all departments through high-speed internet, and digitizing records to improve public service delivery.

This policy aims to foster IT and IT-enabled services in the state, creating a conducive environment for economic growth, job creation, and technological advancement.

Information and Communication Technology Policy for Citizens

To ensure that the state's citizens benefit from information and communication technology (ICT), special efforts are required. A plan has been made to establish Common Service Centers (CSC) in all 8474 Panchayats of the state. The state portal will provide citizens with information about government departments, schemes, orders, tenders, and notices. Complaints and the publication of results of competitive exams will be done through the portal. An e-literacy program will be launched for citizens. Preference will be given to using Hindi and Urdu in all government portals and software applications. The Bihar government will make efforts to initiate pilot projects for the use of information technology and rural development, based on multi-dimensional approaches, including financial and other facilities. Areas such as promoting information technology in developmental and rural works will be encouraged. Mapping of all important infrastructure assets based on Geographic Information Systems (GIS) will be done, and this data will be integrated with various information systems. This information will be used by various departments for long-term planning and monitoring of projects. To assist farmers, a database will be created on various climatic factors such as rainfall, water availability, and soil fertility. A database management system for land use, agricultural work, public health, and multimedia facilities for training and awareness programs related to agriculture will be provided. The state government will link rural areas under the National Broadband Scheme with BSNL. A database of all ICT-trained students will be created with the collaboration of ICT institutions, universities, colleges, and companies. This database will be shared with IT companies established in the state to provide employment opportunities. The plan of this ICT and communication policy is to provide 1 lakh employable youth with opportunities in the IT sector in the next 3 years and create 3 lakh indirect jobs during the same period.

Technology Policy for Business and Social Infrastructure Improvement

Proper availability of infrastructure is the second most important element for the smooth functioning of commercial activities. To meet these needs, significant investment is required in the commercial and social infrastructure of Bihar. In recent years, Bihar has made significant progress in the field of Information and Communication Technology (ICT). The state government has made several innovations and has won the 'Digital India Award' for its achievements. During the recent COVID-19 pandemic, financial assistance was provided to all beneficiaries through direct benefit transfer. Between 2011-12 and 2019-20, ICT has been growing at an annual rate of 7.8%. In 2011-12, the contribution of the communication sector to Gross State Value Added (GSVA) was 2.2%, which increased to 3.0% in 2019-20. During the pandemic, remote work, distance education, e-banking, and e-governance were made possible due to the widespread presence of ICT infrastructure in the state. Under the first phase of the Seven Resolves initiative, the state has provided free Wi-Fi in all government universities and colleges to support their efficient functioning.

The key infrastructure needs for business activities in the context of Information Technology and ICT services include communication, adequate office spaces for world-class offices with regular electricity and water supply, and connectivity to air routes. Other elements include residential real estate, retail, and hospitality. In this regard, the following key plans will be implemented:

1. **Air Connectivity:** To optimize Information Technology and ICT services, air connectivity is essential. The connections from Patna and Gaya will be increased to national and international destinations. Private companies will be encouraged to operate air taxis between various cities of the country.
2. **Road Connectivity:** Roads connecting airports and railway stations with ICT parks will be constructed for quicker access. Road networks

will also be developed to include value-added services like international standard facilities, hotels, restaurants, petrol pumps, emergency services, etc.

3. **Power Supply:** New electricity projects in the public and private sectors will be promoted to meet the needs of ICT industries. ICT units developing captive power plants will be provided with incentives and facilities.
4. **Reliable Communication Links:** The state government will encourage reliable telecom service providers to set up high-power telecom communication links for all ICT parks. Prioritization will be given to setting up West Stations and network enterprises at selected locations. A single-window system will be set up to ensure proper installation of optical fiber and towers.
5. **Residential Real Estate:** High-quality residential complexes with ample open spaces, playgrounds, and parking will be encouraged in ICT parks. Housing units for employees and their families will be constructed near ICT parks.
6. **Retail and Entertainment Centers:** Large departmental stores, malls, cafes, modern restaurants, cinemas, and multiplexes will be promoted. These facilities will cater to the entertainment needs of employees in ICT and related services.

BIHAR RIGHT TO PUBLIC SERVICES ACT, 2011

To provide timely information regarding notified services to the general public, the "Bihar Right to Public Services Act, 2011" was implemented. Under this Act, people are given the right to receive information related to government-notified services within a fixed time frame. Public servants are mandated to provide service-related information. The Act specifies a time limit for this process. The primary goal of the Act is to easily provide certificates like birth certificates, caste certificates, income certificates, and residential certificates.

Under this Act, applications made for notified services are considered valid, and necessary action will be taken by the public servants within the specified time limit. Public servants may approve or reject the application, but reasons must be provided in case of rejection. If a person's application is rejected under Section 5(2) or if the service is not provided within the prescribed time, an appeal can be filed before the appellate authority within 30 days of the rejection or the expiration of the time limit. The appellate authority may accept the appeal after the 30-day period if it is satisfied that the appellant was prevented from filing on time due to sufficient reasons. The appellate authority can either reject the appeal or impose penalties on the public servant while ensuring the service is provided.

If the appellate authority's decision is unsatisfactory, the appellant can file a second appeal with the review authority within 60 days from the date of the decision. The review authority may accept the appeal beyond 60 days if there is a valid reason preventing timely filing. The appellate and review authorities will have the same powers as a civil court while dealing with the matter under the Civil Procedure Code, 1908.

If the appellate authority fails to decide within the specified time without sufficient reason, it will be liable for penalties as per the provisions of the Act. Similarly, if the review authority fails to decide within the given time, penalties can be imposed on the appellate authority. Before imposing any penalty, both the appellate and review authorities will be provided an opportunity to present their case.

BIHAR AGRICULTURAL LAND (CONVERSION FOR NON-AGRICULTURAL PURPOSES) ACT, 2010

The Bihar Legislative Assembly enacted the Bihar Agricultural Land (Conversion for Non-Agricultural Purposes) Act, 2010 to regulate the use of agricultural land for non-agricultural purposes and to address related matters. This Act consists of a total of 15 sections. The Act extends throughout the state of Bihar, excluding areas formed as urban areas under the Bihar Municipal Act, 2007 or any part of it, or areas falling under cantonment regions. The extension of this Act will be as defined in the Bihar Tenancy Act, 1885, meaning it will not apply to areas notified as commercial, industrial, or urban through master planning or any other method, even though these areas may involve agricultural land.

Under this Act, significant powers are conferred upon the Collector and the Competent Authority. "Collector" refers to the District Collector, who has the authority over the agricultural land applied for conversion, and any other officer authorized by the government who is involved in implementing the powers and actions under this Act. "Competent Authority" refers to the Sub-Divisional Officer (SDO), who has the authority over the agricultural land or part of it within their jurisdiction. The SDO will be competent to issue orders for the conversion of agricultural land into non-agricultural use within their jurisdiction. Under this Act, the market value is defined as the value determined by the Collector under the Indian Stamp Act, 1899.

Without prior approval from the Competent Authority, agricultural land in the state cannot be used for non-agricultural purposes. Applications for the conversion of agricultural land for non-agricultural purposes must be submitted in the prescribed form with the prescribed fee under Section 4 of the Act. The competent authority must issue a decision on the application, either granting or rejecting it, within 90 days from the date of receipt of the application or the date of payment of the required fee, whichever is later. If an application is rejected, the reasons for the rejection must be provided in writing to the applicant.

Under Section 8 of the Act, the following land and land uses are exempted from the conversion provisions:

1. Land owned by the state government.
2. Land owned by local authorities, which is being used for community purposes, unless it is being used for commercial purposes.
3. Land used for religious, social, and charitable purposes unless it is used for commercial purposes.
4. Land used for micro-industries of traditional professions under one acre.
5. Land used for small shops under 500 square feet.
6. Land used for any other purposes notified by the government from time to time.

Economic Survey 2025–26 and Bihar Budget 2026–27

ECONOMIC SURVEY 2025-26

Bihar Economic Survey 2025-26 was presented in the Bihar Assembly by Finance Minister **Mr. Bijendra Prasad Yadav** on **2 February 2026.**

KEY POINTS

- This is the 20th Economic Survey of the state, which presents a detailed analysis of Bihar's economic performance, macro trends, sectoral growth, public finance and development priorities.
- **Bihar Economy's Outlook:**
  - o Bihar's economic growth outpaced the national average with growth of 14.9% compared with India's 12.0%.
  - o The **Gross State Domestic Product (GSDP)** for 2024-25 is estimated at **₹ 9,91,997 crore** at current prices and **₹ 5,31,372 crore** at 2011-12 constant prices.
  - o Growth recorded at **13.1% (current prices)** and **8.6% (constant prices)**.
  - o The **Net State Domestic Product (NSDP)** for 2024-25 is estimated at **₹ 8,99,020 crore** at current prices and **₹ 4,71,322 crore** at 2011-12 constant prices.
  - o Bihar's **per capita NSDP** at **constant prices (2011-12) is estimated at ₹ 36,342**, which is **31.7 %** of the all-India average for states.
  - o **Per capita income** rose to **₹ 76,490 (current prices)** and **₹40,973 (constant prices)**.
    - ♦ **Top 3 Districts**: Patna, Begusarai, Munger
    - ♦ **Lowest 3 Districts:** Sheohar, Araria, and Sitamarhi
    - ♦ **Patna:** Highest Petrol, Diesel and LPG consumption.
  - o **The tertiary sector** contributes **54.8%** of GSDP, Secondary sector **26.8%,** Primary sector **18.3%**.
  - o **Sectoral Growth:** At current prices for 2024-25, the **primary sector in the state grew by 9.6%, the secondary sector by 15.5 %, and the tertiary sector by 13.5 %** over the previous year.
  - o **Employment: The tertiary sector** contributes **22%, Secondary sector 24%,** Primary sector **54%**.
  - o The **Gross Fixed Capital Formation** has nearly doubled in the recent five years from **₹ 17,416 crore to ₹ 34,905 crore in 2024-25.**
- **State Finance 2024-25:**
  - o **Total Receipts Revenue Account:** ₹ 2,18,658 crore (22% of GSDP)
  - o **Capital Receipts**: ₹ 66,165 crore (6.7% of GSDP)
  - o **Total Expenditure:** ₹ 2,81,939 crore (28.4% of GSDP)
  - o **Revenue Expenditure:** ₹ 2,19,015 crore (22.1% of GSDP)
    - ♦ 77.7% of Total Expenditure
  - o **Capital Expenditure:** ₹ 62,924 crore (6.3% of GSDP)
    - ♦ 22.3% of Total Expenditure

- o **Total Borrowings:** ₹ 66,049 crore (6.7% of GSDP)
- o **Debt Outstanding:** 3,74,134 crore (37.7% of GSDP)
- o **Gross Fiscal Deficit:** ₹ 41,223 crore (4.2% of GSDP)
- o **Primary Deficit:** ₹ 21,544 crore (2.2% of GSDP)
- o **Revenue Deficit:** ₹ 357 crore

- **Agriculture:**
  - o **Gross Sown Area:** 8,207.27 Thousand Hectare
  - o **Net Sown Area:** 5,411.96 Thousand Hectare
  - o Cropping **Intensity:** 1.52 Thousand Hectare
  - o **Cropping Pattern in Bihar (2020-21 to 2024-25)**: Foodgrains (95.2), Cereals (89.2), Pulses (6.0).
  - o **Milk production** rose by 4.2 percent, egg production by 10.0 percent, and fish production by 9.9 percent.
  - o The **fisheries sector** recorded a total fish production of 960 thousand tonnes with **Madhubani as leading producer.**
    - ♦ **Scheme:** Mukhyamantri Samekit Chaur Vikas Yojana, River Ranching Programme, Jalashay Matsyki Vikas Yojana.
  - o **Government Initiative:** Jaivik Kheti Protsahan Yojana, Jaivik Corridor Yojana Paramparagat Krishi Vikas Yojana (PKVY).
- **Enterprises Sector:**
  - o **Sugar** Industry**:** The Riga Sugar Mill was reopened in 2024-25.
  - o **Dairy** Industry**:** The aggregate daily average milk procurement 2,252.28 thousand kg in 2024-25.
  - o **Textile Industry:** The State government introduced the Bihar Industrial Investment Promotion Policy (Textile and Leather Policy, 2022) under the broader framework of the Bihar Industrial Investment Promotion Policy, 2016.
  - o **Tourism Development:** Takht Sri Harimandir Ji Patna Sahib, Matsyagandha Lake in Saharsa district, Luv-Kush Eco Tourism Park in Valmikinagar.
  - o **Eco-tourism:** In 2024-25, the total outlay for eco-tourism and park development was ₹ 100.00 crore. Bihar's third biological park at Raniganj in Araria.
  - o **Initiative:** Bihar State Khadi and Village Industries Board (KVIB), Industrial Promotion in Bihar, Bihar Industrial Area Development Authority (BIADA),
- **Labour, Employment And Skill:**
  - o In Bihar, the male **labour force participation rate (LFPR)** was 76.8 percent in rural areas and 67.8 percent in urban areas.
  - o Bihar's **female LFPR** being 11.2 percent lower than the all-India average.
  - o In **rural** Bihar**,** the unemployment **rate** for males was 3.3 percent, while the female unemployment rate was just 0.9 percent.
  - o In **urban areas** about 6.9 percent of male workers and 9.1 percent of female workers in urban Bihar are unemployed.
- **Physical Infrastructure:**
  - o Bihar shares **5.5% of** the total road network of India.
  - o A **6**-lane **Bihar** New Ganga bridge is being constructed at an estimate of **₹ 4,988 crore** with the support from ADB.
  - o Construction of expressways and **national** highways continues.
  - o The **road** transport **sector** recorded a high growth of 13.4% annually during the last decade.
  - o Bihar constituted 5.4 percent of the **rail network** of the country.
  - o Bihar has recorded a high growth rate of 20 percent in the **air transport sector.**
  - o **Initiative:** PM e-Bus Sewa, Mukhya Mantri Gram Parivahan Yojana (MMGPY).
- **E-governance:**
  - o **E-governance initiatives: CCTNS, CFMS, Cyber Cell, e-Challan, Bihar Al Mission**
  - o Tele Density coverage 57.23%, Internet density coverage 43.10%.

- o **Initiatives:** Bihar State Data Centre (BSDC 2.0), Bihar State Wide Area Network (BSWAN 3.0), Bihar Aadhaar Authentication Framework (BAAF), Emergency Response Support System (ERSS).

- **Power Sector:**
  - o Per capita energy consumption increased to **374 kilowatt-hours.**
  - o 13 Innovation & Impact Award for DISCOMS 2025 at **19th India Energy Summit** - Won by both **NBPDCL & SBPDCL** in different categories.
  - o **BSPTCL** has been awarded A+ certificate from PFC consecutively for 5 years from the year 2020 to 2025.
  - o **Initiative:** Floating Solar Power Plant, Solar Water Pumps, Mukhyamantri Solar Street Light Scheme, Smart Metering.
- **Rural Development:**
  - o Rural development is fundamental to Bihar's inclusive growth, as nearly 90 percent **of** the population lives in rural areas.
  - o **JEEVIKA:** It implements the **National Rural** Livelihoods Mission **(NRLM)** in Bihar. JEEVIKA has mobilized 1.40 crore families into 11.03 lakh **Self-Help Groups (SHGs),** supported by **Village Organizations** and Cluster-**Level** Federations.
  - o **Initiatives**: Didi-Ki-Rasoi Initiative, Pashu Sakhi Model, One Stop Facility Centre, Satat Jeevikoparjan Yojana, Lohiya Swachh Bihar Abhiyan.
- **Urban Development:**
  - o The **total population growth** rate in Bihar declined to 14.4 per cent during 2021-25.
  - o The **Total Fertility Rate (TFR)** in Bihar will reach the replacement level of **2.1** by **2039**.
  - o **Initiatives:** Mukhyamantri Samagra Shahari Vikas Yojana, Mukhyamantri Shahri Naali-Gali Pakkikaran Nishchay Yojana, Rainwater Harvesting and Artificial Recharge of Ground Water, Solid Waste Management, Smart City Mission, Patna Metro Rail Project.
- **Financial Institutions:**
  - o **Initiatives**: ATM infrastructure in Bihar, Microfinance Institutions (MFI), Kisan Credit Card (KCC), National Bank for Agriculture and Rural Development (NABARD).
- **Human Development:**
  - o **Women Empowerment:** The total expenditure **on women** has increased **3.45 times** between 2018-19 and 2023-24.
    - ♦ Under **Mukhyamantri Kanya Vivah Yojna**, financial assistance of **₹ 5,000** is provided to girls from BPL families who marry at the age of 18 years or above.
    - ♦ **Initiative:** One-Stop Centre, Palna Ghar, Mahila Thana, Pink Bus Initiative, Nayika Apne Jeevan Ki.
  - o **Education & Health Sector:** The **Life Expectancy at Birth** in Bihar in 2019-23 has been **68.9 and 69.7 years for males** and **females** respectively.
    - ♦ Bihar recorded significant improvement in literacy during 2001-11, rising from **47% to 61.8%**, the **highest among all states.**
    - ♦ **Initiatives**: E-Shikshakosh, PM Poshan Scheme, BHAVYA initiative, Janani Suraksha Yojana (JSY), Immunisation, National Health Mission, Samagra Shiksha Abhiyan (SSA), Bihar Student Credit Card Yojana (BSCCY).
- **Child Development:**
  - o **NFHS-5 (2019-21):** Children under 5 Years who are Stunted (42.9%), Wasted (22.9%) and Underweight(**41%**).
  - o **Initiatives**: Anganwadi Services (AS), Poshan Pakhwada, POSHAN Tracker, Mission Vatsalya, Establishment of Child Protection Unit, Juvenile Justice (Care and Protection of Children) Act, 2015.

- **Environment, Climate Change and Disaster Management:**
  - o The forestry sector registered an average annual growth of 10.6% between 2011-12 and 2024-25.
  - o Forest cover increased by **689 sq km** in 12 years.
  - o **Initiative:** Environment Forest and Climate Change Department, Forest Management Information System (FMIS), Bihar-Van Mitra App, e-Parivesh Portal, Hariyali Mission, Bamboo Mission, Wetland Conservation and Development in Bihar, Vikramshila Gangetic Dolphin Sanctuary.
  - o **Disaster Management Initiatives**: State Disaster Response Force (SDRF) in 2010, Bihar Disaster Risk Reduction Road Map (2015-2030), Modernisation of State Emergency Operation Centre (SEOC).

A SYNOPSIS OF ECONOMIC SURVEY, 2024-25

BIHAR ECONOMY: AN OVERVIEW

The Bihar Economic Survey 2024-25 was presented in the state assembly by the Finance Minister on February 28, 2025.

This is the 19th Economic Survey of the State, which discusses in detail the status and trajectory of Bihar's economy.

Bihar has witnessed significant economic growth over the last two decades owing to the State government's initiatives, resulting in notable advancements in education, health, and other social indicators, along with a general increase in the per capita income. Each focusing on different aspects of the Bihar economy.

Gross State Domestic Product (GSDP) of Bihar for the year 2023-24

		At Current Prices	**At Constant Prices (Base year 2011-12)**
Gross State Domestic Product	Estimation	₹ 8,54,429 crore	₹ 4,64,540 crore
	Increase	14.5%	9.2%
Net State Domestic Product	Estimation	₹ 7,71,435 crore	₹ 4,11,359 crore
	Increase	10.7%	5%
Per capita GSDP	Estimation	₹ 66,828	₹ 36,333
	Increase	12.8%	7.6%
Per capita NSDP	Estimation		₹ 32,174
	Increase		7.6%
Gross Fixed Capital Formation (GFCF)	Estimation	₹ 38,986 crore	
	Increase	4.6%	

The share of the different sectors in the Gross State Value Added (GSVA) at constant (2011-12) Prices in 2023-24:

- **Primary: 19.9%**
  - o Crops and livestock are the two major contributors to the state's GSVA, with their contributions estimated to be 9.9% and 6.3%, respectively.
  - o This sector has the largest share in employment (54.2%).
- **Secondary: 21.5%**
  - o The estimated share of manufacturing is 7.6 percent.
  - o Construction activities related to manufacturing are estimated to have contributed the most at 11.3 percent.
  - o 23.6% contribution in workforce participation.
- **Tertiary: 58.6%**
  - o The most significant contributor is estimated to be the Trade and Repair Services, accounting for 14.8 percent.
  - o 22.2% contribution in workforce participation.

Respectively Prosperous and Impoverished Districts of Bihar (2022-23 and 2023-24)		
Criteria / Year	Most Prosperous District	Most Impoverished District
Per Capita GSDP (in ₹)		
2022-23	Patna (121396),Begusarai (49064), Munger (46795)	Sheohar(19561), Sitamarhi (21931), Araria (22204)
Consumption of Petrol per 1000 persons in a year (in MT)		
2023-24	Patna (17.7), Muzaffarpur (11.8), Purnea (10.9)	Lakhisarai (4.9), Banka (5.1), Jehanabad (5.6)
Consumption of Diesel per 1000 persons in a year (in MT)		
2023-24	Patna (35.9), Sheikhpura (34.9), Aurangabad (27.7)	Sheohar (8.9), Siwan (11.2), Gopalganj (11.7)
Consumption of LPG per 1000 persons in a year (in MT)		
2023-24	Patna (24.9), Begusarai (16.5), Muzaffarpur (15.7), Gopalganj (15.7)	Araria (7.5) ,Banka (8.0) , Kishanganj (8.2)

Per capital GSDP in Bihar (2011-12 to 2023-24)

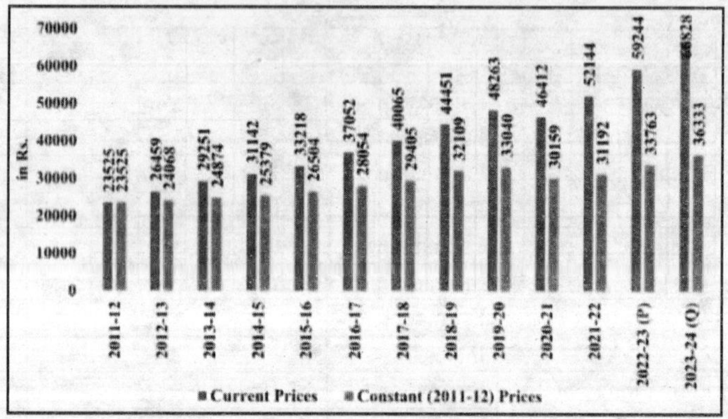

State Finances

The state government's budget has significantly increased over the year and this effectively utilised to improve the infrastructure necessary for economic growth in Bihar. Furthermore, the government has allocated more funds to achieve various developmental goals, resulting in notable improvement across indicators.At the same time, the government has managed its finances prudently, ensuring that the rise in expenditure remains fiscally sustainable. Additionally, its fiscal management has been flexible enough to avoid vulnerabilities.

- **Total Expenditure - 2,52,082 crore**
  - Scheme Expenditure - 1,01,835 crore (40.4%)
  - Establishment and Committed Expenditure - 1,50,247 crore (59.6%)
- **Share of Expenditure (2023-24) -**
  - Social service - 83,225 crore (43.7%)
  - General service - 59,218 crore (31.1%)
  - Economic service - 48,071 crore (25.2%)

Receipts and Expenditure

Item	In Crore		As percentage of GSDP	
	2023-24	2024-25 (BE)	2023-24	2024-25 (BE)
Total Revenue Receipts	1,93,347	2,26,798	22.6	23.2
Total Revenue Expenditure	1,90,514	2,25,677	22.3	23.1
Revenue Deficit	-2833	-1121	-0.3	-0.1
Capital Receipts	60,313	52,127	7.1	5.3
Capital Expenditure	61,568	53,049	7.2	5.4
Total Expenditure	2,52,082	2,78,726	29.5	28.5
Gross Fiscal Deficit	35,660	29,095	4.2	3.0
Primary Deficit	18,054	8,569	2.1	0.9
Total Borrowing	60,218	51,688	7.0	5.3
a. Internal Debt Receipt	49,546	49,188	5.8	5.0
b. Loans from Central Government	10,672	2,500	1.2	0.3
Debt Outstanding	3,32,741	3,48,370	38.9	35.7
GSDP	8,54,429	9,76,514		

- **Revenue Receipts** - The largest share of revenue comes from tax revenue followed by Grants-in-aid and Non-tax revenue.
  - o Tax revenue - 1,61,965 crore (2023-24), 83.8 % of total receipts.
  - o Grants-in-aid - 52,161 crore (2023-24), 13.5 % of total receipts.
  - o Non-tax revenue - 5,257 crore (2023-24), 2.7 % of total receipts.

Component of State's Tax Revenue From Own Source

Source	In Crore		Percentage Share	
	2023-24	2024-25(BE)	2023-24	2024-25(BE)
SGST	27678	31565	57.2	58.1
Taxes on sales, trade etc	9371	10010	19.4	18.4
Stamp and Registration fee	6348	7500	13.1	13.8
Taxes on Vehicle	3358	3700	6.9	6.8
Land Revenue	580	600	1.2	1.1
Taxes and Duties on Electricity	846	750	1.8	1.4

Components of Gross Fiscal Deficit of Bihar - The GFD of 2023-24 of the state government had decreased by 20.4% as compared to its previous year.

Composition	In Crore		Percentage	
	2023-24	2024-25 (BE)	2023-24	2024-25 (BE)
Revenue Deficit / Surplus	-2833	-1121	-7.9	-3.9
Capital Outlay	36453	29416	102.2	101.1
Net Lending	2040	801	5.7	2.8
GFD	35660	29095		

AGRICULTURE AND ALLIED SECTORS

Agriculture remains the backbone of Bihar's economy employing over 75% of the population and making significant contributions to the state's GDP. With its fertile soil, abundant water resources, and favourable climate, Bihar produces a variety of crops, such as rice, wheat, maize, pulses, sugarcane, jute, and oilseeds. The state is also a leading producer of horticultural products such as mango, makhana, and litchi. To enhance agricultural production and yield, the state government adopted the Fourth Agriculture Road Map (2023-28), which focuses on modern infrastructure and allied activities.

- In 2022-23, the crop sector grew by 6.7 percent, fishing and aquaculture by 11.1 percent, and livestock by 2.7 percent.
- The agriculture, forestry, and fishing sector contributed 20.2 percent to the Gross State Value Added (GSVA).
- The Jaivik Corridor Yojana, aimed at promoting organic farming, has nearly achieved its target for 2023-24.
    - In 13 districts, 20,000 acres of land were distributed to farmers under the second phase of the Jaivik Corridor Yojana and the State government allocated ₹ 3192.62 lakh for the purpose.
- Rice production increased by 21% and wheat production by 10.7%.
- Livestock and fisheries sector grew at the rate of 9.50%.
- The Bihar government has implemented the Agricultural Investment Promotion Policy for seven products: makhana, fruits, vegetables, maize, medicinal plants, honey and tea.
- Industrial investment of ₹75,293.76 crore has been proposed.
- The service (tertiary) sector remains the largest contributor to GSDP with 58.6%, followed by industry (secondary) at 21.5% and agriculture (primary) at 19.9%.
- Investment in micro-enterprises increased by 135%, while employment grew by 107%.
- Investment in large-scale industries increased by 131%, leading to a 187% increase in employment.
- The mining sector recorded a growth of 9%.

Sector	Annual Growth Rate (in %)		Share in GSVA in Bihar (in %)	
	2022-23 (Provisional Estimate)	2023-24 (Quick Estimate)	2022-23 (Provisional Estimate)	2023-24 (Quick Estimate)
Agriculture, forestry and fishing	5.4	5.4	20.2	19.5
Crops	6.7	4.7	10.4	9.9
Livestock	2.7	7.6	6.4	6.3
Forestry and Logging	2.1	3.9	1.5	1.5
Fishing and Aquaculture	11.1	3.2	1.9	1.8

Irrigation

- Groundwater irrigation has been the primary source of irrigation in Bihar.
- In 2022-23, irrigation through accessing groundwater using:
  - o Different types of wells was carried out in 64.1% of the gross irrigated area.
  - o Surface irrigation via canals was available in 30.3% of the gross irrigated area.

Dairy Farming

- **Samagra Gavya Vikas Yojana:** In 2024-25, under the state plan, the State government has approved ₹ 48.48 crore to establish dairy units (of 2, 4, 15, and 20) high-breed milk cattle/ heifers.
  - o A provision of 75 percent subsidy has been made for the dairy farmers belonging to the EBC, SC, and ST, while other dairy farmers receive a 50 percent subsidy.
- **Desi Gaupalan Protsahan Yojana:** In 2024-25, under the Saat Nishchay-2, approval has been granted for establishing dairy units of 2 and 4 indigenous cows/heifers under the Desi Gaupalan Protsahan Yojana.
  - o The estimated cost of implementing the scheme was ₹ 25.46 crore.
  - o 75 percent grant to the beneficiaries of EBC, SC, and ST communities, and a 50 percent grant to all others.
- **In 2024-25, under Saat Nishchay-2, an insurance scheme** for milch cattle was approved, with an estimated cost of ₹ 2.99 crore.
  - o The scheme offers financial security through livestock insurance in the event of death, illness, or other reasons.
- **Formation of Milk Products Cooperation Committee:** Under Saat Nishchay-2, approval has been granted to establish milk cooperative societies in 7,000 villages at a cost of ₹ 56 crore over four years (2021-22 to 2024-25).

New Schemes - By Water Resources Department

- **Eastern Gandak Canal System:** The main eastern canal originates from the Valmikinagar Barrage in the West Champaran district and it is targeted for completion by 2025-26.
- **Ganga Water Supply Scheme:** In phase-I 9.91 million cubic meters of water supplied to Rajgir and Nawada in 2023 from the Gangaji Rajgir reservoir. Phase-II includes the Madhuvan reservoir (27 MCM capacity) and related works, with compilation targeted by August 2025.
- **Nikrish Pump Canal Scheme on Karmnasha River:** It addresses water shortages in Rampur distribution canal of the Chausa branch of Son canal system. The project is expected to be completed by February 2025.

ENTERPRISES SECTOR

- Bihar stands at a pivotal moment in its industrial evolution. Despite its rich history and potential, the state faces unique challenges in terms of industrial growth. However, recent government initiatives have emphasized the role of industrialization in Bihar's economic transformation, with a particular focus on attracting large-scale investments and fostering entrepreneurship.
- The secondary sector, particularly construction and manufacturing, has been a major driver of Bihar's industrial growth, with construction contributing 50.2 percent of the Gross State Domestic Product (GSDP) of the secondary sector in 2022-23.
  - o Growth rate of construction activities between 2021-22 and 2022-23 - 22%
  - o Construction activities contribute - 50.2% of the GSDP of the secondary sector
  - o The manufacturing sector contributes - 37% of the GSDP of the secondary sector.
  - o Numerically the most important industry is non-metallic mineral products (1234 units).
  - o The contribution of Bihar to India's GVA - 0.5% (2022-23)
  - o The ratio of GVA to GVO (gross value output)- 11.2

- o Contribution to GVA for the country - 0.7%
- o Share of GCF of India- 1.7%

- The top three states, in terms of GVA contribution of rural market establishments in India, were Uttar Pradesh (14.1 percent), Bihar (8.8 percent), and Maharashtra (8.8 percent).

Tourism

- Bihar Tourism Policy 2023 aims to integrate the tourism industry with the economic progress of the state.
- Bihar branding and Marketing Policy, 2024 promotes national and international tourism. It informs people about the rich tourism heritage including the Ramayana Circuit, the Buddhist circuit and the Jain circuit.

Number of Domestic and Foreign Tourist (2023) in Lakh	
Domestic	815.86
Foreign	5.47
Total	821.33

- 497.71 crore approved in 2023-24 for tourism development works
  - o Gaya Ji dharamshala - 120.16 crore
  - o Punaura dham (Sitamarhi) - 72.47 crore
  - o Construction of pathway cum shed building for the Vishnupad Temple (Gaya) - 61.97 crore.
- 204.99 crore allocated by state government in 2024-25
  - o Budget hotel on premises of Hotel Janki Vihar (Sitamarhi)-29.87 crore
  - o Main building for the service plaza and notch (Supaul)- 29.54 crore
  - o Office building of the Bihar Tourism Development Corporation (Patna)- 28.87 crore

PHYSICAL INFRASTRUCTURE

- Physical infrastructure brings socio-economic development in the society. The state government has considerably invested in this sector. As an outcome during the last one and half decades, the transport and communication sector has proved to be one of the major growth drivers of Bihar's economy. Bihar has also witnessed improvement in rural infrastructure and development has been recorded in the rural area of the state.
- Growth rate of transport, storage and communication sector - 7.6 % (3rd position)
- As a result of high growth recorded in this sector, the contribution of this sector has gradually increased and reached ₹ 47,313 crore in 2023-24 from ₹ 17,545 crore in 2011-12 at constant (2011-12) prices.
- The contribution of this sector in the overall GSVA has also gone up by 3 percentage points from 7.3 percent in 2011-12 to 10.2 percent in 2023-24.
- The state government has achieved the vision of reaching the state capital "Patna" within 5 hours from any corner of the state.

Road Network

- In terms of road network, Bihar has around 3 lakh kms of road network and is placed on 8th rank among all Indian states as of 2019.
- A total of 26 Bharatmala projects have been sanctioned and proposed for Bihar, involving the construction of 1652 kms of road network at an estimated cost of ₹ 49612 crore.

Expressway in Bihar

1. **Varanasi - Ranchi - Kolkata Expressway**

- Connect 4 states i,e UP, Jharkhand, Bihar, W.Bengal.
- Connect Varanasi to Kolkata through NH-19, GT road.
- Passes through Mohania, Rohtas, Sasaram, Aurangabad, Gaya.
- Passes through the Naxalite area and proposed to be greenfield expressway will result in the economic growth of the backward reason.

2. **Gorakhpur - Siliguri**

- Connect Gorakhpur to Siliguri through NH-27. Connect 3 state - UP, Bihar, W. Bengal.
- Passes through - W. Champaran, E. Champaran, Sheohar, Sitamarhi, Madhubani, Supaul, Araria, Kishanganj.

- Enhance the development of under - developed area of Bihar.

3. **Patna-Purnia Expressway**

- Provide direct connectivity between Patna and Purnia.
- Passes through - Patna, Saran, Vaishali, Samastipur, Begusarai, Darbhanga, Saharsa, Madhepura and Purnia.
- Connect approx. 6 proposed Airports in future.

4. **Raxaul - Haldia Expressway**

- Connect Raxaul at the Nepal international border to Haldia port.
- Passes through 3 states - Bihar, Jharkhand and W. Bengal.
- Passes through - Muzaffarpur, Sheohar, East Champaran, Sitamarhi, Samastipur, Begusarai, Lakhisarai, Jamui, Banka.
- This is entirely Greenfield.

POWER SECTOR

Energy plays a crucial role in driving economic and social development. Bihar achieved 100 % household electrification in 2018. The consumer base has now crossed 2.12 crore, with peak power demand reaching a new record of 8005 MW in 2024. Urban areas in Bihar now receive nearly 24 hours power supply, while rural areas get around 22 hours per day on an average.

- Per capita energy consumption - 363 Kwh (2023-24) (increase 229 kwh in 12 years)
- Aggregate technical and commercial losses - 21.74% (2023-24)
- Grid Substation - 170 (in October 2024)
- Length of transmission line - 20393 km (2024)
- Subsidized rate for agricultural sector - ₹ 0.55/ kWh (92%)

Awards

- North Bihar power distribution company - Global CSR
- Bihar state power (holding) Company limited (BSPHCL) - SKOCH Gold award.
- Bihar's state Load Dispatch Centre - 3rd LDC excellence award 2024.

Demand and Supply

- The state recorded an energy surplus of 4034 MU in 2022-23.
- The peak demand increased by almost 1.4 times during 2017-18 to 2023-24.
- Power supply increased by 1.5 times during 2017-18 to 2023-24.
- Average power availability during 2021-22 in urban areas- 23.1 hours and in rural areas 21-22 hours.

Consumption of Power

- The state has witnessed a steady growth in new electricity connections, which has recorded an increase of 17 percent during the period of 2011-12 to 2023-24.
  - o A total of 38 lakh electricity consumers existed in 2012, which increased by nearly 7 times in the same period.
  - o The domestic sector has the largest consumers of electricity that accounts for 88.5% of the total consumers, followed by commercial consumers (7.5%).
- The number of agriculture consumers has also increased appreciably due to implementation of the Mukhyamantri Krishi Vidyut Sambandh Yojana (MKVSY).

  It increased by 289 percent during the four years, from 2.28 lakh in 2018-19 to 6.61 lakh in 2023-24.
- Domestic consumer - 41% of total power consumption.
- Agricultural consumption - 13%.
- Non- domestic consumers (such as industrial & commercial etc) - 46%

Energy Requirement - 2025-26

- Industrial, commercial etc - 22046 Mega unit
- Total domestic requirement -19055 Mega unit
- Agricultural connection - 8297 Mega unit
- Power requirement in 2024 -25 - 49438 MU which is estimated to increase to 53920 MU in 2025-26.

Unincorporated Sector

ASUSE (Annual Survey of Unincorporated Sector Enterprises) categorises establishment into two -

1. Own Account Establishment (OAE)- Run without any hired workers employed on a regular basis.
2. Hired Worker Establishment (HWE) - Employs at least one hired worker on a regular basis.

3. In Bihar, 99.3 percent of the establishments were proprietary. Of all the proprietor ownerships, only 14.5 percent of the proprietors were female workers

- In incorporated non-agricultural enterprises (2022-23)- 59 lakh
  - o In rural establishments - 43.6 lakh
    - ❖ In OAEs - 68%
    - ❖ In HWEs - 32%
  - o In urban establishments - 16.6 lakh
- Among all female workers, 3.3 percent (9.27 lakh, in absolute numbers) were employed in establishments in Bihar.
  - o In rural Bihar, 81.5 percent of all female workers were employed in establishments.
  - o In rural Bihar, OAEs and HWEs have employed 5.6 lakh and 1.9 lakh female workers, respectively.
  - o Total female employment in urban establishments in Bihar was 1.6 lakh.

Education and Health Sector

1. Over the past 18 years, expenditure on education has increased 10 times, health expenditure 13 times, and on social services 13 times.
2. The child welfare budget was introduced in 2013-14 and increased by 19.4% annually between 2016-23.
3. The dropout rate in government secondary schools has declined by 62.25% in the last five years.

Environment and climate change

1. Initiatives such as Green Budget and Jal-Jeevan-Hariyali Mission have been implemented to tackle climate change.
2. In the last 12 years, the forest area in the state has increased by 687 sq. km.

BIHAR BUDGET 2026-27

The Finance Minister of Bihar, Mr Bijendra Prasad Yadav, presented the Budget for the state for the financial year 2026-27 on February 3, 2026.

Budget Highlights

- The **Gross State Domestic Product** (GSDP) of Bihar for 2026-27 (at current prices) is projected to be ₹ 13.1 lakh crore, amounting to growth of 15% over 2025-26. The Union budget has assumed 10% growth for the country in 2026-27.
- **Expenditure (excluding debt repayment)** for 2026-27 is estimated to be ₹ 3,24,925 crore, a decrease of 19% from the revised estimates of 2025-26 (₹ 4,00,465 crore). In addition, debt of ₹ 22,665 crore will be repaid by the state. In 2025-26, as per revised estimates, expenditure (excluding debt repayment) is estimated to be 36% higher than the budget estimate (₹ 2,94,075 crore).
- **Receipts (excluding borrowings)** for 2026-27 is estimated to be ₹ 2,85,813 crore, an increase of 7% over the revised estimate of 2025-26. In 2025-26, receipts are estimated to be 2% higher than budgeted.
- **Revenue surplus** for 2026-27 is estimated to be 0.1% of GSDP (₹ 1,143 crore), as compared to a revenue deficit of 6.7% of GSDP (₹ 76,315 crore) in 2025-26 as per the revised estimates. In 2025-26, revenue surplus of ₹ 8,831 crore was estimated at the budget stage (0.8% of GSDP).
- **Fiscal deficit** for 2026-27 is targeted at 3% of GSDP (₹ 39,112 crore). In 2025-26, as per revised estimates, fiscal deficit is expected to be 11.8% of GSDP, significantly higher than the budget estimate (3% of GSDP).

Policy Highlights

- **Saat Nishchay-3:** The government will implement Saat Nishchay-3 roadmap between 2025 and 2030. Key targets include doubling per capita income, accelerating industrialisation, increasing farmer income, improving education and medical services, new planned cities, and improving ease of living.
- **Income support to farmers:** The state government will launch Jannayak Karpoori Thakur Kisan Samman Nidhi. This state scheme will provide farmers with ₹ 3,000 per year. This will be in addition to ₹ 6,000 per year given under the central government's PM Kisan Samman Nidhi.

Bihar's Economy

- **GSDP:** In 2024-25, Bihar's GSDP (at constant prices) is estimated to grow by 8.6% over the previous year. In comparison, India's GDP is estimated to grow by 6.5% in 2024-25.
- **Sectors:** In 2024-25, agriculture, manufacturing and services sectors are estimated to contribute 23%, and 54% of Bihar's economy, respectively (at current prices).
- **Per capita GSDP:** In 2024-25, Bihar's per capita GSDP (at current prices) is estimated to be ₹ 76,490, an increase of 13% over the previous year. India's per capita GDP is estimated to be ₹ 2,34,859 in 2024-25, an increase of 9% over the previous year.

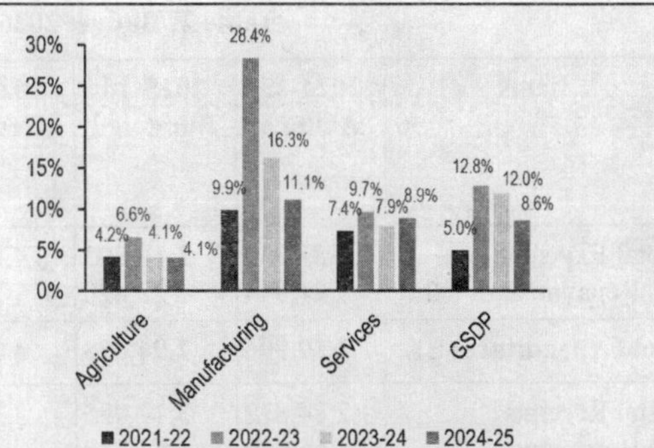

Figure 1: Growth in Bihar's GSDP at constant prices (2011-12)

Note: These numbers are as per constant prices (2011-12) which implies that the growth rate is adjusted for inflation.
Sources: MoSPI; PRS.

- **Industrial hubs:** Phase-2 of the Industrial Manufacturing Cluster (IMC) will be developed in Gaya, as part of the Amritsar-Kolkata Industrial Corridor project. A defence corridor, a pharmaceutical park, and a fintech city will also be developed.
- **Transport:** Five new expressways will be built. Public buses will be converted to CNG and electric buses. More than 2,000 public charging stations will be established.

BUDGET ESTIMATES FOR 2026-27

- **Total expenditure (excluding debt repayment)** for 2026-27 is targeted at ₹ 3,24,925 crore. This is an annualised increase of 12% over 2024-25. This expenditure is proposed to be met through **receipts (excluding borrowings)** of ₹ 2,85,813 crore and net borrowings of ₹ 39,275 crore. Total receipts for 2026-27 (other than borrowings) are estimated to register an annualised increase of 14% over 2024-25.
- The state estimates a **revenue surplus** of 0.1% of GSDP (₹ 1,143 crore) in 2026-27. In comparison, as per the actuals, the state observed a revenue deficit of 0.04% of GSDP in 2024-25.
- **Fiscal deficit** for 2026-27 is targeted at 3% of GSDP (₹ 39,112 crore). This is lower than the actuals for 2024-25 (4.2% of GSDP). The revised estimate for 2025-26 (11.8% of GSDP) is significantly higher than the permitted fiscal deficit limit (3.5% of GSDP, excluding central capex loans).

Variations between Revised Estimates and Actuals

Revised estimate for expenditure has been significantly higher than budgeted amount for last few years. However, actual figures that are released later are significantly lower than the revised estimates (Table 1). We have therefore used annualised increase over two years for our analysis in this document.

Table 1: Total expenditure (excluding debt repayment) — estimates and actuals (₹ Crore)

Year	Budget Estimate	Revised Estimate	Actual
2022-23	2,23,021	2,70,849	2,17,553
2023-24	2,38,327	2,91,392	2,29,103
2024-25	2,56,333	3,27,425	2,59,996
2025-26	2,94,075	4,00,465	-

Source: Bihar Budget Documents of various years; PRS.

Table 2: Budget 2026-27 - Key figures (in ₹ Crore)

Items	2024-25 Actuals	2025-26 Budgeted	2025-26 Revised	% change (25-26 BE to 25-26 RE)	2026-27 Budgeted	% change (25-26 RE to 26-27 BE)	Annualised change from 24-25 to 26-27
Total Expenditure	2,81,939	3,16,895	4,23,284	34%	3,47,590	-18%	11%
(-) Repayment of debt	21,944	22,820	22,820	0%	22,665	-1%	2%
Net Expenditure (E)	**2,59,996**	**2,94,075**	**4,00,465**	**36%**	**3,24,925**	**-19%**	**12%**
Total Receipts	2,84,822	3,17,095	3,29,831	4%	3,47,753	5%	10%
(-) Borrowings	66,049	55,738	63,738	14%	61,939	-3%	-3%
*of which central capex loans**	14,791	0	8,000	-	0	-100%	-100%
Net Receipts (R)	**2,18,773**	**2,61,357**	**2,66,093**	**2%**	**2,85,813**	**7%**	**14%**
Fiscal Deficit (E-R)	**41,222**	**32,718**	**1,34,371**	**311%**	**39,112**	**-71%**	**-3%**
as % of GSDP	4.2%	3.0%	11.8%	-	3.0%	-	-
Revenue Balance**	**-357**	**8,831**	**-76,315**	**-964%**	**1,143**	**-18%**	-
as % of GSDP	-0.04%	0.8%	-6.7%	-	0.1%	-	-
Primary Deficit	**21,544**	**9,704**	**1,11,357**	**1047%**	**13,748**	**-88%**	**-20%**
as % of GSDP	2.2%	0.9%	9.8%	-	1.1%	-	-
GSDP	9,91,997	10,97,264	11,39,595	4%	13,09,155	15%	15%

Note: BE is Budget Estimates; RE is Revised Estimates. *Central government has been providing 50-year interest-free loans to state governments for capital expenditure since 2020-21. These loans are excluded from the calculation of the state's borrowing ceiling.

** (+) indicates a surplus and (-) indicates a deficit.

Sources: Budget at a Glance, Annual Financial Statement, Bihar Budget Documents 2026-27; PRS.

EXPENDITURE IN 2026-27

- **Revenue Expenditure** for 2026-27 is proposed to be ₹ 2,84,134 crore, an annualised increase of 14% over 2024-25. This includes the expenditure on salaries, pension, interest, grants, and subsidies.
- In 2025-26, revised estimate for revenue expenditure is 36% higher than the budget estimate. This is driven by increased allocation for heads such as power subsidy, social security pensions, and cash transfer to women under the Mukhyamantri Mahila Rojgar Yojana.
- **Capital outlay** for 2026-27 is proposed to be ₹ 39,377 crore, roughly same as the actuals for 2024-25 (₹ 38,527 crore). Capital outlay indicates the expenditure towards creation of assets. In 2025-26, capital outlay is estimated to be 37% higher than the initial budget estimate (₹ 15,179 crore higher). Sectors with a higher estimate include transport (₹ 2,901 crore higher) and rural development (₹ 2,450 crore higher).

Mukhyamantri Mahila Rojgar Yojana

The Mukhyamantri Mahila Rojgar Yojana was launched in September 2025. The Scheme aims to provide self-employment and livelihood opportunities to women. Under the scheme, financial support is being provided to one woman from each family. An initial grant of ₹ 10,000 has been provided to 1.56 crore women. Financial support of up to two lakh rupees may be provided upon starting an enterprise.

Table 3: Expenditure Budget 2026-27 (in ₹ crore)

Items	2024-25 Actuals	2025-26 Budgeted	2025-26 Revised	% change (25-26 BE to 25-26 RE)	2026-27 Budgeted	% change (25-26 RE to 26-27 BE)	Annualised change from 24-25 to 26-27
Revenue Expenditure	2,19,015	2,52,000	3,41,883	36%	2,84,134	-17%	14%
Capital Outlay	38,527	40,532	55,711	37%	39,377	-29%	1%
Loans given by the state	2,453	1,543	2,870	86%	1,414	-51%	-24%
Net Expenditure	**2,59,996**	**2,94,075**	**4,00,465**	**36%**	**3,24,925**	**-19%**	**12%**

Sources: Annual Financial Statement, Bihar Budget Documents 2026-27; PRS.

Committed Expenditure: Committed expenditure of a state typically includes expenditure on payment of salaries, pension, and interest. A larger proportion of the budget allocated for committed expenditure items limits the state's flexibility to decide on other expenditure priorities, such as capital outlay. In 2026-27, Bihar is estimated to spend ₹ 1,33,494 crore on committed expenditure items, which is 47% of its estimated revenue receipts. This comprises spending on salaries (26% of revenue receipts), pension (12%), and interest payments (9%). In 2024-25, committed expenditure constituted 39% of revenue receipts. Expenditure on salaries in 2026-27 is estimated to increase at an annualised rate of 38% over 2024-25. Expenditure on salaries by the Education Department is estimated to increase from ₹ 14,561 crore in 2024-25 to ₹ 36,658 crore in 2026-27.

Table 4: Committed Expenditure in 2026-27 (in ₹ crore)

Items	2024-25 Actuals	2025-26 Budgeted	2025-26 Revised	% change (25-26 BE to 25-26 RE)	2026-27 Budgeted	% change (25-26 RE to 26-27 BE)	Annualised change from 24-25 to 26-27
Salaries	38,466	51,690	66,784	29%	72,960	9%	38%
Pension	26,140	33,389	33,391	0%	35,170	5%	16%
Interest payment	19,678	23,014	23,014	0%	25,364	10%	14%
Total	**84,283**	**1,08,094**	**1,23,188**	**14%**	**1,33,494**	**8%**	**26%**

Sources: Budget at a Glance, Annual Financial Statement, Bihar Budget Documents 2026-27; PRS.

- **Sector-wise expenditure:** The sectors listed below account for 69% of the total expenditure on sectors by the state in 2026-27. A comparison of Bihar's expenditure on key sectors with other states is shown in Annexure 1.

Table 5: Sector-wise Expenditure under Bihar Budget 2026-27 (in ₹ crore)

Sector	2024-25 Actuals	2025-26 BE	2025-26 RE	2026-27 BE	% change (25-26 RE to 26-27 BE)	Annualised change from 24-25 to 26-27	Budget Provisions 2026-27 BE
Education, Sports, Arts, and Culture	57,139	63,335	91,254	70,141	-23%	11%	• ₹ 12,107 crore has been allocated towards Samagra Shiksha Abhiyan.
Rural Development	23,151	30,150	35,521	30,387	-14%	15%	• MGNREGS has been allocated ₹ 3,192 crore, and Viksit Bharat-Guarantee for Rozgar and Ajeevika Mission (Grameen) VB-G-RAM-G ₹ 1,890 crore.

Social Welfare and Nutrition	15,862	15,012	51,374	24,710	-52%	25%	• ₹ 9,052 crore has been allocated towards 'Mahila Sashaktikaran' (Rs 21,050 crore in 2025-26 as per revised estimates).
Health and Family Welfare	15,013	19,184	21,150	20,230	-4%	16%	• ₹ 1,495 crore has been allocated towards the PM-ABHIM scheme.
Energy	20,262	13,401	23,535	18,649	-21%	-4%	• ₹ 15,702 crore has been allocated towards subsidy for affordable power.
Police	11,824	14,653	15,495	16,840	9%	19%	• ₹ 9,455 crore has been allocated towards the district police.
Urban Development	8,514	10,928	14,742	14,050	-5%	29%	• ₹ 2,842 crore has been allocated towards the PM Awas Yojana-Urban.
Transport	13,035	9,297	13,181	10,178	-23%	-12%	• ₹ 5,034 crore has been allocated for capital outlay on road and bridges.
Agriculture and Allied Activities	6,251	8,039	10,315	8,463	-18%	16%	• Sub-mission on Agricultural Mechanisation has been allocated ₹ 176 crore.
Irrigation and Flood Control	6,594	9,238	11,284	8,422	-25%	13%	• ₹ 5,814 crore has been allocated towards capital outlay on irrigation and flood control.
% of total expenditure on all sectors	69%	66%	72%	69%			

Sources: Annual Financial Statement, Bihar Budget Documents 2026-27; PRS.

RECEIPTS IN 2026-27

- **Total revenue receipts** for 2026-27 is estimated to be ₹ 2,85,277 crore, an annualised increase of 14% over 2024-25. Of this, ₹ 75,203 crore (26%) will be raised by the state through its **own resources**, and ₹ 2,10,074 crore (74%) will come **from the Central Government.** Resources from the Centre will be in the form of state's share in Central taxes (55% of revenue receipts) and grants (18% of revenue receipts).
- **Devolution:** In 2026-27, the state's share in Central taxes is estimated at ₹ 1,58,178 crore, an annualised increase of 11% over 2024-25.
- **Grants from the Centre** in 2026-27 are estimated at ₹ 51,896 crore, an annualised increase of 32% over 2024-25. This is mainly driven by an increase anticipated in grants for centrally sponsored schemes (CSS). Grants for CSS are estimated to be ₹ 44,003 crore in 2026-27. In 2024-25, as per actuals, grants for CSS were ₹ 21,217 crore, 53% lower than the budget estimate for that year (₹ 45,370 crore).
- **State's own tax revenue:** Bihar's total own tax revenue is estimated to be ₹ 65,800 crore in 2026-27, an annualised increase of 11% over 2024-25. Own tax revenue as a percentage of GSDP is estimated at 5% in 2026-27, lower than the revised estimates for 2025-26 (5.2%) and actuals for 2024-25 (5.4%).

Table 6: Break-up of the state government's receipts (in ₹ crore)

Items	2024-25 Actuals	2025-26 Budgeted	2025-26 Revised	% change (25-26 BE to 25-26 RE)	2026-27 Budgeted	% change (25-26 RE to 26-27 BE)	Annualised change from 24-25 to 26-27
State's Own Tax	53,578	59,520	59,520	0%	65,800	11%	11%
State's Own Non-Tax	5,781	8,221	8,221	0%	9,403	14%	28%
Share in Central Taxes	1,29,435	1,38,516	1,43,069	3%	1,58,178	11%	11%
Grants-in-aid from Centre	29,863	54,575	54,758	0.3%	51,896	-5%	32%
Revenue Receipts	2,18,658	2,60,831	2,65,568	2%	2,85,277	7%	14%
Non-debt Capital Receipts	115	525	525	0%	536	2%	116%
Net Receipts	2,18,773	2,61,357	2,66,093	1.8%	2,85,813	7%	14%

Note: BE is Budget Estimates; RE is Revised Estimates.
Sources: Annual Financial Statement, Bihar Budget Documents 2026-27; PRS.

- In 2026-27, **State GST** is estimated to be the largest source of own tax revenue (58% share). State GST revenue is estimated to register an annualised increase of 14% over 2024-25.
- Revenue from Sales tax/VAT in 2026-27 is estimated to grow at an annualised rate of 1% over 2024-25.
- Revenue from taxes and duties on electricity in 2026-27 is estimated to be ₹ 950 crore, lower than 2024-25 (₹ 1,570 crore).
- In 2025-26, revised estimates for own tax revenue sources are same as the budget estimates. This implies that the government expects to meet its budget targets. In 2024-25, actual SGST revenue was 8% lower than the budget estimate (See Table 12).

Low revenue raised by local bodies

The rural and urban local bodies may be empowered to collect their own sources of revenue (OSR). However, the 16th Finance Commission noted these local bodies depend heavily on grants given by the central and state governments. In Bihar, OSR of rural local bodies was 0.03% of agricultural GDP, significantly lower than states such as Kerala (2.38%) and Maharashtra (1.21%). Similarly, OSR of urban local bodies of Bihar was 0.09% of non-agricultural GDP. This was also significantly lower than states such as Maharashtra (1.4%) and Gujarat (0.84%). The Commission noted that local bodies fail to tap into their own revenue streams due to lack of clear administrative provisions, capacity constraints, and weak enforcement mechanisms.

Source: Report of the 16th Finance Commission Volume-I; PRS.

Table 7: Major Sources of State's Own-Tax Revenue (in ₹ Crore)

Head	2024-25 Actuals	2025-26 Budgeted	2025-26 Revised	% change (25-26 BE to 25-26 RE)	2026-27 Budgeted	% change (25-26 RE to 26-27 BE)	Annualised change from 24-25 to 26-27
State GST	29,003	34,009	34,009	0%	38,000	12%	14%
Sales Tax/ VAT	10,554	11,200	11,200	0%	10,775	-4%	1%
Stamps Duty and Registration Fees	7,976	8,250	8,250	0%	10,000	21%	12%
Taxes on Vehicles	3,678	4,070	4,070	0%	5,000	23%	17%
Taxes and Duties on Electricity	1,570	1,016	1,016	0%	950	-6%	-22%
Land Revenue	571	700	700	0%	800	14%	18%

Sources: Annual Financial Statement, Bihar Budget Documents 2026-27; PRS.

DEFICITS, DEBT, AND FRBM TARGETS FOR 2026-27

The Bihar Fiscal Responsibility and Budget Management Act, 2006 provides annual targets to progressively reduce the outstanding debt, revenue deficit and fiscal deficit of the state government.

Revenue balance: It is the difference of revenue receipts and revenue expenditure. A revenue deficit implies that the government needs to borrow to finance those expenses which do not increase its assets or reduces its liabilities. The budget estimates a revenue surplus of ₹ 1,143 crore (or 0.1% of the GSDP) in 2026-27. Bihar recorded a revenue deficit in 2024-25 (0.04% of GSDP).

Fiscal deficit: It is the excess of total expenditure over total receipts. This gap is filled by borrowings by the government and leads to an increase in total liabilities. In 2026-27, fiscal deficit is estimated at 3% of GSDP. The 16th Finance Commission has recommended the annual fiscal deficit limit for states to be 3% of GSDP for the 2026-31 period. 50-year interest free loans for capital expenditure given by the central government will be excluded to arrive at the borrowing ceiling. In 2024-25, fiscal deficit was 4.2% of GSDP. Excluding central capex loans, fiscal deficit in 2024-25 was 2.7% of GSDP.

> **Regional disparities in economic development**
>
> Bihar's per capita GDP was ₹ 68,624 in 2023-24, the lowest in the country among all states. Per capita GDP at all-India level was ₹ 2,15,935. Per capita GDP also varies widely across districts. In 2023-24, Patna recorded the highest per capita GDP (₹ 2,41,220), followed by Begusarai (₹ 1,05,600). Per capita GDP in all other districts was below one lakh rupees in 2023-24. In 11 districts, per capita GDP in 2023-24 was lower than ₹ 50,000. Sheohar and Araria recorded the lowest per capita GDP, ₹ 38,214 and ₹ 44,134, respectively.
>
> **Source:** Advance estimates of GDP for 2025-26, National Accounts, MoSPI; Bihar Economic Survey 2025-26; PRS.

Outstanding liabilities: Outstanding liabilities is the accumulation of total borrowings at the end of a financial year. It also includes any liabilities on public accounts such as provident funds. At the end of 2026-27, the outstanding debt is estimated to be 34% of GSDP. The 16th Finance Commission noted

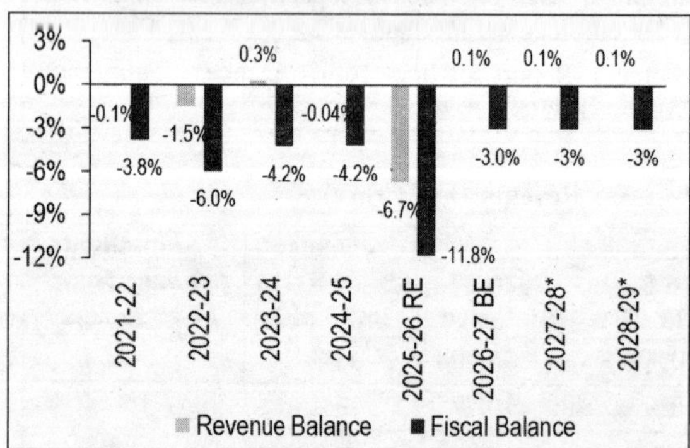

Figure 2: Revenue and Fiscal Balance (% of GSDP)

Note: *Figures from 2027-28 onwards are projections. RE is Revised Estimates; BE is budget estimates. (+) indicates a surplus and (–) indicates a deficit.

Sources: Budget at a Glance, Medium Term Fiscal Policy, Bihar Budget Documents 2026-27; PRS.

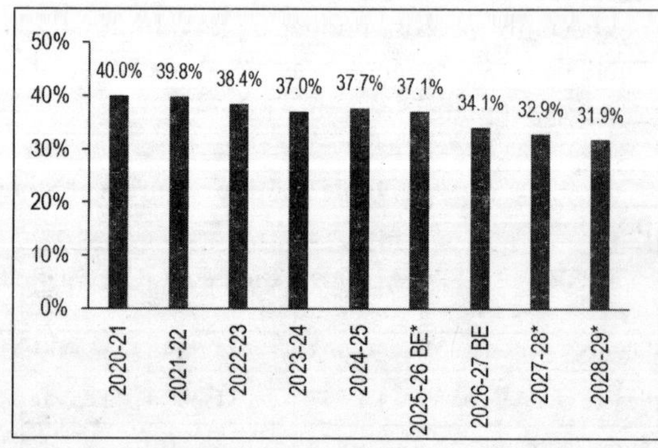

Figure 3: Outstanding Liabilities (as % of GSDP)

Note: *Figures from 2027-28 onwards are projections. BE is budget estimates. RE figure for 2025-26 is not available hence BE.

Sources: Budget at a Glance, Medium Term Fiscal Policy, Bihar Budget Documents 2026-27; PRS.

that Bihar has relatively higher debt to GDP ratio among larger states. It also observed that, given the state's dependence on central transfers and its limited capacity to mobilise own revenue sources, Bihar's debt level is a matter of concern.

Outstanding Government Guarantees: Outstanding liabilities do not include a few other liabilities that are contingent in nature, which states may have to honour in certain cases. State governments guarantee the borrowings of State Public Sector Enterprises (SPSEs) from financial institutions. As of March 2026, the state's outstanding guarantee is estimated to be ₹ 32,008 crore, which is about 2.4% of Bihar's GSDP.

Delay in submission of utilisation certificates

CAG (2025) noted that as of March 2024, 49,649 utilisation certificates (UCs) were yet to be received, amounting to ₹ 70,878 crore. Utilisation certificates are required to be submitted to the Accountant General (Accounts & Entitlements) within a stipulated period. CAG observed that in the absence of these certificates, there is no assurance that funds disbursed have been used for the intended purposes. It further observed that high pendency of certificates increases the risk of misappropriation and diversion of funds.

Source: Report No. 1 of 2025, State Finances Audit Report for the year 2023-24, CAG; PRS.

Annexure 1: Comparison of states' expenditure on key sectors

The graphs below compare Bihar's expenditure in 2026-27 on six key sectors as a proportion of its total expenditure on all sectors. The average for a sector indicates the average expenditure in that sector by 31 states and UTs (including Bihar) as per their budget estimates of 2025-26.[1]

- **Education:** Bihar has allocated 21.7% of its expenditure on education in 2026-27. This is significantly higher than the average allocation for education by states in 2025-26 (14.5%).
- **Health:** Bihar has allocated 6.3% of its expenditure on health in 2026-27. This is marginally higher than the average allocation for health by states in 2025-26 (6.2%).
- **Rural development:** Bihar has allocated 9.4% of its expenditure on rural development in 2026-27. This is significantly higher than the average allocation for rural development by states in 2025-26 (4.9%).
- **Roads and bridges:** Bihar has allocated 2.9% of its expenditure on roads and bridges in 2026-27. This is lower than the average allocation for roads and bridges by states in 2025-26 (4.3%).

[1] The 31 states include the Union Territories of Delhi, Jammu and Kashmir, and Puducherry.

Spending on Education as a % of Total Expenditure

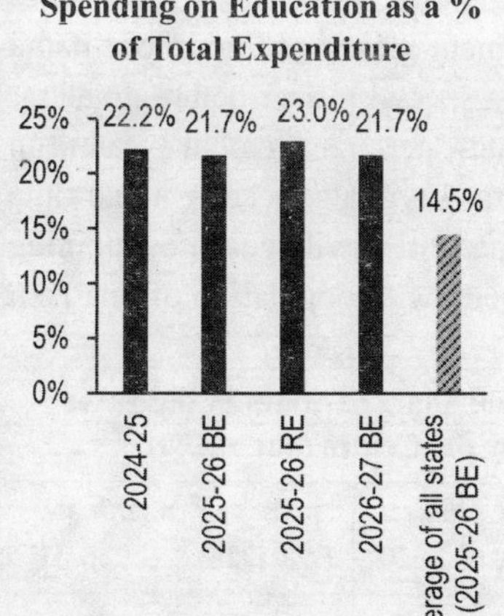

Spending on Health as a % of Total Expenditure

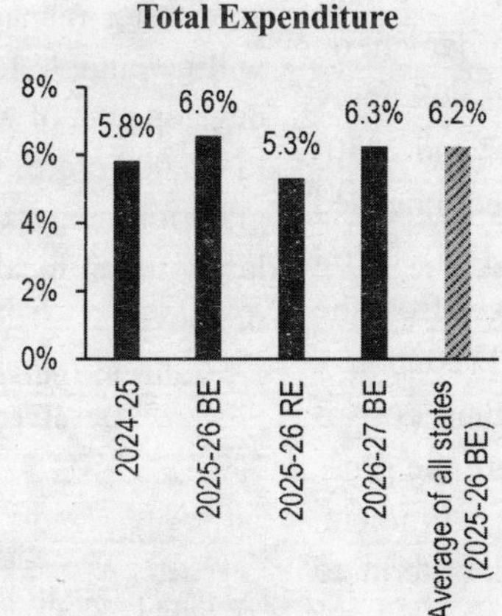

Spending on Rural Development as a % of Total Expenditure

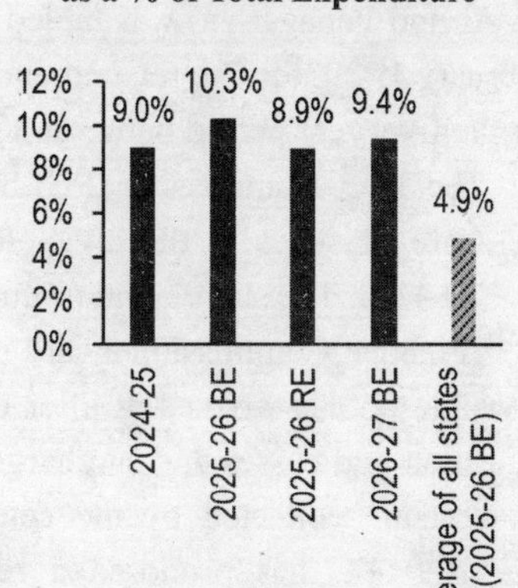

Note: 2024-25, 2025-26 (BE), 2025-26 (RE), and 2026-27 (BE) figures are for Bihar.

Sources: Annual Financial Statement, Bihar Budget Documents 2026-27; various state budgets; PRS.

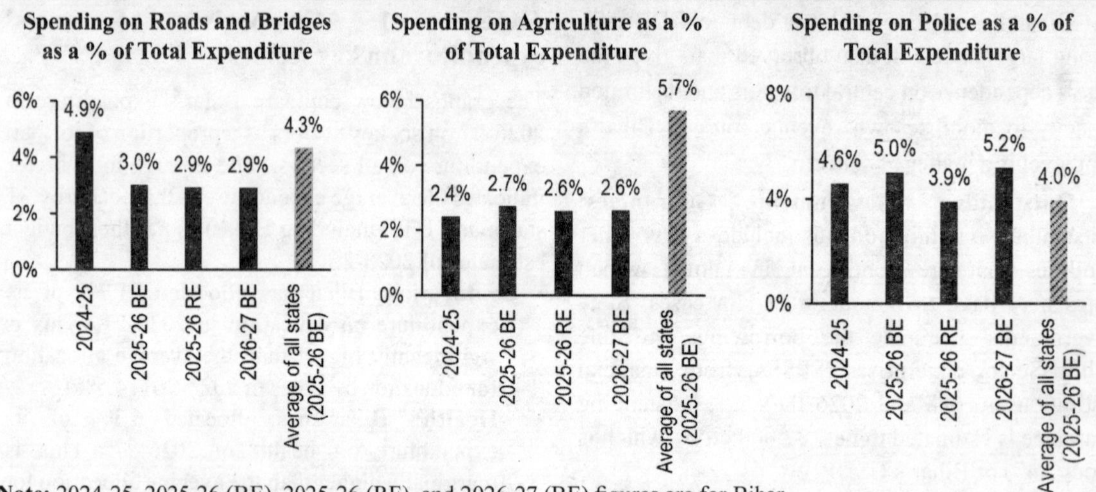

Note: 2024-25, 2025-26 (BE), 2025-26 (RE), and 2026-27 (BE) figures are for Bihar.

Sources: Annual Financial Statement, Bihar Budget Documents 2026-27; various state budgets; PRS.

- **Agriculture:** Bihar has allocated 2.6% of its expenditure on agriculture in 2026-27. This is significantly lower than the average allocation for agriculture by states in 2025-26 (5.7%).
- **Police:** Bihar has allocated 5.2% of its expenditure on police in 2026-27. This is higher than the average allocation for police by states in 2025-26 (4.0%).

Annexure 2: Recommendations of the 16th Finance Commission for 2026-31

The Report of the 16th Finance Commission (Chair: Dr. Arvind Panagariya) was tabled in Parliament on February 1, 2026. The recommendations will apply for the five-year period between 2026-27 and 2030-31. The 16th Commission (FC) has recommended the share of states in the divisible pool of central taxes at 41%. The share remains unchanged from the 15th Finance Commission award period (2020-26). Divisible pool is arrived at after excluding cost of collection and cesses and surcharges from the gross tax revenue collected by the central government. The 16th FC has proposed a revised criteria to determine the share of individual states. See here for a PRS summary of the 16th Finance Commission Report. Based on the recommendations of the 16th FC, Bihar will have a 9.95% share in the divisible pool of central taxes for the 2026-31 period.

The 16th FC has recommended grants worth ₹ 9.47 lakh crore over the five-year period. These comprise grants for: (i) urban and rural local bodies, and (ii) disaster management. It has discontinued the following grants recommended by the 15th FC: (i) revenue deficit grants, (ii) sector-specific grants, and (iii) state-specific grants. Grants recommended for Bihar over the 2026-31 period include: (i) ₹ 9,169 crore for urban local bodies, (ii) ₹ 51,923 crore for rural local bodies, and (iii) ₹ 13,615 crore as disaster management grants. In addition, Patna will be eligible for a special infrastructure grant for development of wastewater management system (up to ₹ 5,000 crore). States will also receive a one-time grant for merger of peri-urban villages into adjoining larger urban local body with population of one lakh or above.

Table 8: Individual Share of States in the Taxes Devolved by the Centre (out of 100)

State	14th FC (2015-2020)	15th FC (2021-26)	16th FC (2026-31)
Andhra Pradesh	4.31	4.05	4.22
Arunachal Pradesh	1.37	1.76	1.35

Assam	3.31	3.13	3.26
Bihar	9.67	10.06	9.95
Chhattisgarh	3.08	3.41	3.30
Goa	0.38	0.39	0.37
Gujarat	3.08	3.48	3.76
Haryana	1.08	1.09	1.36
Himachal Pradesh	0.71	0.83	0.91
Jammu and Kashmir	1.85	-	-
Jharkhand	3.14	3.31	3.36
Karnataka	4.71	3.65	4.13
Kerala	2.50	1.93	2.38
Madhya Pradesh	7.55	7.85	7.35
Maharashtra	5.52	6.32	6.44
Manipur	0.62	0.72	0.63
Meghalaya	0.64	0.77	0.63
Mizoram	0.46	0.50	0.56
Nagaland	0.50	0.57	0.48
Odisha	4.64	4.53	4.42
Punjab	1.58	1.81	2.00
Rajasthan	5.50	6.03	5.93
Sikkim	0.37	0.39	0.34
Tamil Nadu	4.02	4.08	4.10
Telangana	2.44	2.10	2.17
Tripura	0.64	0.71	0.64
Uttar Pradesh	17.96	17.94	17.62
Uttarakhand	1.05	1.12	1.14
West Bengal	7.32	7.52	7.22

Sources: Reports of the 14th, 15th, and 16th Finance Commission; PRS.

Table 9: State-wise Details of Grants-in-Aid for 2026-31 (in ₹ Crore)

State	Rural Local Bodies	Urban Local Bodies	Disaster Management
Andhra Pradesh	16,627	12,158	6,125
Arunachal Pradesh	1,698	233	616
Assam	14,580	3,249	5,243
Bihar	51,923	9,169	13,615
Chhattisgarh	11,664	4,990	2,481
Goa	174	726	112
Gujarat	18,802	23,764	8,459
Haryana	8,270	7,834	2,922
Himachal Pradesh	3,744	435	2,682
Jharkhand	14,231	6,093	2,806
Karnataka	18,889	18,483	6,419
Kerala	3,308	16,683	1,935
Madhya Pradesh	32,033	16,016	11,697
Maharashtra	32,817	46,803	29,619
Manipur	1,262	609	259
Meghalaya	1,479	377	437
Mizoram	567	377	284
Nagaland	697	667	408
Odisha	18,715	5,078	8,900
Punjab	8,486	7,834	2,477
Rajasthan	31,467	12,680	9,211
Sikkim	218	203	455
Tamil Nadu	16,930	25,069	8,486
Telangana	9,968	11,548	2,774
Tripura	1,176	1,016	356

Uttar Pradesh	83,261	33,543	15,321
Uttarakhand	4,047	2,497	4,954
West Bengal	28,203	22,023	6,869

Table 10: Taxes Devolved to States as Per Union Budget 2026-27 (in ₹ Crore)

State	2024-25 Actuals	2025-26 Revised	2026-27 Budget
Andhra Pradesh	51,564	56,374	64,362
Arunachal Pradesh	22,386	24,475	20,665
Assam	39,855	43,572	49,725
Bihar	1,28,151	1,40,105	1,51,832
Chhattisgarh	43,409	47,459	50,427
Goa	4,918	5,377	5,571
Gujarat	44,314	48,448	57,311
Haryana	13,926	15,225	20,772
Himachal Pradesh	10,575	11,562	13,950
Jharkhand	42,135	46,066	51,236
Karnataka	46,467	50,802	63,050
Kerala	24,527	26,815	36,355
Madhya Pradesh	1,00,019	1,09,348	1,12,134
Maharashtra	80,486	87,994	98,306
Manipur	9,123	9,974	9,554
Meghalaya	9,773	10,684	9,631
Mizoram	6,371	6,965	8,608
Nagaland	7,250	7,926	7,341
Odisha	57,692	63,074	67,460
Punjab	23,023	25,171	30,464
Rajasthan	76,779	83,940	90,446
Sikkim	4,944	5,405	5,113
Tamil Nadu	51,971	56,819	62,531
Telangana	26,782	29,280	33,181
Tripura	9,021	9,862	9,783
Uttar Pradesh	2,28,565	2,49,885	2,68,911
Uttarakhand	14,245	15,573	17,415
West Bengal	95,852	1,04,793	1,10,119
Total	12,74,121	13,92,971	15,26,255

Note: Actuals for 2024-25 and Revised Estimates for 2025-26 have been reported in the Union Budget after adjusting for excess or less devolution in previous years.
Sources: Union Budget Documents 2026-27; PRS.

Annexure 3: Comparison of 2024-25 Budget Estimates and Actuals

The following tables compare the actuals of 2024-25 with budget estimates for that year.

Table 11: Overview of Receipts and Expenditure (in ₹ Crore)

Particular	2024-25 BE	2024-25 Actuals	% Change from BE to Actuals
Net Receipts (1+2)	2,27,238	2,18,773	-4%
1. Revenue Receipts (a+b+c+d)	2,26,799	2,18,658	-4%
a. Own Tax Revenue	54,300.00	53,578	-1%
b. Own Non-Tax Revenue	7,326	5,781	-21%
c. Share in central taxes	1,13,012.00	1,29,435	15%

d. Grants-in-aid from the Centre	52,161	29,863	-43%
2. Non-Debt Capital Receipts	439.00	115	-74%
3. Borrowings	51,688	66,049	28%
Of which central capex loans	0	14,791	-
Net Expenditure (4+5+6)	2,56,333	2,59,996	1%
4. Revenue Expenditure	2,25,677	2,19,015	-3%
5. Capital Outlay	29,416	38,527	31%
6. Loans and Advances	1,240	2,453	98%
7. Debt Repayment	22,393	21,944	-2%
Revenue Balance*	1,121	-357	-68%
Revenue Balance (as % of GSDP)	0.10%	-0.04%	-
Fiscal Deficit	29,095	41,222	42%
Fiscal Deficit (as % of GSDP)	2.98%	4.20%	-

* (+) indicates a surplus and (-) indicates a deficit.
Source: Bihar Budget Documents of various years; PRS.

Table 12: Key Components of State's Own Tax Revenue (in ₹ Crore)

Head	2024-25 BE	2024-25 Actuals	% change from BE to Actuals
State GST	31,565	29,003	-8%
Land Revenue	600	571	-5%
Taxes on Vehicles	3,700	3,678	-1%
Sales Tax/ VAT	10,010	10,554	5%
Stamps Duty and Registration Fees	7,500	7,976	6%
Taxes and Duties on Electricity	750	1,570	109%

Source: Bihar Budget Documents of various years; PRS.

Table 13: Allocation Towards Key Sectors

Sector	2024-25 BE	2024-25 Actuals	% change from BE to Actuals
Agriculture and Allied Activities	7,943	6,251	-21%
Water Supply and Sanitation	3,836	3,019	-21%

Urban Development	10,370	8,514	-18%
Rural Development	27,101	23,151	-15%
Police	13,528	11,824	-13%
Welfare of SC, ST, OBC, and Minorities	3,667	3,399	-7%
Housing	5,317	5,096	-4%
Health and Family Welfare	14,488	15,013	4%
Education, Sports, Arts, and Culture	54,605	57,139	5%
Social Welfare and Nutrition	14,718	15,862	8%
Irrigation and Flood Control	5,388	6,594	22%
Transport	8,151	13,035	60%
of which Roads and Bridges	7,723	12,583	63%
Energy	11,334	20,262	79%

Source: Bihar Budget Documents of various years; PRS.

❑❑❑

Partition of Bihar

- Effects of Partition
- Demand of Special Status for the State
- A Game-Changer for Bihar's Economic Transformation in Union Budget 2026

EFFECTS OF PARTITION

Present political shape of Bihar passed through many phases, before it came into existence in its new form on 15 November, 2000. On 1 April, 1912, two new provinces by the name of Bihar and Odisha came into existence, carved out from the Bengal presidency. On 1 April, Odisha was separated from Bihar. Bihar was put in 'A' category of states after independence. States Reorganisation Committee was set up under the chairmanship of Fazal Ali in year 1953, and this committee submitted its report in 1956. In this report, recommendations were made for reorganisation of borders of Bihar. Manbhum, Purulia, some parts of Purnea and Kishanganj were included in the boundary of West Bengal. On 15 November, 2000, Bihar was divided once again and a new state, Jharkhand was formed.

The movement to separate Jharkhand was going on since a long time. Although the central government formed a Committee on Jharkhand Affairs to consider creating a new state by separating the tribal regions from 4 states – Orissa, Bihar, Bengal and Madhya Pradesh, the committee rejected the proposal stating that such a step could promote regionalism and separatism in the country and thus, the demand for a separate Jharkhand was rejected. Therefore, considering the tribal population finally, Jharkhand Autonomous Council was formed in 1995. Finally on 15 November, 2000, Jharkhand was separated from Bihar.

In order to understand the effect of partition on Bihar, it is necessary to ponder upon the situation prior to partition. Area of undivided Bihar was 1,73,476 sq. km. After the partition, the new area of Bihar was reduced to 74,163 sq. km, which was almost 54 per cent of the total area, while 75 per cent population (approx 8.2 crores) of undivided Bihar was left with Bihar. Jharkhand was formed from 18 of the 56 districts of undivided Bihar. About 324 seats of legislative assembly of undivided Bihar were reduced to 243 while 81 seats went to Jharkhand. About 40 out of 54 Lok Sabha constituencies and 75 out of 96 seats of legislative council remained with Bihar. Since there was no arrangement for legislative assembly in Jharkhand, therefore, till the tenure of remaining members was not complete, their responsibility also rested upon Bihar.

Partition had the maximum impact on the economic sector. Major industrial centres, Jamshedpur, Bokaro, Dhanbad, etc. became parts of Jharkhand. Bihar was one of the richest states of the country in terms of mineral resources, but after the partition, major mining regions like Dhanbad, Hazaribagh, Palamu, East Singhbhum, West Singhbhum, etc. went to Jharkhand. Out of all the forest land, 23,605 sq. km area also went to

Jharkhand. Thus, all the primary resources, minerals and forests as well as industrial centres went to Jharkhand, and Bihar was reduced primarily to an agro-economic state.

Only one major industrial centre, Barauni, where oil refinery, thermal power plant and chemical fertiliser plants are established, remained in Bihar. As far as industries are concerned, the sugar industry is either sick or completely closed and cement and paper industries those in Dalmia Nagar are reduced to closed factories. In the field of energy, Bihar got very low share in power generation sector in proportion to the population of the state. Almost 64 per cent the power generation capacity of undivided Bihar has gone to Jharkhand, while Bihar was left with only remaining 36 per cent. Thermal power plants at Barauni and Kanti, that were already sick at the time of partition, remained in Bihar. After the partion, only 21 per cent of total forest area and 6 per cent of total mineral reserves at the time of partition, was left with Bihar. Rate of urbanisation, that was 13.14 per cent prior to partition was reduced to 10.76 per cent after the division. Most of the land and region of Bihar that remained after the partition, is always under the threat of floods or droughts due to which a large part of the earnings of the state is spent in relief works in flood affected area.

Partition of state has also left its impact on distribution of assets and revenue. This has caused a situation of economic crisis in the state. Jharkhand used to contribute around 37.76 per cent of the total revenue in undivided Bihar. Jharkhand's share in total central tax collection for undivided Bihar was around 48.36 per cent. Thus, the lack of resources in Bihar is very evident. Jharkhand has shown better growth, while Bihar has displayed a reverse growth trajectory after the partition. While in undivided Bihar in 1990–1991, the GSDP was ₹26,71,661 lakh and the per capita income was ₹3119, in which the share of regions falling in Jharkhand in GSDP was ₹10,47,824 and per capita income for that region was 4827, for the rest of state it was reduced to GSDP of ₹16,23,837 and per capita income of ₹2,539. These figures showcase the imbalance between the two states from the point of view of area to population ratio.

After the partition, Bihar had to face a grave crisis regarding the distribution of assets, as many large industries and industrial centres of undivided Bihar were located in the Jharkhand region.

Partition also had serious effects on the social structure of the state. Prior to partition tribal regions were abundant in the state. The central government runs many schemes for the Scheduled Tribe community and due to this Bihar used to gain more revenue. After the partition, most of the tribal areas went in Jharkhand and thus, the revenue also went to Jharkhand which had a direct impact on the economy of Bihar. Maximum number of families living below the poverty line remained in Bihar after the partition, which increased the load on economy and affected the development works.

DEMAND OF SPECIAL STATUS FOR THE STATE

Bihar is primarily an agrarian economy. More than 80 per cent population of the state is dependent on agriculture or associated activities for their livelihood. It is categorised as one of the most economically backward states of India due to lack of resources. Lack of basic infrastructure viz., lack of power, scanty development of transport and communications, illiteracy, poverty, unemployment, etc. are some of the major hurdles in the growth of this state. In addition the mineral and wildlife resources of the state. After 2000, majority of these resources went to Jharkhand, while 75 per cent population remained with Bihar. Although there is an abundance of water and land resources in the state, but heavy rainfall and huge stream of rivers cause a situation of floods for one and half to two months.

In these conditions, Bihar needs much support possible from the central government. Bihar has continuously demanded a special status. For this, a resolution passed by general consensus by the

Bihar legislative assembly on 4 April, 2006, has already been sent to the central government for consideration, in which it was demanded that the parametres of backwardness that was applied to 11 states to grant them special status should also be applied to Bihar.

Although there is no provision of special status to any state that is mentioned in the Constitution, but the Planning Commission has set some parametres for border states, states with hilly or plateau regious, states with large tribal population or states that are extremely backward to grant them a special status so that they can be brought on the right trajectory of fast-paced growth. The status of special state is granted under these provisions. The decision to grant special status to any state is done in accordance with the parametres set by the National Development Council (NDC), an ancillary body of the Planning Commission. Although special status to any state is not mentioned in the constitution, still in an affidavit filed in the Supreme Court by the central government, declared four parametres on which special status can be granted to states. These four parametres are as follows:

1. Regions that are geographically disconnected;
2. Regions that are difficult to reach;
3. Regions that are low on resources;
4. Regions that lack basic infrastructure.

The states that are granted special status are given special grant package, by the union government, according to Gadgil Mukherjee Formula. General category states are given financial assistance in a ratio of 70 per cent as loan, and 30 per cent as grant, whereas states with special status receive 90 per cent of the economic package given by the central government in the form of grants and remaining 10 per cent is given as loan.

At present, 11 states in India have been granted special status. From the economical point of view, Bihar is considered as a very backward state. Basic infrastructures like lack of power, issue of coal linkages at the power production plants, grave problems of natural calamities like floods, high rate of poverty and unemployment, extremism, decline in rate of literacy etc. make Bihar fit for grant of special status. Therefore, in order to bring Bihar out of backwardness, it becomes utmost necessity that it is granted a special status because development at fast pace is only possible when problems like lack of resources, and natural calamities like floods are tackled, which is only possible when centre grants special assistance to the state.

Both the Planning Commission as well as the Central Government have not mentioned backwardness as a criterion to grant the special status. So, because of lack of sufficient basis of being backward, the central government has always been denying special status to Bihar. But since the demand for special status was raised continuously by Bihar and other backward states, so in May 2013, Prime Minister Narendra Modi had formed a committee under economic advisor, Raghuram Rajan, to frame new parametres for grant of special status. The committee submitted its report on 26 September, 2013. Shaival Gupta, an economist from Bihar was also a member of this committee. In recommendations, this committee proposed to create a Multidimensional Poverty Index (MPI) to measure the level of poverty in the backward states. Per capita monthly consumption expenditure, level of education, health (includes infant mortality rate), household facilities (drinking water, toilets), level of poverty, female literacy, percentage of scheduled castes and scheduled tribes in total population, rate of urbanisation, financial inclusion and transport connectivity facility, etc., are some of the indicators included in multidimensional poverty index.

The global MPI was developed by Oxford Poverty and Human Index (OPHI) with the UN Development Programme (UNDP) for inclusion in UNDP's flagship Human Development Report in 2010. About 100 developing countries came together to create this index which included health, education and standard of living. It also lists the given indicators:

Dimension	Indicators
Health	Child Mortality Rate, Nutrition
Education	Year of education in the school presence in schools
Standard of living	Use of fuel in cooking
	Toilets
	Water
	Electricity
	Condition of Houses
	Property

Following formula is used to calculate multidimensional poverty index.

$$MPI = k H \times A$$

Here, H indicates the per centage of people living below the poverty line, as per the multidimensional poverty index. I indicates the average intensity of poverty outside the multidimensional index. The states of India have been classified in three categories as per the MPI Those states which have an index of 0.6 and above have been placed under the least-developed states, and it has been mentioned that only these states should be given special status. Bihar is also included in this category as the index for Bihar is 12.04. Those states with an index in between 0.4 and 0.6 are categorised as under-developed, and the states with an index of over 0.4 are placed in the category of relatively developed states. As per this index, Goa, with an index of 0.3, is the most developed state of the country. The Raghuram Rajan Committee in its report also recommended that the index should be reviewed every five years and that its deciding formula should be re-inspected in every ten years. The report of this committee has also mentioned that 0.3 per cent of central financial aid to all the states should be given as constant grant.

A GAME-CHANGER FOR BIHAR'S ECONOMIC TRANSFORMATION IN UNION BUDGET 2026

Bihar stands at the threshold of a transformative era. The Union Budget 2026-27, presented by Finance Minister Nirmala Sitharaman, has ignited fresh hopes for accelerated development across the state. With strategic allocations, infrastructure initiatives, and focused policy measures, this budget could very well be the catalyst that propels Bihar into a new phase of economic prosperity.

The budget's provisions for urban development, infrastructure expansion, and employment generation hold immense promise for Bihar's 130 million residents.

Infrastructure Revolution: The Foundation of Growth

One of the most significant announcements in the Union Budget 2026 is the proposal to develop seven high-speed rail corridors across India. For Bihar, the Varanasi-Siliguri high-speed rail corridor is a game-changer. This corridor will traverse through a significant portion of Bihar, dramatically improving connectivity between the eastern and northern regions of the state.

The impact of this infrastructure project extends far beyond faster travel times. High-speed rail connectivity will facilitate easier movement of goods and people, attract investment, boost tourism, and integrate Bihar more effectively into the national economy. Cities like Patna, Gaya, and Muzaffarpur stand to benefit immensely from this enhanced connectivity.

Industrial Growth and Employment: Addressing Bihar's Core Challenges

Employment generation remains one of Bihar's most pressing challenges, with millions of youth seeking meaningful livelihood opportunities. The Union Budget 2026 addresses this through multiple initiatives that promise to create jobs while fostering industrial growth.

The proposal to establish large textile parks across the country holds particular relevance for

Bihar, where traditional textile and handicraft industries have deep roots. These parks will not only create direct employment but also strengthen the entire value chain, from raw material production to finished goods.

Special Focus on Purvodaya States

The Union Budget 2026 includes a special emphasis on Purvodaya states and the North-Eastern region, reflecting the government's commitment to balanced regional development. This focus is particularly significant for Bihar, which has historically lagged behind western and southern states in industrial development and per capita income.

The budget's provisions for industrial investment and infrastructure expansion in Purvodaya states will help Bihar attract more private sector participation. Improved infrastructure, coupled with policy support, can transform Bihar into an attractive destination for manufacturing, food processing, and service sector industries.

Urban Development: Building Future-Ready Cities

The Union Budget 2026 places strong emphasis on tier-2 and tier-3 city development, which is excellent news for Bihar's urban centres. Cities with populations exceeding 5 lakh—including Patna, Gaya, Bhagalpur, Muzaffarpur, and Darbhanga—will receive focused attention for comprehensive urban development.

This initiative aims to improve urban infrastructure, expand public transport, enhance civic amenities, and create employment opportunities in these cities. For Bihar, which has one of the highest urban growth rates in India, this investment in urban infrastructure is crucial for sustainable development.

The state government's own budget allocation of ₹3.47 lakh crore for 2026-27 complements the Union Budget's initiatives. Bihar's budget includes ambitious plans for affordable housing across the state and the construction of five new expressways to boost connectivity and economic growth.

Healthcare and Education: Building Human Capital

The Union Budget's provisions for healthcare and education strengthen Bihar's efforts to build quality human capital. The announcement that girls' hostels will be constructed in every district of the country is particularly significant for Bihar, where female literacy and higher education participation remain critical development priorities.

Improved access to quality education, especially for girls from rural areas, will have multiplier effects on Bihar's social and economic development. An educated population is essential for attracting knowledge-based industries and creating high-value employment opportunities.

The budget's focus on making essential medicines more affordable, particularly for diabetes and cancer treatment, will reduce the healthcare burden on Bihar's families. With 17 cancer medicines and 7 drugs for serious illnesses becoming cheaper, quality healthcare becomes more accessible to common citizens

Bihar's State-Level Initiatives Complement Central Budget

Bihar's state budget for 2026-27, at ₹3.47 lakh crore, demonstrates the government's commitment to accelerating development. The budget outlines a development model based on five elements: knowledge, integrity, science, aspirations, and respect.

The state is simultaneously pushing forward with 10 mega infrastructure projects spanning roads, bridges, healthcare, renewable energy, education, and urban infrastructure. These projects include the Kacchi Dargah-Bidupur six-lane bridge over the Ganga, the Gaya-Biharsharif four-lane road, and various urban development initiatives across Patna and other cities.

The approval for constructing two five-star hotels in Rajgir and a resort in Vaishali demonstrates the government's focus on developing tourism infrastructure. These projects will not only improve accommodation facilities for tourists but also create significant employment opportunities in the hospitality sector.

Tourism Development: Unlocking Bihar's Heritage Potential

Bihar's rich historical and spiritual heritage remains a largely untapped economic resource. The state is home to Nalanda, Rajgir, Bodh Gaya, and numerous other sites of immense significance to Buddhist, Jain, and Hindu pilgrims from around the world.

The Union Budget's provisions for tourism development, combined with state-level initiatives, can transform Bihar into a major tourist destination. Improved connectivity through high-speed rail and expressways will make it easier for domestic and international tourists to visit Bihar's heritage sites.

Rajgir, in particular, holds tremendous potential for tourism-led development. This ancient city, surrounded by seven hills and rich in historical significance, is witnessing significant infrastructure development. The proposed five-star hotels, improved road connectivity to the Rajgir Sports Complex and International Cricket Stadium, and development of eco-tourism facilities position Rajgir as an emerging hub for tourism, sports, and spiritual activities.

Technology and Digital Infrastructure

The Union Budget 2026 also brings relief on the technology front. Mobile phones becoming cheaper will improve digital penetration, essential for Bihar's Digital India initiatives. Similarly, more affordable electric vehicle batteries will support Bihar's clean mobility goals and reduce urban pollution.

These technology-focused provisions align well with Bihar's push toward digital governance, e-learning platforms, and technology-enabled service delivery. As internet penetration increases and digital devices become more affordable, Bihar's youth can access better educational resources and participate more effectively in the digital economy.

Road Infrastructure: The Backbone of Connectivity

2026 is set to become a landmark year for road infrastructure in Bihar. Several highway, expressway, and bridge projects are either nearing completion or set to begin construction. Bihar's first six-lane national highway, the Varanasi-Aurangabad road project, is in its final stage and scheduled for completion in 2026.

The state's first access-controlled highway, connecting Amas and Darbhanga, is also expected to open in 2026. These modern roadways will offer controlled entry and exit points, improving safety and allowing faster travel across central and northern Bihar.

Looking ahead, Bihar is preparing to enter the expressway era with the Patna-Purnea road receiving expressway status from the central government. Construction may begin in 2026 for what will become Bihar's first expressway, marking a significant milestone in the state's infrastructure development journey.

Conclusion

The Union Budget 2026 represents more than just fiscal allocations it's a vision for Bihar's transformation. With strategic investments in infrastructure, focus on employment generation, support for industrial growth, and emphasis on urban development, this budget can indeed change Bihar's economic trajectory.

As the state prepares for this transformative journey, opportunities abound for those ready to invest in Bihar's future. The convergence of favorable policies, infrastructure development, and economic momentum creates an environment ripe for growth and prosperity.

Naxalism

Naxalism is an ideology according to which the marginalised and exploited sections of the society, while demanding their rights, start to indulge in rageful and violent activities. This ideology is inspired by the ideas of communists like Marx, Lenin, and Mao-Tse-Tung. In India, the naxal movement began from a village named Naxalbari, in Silliguri District in West Bengal, under the leadership of Charu Majumdar in 1967. Charu Majumdar had joined the Communist Party of India to start an armed revolt against the government along with Kanhu Sanyal. Majumdar was inspired by the ideas of Chinese leader Mao-Tse-Tung.

From the decade of 1980, naxalism began to show its impact in Bihar as well. At first, the ideology began to spread in Bihar. Political parties inspired by communist ideologies and with support from farmers and workers, began to gain more and more votes in elections. This caused an impact on landless farmers and workers. They began to rise in numbers. These landless farmers and workers started getting united which gave rise to situations of class clashes. Taking an advantage of this situation, an extremist ideology like naxalism began to spread in the region. More than 15 out of 38 districts of the state: Jamui, Kaimur, Motihari, Sitamarhi, Munger, Jehanabad, Nawada, Bhojpur, Aurangabad, Muzaffarpur, Vaishali, Sheohar, Gaya and Rohatas were under the impact of this ideology. As time passed, naxalism emerged in the new form of caste clashes in Bihar. In between 1980 and 2010, many massacres took place in Bihar. First incident of massacre occurred in Rupaspur village in Purnea District.

As a result of these incidents of massacre, many caste-based armed private services found courage for their establishment with the motive to protect their castes as well as to establish their domination. The communist organistions that played very important role in spreading the naxal ideology in the state were—Maoist Communist Centre (MCC), Communist Party of India (Marxist-Leninist) Liberation, Communist Party of India (ML) Unity, MCC backed Red Army party unity backed Red Squad. Champaran, Jehanabad, Gaya, Aurangabad districts were under the influence of People's War backed Maoist Communist Centre of Andhra Pradesh as well. Communist Party of India liberation has a major impact in the rural areas especially in districts of Bhojpur, Jehanabad, Rohtas, Nalanda, Aurangabad and Siwan. Communist Party of India (ML) has influence in the rural areas of Gaya, Jehanabad, Aurangabad and Gaya districts. In order to curb the rising influence of these organisations, land owners also started forming private armies with different names all across the state. Among these, Ranveer Sena in 1994, Sunlight Sena in 1989, Laurik Sena in 1985, Brahmarshi Sena in 1981, Bhumi Sena in 1979 and Kunwar Sena in 1978 were established in the state. With the rise of these organisations, events of violence and counter-violence became rampant and even the incidents of massacre rose sharply.

Some of the major factors for the rise of naxalism in Bihar include uneven distribution of land, excess pressure of population on the available land, low wages to landless workers, relatively low growth of villages in the state, etc. More than

80 per cent population of Bihar is dependent on farming. Population of marginalised and small farmers in the state is more than 90 per cent. These farmers own less than one acre land on average. Landless workers were getting wages lower than what was prescribed by the government, which was one of the foremost reasons for increase in naxal activity in the state. The land distributed to the landless people during the Bhoodan movement were either barren or were forcefully taken back by the previous owners. Most of the 'gair majarma' lands of the state are under the control of landowners.

Additionally, naxal organisations are targeting government buildings like schools, community halls, railway stations and railway tracks in the affected areas for past few years. A maoist organisation by the name of People's Liberation Gorilla Army is very active in Kaimur and Rohtas region. To solve this problem, the state government has formed Commando Battalions for Resolute Action (CoBRA) force with an objective to provide security to the people and to bring deviant elements to the mainstream of society.

In order to tackle the menace of naxalism, state government has taken many significant steps. An armed squad by the name of Quick Response Team has been formed in every district of the state. Efforts like reforms in police force, formation of land reforms committee, formation of SAP, etc., has proved very effective in curbing the influence of naxalism in source parts of the state. It has been decided to build a model police station in every district. In order to ensure seamless and swift development in naxal affected districts, the state government launched the 'government at your doorstep' (Sarkar Apke Dwaar) Programme on 21 January, 2006 from Jehanabad District. This programme launched by the government is now operational in 25 blocks and 65 villages of 8 districts. Grand cultural programmes are organised by the government in these areas. To ensure effective action against naxalism, State Auxiliary Police (SAP) was formed in March 2006. At present total number of personnels in SAP force is around 6,500. Women police stations have been established in all 38 districts of Bihar.

Under the integrated action plan, complete focus was laid upon swift completion of development works in 11 naxal affected districts of Arwal, Aurangabad, Gaya, Jamui, Jehanabad, Nawada, Rohtas, Munger, Kaimur, West Champaran and Sitamarhi. In order to fight naxal militancy, police building construction corporation has been authorised to build police buildings for upgradation of police force in these areas under the special fundamental framework plan. With the funds available with the corporation, training centres for special forces, housing, barracks, watch towers, helipads, magazine rooms and fronts etc. are being developed.

Special Task Force was formed (STF) in year 2000, in the direction of preparing elaborate and collaborated plan to curb the menace of naxalism in the state. With an expansion in their size and increase in their capacity, the mission against militants and organised criminal groups has progressed at a very fast pace. At present, their 33 cheeta units are operational. About 11 bomb diffusal squads are operational under the Special Task Force. Out of these, 9 squads have been posted with special forces of Bihar Military Police and Special Branches. One bomb diffusal squad each has been posted with Patna District Police Force and Rail District Police force. STF training college is being built in Bodh Gaya under the special fundamental frameworks plan for the upgradation of this force.

A proposal to raise a dog squad has been approved by the state government. It aims to establish a dog squad for all district police in the state including railway police that will consist of two trackers, two sniffers and eight handler dogs. Apart form this, reserved dog squads have also been arranged at the level of Inspector General of Police, Range and Director General of Police. Construction buildings for these dog squads in every district has also been approved by the state government.

Skill development programmes have been initiated in 34 naxal affected districts of Bihar with an aim to provide skill training and employment opportunities to the youth of these naxal-affected districts and make them self-dependent. Under this scheme, one industrial technology institute and two skill development centres, each in the districts of Jamui, Aurangabad, Arwal, Gaya, Rohtas and Jehanabad districts have been set up.

New policies have been framed regarding surrender and rehabilitation schemes for the communist militants. For high-level communist militants, an amount of ₹2,50,000 and for mid or low level communist militants a sum of ₹1,50,000 will be given to them, after they surrender. Apart from this, extra cash rewards have been announced for militants surrendering their arms, explosives etc. There is a provision to give a monthly pension of ₹4,000 (for a maximum of 36 months) to the militants during employment-oriented training as per the liking of the militant. Under this scheme a sum of ₹1.4 crores was given to 270 militants who surrendered. The compensation of ₹1 lakh that was given to the dependents of those who lost their lives in militant/terrorist attacks or caste clashes has been increased to ₹5 lakhs in September 2014. The dependents of home guards who lost their lives in militant attacks or other violent attacks will be given a grace grant of ₹10 lakhs under special assistance scheme. With these consolidated efforts by the state government, there has been a continuous decrease in militant–induced incidents in the state.

❑❑❑

Good Governance and Bihar "Saat Nishchay-3" Programme (2025-2030): A State-Level Welfare and Development Model

Bihar was among the states that showed fast-paced economic growth after independence. Bihar was a forerunner in agricultural growth and industrial growth rate. Many large industries were established in Bihar during the first four Five Year Plans. Canals were constructed for better irrigation facilities that resulted in increase in agricultural productivity. In addition to establishment of mineral-based industries in South Bihar, agriculture-based industries, especially jute industry and sugar industry, also developed simultaneously in North Bihar. But after the decade of 1980, the growth rate of Bihar started to go on a downhill. Rise in many negative trends like lack of political will, corruption, rise in crimes, ciminalisation of politics began to adversely impact the growth of agriculture and other industries in the state, and Bihar joined the club of BIMARU states of India.

Amidst the environment of uncertainity hindering the growth of state, there was a change in regime in the year 2005. The government gave the slogan of good governance to make the state free of crimes and corruption. In order to achieve this, control over crime and corruption, eradication of naxalism, and castes-based animosity and removal of criminals from politics were considered utmost priorities. Therefore, reforms and improvement in administration, health services and educational environment as well as empowerment of women were stressed upon. Government has enacted many new laws that include Public Services Rights Act, Public Grievances Redressal Act, Land Reforms Programmes, Prohibition Act, etc.

In order to reform the law and order situation, the police force is being modernised. Special Task Force (STF) and Special Auxiliary Force (SAF) have been formed. A fast track court has been established in year, 2000, to conduct swift trials on the criminals and punish them accordingly. Fast track courts were established by the central government for five years, but then its tenure had been extended till 2011. However, states like Bihar, Himachal Pradesh, and Maharashtra have continued with this system of fast track courts in accordance with their resources. About 179 fast track courts were functional in Bihar till March 2019, which is more than any other state in India. The capital police has started programmes like police–public dialogue and dual power in order to establish direct connect with the public. Bihar is the first state in India to develop fully computerised Prison Enterprise Resource and Planning System to strengthen and upgrade the prison system. Crime and Social Media Lab has been formed with an objective to curb the rising cyber crimes in the state.

Special Task Force (STF) was formed by the state government in 2003, and now it has become an important tool of crime control in the state. In 2003,

Special Task Force was formed with 15 squads, and now this number has risen to 25. In 2005, Special Auxiliary Force was formed by including the retired officers. It was formed with a primary objective to control the naxal and criminal elements, a task in which it has been successful to a large extent. Women police stations have been established in all 38 districts of the state. A resolution has already been passed for the formation of Swabhiman Police Battalion for women from the Scheduled Castes.

In the decade of 1980, naxalism spread out rampantly in Bihar. Reforms in administration and law and order, and swift implementation of development programmes in naxal-affected districts has been carried out as an attempt to curb the problem.

In order to improve the educational environment, attempts have been made for institutional and structural reforms. This includes actions and implementation like construction of school buildings, appointment of teachers, cycle scheme, uniform scheme etc. Good quality education has also been stressed upon in addition to literacy. A mobile application named DISHA was launched in the year 2015 for digital literacy with goals to teach computer and Internet to the people through self-educating modules. A scheme named 'Akshar Anchal Yojana' is being run by the government to educate women. In order to connect the children with mainstream education many centres like Vidyalay Chalo Kendra, Prayas Kendra, Maktab-Madarsa Navachari Kendra, Talimi Markaj Kendra, Utthan Kendra, Utpreran Kendra, etc. are being run by the government. It has been decide to open one engineering college in every division, one polytechnic college in every district and ITI institute in every sub division.

Bihar Mahadalit Vikas Mission has launched many programmes in the state. Among these, the objective of Dashrath Manjhi Skill Development Scheme is to provide free professional training to young boys and girls from the Mahadalit community, and ensure employment for them so that their educational and economical growth is ascertained. In order to implement all the programmes associated with the development of Mahadalits, one Vikas Mitra each at the Panchayat level and ward level each is selected, and there is a reservation of 52 per cent for the women from the Mahadalit community. Many other programmes like Mahadalit Uniform Scheme, Mahadalit Construction of Toilets Scheme, Chief Minister Mahadalit Radio Scheme, Establishment of Community Hall and Call Centre Scheme, Mahadalit Land Residence Scheme, Mahadalit Water Supply Scheme etc. have also been implemented.

Women constitute 48 per cent of the total population of the state. Women empowerment becomes one of the primary conditions for the growth of the state. The state government has taken many steps towards women empowerment. As per the data of Census 2011, gender ratio in the state is 918. In this direction many steps have been taken by the government like Mukhyamantri Nari Suraksha Yojana, Establishment of Women Self Help Groups, Akshar Aanchal Yojana, Chief Minister Girl Cycle Scheme, Mukhyamantri Kanya Suraksha Yojana, Jananai in Suraksha Yojana etc. In order to include women in the mainstream of development, Bihar State Women Empowerment Policy 2015 was enacted by the government on the occasion of Bihar Day. Hunar Yojana is also being implemented by the state government for the women of scheduled castes, scheduled tribes and extremely backward sections of the society.

Government has made a provision of 50 per cent reservation for women in the institutions of Panchayat level. On 1 April, 2016, 35 per cent reservation has been made for women in all types of government jobs. Self-help groups have been formed in order to make them economically self-dependent. Women helpline numbers have been issued to ensure the safety of women from Domestic Violence and ensure proper implementation of Domestic Violence Act. The objective of Mukhyamantri Kanya Suraksha Yojana is to end female foeticide, which is a crime both socially as well as constitutionally, and to improve the gender ratio by curbing female foeticide.

Right to Information Act, Right to Public Services Legislation Act, Public Grievances Redressal Act etc. have been enacted to ensure transparency in the state administration as well as to ensure that everyone can approach the administration. The Right to Information Act was enacted by the government in the year, 2006. Under the provisions of this Act, Right to Seek Information through telephone has also been granted on 29 January, 2007, which is also known as information Call Centre. Under the provisions of Right to Bihar Public Services Act, 2011, it has been arranged that a public servant must ensure availability of services to common people within a defined time frame. Under this Act, the common people have been granted the right to avail public services within a fixed time period. The objective of this Act is to provide birth certificates, castes certificates, income certificates, etc. to the public in a swift and timely manner.

Public Grievance Redressal Act has been implemented in Bihar since 5 June, 2016. Under the provisions of this act, an effective mechanism has been developed for smooth redressal of public grievances.

On the occasion of Prohibition Day on 26 November, 2015, the government announced complete prohibition in the state. The state legislature passed the Prohibition Act with unanimity. On 1 April, 2016, all country-made liquors were banned in the state, and with a ban on foreign-made liquor on 5 April, 2016, complete prohibition was implemented in the state.

Seven Resolutions

In a significant policy move, the Bihar Cabinet has approved the "Saat Nishchay-3" Programme (2025–2030), outlining seven priority resolutions to guide Bihar's development over the next five years. The programme builds upon earlier phases of Saat Nishchay and seeks to address employment generation, inclusive growth, human development, and quality of life in a coordinated manner.

What is Saat Nishchay-3?

Saat Nishchay-3 Programme is Bihar's third multi-year development agenda, covering the period 2025–2030. It represents a mission-mode governance framework, under which sectoral policies are aligned to a fixed set of development priorities ("nishchays" or resolves).

The Seven Resolves (Saat Nishchay-3)

The programme is structured around seven core resolves, each addressing a key development challenge:

1. **Double Employment, Double Income**
   - Focus on job creation for youth
   - Promotion of skill development and employability
   - Support for entrepreneurship and local employment opportunities
2. **Prosperous Industry – Empowered Bihar**
   - Encouragement of MSMEs and local industries
   - Investment facilitation and industrial clusters
   - Linking industrial growth with job creation
3. **Prosperity of the State through Progress in Agriculture**
   - Productivity enhancement and diversification
   - Support to farmers through infrastructure, irrigation, and markets
   - Promotion of agri-based industries and value chains
4. **Advanced Education – Bright Future**
   - Improvement in learning outcomes
   - Strengthening school and higher education infrastructure
   - Skill-linked education to meet labour market needs
5. **Accessible Healthcare – Secure Life**
   - Expansion of primary and secondary healthcare services
   - Focus on preventive healthcare and nutrition
   - Strengthening public health institutions
6. **Strong Foundation – Modern Expansion**
   - Roads, power, water supply, and digital connectivity
   - Urban and rural infrastructure expansion
   - Support for economic and social mobility
7. **Ease of Living through Dignity/Respect for All**
   - Housing, sanitation, and basic amenities
   - Social security for vulnerable sections
   - Emphasis on quality of life and human dignity

Bihar Foundation Day

On 22 March, 2020, Bihar celebrated its 108th foundation day. The tradition to celebrate 'Bihar Day' or 'Bihar Foundation Day', began in year 2010, when Chief Minister of Bihar, Nitish Kumar inaugurated the first Bihar Day on 22 March, 2010 at the historic Gandhi Maidan in Patna. Since then, it is celebrated every year on this day. The reason behind celebrating Bihar Day on 22 March is that, it was on 22 March, 1912 when the British Gazette was published announcing separation of Bihar from Bengal, and Bihar was separated on 1 April, 1912. The announcement to separate Bihar from Bengal came on 12 December, 1911 when the official capital of India was shifted to Delhi from Calcutta. Sir Charles Stuart Bayley was appointed the first governor. Satyendra Prasad Sinha was appointed the first Indian Governor of Bihar.

State government has declared a state holiday on the occasion of 'Bihar Day'. At present, Bihar Day is observed in many cities across India as well the world. Bihar day was observed in USA, Australia, Canada, Bahrain, Qatar, Trinidad & Tobago, Mauritius and UAE on 22 March, 2016. This program is conducted outside the state and other countries by an organisation named 'Bihar Foundation'. Bihar foundation is a single window system of the state government that encourages the non-resident Biharis to invest in the state.

In order to celebrate their glorious past, every year since 2010 the Government of Bihar organises Bihar Day on 22 March. Its goal is to awaken the self-pride among the people of Bihar. This step will create a sense of culture, traditions and gratitude and respect towards our great ancestors. Bihar has been the land of Janaka, the king of Videha, Vishvamitra, Chanakya and Chandragupta. Many great scholars, philosophers, thinkers and litterateur have been associated with Bihar. The land of Bihar has a glorious past historically, culturally, and politically. The kingdom of Mauryan Empire under the reign of Ashoka found its expanse up till Afghanistan and Shershah Suri also hailed from Bihar. This is the pious land of Bhagwan Biddha, Bhagwan Mahavir and Guru Gobind Singh. This land has also heard the voices of sufi saints. Out of 3 ancient universities, Nalanda and Vikramshila were situated in Bihar. The greatness of the tales of Bihar can never be praised enough.

The most important objective behind celebrating Bihar Day is to develop a sense of emotional attachment among the people of Bihar, and to strengthen the unity of Bihar. The aim to celebrate this day is to showcase the historical prosperity of Bihar to the whole world, and also to put forward a glimpse of hope for the states' resources and opportunities so that the image of the state can be changed. Through this celebration, it is also attempted to attract maximum investment from the people living outside the state or country, the businessmen of Bihar as well as other states, for the development of the state.

Coming generations will learn and take pride in the civilisation, culture and tales of greatness through this celebration. In the coming years, the name and image of Bihar will be seen spread across the world, leading to an overall growth of the state.

❑❑❑

Bihar: A Diverse Perspective

Major Fairs of Bihar

Baba Brahmeshwar Nath Mela	Buxar
Malmas Mela	Rajgir
Muzaffarpur Mela	Muzaffarpur
Mandar Mela	Banka
Bounsi Mela	Bhagalpur
Sitamarhi Mela	Sitamarhi
Sonpur Animal Fair	Sonpur
Sorath Mela	Madhubani
Vaishali Mela	Vaishali
Singheshwar Mela	Madhepura
Buxar Fair	Buxar
Patna Sahib Gurudwara Mela	Patna
Badgaon Mela	Nalanda
Simaria Mela	Begusarai
Patna Book Fair	Patna
Sahodra Mela	West Champaran
Makar Sankranti Mela	All Parts of Bihar
Munger Sharif & Makhdoom Shah's Urs	Bihar Sharif (Nalanda)
Sabaur Mela	Bhagalpur

Industries Contributing to Pollution in Bihar

Industry	Number
Textile/Handloom	40
Sugar Industry	28
Pharmaceutical/Medicine	10
Alcohol Related	2
Cement Industry	3
Fertilizer	1
Thermal Power Plant	5
Pesticides	5
Leather	5
Dyes	6

Source: Economic Review, Bihar Government

Major Crops of Bihar's Districts

Nalanda	Rice, Maize, Gram, Onion, Potato, etc.
Rohtas	Rice, Wheat, Guava, Fenugreek, Gram.
Kaimur	Rice, Wheat, Maize.
Bhojpur	Rice, Wheat, Maize, Gram, etc.
Buxar	Wheat, Rice, Gram, Mustard, Tomato, etc.
Gaya	Rice, Wheat, Maize, Sugarcane, etc.
Jehanabad	Rice, Wheat, Maize, Khesari, etc.
Aurangabad	Rice, Wheat, Gram, Maize.
Arwal	Rice, Wheat, Gram, Maize.
Munger	Rice, Wheat, Gram, Barley, Arhar.
Lakhisarai	Rice, Wheat, Maize, Gram, Lentils, etc.
Sheikhpura	Rice, Wheat, Gram, Potato, etc.
Jamui	Rice, Wheat, Gram, Barley, etc.

Khagaria	Rice, Wheat, Jute, etc.
Begusarai	Maize, Wheat, Rice, Sugarcane, Red Chili, etc.
Muzaffarpur	Rice, Wheat, Sugarcane, Maize, Litchi, Mango, etc.
Vaishali	Rice, Wheat, Banana, Maize, Tobacco, Litchi, etc.
Sitamarhi	Rice, Wheat, Maize, Khesari, etc.
East Champaran	Rice, Wheat, Sugarcane, Maize, Jowar, Khesari, Arhar, Jute, etc.
West Champaran	Rice, Wheat, Sugarcane, Maize, Jowar, etc.
Sheohar	Rice, Wheat, Sesame, Maize, Tobacco, Red Chili, etc.
Saran	Rice, Wheat, Maize, Sugarcane, etc.
Siwan	Rice, Wheat, Sugarcane.
Gopalganj	Rice, Wheat, Maize, Sugarcane, Arhar, etc.
Darbhanga	Rice, Wheat, Maize, Jute, Tobacco, Makhana, Mango, etc.
Madhubani	Rice, Wheat, Maize, Khesari, Mango, etc.
Samastipur	Rice, Wheat, Maize, Tobacco, Red Chili, etc.
Saharsa	Rice, Wheat, Maize, and Jute.
Supaul	Rice, Wheat, Maize, Jute, etc.
Madhepura	Rice, Maize, Jute, etc.
Purnia	Rice, Jute, Wheat, Maize, Banana, etc.
Araria	Rice, Wheat, and Jute, etc.
Kishanganj	Rice, Wheat, Jute, etc.
Katihar	Rice, Jute, Wheat, Maize, etc.
Bhagalpur	Rice, Wheat, Maize, Gram, Sugarcane, etc.
Banka	Rice, Wheat, Gram, Maize, Khesari, Potato, Sugarcane, etc.

Districts-wise Blocks of Bihar

Gaya	Atri, Belaganj, Mohanpur, Konch, Barachatti, Mohra, Manpur, Gurua, Tekari, Imamganj, Gaya Sadar, Wazirganj, etc.
Katihar	Katihar, Barsoi, Kadwa, Amadabad, Manihari, Balrampur, etc.
Aurangabad	Aurangabad, Barun, Obra, Dev, Goh, Nabinagar, etc.
Gopalganj	Bhor, Gopalganj, Kataiya, Vijaypur, Barouli, Kuchaikot, etc.
Vaishali	Mahnar, Vaishali, Bidupur, Garoul, Raghopur, etc.
Siwan	Panchruchi, Raghunathpur, Ander, Ukari, Guthani, Maharajganj, etc.
Rohtas	Nohatti, Chenari, Nasirganj, Rohtas, Shivsagar, etc.
Darbhanga	Bahadurpur, Jale, Hayaghat, Singhwara, Benipur, etc.
Sitamarhi	Surasand, Bathnaha, Parihar, Sonbarsa, Runnisidpur, etc.
Kishanganj	Kishanganj, Kauchadhaman, Bahadurganj, etc.
Purnia	Purnia East, Amour, Bhawanipur, Banmankhi, Kothi, etc.
Banka	Rajoun, Dhoraiya, Bounsi, Barahat, Boka, etc.
Begusarai	Bhagwanpura, Teghra, Bakhri, Barauni, etc.
Bhojpur	Ara Sadar, Udwantnagar, Jagdishpur, etc.
Nawada	Kavakol, Warsaliganj, Rajouli, etc.
Araria	Araria, Karbisganj, RaniGanj, etc.
Bhagalpur	Pirpanti, Kahalgaon, Sanhoula, Sabour, Nathnagar, etc.
East Champaran	Keshariya, Kalyanpur, Motihari, etc.

Madhubani	Jayanagar, Pandoul, Rahika, etc.
Saharsa	Nohatta, Simri-Bakhtiarpur, Salakhua, etc.
Supaul	Supaul, Triveniganj, Pipra, etc.
Jehanabad	Ghosa, Jehanabad, Kakau, etc.
Munger	Haveli, Khadgapur, Jamalpur, etc.
Samastipur	Jitwarpur, Kalyanpur, Rosra, etc.
Nalanda	Giriak, Rahoi, Tharthari, etc.
Saharsa	Nohatta, Simri-Bakhtiarpur, Salakhua, etc.
Sheohar	Sheohar, Tariyani, Pipradhahi, etc.
Muzaffarpur	Mural, Musahari, Gayghat, etc.

Area and Population of Bihar's Districts (as per 2011 Census)

District	Area (sq. km.)	Population
Araria	2830	2,811,569
Arwal	638	700,843
Aurangabad	3305	2,540,073
Banka	3020	2,034,763
Begusarai	1918	2,970,541
Bhagalpur	2569	3,037,766
Bhojpur	2395	2,728,407
Buxar	1703	1,706,352
Darbhanga	2279	3,937,385
Gaya	4976	4,391,418
Gopalganj	2033	2,562,012
Jamui	3098	1,760,405
Jehanabad	931	1,125,313
Kaimur (Bhabua)	3352	1,626,384
Katihar	3057	3,071,029
Khagaria	1486	1,666,886
Kishanganj	1884	1,690,400
Lakhisarai	1228	1,000,912
Madhepura	1788	2,001,762
Madhubani	3501	4,487,379
Munger	1419	1,367,765
Muzaffarpur	3172	4,801,062
Nalanda	2355	2,877,653
Nawada	2494	2,219,146
West Champaran	5228	3,935,042
Patna	3202	5,838,465
East Champaran	3968	5,099,371
Purnia	3229	3,264,619
Rohtas	3881	2,959,918
Saharsa	1687	1,900,661
Samastipur	2904	4,261,566
Saran	2641	3,951,862
Sheikhpura	689	636,342
Sheohar	349	656,246
Sitamarhi	2294	3,423,574
Siwan	2219	3,330,464
Supaul	2425	2,229,076
Vaishali	2036	3,495,021

Bihar's Districts and Sub-divisions

Gaya	Gaya Sadar, Neemchak, Bathani, Sherghati, Tekari
Katihar	Barsoi, Katihar Sadar, Manihari
Aurangabad	Aurangabad, Daudnagar (Incomplete)
Gopalganj	Gopalganj, Hathua
Vaishali	Hajipur, Mahnar, Mahua
Siwan	Siwan, Maharajganj
Rohtas	Sasaram, Buxar, Dehri
Darbhanga	Darbhanga Sadar, Benipur, Biraul
Sitamarhi	Sitamarhi Sadar, Pupri, Sheohar
Kishanganj	Kishanganj

Purnia	Banmankhi, Dhamdaha, Purnia, Baisi
Begusarai	Bakhari, Ballia, Begusarai, Manjhaul, Teghra
Bhojpur	Ara Sadar, Jagdishpur, Piro
Nawada	Nawada, Rajouli
Araria	Araria, Farbisganj
Bhagalpur	Bhagalpur, Kahalgaon, Naugachhia
East Champaran	Motihari Sadar, Areraj, Raxaul, Sikrahna, Pakridayal
Madhubani	Madhubani, Jayanagar, Benipatti, Jhanjharpur, Qalparas
Supaul	Supaul, Veerpur, Nirmali, Triveniganj
Jehanabad	Jehanabad
Munger	Haveli Khargpur, Tarapur
Samastipur	Dalsinghsarai, Patory, Rosda, Samastipur Sadar
Nalanda	Bihar Sharif, Rajgir, Hilsa
Saharsa	Saharsa Sadar, Simri-Bakhtiarpur
Arwal	Arwal
Kaimur	Bhabua, Mohania
Khagaria	Khagaria, Ghoghari
Sheikhpura	Sheikhpura
Saran	Chapra, Marhaura, Sonpur
Buxar	Buxar, Dumraon
Madhopur	Madhopur, Uday Kishanganj
Sheohar	–
Muzaffarpur	East Muzaffarpur, West Muzaffarpur
Jamui	Jamui
Lakhisarai	Lakhisarai
Patna	Barh, Danapur, Masaudhi, Paliganj, Patna City, Patna Sadar
West Champaran	Betiah, Bagha, Narkatiaganj
Banka	Banka

Years of Formation of Districts in Bihar

Gaya	3rd October, 1865
Katihar	1973
Aurangabad	26th January, 1973
Gopalganj	2nd October, 1973
Vaishali	12th October, 1972
Siwan	11th December, 1972
Rohtas	10th November, 1972
Darbhanga	1875
Sitamarhi	11th December, 1972
Kishanganj	1990
Purnia	1770
Begusarai	2nd October, 1972
Bhojpur	1972
Nawada	26th January, 1973
Araria	1990
Bhagalpur	1773
East Champaran	1971
Madhubani	1972
Supaul	14th March, 1991
Jehanabad	1st August, 1986
Munger	1832
Samastipur	1972
Nalanda	9th November, 1972
Saharsa	1st April, 1954
Arwal	1st August, 2001
Kaimur	1991
Khagaria	1980
Sheikhpura	31st July, 1994
Saran	1981
Buxar	1991
Madhopur	9th May, 1981
Sheohar	6th October, 1994
Muzaffarpur	1875
Jamui	21st February, 1991

Lakhisarai	3rd July, 1994
Patna	Ancient City
West Champaran	1971
Banka	1991

District-wise Rivers of Bihar

Gaya	Ganga
Katihar	Mahananda, Ganga
Aurangabad	Son, Punpun, Auranga, Batane, Morhar
Gopalganj	Gandak
Vaishali	Ganga, Gandak
Siwan	Daha, Jhari
Rohtas	Son, Kawar
Darbhanga	Kamla, Balan
Sitamarhi	Bagmati, Lakshman, Rato Singhi, etc.
Kishanganj	Mahananda
Purnia	Koshi, Mahananda, Suara Kali, and Kohli
Begusarai	Ganga, Kamla
Bhojpur	Ganga, Son
Nawada	Sakri
Araria	Koshi, Sura, Kali, and Kohli
Bhagalpur	Ganga
East Champaran	Gandak, Sikrahna
Madhubani	Kamla, Bhutahi, Balan
Supaul	Koshi
Jehanabad	Ganga, Dardha, Yamunia
Munger	Ganga, Mohani, Harohar, etc.
Samastipur	Budhi Gandak, Kamla, Balan
Nalanda	Ganga, Mohani
Saharsa	Koshi
Arwal	Ganga
Kaimur	Karmanasha, Durgawati
Khagaria	Ganga, Koshi
Sheikhpura	Ganga, Mohane, Harohar, etc.
Saran	Ganga, Ghaghara, Gandak
Buxar	Ganga, Karmanasha
Madhopur	Koshi
Sheohar	Bagmati
Muzaffarpur	Bagmati, Budhi Gandak
Jamui	Ganga, Mohane, Harohar, etc.
Lakhisarai	Ganga, Mohane, Harohar, etc.
Patna	Ganga, Son, Punpun
West Champaran	Gandak
Banka	Chandani, Chiar, Orhani, Belharani, and Barla

Major Lok Sabha Constituencies of Bihar

Patna	Patliputra, Patna Sahib (2)
Nalanda	Nalanda (1)
Gaya	Gaya (1)
Jehanabad	Jehanabad (1)
Nawada	Nawada (1)
Aurangabad	Aurangabad (1)
Arwal	Under Jehanabad Constituency
Munger	Munger (1)
Lakhisarai	Under Munger Constituency
Sheikhpura	Under Jamui and Nawada Constituencies
Jamui	Jamui (1)
Khagaria	Khagaria (1)
Begusarai	Begusarai (1)
Muzaffarpur	Muzaffarpur (1)
Vaishali	Vaishali, Hajipur (2)
Sitamarhi	Sitamarhi (1)
East Champaran	East Champaran (1)
West Champaran	West Champaran, Valmiki Nagar (2)

Sheohar	Sheohar (1)
Saran	Saran (1)
Siwan	Siwan, Maharajganj (2)
Gopalganj	Gopalganj (1)
Darbhanga	Darbhanga (1)
Madhubani	Madhubani, Jhanjharpur (2)
Samastipur	Ujiarpur, Samastipur (2)
Saharsa	Madhepura (1)
Supaul	Supaul (1)
Madhepura	Madhepura (1)
Purnia	Purnia (1)
Araria	Araria (1)
Kishanganj	Kishanganj (1)
Katihar	Katihar (1)
Bhagalpur	Bhagalpur (1)
Banka	Banka (1)
Rohtas	Sasaram, Karakat (2)
Kaimur	Sasaram (1)
Bhojpur	Ara (1)
Buxar	Buxar (1)

Major Districts of Bihar

The list below provides the names of districts in Bihar with there corresponding cities:

Buxar	Buxar
Gaya	Gaya
Jehanabad	Jehanabad
Nawada	Nawada
Aurangabad	Aurangabad
Arwal	Arwal
Munger	Munger
Lakhisarai	Lakhisarai
Sheikhpura	Sheikhpura
Jamui	Jamui
Khagaria	Khagaria
Begusarai	Begusarai
Muzaffarpur	Muzaffarpur
Vaishali	Hajipur
Sitamarhi	Sitamarhi
East Champaran	Motihari
West Champaran	Bettiah
Sheohar	Sheohar
Saran	Chapra
Siwan	Siwan
Gopalganj	Gopalganj
Darbhanga	Darbhanga
Madhubani	Madhubani
Samastipur	Samastipur
Saharsa	Saharsa
Supaul	Supaul
Madhubani	Madhubani
Purnia	Purnia
Araria	Araria
Kishanganj	Kishanganj
Katihar	Katihar
Bhagalpur	Bhagalpur
Banka	Banka

Major Assembly Constituencies in Bihar

This section details the constituencies within each district of Bihar, which play a crucial role in the state's political landscape:

Patna	Mocama, Barh, Bakhtiyarpur, Digha, Bankipur, Kumharar, Patna Sahib, Fatuha, Danapur, Maner, Phulwari, Masoudhi, Paliganj, Vikram
Nalanda	Bihar Sharif, Rajgir, Islamapur-Nalanda, Harnaut, Nalanda, Asthwan, Hilsa
Rohtas	Karakat, Nokha, Dinara, Kargahar, Chenari, Dehri, Sasaram
Kaimur	Ramgarh-Kaimur, Chainpur, Bhabhua, Mohaniya

Bhojpur	Ara, Jagdishpur, Barahra, Tarari, Sandesh, Agiawan, Shahpur
Buxar	Buxar, Brahmpur, Rajpur, Dumraon
Gaya	Gaya Sadar, Velaganj, Atari, Tekari, Sherghati, Gushra, Bodhgaya, Imamganj, Vijerganj, Barachatti
Jehanabad	Jehanabad, Makhdumpur, Ghosi
Nawada	Nawada, Warisliganj, Kashichak, Pakri Barawan, Kauakol, Hisua, Narhat, Meskaun, Siradla, Rajouli, Akbarpur, Govindpur, Roh, Nardiganj
Aurangabad	Aurangabad, Nabiganj, Rafiganj, Kutumba, Obra, Goh
Arwal	Arwal, Kurtha
Munger	Munger, Jamalpur, Tarapur
Lakhisarai	Lakhisarai, Surygarh
Sheikhpura	Sheikhpura, Barabigha
Jamui	Jhajha, Jamui, Sikandra, and Chakai
Khagaria	Khagaria, Alouli, Parbatta, Beldour
Begusarai	Cheria-Beriarpur, Bachwara, Teghra, Matihani, Sahebpur Kamal, Begusarai, Bakhri
Muzaffarpur	Muzaffarpur, Sahebganj, Aurai, Kanti, Bochaha, Meenapur, Gaighat, Paru, Sakra, Baruraj, Kudhani
Vaishali	Hajipur, Mahua, Lalganj, Vaishali, Mahnar, Rajapakar, Radhopur, Patepur
Sitamarhi	Sitamarhi, Parihar, Righa, Runnisse Darpur, Belsand, Bathnaha, Bajpatti, Surasand

East Champaran	Motihari, Dhaka, Pipra, Govindganj, Raxaul, Harsidhi, Sugouli, Chiraiya, Narkatiya, Keshariya, Madhuban, Kalyanpur
West Champaran	Narkatiyaganj, Bettiah, Ramnagar, Lauriya, Bagaha, Chanpatiya, Sikta, Nautan, Valmikinagar
Sheohar	Sheohar
Saran	Para, Ekma, Manjhi, Baniyapur, Marhura, Sonpur, Taraiya, Gadhka, Parsa, Amanour
Siwan	Siwan, Barharia, Goriakothi, Jeeradei, Raghunathpur, Daroundha, Maharajganj, Darouli
Gopalganj	Gopalganj, Kuchai Kot, Hathua, Barouli, Bhor, Baikunthpur
Darbhanga	Darbhanga, Shari, Darbhanga Gramin, Kevati, Alinagar, Jale, Kuseshwar Sthan, Hayaghat, Gora Bauram, Benipur, Bahadrapur
Madhubani	Madhubani, Khajouli, Bisfi, Jhanjharpur, Harlakhi, Benipatti, Rajnagar, Babubarhi, Laukha, Phulparas
Samastipur	Samastipur, Rosda, Kalyanpur, Morwa, Sarairanjan, Ujiarpur, Vibhutipur, Warisnagar, Mohiuddin Nagar, Hasanpur
Saharsa	Saharsa, Mahishi, Sonbarsa, Simri-Bakhtiarpur
Supaul	Nirmali, Triveniganj, Supaul, Chhatapur, Pipra
Madhubani	Alamnagar, Bihari Ganj, Sindheswar, Madhubani
Purnia	Purnia, Roupouli, Dhamdaha, Banmankhi, Kaswa, Amour, Baisi

Araria	Narpatganj, Raniganj, Farbisganj, Araria, Jokihat, and Sikti
Kishanganj	Kishanganj, Bahadurganj, Thakurganj, Konchadhaman
Katihar	Katihar, Kadwa, Balrampur, Pranpur, Manihari, Barari, Korha
Bhagalpur	Nathnagar, Sultan Ganj, Kahalgaon, Pirpanti, Bihpur, Bhagalpur, Gopalpur
Banka	Banka, Katoria, Belhar, Amarpur, Dhoraiya

Sex Ratio in Bihar
(According to Census 2011)

District	Sex Ratio
Patna	897
Nalanda	922
Rohtas	918
Kaimur	920
Bhojpur	907
Buxar	922
Gaya	960
Jehanabad	922
Nawada	939
Aurangabad	926
Arwal	928
Munger	876
Lakhisarai	902
Sheikhpura	930
Jamui	922
Khagaria	886
Begusarai	895
Muzaffarpur	900
Vaishali	895
Sitamarhi	899
East Champaran	902
West Champaran	909
Sheohar	893
Saran	964
Siwan	988
Gopalganj	1021
Darbhanga	911
Madhubani	926
Samastipur	911
Saharsa	906
Supaul	929
Madhubani	911
Purnia	921
Araria	921
Kishanganj	950
Katihar	919
Bhagalpur	880
Banka	907

Bihar: A Snapshot
(According to Population Census 2011)

Scheduled Tribe Population Growth (2001-2011)	76.2%
Percentage of Children Aged 0-4 Years	12.3%
Percentage of Children Aged 5-9 Years	14.4%
Percentage of Children Aged 10-14 Years	13.4%
Percentage of Adolescents Aged 10-19 Years	22.5%
Percentage of Youth Aged 15-24 Years	16.8%
Percentage of Adults Aged 18 or More	54.0%
Percentage of Working-Age People (15-59 years)	52.1%
Percentage of People Aged 60 or More (Elderly)	7.4%
Child Dependency Ratio (YDR)	769

Number of Workers (in Million)	34.7
Work Participation Rate (WPT)	33.4%
Male Work Participation Rate (WPR)	46.5%
Percentage of Agricultural Workers	52.8%
Percentage of Agricultural Laborers	73.5%
Percentage of Other Workers	22.4%
Percentage of Families with Female Heads	7.4%
Percentage of Population in Slums	1.9%
Work Participation Rate in Slums	29.0%
Literacy Rate in Slums	68.2%
Number of Cities with a Population of 1 Lakh or More	26
Total Literacy Rate (Population Aged 7 and Above)	52,504,553 (61.8%)
Literacy Rate of Rural Population Aged 7 and Above	44,812,152 (59.8%)
Literacy Rate of Urban Population Aged 7 and Above	7,692,401 (76.9%)
Male Literacy Rate of Population Aged 7 and Above	31,608,023 (71.2%)
Rural Male Literacy Rate	27,241,830 (69.7%)
Urban Male Literacy Rate	4,366,193 (82.6%)
Female Literacy Rate of Population Aged 7 and Above	20,896,530 (51.5%)
Rural Female Literacy Rate	17,570,322 (49.0%)
Urban Female Literacy Rate	3,326,208 (70.5%)

Population Statistics of Bihar (1901-2011)

Year	Population (in Crores)	Growth Period	10-Year Growth Rate (%)
1901	2.73	...	...
1911	2.83	1901-11	+3.69%
1921	2.81	1911-21	(-)0.66%
1931	3.13	1921-31	+11.45%
1941	3.52	1931-41	+12.20%
1951	3.88	1941-51	+10.27%
1961	4.65	1951-61	+19.78%
1971	5.63	1961-71	+21.07%
1981	6.99	1971-81	+24.11%
1991	8.63	1981-91	+23.49%
2001	8.29	1991-2001	+28.62%
2011	10.41	2001-2011	+25.42%

Major Languages in Bihar - District-wise

District	Major Languages
Patna	Magahi, Bhojpuri, Maithili, Hindi, and Urdu
Nalanda	Hindi, Magahi
Rohtas	Bhojpuri, Hindi
Kaimur	Hindi, Bhojpuri
Bhojpur	Bhojpuri, Hindi, Urdu, Magahi
Buxar	Bhojpuri, Hindi
Gaya	Magahi, Hindi
Jehanabad	Magahi, Hindi
Nawada	Magahi, Hindi, Urdu
Aurangabad	Magahi, Hindi
Arwal	Magahi, Hindi
Munger	Angika, Hindi
Lakhisarai	Angika, Maithili, Hindi
Sheikhpura	Hindi, Urdu, Magahi
Jamui	Angika, Hindi
Khagaria	Angika, Maithili, Hindi, Urdu
Begusarai	Angika, Hindi
Muzaffarpur	Vajjika, Hindi
Vaishali	Urdu, Hindi, Vajjika

Sitamarhi	Hindi, Maithili, Vajjika
East Champaran	Bhojpuri, Hindi
West Champaran	Bhojpuri, Hindi
Sheohar	Hindi, Urdu, Maithili
Saran	Bhojpuri, Hindi, Urdu
Siwan	Bhojpuri, Urdu, Hindi
Gopalganj	Hindi, Bhojpuri, Urdu
Darbhanga	Maithili, Hindi, Urdu
Madhubani	Maithili, Hindi
Samastipur	Hindi, Maithili
Saharsa	Hindi, Maithili, Angika, Urdu, Bengali
Supaul	Hindi, Maithili
Madhubani	Hindi, Maithili
Purnia	Maithili, Bengali, Santhali, Hindi
Araria	Hindi, Maithili, Urdu
Kishanganj	Hindi, Urdu, Bengali, Maithili
Katihar	Angika, Maithili, Hindi, Marwari, Bengali, Urdu
Bhagalpur	Hindi, Maithili, Angika, Urdu
Banka	Angika, Hindi

Latitude Extension of Districts of Bihar

District	Latitude Extension
Patna	25°12' to 25°44' North
Nalanda	24° to 25°27' North
Rohtas	24°30' to 25°20' North
Kaimur	25°02' North
Bhojpur	25°10' to 25°40' North
Buxar	25°33' North
Gaya	24°05' to 24°10' North
Jehanabad	25°00' to 25°15' North
Nawada	25°31' to 25°08' North
Aurangabad	24°19' to 26°10' North
Arwal	25°00' to 25°15' North
Munger	25°45' to 25°15' North
Lakhisarai	25°00' to 25°20' North
Sheikhpura	24°45' to 25°00' North
Jamui	24°55' North
Khagaria	25°15' to 25°44' North
Begusarai	25°15' to 25°45' North
Muzaffarpur	25°54' to 26°23' North
Vaishali	25°00' to 25°30' North
Sitamarhi	25°36' to 26°06' North
East Champaran	26°16' to 27°01' North
West Champaran	26°16' to 27°31' North
Sheohar	26°24' to 26°18' North
Saran	25°36' to 26°13' North
Siwan	25°53' to 26°23' North
Gopalganj	26°12' to 26°39' North
Darbhanga	25°53' to 26°27' North
Madhubani	25°59' to 26°39' North
Samastipur	25°51'39" North
Saharsa	25°53' to 25°88" North
Supaul	25°37' to 26°00' North
Madhepura	25°31' to 26°20' North
Purnia	25°13'-80" to 27°07'-59" North
Araria	25°46' North
Kishanganj	25°20' to 26°30' North
Katihar	25°42' to 26°22' North
Bhagalpur	25°07' to 25°30' North
Banka	22°30' to 25°09' North

Longitude Extension of Districts of Bihar

District	Longitude Extension
Patna	84°42' to 84° East
Nalanda	85°18' to 85°65' East
Rohtas	83°14' to 83°20' East
Kaimur	83°33' East
Bhojpur	83°45' to 84°45' East
Buxar	83°58' East

Gaya	84°04' to 84°05' East
Jehanabad	84°31' to 85°15' East
Nawada	84°00' to 86°30' East
Aurangabad	84°00' to 84°55' East
Arwal	84.7° to 85°15' East
Munger	85°45' to 86°45' East
Lakhisarai	85°55' to 86°25' East
Sheikhpura	85°45' to 86°45' East
Jamui	86°13' East
Khagaria	85°17' to 86°52' East
Begusarai	86°45' to 86°36' East
Muzaffarpur	84°53' to 85°45' East
Vaishali	84°00' to 85°00' East
Sitamarhi	85°29' to 85°48' East
East Champaran	84°30' to 85°16' East
West Champaran	83°50' to 85°18' East
Sheohar	85°21' to 85°30' East
Saran	84°24' to 85°15' East
Siwan	84°01' to 85°47' East
Gopalganj	83°54' to 84°55' East
Darbhanga	85°45' to 86°25' East
Madhubani	85°43' to 86°42' East
Samastipur	85°46'45" East
Saharsa	86°06' to 86°36' East
Supaul	86°22' to 87°10' East
Madhepura	86°36' to 87°07' East
Purnia	86°59'-06" to 87°52'-35" East
Araria	87°28' East
Kishanganj	87°07' to 88°19' East
Katihar	87°10' to 88°05' East
Bhagalpur	86°37' to 87°30' East
Banka	84°30' to 87°12' East

Average Annual Rainfall in Bihar's Districts

District	Average Rainfall
Patna	1052.6 mm
Nalanda	858.11 mm
Rohtas	952 mm
Kaimur	777 mm
Bhojpur	1166.2 mm
Buxar	774.82 mm
Gaya	1242 mm
Jehanabad	1074.5 mm
Nawada	1037 mm
Aurangabad	1231 mm
Arwal	817 mm
Munger	1273.2 mm
Lakhisarai	858 mm
Sheikhpura	1200 mm
Jamui	1102 mm
Khagaria	1056 mm
Begusarai	1384 mm
Muzaffarpur	118.7 mm
Vaishali	1168 mm
Sitamarhi	1200 mm
East Champaran	1242 mm
West Champaran	1422 mm
Sheohar	956 mm
Saran	818.87 mm
Siwan	1200 mm
Gopalganj	290 mm
Darbhanga	1143 mm
Madhubani	273.2 mm
Samastipur	926.36 mm
Saharsa	948.48 mm
Supaul	1084 mm
Madhepura	1300 mm
Purnia	1470 mm
Araria	1195 mm
Kishanganj	2250 mm
Katihar	1032 mm
Bhagalpur	1166.2 mm
Banka	1200 mm

This provides the latitude and longitude ranges of each district in Bihar, along with there average annual rainfall.

Elevation of Districts in Bihar from Sea Level

District	Elevation from Sea Level
Patna	53 meters
Nalanda	67 meters
Rohtas	107.78 meters
Kaimur	76 meters
Bhojpur	193 meters
Buxar	55 meters
Gaya	111 meters
Jehanabad	113 meters
Nawada	80 meters
Aurangabad	30 to 65 meters
Arwal	67.9 meters
Munger	52 meters
Lakhisarai	53 meters
Sheikhpura	47 to 69 meters
Jamui	1000 meters
Khagaria	36 meters
Begusarai	41 meters
Muzaffarpur	170 meters
Vaishali	52 meters
Sitamarhi	56 meters
East Champaran	113 meters
West Champaran	113 meters
Sheohar	80 meters
Saran	36 meters
Siwan	77 meters
Gopalganj	65 meters
Darbhanga	52 meters
Madhubani	80 meters
Samastipur	35 meters
Saharsa	1661.30 meters
Supaul	34 meters
Madhepura	43 meters
Purnia	171 meters
Araria	47 meters
Kishanganj	173 meters
Katihar	31 meters
Bhagalpur	43 meters
Banka	79 meters

Scheduled Castes in Bihar - Districtwise

No.	District	Population	Percentage
1	West Champaran	553,944	14.2%
2	East Champaran	649,726	12.7%
3	Sheohar	96,655	14.7%
4	Sitamarhi	405,714	11.9%
5	Madhubani	587,158	13.1%
6	Supaul	354,249	15.9%
7	Araria	382,654	13.6%
8	Kishanganj	113,118	6.7%
9	Purnia	390,991	12.0%
10	Katihar	263,100	8.6%
11	Madhepura	346,275	17.3%
12	Saharsa	317,249	16.7%
13	Darbhanga	615,688	15.6%
14	Muzaffarpur	751,975	15.7%
15	Gopalganj	320,064	12.5%
16	Siwan	386,685	11.6%
17	Saran	474,066	12.0%
18	Vaishali	738,031	21.1%
19	Samastipur	803,128	18.9%
20	Begusarai	432,270	14.6%
21	Khagaria	247,161	14.8%
22	Bhagalpur	318,569	10.5%
23	Banka	247,858	12.2%
24	Munger	183,849	13.4%
25	Lakhisarai	153,209	15.3%
26	Sheikhpura	131,115	20.6%
27	Nalanda	607,672	21.1%

28	Patna	920,918	15.8%
29	Bhojpur	425,402	15.6%
30	Buxar	251,737	14.8%
31	Kaimur (Bhabhua)	369,088	22.7%
32	Rohtas	549,546	18.6%
33	Aurangabad	612,064	24.1%
34	Gaya	1,334,351	30.4%
35	Nawada	565,112	25.5%
36	Jamui	302,649	17.2%
37	Jehanabad	222,974	19.8%
38	Arwal	141,314	20.2%
Total	**All Districts**	**16,567,325**	**15.9%**

Scheduled Tribes in Bihar - Districtwise

No.	District	Population	Percentage
1	West Champaran	250,046	6.4%
2	East Champaran	12,461	0.2%
3	Sheohar	318	NI
4	Sitamarhi	2,989	0.1%
5	Madhubani	3,990	0.1%
6	Supaul	10,168	0.5%
7	Araria	38,848	1.4%
8	Kishanganj	64,224	3.8%
9	Purnia	139,490	4.3%
10	Katihar	179,971	5.9%
11	Madhepura	12,532	0.6%
12	Saharsa	6,009	0.3%
13	Darbhanga	2,772	0.1%
14	Muzaffarpur	5,979	0.1%
15	Gopalganj	60,807	2.4%
16	Siwan	87,000	2.6%
17	Saran	36,786	0.9%
18	Vaishali	2,274	0.1%
19	Samastipur	1,884	NI
20	Begusarai	1,597	NI
21	Khagaria	675	NI
22	Bhagalpur	67,180	2.2%
23	Banka	90,432	4.4%
24	Munger	21,404	1.6%
25	Lakhisarai	8,333	0.8%
26	Sheikhpura	617	0.1%
27	Nalanda	1,442	0.1%
28	Patna	9,069	0.2%
29	Bhojpur	13,977	0.5%
30	Buxar	26,824	1.6%
31	Kaimur (Bhabhua)	57,981	3.6%
32	Rohtas	31,650	1.1%
33	Aurangabad	1,033	NI
34	Gaya	3,098	0.1%
35	Nawada	2,045	0.1%
36	Jamui	78,793	4.5%
37	Jehanabad	1,285	0.1%
38	Arwal	590	0.1%

Major Museums in Bihar

Archaeological Museum in Bodh Gaya – Established in 1956

Archaeological Museum in Vaishali – Established in 1945

Shri Krishna Science Center in Patna – Established in 1981

Jalan Museum in Patna – Established in 1954

Gandhi Museum in Patna – Established in 1967

Rajendra Memorial Museum in Patna – Established in 1963

Districts Affected by Groundwater Quality in Bihar

Contaminant	Affected Districts
Arsenic (μg/l)	Begusarai, Bhagalpur, Bhojpur, Buxar, Darbhanga, Katihar, Khagaria, Lakhisarai, Munger, Samastipur, Saran, Sitamarhi, Patna, and Vaishali (14 districts)

Fluoride (μg/l)	Aurangabad, Banka, Bhagalpur, Gaya, Jamui, Kaimur, Munger, Nalanda, Rohtas, Sheikhpura, and Nawada (11 districts)
Iron (μg/l)	Araria, Begusarai, Bhagalpur, Katihar, Khagaria, Kishanganj, Madhepura, Munger, Purnia, Saharsa, and Supaul (11 districts)

Source: Public Health Engineering Department, Bihar Government

Bihar Hydroelectric Projects

New Projects:

1. Nabinagar Phase-1 Plant
2. Buxar Electric Project
3. Ultra-Mega Electric Project (Banka)

Small Hydroelectric Projects (Installed Capacity)

Main Hydroelectric Projects	Status	Capacity
Koshi Hydroelectric Center (KHPS), Katia, Birpur	Transferred to Bihar State Hydroelectric Corporation in Nov 2003, Renovation completed	4.8 MW (4 units)
Eastern Gandak Canal Hydroelectric Project	Started in 1996-97, located in West Champaran	5 MW (3 units)
Son Western Link Canal Hydroelectric Project	Started in 1991-92, located in Dehri-on-Son, Rohtas	1.65 MW (4 units)
Son Eastern Link Canal Hydroelectric Project	Started in 1996-97, located in Barun, Aurangabad	1.65 MW (2 units)
Agnur Hydroelectric Project	Started in 2004-05, located in Arwal	0.5 MW (2 units)
Dhelabag Hydroelectric Project	Started in 2006-07, located in Rohtas	0.5 MW (2 units)
Triveni Link Canal Hydroelectric Project	Started in 2007-08, located in West Champaran	1.5 MW (2 units)
Nasriganj Hydroelectric Project	Started in 2007-08, located in Rohtas	0.5 MW (2 units)
Sebari Hydroelectric Project	Started in 2008-09, located in Rohtas	0.5 MW (2 units)
Jaynagara Hydroelectric Project	Started in 2007-08, located in Rohtas	0.5 MW (2 units)
Sirkhanda Hydroelectric Project	Started in 2009-10, located in Rohtas	0.35 MW (2 units)
Belsar Hydroelectric Project	Started in 2011-12, located in Arwal	0.5 MW (2 units)
Arwal Hydroelectric Project	Started in 2011-12, located in Arwal	0.5 MW (2 units)

Famous Festivals of Bihar

Festival	Location
Valmiki Mahotsav	Bettiah, West Champaran
Nandangarh Mahotsav	Bettiah, West Champaran
Kesariya Mahotsav	Motihari, East Champaran
Vidyapati Mahotsav	Vidyapati Nagar, Samastipur
Dashrath Manjhi Lok Utsav	Gaya

Veer Kunwar Singh Vijayotsav	Ara
Ang Mahotsav	Munger
Harihar Kshetra Mahotsav	Sonpur
Vishwamitra Mahotsav	Buxar
Brahmapur Mahotsav	Buxar
Ambe Utsav	Aurangabad
Jayaprakash Narayan Mahotsav	Sitab Diara, Saran
Dinkar Sahitya Utsav	Simriya, Begusarai
Kinnar Mahotsav	Patna
Mahanar Mahotsav	Vaishali
Jaymangla Garh Mahotsav	Begusarai
Ustad Bismillah Khan Mahotsav	Dumraon
Pawapuri Mahotsav	Nalanda
Holika, Dinabhadri, Purania Mahotsav	Purnia
Manjusha Mahotsav	Bhagalpur
Vachaspati Mahotsav	Madhubani
Sita Kund Mahotsav	Sita Dham, East Champaran
Gajna Mahotsav	Navinagar, Aurangabad

Operations/Campaigns in Bihar

Sl. No.	Operation/Campaign	Objective
1	Operation Siddharth	Initiated to tackle left-wing extremism. Involves providing infrastructure like schools, hospitals, and roads in Naxal-affected areas.
2	Operation Ujala	Aimed at bringing about significant changes in the lives of women involved in prostitution in Muzaffarpur's infamous red-light area.
3	Operation Cobra	Focused on eradicating mafia gangs operating in Bihar.
4	Operation Chanakya	Aimed at preventing adulteration of daily consumables in the market.
5	Operation Todarmal	Focused on land reforms and distribution of land to the landless.
6	Operation Panther	Aimed at eliminating the dacoit problem in Western Champaran.
7	Operation Dashak	Focused on improving the socio-economic status of weaker sections and ensuring social justice.
8	Operation Dhanwantri	Aimed at controlling illegal and counterfeit drugs.
9	Operation Chara	Focused on investigating and apprehending those involved in the fodder scam.
10	Operation Jaguar	Aimed at eliminating criminals operating in the Diyara region of the Anga and Koshi areas.
11	Operation Mudgal	Focused on stopping stone smuggling from forests.
12	Operation Combing	Focused on capturing the culprits of the infamous Dhamariya massacre.

Firsts in Bihar

- First Chief Minister of Bihar: **Sri Krishna Singh** (1946-1961)
- First Hindi Newspaper in Bihar: **Bihar Bandhu** (1872)
- First English Newspaper in Bihar: **The Bihar Herald** (1875)
- First English Daily in Bihar: **Searchlight**
- First Hindi Daily in Bihar: **Sarvahitshi**
- First TV Station in Bihar: **Muzaffarpur** (1978)
- First Medical College in Bihar: **Patna Medical College** (1925)
- First University in Bihar: **Nalanda University** (5th century)

- First Modern University in Bihar: **Patna University** (1917)
- First Open University in Bihar: **Nalanda Open University**
- First Independent Chief Minister of Bihar: **Mahamaya Prasad Singh** (1967-1968)
- First Speaker of Bihar Legislative Council: **Rajiv Ranjan Prasad Singh**
- First Chairperson of Bihar Women's Commission: **Manju Prakash**
- First Speaker of Lok Sabha from Bihar: **Baliram Bhagat**
- First Deputy Prime Minister of India from Bihar: **Jagjivan Ram**
- First Chief Justice of the Supreme Court from Bihar: **Bhupeshwar Prasad Sinha**
- First Winner of the Jnanpith Award from Bihar: **Ramdhari Singh Dinkar**
- First Deputy Commander-in-Chief from Bihar: **Lt. General S.K. Sinha**
- First Hindi Film in Bihar: **Kal Hamara Hai**
- First Bhojpuri Film in Bihar: **Ganga Maiya Tohe Piyari Chadhaibo**
- First Maithili Film in Bihar: **Kanyadan**
- First Magahi Film in Bihar: **Bhaiya** (1961)
- First Bank in Bihar: **Allahabad Bank**
- First Oil Refinery in Bihar: **Barauni Oil Refinery**
- First Sugar Mill in Bihar: **Madhoura** (1904)
- First Municipality in Bihar: **Ara** (1865)
- First Stadium in Bihar: **Moinul Haque Stadium** (Patna)
- First Dance Hall in Bihar: **Indian Dance Arts Center** (Patna)
- First Bio-Village in Bihar: **Kothia** (Samastipur, 2006)
- First E-Service Center in Bihar: **Vasudha** (Danapur, 29 August 2008)
- First Hindi Printing Press in Bihar: **Bihar Bandhu Press** (1874)
- First Person from Bihar to Receive Ashok Chakra: **Randhir Verma**
- First English Visitor to Bihar: **Ralph Fitch**
- First Muslim Invader to Bihar: **Bakhtiyar Khilji**
- First Science Center in Bihar: **Patna Science Center**

Largest in Bihar

- The largest airport of Bihar is **Jayaprakash Narayan Airport** of Patna.
- The largest rail bridge of Bihar is **Loknayak Jayaprakash Setu**.
- The largest road bridge of Bihar is **Mahatma Gandhi Setu**.
- The largest railway junction of Bihar is **Patna Junction**.
- The largest pilgrimage place of Bihar is **Bodh Gaya**.
- The largest city of Bihar is **Patna**.
- The largest platform of Bihar is **Sonpur Platform**.
- The largest fair of Bihar is **Sonpur Fair**.
- The largest university of Bihar is **Magadh University**.
- The largest planetarium of Bihar is **Indira Gandhi Planetarium** (Patna).
- The largest river of **Bihar is Ganga**.
- The largest tributary of **Bihar is Kosi**.
- The largest river valley project of Bihar is **Gandak Project**.
- The largest bank of Bihar is **State Bank of India**.

Birth Place of Important Persons

- **Vidyapati:** Bisfi (Madhubani)
- **Rajendra Prasad :** Jiradei (Siwan)
- **Jaiprakash Narayan :** Sitabdiara (Chhapra)
- **Kunwar Singh :** Jagdishpur (Bhojpur)
- **Mandan Mishra :** Mahisi (Saharsa)
- **Shri Krishna Singh :** Barbigha (Munger)
- **Shiv Pujan Sahay :** Unnavas (Bhojpur)
- **Jagjivan Ram :** Chandwa (Bhojpur)
- **Janaki Vallabh Shastri :** Maigra (Gaya)

- **Ramdhari Singh Dinkar :** Simaria (Begusarai)
- **Raja Radhika Raman Prasad Singh :** Suryapura (Rohtas)
- **Hans Kumar Tiwari :** Bhagalpur
- **Mohanlal Mahto 'Viyogi' :** Gaya
- **Anugrah Narayan Singh :** Poiawan (Aurangabad)
- **Phanishwar Nath 'Renu' :** Aurahi - Hingna (Araria)
- **Nagarjun :** Tarauni (Darbhanga)
- **Pt. Ramchatur Mallick :** Amta (Darbhanga)
- **Shatrughan Sinha :** Patna
- **Bhikhari Thakur :** Qutubpur (Saran)
- **Ishwari Prasad :** Lodikatra (Patna)
- **Ashvaghosha :** Pataliputra (Patna)
- **Nandlal Basu :** Kharagpur (Munger)
- **Gopal Singh 'Nepali' :** Bettiah (P. Champaran)
- **Ramvriksha Benipuri :** Benipur (Muzaffarpur)
- **Devaki Nandan Khatri :** Pusa (Muzaffarpur)
- **Vachaspati Mishra :** Thadhi (Madhubani)
- **Guru Gobind Singh :** Patna City
- **Majrul Haq :** Bahpura (Patna)
- **Sachchidanand Sinha :** Ara (Bhojpur)
- **Ali Imam :** Neura (Patna)
- **Baikunth Shukla :** Jalalpur (Vaishali)
- **Yogendra Shukla :** Lalganj (Vaishali)
- **Abdul Bari :** Koilwar (Bhojpur)
- **Ganesh Dutt Singh :** Chhatiyana (Nalanda)
- **Jaglal Chaudhary :** Garkha (Saran)
- **Karpoori Thakur :** Pithaunjhia (Samastipur)
- **Lalu Prasad Yadav :** Chhoti Phulwaria (Gopalganj)
- **Nitish Kumar :** Kalyanpur (Bakhtiarpur, Patna)
- **RC Prasad Singh :** Rosera (Samastipur)
- **Bidhan Chandra Rai :** Bankipur (Patna)
- **Collector Singh Kesari :** Ara
- **Anuplal Mandal:** Purnia
- **Sahajanand Saraswati :** Bihta (Patna)
- **Chunchun Pandey :** Bhagalpur

Water Management in Bihar

- **Flood-Prone Areas:** 28 districts in Bihar are affected by floods, mainly in the upper Ganges plains.
- **Drought-Prone Areas:** Some areas like Aurangabad, Gaya, and Nawada face droughts once every two years.
- **Agricultural Potential:** With proper water management, Bihar could become one of the most productive agricultural regions globally.
- **Water Resources:** About 85% of the population is engaged in agriculture.
- **Irrigation Facilities:** By 2019, 71.03 lakh hectares (approximately 62%) of land had irrigation facilities.
- **Important Projects:** The Son River dam helps irrigate southern Ganges plains.

❑

Appendices

APPENDIX I

Historical

Sixteen Mahajanapadas of the 6th Century BCE

Mahajanapada	Main Ruler	Capital	Present Location
Anga	Brahmadatta	Champa	Bhagalpur, Munger (Bihar)
Kashi	Ajatashatru	Varanasi (UP)	Allahabad (Merged into Magadh)
Kosala	Prasenjit	Shravasti/Saketa	Awadh (UP)
Vatsa	Udayana	Kaushambi (UP)	Allahabad
Chedi	Shishupala (Mahabharata period)	Sothivati	Bundelkhand (UP), Southern Rajasthan
Magadha	Bimbisar, Ajatashatru	Girivraja/Rajagriha	Patna, Gaya, Shahabad (Bihar)
Vajji	-	Vaishali	Vaishali and Northern Bihar
Avanti	Chandra Pradyota	Northern Avanti-Ujjain, Southern Avanti-Mahishmati	Southern Madhya Pradesh
Malla	-	Pava/Kushinara	Deoria (UP)
Panchala	-	Ahicchatra, Kampilya	Bareilly, Badaun, Farrukhabad (UP), Rohilkhand
Surasena	-	Mathura	Brajmandal Region (UP)
Kuru	-	Hastinapur/ Indraprastha	Delhi, Meerut, Haryana
Matsya	Founder-Virata	Viratnagar	Jaipur (Rajasthan), Bharatpur
Asmaka	-	Potali/Potan	Narmada-Godavari River Region (South India)
Gandhara	Pushkarasarin	Taxila	Kashmir and UP (Pakistan), (Educational Center)
Kamboja	-	Poonch	Rajouri and Hazara Region (Pakistan)

Facts Related to Lord Buddha

Mahamaya	Mother of Gautama Buddha
Rahul	Son of Gautama Buddha
Chandaka	Charioteer of Buddha
Cunda	The son of the village goldsmith whose food led to Buddha's death
Kanthaka	Buddha's favorite horse
Sujata	The village woman who offered milk-rice to Buddha
Mahaprajapati Gautami	Buddha's aunt, first female Buddhist nun
Alara Kalama and Uddaka Ramaputta	Buddha's teacher of Yoga and Upanishadic philosophy
Subhadda	The last person to receive Buddha's final teaching
Devadatta	Buddha's cousin
Ashvattha (Tree at Bodhgaya)	The pipal tree under which Buddha attained enlightenment
Stupa	Symbol of Buddha's Mahaparinirvana
Vaishali	Place where Buddha spent his last monsoon
Sal Tree	The tree under which Buddha died
Suddhodana	Father of Buddha and head of the Shakya clan
Yashodhara	Buddha's wife

Major Buddhist Texts

Buddhist Text	Author	Description
Jatak Tales	-	Collection of 549 stories about Buddha's past lives.
Milindapanho	Nagasena	The text records a series of discussions on Buddhist doctrine and is in Pali language.
Visuddhimagga	Acharya Buddhaghosa	Philosophical summary of Buddhist doctrine.
Nidana Katha	Acharya Buddhaghosa	The only biography of Buddha in Pali language.
Atthakathas	Various authors namely, Acharya Buddhaghosa Dhammapala, Mahanama, Upasena and Buddhadatta	Commentary on the Tripitaka.
Abhidharma Kosha	Vasubandhu	Provides information about time calculation and year calculation.
Samdhinirmochana Sutra	-	Related to Mahayana Buddhism, describes Buddha as Amitabha, the one sitting in heaven.
Prajnaparimata Sutras	Nagarjuna	Discusses the theory of Emptiness.
Lalitavistara		It is a Mahayana Buddhist Sutra
Mahavibhasa	Vasumitra	It is a Buddhist philosophy encylopaedia
Saundarananda	Ashvagosa	Describes the conversion of Buddha's half-brother, Saundarananda, to Buddhism.

Buddha Charita	Ashvagosa	The epic of Buddha's life.
Dipavamsa	-	History of Sri Lanka.
Mahavamsa	Mahānāma	Details the reign of King Ashoka as Viceroy of Ujjain and the Third Buddhist Council conducted by him.
Divyavadana	-	Nepali literature, consisting of two parts: Ashokavadana and Kunalavadana.

Jain Tirthankaras and Their Symbols

Rishabhanatha	Bull
Ajitanatha	Elephant
Sambhavanatha	Horse
Abhinandanatha	Monkey
Sumatinatha	Heron
Padmaprabha	Red Lotus
Suparshvanatha	Swastika
Chandraprabha	Moon
Pushpadanta	Crocodile
Shitalnatha	Shrivatsa
Shreyanasanatha	Rhinoceros
Vasupujya	Buffalo
Vimalanatha	Boar
Anantanatha	Falcon
Dharmnatha	Vajra Danda
Shantinatha	Horned Deer
Kunthunatha	Goat
Arahanatha	Fish
Mallinatha	Kalasha
Munisuvrata	Tortoise
Naminatha	Blue Lotus
Arishtanemi (related to Krishna)	Conch
Parshvanatha	Snake
Mahavir Swami	Lion

Mauryan Inscriptions

Inscriptions	Discovery Year	Script
Shahbazgarhi	1836	Kharoshthi
Mansehra	1889	Kharoshthi
Girnar	1822	Brahmi
Dhauli	1837	Brahmi
Kalsi	1837	Brahmi
Jogadh	1850	Brahmi
Sopara	1882	Brahmi
Erragudi	1916	Brahmi

Ashoka's Inscriptions and Their Locations

Shahbazgarhi	Peshawar (Pakistan)
Mansehra	Hazara (Pakistan)
Kalpi	Dehradun (Uttarakhand)
Girnar	Junagadh (Gujarat)
Dhauli	Puri (Odisha)
Jogadh	Ganjam (Odisha)
Sopara	Thane (Maharashtra)
Erragudi	Kurnool (Andhra Pradesh)
Maski	Raichur (Karnataka)
Gurjara	Datiya (Madhya Pradesh)
Brahmagiri	Mysore (Karnataka)
Bhabru	Bairat (Rajasthan)
Ahorora	Mirzapur (Uttar Pradesh)
Jatinga Rameshwara	Karnataka
Sasaram	Bihar
Rajula Mandagiri	Kurnool (Andhra Pradesh)
Govimath	Mysore (Karnataka)
Saro-Bharo	Madhya Pradesh
Nittur	Karnataka
Udegolam	Bellary (Karnataka)
Sannati	Karnataka

Mauryan Administrative Divisions

Position	Department
Purohita	Prime Minister and Chief Religious Officer
Samaharta	Chief Revenue Collector
Sannidhata	Chief Treasurer
Pradeshta	Provincial Governors or District Magistrates
Nayaka	Military Leader
Karmantika	Chief Inspector of Industries
Vyavaharika	Chief Judge of Civil Court
Danpal	Police Officer or person responsible for enforcing the law
Atavika	Head of Forest Department
Antapala	Protector of Border Forts
Dauvarika	In-charge of Palace Maintenance
Antarvedi	A group of officials, advisors who were part of the king's inner circle
Nagarka	Head of the City or City Watchman (Police Chief)
Durga-Pala	Chief of the State Fort Defenders
Yuvraj	Heir to the King
Senapati	Minister of the War Department
Mantri Parishad Adhyaksha	President of the Council of Ministers

Subedars of Bihar during the Reign of Jahangir

Year	Subedars of Bihar
1605	Baz Bahadur (Lal Beg)
1607	Islam Khan
1608	Afzal Khan (Abdurrahim)
1613	Zafar Khan
1615	Ibrahim Khan Kakar
1617	Kuli Khan II
1618	Mukarrab Khan
1621	Shahzada Parvez
1622	Khan-e-Durran (Bairam Beg)
1626	Mirza Rustam Safabi
1627	Khan-e-Alam
1628	Saif Khan

Important Centers of the 1857 Revolt

Center	Revolt Date	Indian Leaders	Suppression Date	British Leaders
Delhi	11–12 May, 1857	Bahadur Shah Zafar, General Bakht Khan (Military Leadership)	21 Sep, 1857	Nicholson and Hudson
Kanpur	5 June, 1857	Nana Sahib, Tantiya Tope (Military Leadership)	6 Sep, 1857	Campbell
Lucknow	4 June, 1857	Begum Hazrat Mahal, Birjis Qadir	March, 1858	Campbell
Jhansi	June, 1857	Rani Lakshmi Bai	March, 1858	General Havelock
Allahabad	1857	Liaqat Ali	1858	Colonel Neil
Jagdishpur	August, 1857	Kunwar Singh, Amar Singh	1858	William Taylor & Vincent Ayr
Bareilly	1857	Khan Bahadur Khan	1858	Colonel Neil
Faizabad	1857	Maulvi Ahmadullah	1858	General Renard
Fatehpur	1857	Azimullah	1858	General Renard

Leaders of the Salt Movement in Bihar

Location	Leader
Champaran	Bipin Bihari Verma
Baireja	Girish Tiwari
Goriya Kothi	Chandrika Singh
Hajipur	Bharat Mishra
Patna	Ambika Kant Singh
Munger	Shri Krishna Singh
Lakhisarai	Nand Kumar Singh
Darbhanga	Satyanarayana Singh

Role of Bihar in the National Movement: An Overview

Year	Region/Centre	Activities
12 June, 1857	Deoghar, Rohini Village	The killing of the local Major by the 30th Regiment's troops, marking the beginning of the rebellion in Bihar.
	Patna	Led by Peer Ali Khan (bookseller).
25 July, 1857	Danapur Cantonment	The landlord of Jagdishpur took control of Ara.
1905	Deoghar	Establishment of the Golden League during the Swadeshi Movement.
1906		Spread of revolutionary ideas through the Ramkrishna Society.
1908	Muzaffarpur	Khudiram Bose and Prafulla Chaki attempted to assassinate Chief Presidency Magistrate Douglas Kingsford's carriage by throwing a bomb.
1913	Patna	Formation of the Anushilan Samiti by Sachindra Nath Sanyal.

APPENDIX-II

Geographical

Agricultural Climatic Zones of Bihar

Agricultural Climatic Zone	Crop Pattern	Relevant Districts	Soil Type
1. North-West Floodplain (Zone-I)	Rice, Wheat, Maize, Potato, Sugarcane, Mango, Banana, Litchi	West Champaran, East Champaran, Siwan, Saran, Sitamarhi, Sheohar, Vaishali, Muzaffarpur, Madhubani, Darbhanga, Samastipur, Gopalganj, Begusarai	Medium acidic, heavy texture, sandy loam to clay loam, flood-prone
2. North-East Floodplain (Zone-II)	Rice, Maize, Jute, Tea, Pomegranate	Purnia, Katihar, Saharsa, Supaul, Madhepura, Khagaria, Araria, Kishanganj	Light to medium texture, slightly acidic, sandy to silty loam
3. South-East Plateau Region (Zone-IIIA)	Rice, Wheat, Potato, Onion, and other Vegetables	Sheikhpura, Jamui, Lakhisarai, Banka, Munger, Bhagalpur	Sandy loam
4. South-West Floodplain (Zone-IIIB)	Rice, Wheat, Guava, Maize, Gram	Rohtas, Bhojpur, Buxar, Kaimur, Arwal, Patna, Nalanda, Nawada, Jehanabad, Aurangabad, Gaya	Floodplain and sandy loam

Features of Agricultural Climatic Zones of Bihar

Agricultural Climatic Zone	Soil	pH	Organic Matter	Available Nitrogen (kg/ hectare)	Available Phosphorus (kg/ hectare)	Available Potash (kg/ hectare)	Average Annual Rainfall (mm)	Temperature	Maximum
North-Western Floodplain	Sandy loam, clay loam	6.5-8.4	0.2-1.0	150-350	5-50	100-300	1040-1450 (1245)	36.6°C	7.7°C
North-Eastern Floodplain	Sandy loam, clay loam	6.5-7.8	0.2-1.0	150-300	10-35	150-250	1200-1700 (1450)	33.8°C	8.8°C
South-Eastern and Western	Sandy loam, clay loam	6.8-8.0	0.5-1.0	200-400	10-100	150-350	990-1240 (1150)	37.1°C	7.8°C

Soils of Bihar and Their Major Areas

Soil Type	Physical/Chemical Characteristics	Major Areas	Crops
Terai Soil	Sandy and gravelly, brown and light yellow in color, medium fertility	North Nepal, West Champaran Hills to East Kishanganj	Rice, jute, mango, litchi, sugarcane
Floodplain or New Alluvial Soil	Lacks lime and alkali, dark brown to black in color, high fertility	Koshi region (Purnia, Saharsa, Darbhanga, Muzaffarpur, and North-Western Champaran)	Rice, jute, sugarcane, maize, chickpea, wheat, pigeon pea
Balasundari or Loam Soil	Contains lime and alkali, light brown to dark brown, white	South Purnia, Saharsa, Southern Darbhanga, Muzaffarpur, Southern Saran, Southern West Champaran	Rice, sugarcane, wheat, maize, tobacco, mango, litchi, banana
Tal Soil	Grey in color, heavy soil, high fertility	Found in flood-prone areas in districts like Patna, Muzaffarpur, Bhagalpur	Only rabi crops as kharif crops cannot grow
Old Alluvial or Banger Soil	Alkaline and acidic, dark brown in color, high fertility	Southern parts of Ganga plains like Rohtas, Gaya, Patna, Munger	Rice, wheat, pigeon pea, maize, sugarcane
Red and Yellow Soil	Contains sand and gravel, acidic, reddish-yellow color, low fertility	Hills, foothills, and areas between West Kaimur and East Rajmahal	Pigeon pea, millet, sorghum, coarse grains

Major Waterfalls of Bihar

Waterfall Name	River	Location/District
Kankolat	Stream descending from Koderma Plateau	Kankolat (Navada)
Sukhladri	Kanhar	Rohtas
Dhuan Kund (30 meters)	Kaw, Dhoba	Tarachandi (Rohtas)
Durgawati (Khadar Koh) (80 meters)	Durgawati	Chanpapar (Rohtas)
Jiarakhund	Fulwariya	Jiarakhund (Bhojpur)
Tamasin	Mahane	-
Khuwari Dah (180 meters)	Asane	Rohtas
Rakim Kund	Gayghat	Rohtas
Okharin Kund (90 meters)	Gopth	Rohtas
Suara (120 meters)	Eastern Suara	Rohtas
Devdari (58 meters)	Karmanasa	Rohtas Plateau (Rohtas)
Telhar Kund (80 meters)	Western Suara	Rohtas Plateau (Rohtas)

Livestock (2012 and 2019)

Livestock and Poultry	2012	2019
Cow & Bull	122.3	154.0
Male > 3 years	19.2	13.5
Female > 3 years	59.8	71.5
Calves	43.3	69.0
Buffalo & Bullock	75.7	77.2
Male > 3 years	3.0	4.6
Female > 3 years	40.2	36.7
Calves	32.5	35.9
Sheep	2.3	2.1
Goat	121.5	128.2
Pigs	6.5	3.4
Horses	0.5	0.3
Others	0.6	0.1
Total Livestock	329.4	365.4
Total Poultry Birds	127.5	165.3

Major Minerals of Bihar

Mineral	Region
Coal	Rajmahal
Limestone	Kaimur (Bhabua), Munger, Rohtas
Mica	Nawada
Quartz & Silica	Bhagalpur, Jamui, Munger, Nalanda
Quartzite	Lakhisarai, Munger, Nalanda
Talc, Soapstone, Steatite	Munger
Bauxite	Munger, Rohtas
China Clay	Bhagalpur, Munger
Feldspar	Gaya, Jamui, Munger
Fire Clay	Bhagalpur, Purnia
Gold	Jamui
Granite	Bhagalpur, Gaya, Jehanabad, Jamui
Iron Ore (Hematite)	Bhagalpur
Iron Ore (Magnetite)	Gaya, Jamui
Lead-Zinc	Banka, Rohtas
Pyrites	Rohtas

Industrial Cities and Related Industries of Bihar

No.	City	District	Industry Description
1	Bihta	Patna	Sugar Industry
2	Mokama	Patna	Shoe Factory & Freight Train Coaches
3	Digha	Patna	Leather Shoes & Liquor Industry
4	Bhagalpur	Bhagalpur	Tassar (Silk) Industry, Handloom Industry
5	Patna City	Patna	Sindoor, Gulal, and Firecracker Manufacturing Industry
6	Obra	Aurangabad	Carpet Manufacturing Industry
7	Dalmianagar	Rohtas	Paper, Cement & Vegetable Oil Industry
8	Munger	Munger	Gun and Cigarette Factory
9	Bihar Sharif	Nalanda	Beedi Industry
10	Dumraon	Buxar	Cotton Fabric & Lantern Industry
11	Gaya	Gaya	Sugar, Lac, Cotton Fabric & Leather Industry
12	Hathua	Gopalganj	Ganga Vegetable Oil Factory

13	Madhoura	Saran	Sugar & Chocolate Factory
14	Tandiwa	Aurangabad	Blanket Manufacturing Industry
15	Kanti	Muzaffarpur	Thermal Power Plant
16	Narayanpur	Muzaffarpur	Pharmaceutical Manufacturing Industry
17	Rega	Sitamarhi	Sugar Mill
18	Bagha	West Champaran	Paper Mill
19	Mehasi	East Champaran	Button Manufacturing Industry
20	Darbhanga	Darbhanga	Paper Mill
21	Lohat	Madhubani	Sugar Mill
22	Samastipur	Samastipur	Paper & Sugar Mill
23	Katihar	Katihar	Jute Factory
24	Jamalpur	Munger	Railway Engine Repair Factory
25	Lakhisarai	Lakhisarai	Sindoor Factory

BIADA Industrial Zones, Estates, Development Centers & Mega Parks

Region	Type	Location
Patna	IA	Patliputra, Fatuha, Hajipur, Nawada, Gaya, Jehanabad, Barun, Aurangabad, Dehri, Vikramganj, Bihia, Bihta
	EPIP	Hajipur
	IE	Bihar Sharif, Kopakla, and Barauni
	GC	Aurangabad and Buxar
	MIP	Gidha
Darbhanga	IA	Bela, Khagaria, Samastipur
	IE	Saharsa, Udakishanganj, Pundol, Murliganj, Jhanjharpur, Dharampur
	GC	Shonar
Muzaffarpur	IA	Muzaffarpur, Kumarbagh, Ramnagar, Sitamarhi, and Raxaul
	IE	Bettiah and Siwan
Bhagalpur	IA	Barari, Munger, Lakhisarai, Purnia, Farbisganj, Katihar, and Khagra
	IE	Maranga, Kahalgaon, Bhediyadangi
	GC	Sitakund, Jamalpur

Bihar in a Glimpse

Total Area	94,163 square kilometers
Percentage of India's Total Area	2.86%
Latitude Extent	21°058' 10"N – 27°31'15"N
Longitude Extent	82°19'50"E – 88°17'40"E

Length (North to South)	345 km
Width (East to West)	483 km
Average Height above Sea Level	173 feet (53 meters)

State Border	North – Nepal, South – Jharkhand, East – West Bengal, West – Uttar Pradesh
Climate	Tropical Monsoon
Average Annual Rainfall	109 cm
Region with Maximum Vegetation	Deciduous Forests / Monsoon Forests
District with Highest Ranfall	Kishanganj
District with Minimum Rainfall	Aurangabad
Population (2011)	10,40,99,452
Percentage of India's Population	8.58%
Male Population	5,42,71,857
Female Population	4,98,21,295
Rural Population	9,23,41,436
Urban Population	1,17,58,016
Population Density	1102
Literacy Rate	61.80%
Male Literacy	71.20%
Female Literacy	51.50%
Sex Ratio	918 females per 1000 males
Official Language	Hindi
Second Official Language	Urdu
State Formation Day	March 22
State Animal	Bull
State Bird	House Sparrow
State Tree	Peepal
State Emblem	Bodhi Tree (Between Two Swastikas)
State Flower	Marigold

Major Cities of Bihar Located on Rivers

City	River	City	River
Patna	Ganga	Bhagalpur	Ganga
Muzaffarpur	Budhi Gandak	Darbhanga	Bagmati
Chhapra	Ganga	Khagaria	Budhi Gandak
Hajipur	Gandak	Jehanabad	Dardha
Samastipur	Budhi Gandak	Bettiah	Budhi Gandak
Gaya	Phalgu		

Airways in Bihar

Name	Location	Type
Jay Prakash Narayan International Airport	Patna	International
Gaya International Airport	Gaya	International
Bhagalpur Airport	Bhagalpur	Domestic
Darbhanga Airport	Darbhanga	Military
Jogbani Airport	Jogbani	Domestic
Chunapur Airport	Purnia	Military

Forest Product-Based Industries

Catechu (Katha) Plywood Industry	Hajipur, Bettiah, Patna, Muzaffarpur
Catechu (Katha) Industry	Bettiah
Silk Industry	Bhagalpur

Major Crops and Their Production Areas in Bihar

Crop	Production Areas
Rice	Rohtas, West Champaran, East Champaran, Arwal, Buxar
Wheat	Rohtas, Gaya, Darbhanga
Maize	Saran, Muzaffarpur, Khagaria, Begusarai, Munger
Barley	West Champaran, Saharsa, Purnia
Millet	Saharsa, Muzaffarpur, Saran
Sorghum	Patna, Munger, Gaya
Groundnut	Patna, Bhojpur, Gaya

Bihar's River Interlinking Projects

Name of Rivers	Districts Receiving Benefits	Achievements
Budhi Gandak-Nuun via Ganga	Samastipur, Begusarai, Khagaria	1.26 lakh hectares of irrigation capacity.
Sakri-Nata River	Nawada, Nalanda, Sheikhpura	68 thousand hectares of irrigation capacity.
Kosi-Mechi	Araria, Saharsa, Supaul, Kishanganj, Purnia	2.11 lakh hectares of irrigation capacity.

Key Industries in Bihar

Silk Industry	Bhagalpur, Katihar, Manoharpur, Purnia
Leather Industry	Mokama, Gaya, Digha
Iron Industry	Purnia, Gaya
Liquor Industry	Munger, Madhoura, Manpur, Patna, Panchrukhi
Fertilizer Industry	Barauni
Mining Industry	Aurangabad
Tobacco Industry	Munger, Ara, Gaya, Bihar Sharif, Lakhisarai, Buxar, Jhajha, Jamui, Ara, Dalsingh Ray, Shahpur, Ayodhyaganj
Cement Industry	Dalmianagar
Jute Industry	Katihar, Samastipur, Darbhanga, Saharsa, Champaran, Saharsa, Purnia
Blanket Industry	Purnia, Aurangabad, Gaya, Motihari
Rubber Industry	Ara, Patna, Gaya, Muzaffarpur
Utensil Industry	Bihta, Siwan
Beedi Industry	Jamui, Jhajha, Bihar Sharif
Handloom Industry	Bhagalpur, Madhubani, Gaya, Bihar Sharif, Patna, Muzaffarpur
Cotton Textile Industry	Gaya, Phulwari Sharif, Mokama, Muzaffarpur, Dumraon, Muzaffarpur, Bhagalpur, Madhubani, Kishanganj, Bihar Sharif
Glass Industry	Barauni, Bhawani Nagar, Patna, Hajipur
Firecracker Industry	Patna City
Button Industry	Mehsi
Sindoor Industry	Lakhisarai
Glass Industry	Patna
Sugar Industry	Bhojpur, Siwan, Darbhanga, Samastipur, Harinagar, Motihari, Muzaffarpur, Dalmianagar, Mirganj, Sugouly, Warislaiganj, Bihta, Gaya, Madhoura, Naraktiyaganj, Gopalganj, Motipur, Banmakhni, Panchrukhi, Sashamusa, Majholia, Sidhwaliya, Betia, Chhapra, Guraaru, Maharajganj, Lohat, Hasanpur, Lauria, Sakri, Raiyam etc. are major areas.
Paper Industry	Samastipur, Patna, Barauni, Darbhanga, Dalmianagar
Vegetable Oil Industry	Dalmianagar
Wood Industry	Naraktiyaganj, Jogbani, Gopalganj, West Champaran, Patna, Muzaffarpur, Samastipur, Bhagalpur, Katihar

Major River/Rail Bridges in Bihar

Bridge	River	Mode of Transport
Mahatma Gandhi Setu	Ganga	Road
Rajendra Birdge	Ganga	Rail & Road
Son Birdge	Son	Rail & Road
Abdul Bari Bridge	Son	Rail & Road
Vashistha Narayan Bridge	Son	Road
Bagaha-Chhitouni Bridge	Gandak	Rail & Road
Vikramshila Bridge	Ganga	Road
Jai Prakash (JP) Setu	Ganga	Rail & Road
Kosi Rail Mahasetu	Kosi	Rail

Census Data of Bihar - 2011

S.No.	Name of the District	Total Sum	Male	Female	Sex Ratio	Population Density	Decadal Growth
1.	E. Champaran	3,922,780	2,057,669	1,865,111	906	750	28.89
2.	W. Champaran	5,082,868	2,674,037	2,408,831	901	1281	29.01
3.	Sheohar	656,916	347,614	309,302	890	1882	27.32
4.	Sitamarhi	3,419,622	1,800,441	1,619,181	899	1491	27.47
5.	Madhubani	4,476,044	2,324,984	2,151,060	925	1279	25.19
6.	Supoul	2,228,397	1,157,815	1,070,582	925	919	28.62
7.	Araria	2,806,200	1,460,878	1,345,322	921	992	30.00
8.	Kishanganj	1,690,948	868,845	822,103	946	898	30.44
9.	Purnia	3,273,127	1,695,829	1,577,298	930	1014	28.66
10.	Katihar	3,068,149	1,601,158	1,466,991	916	1004	28.23
11.	Madhepura	1,994,618	1,042,373	952,245	914	1116	30.65
12.	Saharsa	1,897,102	995,502	901,600	906	1125	25.79
13.	Darbhanga	3,921,971	2,053,043	1,868,928	910	1721	19.00
14.	Muzaffarpur	4,778,610	2,517,500	2,261,110	898	1506	27.54
15.	Gopalganj	2,558,037	1,269,677	1,288,360	1,015	1258	18.83
16.	Siwan	3,318,176	1,672,121	1,646,055	984	1495	22.25
17.	Saran	3,943,098	2,023,476	1,919,622	949	1493	21.37
18.	Vaishali	3,495,249	1,847,058	1,648,191	892	1717	28.58
19.	Samastipur	4,254,782	2,228,432	2,026,350	909	1465	25.33
20.	Begusarai	2,954,367	1,560,203	1,394,164	894	1540	25.75
21.	Khagaria	1,657,599	880,065	777,534	883	1115	29.46
22.	Bhagalpur	3,032,226	1,614,014	1,418,212	879	1180	25.13
23.	Banka	2,029,339	1,064,307	965,032	907	672	26.14
24.	Munger	1,359,054	723,280	635,774	879	958	19.45
25.	Lakhisarai	1,000,717	526,651	474,066	900	815	24.74
26.	Sheikhpura	634,927	329,593	305,334	926	922	20.82
27.	Nalanda	2,872,523	1,495,577	1,376,946	921	1220	21.18
28.	Patna	5,772,804	3,051,117	2,721,687	892	1803	22.34

29.	Bhojpur	2,720,155	1,431.722	1,288,433	900	1136	21.27
30.	Buxar	1,707,643	888,356	819,287	922	1003	21.77
31.	Kaimur	1,626,900	847,784	779.116	919	488	27.54
32.	Rohtas	2,962,593	1,547,856	1,414,737	914	763	20.22
33.	Aurangabad	2,511,243	1,310,867	1,200,376	916	760	24.75
34.	Gaya	4,379,383	2,266,865	2,112,518	932	880	26.08
35.	Nawada	2,216.653	1,145,123	1,071,530	936	889	22.49
36.	Jamui	17,56,078	914,368	841710	921	·567	25.54
37.	Jehanabad	1,12,4176	5,86,202	537974	918	1206	21.34
38.	Arwal	699563	362,945	336618	927	1099	19.01
	Total	103,803,637	54,185 347	49,619,290	916	1102	25.07

APPENDIX III

Political

Bihar's Divisions, Districts, and Sub-divisions

Division	District	Sub-division
Patna	Patna	Patna Sadar, Danapur, Baid, Patna City, Masaurhi, Paliganj
	Nalanda	Bihar Sharif Sadar, Hilsa, Rajgir
	Rohtas	Sasaram Sadar, Vikramganj, Dehri
	Kaimur (Bhabhua)	Bhabhua Sadar, Mohania
	Bhojpur (Ara)	Ara Sadar, Jagdishpur, Piro
	Buxar	Buxar Sadar, Dumraon
Magadh	Gaya	Gaya Sadar, Sherghati, Tekari, Neemchak, Bathani
	Jehanabad	Jehanabad Sadar
	Arwal	Arwal Sadar
	Nawada	Nawada Sadar, Rajouli
	Aurangabad	Aurangabad Sadar, Daudnagar
Saran (Chapra)	Saran (Chapra)	Chapra Sadar, Madhura, Sonpur
	Siwan	Siwan Sadar, Maharajganj
	Gopalganj	Gopalganj Sadar, Hathua
Tirhut (Muzaffarpur)	Muzaffarpur	Muzaffarpur East, Muzaffarpur West
	Sitamarhi	Sitamarhi Sadar, Pupi, Belsand
	Sheohar	Sheohar Sadar
	West Champaran (Bettiah)	Bcttiah, Bagaha, Narkatiaganj

	East Champaran	Motihari Sadar, Areraj, Chakia, Pakhri Dayal, Raxaul, Sikharna
	Vaishali	Hajipur, Mahua, Mahanar
Darbhanga	Darbhanga	Darbhanga Sadar, Benipur, Biroul
	Madhubani	Madhubani Sadar, Jayanagar, Benipatti, Jhanjharpur, Phulparas
	Samastipur	Samastipur Sadar, Dalsinghsarai, Patori, Rosra
Kosi (Saharsa)	Saharsa	Saharsa, Simri Bakhitiyarpur
	Supaul	Veerpur, Nirmali, Supaul, Triveniganj
	Madhubani	Madhubani, Udakishunganj
Purnia Division	Purnia	Purnia Sadar, Banmankhi, Baisi, Dhamdaha
	Araria	Araria Sadar, Farbisganj
	Kishanganj	Kishanganj
	Katihar	Katihar Sadar, Barsoi, Manihari
Bhagalpur	Bhagalpur	Bhagalpur Sadar, Kahalgaon, Navgachhia
	Banka	Banka Sadar
Munger	Munger	Munger, Haveli Khargpur, Tarapur
	Lakhisarai	Lakhisarai
	Jamui	Jamui
	Khagaria	Khagaria, Gogri
	Sheikhpura	Sheikhpura
	Begusarai	Begusarai, Teghra, Ballia, Manjholi, Bakhri

Chief Justices of Bihar High Court

Justice Sir Edward Mayward Champs Chamier	March 1, 1916 to October 30, 1917
Justice Sir Arthur Trevor Harris	October 10, 1928 to January 19, 1943
Justice Sir Syed Fazal Ali	January 19, 1943 to October 14, 1946
Justice Sir Clifford Manmohan Agarwal	January 9, 1948 to January 24, 1950
Justice Sir Herbert Ribton Meredith	January 25, 1950 to April 8, 1950
Justice Lakshmikanth Jha	April 8, 1950 to June 1, 1952
Justice David Ezra Reuben	June 1, 1952 to September 2, 1953
Justice Sir Syed Jafer Imam	September 3, 1953 to January 10, 1955
Justice Sudhanshu Kumar Das	January 10, 1955 to April 30, 1956
Justice Vidyanathier Ramaswamy	April 30, 1956 to January 4, 1965
Justice Ramaswamy Lakshmi Narasimhan	January 4, 1965 to August 2, 1968
Justice Satish Chandra Mishra	November 9, 1968 to September 5, 1970
Justice Ujjwal Narayan Sinha	September 5, 1970 to September 29, 1972

Justice Nandlal Untwalia	September 29, 1972 to October 3, 1974
Justice Shyam Nandan Prasad Singh	October 3, 1974 to May 1, 1976
Justice Krishnavallabh Narayan Singh	July 19, 1976 to March 12, 1983
Justice Surjeet Singh Sanghawalia	November 29, 1983 to July 27, 1987
Justice Bhagwati Prasad Jha	January 2, 1988 to May 1, 1988
Justice Deepak Kumar Sen	May 1, 1988 to May 1, 1989
Justice Sushil Kumar Jha	October 19, 1989 to October 23, 1989
Justice Gangadhar Ganesh Sahani	October 24, 1989 to December 17, 1990
Justice Vimal Chandra Basaak	March 18, 1991 to October 21, 1994
Justice Krishnaswami Sundar Paripurnan	January 24, 1994 to June 11, 1994
Justice K. Venkataswamy	September 19, 1994 to March 6, 1995
Justice Govind Vallabh Pattanayak	May 19, 1995 to September 11, 1995
Justice Devinder Pratap Badhwa	September 29, 1995 to March 21, 1997
Justice Brijmohan Lal	July 9, 1997 to October 6, 1999
Justice Ravi Swaroop Dhawan	January 25, 2000 to July 22, 2004
Justice J. N. Bhatt	July 18, 2005 to October 10, 2007
Justice Rajesh Walia	January 5, 2008 to March 3, 2008
Justice Rajendramal Lodha	May 13, 2008 to December 16, 2008
Justice J. B. Koshi	March 16, 2009 to May 13, 2009
Justice Prafull Kumar Mishra	August 12, 2009 to September 17, 2009
Justice Deepak Kumar Mishra	December 23, 2009 to May 24, 2010
Justice Rekha Manhar Lal Dixit	June 21, 2010 to December 12, 2014
Justice L. Narasimha Reddy	December 13, 2014 to July 31, 2015
Justice Iqbal Ahmad Ansari	August 29, 2016 to October 28, 2016
Justice Rajendra Menon	March 15, 2017 to June 8, 2018
Justice Mukesh Sah	September 12, 2018 to November 1, 2018
Justice Armeshwar Pratap Sahi	November 10, 2018 to November 10, 2019
Justice Sanjay Karol	November 11, 2019 to February 5, 2023
Justice Chakradhari Sharan Singh (Acting)	February 6, 2023 to March 28, 2023
Justice K. Vinod Chandran	March 29, 2023 to January 15, 2025
Justice Vipul Manubhai Pancholi	July 21, 2025 to August 28, 2025
Justice Pavankumar Bhimappa Bajanthri (Acting)	September 21, 2025 to October 22, 2025
Justice Sangam Kumar Sahoo	January 7, 2026 to till date

President's Rule in Bihar

1.	June 29, 1968 - February 26, 1969	Nityanand Kanungo
2.	July 6, 1969 – February 16, 1970	Nityanand Kanungo
3.	January 9, 1972 – March 19, 1972	Devkant Baruah
4.	April 30, 1977 – June 22, 1977	Jagannath Kaushal
5.	February 17, 1980 – June 8, 1980	Dr. A. R. Kidwai

6.	March 28, 1995 – April 4, 1995	Dr. A. R. Kidwai
7.	February 12, 1999 – March 8, 1999	Sundar Singh Bhandari
8.	March 7, 2005 – November 24, 2005	Sardar Buta Singh

List of Chief Ministers of Bihar

Chief Minister	Chief Minister's tenure
Shri Krishna Sinha	26 January 1950 - 31 January 1961
Deep Narayan Singh	1 February 1961 - 18 February 1961
Binodanand Jha	18 February 1961 - 2 October 1963
K B Sahai	2 October 1963 - 5 March 1967
Mahamaya Prasad Sinha	5 March 1967 - 28 January 1968
Satish Prasad Singh	28 January 1968 - 1 February 1968
B. P. Mandal	1 February 1968 - 22 March 1968
Bhola Paswan Shastri	22 March 1968 - 29 June 1968
President's Rule	29 June 1968 - 26 February 1969
Harihar Singh	26 February 1969 - 22 June 1969
Bhola Paswan Shastri	22 June 1969 - 4 July 1969
President's Rule	6 July 1969 - 16 February 1970
Prasad Rai	16 February 1970 - 22 December 1970
Karpoori Thakur	22 December 1970 - 2 June 1971
Bhola Paswan Shastri	2 June 1971 - 9 January 1972
President's Rule	9 January 1972 - 19 March 1972
Kedar Pandey	19 March 1972 - 2 July 1973
Abdul Gafoor	2 July 1973 - 11 April 1975
Jagannath Mishra	11 April 1975 - 30 April 1977
President's Rule	30 April 1977 - 24 June 1977
Karpoori Thakur	24 June 1977 - 21 April 1979
Ram Sundar Das	21 April 1979 - 17 February 1980
President's Rule	17 February 1980 - 8 June 1980
Jagannath Mishra	8 June 1980 - 14 August 1983
Chandrashekhar Singh	14 August 1983 - 12 March 1985
Bindeshwari Dubey	12 March 1985 - 13 February 1988
Bhagwat Jha Azad	14 February 1988 - 10 March 1989
Satyendra Narayan Sinha	11 March 1989 - 6 December 1989
Jagannath Mishra	6 December 1989 - 10 March 1990
Lalu Prasad Yadav	10 March 1990 - 28 March 1995
President's Rule	28 March 1995 - 4 April 1995
Lalu Prasad Yadav	4 April 1995 - 25 July 1997
Rabri Devi	25 July 1997 - 11 February 1999
President's Rule	11 February 1999 - 9 March 1999
Rabri Devi	9 March 1999 - 2 March 2000
Nitish Kumar	2 March 2000 - 10 March 2000
Rabri Devi	11 March 2000 - 6 March 2005
President's Rule	7 March 2005 - 24 November 2005

Nitish Kumar	24 November 2005 - 20 May 2014
Jitan Ram Manjhi	20 May 2014 - 22 February 2015
Nitish Kumar	22 February 2015 - 14 April 2026
Samrat Choudhary	15 April 2026 - till date

List of Honourable Speakers of the Bihar Legislative Assembly

Shri Ramdayalu Singh	23.07.1937 to 11.11.1944
Shri Bindeshwari Prasad Verma	25.04.1946 to 14.03.1962
Shri Laxmi Narayan Sudhanshu	15.03.1962 to 15.03.1967
Shri Dhaniklal Mandal	16.03.1967 to 10.03.1969
Shri Ram Narayan Mandal	11.03.1969 to 20.03.1972
Shri Harinath Mishra	21.03.1972 to 26.06.1977
Shri Tripurari Prasad Singh	28.06.1977 to 22.06.1980
Shri Radhanandan Jha	24.06.1980 to 1.04.1985
Shri Shivchandra Jha	4.04.1985 to 23.01.1989
Shri Mohammad Hidayatullah Khan	27.03.1989 to 19.03.1990
Shri Ghulam Sarwar	20.03.1990 to 9.04.1995
Shri Dev Narayan Yadav	12.04.1995 to 6.03.2000
Shri Sadanand Singh	9.03.2000 to 28.06.2005
Shri Uday Narayan Chaudhary	30.11.2005 to 29.11.2010 2.12.2010 to 28.11.2015
Shri Vijay Kumar Chaudhary	2.12.2015 to 15.11.2020
Shri Vijay Kumar Sinha	25.11.2020 to 24.8.2022
Shri Avadh Bihari Chaudhary	26.08.2022 to 12.02. 2024
Shri Nand Kishore Yadav	16.02. 2024 - Incumbent

List of Deputy Governors / Governors of Bihar (1912-1920)

Sir Charles Stuart Baillie	1.04.1912 to 19.11.1915
Sir Edward Albert Gate	19.11.1915 to 04.04.1918
Sir Edward Vere Leving	5.04.1918 to 12.08.1918
Sir Edward Albert Gate	12.08.1918 to 29.12.1920

List of Governors of Bihar (1937-1947)

Sir Maurice Garnier Hallet	11.03.1937 to 15.05.1938
Sir Thomas Alexander Stewart	15.05.1938 to 16.09.1938
Sir Maurice Garnier Hallet	17.09.1938 to 5.08.1939
Sir Thomas Alexander Stewart	6.08.1939 to 2.02.1943
Sir Thomas George Rutherford	3.02.1943 to 6.09.1943
Shri Robert Francis Moody (later Sir)	7.09.1943 to 23.04.1944
Sir Thomas George Rutherford	24.04.1944 to 12.05.1946
Sir Hugh Dow	13.05.1946 to 14.08.1947

List of Post-Independence Bihar Governors

Shri Jairamdas Doulatram	15.08.1947 to 11.01.1948
Shri Madhav Shreehari Aney	12.01.1948 to 14.06.1952
Shri Ranganath Ramachandra Diwakar	15.06.1952 to 5.07.1957
Dr. Zakir Husain	6.07.1957 to 11.05.1962

Shri Madhbhushi Anant Shayanam Ayyangar	12.05.1962 to 6.12.1967
Shri Nityanand Kanungo	7.12.1967 to 20.01.1971
Justice Ujjwal Narayan Sinha (Acting)	21.01.1971 to 31.01.1971
Shri Devkant Barua	1.02.1971 to 4.02.1973
Shri Ramchandra Dhondiba Bhandare	4.02.1973 to 15.06.1976
Shri Jagannath Kaushal	16.06.1976 to 31.01.1979
Justice Krishnavallabh Narayan Singh (Acting)	27.05.1978 to 26.06.1978 31.01.1979 to 19.09.1979
Shri Jagannath Kaushal	26.06.1978 to 31.01.1979
Justice Krishnavallabh Narayan Singh (Acting)	31.01.1979 to 20.09.1979
Dr. Akhlaqurrahman Kidwai	20.09.1979 to 15.03.1985
Shri P. Venkatasubiah	15.03.1985 to 25.02.1988
Shri Govind Narayan Singh	26.02.1988 to 24.01.1989
Justice Deepak Kumar Sen (Acting)	24.01.1989 to 28.01.1989
Shri R. D. Pradhan (Acting)	29.01.1989 to 2.03.1989
Shri Jagannath Pahadiya	3.03.1989 to 2.02.1990
Justice G. G. Sohoni (Acting)	2.02.1990 to 16.02.1990
Shri Mohammad Yunus Saleem	16.02.1990 to 13.02.1991
Shri B. Satyanarayana Reddy	14.02.1991 to 18.03.1991
Shri Mohammad Shafi Qureshi	19.03.1991 to 13.08.1993
Dr. Akhlaqurrahman Kidwai	14.08.1993 to 26.04.1998
Shri Sundar Singh Bhandari	27.04.1998 to 15.03.1999
Justice Brijmohan Lal (Acting)	15.03.1999 to 5.10.1999
Shri Surajbhan	6.10.1999 to 22.11.1999
Shri Vinod Chandra Pandey	23.11.1999 to 12.06.2003
Shri M. Rama Jois	12.06.2003 to 31.10.2004
Shri Ved Prakash Marwah	1.11.2004 to 4.11.2004
Dr. Sardar Buta Singh	5.11.2004 to 30.01.2006
Shri Gopalkrishna Gandhi	31.01.2006 to 21.06.2006
Shri Ramkrishna Surajbhanji Gavai	22.06.2006 to 10.07.2008
Shri R. L. Bhatia	10.07.2008 to 28.06.2009
Shri Debanand Kunwar	29.06.2009 to 21.03.2013
Dr. D. Y. Patil	22.03.2013 to 26.11.2014
Shri Kesharinath Tripathi	27.11.2014 to 15.08.2015
Shri Ram Nath Kovind	16.08.2015 to 21.06.2017
Shri Kesharinath Tripathi (Acting)	22.06.2017 to 3.10.2017
Shri Satyapal Malik	04.10.2017 to 22.08.2018
Shri Lalji Tandon	23.08.2018 to 28.07.2019
Shri Fagu Chauhan	29.07.2019 to 16.02.2023
Shri Rajendra Vishwanath Arlekar	17.02.2023 to 1.01.2025
Shri Arif Mohammad Khan	2.01.2025 to 14.03.2026
Lieutenant General (Retd.) Syed Ata Hasnain	14.03.2026 – till date

APPENDIX IV

Economic Data

Major Schemes Related to Women Empowerment

Economic Empowerment	Social Empowerment	Cultural Empowerment
Bihar Rural Livelihood Promotion Committee	Chief Minister's Kanya Vivah Yojana	Didi Ki Rasoi
Digital Financing	Chief Minister's Kanya Utthan Yojana	Saras Mela
Sustainable Livelihood Scheme	Alpavasa Griha	Mama Kans
Reserved Employment Rights for Women	Interventions Related to Gender Mainstreaming	
Empowered Women, Capable Women	Chief Minister's Nari Shakti Yojana	
Micro Insurance	Swarakarya Center and Helpline	
Alternative Banking – Bank in Our Village	Adolescent Girl Scheme	
Agriculture Value Chain	Lakshmibai Social Security Pension Scheme	
Women Development Corporation	Chief Minister's Girl Cycle Scheme	
Cattle Producer Company	Chief Minister's Girl Security Scheme	

Prominent Banks

Allahabad Bank	1865
Punjab National Bank	1894
Bank of India	1906
Canara Bank	1906
Indian Bank	1907
Bank of Baroda	1908
Central Bank of India	1911
Union Bank	1919
Syndicate Bank	1925
Bank of Maharashtra	1935
Indian Overseas Bank	1936
Dena Bank	1938
United Commercial Bank	1943
United Bank	1950

State Specific Libraries

Name	Establishment Year
Gopal Narayan Library, Patna	1912
Shri Sharda Sadan Library, Lalganj (Vaishali)	1914
Great Public Library, Patna	1916
Shri Hindi Library, Sohsarai, Nalanda	1924
Mahant Ramsharan Das Library, Samastipur	1939
Gyan Niketan Library, Sitamarhi	1946
Prabhavati Women's Library, Patna	1973
Ghatapurak Grant Library (Sinha Library), Patna	1924
Shri Krishna Seva Sadan, Munger	-

Key Schemes Running in Bihar

Skills Programme	Tools Scheme
Chief Minister's Bihar Darshan Scheme	Chief Minister's Labor Force Scheme
Muskaan Campaign	Apna Ghar Scheme
Prime Minister's Rural Housing Scheme	SC/ST Entrepreneur Scheme
Chief Minister's Electrical Connections Assurance Scheme	Bihar Student Credit Card Scheme
Bihar State Crop Assistance Scheme	Bihar Skilled Youth Program
Prime Minister's Mother and Child Welfare Scheme	Kasturba Gandhi Municipal Residential Schools
Lohia Swachhata Scheme / Swachh Bharat Mission	Inter-caste Marriage Scheme
Disability Social Security Pension Scheme	State Social Security Pension Scheme
Bihar Rural Livelihood Project	Chief Minister's Food Security Scheme
Maa-Bap Seva Scheme	Poor Welfare Employment Campaign
Bihar State Migrant Accident Relief Scheme	Bihar Toilet Scheme
E-Kalyan Portal	Jal Jeevan Hariyali Scheme
Bihar Unemployment Allowance	Crop Assistance Scheme
Chief Minister's Rural Transport Scheme	Ganga Udbhav Scheme
Bihar Chief Minister Youth Entrepreneur Scheme	Bihar Chief Minister Women Entrepreneur Scheme
Bal Hriday Scheme	Sunandini Scheme

Percentage Distribution of Government Expenditure (2018-19 to 2023-24 Budget Estimates)

Expenditure Category	2018-19	2019-20	2020-21	2021-22	2022-23 (Budget Estimates)	2023-24 (Budget Estimates)
General Services	25.0	28.5	27.9	25.3	24.2	26.7
Social Services	37.7	39.6	38.5	39.4	38.1	35.9
Economic Services	18.1	18.2	17.8	17.7	17.1	16.7
Capital Expenditure	13.6	8.4	11.0	12.3	13.6	11.2
Payment of Public Debts	4.7	4.9	4.2	4.5	6.2	9.0
Loans and Advances	1.0	0.5	0.7	0.8	0.9	0.5
Total	100.0	100.0	100.0	100.0	100.0	100.0

Percentage Share of Different Expenditure Categories (2018-19 and 2022-23)

Sector-wise Contribution to Gross Value Added and Employment in Bihar and All of India (2017-18 and 2021-22)

(Percentage)

Sector	Gross Value Added Share (2017-18)	Employment Share (2017-18)	Gross Value Added Share (2021-22)	Employment Share (2021-22)
Agriculture, Livestock, Forestry & Fisheries	Bihar: 21.48%, India: 15.29%	Bihar: 45.10%, India: 44.14%	Bihar: 20.56%, India: 15.58%	Bihar: 7.64%, India: 45.46%
Mining & Quarrying	Bihar: 0.10%, India: 2.74%	Bihar: 0.07%, India: 0.41%	Bihar: 0.11%, India: 2.25%	Bihar: 0.13%, India: 0.33%

Primary Sector	Bihar: 21.57%, India: 18.03%	Bihar: 45.17%, India: 44.55%	Bihar: 20.67%, India: 17.83%	Bihar:47.77%, India: 45.79%
Manufacturing	Bihar: 9.14%, India: 18.36%	Bihar: 8.93%, India: 12.13%	Bihar: 9.47%, India: 18.72%	Bihar: 6.82%, India: 11.57%
Electricity, Gas, Water Supply & Other Utility Services	Bihar: 1.49%, India: 2.27%	Bihar: 0.09%, India: 0.59%	Bihar: 2.00%, India: 2.29%	Bihar: 0.48%, India: 0.55%
Construction	Bihar: 9.47%, India: 8.01%	Bihar: 16.30%, India: 11.67%	Bihar: 9.26%, India: 8.18%	Bihar: 18.64%, India: 12.43%
Secondary Sector	Bihar: 20.10%, India: 28.64%	Bihar: 25.32%, India: 24.39%	Bihar: 20.72%, India: 29.19%	Bihar: 25.94%, India: 24.55%
Trade, Repair, Hotels & Restaurants	Bihar: 18.20%, India: 19.68%	Bihar: 13.68%, India: 11.96%	Bihar: 15.00%, India: 17.80%	Bihar: 11.15%, India: 10.35%
Transport, Storage, Communication & Broadcasting Services	Bihar: 9.66%, India: 4.13%	Bihar: 5.92%, India: 10.57%	Bihar: 6.51%, India: 7.38%	–
Financial, Real Estate & Professional Services	Bihar: 13.73%, India: 21.08%	Bihar: 1.94%, India: 2.09%	Bihar: 14.24%, India: 22.46%	Bihar: 0.92%, India: 1.90%
Public Administration & Other Services	Bihar: 16.74%, India: 12.57%	Bihar: 9.76%, India: 11.07%	Bihar: 18.79%, India: 12.72%	Bihar: 7.70%, India: 10.03%
Tertiary Sector	Bihar: 58.32%, India: 53.33%	Bihar: 29.51%, India: 31.05%	Bihar: 58.60%, India: 52.98%	Bihar: 26.29%, India: 29.66%
Total	100.00%	100.00%	100.00%	100.00%

State Government's Revenue Components (2018-19 to 2023-24 Budget Estimates)

(in Crore)

Revenue Source	2018-19	2019-20	2020-21	2021-22	2022-23	2023-24 (Budget)
State's Own Revenue	33,539	33,858	36,543	38,839	48,153	56,212
(a) Tax Revenue	29,408	30,158	30,342	34,855	44,018	49,700
(b) Non-Tax Revenue	4,131	3,700	6,201	3,984	4,135	6,512
Revenue from Center	98,255	90,375	91,625	1,19,958	1,24,535	1,56,115
(a) Share of Divisible Taxes	73,603	63,406	59,861	91,353	95,510	1,02,737
(b) Grants & Assistance	24,652	26,969	31,764	28,606	29,026	53,378
Total Revenue	1,31,793	1,24,233	1,28,168	1,58,798	1,72,688	2,12,327
State's Own Revenue as % of Total	25.4	27.3	28.5	24.5	28	28

State Government's Expenditure Pattern (2018-19 to 2023-24 Budget Estimates)

(in Crore)

Expenditure Category	2018-19	2019-20	2020-21	2021-22	2022-23	2023-24
General Services	38,691	41,628	46,239	48,939	56,029	70,049

Social Services	58,284	57,816	63,808	76,115	88,348	93,932
Economic Services	27,918	26,571	29,445	34,166	39,598	43,861
Grants & Assistance	4	2	2	0	0	7
Capital Expenditure	21,058	12,304	18,209	23,678	31,520	29,257
Public Debt Repayment	7,230	7,110	6,880	8,746	14,351	23,559
Loans & Advances by State	1,471	666	1,114	1,479	2,057	1,221
Total Expenditure	1,54,656	1,46,097	1,65,697	1,93,123	2,31,904	2,61,885

Percentage Increase in State Government Expenditure (2018-19 to 2022-23) (Percentage)

Expenditure Category	2018-19	2019-20	2020-21	2021-22	2022-23
General Services	15.9%	7.6%	11.1%	5.8%	14.5%
Social Services	27.3%	-5.1%	15.3%	19.3%	16.1%
Economic Services	18.9%	-4.8%	10.8%	16.0%	15.9%
Grants & Assistance	0.0%	-50.0%	0.0%	-100.0%	-63.8%
Capital Expenditure	-27.2%	-41.6%	48.0%	30.0%	33.1%
Public Debt Repayment	55.4%	-1.7%	-3.2%	27.1%	64.1%
Loans & Advances by State	505.7%	-54.7%	67.2%	32.7%	39.1%
Total	13.4%	-7.1%	15.4%	16.6%	20.1%

Per Capita Expenditure on Social, Economic, and General Services (2018-19 to 2023-24)

Year	2018-19	2019-20	2020-21	2021-22	2022-23	2023-24
Estimated Population (in crore)	11.7	12.5	12.8	13.0	13.3	13.1
Total Expenditure (in crore)						
Education, Sports, Art & Culture	28080	26353	27347	35530	42810	42381
Medical & Public Health	7318	7674	9152	11510	11810	16704
Water Supply & Sanitation	15638	11949	16329	15617	21752	21024
Social Services	94316	62346	60619	70139	81268	99878
Economic Services	41603	33684	39935	49183	61896	62888
Capital Expenditure	21058	12304	18209	23678	31520	29257
General Services	42002	44016	47626	52447	59284	74332
Per Capita Expenditure (in ₹)						
Education, Sports, Art & Culture	2400	2108	2136	2724	3209	3243
Medical & Public Health	625	614	715	882	885	1278
Water Supply & Sanitation	1337	956	1276	1197	1630	1609
Social Services	5329	4849	5480	6231	7069	7642
\Economic Services	3556	2695	3120	3771	4639	4812
Capital Expenditure	1800	984	1423	1815	2362	2239
General Services	3590	3521	3721	4021	4443	5687

Livestock and Fisheries Production in Bihar (2018-19 to 2022-23)

Year	Milk (Lakh Ton)	Eggs (Crore)	Wool (Lakh Kg)	Meat (Lakh Ton)	Fish (Lakh Ton)
2018-19	98.18	176.33	3.12	3.64	6.02
2019-20	104.83	274.08	3.10	3.83	6.41
2020-21	115.01	301.32	1.70	3.85	6.83
2021-22	121.19	306.66	1.72	3.92	7.62
2022-23	125.03	327.43	1.75	3.96	8.46
Annual Growth Rate (%)	6.49	14.46	-16.02	1.94	8.91

District-wise Concentration of Handloom Products in Bihar

District	Products
Bhagalpur	Silk, Cotton, Decorative Fabrics, Staple Sheets, Export Quality Silk & Cotton Fabrics
Banka	Tassar Silk, Export Quality Silk Fabrics, Cotton Towels and Gamchas
Gaya	Cotton Cloth, Bed Sheets, Towels and Gamchas
Nalanda	Cotton, Silk, Linen Sarees, Bawanbooti Sarees, Bed Covers, Towels-Gamchas, Tassar & Mulberry Silk Kurta Fabric, Tassar & Moonga Shirt Fabric, Mercerized Katia Tassar Kurta Fabric
Navada	Tassar Silk & Linen Fabrics for Men's and Women's Wear
Madhubani	Fine Cotton Fabric, Dhoti, Shirt Fabrics
Aurangabad, Rohtas	Towels-Gamchas, Woolen Blankets, Woolen Carpets
Kaimur	Woolen Carpets, Banarasi Sarees
Patna, Siwan	Cotton Fabrics, Bed Sheets, Shirt Fabrics, Towels-Gamchas, Dusters, Plain Fabrics
Purnia, Katihar	Jute Bags, Jute Blended Products, Interior Decor Items
West Champaran	Shawls, Mufflers, Towels-Gamchas, Bed Covers

Status of Ongoing Schemes in Handloom and Powerloom Sector in Bihar (2022-23)

Scheme	Objective	Financial Target (in Crore)	Financial Achievement (in Crore)
Electricity Subsidy Grant	Provide electricity subsidy to powerloom weavers at ₹3 per unit	15.0	15.0
Working Capital Scheme	Provide ₹10,000 as working capital to handlooms with UID marks	2.0	2.0
Total		17.0	17.0

Status of Industrial Units in Bihar as of 30th September 2023

Sector	No. of First Stage NOCs Issued	Investment (in Crore)	No. of Operational Units	Investment (in Crore)
Food Processing	1157	12166.32	233	1869.45
General Manufacturing	603	3103.71	111	489.26
Plastic & Rubber	277	1176.40	76	297.07
Tourism	79	968.41	21	163.07
Health Care	106	1436.86	30	224.28
Textiles	116	631.90	7	106.42
Renewable Energy	59	10397.29	6	294.83
Small Machine Manufacturing	26	156.68	5	7.52
Information Technology & IT-enabled Services	22	146.82	12	29.12
Technical Education	12	94.40	1	1.24
Electrical & Electronic Hardware	12	56.97	0	0
Leather Industry	8	172.82	3	3.18
Wood Industry	25	95.66	7	16.64
Ethanol	164	30747.55	6	686.74
Cement	12	3616.92	4	503.84
Sugar Mill (Expansion)	5	1922.34	0	0
Private Industrial Park	3	683.94	0	0
Others	9	39.95	2	20.31
Total	2695	67614.94	524	4712.97

Source: Department of Industries, Government of Bihar

Revenue Collection from Minerals in Bihar (2018-19 to 2022-23)

(In Lakhs)

Source	2018-19	2019-20	2020-21	2021-22	2022-23
1. Main Minerals	588.6	1004.1	1079.9	710.4	758.53
2. Minor Minerals					
i. Bricks	4154.6	6218.3	7308.5	7104.6	7793.88
ii. Sand	76740.7	87431.4	67865.5	74544.5	138446.85
iii. Stone + Crusher	16283.6	9104.26	7936.9	5140.2	7348.5
iv. Soil	702.4	417.2	677.6	1399.5	2210.86
v. Public Works Department	43687.7	52912.0	77207.0	70754.2	85792.99

vi. Others	6382.7	4355.6	5803.6	16960.6	30621.46
3. Arrears	7137.0	182.9	3014.1	0.0	0.0
Total	155677.3	161625.8	170893.0	176614.0	272973.07

Existing Installed Capacity (2022 and 2023)
(In Megawatts)

Ownership	March 2023	March 2022
	Thermal (Coal)	Hydroelectric (Renewable)
Electric	0	54
Producer	688	0
Central	4675	754
Total	5363	808

Source: Department of Energy, Government of Bihar

Daily Newspapers in Bihar

Hindi Dailies		
Newspaper Name	**Establishment Year**	**Publication Place**
Bihar Bandhu	1874	Patna
Aryavart	1941	Darbhanga
Pradeep	1947	Patna
Naveen Bharat	1948	Patna
Jan Shakti	1960	Patna
Aaj	1979	Patna
Begusarai Times	1981	Begusarai
Patliputra Times	1985	Patna
Navbharat Times	1986	Patna
Hindustan	1986	Patna
Maurya Bihar (Evening)	1988	Patna
Dainik Jagran	2000	Patna
Dainik Bhaskar	2013	Patna

English Dailies		
Newspaper Name	**Establishment Year**	**Publication Place**
Searchlight	1918	Patna
Hindustan Times	1986	Patna
Times of India	1986	Patna

Editorial office shifted from Calcutta to Patna in 1874.

APPENDIX V

Cultural

Symbols of Madhubani Painting Style

Symbol	Meaning
Banana	Fertility
Fish	Sensuality
Parrot	Love Messenger
Bamboo	Family Growth
Lion	Power
Elephant-Horse	Prosperity
Swan-Peacock	Peace
Sun-Moon	Longevity

Main Museums of the State

Sl. No.	Name	Establishment	Specialization
1.	Patna Museum, Patna	1915	Famous artifacts like the Didarganj Yakshini statue, ancient relics from the Maurya to Pala period, fossilized trees (20 million years old), Mughal paintings, and beautiful bronze statues.
2.	Nawada Museum, Nawada	1974	Pala period, Sultanate period relics
3.	Gaya Museum, Gaya	1970	Black stone sculptures from the Maurya period, coins, and manuscripts
4.	Chhathbhari Museum, Darbhanga	1957	Historical relics in metal, wood, stone, and ivory, along with manuscripts
5.	Archaeological Museum, Bodhgaya	1956	Artifacts and relics excavated from Bodhgaya
6.	Archaeological Museum, Vaishali	1945	Relics from the Maurya to Pala period
7.	Archaeological Museum, Nalanda	1917	Gupta and Pala period relics

Important Folk Songs

Folk Song	Specialty
Nachari	Devotional songs dedicated to Lord Shiva, sung in a special melody. This melody was created by the great poet Vidyapati.
Lagni Rag	Songs sung during marriages in the Mithila region.
Phag	Songs sung during the festival of Holi.
Chaita	A specific ragam sung in the month of Chaitra, related to separation and love.
Purbi Rag	Songs sung by women.

Major Folklore of Bihar

Folk Story	Speciality
Historical Stories	Related to the origin of individuals, places, famous dynasties, and the origin of castes and sub-castes.

Humorous Stories	Related to characters like Barons, Makhsha, etc.
General Stories	Related to Kings and Queens.
Creation Stories	Related to the origin of the Sun, Moon, Sky, Earth, rivers, Animals, Birds, and Humans.
Anecdotal Stories	Related to sexual matters, ghosts, and spirits.

Theatre Organizations and Institutions in Bihar

Location	Theatre Organizations & Institutions
Patna	Akshara Arts, Roopakshar, Kala-Nikunj, Kala-Triveni, Bhangima, Prayas Arpan, Anamika, Prangan, Sarjana, Madhyam, Bihar Art Theatre, Kala Sangam, Bharatiya Jan-Natyasangh, etc.
Begusarai	Zilla Naty Parishad, Saraswati Kala Mandir, etc.
Buxar	Navrang Kala Manch
Bihiya	Bharat Natya Parishad
Bhagalpur	Sarjana, Sagar Natya Parishad, Disha, Prem Art, Adarsh Natya Kala Kehn, Abhinay Kala Mandir, etc.
Ara	Kamayani, Yavnika, Bhojpur Manch, Yuva-Niti, Nati, Navodaya Sangh, etc.
Aurangabad	Natya Bharti, Actors Group, etc.
Khagual	Bhumika, Darpan Kala Kehn, Sutradhara, Theatresia, Manthan Kala Parishad, etc.
Gaya	Kala-Nidha, Shabnam Arts, Lalit Kala Manch, Natya Stuti, etc.
Chhapra	Mayur Kala Kehn, Shivam Sandbratik Manch, Hind Kala Kehn, Ihnjal, Manorama Sandbratik Dal, etc.
Jamalpur	Utsav
Nawada	Shobhadi Rang Sanstha
Mahnar	Anant Abhinay Kala Parishad

Major Festivals Organized in Bihar

Festival Name	Location
Valmiki Mahotsav	Bettiah, West Champaran
Nandangarh Mahotsav	Bettiah, West Champaran
Kesariya Mahotsav	Motihari, East Champaran
Vidyapati Mahotsav	Vidyapati Nagar, Samastipur
Dashrath Manjhi Lok Utsav	Gaya
Veer Kunwar Singh Vijayotsav	Bhojpur
Ang Mahotsav	Munger
Harihar Kshetra Mahotsav	Sonpur
Vishwamitra Mahotsav	Buxar
Brahmapur Mahotsav	Buxar
Ambe Utsav	Aurangabad
Jai Prakash Narayan Mahotsav	Sitab Diara, Saran
Dinkar Sahitya Utsav	Simaria, Begusarai
Kinnar Mahotsav	Patna

Mahnar Mahotsav	Vaishali
Jai Mangla Garh Mahotsav	Begusarai
Ustad Bismillah Khan Mahotsav	Dumraon
Pawapuri Mahotsav	Nalanda
Holika, Dinabhadri, Purainiya Mahotsav	Purnia
Manjusha Mahotsav	Bhagalpur
Singheswar Mela	Madhepura
Simaria Mela	Begusarai
Vachaspati Mahotsav	Madhubani
Sita Kund Mahotsav	Sita Dham, East Champaran
Gajna Mahotsav	Navinagar, Aurangabad

Famous Writers of Bihar

Writer	Famous Works
Banbhatt	Kadambari, Harshcharitam
Vishnu Sharma	Panchatantra
Kautilya	Arthashastra
Ashvagosa	Mahayana Shraddhotpad Samhita, Buddhacharita, Vajra Suchi
Aryabhatt	Aryabhatiyam
Vatsyayana	Kamasutra
Mandan Mishra	Bhav Vivek, Vidhi Vivek
Vidyapati	Padavali, Kirtilata, Kirtipataka, Gau-Raksha Vijay, Bhoo-Parikrama
Mulla Daud	Chandayan
Jyotishwar Thakur	Varn Ratnakar, Darshan Ratnakar
Phanishwar Nath 'Renu'	Maila Aanchal, Julous, Paltu Babu Road, Deerghatapa
Ramdhari Singh 'Dinkar'	Pranbhanga, Urvashi, Renuka, Dvadhvageet, Hunkar, Raswanti, Chakravaat, Dhoop-Chaav, Kurukshetra
Baba Nagarjuna	Baba Bateshwar Nath, Hazaar-Hazaar Baho Wali, Paro Kumbhipak, Tumne Kaha Tha, Ratinath Ki Chachi, Dukhharja Master
Devkinandan Khatri	Chandrakanta Santati, Bhutnath, Kajal Ki Kothari, Naulakhahaar
Rahul Sankrityayan	Buddhacharya, Vinaypitak, Dhammapad, Darshan-Iddarshan
Shah Azimabadi	Nakshapaydar
Dr. Rajendra Prasad	India Divided, Champaran Mein Satyagrah, Bapu Ke Kadmon Mein
Kedarnath Mishra 'Prabhat'	Jwala, Kaikeyi, Ritu Vansh
Shivsagar Mishra	Doob Janam Chhayi
Ramvriksh Benipuri	Amrapali, Maati Ki Muratein, Chita Ke Phool, Sanghamitra
Vachaspati Mishra	Bhashya Bhamati, Brahmsiddhi Ke Teekakar

Major Magazines Published in Bihar

Name	Location	Established Year	Medium of Publication
Dharmniti Tatvatham	Patna	1880	Sanskrit
Kshatriya Patrika (Monthly)	Patna	1881	Hindi
Lakshmi (Monthly)	Gaya	1903	Hindi
Balak (Monthly)	Patna	1926	Hindi
Yuvak (Monthly)	Patna	1929	Hindi
Bhookhe (Monthly)	Patna	1933	Hindi
Aarti (Monthly)	Patna	1940	Hindi
Parijat	Patna	1946	Hindi
Jyotsna	Patna	1948	Hindi
Nai Dhara	Patna	1950	Hindi
Avantika (Monthly)	Patna	1952	Hindi
Patal (Monthly)	Patna	1952	Hindi
Devvani	Munger	1960	Sanskrit
Chunnu-Munnu	Patna	1950	Hindi
Vidyarthi	Patna	1978	Sanskrit
Avkash (Monthly)	Patna	1979	Hindi
Janmat	Patna	1981	Hindi
Shiksha Digest (Monthly)	Patna	1984	Hindi

Major Daily Newspapers Published in Bihar

Name	Location	Established Year	Medium of Publication
Sarv Hitayshi	Patna	1880	Hindi
Searchlight	Patna	1918	English
Indian Nation	Patna	1931	English
Sada-e-Watan	Patna	1942	Urdu
Ittehad-e-Watan	Patna	1946	Urdu
Pradeep	Patna	1947	Hindi
Naveen Bharat	Patna	1948	Hindi
Vishwamitra	Patna	1948	Hindi
Sangam	Patna	1952	Urdu
Janashakti	Patna	1960	Hindi
Qoumi Tanmeen	Patna	1964	Urdu
Aatmkatha	Patna	1970	Hindi
Bihar Bandhu	Patna	1974	Hindi

Aaj	Patna	1979	Hindi
Begusarai Times	Begusarai	1981	Hindi
Patliputra Times	Patna	1985	Hindi
Hindustan Times	Patna	1986	English
Times of India	Patna	1986	English
Amrit Varsha	Patna	1986	Hindi
Hindustan	Patna, Muzaffarpur, Bhagalpur	1986	Hindi
Navbharat Times	Patna	1986	Hindi
Aryavart	Patna	1987	Hindi
Maurya Bihar (Sandhya)	Patna	1988	Hindi
Saathi	Patna	1989	Urdu
Sandhya Prahari	Patna	1992	Hindi
Dainik Jagran	Patna	2000	Hindi
Dainik Bhaskar	Patna	2013	Hindi
Qaumi Awaz	Patna	-	Urdu
Pindar	Patna	-	Urdu

Other Islamic Holy Sites in Bihar

Religious Site	Location
Shahi Masjid	Hajipur
Jama Masjid	Sasaram
Patthar Ki Masjid	Vaishali
Malsalami Masjid	Patna
Shah Kale Ka Maqbara	Patna
Amzhar Sharif	Aurangabad
Sheesh Mahal Masjid	Patna

Religious Sites of Sikh Followers in Bihar

Religious Site	Location
Gurudwara Govind Ghat	Patna City
Takht Sri Harminder Sahib	Patna
Gurudwara Gai Ghat	Patna
Gurudwara Handi Sahib	Danapur
Gurudwara Guru Ka Bagh	Patna
Gurus Singh Sabha Gurudwara	Gaya
Gurudwara Guru Singh Sabha	Purnia

Prominent Buddhist Pilgrimage Sites in Bihar

Religious Site	Location
Venuvan Vihar	Rajgir
Jeevak Amravan	Rajgir
Bodhi Tree	Bodh Gaya
Vajrasana	Bodh Gaya
World Peace Stupa	Rajgir
Trikuta Mountain	Rajgir
Mahabodhi Temple	Bodh Gaya

Prominent Jain Pilgrimage Sites in Bihar

Religious Site	Location
Rajgir	Nalanda
Kundalgram	Vaishali
Kamaldah	Patna
Gunawa Ji	Nawada
Champa, Nathnagar	Bhagalpur
Ara	Bhojpur
Lachhuar	Jamui
Pawapuri	Nalanda

Protected Monuments Declared by the Archaeological Survey of India in Bihar

Protected Monument	Village/Location	District
Patalpuri Cave	Patharghat Hill	Bhagalpur
Stone Sculpture Group	Patharghat Hill	Bhagalpur
Remains of Vikramshila Mahavihara	Antichak, Oriyap	Bhagalpur
Stone Temple	Kahalgaon, Adjacent to Vikramshila Mahavihara	Bhagalpur
Ashoka Era Stone Pillar	Lauria Areej	East Champaran
Ashoka Era Lion-Topped Stone Pillar	Lauria Nandangarh	West Champaran
Remains of Two Ashoka Era Stone Pillars	Rampurwa	West Champaran
Vedic Cremation Site Mound	Marhiya	West Champaran
Buddhist Stupa	Tajpur (Kesariya)	East Champaran
Remains of Fort, Lake & Ruins	Sagardei	East Champaran
Remains of Fort	Chan Ki Garh	West Champaran
Fort Ruins and Stupa	Marhiya	West Champaran
Vedic Cremation Mound	Lauria Nandangarh	West Champaran
Vedic Cremation Mound	Pakri	West Champaran
Ancient Fort Remains	Balirajgarh	Madhubani
Shobhanath Hill Ancient Mound	Hasra, Jagdishpur	Gaya
Ancient Buddhist Statue Group	Ghezan	Jehanabad
Group of Ancient Buddhist and Other Statues	Guneri Village	Gaya
Sapt Gufa (Seven Caves) Group	Barabar-Nagarjuna Hills	Jehanabad
Shamsher Kshan's Mausoleum	Shamshernagar	Aurangabad
Ancient Fort	Kurkihar	Gaya
Raja Vishal's Fort	Basadh	Vaishali
Jama Masjid	Hajipur	Patna
Archaeological Site	Kumhrar	Patna
Archaeological Site	Bulandibagh	Patna
Excavated Archaeological Site (Including Stupa)	Harpur Basant	Vaishali
Small Hill Mound	Chhoti Pahadi	Patna
Five Mound Group	Pahari Dih	Patna
Group of Statues	Datiyana	Patna
Fort Walls	Rajgir	Nalanda
All Archaeological Sites, Monuments, and Statues in Rajgir	Rajgir	Nalanda
Excavated Remains	Nalanda Village	Nalanda

Malik Ibrahim Bayan's Mausoleum	Bihar Sharif	Nalanda
Buddha Statue	Jagdishpur	Nalanda
Makhdum Shah Daulat Maneri & Ibrahim Khan's Mausoleum	Maner	Patna
Remains of Ancient Wooden Mauryan Wall	Sandalpur	Patna
Mir Ashraf's Jumma Mosque	Patna City	Patna
Ancient Ruins	Ghor Katora	Nalanda
Ancient Pond	Maner	Patna
Ancient City, Ruins & Other Ancient Sites	Manjhi	Saran
Hasan Shah's Mausoleum	Sasaram City	Rohtas
Sher Shah Suri's Mausoleum	Sasaram City	Rohtas
Ashoka's Rock Edict	Ashikpur Chandan Shaheed Hill	Rohtas
Ancient Fort	Rohtas Hill	Rohtas
Bakhitiyar Khilji's Mausoleum	Malik Sarai (Chainpur)	Bhabua
Ancient Mundeshwari Temple	Pavra (Ramgarh)	Bhabua
Ashoka Pillar and Stupa	Kolhua	Muzaffarpur
Shiva Temple	Konch	Gaya
Single Stone Pillar	Lat	Jehanabad
Stone Inscription in Nagari Script	Near Tarachandi Temple, Sasaram City	Rohtas
Ancient Mound	Buxar City	Buxar
Ancient Ruins & Statues	Near Khijarsarai, Kauadola	Jehanabad
Dr. Rajendra Prasad's Ancestral House	Jeeradahi	Siwan

Protected Monuments Declared by the Department of Archaeology, Government of Bihar

Protected Monument	Village/Location	District
Golghar	Patna	Patna
Agam Kuan	Gulzar Bagh	Patna
Begu Hajjam's Mosque	Patna City	Patna
Jain Temple	Kamaldah, Gulzar Bagh	Patna
Dorukhi Statue	Kankarbagh	Patna
Small Patna Devi Temple	Patna City	Patna
Shergarh Fort	Sabzi Bazar, Sasaram	Rohtas
Alawal Khan's Tomb	Sasaram	Rohtas
Sun Temple, Kandaha	Mahawara, Mahishi	Saharsa
Katra Fort	Muzaffarpur	Muzaffarpur
Nepali Temple	Hajipur	Vaishali

Kheri (Archaeological Site)	Shahkund	Bhagalpur
Jalalgarh Fort	Kasba	Purnia
Ara House	Ara	Bhojpur
Chousgarh	Narwatpur	Buxar
Dawood Khan's Fort	Dawood Nagar	Aurangabad
Ramshila Mountain	Gaya City	Gaya
Vishnupad Temple	Gaya City	Gaya
Pretshila Mountain	Bahadur Wigha, Hill Range	Gaya
Brahmyoni Hill	Gaya	Gaya
Hazari Mal Old Dharmshala	Bettiah	West Champaran

This translation covers the religious and archaeological sites of significance in Bihar across various religions and their historical importance.

Important Tourist Destinations in Bihar

Patna	Golghar, Harmandir, Jalan Museum, Shaheed Smarak, Pathar Ki Masjid, Patna Museum, Khuda Bakhsh Oriental Library, Agam Kuan, Gandhi Setu, Zoo, Padhari Ki Haveli, Biological Garden, Nawab Shahid's Tomb, Birla Mandir, Western Gate, Maner Sharif Dargah, Sadakat Ashram, Kumhrar, Saif Khan's Mosque, Bihar Institute of Handicraft and Design, Sonpur Fair, Gandhi Maidan, Malsalami, Ghavalpura, Begampur, Chimney Ghat, Bansghat, Mangal Talab, Kaladari Mahal, Nepali Kothi, Maharaj Ghat, Kowaso Ghat, etc.
Gaya	Mahabodhi Tree, Mahabodhi Temple, Barabar Caves, Tibetan Temple, Myanmar Temple, Bhutanese Temple, Vishnupad Temple, Pind Daan Sites, Vajrasana, Chankramana, Animation Lochan, Lotus Tank, Ancient Enclosure, Ratnasagar, Archaeological Museum, Thai Temple, Chinese Temple, Sri Lankan Temple, Ancient Temples on the banks of the Falgu River, Vishnupad Temple, Chankramana, Buddha's Dhyana Mudra, Handicraft Items, etc.
Rajgir	Bimbisar's Jail, Ajatashatru's Fort, World Peace Stupa, Amravan, Vaibhav Hill, Pimple Caves, Maniyar Math, Brahakund, Saptaparnika Caves, Virayatan Jain Temple, Water Temple, Samosharan Temple, Malmas Mela, Kundalvan Temple, Pushpkarni, Museum, Markkukshi, Cheryath Marks, Buddha's Bathing Place, Karnad Tank, Chariot Marks, Cyclopean Walls, Rajju Marg, Hot Water Springs, Kundalpur, Temples & Lotus Lake, Dheergh Pushpkarni, Pandav Pushpkarni.
Nalanda	Ruins of the Ancient Buddhist University.
Pawapuri	Nirvana Site of the 24th Tirthankara Mahavira in Jainism, Water Temple, Samo Sharan Temple.
Vaishali	Birthplace of the 24th Tirthankara Mahavira, Republic of the Licchavis.
Bhagalpur	Barari Caves, Ajgaibinath's Shiva Temple.
Purnia	Narasingh Avatar Pillar (Banmankhi), Poorandevi Temple.
Saharsa	Tarapeeth (Mahishi).

Munger	Barari Cave, Bahlgaon Temple, Mandar Hill, Bhim Bandh, Garbhjal Springs.
Maner	Sufi Saint Peer Hazrat Yahya Maneri's Dargah.
Bihar Sharif	Sufi Saint Peer Makhdum Shah Sharifuddin's Tomb.
Sasaram	Sher Shah Suri's Fort and Tomb.
Barouni	Oil Refinery.
Sitamarhi	Maa Janaki Temple.
Madhubani	Famous for Madhubani Paintings.

❑

Maps of Bihar

• Geographical Introduction of Bihar • Climate Zones of Bihar • Forests of Bihar • Agriculture of Bihar • Major Rivers of Bihar • Waterfalls and Lakes of Bihar • River Valley Projects of Bihar • Mineral Resources of Bihar

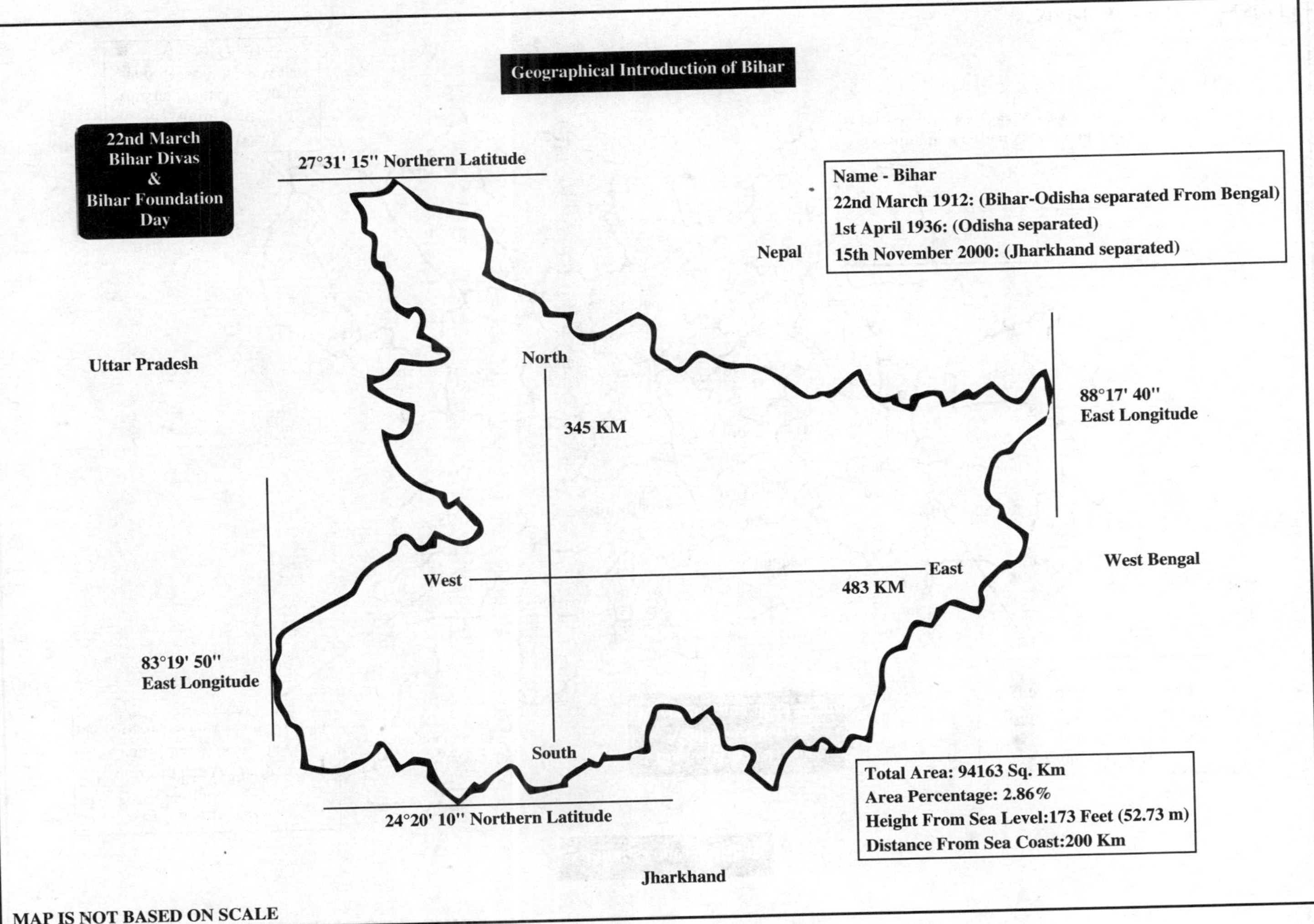
Geographical Introduction of Bihar
22nd March
Bihar Divas
&
Bihar Foundation
Day
27°31' 15'' Northern Latitude
Name - Bihar
22nd March 1912: (Bihar-Odisha separated From Bengal)
1st April 1936: (Odisha separated)
15th November 2000: (Jharkhand separated)
Nepal
Uttar Pradesh
North
345 KM
88°17' 40''
East Longitude
West
East
483 KM
West Bengal
83°19' 50''
East Longitude
South
24°20' 10'' Northern Latitude
Total Area: 94163 Sq. Km
Area Percentage: 2.86%
Height From Sea Level:173 Feet (52.73 m)
Distance From Sea Coast:200 Km
Jharkhand
MAP IS NOT BASED ON SCALE

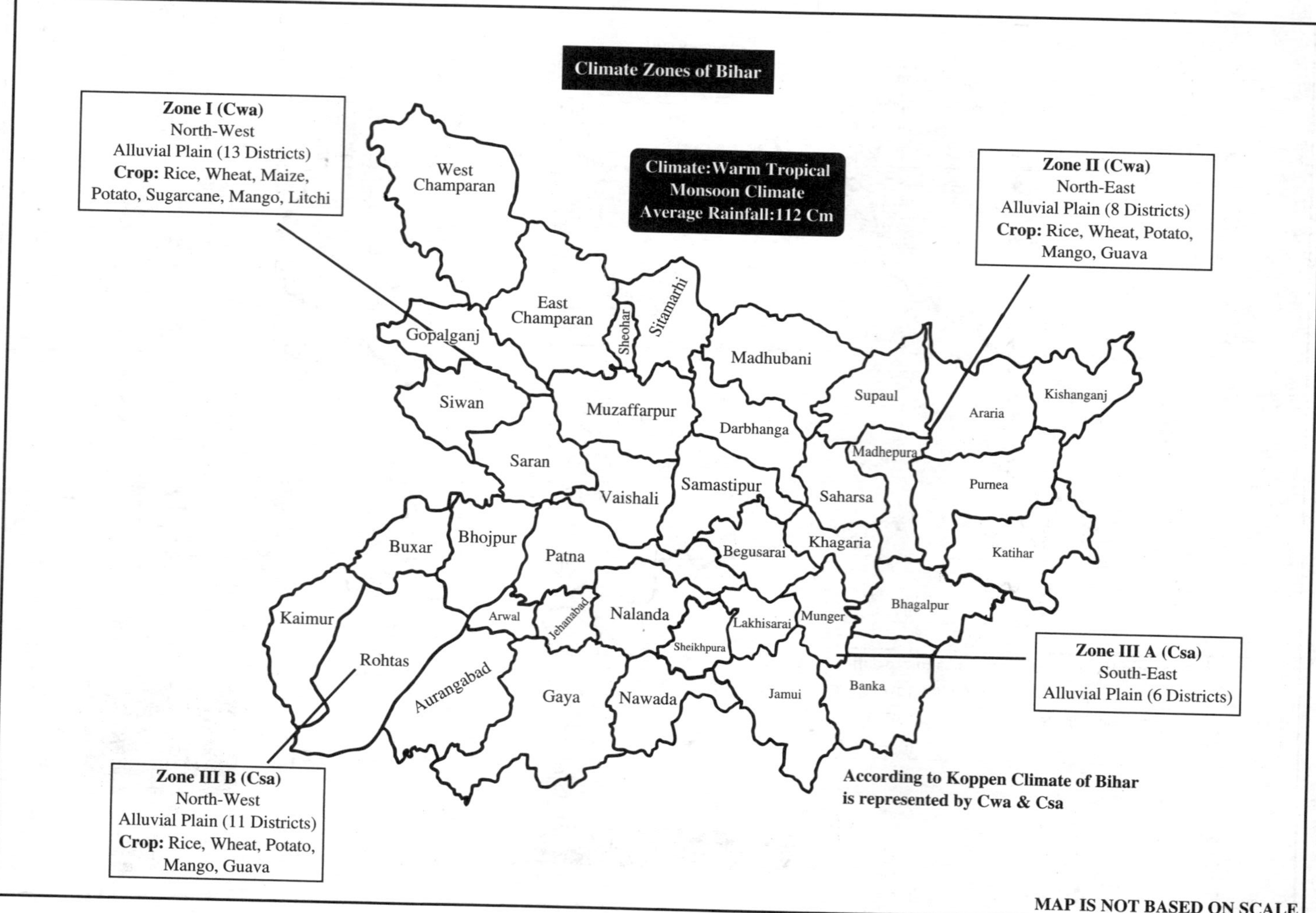
Climate Zones of Bihar
Zone I (Cwa)
North-West
Alluvial Plain (13 Districts)
Crop: Rice, Wheat, Maize, Potato, Sugarcane, Mango, Litchi
Climate:Warm Tropical Monsoon Climate
Average Rainfall:112 Cm
Zone II (Cwa)
North-East
Alluvial Plain (8 Districts)
Crop: Rice, Wheat, Potato, Mango, Guava
West Champaran
East Champaran
Gopalganj
Sheohar
Sitamarhi
Madhubani
Supaul
Araria
Kishanganj
Siwan
Muzaffarpur
Darbhanga
Madhepura
Purnea
Saran
Vaishali
Samastipur
Saharsa
Buxar
Bhojpur
Patna
Begusarai
Khagaria
Katihar
Kaimur
Arwal
Jehanabad
Nalanda
Sheikhpura
Lakhisarai
Munger
Bhagalpur
Rohtas
Aurangabad
Gaya
Nawada
Jamui
Banka
Zone III A (Csa)
South-East
Alluvial Plain (6 Districts)
Zone III B (Csa)
North-West
Alluvial Plain (11 Districts)
Crop: Rice, Wheat, Potato, Mango, Guava
According to Koppen Climate of Bihar is represented by Cwa & Csa
MAP IS NOT BASED ON SCALE

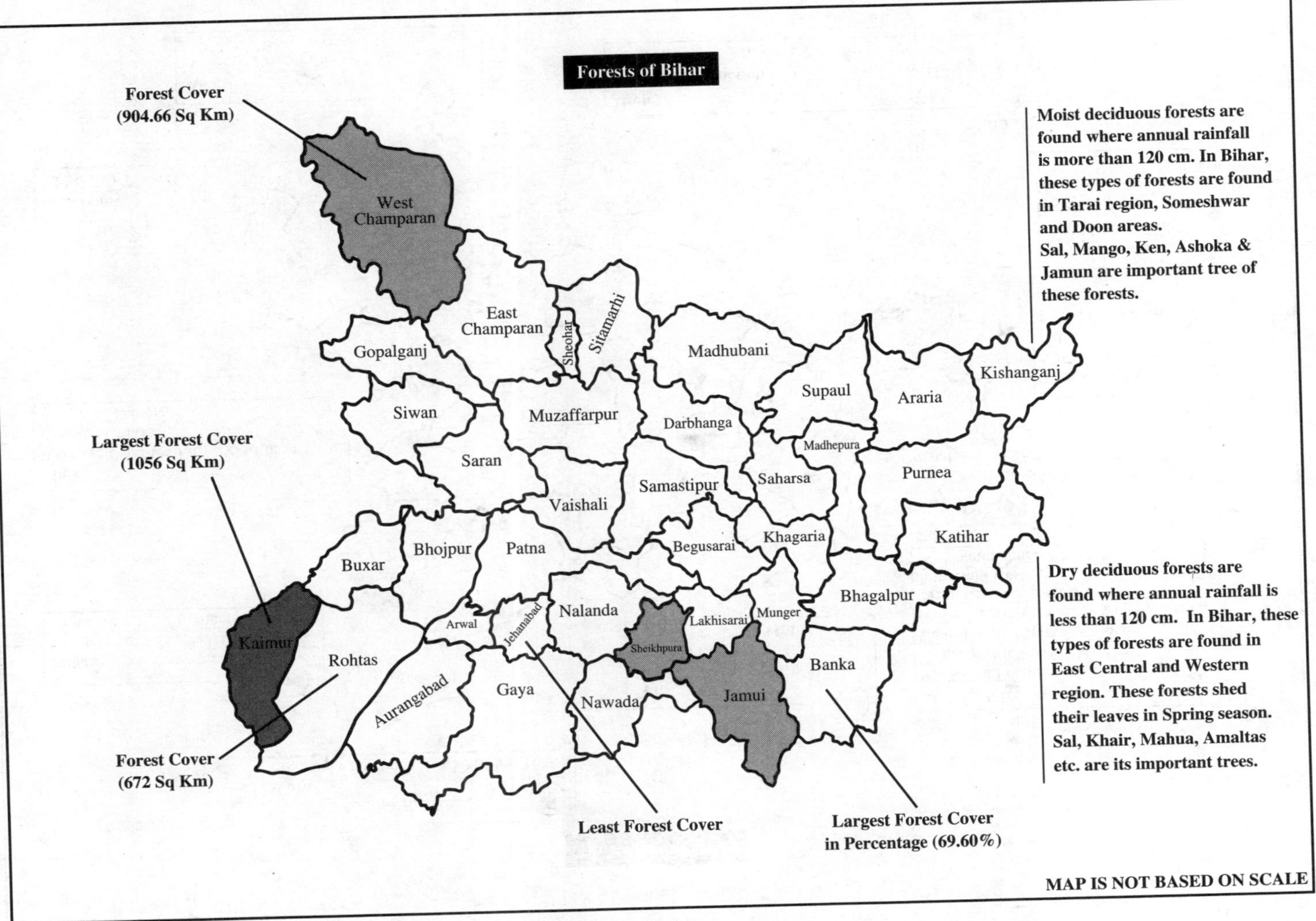
Forests of Bihar
Forest Cover
(904.66 Sq Km)
Largest Forest Cover
(1056 Sq Km)
Forest Cover
(672 Sq Km)
Least Forest Cover
Largest Forest Cover
in Percentage (69.60%)
West Champaran
East Champaran
Gopalganj
Sheohar
Sitamarhi
Madhubani
Supaul
Araria
Kishanganj
Siwan
Muzaffarpur
Darbhanga
Madhepura
Purnea
Saran
Samastipur
Saharsa
Vaishali
Katihar
Buxar
Bhojpur
Patna
Begusarai
Khagaria
Bhagalpur
Arwal
Jehanabad
Nalanda
Lakhisarai
Munger
Kaimur
Sheikhpura
Rohtas
Banka
Aurangabad
Gaya
Nawada
Jamui
Moist deciduous forests are found where annual rainfall is more than 120 cm. In Bihar, these types of forests are found in Tarai region, Someshwar and Doon areas.
Sal, Mango, Ken, Ashoka & Jamun are important tree of these forests.
Dry deciduous forests are found where annual rainfall is less than 120 cm. In Bihar, these types of forests are found in East Central and Western region. These forests shed their leaves in Spring season. Sal, Khair, Mahua, Amaltas etc. are its important trees.
MAP IS NOT BASED ON SCALE

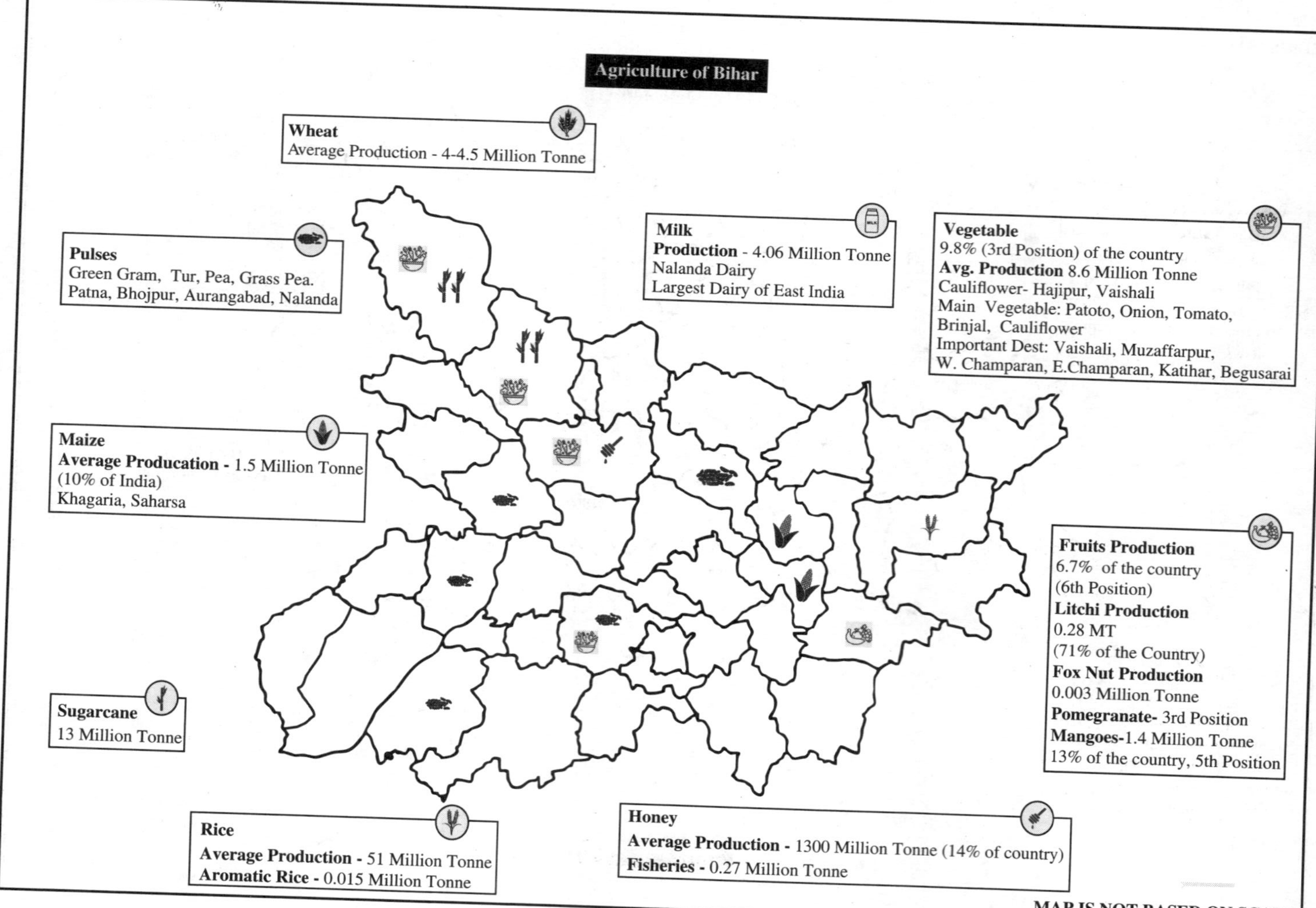
Agriculture of Bihar
Wheat
Average Production - 4-4.5 Million Tonne
Pulses
Green Gram, Tur, Pea, Grass Pea.
Patna, Bhojpur, Aurangabad, Nalanda
Milk
Production - 4.06 Million Tonne
Nalanda Dairy
Largest Dairy of East India
Vegetable
9.8% (3rd Position) of the country
Avg. Production 8.6 Million Tonne
Cauliflower- Hajipur, Vaishali
Main Vegetable: Patoto, Onion, Tomato,
Brinjal, Cauliflower
Important Dest: Vaishali, Muzaffarpur,
W. Champaran, E.Champaran, Katihar, Begusarai
Maize
Average Producation - 1.5 Million Tonne
(10% of India)
Khagaria, Saharsa
Fruits Production
6.7% of the country
(6th Position)
Litchi Production
0.28 MT
(71% of the Country)
Fox Nut Production
0.003 Million Tonne
Pomegranate- 3rd Position
Mangoes-1.4 Million Tonne
13% of the country, 5th Position
Sugarcane
13 Million Tonne
Rice
Average Production - 51 Million Tonne
Aromatic Rice - 0.015 Million Tonne
Honey
Average Production - 1300 Million Tonne (14% of country)
Fisheries - 0.27 Million Tonne
MAP IS NOT BASED ON SCALE

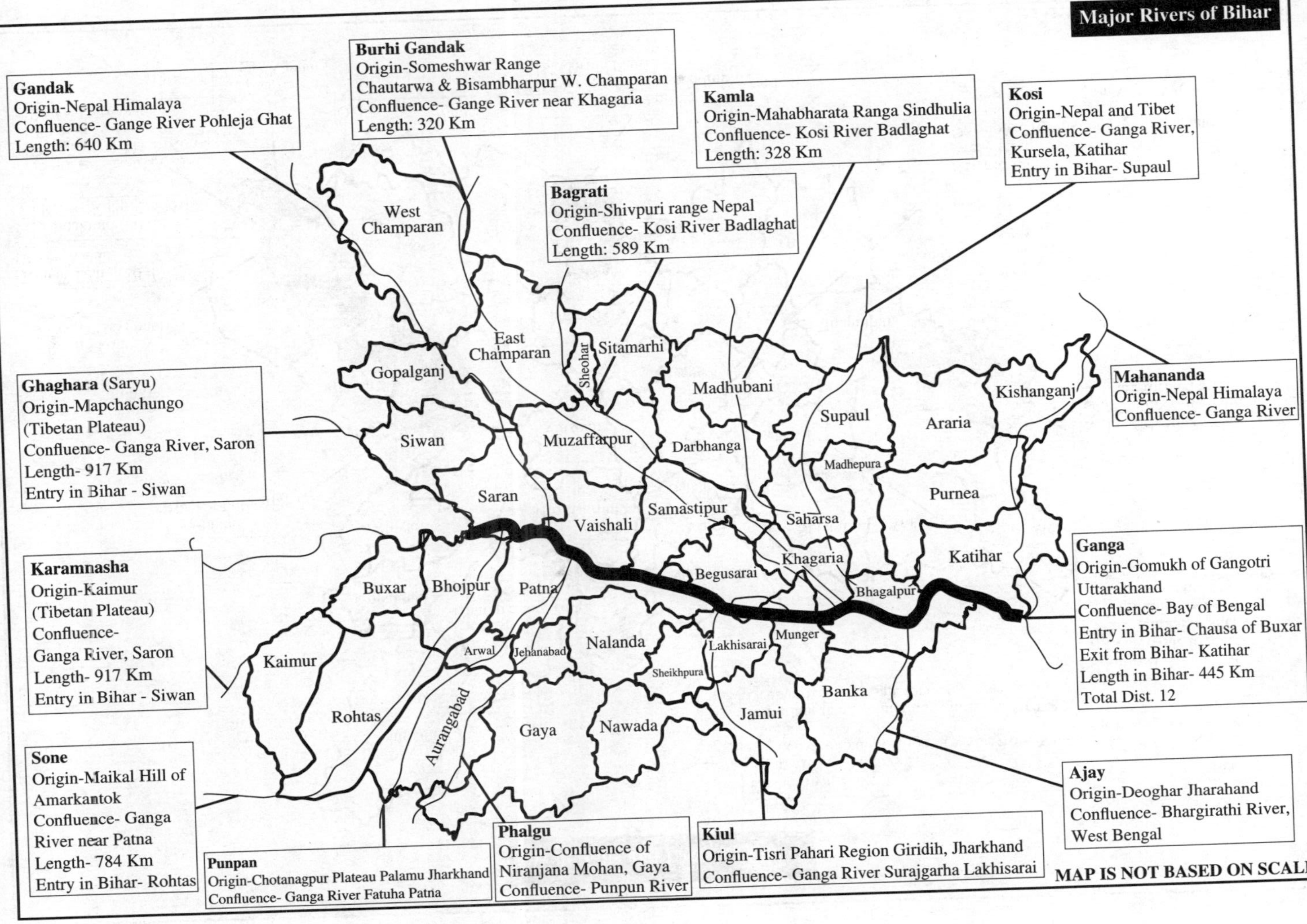
Major Rivers of Bihar
Gandak
Origin-Nepal Himalaya
Confluence- Gange River Pohleja Ghat
Length: 640 Km
Burhi Gandak
Origin-Someshwar Range
Chautarwa & Bisambharpur W. Champaran
Confluence- Gange River near Khagaria
Length: 320 Km
Kamla
Origin-Mahabharata Ranga Sindhulia
Confluence- Kosi River Badlaghat
Length: 328 Km
Kosi
Origin-Nepal and Tibet
Confluence- Ganga River,
Kursela, Katihar
Entry in Bihar- Supaul
Bagrati
Origin-Shivpuri range Nepal
Confluence- Kosi River Badlaghat
Length: 589 Km
Ghaghara (Saryu)
Origin-Mapchachungo
(Tibetan Plateau)
Confluence- Ganga River, Saron
Length- 917 Km
Entry in Bihar - Siwan
Mahananda
Origin-Nepal Himalaya
Confluence- Ganga River
Karamnasha
Origin-Kaimur
(Tibetan Plateau)
Confluence-
Ganga River, Saron
Length- 917 Km
Entry in Bihar - Siwan
Ganga
Origin-Gomukh of Gangotri
Uttarakhand
Confluence- Bay of Bengal
Entry in Bihar- Chausa of Buxar
Exit from Bihar- Katihar
Length in Bihar- 445 Km
Total Dist. 12
Sone
Origin-Maikal Hill of
Amarkantok
Confluence- Ganga
River near Patna
Length- 784 Km
Entry in Bihar- Rohtas
Punpan
Origin-Chotanagpur Plateau Palamu Jharkhand
Confluence- Ganga River Fatuha Patna
Phalgu
Origin-Confluence of
Niranjana Mohan, Gaya
Confluence- Punpun River
Kiul
Origin-Tisri Pahari Region Giridih, Jharkhand
Confluence- Ganga River Surajgarha Lakhisarai
Ajay
Origin-Deoghar Jharahand
Confluence- Bhargirathi River,
West Bengal
MAP IS NOT BASED ON SCALE
West Champaran
East Champaran
Gopalganj
Sheohar
Sitamarhi
Madhubani
Supaul
Araria
Kishanganj
Siwan
Muzaffarpur
Darbhanga
Madhepura
Purnea
Saran
Vaishali
Samastipur
Saharsa
Katihar
Khagaria
Begusarai
Bhagalpur
Buxar
Bhojpur
Patna
Kaimur
Arwal
Jehanabad
Nalanda
Lakhisarai
Munger
Sheikhpura
Banka
Rohtas
Aurangabad
Gaya
Nawada
Jamui

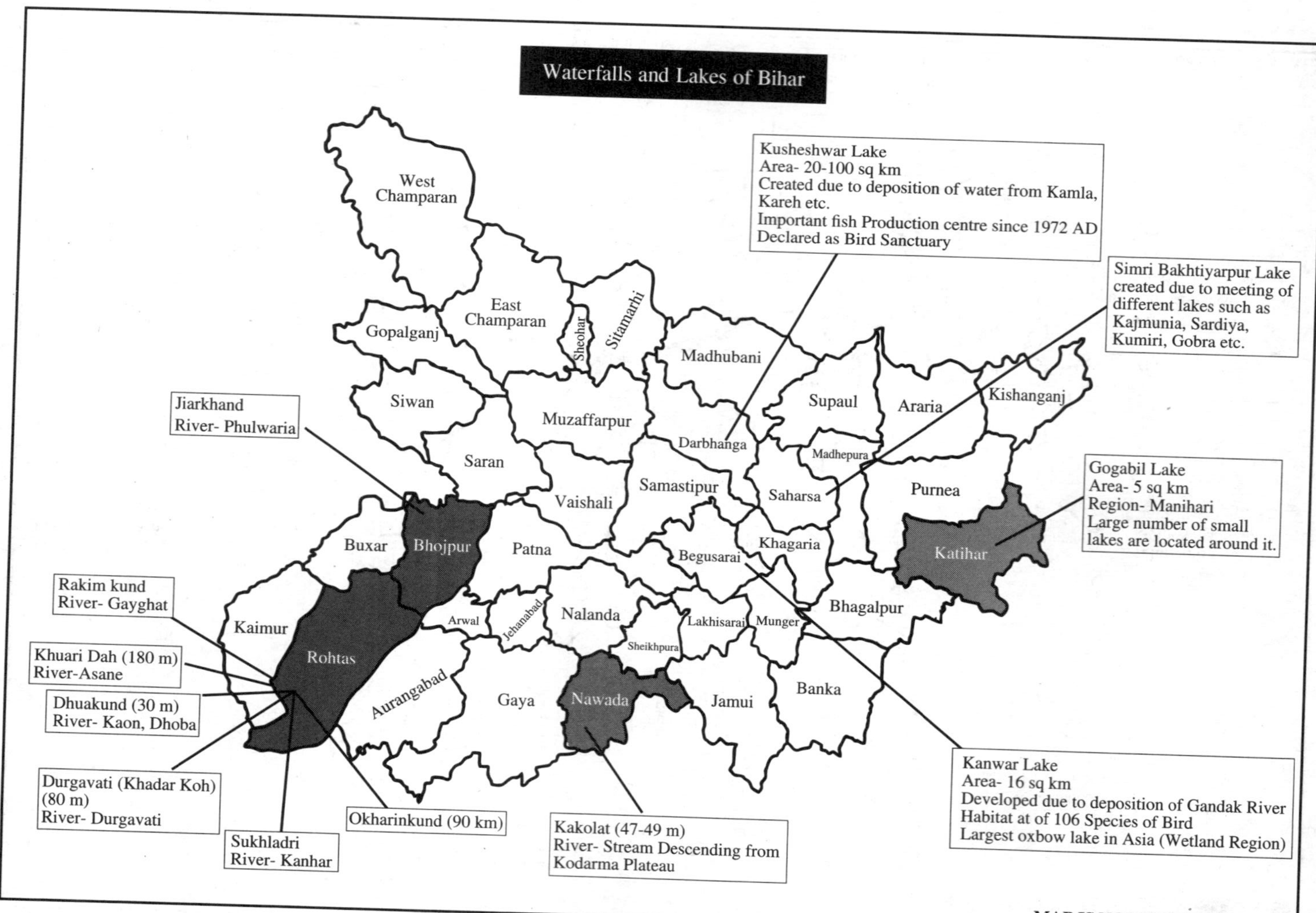
Waterfalls and Lakes of Bihar
Kusheshwar Lake
Area- 20-100 sq km
Created due to deposition of water from Kamla, Kareh etc.
Important fish Production centre since 1972 AD
Declared as Bird Sanctuary
Simri Bakhtiyarpur Lake
created due to meeting of different lakes such as Kajmunia, Sardiya, Kumiri, Gobra etc.
Gogabil Lake
Area- 5 sq km
Region- Manihari
Large number of small lakes are located around it.
Kanwar Lake
Area- 16 sq km
Developed due to deposition of Gandak River
Habitat at of 106 Species of Bird
Largest oxbow lake in Asia (Wetland Region)
Kakolat (47-49 m)
River- Stream Descending from Kodarma Plateau
Okharinkund (90 km)
Sukhladri
River- Kanhar
Durgavati (Khadar Koh) (80 m)
River- Durgavati
Dhuakund (30 m)
River- Kaon, Dhoba
Khuari Dah (180 m)
River-Asane
Rakim kund
River- Gayghat
Jiarkhand
River- Phulwaria
West Champaran
East Champaran
Gopalganj
Sheohar
Sitamarhi
Madhubani
Siwan
Muzaffarpur
Saran
Darbhanga
Supaul
Araria
Kishanganj
Madhepura
Purnea
Samastipur
Saharsa
Vaishali
Katihar
Buxar
Bhojpur
Patna
Begusarai
Khagaria
Bhagalpur
Kaimur
Rohtas
Arwal
Jehanabad
Nalanda
Lakhisarai
Munger
Sheikhpura
Aurangabad
Gaya
Nawada
Jamui
Banka
MAP IS NOT BASED ON SCALE

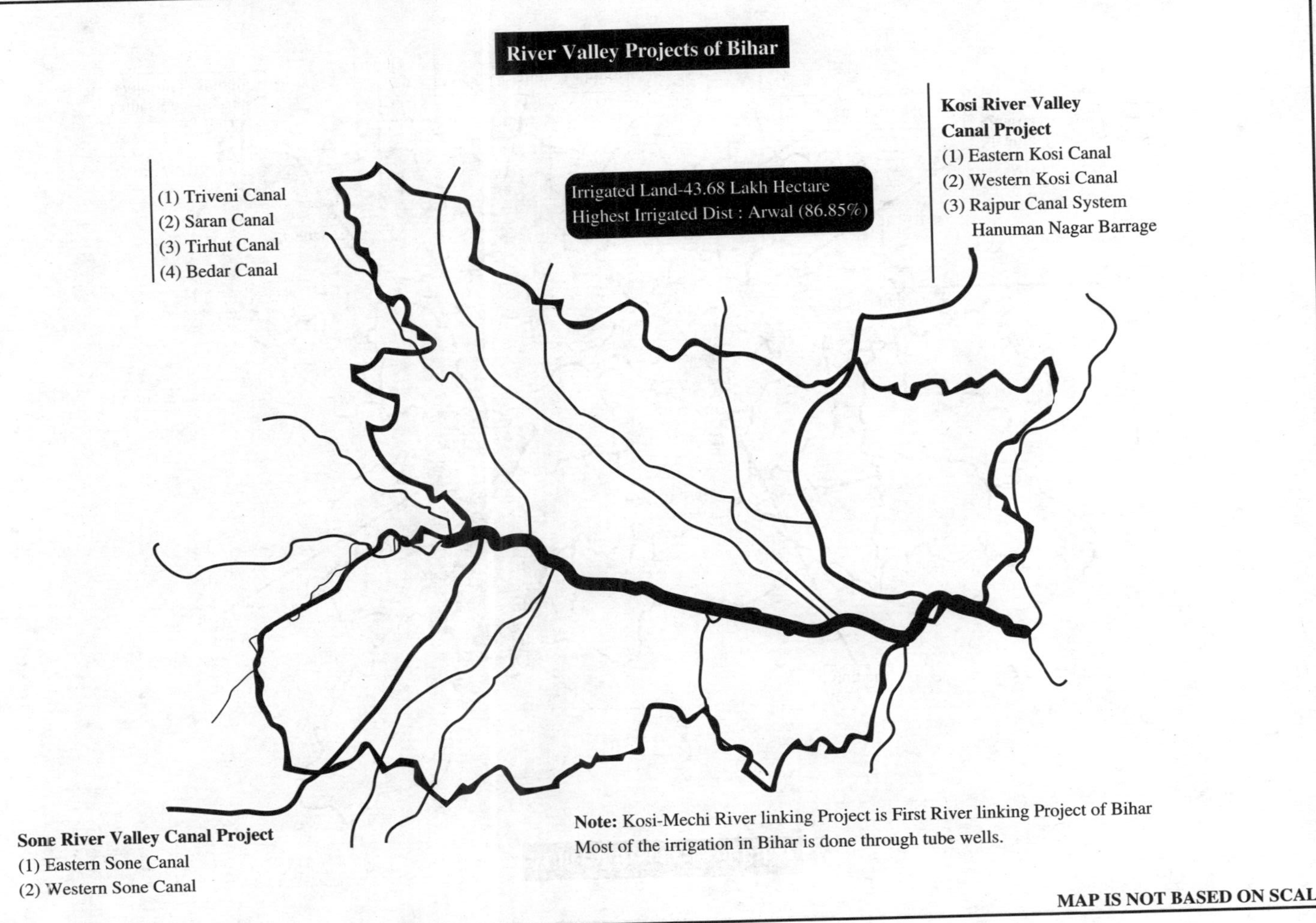
River Valley Projects of Bihar
(1) Triveni Canal
(2) Saran Canal
(3) Tirhut Canal
(4) Bedar Canal
Irrigated Land-43.68 Lakh Hectare
Highest Irrigated Dist : Arwal (86.85%)
Kosi River Valley
Canal Project
(1) Eastern Kosi Canal
(2) Western Kosi Canal
(3) Rajpur Canal System
Hanuman Nagar Barrage
Sone River Valley Canal Project
(1) Eastern Sone Canal
(2) Western Sone Canal
Note: Kosi-Mechi River linking Project is First River linking Project of Bihar
Most of the irrigation in Bihar is done through tube wells.
MAP IS NOT BASED ON SCALE

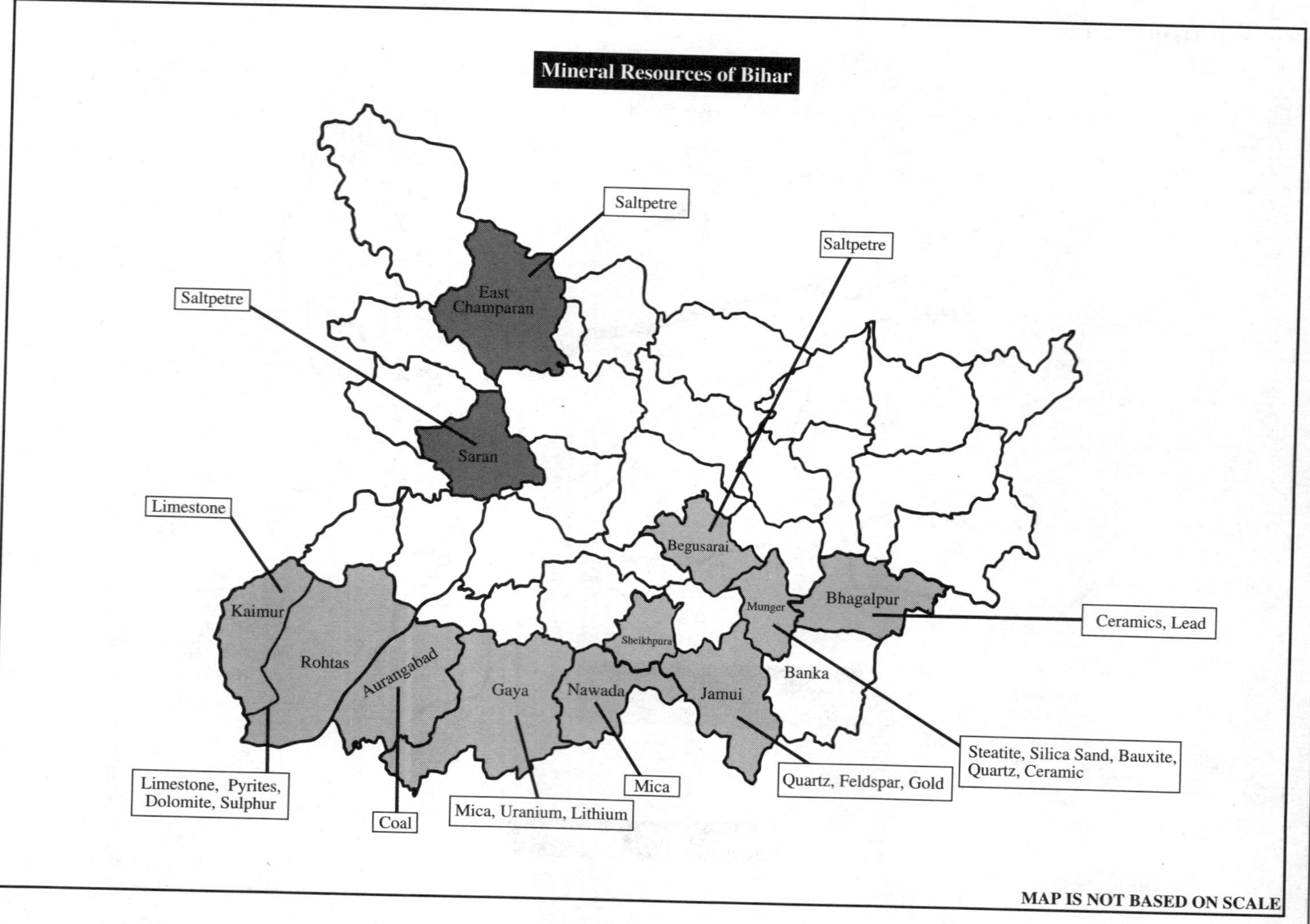
Mineral Resources of Bihar
Saltpetre
East Champaran
Saltpetre
Saran
Saltpetre
Limestone
Begusarai
Kaimur
Munger
Bhagalpur
Ceramics, Lead
Sheikhpura
Rohtas
Aurangabad
Gaya
Nawada
Jamui
Banka
Steatite, Silica Sand, Bauxite, Quartz, Ceramic
Limestone, Pyrites, Dolomite, Sulphur
Mica
Quartz, Feldspar, Gold
Coal
Mica, Uranium, Lithium
MAP IS NOT BASED ON SCALE